THE RISE OF THE CHINESE COMMUNIST PARTY 1921-1927

Volume One of
the Autobiography of Chang Kuo-t'ao

by Chang Kuo-t'ao

THE UNIVERSITY PRESS OF KANSAS
Lawrence, Manhattan, Wichita

PUBLISHER'S ACKNOWLEDGMENTS

Since this publication has been in preparation for some years, there are several acknowledgments to be made. First of all, it should be made clear that this English edition of Chang Kuo-tao's autobiography is not a translation from the Chinese version published in Hong Kong. For the most part it dates initially from the 1950's, when Robert A. Burton, presently Lecturer in Oriental Languages and Literatures at the University of Kansas, assisted Mr. Chang in preparing an English version. Acknowledgment should also be made to the Ford Foundation for its financial support during the early years of the project and to George E. Taylor, then Director of the Far Eastern and Russian Institute at the University of Washington, who administered the grant.

In 1964 a draft of the present volume was made available, which, with Mr. Chang's permission and under his supervision, became the basis for further editorial work. John K. Fairbank and Roy Hofheinz, Jr., of the East Asian Research Center at Harvard University reviewed the work and gave helpful advice. Walter E. Gourlay of Michigan State University and William Hsu of Union Research Institute, Hong Kong, gave the manuscript careful editorial reviews. Additional support was provided from General Research Funds of the University of Kansas and also from a Ford Foundation Grant administered at the university by George M. Beckmann. Finally, during this period many of the arrangements with regard to the manuscript and initial discussions between the author and the Press were arranged by Thomas R. Smith, then Director of the Center for East Asian Studies at the University of Kansas.

FOREWORD

The publication in English of the first volume of Chang Kuo-t'ao's memoirs is an important event. This long-awaited book, in preparation for over a decade, provides an intimate, detailed first-hand account of the founding and early development of the Chinese Communist Party. No comparable account has been written by any other major participant in the Party's early history. Consequently, the book provides a unique insider's view of the early stages of a revolutionary movement which has resulted in one of the most far-reaching and momentous upheavals in history. It should be of extraordinary interest not only to students of modern China but to all who strive for better understanding of the revolutionary forces at work in the contemporary world.

Chang Kuo-t'ao was one of the dozen founders of the Chinese Communist Party, and he played a central role in the development of the Party during the 1920's and early 1930's. In the mid-1930's, in fact, it was possible that he, rather than Mao Tse-tung, might emerge as the Party's predominant leader, and Mao achieved primacy only after a power struggle in which he defeated Chang.

Born in the late nineteenth century, into the landlord family of a Hakka community in Kiangsi Province, near the border of Hunan—the province that produced Mao and many other Chinese Communist leaders—Chang grew up in a time of rapid change and confused turmoil. The Chinese revolution, if one uses this term in a broad sense, was well under way, and he became involved in it at an early age. The first part of his book might well be labeled "The Making of a Revolutionary."

He vividly portrays the impact on him of varied revolutionary forces, ideas, and influences: anti-Manchu secret societies' activities which swept his home district when he was a child; new ideas to which he was exposed by modern-minded, Western-influenced teachers in county and provincial schools; economic forces for modernization and change that emanated from a nearby Anyuan coal mine; revolutionary activities associated with Sun Yat-sen's political movement; enthusiasm generated by the 1911 revolution, which toppled the Ch'ing Dynasty; subsequent disillusionment during the Republican period; intense patriotic and nationalistic feelings that grew in response to increasing Japanese pressure on China during World War I; new newspapers and journals which spread ideas on a nationwide basis; early contacts with revolutionaries and secret agents of a variety of sorts; the patriotic anti-Japanese student movement, centered at Peking National University (where he had enrolled to study science), which exploded after World War I in the May Fourth Movement of 1919; and the radical ideas and influences that reached China in the wake of the Bolshevik Revolution in Russia. All of these contributed to making Chang and many other young Chinese of the period revolutionaries.

Chang played a major role as a student leader in the May Fourth Movement. This patriotic outburst was a milestone in the development of modern nationalism in China, and a startling number of China's future revolutionaries, both Communist and non-Communist, began their actual careers as a result of the Movement. The primary initial motivating force for most of them, including Chang, was nationalism. Dedication to other ideologies, including communism, only came later; for a while innumerable ideologies and philosophies competed for attention—liberal democracy, parliamentarianism, Christianity, anarchism, syndicalism, guild socialism, and others, as well as Marxism.

Chang describes how, out of this milieu, the Communist Party emerged and grew. Consisting of only a handful of intellectuals and students at the start, it grew within a few years into a significant revolutionary movement and began to acquire a mass base. In the early years, labor provided its first mass following; only later, after numerous failures and setbacks, did it turn seriously to the peasantry for support. In this volume, Chang pays special attention to the labor movement in China; this is in part because of the importance of labor in the Party's strategy in the 1920's but in part, no doubt, because Chang himself played such a key role in organizing labor.

Chang's role was extremely important in the operation of the Party as a whole, and his book adds rich detail and throws a great deal of new light on most of the major events in the Party's early history: the formation of the first Party groups in 1920, the founding Congress in 1921, the principal meetings of Party leaders thereafter, the February Seventh Strike in 1923, the formation of a united front with the Nationalists, the May Thirtieth Movement in 1925, the Northern Expedition, the Nationalist-Communist split in 1927, and so on.

The book analyzes in great detail the shifting policies, strategies, and tactics of the Party in its early years, the debates and disputes that took place among its leaders, and the specific views of the individuals involved. What emerges is a fascinating picture not only of the multitude of issues that the leadership had to face but also of how and when decisions were made and the personalities involved. In short, it gives the story a human dimension which most historians are hard put to provide. Included throughout the book are revealing characterizations and vignettes of almost all the early leaders of the Party.

Chang's personal views on the key problems and issues facing the Communist Party in those years are, of course, strongly presented in the book. Chang believes that one of the Party's basic errors in that period was the adoption of the particular kind of united-front policy that it pursued in the 1920's, a policy that he opposed. In his view, while a united front between the Communists and Nationalists was essential for revolutionary success, it should have been a united front "from without," enabling the Communist Party to maintain maximum independence and freedom of action, rather than a united front "from within," in which Communist Party members actually joined the Kuomintang. He believes that adoption of a wrong united-front strategy was a basic factor leading to the subsequent split with the Nationalists and the debacle of 1927. He blames the adoption of the wrong strategy primarily on the representatives of the Comintern in China—and most specifically on a particular advisor: Maring.

One underlying, recurring theme throughout Chang's account, in fact, is the view that Comintern and Soviet advisors in China in the 1920's played too great a role, and one characterized by lack of understanding and frequent ineptitude and error. Despite the value to the Chinese Communists of the assistance that Moscow provided at the start, he seems to feel that, on balance, Chinese revolutionaries would have done better if they had been more on their own and had acted independently.

One of the greatest values of these memoirs derives from the fact that they not only provide important new facts on the key issues and events in the Chinese Communist Party's early history but also reveal the human elements in the story. History sometimes is reduced to analysis of seemingly abstract "social forces"; an account of this sort highlights the fact that the Chinese Communist movement—like all important historical movements—was also the result of the activities of individual human beings moved by various motives, possessing various capabilities, and having a potential for various accomplishments and follies.

Chang Kuo-t'ao would be the first, I am sure, to say that his memoirs do not constitute a complete history of the period he covers. No individual participant in a revolutionary movement is capable of writing such a history; the attempt to do so must be a continuing task involving many historians using a multiplicity of sources. But Chang's account is clearly the most important first-person account that we have of the formative years of the Communist Party in China, written by a major participant. As such, it will be an indispensable primary source for all future historians who try to analyze and understand the Chinese revolution.

Chang would also freely admit, I believe, that any such first-person account inevitably must reflect the author's personal perspectives—and biases—and that different participants in the same events might vary somewhat in their interpretations. Despite this fact, his book is remarkably free of polemics. I was fortunate in knowing Chang in Hong Kong throughout most of the period when he was writing these memoirs, and I became convinced then, and am confident now, that his primary aim has been to place in the record the most honest and accurate account that he is capable of writing. Not surprisingly, his strong feelings on many questions are clearly reflected in the book—including, for example, his antipathy toward Mao and his belief that the original promise of the Chinese revolution has been betrayed; one would not expect otherwise. But on balance the book represents a remarkable combination of involvement and dispassionate observation. Chang's personal participation in most of the events he describes gives the account the unique flavor of an authentic inside view. Yet the fact that three decades have passed since he broke with the Party has made it possible for him to analyze past events with a detachment that is impossible for those who have continued to be involved.

In preparing this English version of his memoirs, which were originally published in Chinese, Chang was assisted by a number of people, and in particular by Robert Burton of the University of Kansas.

In this first volume, Chang ends with the events surrounding the Kuomintang-Communist split in 1927, and therefore the story is only half-complete. The second volume will cover the equally important period of the Kiangsi Soviet—when the Chinese Communist Party moved into the countryside—and the subsequent struggle and split between Chang and Mao. All those who read this first volume will eagerly await the second, at least if they feel, as I do, that Chang Kuo-t'ao adds a great many new and revealing dimensions to an understanding of one of the most enormous and important revolutionary movements of our time.

A. Doak Barnett
The Brookings Institution
Washington, D.C.

A Biographical Sketch of
CHANG KUO-T'AO

The author of this sketch, Yang Tzu-lieh, is the
wife of Mr. Chang Kuo-t'ao. For several decades she
and her husband led active lives which involved many
difficulties and dangers. Then, until they moved to
Canada late in 1968, they lived in seclusion in Hong
Kong's suburbs, leading peaceful lives and spending
their time with their grandchildren. They are now
observers of the political scene, rather than participants in it.

This book, by Mr. Chang
Kuo-t'ao, traces the development of a radical young
man during the May Fourth Movement and describes
the true history of the early life of the Chinese Communist Party. Much of his experience in the Party is
unknown not just to outsiders but even to such con-
temporaries of his as Mao Tse-tung, Tung Pi-wu, Liu
Shao-ch'i, Li Li-san, and Chou En-lai, who may not
know as much about the initial policies and strategies
involved in the formation of the Party or the activities
of the Party center in its early days. Mr. Chang's book
is an objective and temperate presentation of the life
and times of one of the founders of the Chinese Communist Party that is meticulously truthful in every
detail. By reading this representative radical's account
of China in the past half-century and by looking at
the realities of China through his eyes, the reader may
not only gain knowledge of modern Chinese history,
but also gain certain insights that, perhaps, will enable
him to better understand the political drama of pres-
ent-day China.

I feel that I am the best witness to the importance
of this work by Mr. Chang Kuo-t'ao. I, too, was
among the earliest Chinese Communists. In the autumn of 1921, not long after the Hupeh regional
organization of the Communist Party was inaugurated,
I became a full-fledged Party member. I met Mr.
Chang in Peking in 1922 and worked with him for a
common cause. We were married in the spring of

1924. We have never been separated from that time on. Together we have experienced many hardships and perils, and it goes without saying that I know a great deal about his experiences. Every time I read this book, things from the past come back to me as if they had occurred only yesterday. Historical events vividly recreate themselves in my mind, often causing me to heave a sigh or even to shed tears.

It is not my intention, however, to make an appraisal of Mr. Chang's work here. At this point I shall merely present a biographical sketch of Mr. Chang.

Born in 1897 in Kiangsi Province, Chang Kuo-t'ao was brought up in one of the typical families of farming gentry in central China. His father was a judge and later a county magistrate. After attending primary and secondary schools in Kiangsi, Mr. Chang went to Peking University in 1916. He was one of the most important student leaders of the May Fourth Movement in 1919. Arrested in the June Third Incident and constantly persecuted by the Peking government, he became a radical inclined towards socialism, and he maintained frequent contacts with two professors then at Peking University—Ch'en Tu-hsiu and Li Ta-chao. His zeal in "going into the masses" made him a center of attraction for leftist students.

In the summer of 1920 Ch'en Tu-hsiu, Li Ta-chao, and Mr. Chang started to plan for the organization of the Chinese Communist Party. In the summer of 1921 he took part in preparations for the First Congress of the Chinese Communist Party, which elected him chairman of the Congress. The Congress later elected three members to be responsible for directing programs at the central level—actually a three-member Politburo, though the name was not used. The three members were Ch'en Tu-hsiu, secretary; Li Ta, propaganda; and Chang Kuo-t'ao, organization. It would be fair to say that it was Mr. Chang who started the Party construction and set in motion the Communist labor movement, which at the time absorbed most of the cream of the Communist Party—such currently eminent Communists as Mao Tse-tung, Liu Shao-ch'i, Li Li-san, and Ch'en Yun being his comrades-in-arms. In late 1921 Mr. Chang went to Moscow as a delegate of the Chinese Communist Party to the Congress of the Toilers of the Far East. He was the only Chinese Communist leader whom Lenin even received.

Mr. Chang returned to Shanghai early in 1922. At the Third Congress of the Chinese Communist Party, in 1923, he was relieved of his post as a member of the Central Committee because of his opposition to the policy requiring Communists to become full members of the Kuomintang; but he retained his important position in the labor movement. Early in 1924 Mr. Chang attended the First Congress of the Kuomintang as a delegate of the Kuomintang's Peking Municipal Party Headquarters and was elected an alternate member of the Central Executive Committee of the Kuomintang. His election to this post was due chiefly to the influence of Dr. Sun Yat-sen, who held him in high esteem.

At the Fourth Congress of the Chinese Communist Party, early in 1925, Mr. Chang was once again elected a member of the Central Committee and a member of the Political Bureau of the Central Committee. He participated in Communist policy-making from then until the Party's August Seventh Conference in 1927. At the time the Chinese Communists had suffered many failures, especially the failure of the Nanchang Uprising. Mr. Chang was branded a rightist opportunist, and in November, 1927, he was once again dismissed as a member of the Central Committee and as a member of its Political Bureau. But in the summer of 1928 the Chinese Communist Party's Sixth Congress reinstated him in these positions and appointed him a delegate of the Chinese Communist Party to the Communist International. Consequently, he stayed in Moscow for two and one-half years.

Returning to China in the spring of 1931, Mr.

Chang made significant contributions toward solving the grave crisis that confronted the Chinese Communists. Party work at that time shifted to the soviet areas, and Mr. Chang was appointed secretary of the Central Committee's bureau in the Hupeh-Honan-Anhwei region and, concurrently, chairman of the Military Council there. Later he was named vice-chairman of the Chinese Soviet Republic. In 1932 the Red Army's Fourth Field Army, under his command, moved to northern Szechwan, at which time Mr. Chang was appointed the fully accredited representative in Szechwan of the Party's Central Committee, of the Central Military Council, and of the Central Soviet government. This meant that wherever he went, Party, army, and government organizations were under his command.

In 1935 his Fourth Field Army joined forces at Maokung in western Szechwan with the First Field Army led by Mao Tse-tung. Political differences split the two. In 1936 Mr. Chang again met Mao in northern Shensi. At that time, although Mr. Chang still carried on as a member of the Political Bureau of the Party's Central Committee, he experienced a sense of frustration as a result of being discriminated against. At the outbreak of the War of Resistance against Japan in 1937, however, a sense of mission to save the nation impelled him to take up the post of acting chairman of the Border Region government. But an increasing deterioration in the situation caused him to despair and finally made him leave Yenan in 1938.

During the War of Resistance, Mr. Chang became a member of the National Assembly in order to show his determination to join his people in resisting the Japanese invaders. After the war he increasingly disengaged from party and national politics. In his words, "My radical ideas and patriotism are the same as always. I only hope that we will be far, far away from this or that dictatorship." A man who has had long and varied experience, Mr. Chang, now seventy, is content with a poor but happy life; and he looks back not with a sense of grief, but with a sense of relief. As he frequently says, "I used to be an actor on the Chinese stage. Now I am merely a spectator who always hopes to see fewer tragedies."

ABBREVIATIONS

CC: Central Committee
CCP: Chinese Communist Party
CEC: Central Executive Committee
CSC: Central Standing Committee
CYC: Communist Youth Corps
ECCI: Executive Committee of the Communist International
KMT: Kuomintang (The Nationalist Party of China)
SYC: Socialist Youth Corps
The shortened form Comintern is used for the Communist International

CONTENTS

GROWING UP IN THE MIDST
OF REVOLUTIONARY UPHEAVAL

CHAPTER

The Hung Chiang Rebellion

One winter afternoon in 1906 the usually placid town of Shanglishih in P'inghsiang County, Kiangsi Province, erupted with excitement as terrifying news swirled through it. Country people hastily packed the wares they were selling at this market town and, jostling one another, rushed toward home. Panic-stricken women and children hurried out of town. Shopkeepers closed their shops and packed their displays safely away. About five o'clock that afternoon wooden gates on the streets leading out of town swung closed, isolating Shanglishih from the surrounding countryside. Watchmen dashed about, warning residents to guard against fires.

I was quite ignorant of the town's affairs, as I was only a nine-year-old pupil in a private school there. The school was run by Liao Shih-hsi, a friend of my father's. Attending the school were the sons of Liao and of his friends, a dozen or so in all, the oldest not more than seventeen years old. We all boarded there.

When panic struck the town, Liao was away on business; and we were working on the assignments he had left with us. Several older boys, goaded by curiosity, slipped out to watch the excitement. Most of the other students were whisked home by their families; but a few like

1

me were stranded in the school because our families lived too far away to fetch us. We did not know what to do.

Some time after the gates closed, my young fourth uncle, a fellow student, darted back. He bundled me and two schoolmates named Wen off to a beancurd shop at the edge of town, shoved us through a window in its rear, and told us to wade the stream on which the window opened and to follow the road on the far side to the home of the Wens.

"Hurry along," he admonished. "No matter what happens, don't stop on the way. It's getting dark." He watched as we waded the wide, shallow stream, and then his figure vanished from the window.

People came and went on the road—some empty-handed, others carrying things—all in silent haste. But we three youngsters encountered nothing exceptional as we trudged along. After five *li** we arrived at a small general store that the Wens owned. There was still one li to go, but the shopkeeper cautioned us against walking it alone because, he warned, the winds blew ill that night. Since he tended the shop alone and could not leave it to accompany us, he suggested that we eat there and spend the night. We were only too happy to accept his warm invitation.

It must have been about midnight when a crowd of hefty drunken men carrying sabers dragged us from bed and stood us on a counter. We awoke suddenly to see them brandishing sabers at us.

"Chop off the kids' heads and wet our battle flags in their blood," some yelled. "They'd be nice to try our sabers on," bawled others. "Don't kill them," still others suggested. "Tie them up and cart them off, and let their families ransom them back with big shiny silver dollars."

The shopkeeper tried desperately to save us. Pleading that we be allowed to go back to sleep, he promised them wine, food, and everything else in the shop. And because he belonged to their gang, as we learned later, they listened to him. Pandemonium continued for a while; but they left us alone at last, and we crept back to the bedroom. As our terror gradually subsided, we reentered the village of slumber.

We awoke early the next morning to find the door gaping open. There was no sign of the shopkeeper. Gone, too, were the bolts of cloth, the food, the grass sandals, and everything else. Outside, a long line of shabby peasants filed in disorderly fashion down the road, carrying spears, flintlock bird guns, rakes, huge broad-bladed swords, sabers, clubs, and for shields, black iron pans and pot covers. They showed no

---

* One *li* is 576 meters, about one-third of a mile.

enthusiasm; there was no flag-waving or shouting as they marched toward Liuyang County in nearby Hunan Province. We just gawked as
they scuffed past, too innocent and artless to fear them, and nobody paid
any attention to us.

After some time we tired of staring and took a path off the main
road to the Wen mansion. It was deserted. We scoured the house,
shouting at the top of our lungs. Not until we reached the hillside
behind it, still shrieking, did we notice with relief a man clambering
down the wooded hillside toward us. He guided us deep into the forest
to the Wen family. They asked anxiously why we had risked coming
home at such a time and what was happening in town and along the
road. And when we had recounted what we knew, they told us that they
had learned only the night before that the Hung Chiang Society Rebellion had broken out. By then it was too late to fetch us. Thus we discovered that we had wandered through the storm center of a rebellion,
which was, I learned later, actually the first of a series of eight rebellions
associated with Dr. Sun Yat-sen's T'ung-meng Hui between 1906 and
1911.

Although the Wens had been close friends of my family for generations, I wanted to go home. But they were especially kind, soothing me
with assurances that there was nothing to worry about. It was impossible to reach my home, which was twenty li away, and they reminded
me that I was as safe with them as with my own family. So I stayed
with them for about ten days.

During the first few days scattered bands of "secret society bandits"
honored the Wen home below us with their attention. They were not
particularly destructive, nor did they commit many major thefts, yet the
Wens reacted as birds startled by a flight of arrows. With me in tow,
they retreated further up the hill. There, deep in a hilly recess, shrinking
like snails into their shells, we hid in tents. Not until the winds of rumor
eased did we return quietly to their mansion, where I stayed three or
four more nights.

The Wens thought of nothing but the rebellion the whole time.
Neighbors and friends ran back and forth trying to keep them informed
of the latest developments. But they had little to report other than that
so-and-so had joined the "society bandits," how the rebellious march was
organized, and finally, that it had encountered defeat.

In this way the Wens learned that their trusted shopkeeper was
leader of a one-hundred-man Hung Chiang unit—news that intensified

their nervous uncertainty. They feared it might get them into trouble with the authorities. No doubt the shopkeeper joined the Society, they decided, in order to protect himself from local scoundrels. But they found it less easy to explain the motives of other neighboring villagers who had joined the rebellious march. "Why do you suppose this conservative and contented man is rebelling?" they would muse, picking a name here and there. Needless to say, a family of gentry like the Wens stood against rebellion. The fact that so many villagers were swept into this rebellion truly puzzled them.

Ten days after we went into hiding, the turmoil seemed to subside, communications were restored, and my family sent for me. The stormy incident had meanwhile implanted many strange new ideas in my young mind. I began to see what this so-called Hung Chiang Society Rebellion amounted to and to understand for the first time what a rebellion really was.

Safe and sound, I returned home to Chihmushan, to the great relief of my family and especially of my mother. Their experiences had differed from those of the Wens, I learned. They first heard the winds of rumor on the evening of the nineteenth day of the tenth moon (December 6, 1906). They immediately scurried with our valuables into the wooded hills. That same night the leader of a one-thousand-man Hung Chiang Society unit assembled more than a thousand Society villagers in the open space before our house. After slaughtering a good many of our pigs, they feasted inside, leaving the place a shambles. They did not, to be sure, really loot the house. Yet they made off with a number of things and did some damage. Then, while torches blazed throughout the house, they hoisted a flag in front of it and shouted their "onward march" oath.

Meanwhile, Hung Chiang Society men discovered my fifth granduncle, who had not fled in time, and carted him away. They demanded a ransom of two thousand silver dollars as a levy for the troops. One week later, however, by the time his frantic family had scraped together a thousand dollars, he returned unharmed, for by then the Hung Chiang Society Rebellion was crumbling.

The Hung Chiang Society, which stretched like a spider web over Hunan and Kiangsi provinces, started as a small branch of the Hung Men Society. Formed by Ming dynasty loyalists in the early days of the Ch'ing dynasty, the Hung Men Society was a secret organization dedicated to overthrowing the Ch'ing. The Heaven and Earth Society (T'ien-ti Hui), the Big Brother Society (Ko-lao Hui), and the Three Dot Society (San-t'ien Hui), which was also known as the Triad Society (San-ho Hui), were all prominent offshoots of the Hung Men Society with tremendous underground power. They had contributed a great deal to the Taiping Rebellion. For, as such things go, the Hung Men Society was the most progressive and powerful secret society during the Ch'ing dynasty. From its inception its political aim was summarized by the slogan "Overthrow the Ch'ing and Restore the Ming." In addition, it promoted mutual help among members and stood for a "brotherhood of those who roam the rivers and lakes." By binding members to assist one another, it offered protection against lawless elements to those who traveled frequently. In its ranks were people from all walks of life and every social stratum.

During its early days the Hung Men Society fabricated numerous myths about itself and adopted superstitious rites as a means of hiding its political objectives. After two hundred years, however, regionalism, as well as the very superstitious practices it had adopted as camouflage, diluted its political aims; and gradually its ranks came to include unscrupulous elements. It deteriorated into a typical secret society, indulging in questionable activities that brought it almost universal condemnation. The Society lost its prestige, and its branches were belittled. They were generally known disparagingly as "Hung bands" (pang), while local authorities dubbed them "bandit bands" (pang fei) or "society bandits" (hui fei).

It was no coincidence that the P'inghsiang-Liuyang region, in which my home was located, became an important Hung Chiang Society stronghold. Take as an example Shanglishih, the marketing center of northern P'inghsiang County in Kiangsi Province. Eighty li from the city of P'inghsiang, our county seat, it was less than twenty li from both Liling and Liuyang counties in adjoining Hunan Province. A waterway connected it with Changsha and Hankow. The crest of the Lohsiao Mountains ran along the Hunan-Kiangsi border there, and bamboo groves and forests thrived on the mountainous terrain. Handicrafts that flourished there included papermaking, firecrackers, and linen. They supplied a heavy traffic of peddlers and merchants who wandered throughout Hunan, Kiangsi, and Hupeh. The Lohsiao Mountains also cradled numerous primitive little coal mines, and armed feuds between individual miners and between rival mines were commonplace. Trouble also came from the small bandit gangs that roamed the forests. It was lawless conditions such as these that encouraged the development of secret societies, for people felt a need to organize themselves for mutual protection.

Several years before the Hung Chiang Society Rebellion, the Hung Chiang Society established numerous gambling dens along this rugged Hunan-Kiangsi border. The gambling system, known locally as *k'ai piao*,* resembled the one used by the flower societies in Shanghai. Runners ranged through the villages every morning soliciting bets for the daily drawings, which actually took place before the placement of bets. The results were announced at four or five o'clock every afternoon.

Hung Chiang Society leaders used the gambling runners to recruit members. If the Hunan authorities moved against them, they simply shifted their headquarters across the border into Kiangsi. They slipped back into Hunan when the Kiangsi authorities cracked down. Because the Kiangsi and Hunan authorities never seemed able to coordinate their actions, the Hung Chiang Society was free to develop pretty much as it wished. Within three to five years the gambling network grew large and strong, and more and more villagers joined the Society.

This occurred almost exclusively among the lower social strata. Most Hung Chiang Society members were peasants, handicraft workers, miners, traveling peddlers, and coolies. One characteristic of the Hung Chiang Society in this region was that scarcely any landlords, intellectuals, or gentry joined it. Moreover, most Hung Chiang leaders in the area came from the lower social strata themselves, and as time went on they were less and less able to attract members from above those strata.

They recruited members with promises of a brotherhood devoted to the righting of wrongs. People joined in the hope of gaining protection from being victimized in their produce businesses and their traveling occupations, and they expected a certain amount of aid in the face of difficulties. Since they were not bound by concrete obligations or strict regulations, most people that were not very well-off financially were happy to join the Society.

Furthermore, the gambling network, the nerve center of the Hung Chiang Society in our region, was well organized. While making a good deal of money, it achieved a reputation for reliability. It never cheated or bullied the villagers, and even wealthy families found nothing wrong

---

* In *k'ai piao* a bettor may select any one of thirty-six Chinese characters. The one character that wins pays thirty times the bet.

with participating in the gambling. Also reassuring was the fact that robberies diminished as the Hung Chiang Society appropriated the region as its own sphere of influence. Outside bandits dared not enter. On the whole, people did not regard the Hung Chiang Society as harmful to the community, but neither did they expect it to give birth to any dynamic action.

Several months before the 1906 rebellion, nevertheless, the political intent of the Hung Chiang Society leaders began to reveal itself. Winds of rumor blew, gradually intensifying. At first only anti-Manchu tales and myths were spread. But eventually specific instructions came, such as: "Should the day of Hung Chiang Society action arrive, every household must paste on its gate a sheet of yellow paper with the character 'Ming' written prominently on it. Households without the Ming sign on their gates belong to scum." Soon the Hung Chiang Society was emboldened to make public two slogans stating its objectives: "Overthrow the Ch'ing and Restore the Ming" and "Uproot the Rich and Succor the Poor."

"Overthrow the Ch'ing and Restore the Ming" was an old Hung Men Society slogan. By this time, of course, there was no Ming dynasty to restore; and the Society's main purpose was to stir up nationalistic feelings against the Manchus. "Uproot the Rich and Succor the Poor" was an even older slogan. Every rebellion throughout Chinese history has used a similar slogan. It was rather vague, to be sure, but generally it implied the distribution to the poor of money and grain confiscated from the rich.

As rebellion approached, the Hung Chiang Society invoked disciplinary measures to tighten its organization. A threat of truly severe punishment was contained in the old Hung Chiang slogan "Three Thrusts and Six Holes." It received such prominence shortly before the rebellion that even quarreling village children threatened their opponents with it. It warned that traitors, those who broke discipline, and those who violated important regulations would be run clear through with a sword three times. While such measures were seldom actually used, they sounded brutal enough to intimidate the villagers and keep Society members well under control.

In preparation for the rebellion, Hung Chiang Society members were organized in much the same way as troops. The smallest unit was composed of ten men living in the same locality, one of whose number was placed in command by the Hung Chiang Society leaders. A leader of one hundred men commanded each group of ten units, and over every ten of those groups was a commander. At the top were other ranking officers.

When the local Hung Chiang Society leaders decided that their ranks were large enough and that everything was in readiness, they planned a surprise attack.[1] The date was a carefully guarded secret. People in general had no knowledge of it, nor did the local authorities. The day that panic convulsed Shanglishih was the day the Hung Chiang leaders suddenly issued orders to assemble. Leaders of the units of ten, one hundred, and one thousand were ordered to marshal their men, who were instructed to bring along whatever weapons they had and march on given locations. The line of peasants that we three youngsters saw passing the Wen's shop was a column of these troops.

What the rebellious troops called themselves and the names and titles of their leaders were heard in many versions.[2] The only piece of information that was generally accepted was that Kung Ch'un-t'ai was the real head of the rebellion. He was known as the Great Commander-in-Chief of the Hung Chiang Society (Ta T'ou-mu or Ta T'ung-ling), and it was reportedly over his name that official notices were posted.

Kung Ch'un-t'ai, however, was Great Commander only in the P'inghsiang-Liuyang region and not the highest ranking leader of the Hung Chiang Society as a whole. It was said that he stood behind the most important gambling network. Seeing the rising revolutionary tide elsewhere in China and wanting to be acknowledged as a hero, he touched off the Hung Chiang Society Rebellion. It was rumored that he planned to assemble all of his forces at a point south of Liuyang, where he would take command and swoop down on the city. No doubt he expected to take it with ease. Once he had occupied Liuyang and unfurled the flag of rebellion there, he assumed that Hung Chiang Society branches spread out over the other counties would rise up in response.

Between the summer and autumn of 1906 drought had withered the Hunan-Kiangsi border region. By October people found rice selling at the price of pearls and firewood taking on the value of cinnamon; and a terrible insecurity gripped them. Kung Ch'un-t'ai, exploiting this famine, assured his followers that there would be rice for all when they took Liuyang and confiscated the wealth and grain of the rich people there. It was reported that among the troops marching on Liuyang, there were impoverished people carrying baskets to hold the grain that they expected to get. This factor was instrumental in gaining followers for Kung.

Kung Ch'un-t'ai and the other Hung Chiang Society leaders demonstrated a marked talent for recruiting members and managing their gambling network; but they fell far short when it came to making battle preparations. Kung assembled a column said to be twenty thousand strong—in itself a remarkable show of strength. Yet he failed to organize an effective command structure. At the last minute, commanders of all ranks, inexperienced to begin with, were pitched together for the first time. Moreover, logistic problems went unconsidered. As a result, during its two-day march the huge column was not fed at reasonable intervals; facilities for shelter were forgotten altogether; and hunger, cold, and fatigue bedeviled the troops. Nor was the morale of this column of peasants, who knew nothing about what was happening, ever boosted high enough. When they encountered difficulties, thoughts of desertion clogged their minds too easily, for they did not realize the serious consequences of defeat. So they returned home.

On the twenty-first day of the tenth moon (December 8, 1906) the rebellious column ran into resistance from a small rifle corps as it neared the city of Liuyang. The Liuyang County authorities, it turned out, had learned of the rebellion. Making frenzied efforts to defend the city, they closed its gates and tried to intercept the column by dispatching several dozen soldiers, armed with every rifle the city contained—twenty-six. The mission seemed hopeless, but there was nothing else to do. Yet sporadic shots from this rifle corps, firing across a river, halted the column. Rebel troops piled up in disorder, spreading out on both sides of the road down which they were marching. Before long, its faith shaken, the column went out of control. Rebel troops fled in batches until, it was said, desertions reached the proportion of a flood breaching an embankment. Officers tried to regroup and deploy the remaining troops. The avalanche of desertions made the troops feel isolated, however, and their morale was shattered. Sporadic activities continued for several days under the mounting threat of an all-out campaign by the government troops. But finally Society leaders conceded that the tide had turned irrevocably against them, and they disbanded their forces. The government then launched a shrill propaganda campaign. "One hundred thousand Hung Chiang Society rebels collapsed before twenty-six rifles," it bragged.

The attack on Liuyang was the rebellion's main act, and the column commanded by Kung Ch'un-t'ai was its leading actor.[3] At first, branches of the Hung Chiang Society in nearby northern P'inghsiang and southern Liuyang did stage uncoordinated uprisings in response. But when they learned that Liuyang had not been taken as planned and that the rebellion's mainstay had collapsed, they turned their rudders with the wind, disbanded, and went into hiding. Because they had never known unified leadership, the other Hung Chiang Society branches, which were numerous and widespread, did not even stage simultaneous uprisings. Thus the Hung Chiang Society Rebellion in 1906 miscarried as had so many other abortive Chinese uprisings led by secret societies or religious sects.

When the storm of the rebellion ended, government troops started a campaign to suppress the bandits. While my family realized that the rebellion was over, they were also fully aware that misery would continue to stalk the area for some time, for nobody knew quite what to expect from the government troops. To avoid trouble we children were sternly warned to guard our words, not even to mention the rebellion, and not to leave the house.

Several days after I returned home, a vengeful detachment of government troops arrived in our village. Typical of the old-style army of the Manchu dynasty, they were called "Green Braves" (Lui Yung). Every soldier wore a green vest emblazoned on the back with the large character for a "brave." Soldiers were called "braves" in those days.

That morning a platoon of more than twenty of them strode into our house, each carrying a saber and a few carrying rifles. As they ferociously barged in, one of them chopped the corner off an antique table in our hall with one fierce cut of his saber.

"You are in the center of the rebellious district," the platoon leader barked. "Why didn't you warn the government? The Imperial Court has decreed summary execution for all rebels, and the same punishment applies to people that withheld information. Any more of these damnable rebellions here, and we'll wipe out the entire population and burn every house to the ground."

My family elders, along with everyone else in our village, had always despised troops. To them, troops were a perverse crew of monstrous barbarians, too weak to suppress bandits but quite strong enough to bully the people; and the mere presence of the Green Braves left them stupefied with fear. Receiving the braves in hastily-donned court robes, our elders tried to pacify them by being humble.[4] Nobody dared to protest the soldiers' belligerence. It was a perfect illustration of the Chinese saying "When a scholar and a soldier meet, reason is on the soldier's side." Our elders put on court dress, naturally, to demonstrate their allegiance to the Manchus. More importantly, however, court dress afforded the wearer a certain immunity, for Manchu law decreed that not even officials and soldiers could humiliate the holders of Imperial degrees. And ours was a home of poetry and books.

For generation upon generation our people had been scholars. We were at the same time landed gentry; and in our vast, rambling house lived my grandfather and his five brothers and the families of all six of them, each with land that supplied an annual income from rent of between five hundred and one thousand *piculs** of grain. Four of these six brothers were qualified to wear Imperial hat buttons and court robes. Two had gained their Imperial degrees by passing the Hsiu Ts'ai examination,[5] while the other two had bought theirs by making donations to the State.[6] Abolition of the Imperial examination system began in my father's generation, however, when most people turned to modern schools for a better stepping stone to a career. My father was in the last group of students especially selected to sit for the provincial examinations, which he passed to become a *pa kung*.[7] But only two or three members of the family in his generation took Imperial degrees. (When the rebellion occurred, he was studying law at the Chekiang Institute of Legal Administration.)

Scholars, such as members of my family, cultivated an apathy toward local affairs and never even deigned to enter a government office. Truly, they did not know how to cope with the pugnacious Green Braves.

Fortunately, local officials—*pao cheng* and *lu cheng*—arrived hot on the heels of the Braves.[8] It was their official responsibility to receive the Green Braves in any case, and they were old hands at handling officials and soldiers. Their reception and the negotiations that followed changed the attitude of the Braves markedly—a change my family doubtless helped along with a considerable amount of money. In addition, we slaughtered pigs and lambs and feasted the soldiers as honored guests. Drunk and well fed, they lost their arrogance.

After dallying in our home for some time, the Green Braves left in search of "Society bandits." They rounded up every able-bodied man they could lay their hands on. Men in the fields and on the road and those found in a house-to-house search—peasants, handicraftsmen, and

---

* A weight equal to about 133 to about 143 pounds avoirdupois.

carrying coolies—were confined in a temple five li from our house. There the platoon leader ordered the gentry and local officials to pick out the rebels, who were to be executed on the spot.[9]

Once again a weighty problem confronted our family elders. They could not attend this ceremony in person, because if they did not identify anyone, they risked the accusation of withholding information and covering up for the rebels. On the other hand, they did not want to be put in a position of causing any deaths. Even more disturbing was the realization that for every man identified, others associated with him might also be victimized. This was something they had neither the heart nor inclination to cause. But here again a saying applied to the situation: "Money buys approval even from the gods." An arrangement was somehow made whereby the platoon leader agreed that children might identify the rebels; apparently this was the best bargain that could be struck. So our elders had no choice but to select several of the brighter children in the family to attend to this risky business. I was one of them.

Our parents carefully coached us in what to do. Then we followed the local officials and Green Braves to the temple. It was filled with terrorized prisoners. The Braves pointed to one man after another and demanded gruffly: "Is he a rebellious bandit? Speak up."

In front of each man we children shook our little heads and said no. Although our act continued for same time, the Braves were finally satisfied. Their knapsacks were no doubt already stuffed full with the fruits that they had harvested during three or four days in our village from wealthy families and from the arrested men. In any event, they had acquired enough to report fulfillment of the mission to their superiors. The prisoners were placed in the custody of local authorities, who released them on bail. But neighboring villages had a different experience. "Society bandits" were identified in some and were summarily executed. Their heads hung from the trees as a public warning.

Thus the curtain came down on an act filled with the menacing tenseness and terror of search, with suppression, arrest, and execution. The villagers all praised the way my family handled the incident, and they flocked to our house to express gratitude. Because I was among the children who had saved them, I was warmly embraced on many occasions. Actually, however, this was merely typical village-gentry behavior during the last days of the Manchus—minimization of large issues and mollification of everybody.

True peace did not return to our region for a long time after the rebellion. Government agents and troops continued to frequent the village, snooping about for hidden "Society bandits"; and unscrupulous members of the gentry and local despots capitalized on their visits to blackmail the villagers. Indeed not even the chickens and dogs of our village knew peace. For the Manchus in their last days understood only arbitrary suppression as a means of governing the country.

Of the revolutionary movements during the latter part of the Manchu dynasty, the Hung Chiang Society Rebellion had a relatively large mass base and its influence as a result was relatively broad. It was an important personal experience for people in the remote P'inghsiang-Liuyang region, and it remained the topic of conversation for many years. Time and again the curious pressed me to recount my dramatic experience.

Monarchists and other village conservatives could not but shake their heads sadly and sigh, "It looks as though the heavenly number of the Great Ch'ing is almost up." For they had seen the Hung Chiang Society create a large-scale rebellion overnight. They had seen, too, the inept fashion in which a fumbling officialdom had handled it.

Yet modern-minded people harbored radical thoughts. A majority of them were teachers and young intellectuals, of whom I was soon to meet many at the P'inghsiang County Public School. In their eyes the main cause of the rebellion was Manchu corruption. The government did nothing more than squeeze out our region's wealth by such means as a farm tax, *likin*,* other taxes, and assorted underhanded means. Government officials looked the other way while their agents stirred up trouble among the people. Officials seemed incapable of differentiating the bad from the good elements, nor were they moved by the people's suffering. Government officials drove the people to rebel.

Modern-minded people, moreover, blamed the failure of the Hung Chiang Society on its unsound leadership. They believed that it lacked sophisticated and capable men. It also lacked an inspiring manifesto. Even worse was its slogan "Overthrow the Ch'ing and Restore the Ming." The Ming dynasty had ceased to exist more than 260 years earlier. Where would they find a Ming dynasty to restore?[10] Furthermore, insufficient preparations had been made for the uprising. Its leaders lacked the foresight to buy up arms and ammunition. What could they hope to accomplish with a handful of bird guns, knives, and spears?

* A provincial duty placed upon articles of trade that are in transit.

As to strategy, they had failed to make the attack on Liuyang a surprise, nor had they cut the railway so as to block the arrival of Ch'ing reinforcements. Criticisms such as these, however, showed not that modern-minded men opposed the rebellion, as such, but that they regretted its failure.

The Manchu government classified rebellion as the most serious crime in the land and threatened to exterminate every rebel along with all his relatives. It worked desperately to put down rebellions. Nevertheless, popular pessimism, disheartenment, contempt, and hatred continued to mount against Manchu rule. These increased relentlessly until the Manchus fell.

Three years later I came to know a seventy-year-old watchman at the P'inghsiang County Public School who typified popular sentiments of the time. He had taken part in the Taiping Heavenly Kingdom Movement as a youth. In order to escape Manchu reprisals, he had changed his name and buried his past. But as anti-Manchu feelings again surged up, the defiant spirit of this husky, still able-bodied old soldier came to life once more. Throwing caution to the winds, he recounted to trusted students tales of the rebellion in which he had taken part. He told us how he had joined the Taiping Heavenly Kingdom Movement as a youth and how he had gone to war. And the telling of these tales so excited him that his eyebrows flew and his whole face danced. He thought that the leaders of the Hung Chiang Society Rebellion were incompetent. They were farcical compared to the Taipings. The Hung Chiang Society leaders, he assured us, had neither system nor method, nor was the face they presented to the world as impressive as that of the "Long Hairs."[11] We youngsters showed enormous respect for this "Long Hair" warrior and treated him as an old hero who had survived at least one hundred battles. In the school's tiny gatehouse we frequently bought him wine and food in exchange for thrilling anecdotes.

In KMT revolutionary records the Hung Chiang Society Rebellion is called the P'ing-Liu Campaign of 1906, the first of eight revolutionary movements started by the T'ung-meng Hui. It was also the third of ten unsuccessful rebellious movements instigated by Sun Yat-sen before the 1911 Revolution.[12] Dr. Sun himself pointed out that the T'ung-meng Hui exerted only a feeble influence over the P'ing-Liu Campaign.[13] Yet since Huang Hsing,[14] number two leader of the T'ung-meng Hui, conferred with Ma Fu-i, Great Dragon Head (Ta Lung T'ou) of the Hung

Chiang Society, in 1904 to plan an uprising,[15] the Hung Chiang Society Rebellion obviously did receive encouragement from the revolutionaries. Nevertheless, the Hung Chiang Society's approach to rebellion demonstrated a far stronger heritage of old Hung Men Society traditions than of modern revolutionary techniques. Revolutionary propaganda had yet to reach the people, and "Sun Yat-sen," "Huang Hsing," and "The Republic of China" were still unheard-of in the P'inghsiang-Liuyang region.

In P'inghsiang County Public School

In the spring of 1908 I entered P'inghsiang County Public School, which was one hundred li (about thirty-six miles) from my home, the only public school in the county. There I turned over another page of my childhood.

P'inghsiang County Public School was established following the campaign to "abolish [Imperial] examinations and set up schools."[16] A group of well-known old-style scholars ran it. Stressing the study of the Classics, they were extremely strict disciplinarians who would rather have died than allow heretical thoughts to enter the minds of their students. For it was their consuming wish that all students devote themselves to the accepted teachings of the ancients and observe in all matters the forms handed down through the ages.

Yet our science teachers were on the whole younger men with more modern minds. Their concept of education differed sharply from that of the men that ran the school. It was on the understanding of new things that they placed greatest emphasis. We were made to see that the earth was not flat after all, but a round, ball-like thing. We learned not only of Confucius but also of Napoleon, Washington, Newton, Watt, Rousseau, and others. Sages, it seemed, were born in the West as well as in the East, and curiously they did not necessarily always agree with one another. Thus in primary school the clashing intellectual currents of China and the West swirled about us.

The Manchu government established an additional military command (ping pei tao) in the district to suppress any further uprisings. A new official came to oversee it, a new office went up, and a military encampment was built. Modern rifle corps were stationed at the county seat and at adjoining strategic points. These new arrivals ran roughshod over the people, increasing their burdens and disrupting their lives in hundreds of scattered incidents. The new official regularly promulgated warnings against rebellion and, to show that they had teeth, executed revolutionists from time to time. Some students, myself among them, viewed these actions with smoldering indignation, calling them the last convulsions of the dying Manchus, whom we hated.

Change was inevitable. The mechanized Anyuan Coal Mine, sixteen li from P'inghsiang's county seat, was started by German interests in 1898, the twenty-fourth year of Kuang Hsü. In 1905 the railroad from Anyuan to P'inghsiang was extended to Chuchow and then on to Changsha soon afterward. Modern transportation and mining brought with them many social changes, the most distinctive of which was the transformation of a tiny shop selling foreign goods into P'inghsiang's largest store. Foreign cloth, foreign oil (kerosene), manufactured metal items, and other foreign products gradually spread over the countryside, posing a direct threat to the handicraft industries.

The invasion of backward areas by modern enterprises and imported goods often evokes general resistance from the established forces. So it happened in P'inghsiang. A weird variety of rumors circulated through the county seat and countryside. Some contended that the railroad destroyed *feng shui* (the mystic balance of nature), thereby disturbing ancestral graves. Others insisted that a child had to be fed into the locomotive's smokestack each day before it would run, and the same was reportedly true of the chimney at the coal mine. There was deep-seated hatred for such new monsters as trains and mechanized coal mines.

Foreign cloth, kerosene, and foreign lamps, moreover, were viewed as contemptible fads. Grandfather was outraged when I returned home one day dressed in a gown of foreign cloth; and the lamps and other foreign goods that my father brought with him from Shanghai deeply offended the eyes of our elders. They regarded foreign products with an uncompromising hatred; and they deplored their children's seeking after modern things while abandoning the old ones. For them the large-flowered Suchow and Hangchow silks and satins were still the only civilized garb. Before the changes taking place under their eyes, however, they could do little more than shake their heads and sigh, "The ancient ways are no longer enshrined in the hearts of men, and the world sinks deeper into damnation every day."

But a wise geography teacher at our school, Mr. Huang, saw things differently. He saw that the railroad had indeed broken the rice bowls of numerous coolies, sedan-chair bearers, and boatmen. It was also true that the mechanized coal mine had seriously hurt many little native mines and that imported goods had displaced native products. Yet what good was accomplished merely by hating and cursing? China could no longer isolate herself by closing her gates. China had to build herself up. There was nothing wrong with railroads, mines, and foreign goods, he assured us; not if the Chinese could build their own machines and manage their own enterprises. We students, seeing with our own eyes the advantages of the new things, could no longer accept the validity of the old thinking. Daily we became more enamored of Huang's position.

To fight all that was old, rotten, and senseless; to make China wealthy and powerful; to stop Chinese from being the sick men of East Asia became the goals of aspiring young men. Bound feet, opium, superstition, and bureaucracy became the targets we hit hardest.

The binding of women's feet was an evil tradition with long roots in China. Now, when girls in our homes or in other families were forced to bind their feet, we charged furiously in and created a scene. Denouncing the practice as cruelty toward women, we insisted it would weaken the race and the country.

There were few opium smokers in P'inghsiang. There were, nevertheless, occasions when we students stealthily destroyed the opium-smoking apparatus of relatives and friends.

Thunderously we stormed temples, smashed images of the gods, and campaigned against medical cures dispensed by clay idols. Naturally we were in constant conflict with pious and religiously faithful people.

The belligerant way in which officials and agents went about extorting money and bullying the people also infuriated us; and at the slightest excuse we mocked and humiliated them. Purposefully we went about shattering the prestige and dignity of the government agencies.

These were the acts of a rudimentary social reform movement. But they were neither widespread nor organized, and more often than not they flared up on the spur of the moment.

Far better organized—and more nationalistic than social—was the movement against wearing a queue. This symbolized an important anti-Manchu position; and youths supported it with special enthusiasm.[17] In November, 1908, the Emperor Kuang Hsü and the Empress Dowager departed this world. That month I returned to school from a visit home wearing the traditional badge of mourning on my queue.[18] Such a shower of mockery descended on me from my schoolmates, however,

that I tore it off as fast as I could. Yet it was not merely that my schoolmates opposed wearing mourning for the Throne. They despised having
to wear a queue as well. At first they complained that queues soiled
their clothes, that they were ugly and inconvenient. Later, however,
queues were reviled as the tails of pigs and were secretly referred to as
a symbol of Han Chinese enslavement by the Manchus.

One night in 1909 a handful of my schoolmates produced several
pairs of sharp scissors with which they first cut their own queues. Their
plan called for cutting the queue of every other student in school; and
if they got away with that, they intended to cut the queues of our sleeping teachers and headmaster. Before their naive minds, no doubt, floated
the tantalizing picture of four hundred tailless teachers and students.
They were caught, however, after disposing of the twenty-ninth queue.
The headmaster and our dormitory proctor wailed as though they had
just lost their parents. For this deed was close enough to rebellion to
make them fear not only that they would be charged with lax teaching
but that they would lose their heads.

Our school fell under the jurisdiction of the P'inghsiang Board of
Education, whose chairman assumed ultimate responsibility for the
queue-cutting incident. His name was Yü Chao-fan, and he was a Han-
lin.[19] A well-known monarchist, who had been Deputy Governor (Pu-
cheng Shih)[20] of Chekiang Province, he was living at home, observing
the traditional period of mourning for his dead father. This was why he
was available for work on the local board of education. The old gentleman rushed to our school from his country home when he heard the
shocking news. In a pained but coldly severe voice he excoriated us,
"Queue-cutting is rebellion. It is absolutely forbidden."

The board chairman was related to our family; and he showed
especial concern for me and several other relatives by scolding us with
particular harshness. Fortunately this Manchu bureaucrat maintained
very close relations with the local government. By shrewd, capable
maneuvering, he was able to smooth over the catastrophe.

The twenty-nine queueless students each received two large and
two small demerits—just one small demerit short of expulsion—and were
confined to school until their queues had grown back. After that the
school became even more strict, as its administrators did everything
possible to keep heresy from creeping into it again. Students were forbidden to discuss current events. We were expected to turn our hearts
and minds entirely toward studying the classics.

We managed, nevertheless, to garner from a few teachers and relatives news of the monarchical reform movement and of the anti-Manchu revolutionary movement. The "new" publications from Shanghai and Tokyo were banned throughout the area, as in my school. Spotty transportation, furthermore, made it difficult for them to reach the area; and they were most difficult to get. But some of my schoolmates would occasionally get clippings from them from Shanghai or Changsha. They were like supreme treasures. We read them secretly and passed them along; and with our heads close together, we whispered about them.

For the thinking of youths in general was moving from scattered social reforms to more radical political reform. Japan, under the Meiji Restoration, defeated China in 1894 and went on to defeat a far more powerful Russia next. This example of a country grown strong through reform greatly stimulated the youth of China. Certainly it increased their hatred of the Manchu government's insupportably stubborn conservatism and rottenness, which would clearly lead to the eventual extinction of China and the Chinese. This soul-searing belief was shared by most young people. But as in all things under the sun, the same stimulus in the same setting can result in different conclusions. The school of reformism held that China could grow strong through a constitutional monarchy patterned after the Meiji Restoration. Revolution against the Manchus, they believed, would produce a period of prolonged chaos, which would result in the catastrophe of China being cut up like a melon and devoured. The revolutionary school, however, held that talk of reform within the monarchical framework was like a fool's raving about his dreams. There could be no salvation for China short of totally overthrowing the Manchus. As Sun Yat-sen's revolutionary concepts and the reformism advocated by K'ang Yu-wei and Liang Ch'i-ch'ao circulated among us, arguments boiled up.

Since the Emperor Kuang Hsü, imprisoned as a result of the Hundred Days of Reform, died only one day before the Empress Dowager, almost everyone was convinced that his death was the result of a venomous conspiracy by the Empress Dowager's clique.[21] In any event, this shameful court tragedy robbed the reformists of the basis for their program of preserving the monarchy. P'u Yi ascended the throne at the age of three, and Tsai Li became regent. Contrary to what was expected, with Tsai Li as regent the power of the court nobles increased.[22] All pretense of setting up a constitutional monarchy became an obvious hoax. Then the government announced the nationalization of railroads in order to use them as collateral for foreign loans. This not only robbed those who had invested in the railroads but also gave people the impression that the loss of the railroads would eventually lead to the loss of the whole country. This finally touched off the "Save the Railroads" campaign in Szechwan, Hunan, Hupeh, Kwangtung, and other provinces.[23] These signs clearly pointed toward the end of the Manchu dynasty; and each day they pushed the youths in my school closer to the revolutionary school of thought.

The revolution in those days was a movement of the youth, with modern-minded intellectuals as its backbone. Students that had returned from abroad and students from the modern schools in China made up a hotbed of revolution. A step forward was taken when Sun Yat-sen's revolutionists encouraged young people to join the New Army of the Manchus in order to gain military experience. As they did so, revolutionary activities expanded from attempts to win over secret societies to include attempts to win over troops.

In the years 1910 and 1911 a majority of my schoolmates even went so far as to break with the traditional concept that "good men are no more used as soldiers than good iron is used for nails." They came to accept the idea that "the body of a real man should be sent home wrapped in horse hide"[24]—in other words, that death in battle was a glorious death. They considered it an honor to join the New Army. Hiding their feelings from both their families and the school authorities, they secretly filled out application forms, even forging the seals of guarantors; and off they went to sit for the enlistment examinations. Some of my underage schoolmates joined them. Some, but not all, acted with the clear belief that "only if you join the New Army and take up arms can the revolution be carried out."

The school authorities were naturally shocked to discover that so many radicals had suddenly disappeared. To absolve themselves from the possibility of being held responsible for these disappearances, they investigated all cases thoroughly and did everything possible to prevent further disappearances.

I was among the youngest in school, only thirteen or fourteen years of age—too young to join the New Army. The school authorities regarded me as a model student. Actually, however, I was as enthusiastic about joining the New Army as those who disappeared; and I secretly helped them to raise money for the trip and to forge the necessary documents. Such things often had to be done after the school's lights were out and everybody had gone to bed. By the light of tiny wax candles, carefully shielded beneath mosquito nets and blankets, we would work in bed. As an extra precaution, student lookouts were posted inside and outside the bedrooms to send and receive coded warning knocks at the approach of a dormitory proctor.

Amidst such developments as these the Double Ten insurrection at Wuchang occurred, shaking the entire country. It was 1911. Revolutionists at Wuchang, who had close connections with New Army elements there, originally planned the uprising for the twenty-fifth day of the eighth moon (October 16). But on the eighteenth day there was an explosion in a secret revolutionary hideaway where bombs were being manufactured. In the search that followed, Manchu agents got hold of a book containing the names of revolutionists. For this reason the revolutionists decided to start the insurrection the following day, October 10.

Hsiung Ping-k'un, a revolutionist member of the Left Corps of the Engineering Regiment of the New Army, fired the first shot. He and the comrades in his unit killed their regimental commander, staged a fierce attack on the Ch'u Wang T'ai arsenal, and then charged into the walled city and attacked the governor's headquarters. Jui-cheng, the incompetent and cowardly governor of Hupeh, and Chang Piao, the ill-informed commander of the New Army there, fled headlong. Thus, Wuchang was unexpectedly captured by the revolutionary army.[25] Hankow and Hanyang were also occupied; yet the leader of the revolution, Sun Yat-sen, was still in the United States, while Huang Hsing was in Hong Kong. In this action the revolutionists and the rebellious troops, in an unpremeditated move, forced Li Yuan-hung, deputy commander of the New Army at Wuchang, to become commander (tu tu) of the "Hupeh Army of the Revolutionary Army of the Military Government of the Republic of China."[26] That was how the uprising started.

P'inghsiang was as startled as the rest of the country by the Wuchang Uprising. My father made a special trip to the county seat to bundle me home. On the twenty-second of October the city of Changsha in Hunan Province announced its independence of the throne. Kiukiang and Nanchang in Kiangsi Province followed suit on the twenty-third and the thirty-first of October, respectively. Other cities also responded to the revolution. P'inghsiang declared for the revolution on the third of November.[27] Yang Hui-k'ang, the ranking military affairs official (ping pei tao) there, and Ch'i Pao-chan, the commander under him, fled. Hu Piao, commander of the Second Regiment of the 54th Battalion (piao), became military governor (tu tu) as a result of support from the revolutionists; and headquarters for the tu tu were set up. Notices were posted everywhere to solicit funds and recruit soldiers. Though some chaos and confusion were unavoidable, nevertheless the revolutionary acts were in the main colorful and high-sounding.

My family adopted a wait-and-see attitude toward the revolution, however. Our elders maintained a tight rein on the younger set and insisted that we keep our queues. While the situation had clarified itself, there would be time enough for decision. On the one hand, they knew that they could no longer rely on the great Ch'ing Empire; but on the other hand, rumor had it that Sun Yat-sen was no more than a traveling political herbalist, a fast-talking quack.

My young uncles, brothers, and cousins, however, frequently gathered in the family hall for heated discussions of current affairs. Inclining more and more toward revolution, we were disgruntled by the discipline imposed on us by our elders. And one day twenty youngsters in the family assembled in the family hall and defiantly cut their queues. I was one of them. This was a dramatic and very important act; and it placed our helpless family elders in a most awkward position. Yet at the bottom of their hearts they may have endorsed such deeds, while considering them perhaps a bit premature. Feeling that we had got the upper hand in any event, the younger set went on to demand permission to join the revolutionary army, to publicize the revolution, or to work for it. Our joy at the Manchus' downfall and the birth of the Republic of China, now irrepressible, burst forth without reserve.

The tidal wave of revolution battered my old family. Something my mother said years later may best illustrate the effect of its impact. It was on a moonlit winter night in 1938 at Liutangchen, a suburb of Kweilin. Japanese planes were bombing Kweilin. My aging mother, reminiscing about our old home, was talking to me of family affairs.

"My son, do you still remember your maternal grandmother's home?" she asked. "You were there when you were eight."

"I remember a little, Mother," I replied.

"Do you remember Grandmother's garden with its crescent-shaped pool, the profusion of flowers and trees? It was in beautiful taste. At the front gate was a tall flagpole, and banners festooned the main hall.[28] That large family at Wenchiashih, in Liuyang County, was kind and scholarly. Just and honorable, they never wanted for food or clothes. But these thirty years of change and chaos have brought the Liu family to the verge of utter collapse. All that remains now is a young man, your cousin, who has gone away to make his living as a manual laborer.

"Our family has not fared much better than Grandmother's. In the late Ming or early Ch'ing, our ancestors moved to the mountain region between the two provinces, although I don't know why. We settled down easily and got along fine even though we were 'guest people' (K'o-chia). The Long Hairs came, and other rebellions occurred; but our elders say we never suffered serious losses. Our six families living together included more than one hundred people. We worked hard, farmed hard, studied hard, and led a frugal life. Not one of us smoked opium or gambled or got into trouble. On the contrary, we did much charitable work. Relatives, clansmen, neighbors, and local villagers felt free to visit us often, for we liked and respected each other. Everything went so smoothly that we enjoyed settling there.

"And then the Hung Chiang Society Rebellion brought both soldiers and bandits to our house; and from then on there were no peaceful days. There was the anti-Manchu revolution, the battles between warlords, the Northern Expedition, the Peasant Associations, and the Communists— each one more violent than the last. One sentence could not contain the sufferings our family endured. When the Nationalists and Communists started fighting each other, more often than not it was the area around our home that they most wanted to take. One day what you call the Red Army guerrillas would come; and their headquarters would always be set up in our house. What you call the Political Defense Bureau was always set up there, too. People were imprisoned in our house; reactionaries were executed there. And the next day the Bandit Suppression Armies would come. They also were stationed in our house. In the same way, they imprisoned people and executed them. Each has come and gone away and returned again. I don't know how many times that has happened. A curse has almost literally fallen on our old house. The ancient furniture, the old books, the paintings, are all gone. The floors have been dug up to a depth of three feet by people searching for gold, silver, and other treasures. The hills around our home are all barren now, for our precious tea oil trees have all been cut down for firewood."

My mother recalled the suffering caused our family by both Nationalists and Communists. She recalled the outrage that my eighty-nine-year-old grandfather felt when he was subjected to public trial by the Peasant Association, when he had to flee the house in his old age, and when the guerrillas kidnapped his second daughter. She also reminisced about my father, who had been dead for eight years. Although he underwent years of grinding torment and was terribly unhappy in his later years on my account, he still loved his Communist son without bitterness or complaint. She further recalled that because I was a prominent Communist, National Government officials and agents time after time trampled over our family. Briefly she touched upon the facts that of her six children, two sons and one daughter died during this period of chaotic change and that she had almost lost her life one time while escaping the scene of battle.

Sadness weighed her down as she relived these events. Gamely, however, she fought back her feelings and continued brokenly, "This chaos dispersed our big family. Some abandoned their ancestral home and settled down elsewhere. Although I too have spent much time away from that house, there was no time when I did not long for it; and I have spent more time than anyone else watching over it. Now, among those of you who survive, some are opium addicts, some are gamblers, some have joined secret societies, some are Nationalists, and some are Communists. There are among you those who get along very well indeed, but there are others who are hopelessly impoverished. Each flies in his own personal direction, pursuing his own career irrespective of the others. Only once a year, on my birthday, when twenty or so of you come to congratulate me, do I glimpse what remains of the imposing family we once had."

I tried my best to soothe my seventy-two-year-old mother, pointing out that there had indeed been an excess of things that could cause grief, among them my own adventures and experiences. With a heavy heart I said, "If I could return to my childhood and live life over again, there would be much less cause for regret."

Then my mother said, "I don't like to mention the heartbreaking past, but you have been away from our old home for twenty-six years, and there has been no way for us to send word to each other. I recount these things now only because you do not know what went on at home. I have often heard people say that all these sufferings are caused by circumstances, by the fact that times change too quickly, because the struggle between new and old is too violent. Suffering, fear, and danger are inevitable if one wishes to live in this epoch. That's all right. If only the war against Japan is won, maybe better days will follow."

It was with a mixture of despair, sadness, and regret that my old mother hoped.

The Republic

Formal establishment of the Republic of China took place on New Year's Day, 1912. Thinking people all over the country were exuberant, believing that the country and its people would experience a vital turn for the better merely because several thousand years of dictatorship had ended. The exalted revolutionists of the time had aimed only at overthrowing the Manchus. Loudly had they sung their anti-Manchu chorus, for most of them assumed that the end of the Manchu dynasty would automatically solve all problems. Yet the monarchy in its last days was a rotting ship which was incapable of withstanding the slightest revolutionary winds and waves. The salvation of this vast, old, debilitated China from the silkworm-like nibblings and whale-sized gulps of the foreigners and from its own backwardness and restrictive traditionalism was not to be accomplished in one day. Still, it was precisely this fact that thoughtful people did not realize and that they were utterly unprepared for. Nor was the revolutionary camp strong enough. Nourished as an embryo under such circumstances, the Republic of China had to struggle against suffering and difficulties from its very first birth cry.

On December 29, 1911, representatives from seventeen provinces met at Nanking to elect a provisional president and to organize a provisional central government of the Republic of China.[29] They elected Sun Yat-sen president by sixteen votes. Arriving in Nanking from Shanghai, he took the oath of office on January 1, 1912, organized a government, and issued the Republic's declaration of establishment. On January 28 the conference of provincial representatives was renamed the Provisional Senate, and it went to work on a provisional constitution.

Circumstances following the Wuchang Uprising had meanwhile forced the Manchu court to lean heavily upon Yuan Shih-k'ai, for he had created a special position for himself through the New Army, which he headed. The court decreed Yuan governor of Hunan, Hupeh, Kwangtung, and Kwangsi provinces on October 14, 1911. His assignment was to squash the revolution. On November 2 another decree made him premier of the cabinet, giving him sole administrative and military authority. With full military power and a court utterly dependent upon him, Yuan on the one hand made exorbitant demands of the Manchus and began to put pressure on the Emperor to abdicate. On the other hand, after defeating the revolutionary armies at Hsiaokan, Hankow, and Hanyang, he halted. He had demonstrated that his power could bring victory to either side. Then he proceeded to negotiate a truce with the revolutionary armies. As a condition for supporting the Republic, he insisted upon the presidency for himself and command of the army in the new government for his right-hand man.

The great revolutionists in Nanking seemed to think that the most important thing was that a Republican signboard be hoisted even though it might not be hoisted entirely in their way. So they assumed a compromising attitude toward Yuan Shih-k'ai. Under these circumstances, on February 13, 1912, Sun Yat-sen handed his resignation to the Provisional Senate and recommended Yuan Shih-k'ai as his successor. The next day the Senate unanimously elected Yuan Shih-k'ai president. Meanwhile, the Emperor accepted the Terms of Special Treatment agreed to in the North-South truce negotiations[30] and decreed his own abdication on February 12.[31] Having achieved exactly what he wanted, Yuan Shih-k'ai assumed the provisional presidency.

Modern-minded people in our village were rather at a loss about what to make of these events. On the one hand they recognized the great power of Yuan Shih-k'ai, and yearning for peace, they strongly hoped that he could unify China so that they might stroll into a prosperous republican period. On the other hand, however, they had no praise for Yuan's past. Some regarded him as just another powerful minister of the Manchu dynasty and jokingly called him Lord Yuan, the honored title he had enjoyed in the Ch'ing court. Moreover, Yuan had betrayed T'an Ssu-t'ung[32] during the Hundred Days of Reform—an act that was condemned as truly contemptible and that had long given Yuan a bad name in our village. For T'an Ssu-t'ung, a well-known reformist, was born in Liuyang, a neighboring county. Quite a few people, in our village knew some personal anecdote or other about him, and he was universally respected for his scholarly achievements and exemplary life. Because of Yuan, T'an was executed. Yet overnight Yuan Shih-k'ai had become the head of the Republic. People did not know whether to rejoice or cry.

Although it seemed that China had merely tacked up a new signboard on its old structure, some reforms were achieved. The resented queues were openly cut, a majority of the tyrannical ceremonies were abolished, and speech became relatively free. County magistrates were no longer called the "official parents of the people." No longer were the populace the "lowly people" or the "sons of officialdom." Instead they were called great citizens of the Republic of China. And, amazingly, the great citizens had voting rights. These visible benedictions were bestowed by the Republic.

The 1911 Revolution caused no major destruction to the country; yet the government and people, impoverished for years and years, remained poor. Take, for example, the financial condition of the Peking government, which had to use more than half of its total annual income to repay foreign debts and indemnities.[33] Still in the process of establishing its authority, the government increased its expenditures while its income dwindled. In addition to raising loans to meet daily expenditures, the Peking government created new taxes and increased the rates of existing taxes. Since most provinces were semiautonomous, raising their own funds to meet their own needs, they followed accepted practice and issued their own currency. As a result the people were faced with all sorts of coins and notes that had little real value and with ever-increasing taxation. Furthermore, Yuan Shih-k'ai kept the country under his thumb by scattering over it large and small warlords that owed him allegiance; and they ran wild.

In March or April, 1912, I returned to P'inghsiang County Public School to continue my studies. The primary school had changed its name to P'inghsiang Public Middle School, and it had been taken over by so-called modern-minded persons. By that time P'inghsiang County's own tu tu office was dissolved, and county administration had been restored to the control of the Kiangsi provincial tu tu. Order in the city had been restored, but a special revolutionary atmosphere still permeated it. Numerous people left-over from the Manchu dynasty modernized themselves overnight, spitting out new expressions at the slightest opportunity. Nor was our school free from the curious spectacle that the change of government brought about. The modernists in charge of our school, while they realized that the traditions of the past were now outmoded, did not really understand what the new things were that were supposed to accompany this new term—the Republic of China—and some confusion in these matters was evident.

Soon afterwards Huang Hsing, the great revolutionist, honored our city with a visit. He was touring his native Hunan Province. Assuming a personal relationship to the P'ing-Liu Campaign, he made a special pilgrimage to this revolutionary landmark where the first uprising took place. Faculty and students at my school welcomed him at a rally that was crowded with many modern-minded outsiders. They were all delighted to look upon this great revolutionist and to hear his exalted revolutionary theories. His bearing was impressive, and the stumps of his two missing fingers, an honorable badge of his revolutionary past, made him seem even more impressive. But his speech made no impression on me at all, perhaps because his Hunan accent was not easily understood.

Generally speaking, peace followed Yuan Shih-k'ai's assumption of the provisional presidency. The senate convened on April 29, 1912, at Peking. It drafted organizational regulations for a two-house parliament and rules for the election of senators and representatives. These were announced by the Peking government on August 10, and they were greeted optimistically as a suitable foundation for the Republic of China. Most revolutionists, assuming that the destructive phase of the revolution had ended, believed that the constructive phase was now beginning and that emphasis quite properly belonged upon electing a parliament. Our school, too, was influenced by this attitude. Teachers and students alike viewed the country's future with optimism and passed their time happily, at peace with the world. The only exception came when we students stormed the city's largest temple, the temple of the city god. That was the most drastic revolutionary action we took during this period, and it evoked uniform public indignation. The school authorities also frowned upon such destructive activities now that the Republic had been established; and we were cautioned against doing such things again.

The KMT (Kuomintang) was formed in August, 1912, to take part in the parliamentary election. It was an amalgamation of the Alliance Association (T'ung-meng Hui), the United Republican Party (T'ung-i Kung-ho Tang), the Association for National Advancement (Kuo-min Kung-chin Hui), the National Public Party (Kuo-min Kung Tang), and the Association for the Actual Advancement of the Republic (Kung-ho Shih-chin Hui). But Sun Yat-sen, the man who had resigned the presidency, took no part in these practical politics. He announced that he would devote himself instead to promoting his ambitious plan for constructing one hundred thousand kilometers of railroad. This plan, however, was generally regarded as not immediately realizable, and the derisive nickname "Big Gun Sun" achieved even wider currency.

Sun Yat-sen had always been a farsighted man of large visions, but his followers did not generally understand his radical stand. While Sun refused to make the disastrous compromises entailed in party politics of the day, Huang Hsing became politically active, and Sung Chiao-jen even more so.[34] Sung, with his roseate dreams of what would be accomplished by party politics in China at that time, differed sharply with Sun. It was he who was chiefly responsible for forming the KMT. He believed a KMT cabinet could control Yuan Shih-k'ai and thereby realize the ideals of the revolution.

When the results of the parliamentary election were announced in February, 1913, moreover, the KMT did hold a majority.[35] As a result of this victory, Sung Chiao-jen seemed certain to head the first cabinet to be formed by an elected political party.

But this reckoned without Yuan Shih-k'ai, who had all along fought the KMT both openly and in secret. The election made the KMT and the parliament it controlled nails in his eye. Sung Chiao-jen loomed up as his arch political enemy; and this led to the assassination of Sung Chiao-jen in Shanghai's North Station on March 20, 1913, shortly before Parliament was scheduled to convene for the first time. Everything indicated that Yuan Shih-k'ai and his prime minister, Chao Ping-chun, were behind the move.[36] The incident shocked China and the world. Naturally, revolutionists made the loudest cries of outrage. The Sung case marked the beginning of an open split between the KMT and Yuan Shih-k'ai.

Yuan, intoxicated by dreams of becoming emperor, was incapable of fitting into the mold of modern democratic politics. He had earlier appointed a tu tu of Chihli without the countersignature of the cabinet that had been formed by T'ang Shao-yi, thereby destroying the cabinet system. Yet even then he could not act entirely as he had wished, but had to cloak his deeds in quasi-legal forms. Growing bolder after the Sung case, however, he turned openly toward destruction of the KMT. He had strengthened his financial position by signing the huge Rehabilitation Loan with the Five Power Consortium,[37] and after bolstering his military position, he moved to replace the three tu tu in Kiangsi, Anhwei, and Kwangtung. All three of the incumbents were KMT members. Sun Yat-sen retaliated by calling for resistance. The result was the first open battle against Yuan—the Kiangsi-Nanking Campaign.[38] On July 12, 1913, Li Lieh-chün, the Kiangsi tu tu, fired the first shot at Hukou in Kiangsi. Although Anhwei, Kiangsu, Kwangtung, Hunan, and Fukien responded, they were rapidly defeated by the superior military strength of Yuan Shih-k'ai.

With Yuan Shih-k'ai's power at its height, some hypocritical revolutionists in our city and in our school suddenly began praising him. Nevertheless, radical elements among the students and some of the teachers despised Yuan. A majority of my schoolmates that joined the army around the time of the revolution were under the command of Li Lieh-chün; and most of them were missing after the Hukou battle. Sadly we thought of them.

Revolution was rooted in P'inghsiang, and revolutionaries had always been active there. While my sympathies were all with the revolution, however, I knew nothing of the inner workings of the KMT and did not join it. Now I was introduced to it by an older schoolmate nicknamed "Dwarf" Ch'en, who turned out to be an underground KMT agent in the struggle against Yuan Shih-k'ai. He lived in the Ch'en clan's temple, where he had two rooms of his own. Often he gave shelter there to transient revolutionists. Since we saw eye to eye on most things and since I shared my views with him, he accepted me as a trusted friend from whom he hid nothing. More than that, I often joined him in meeting clandestine visitors and seeing them off. I helped him to handle secret shipments of arms, ammunition, and other revolutionary appurtenances. We would have been executed had we been caught. But by working under the cover of our student uniforms, we lessened the risk of this. In any event, I began to learn the practical work of revolution.

An open-hearted youth, I was as outspoken as I was naive; and sympathy for Sun Yat-sen and his revolutionary group involved me in numerous arguments. Antirevolutionists kept their eyes on me as a result.

Deportment in P'inghsiang Public Middle School during this chaotic time was far from good. Students grew unruly and riotous, and they frequently defied regulations by gambling. And when during the Lunar New Year in February, 1914, several primary school students were caught playing a harmless New Year's game of chance, they were severely punished. I stepped forward in their defense, arguing about it with the dormitory proctor. Proctor Yen promptly charged me with using impertinent language and insulting him. He demanded my dismissal. Several students and teachers urged me to lighten my punishment by repenting before the headmaster; but I refused. In any case, I had decided to enter a better middle school, which I had always wanted to attend, in the provincial capital. So I left P'inghsiang Public Middle School for Nanchang to continue my studies in Hsinyuan Middle School.

Hsiung Yu-hsi originally started Hsinyuan Middle School to teach his own children and those of his relatives. But it attracted so many other students that it quickly became a very famous Kiangsi institution. Emphasizing science and English, it encouraged graduates to continue their studies at Tsinghua, other modern universities, or abroad. Mr. Hsiung, a well-known educator in his own right, was a good friend of Yen Fu—the scholar famous for introducing Western studies to China; and Hsinyuan students especially admired the great name of Yen Fu and the Western ideas that he had introduced.[39] This was indeed a vast improvement over P'inghsiang Public Middle School. Teachers and students got along well with each other; and everyone willingly buried himself in study. Typical of the atmosphere was the fact that we all called our headmaster "Monkey" Hsiung, an affectionate nickname obviously inspired by his face.

As a new arrival from P'inghsiang Public Middle School, I busied myself catching up to a much higher level in English and science. Under the school's influence, my chief interest settled upon science courses. I began preparing for college engineering studies. At the same time I poured over Yen Fu's translation of *On Evolution,* the first translation of any kind that I had read carefully. Here it was that my intellectual life passed beyond merely studying the classics. I began to knock at the door of modern knowledge.

When the European war broke out in July of that year, however, it disrupted the atmosphere of quiet study in our school. Japan declared war on Germany on August 23; and on September 2 Japanese forces landed in Shantung Province. Ignoring a protest from our Minister of Foreign Affairs, they occupied the Tsinan railway station on October 6 and took over management of the German-operated Chiao-Chi Railroad. On November 7 Japan occupied the German-leased territory of Tsingtao. These moves roused the indignation of us students. As we saw it, Japan was merely making use of this wartime opportunity to realize her pent-up aggressive ambitions in China.

Then on January 18, 1915, the Japanese minister to Peking, Hioki, presented secretly and in person the Twenty-one Demands to Yuan Shih-k'ai.[40] Newspapers all over the country published this news in large headlines, treating it as the first important Japanese step toward the annexation of China at a time when the Powers were too preoccupied to look eastward. Japan had used her declaration of war on Germany as a pretext for carrying out her plan. This news aroused everyone—

from headmaster to youngest pupil—more than anything before had. All of us believed that the life or death of China hinged on the Twenty-one Demands and that we had no alternative but to rise up and fight.

Consumed now by an interest in current events, I began reading newspapers and magazines regularly. At the same time I began to see myself as a grown man with a mind of my own; and a battle arose between my desire to learn more about science and my enthusiasm for national affairs. My enthusiasm for national affairs won. Ultimately it made me a zealous patriot.

At three o'clock on the afternoon of May 7, Japan had the effrontery to present an ultimatum to our country. It insisted upon a satisfactory reply to the Twenty-one Demands before six o'clock on the evening of May 9. The Peking government was forced to its knees; and the whole country considered this event the greatest humiliation China had ever suffered.

Many of my schoolmates and I were naturally crushed and outraged by this event. Although there was no student-body organization, we frequently went out in groups to preach against Japan and to advocate an embargo on Japanese goods, an idea that we had picked up from the newspapers.[41] A fanatical patriotic zeal got hold of me, and I began to pore over the modern history of China and accounts of how India and Korea had lost their sovereignty. Many were the discussions I had with teachers and friends about how to save our country. Sometimes I believed that Christianity offered a solution. At other times I was convinced that physical education, a new idea in China then, was the key to national salvation. With all of my heart and mind I sought a way to save my country.

Misfortune and suffering had haunted China for years. One calamity had followed closely upon another. And now, instead of seeking ways to defend China against Japan, Yuan Shih-k'ai was openly betraying the Republic while scheming to make himself emperor. This scheming went as far back as October 6, 1913, when in his high-handed way he had forced Parliament to officially elect him president. After that he trampled Parliament under foot, outlawed the KMT, and set up a State Council. He scrapped the provisional constitution that had been drawn up during the first year of the Republic, arbitrarily replacing it with the "New Constitution," which made Yuan the so-called Lifetime President. Under it he not only had power and authority comparable to an emperor but also had the sole say in appointing a successor. Yet Yuan and his eldest son were still not satisfied. The only way to ensure that a Yuan empire would pass from generation to generation was to have an enthronement. Hence, in August of 1915 a plot to restore the monarchy, secretly masterminded by Yüan K'e-ting, the eldest son of Yuan Shih-k'ai, began to be staged, act after act.

At first F. J. Goodnow, Yuan's American advisor, and a Japanese named Ariga Nagao wrote articles advocating a constitutional monarchy. Then, on August 14, Yang Tu, Sun Yu-yun, Yen Fu, Liu Shih-p'ei, Li Hsieh-ho, and Hu Ying—the so-called Six Gentlemen[42]—proposed organizing the Ch'ou An Society in Peking. They used the pretext of studying the question of the most suitable form of government for China, but actually they designed the society in order to promote the establishment of Yuan's dynasty. On August 23 the Ch'ou An Society was founded. To all ruling provincial military and civil officials and to civil organizations it sent telegrams advocating a constitutional monarchy. On October 8 Yuan Shih-k'ai announced regulations for organizing a national assembly. Its members were delegates in the provinces. They would vote upon the form of national government by sending ballots to Peking, where Yuan would count them and announce the results. This farce began in the provinces on October 28, and, not unexpectedly, when the 1,993 ballots were counted in Peking, they were declared to unanimously favor a constitutional monarchy. On December 11 Yuan's State Council blatantly played the role of a body "representing all the citizens of China" and openly urged Yuan to accept the throne. On the twelfth, after having once declined in order to carry out the forms of modesty, Yuan accepted.

During that period branches of the Ch'ou An Society, the Joint Association for a Petition (Ch'ing-yuan Lien-ho Hui), and similar bodies, which were designed to create support for Yuan's enthronement, sprang up throughout the provinces. These sleight-of-hand performances were intended to present the illusion of popular support for "Emperor Yuan." In the farcical scenes of collecting signatures from men pleading that Yuan assume the emperorship, some people were forced by circumstances to act against their own better judgment, while others willingly subscribed to the movement in a bid for honors and power. Hsiung Yu-hsi, our headmaster, dramatically refused to sign a petition from Kiangsi Province in spite of a welter of threats and enticements. But this was a rare occurrence. My fellow students and I were so highly indignant at the shameful things that were done in an effort to set up

Yuan's dynasty that we unanimously acclaimed Hsiung's upright action in refusing to recognize Yuan as emperor. Frequently we stuck our thumbs up and reminded one another that, after all, this "Monkey" Hsiung was a fine man.

The scheme of Yuan Shih-k'ai and his son was anachronistic. While Yuan, who confidently expected to become emperor on February 9, excitedly prepared for the grand enthronement ceremonies and changed the fifth year of the Republic into the first year of Emperor Hung-hsien (Great Constitution), revolts against him burst out one after another in the provinces. First, on December 6 the gunboat *Shao-ho* at Shanghai hoisted the anti-Yuan flag. Then, on December 25 General T'ang Chi-yao of Yunnan, influenced by Ts'ai O and Li Lieh-chün, announced a campaign against Yuan, to which the southwestern provinces eagerly responded. Yuan Shih-k'ai was thus confronted by a broad united front directed against him. Needless to say, youths in general and the impartially-minded public all actively opposed him. In addition, the China Revolutionary Party (Chung-hua Ko-ming Tang)—or KMT—and the Progressive Party (Chin-pu Tang) cooperated in seeking to overthrow Yuan. Even the powerful generals and elder statesmen that stayed with Yuan showed varying degrees of dissatisfaction, some going so far as to rebel. Nor did the diplomatic corps lend him support. Yuan was thus forced on March 22, 1916, to announce dissolution of the "Great Constitution Dynasty." His enticing dreams of becoming emperor evaporated. Yet he lingered on as President in the face of continuing opposition until finally, on June 5, 1916, he died, a disappointed man.

The entire country rejoiced at Yuan's death. It was the end of the first military dictator to arise after the establishment of the Republic of China. Li Yuan-hung, the vice-president, succeeded Yuan in the presidency, restored the provisional constitution of the first year of the Republic, which Yuan had abolished, and recalled the first Parliament, which Yuan had disbanded. China seemed to have survived its worst crisis. My schoolmates and patriotic youths in general at Nanchang embraced the hope that the country would take a turn for the better and that one might concentrate on study once more.

My Earliest Contact with Revolutionaries

It was July, 1916, during summer vacation. After visiting my father in Hsiangshan County, Chekiang Province—he had been a judge for

many years and was then county magistrate there—I went to Shanghai
to take the entrance examination for National Peking University. Ts'ai
Yuan-p'ei, the progressive educator, had become its chancellor; and I
wanted to study in the fresh intellectual atmosphere his chancellorship
promised. On an introduction from my second uncle, I stayed in Shanghai with a revolutionist named Yeh Po-heng. I actually lived among
revolutionists throughout my Shanghai stay.

Yeh lived in the front room of a house on Shoushan Lane, a cluttered tenement area at the Bridge of the Eight Gods in the French
Concession. His shabby room contained only a few pieces of dilapidated
old furniture and a bed of taut woven cord on top of which was a
tattered reed mat. Newspapers and books stood in untidy piles on a
desk. Although his clothes were little more than rags, he bore himself
with the dignity of a traditional scholar. He seemed both pleased and
apprehensive upon reading my uncle's letter of introduction. He con-
fided that he led the impoverished, rugged, and dangerous life of a
revolutionary and that such a life would not suit a youth studying for
his college entrance examinations. But when I assured him that I liked
revolutionists and that I would love to taste his kind of life, he laughed
with delight. He managed to get a bed for me; and the hospitality he
extended to his uninvited guest was warm.

Yuan Shih-k'ai, after the 1913 Kiangsi-Nanking Campaign against
himself, had furiously stepped up his drive against revolutionists; and
the KMT had been very badly trampled. Quite a few members, their
determination never very strong, had deserted the revolutionary front
for a life of passive disillusionment. Some went so far as to capitulate to
Yuan Shih-k'ai. Then, on July 8, 1914, Sun Yat-sen regrouped the revolutionary front and reorganized the KMT into the Chinese Revolutionary
Party (Chung-hua Ko-ming Tang).[43] Its members were required to take
an oath of allegiance to Sun Yat-sen personally and to sign it with their
fingerprints. This antagonized several influential revolutionists, and
they refused to join the party.[44] By the time I reached Shanghai, the
anti-Yuan insurrection that started in Yunnan Province had, of course,
ended. Yet many of Sun Yat-sen's faithful followers were still forced to
seek refuge in the French Concession of Shanghai. Though Yuan Shih-
k'ai had died, his lackeys still continued to oppress the members of the
Revolutionary party in Shanghai.

Yeh Po-heng was, I believe, a member of Sun's Revolutionary party.
He warned me that in spite of Yuan Shih-k'ai's death, his claws and fangs

were still ferociously active in Shanghai; and he advised that I immediately get to know the streets and lanes connecting the French Concession with the British Settlement. For the British Settlement crawled with spies and agents sent by the king of bloodthirsty devils, Lu Chien-chang.[45] Although they dared not start trouble in the French Concession, they often lured revolutionists into the British Settlement and kidnapped them. Those seized were in danger of losing their heads. He warned me especially against being seen on the streets with revolutionists too often and against going into the British Settlement.

Yeh also told me of his way of life in Shanghai. Trapped in the French Concession, he had pawned or sold his clothes and every other decent thing he owned. Often he could not afford even a meal, and very frequently, of course, he had to borrow money. Many refugee revolutionists in the French Concession, he told me, were so poor they did not own even a pair of trousers. Often two or three of them shared one pair, each waiting to go out until it was his turn to wear them. Yet their vigor in the cause of the revolution remained high. Smiling, he told me that he, too, was fast approaching the stage at which he would lose his trousers. His story filled me with sympathy and admiration for the revolutionists' spirit of struggle and endurance.

Revolutionists often came to Yeh's room to talk, and I often trailed along after him when he called on revolutionary friends. Most of them came from Kiangsi, Hunan, and Hupei provinces; and they were on the whole an impoverished lot. Those who were a little better-off frequently passed the long, long days of a refugee playing mah-jongg for the lowest possible stakes. Some later became important National Government officials. In those days, however, we often walked barefooted through the streets at night in search of a breath of cool air. And occasionally we would buy cheap wine and food and enjoy it at home. Most of them solicited the help of wine to cool the heat of their sorrows, and after several glasses a torrent of grumbling would burst from them. They would belabor current events, and out would come their bitter hatred for Yuan Shih-k'ai and his lackeys. They were particularly outraged by his massacre of party members. They never tired of repeating scandalous stories about Yuan and his family.

Usually I just listened to them, but sometimes I threw in my own questions. If they were that despicable, I asked, what were the revolutionists going to do about Yuan Shih-k'ai's warlord clique?

"We have Dr. Sun to lead the revolution," was their usual reply.

"How?" I would ask. And generally they answered, "By infiltrating their armies and secret societies and by using guns and bombs."

But when I inquired about what would happen after the revolution succeeded, they could not provide a consistent answer. When I asked about the attitude of the Revolutionary party towards Japan's ambition to annex China, they would stick to their approach of dwelling on the May 9 National Humiliation Incident and of castigating the treasonous Yuan Shih-k'ai. This made me feel that they attached insufficient importance to Japanese aggression.

After I had stayed with Yeh for more than a month, which I spent mainly in preparing for the entrance examinations, he left Shanghai. He was too uncompromising even to have many really close friends; and his disillusionment with the course of the revolution was inevitable. With the help of Li Jui-ch'ing, a famous caligrapher better known as Ch'ing Tao-jen, he went to Djakarta and taught at an overseas Chinese school. I have heard nothing about him since.

Just at this time a cousin of mine named Tu, whom I had not seen for years, arrived in Shanghai. He had devoted himself to the revolution and had once been a regimental commander in the Revolutionary Army. He and seven other youths lived together in one small room of a boardinghouse. All of them slept on the floor, packed in like sardines. Meeting as we did, far from home, we were especially glad to see one another; and when Yeh departed, Tu pressed me to move in with them, which I was happy to do. Still another sardine was crammed into that tiny room.

The eight young revolutionary soldiers with whom I stayed all came from around Wuhan, Changsha, and P'inghsiang. They had been ordered to stop their military activities, no doubt, because Yuan Shih-k'ai was dead and the battles against him had ended. Sun Yat-sen's headquarters in Shanghai, in any event, was sending them to Japan to study. There they were to wait until the time was right to resume their activities in China. Sun's headquarters was giving them travel money in installments, and they invested each installment in having a fine time in Shanghai. Enthusiastic, energetic, naive, and very active, they loved to brag about their heroic experiences, beside which nothing else in the world seemed of any importance. With special energy, moreover, they pursued wine and women. We had little in common, despite the fact that I lived with them, for I was given to browsing through bookstores, searching for my favorite books.

"You heroes," I sometimes asked them jokingly, "why don't you dip into a few books?"

"Everything will be all right when Sun Yat-sen becomes our great president," they generally replied.

While they had no definite date of departure, they were supposed to leave as soon as they were given their tickets. Therefore, one day I returned from browsing in a bookstore to discover that they had all boarded a ship. My cousin had left a note explaining that they could not wait for my return, because they had had to rush to catch the ship. Having spent their last cent, he wrote, they had no choice but to borrow the silver dollars and clothes in my trunk. He promised to return them when we met again. Upon opening my trunk, I found only twenty silver dollars left of the one hundred dollars I kept there. Most of my clothes were gone, and their cast-off belongings were jammed in the trunk instead. My cousin's behavior was typical of Revolutionary soldiers in reduced circumstances.

I passed my entrance examination to Peita (Peking University), but I no longer had the money to get to Peking. I had to visit my father again and replenish my purse.

During those two months I had enjoyed a grand tour of the small world of the French Concession revolutionists. It was a world filled with revolutionary idealism and unharnessed romanticism. There was a willingness to take risks and stand up against hardship. There was optimism, energy, and a willingness to share both the good and the bad. Influenced by these things, I came to believe that if such people could have a better understanding of the forces at work in China and the world, there would be no limit to what could be accomplished. I began to think that if I were to take part in the revolution, I could not neglect any of these things.

Peita, Hotbed of the New Culture Movement

Early in October of 1916 I arrived at Peking for the first time. Generally speaking, Shanghai, which I had just left, differed entirely from inland cities. It had become what you might call a modernized international port. The capital of the country was at Peking, a striking and purely Chinese metropolis, grand and colorful. The Gate of Heavenly Peace, the Forbidden City, Chung-nan Hai, the Temple of Heaven, the many sublime palaces and temples, the court residences with their red walls and green-tiled roofs ornamented by dragons and phoenixes were all there. Without immodesty it could claim to represent the very cream of Classical architecture.

Peking also displayed the atmosphere of the late monarchical period. On the first and fifteenth day of each lunar month fallen nobles and once-ranking ministers, sitting in their sedan chairs and wearing scarlet hat buttons, still waited at the Gate of Godlike Courage to be called to an audience by the fallen Emperor P'u Yi. Manchus still greeted one another in their traditional way—on one knee with long sleeves drawn over their hands. Rickshaw pullers respectfully hailed all potential male customers as *lao yeh* (my lord) and women as *t'ai-t'ai* (my lady). Shopkeepers still greeted shoppers with elaborate ceremony. These were all remnants of a paternalistic tradition that was not far from feudalism.

The Legation Quarter stood as an obviously separate district of the city of Peking. Legations, banks, and foreign firms were housed there in a forest of mansions. It was surrounded by a wall lined with barracks, each section of the Quarter being guarded by troops of the foreign country occupying that section. It was a small-scale example of the foreign aggrandizement and of the spheres of influence in China. This seemed especially true of the monument to Baron von Ketteler, the German minister killed in the Boxer Incident, which towered over Hatamen Street. It was a painful sight which evoked tormenting memories of the humiliations to China that attended the Boxer Incident.

The President's office, the Premier's office, Parliament, and other buildings bearing the Republic of China insignia were scattered about the city, all retaining the aura of official residences of past dynasties. They displayed nothing new. This applied also to Peking University, which retained much of the atmosphere of the old Imperial Capital Academy.[46] Right beside it was stationed a small contingent of the pigtailed troops of Chang Hsün, the swashbuckling Kiangsi warlord. It was impossible to foretell then that this school would become the hotbed of China's New Culture Movement.

Peking was truly a city of many faces and colors. Things characteristically ancient and modern, Chinese and foreign, Han Chinese, Manchu, Mongol, Moslem, and Tibetan were all there. Yet it could not accurately be called China in miniature. For in the eyes of a Southerner like myself it was more in the nature of a conservative Northern city.

The Imperial Capital Academy was the predecessor of Peking University, commonly called Peita. While it dated back to 1898, its equipment was still inadequate, and a majority of its professors were of the old classical type. Others, although they had been exposed to Western education, were also traditionalists. Prominent among these were the formidable Ku Hung-ming,[47] who retained his queue, and Liu Shih-p'ei, famed for his command of Classical Chinese and one of the Six Gentlemen in the Ch'ou An Society. The students tended to view themselves more or less as candidates for Imperial degrees. There were among them scholars in the romantic Bohemian tradition, youths who attended the university chiefly for ornamental reasons or because they sought a government sinecure. Schools elsewhere, and even other schools in Peking, by then showed the effects of at least some modern influence. But Peita still retained its ancient aura and remained staunchly conservative.

The atmosphere at Peita changed only after Ts'ai Yuan-p'ei assumed the chancellorship in the autumn of 1916. He did not regard himself as a high official but rather as a person whose task it was to promote scholarship; and he worked with quiet determination to remake senile old Peita into a ranking educational institution. Beside the old-style professors he installed such advanced thinkers as Ch'en Tu-hsiu and Hu Shih, champions of the New Culture Movement; Ch'ien Hsuan-t'ung, Lu Hsün, Shen Yin-mo, and Shen Chien-shih, literary titans; Wu Chih-hui and Li Shih-tseng, anarchists; Ma Chun-wu and Wang Ch'ung-hui, important figures in the KMT; and Li Ta-chao, the Socialist. All of them taught there at one time or another, each making his own special contribution to this unique institution. Chancellor Ts'ai's policy of academic freedom offered room for all; and under it the scholastic atmosphere at Peita improved by the day.

I went to Peita hoping that the political situation in Peking would take a turn for the better and that Chancellor Ts'ai would as a result bring about great improvements in the university. Many of the students that flocked there went for the same reason. Peita operated then under a system of three years of preparatory school followed by three years of university study in some major field. I enrolled in the third class of the first year in the preparatory school of science and engineering, and I lived in the Third Dormitory on *Pei-ho yen*. There were several students to each room, with new and old students generally mixed.

The first problem I encountered was a clash between the old and new students over their ways of living. Of the eight of us in my room, two were about to graduate. Their major concern seemed to be with putting out a tabloid newspaper containing poems and articles that they wrote to enhance the reputation of their favorite actresses. Often they were very drunk when they returned to the dormitory in the dead of night, making a horrendous din, asserting their self-importance as seniors, and utterly ignoring the plight of lower students. Finally, however, most of us new students closed ranks and forced our haughty roommates to observe dormitory regulations.

Peita, when I first entered it, was in confusion. There was no communication between professors and students; they were scarcely on speaking terms outside the classroom. Outside the classroom, students could do whatever they pleased. They were given freedom in its worst sense.

It was at this time, however, that a new tide began to come in. Lower students often ridiculed the *lao yeh* gentry ways of senior students, their romantic Bohemian traditionalism, and their outmoded conservative approach to things. We demanded that they have greater respect for communal interests and hard study and that they put an end to the concept that one studied merely as a stepping stone to high official position. We introduced three concepts: Study in order to really learn something; study for a practical purpose; and study in order to save the country. And this was an extremely important change for Peita. The change was spurred on by the policy of Ts'ai Yuan-p'ei, and in turn it bolstered his policy as well.

Ch'en Tu-hsiu became dean of the College of Arts early in 1917, when *Hsin Ch'ing-nien* (New Youth), which he edited, became available on campus and in the bookstores. Very few Peita students had heard of the magazine before this time, although it had begun publication on September 15, 1915. In January, 1917, the fifth issue of the second volume of *New Youth* contained an article by Hu Shih entitled "Tentative Suggestions for the Improvement of Literature." The following issue carried Ch'en Tu-hsiu's "On the Literary Revolution." The magazine promptly attracted wide attention from my schoolmates. For the vernacular language (pai hua) that these articles advocated was to thought and scholarship what the abolition of bound feet was to women. Hu Shih called it "the birth of a living literature," and Ch'en Tu-hsiu hoisted high the banner of the literary revolution. Thus began the great debate between new and old literatures.

The New Culture Movement, beginning with literary reform, offered vital liberation to Chinese scholarship and thought. Western culture had moved steadily into China since the Opium Wars battered in the front gate of the country. One tidal wave after another had crashed against the bulwarks of traditionalism. The Foreign Affairs Movement of Tseng Kuo-fan and Li Hung-chang, the translations of Timothy Richards, the reform movement of K'ang Yu-wei and Liang Ch'i-ch'ao, and the revolutionary movement of Sun Yat-sen had all shaken the foundations of academic orthodoxy. But in 1917 the New Culture Movement began to bring about a brilliant cultural renaissance. While storming the fortress of classical literature, it promoted in plain understandable words democracy and science and the various schools of modern Western thought.

It would not be entirely correct to say that the New Culture Movement was bound by any single school of thought. Take, for example, *New Youth,* which led the movement. Its stand on literary reform was, to be sure, unanimously accepted by supporters of the movement. But there was little unanimity behind the many other things it promoted and introduced. For in those days the war between the Old and the New was total. Everything new battled against everything old. And the "New" was armed with the modern Scientific Method as its main weapon. Moreover, as backward people in the twentieth century awakened and began to catch up, they often tended to be radical; and radicalism was the main trend of the New Culture Movement. This applied also to the "cosmopolitan society"[48] of K'ang Yu-wei and to Sun Yat-sen's Principle of Livelihood.

I was among the first of the Peita students to support the New Culture Movement. Upon arriving, I had buried myself in study and got high marks. But then, like many other youngsters, I came to view myself as a youth of the new times, refusing to remain backward, struggling to march forward more rapidly. Previously, in addition to assigned work, I had enjoyed reading regularly *Tung-fang Tsa-chih* (Eastern Magazine), *Ta Chung-hua* (Great China), and other magazines, hoping to find therein new ways of saving the country and of broadening myself intellectually. Early in 1917, however, I began reading *New Youth.* I decided that even its name applied to me and that it fulfilled the needs of most young people. Overjoyed at discovering it, I immediately became one of its most zealous supporters.

Many were the arguments I had with detractors of the magazine. For at the time a majority of students still clung to Confucianism and opposed pai hua. Even the names "New Youth" and "Ch'en Tu-hsiu" were as frightening to them as monsters. While students that supported the new current and pai hua unconditionally and that took violent exception to Confucianism were in the minority, they were determined and zealous. And because of the endless heated arguments that they instigated in classrooms, dormitories, and elsewhere, defenders of the Old began to founder. In this way students were gradually converted into supporters of the New Culture Movement, and the movement gained a stronghold at Peita. The influence of the New Culture Movement grew more extensive daily. So also did the circulation of *New Youth* increase, and each issue sold out at Peita as soon as it appeared.

Then, in December, 1918, Ch'en Tu-hsiu began publishing another magazine, *Mei-chou P'ing-lun* (Weekly Review), which was more political in its orientation than *New Youth*. In January, 1919, furthermore, Fu Ssu-nien, Lo Chia-lun, and other Peita students started *Hsin Ch'ao Yueh-k'an* (Renaissance, or literally New Tide Monthly) in response to the New Culture Movement. These two magazines were regarded as the chief satellites of *New Youth*. Some newspapers in Shanghai and Peking also swung support behind the movement, and in due time small literary magazines and groups dedicated to the New Culture Movement sprang up all over the country.

An active movement for socialism developed together with the New Culture Movement. Anarchism had been the earliest of the Socialist movements to appear in China; consequently its activities were more obvious. On June 22, 1907, Li Shih-tseng, Wu Chih-hui, Chang Ching-chiang, and others had started publishing *Hsin Shih-chi* (New Century Weekly) at Paris in order to promote anarchism in China. Later Ts'ai Yuan-p'ei became an important figure in this Chinese-language magazine. During 1917 and 1918, moreover, anarchists in Peking, Canton, and other cities stepped up their activities; and their small publications grew quite popular. While these people remained anarchists, they were also earnest supporters of the New Culture Movement.

But socialism in China had other early roots. In 1906 the *Min Pao* (People's Journal) of the T'ung-meng Hui published an abridged translation of the *Communist Manifesto* done by Chu Chih-hsin. At the same time articles eulogizing socialism often appeared in other small publications. Around the time of the 1911 Revolution, furthermore, Chiang K'ang-hu organized the Chinese Socialist Party (Chung-kuo She-hui Tang) and entered practical politics. Gradually pushed aside by the hectic political situation, however, it faded away completely. It was not until after

World War I ended in November, 1918, and the influence of the Russian Revolution was felt in China that socialism began to rise once again. Following the armistice, *Weekly Review, New Youth,* and *Hsing-ch'i P'ing-lun* (Sunday Review) in Shanghai at one time or another published articles on Marxism and ones sympathetic to the Russian Revolution.

The new thought that swept like a torrent over China swept over my family, too. After getting to Peking, I regularly sent my father newspapers, magazines, and books after I finished reading them. It became a habit. They came to include *New Youth* and similar magazines and even anarchist publications. At the same time in frequent letters to my father I pleaded the cause of the New Culture Movement. Father kept quiet for almost a year, his replies cautiously avoiding the subject. When finally he spoke up, his letter was a long essay denouncing the new thought and especially vernacular language. He called for the preservation of China's traditional culture. This touched off a heated debate between a stubborn father and a stubborn son.

Nor was the clash between new and old merely an intellectual exercise. It reached deeply into one's life. Somewhat earlier, in the spring of 1917, my family blandly arranged my engagement. It was Grandfather's idea, and my parents acquiesced. In keeping with practice, they found me a fiancée whose family background matched my own. But I was not consulted. I shot back a letter of protest. Although she might be a fine girl, how could I be expected to agree to the marriage when I didn't even know her? To my postal debate with Father over the new thought was now added this running argument. I expressed absolute determination to break the engagement, which placed Father in a most difficult position. But with the mediation of relatives the deadlock finally was broken and the engagement was called off.

Father came to Peking in the spring of 1919, by which time I had became a rather notorious radical. I visited him weekly during his stay and sent him books as usual. The old warm relationship between father and son still existed when we discussed everyday affairs. My father knew that I had already become an active radical, and feeling anxious, he often made it clear that he did not approve. But the broken engagement and the issue of the new thought were not once mentioned.

He left after a short stay, and I saw him off at the railway station. With deep sincerity I told him, "Father, you are always very cautious about the things you do or say. But your son has accepted a challenge to fight the old society. For your own sake you had better adopt the position that you are not responsible for your son's actions."

My father kept a grieved silence. Then we parted.

"Save the Country First"

During World War I, Japan monopolized East Asia. Her aggressive designs on China grew more obvious daily. Still trying to realize the Twenty-one Demands of 1915, she intervened extensively in China's internal politics, attempting to create a legal government in Peking that would be subservient to Japan. This roiled the already restless political situation. It also fostered the growth of a clamorous and widespread anti-Japanese sentiment. If the New Culture Movement, the hallmark of which was internal reform, led to a dispute between the old and the new, the anti-Japanese sentiment, which was the main content of the patriotic movement of the day, in its turn brought about unity among the people irrespective of their ideological differences. The cry "Save the Country First" arose to become the prelude to the May Fourth Movement.

Yuan Shih-k'ai was dead, to be sure, but the Peiyang military clique he had built up continued to control the Peking government. Tuan Ch'i-jui succeeded to Yuan's power. He controlled the political situation. With neither Yuan's prestige nor his power, Tuan acted no less tyrannically and dictatorially, and he maintained closer relations with Japan than Yuan had done. Resistance to his reign popped up constantly; and to defeat his political enemies he sought to "unify China by force." In order to do this he became more reliant than ever upon Japanese support.

In 1916, when after Yuan's death Tuan Ch'i-jui became Premier, he came into frequent conflict with President Li Yuan-hung and Parliament. He clashed openly with Li during November of that year in what was the beginning of a power struggle between them.[49] There followed a prolonged battle with Parliament over whether or not China should join the Allies in World War I, a move that Tuan favored. Making no headway, in May of 1917 Tuan summoned a corps of provincial warlord governors,[50] who had the troops to enforce their wishes, and tried to intimidate Li Yuan-hung and Parliament with them. He also organized numerous groups of people for petitions. They surrounded Parliament, attacked members of Parliament, and demanded that war be declared.

Yet these crude, high-handed actions failed to bring the results Tuan sought. On the contrary, they forced the angry Li Yuan-hung to dismiss him, whereupon the militarists of Tuan's clique one after the other declared themselves independent of the government. With no military power to back him, the best Li Yuan-hung could do to save the situation was to request mediation by Chang Hsün, the senior member of the Tuchun Corps. Chang arrived in Peking with his troops and on June 13, 1917, forced Li to decree the disbandment of Parliament. On July 1, moreover, Chang forced Li Yuan-hung himself out of office and restored the abdicated emperor, P'u Yi, to the throne.

Tuan Ch'i-jui, in trying to take over the government, had lost power himself. But Chang Hsün's enthronement of P'u Yi gave Tuan the excuse to make another bid for power. He rallied his loyal warlords at Ma-ch'ang, marched on Peking, and defeated the troops of Chang Hsün. The Emperor went back into retirement, and Tuan claimed that he had re-created the Republic. On July 15 Tuan again became Premier. On August 1 he invited Feng Kuo-chang, who had been vice-president under Li Yuan-hung, to succeed Li as president; and Feng accepted. Ignoring the fact that Li Yuan-hung had been forced to resign and that Parliament had been forced to disband, Tuan did nothing to reinstate either. In order to gain support of the monarchists that had betrayed the Republic, he decided not to punish them. On the contrary, he sheltered them, giving important jobs to some militarists that had actually taken part in the monarchist coup.[51]

Out of all this political juggling, Tuan somehow emerged the victor. Yet he did not have quite enough strength to control the situation completely, and this eventually led to further turmoil.

Sun Yat-sen and Ch'eng Pi-kuang, the Minister of the Navy in the Peking government, led the Navy and some members of Parliament to the South to organize opposition to Tuan and the Peking government. Their slogans were "Protect the Constitution," "Reinstate Parliament," and "Punish those chiefly responsible for the Manchu restoration." On September 1 the Southwestern Military Government for the Protection of the Constitution was established in Canton, resulting in a split between the North and the South.

Meanwhile a power struggle flared up in Peking between Tuan Ch'i-jui and Feng Kuo-chang, who had succeeded to the presidency. Tuan advocated national unification by force, while Feng declared for a policy of peaceful settlement of national issues. The dispute over the question of whether or not a punitive campaign should be undertaken against the Southwest caused Tuan and Feng to break apart, leading to an open split of the Peiyang militarists into the Chihli clique and the Anhwei clique, the former led by Feng and the latter by Tuan. The two struggled against each other overtly and covertly until their cleavage became irreparable and their controversy had to be settled on the battle-field.

Tuan Ch'i-jui's struggle for power pushed him further into the waiting arms of Japan. On August 14, 1917, he declared war on Germany and Austria as part of a silent understanding with the Japanese. Japan sought to use the resulting wartime alliance to extend her control in China, while Tuan's aim was to gain Japanese financial support and assistance in expanding his military strength.

Tuan created the Anfu Parliament, over which he had absolute control.[52] This Parliament and the State Council were packed with members of his Anfu clique and of its ally, the New Communications clique, which was more and more openly engaging in traitorous pro-Japanese activities.[53] Pressure by Tuan forced Feng Kuo-chang to abandon the presidency when his term of office expired. In his place Tuan put an old bureaucrat named Hsu Shih-ch'ang. Under his title of War Participation Supervisor, Tuan also saw to the organization and training of a "War Participation Army," which was to serve his own political ends. During 1917 and 1918 Tuan received a total of $150,000,000 in loans from Japan under conditions extremely unfavorable to China.[54]

The young people of China, generally speaking, felt only hatred for this Japanese aggression. The traitorous pro-Japan activities of Tuan Ch'i-jui's Anfu clique and of the New Communications clique were especially resented. But most young people also saw the confusion and corruption that characterized practical politics, which most of them found so distasteful that they would take no part in them. Some of the youths that engaged in the New Culture Movement, for example, tended to have little contact with practical politics. Indeed, political parties at that time left the general public with a feeling of disillusionment. The general public did not even pin much hope on the KMT, led by Sun Yat-sen, because of its internal chaos and because it did not have a clear anti-Japanese stand. While most young people felt that opposing Japan and being patriotic were inescapable obligations, there was no way to mobilize them without some form of organization; and some remained fearful that any organization would drag them down into the unsavory whirlpool of practical politics.

On May 7, 1918, Chinese students in Tokyo met to protest the China-Japan Mutual Defense Agreement which had been drawn up in a series of conferences there. Japanese police disbanded the meeting and made numerous arrests. In protest, more than a thousand Chinese students in Japan returned to China. Some came to Peking and told us with a good deal of bitterness of the humiliations they had experienced in Japan, and this roused widespread sympathy among Peking students.

As a result of a large student rally that was called by sympathetic students on the third campus of Peita on May 21, 1918, more than a thousand of us marched to the office of the President of China and presented a petition. Most of us were college students from Peking, with some Tientsin student delegates. The petition objected to the signing of the China-Japan Agreement and to the Japanese loans. It asked that the Twenty-one Demands be rejected once and for all and that Japanese privileges and interests in Shantung Province be returned to China. The petition was mildly worded, however, and was similar to the petition that K'ang Yu-wei tendered to Emperor Kuang Hsü.[55] Four student delegates, bearing the petition with traditional demonstrations of respect, sought an audience with President Hsu Shih-ch'ang. The rest of us waited, solemn and quiet, outside the Hsin Hua Men (New China Gate). There were no speakers, no banners, and no slogan-shouting. The citizens of Peking had no way of knowing what the students were up to, for it was a truly silent petition. Nothing at all came of it. The President delivered himself of inconsequential evasions to our four awed delegates, and the assembled students accepted their report of the audience in meek silence. The only remotely revolutionary aspect of it was when Miss Kuo Lung-chen, a student representative from Tientsin, burst into hysterics in front of the President's office as a protest.

Yet this petition did stir up the Peking students. Some schoolmates and I believed it was much too gentle, and we thundered that Peking students were practically lifeless, like dumb animals. Their patriotism could not approach that of Chinese students in Japan, we said. Even Kuo Lung-chen, the girl from Tientsin, was more patriotic than they. By persistent badgering we won over a number of students.

The students at Peita still could not agree on how to go about saving the country. Roughly, there were three schools of thought. First, quite a number of my schoolmates believed that patriots should seek popular support that would vote them into Parliament and allow them to gain control of the government machinery. Only then, when they were able to establish a new political trend, could methods be devised to save the country. Secondly, those who were devoted to the New Culture Movement felt that the proper way to save the country was simply to strengthen the New Culture Movement. Thirdly, radicals like myself believed that we should work for a complete revolution that would overthrow the pro-Japan regime. In little groups throughout the dormitories students thrashed out these problems, and my room was one of the storm centers of argument. The conclusion most students finally reached was: "The whole student body should take part in a Save-the-Country Movement. Saving the country is more important than anything else. From the deepest conservatives to the anarchists, everyone should rise up and unite to save the country. 'Save the country first.'"

Since we wanted to save the country, the obvious first step in the march forward was to form groups and put out publications. The idea of organizing groups was widespread at that time, and many ambitious youths sought to try their talents in them and thus to rise in the world. Some fellow students and I organized the Kuo-min Tsa-chih (National Magazine) group. More than a hundred students took part in the venture, most of them from Peita, with a few from other Peking institutions of higher education. We published a monthly periodical called *National Magazine,* whose circulation department I was elected to head from the start. I became busy raising funds from members and looking after management, publication, and circulation affairs. The first issue of the magazine came out on January 1, 1919. About four issues appeared before the May Fourth Movement broke out. Then our members, all of whom became active in that movement, had no time to look after its publication; and the magazine was suspended.

Members of the National Magazine group were the prime movers and organizers of the May Fourth Movement. The fact that they were all fervent patriots often led them into disputes. The groups could be roughly divided into three sections. One was a small minority of conservatives whose spokesmen were Ch'en Chung-fan and Huang Chien-chung. They advocated preserving the traditional culture and they opposed *pai hua.* The second section, which numbered nearly half the membership, was composed of moderates. I K'e-i was its chief spokesman. A leading sponsor of *National Magazine,* he advocated unity for national salvation while championing the parallel development of both "old" and "new" thought. He laid equal stress on both Eastern and Western cultures. The third section, which about equaled the second in strength, consisted of radicals. Hsü Te-heng and I were its spokesmen. We stood for national salvation through revolution and unqualified support to the New Culture Movement.

Although as a major figure in the National Magazine group I served it enthusiastically, the divergent views of its members left me feeling dissatisfied. At the close of the European war, I developed a close relationship with Li Ta-chao, who was then Director of the Library at Peita. My interest in socialism increased as a result of his influence. At the same time I began to have a close association with two anarchist schoolmates, Huang Ling-shuang and Au Sheng-pai, and I began to read in Chinese such anarchist works as the writings of Kropotkin, Bakunin, and others. Such concepts as social reform and going into the masses were added to my thinking. Apart from patriotic zeal, it seemed, I developed some sense of social revolution.

Prompted by such ideals, I gathered together Teng Chung-hsia, Lo Chang-lung, and other schoolmates and organized the P'ing-min Chiao-yu Hui (Society for Mass Education). It advocated social reform through the education of the common man. The charter participants in this organization included more than sixty Peita students who came from the National Magazine group. Bent on social reform work, some of them were dissatisfied with *National Magazine*'s purely patriotic stand.

Such small organizations devoted to the promotion of social reform were coming into vogue in Peking at the time. A leading one among them was the Work-Study Mutual Aid group which hoisted the slogan "Experiment in New Living" in its quest for a Utopian way of life.

Though anarchists did not join the Society for Mass Education, it was established under the influence of their slogan "Go into the masses." When before long it received support from the Peita authorities, it was reorganized as the Peking University Public Speaking Group for Mass Education. Under it were maintained such organizations as the Peita Institute of Mass Education Through Public Speaking and the Common Man's Night School. Similar groups were formed in other Peking educational institutions also. Members of all these organizations were regularly sent to suburban Peking areas, where they made street speeches. Soon afterward we had the added support of the Peking Education Bureau, which supplied us with lecture halls scattered throughout Peking and arranged special hours each week for us to speak in them. Our speeches were primarily concerned with "national salvation," "the sufferings of the common man," and "popular culture," all of which were then novel subjects for public attention. Our speeches attracted considerable notice and our audiences grew markedly. Since few Chinese intellectuals had ever thought of trying to communicate with the masses, ours was a very exceptional activity. It was there that I began to gain experience in effective public speaking and to grasp the dramatic possibilities of appealing directly to the masses.

Each week we also sent teams into the slum areas to investigate the plight of the poor and to carry on a limited amount of relief work. Members of our Society, or people sympathetic to it, wrote accounts for the Peking press of the conditions under which the average man lived. Such reporting was quite an innovation, and it attracted widespread attention. In addition, the organization called upon members to develop similar groups in their home villages throughout the provinces when they returned there for summer and winter vacations.[56] In this way we hoped to spread social reform throughout the country.

The European war ended on November 11, 1918; and China, having declared war on Germany, was apparently one of the victorious nations. Then the victors were trumpeting a fanfare to the effect that right had triumphed over might; and in this vein Peking also celebrated the victory. The monument to Baron von Ketteler was torn down, moved to Central Park, and renamed the "Monument to the Victory of Right over Might." We all turned out approvingly to watch the foundation-laying ceremony, brimming with vague hopes that China would now shed her weakness and that there would be a turn for the better. For the realists' axiom "right is might" appeared to call for a bit of revision. At a victory rally at Tien An Men (Gate of Heavenly Peace), Ts'ai Yuan-p'ei spoke on "The Sanctity of Labor" and Li Ta-chao on "The Victory of the Common Man." A student delegate gave a speech on "The French Revolution and the Russian Revolution," openly declaring that twentieth-century revolutions would follow the pattern of the Russian Revolution, which he commended as a model to the general public of China.

On January 18, 1919, the Conference of Paris opened. President Wilson of the United States had already advocated a league of nations and peace without reparations or ceding of territory. In an address to the U.S. Congress on January 8, 1918, he had enunciated the famous

Fourteen Points, stressing the principle of national self-determination. The youth of China generally greeted Wilson's declarations with great respect and voiced unanimous support for them, reacting rather as someone that had been unjustly imprisoned would react upon finding that there was now an opportunity for the wrong that had been done to him to be righted. Among the people and in the press there was talk of the major role that the United States would play in the peace talks and of the belief that her policy would not prove to be empty talk. Though the United States enjoyed in China the special privileges conferred by the unequal treaties, it was pointed out that she did not possess a sphere of influence. The United States had advocated the Open Door policy and a policy of equal opportunity in China from the standpoint of her own national interest, to be sure; but the effect of this was to frustrate Japan's plans to annex China. The United States had also returned the Boxer indemnity payments to China for the establishment of Tsinghua University, a gesture which had won the goodwill of the general public. And the fact that she now supported the restoration of China's rights and interests in Shangtung was naturally heartening. All of these things led the Chinese people in general to pin high hopes on President Wilson and the Conference of Paris.

But news soon came that the Peace Conference was turning more and more against the interests of China. China, as an Ally, raised seven demands for abolition of the special privileges that the Powers enjoyed in the country; but the Peace Conference paid absolutely no attention to them. Even the demand that Japan's Twenty-one Demands be renounced was not included on the agenda. As to the Shantung issue, in the middle of April, because of a private agreement between Japan and the Anglo-French powers, articles 156, 157, and 158 of the peace treaty gave everything that Germany had plundered in Shantung to Japan. President Wilson opposed this; but force of circumstances led him to abandon his promises to China, and he also openly compromised.

Japan was doing her utmost to gain control of China. In both Paris and Peking she played games of diplomatic treachery[57] to create a situation so unfavorable to China that the Peking authorities would have to accept the Peace Conference conditions that disposed of her Shantung interests. This aroused great indignation among the students in Peking. Filled with despair and wrath, as though awakened from a beautiful dream, they adopted the attitude that there was no justice in the world and that the Chinese people had no alternative but to rouse themselves to save their own country.

The May Fourth Movement

It was under the circumstances described in the previous section that the May Fourth Movement erupted.

On May 2, 1919, at seven o'clock in the evening, the National Magazine group held a routine meeting, which was attended by more than ten staff members. The agenda contained only matters connected with the publication. Without any prearrangement everyone began talking about the humiliations China was suffering at Versailles, the despicable attitude of Ts'ao Ju-lin and others that toadied to the Japanese, and the rising patriotic spirit of organizations in Shantung and elsewhere. The talk grew fiery.

Making the first proposal that we do something about the situation, I said that the National Magazine group ought to initiate a demonstration of students from all Peking schools. And I pointed out that the demonstration must not repeat the mistakes of the previous year's petition. A loud fanfare must accompany it, and it must achieve satisfactory results. It should be held, furthermore, as soon as possible, instead of being delayed until National Humiliation Day, when a rally was scheduled.[58] One phase of the demonstration would be to go to the Japanese Legation in order to protest on behalf of the Chinese people. Another purpose would be to arouse the masses to take united action that would force the government, which was already preparing a foreign policy of capitulation, to refuse to sign the peace treaty. This would break ground for the ultimate restoration of Chinese rights and interests in Shantung and the renunciation of the Twenty-one Demands. It also would strike a blow against the traitorous pro-Japanese clique of Ts'ao Ju-lin, Lu Tsung-yü, Chang Tsung-hsiang, and the others. And it would, I said, bolster the morale of the people while it upheld a righteous cause.

The others immediately supported my proposal with enthusiasm and added many valuable suggestions. Some pointed out that since there was no student federation for Peking students as a whole, it would be difficult to launch common action; so we should take advantage of this opportunity to form a student union in every school in Peking. Others supplied the immediate objective of the demonstration, which was to bring Ts'ao Ju-lin and the others to account; for only in this way could we give concrete expression to public indignation.

Assuming the responsibility for patriotic action, we decided that the National Magazine group would call a rally of all Peita students for the following evening at seven o'clock in the auditorium of the university's third campus. Students from the Higher Normal School, the Institute of Technology, the School of Agriculture, and the Law School also would be invited. We elected I K'e-i, a schoolmate, to serve as chairman of the rally, at which we planned to work out the steps that this movement to save the country would take. Some group members were assigned to deliver speeches in which they would propose concrete measures, and others were assigned to carry on liaison with students from other schools.

As a result of our meeting, inflammatory notices of the rally appeared on Peita bulletin boards early the next morning. The news spread like wildfire among the students. Their patriotic feelings mounted throughout the day.

At seven o'clock on the evening of May 3 the auditorium of the third campus was filled to capacity. Almost all of the more than one thousand students at Peita were there. Several scores of enthusiasts from other schools also attended.

After Chairman I K'e-i had opened the meeting and explained its objectives, I mounted the platform to expound the views that I had raised the previous evening. This was my first experience before an important mass meeting. I felt rather tense; and to make matters worse, my speech was heavy with the accent of my native P'inghsiang. The way I pronounced the all-important term "mass movement," for example, varied drastically from the standard Mandarin. Even so, the students endorsed my ideas and applauded vigorously. But afterward some of them kidded me so much about the way I had pronounced "mass movement" that it nearly became my nickname.

Hsü Te-heng, who was well known as a "big gun" because of his speaking virtuosity, followed me. He stirred up the students tremendously. Another student, Hsieh Shao-min, bit his index finger; and on a white banner he wrote in blood the words "Return our Tsingtao." This raised the indignant temper of the meeting still higher. It was unanimously agreed at the rally that students from all schools would be called upon to assemble before the Gate of Heavenly Peace at noon the next day—the fourth of May—for a demonstration. Students from all the schools represented at the meeting declared their support. This was the first truly provocative rally I had ever attended.

About eleven o'clock on the morning of May 4 Peita students were assembled in the mall of the first campus at Ma-shen-miao, ready to start for the Gate of Heavenly Peace, when Chancellor Ts'ai Yuan-p'ei tried to prevent us from marching. In a moving address he declared that the demonstration would not improve the situation. Because of Peita's insistence upon academic freedom, he said, it had earned the hatred of the government and of conservatives in general. It was looked upon as some sort of heretical monster. And now, if the students staged their demonstration and trouble ensued, opponents of the university would have the pretext they had been looking for. Then Peita, built up with such difficulty, its foundations not yet firmly set, would be destroyed.

I K'e-i, who looked very gentle and scholarly, bluntly told the chancellor that the students could no longer contain their wrath. He appealed to him not to try to stop them. Many other students, growing impatient, began protesting loudly. Hissing and other sounds of derision arose from all corners. Noon was approaching, so I strode up to the chancellor and said, "The demonstration cannot be called off. You knew nothing of it beforehand, and so you are not compelled to interfere now. Please return to your office."

In this fashion a few other students and I half cajoled and half pushed Chancellor Ts'ai back to his office. Then, on a wave of applause, the students surged toward the Gate of Heavenly Peace.

We reached it last. Students from all other institutions of higher education in Peking had kept their promise and were waiting. There were more than three thousand students altogether. Promptly after a brief announcement of the objectives of the demonstration, we marched off in force to the Legation Quarter, intending to demonstrate before the Japanese Legation first of all. We shouted a wide variety of slogans and carried many different banners. Chief among them were "Return our Tsingtao," "Abolish the Twenty-one Demands," "Punish the Traitors," "Refuse to Sign the Peace Treaty," and "China for the Chinese." A formidable contingent of soldiers and policemen, drawn up at the entrance to the Legation Quarter, prevented the body of students from going in. Some representatives were sent to visit the legations of the United States and a few other countries to explain to them the goal of the demonstration. Keeping to our schedule, we next marched off to the residence of Ts'ao Ju-lin in Chao-chia-lou.

A group of more than ten youths broke into Ts'ao's residence ahead of the demonstrators. Led by a Hunanese named Chung Wei, a Peita student friend of mine, they climbed through its windows, flung open the front gate, and admitted the rest of the students. Everyone scoured the house for Ts'ao Ju-lin, the Minister of Communications, but he had fled. Nor was Lu-Tsung-yü, the Director of the Currency Bureau, to be found anywhere. However, another leading pro-Japan official—Chang Tsung-hsiang, who was then Minister to Japan—happened to be in the house. He had not managed to escape in time, so the students gave him a harsh beating.[59] Meanwhile they turned their wrath against the house's furnishings and recklessly destroyed things. Some students set fire to a pile of this wreckage in one of the courtyards.

Several other students and I, who were directing the operation, felt that by then our objectives had been achieved; and we individually went about telling the disorganized crowd to form into their own groups and to start the trip back to their schools. The large detachment of police and soldiers that soon arrived quickly put out the fire, which fortunately had not spread. Immediately the extensive arrest of people in the area began. Thirty-two students that had failed to rejoin the main body of students were seized. And that was the stirring May Fourth Movement episode known as "the fire at Chao-chia-lou."

Dusk had nearly fallen before the Peita students got back from the demonstration. Hungry and tired, we were nevertheless still in high spirits, and we clotted into little groups to discuss ways of coping with the expected government retaliation. We were elated by the stirring episode at Chao-chia-lou, to be sure; but we were worried about the thirty-two schoolmates that had been arrested and also about the oppression that we could soon expect. We all agreed that a crisis faced us. The only thing to do now was to intensify our efforts; it was too late to draw back. As a result, it was decided to hold another student meeting at ten o'clock the following morning, May 5, at which a Peita student union and a Peking student federation would be organized. The meeting also was to take steps to extend this movement throughout the entire country.

Early on the morning of May 5 the metropolitan garrison commander, Tuan Chih-kuei, an old warlord and trusted subordinate of Tuan Ch'i-jui and the real instigator of the policy of cracking down hard on the students, acted. He sent Yü Wei-to, director of the Office of the Advocate-General, to Peita. Yü, a bureaucrat, did not really want to cause trouble. He began threatening us the moment he arrived. The students had created a great deal of trouble, he pointed out. Unless they desisted, the university would be dissolved on official order and the agitators would be severely punished.

Tuan Hsi-p'eng, a student who later became an important KMT official, challenged him. The students would be cowed neither by threats nor oppression, Tuan declared. They were determined to continue their struggle even more vigorously. If the government did not change its policy as the students demanded, the whole country would be thrown into chaos. Before this force which Yü obviously could not control, he decided to switch to more moderate tones, expressing the hope that the students would create no further trouble in the streets and that they would peacefully attend classes while awaiting government disposal of the case. Then he meekly withdrew.

At about ten o'clock on the morning of May 5 Peita students, at a very enthusiastic meeting, decided to organize a Peita student-union secretariat forthwith. They decided also to initiate a federation of students of all middle schools and institutions of higher learning in Peking, and they called upon all such institutions to participate in the federation. Tuan Hsi-p'eng and Fang Hao were the representatives elected by the Peita Student Union to it. At the same time Lo Chia-lun, Ti Chun-wu, K'ang Pai-ch'ing, Chou P'ing-lin, Ch'en Chien-hsiu, Lu Shih-i, Chung Wei, and I myself were elected to take charge of documents, general affairs, speechmaking, and other activities of the Peita Student Union.

That same afternoon at Peita, representatives of the various student bodies to the federation held their first meeting. More than twenty institutions were represented. It was at this meeting that the Federation of Students in Middle and Higher Schools in Peking was officially formed. Tsinghua University, some missionary institutions, the Senior Normal College for Girls, and other institutions soon afterward organized student unions and joined the Peking Student Federation, as it was generally called. The Federation, then, was both in name and in fact an organization of the student bodies of all middle schools and institutions of higher education in Peking.

The first meeting of student-body representatives adopted as the aim of the Federation "To resist the foreign aggressors and destroy the national traitors." It produced such concrete demands as "Restore Tsingtao" and "Punish the traitors." And it issued a manifesto calling upon all groups throughout the country to support its demands. This representative student body was later reorganized according to the constitution of the Peking Student Federation into its Senate Council, which was composed of two representatives from each school and was responsible for making major policy decisions. By following the democratic procedure of free discussion and by efficiently disposing of matters, it truly functioned as the hub of the entire national movement. The Senate Council built a public reputation for being a "miniature parliament" of an excellence unprecedented in Chinese history.

In order to get on with urgent matters at hand, furthermore, at its initial meeting the Federation deputized the Peita Student Union secretariat to act as its executive branch. The whole movement came, in this way, to pivot around Peita. And in this way, too, I—a person who had always attached great importance to mass education and had advocated speaking directly to the public—became the first director of the Federation's Department for Public Speaking. My department organized and supervised the Federation's teams of public speakers. It promoted the "use native goods" movement and the boycott of Japanese goods, it formed organizations among the populace, and it distributed pamphlets and other publications. As a matter of fact, this committee constituted the pivotal body in promoting the innumerable explosive activities carried out by the Student Federation.

The dramatic events of May 4 in Peking reverberated through the country like a tempest. The Movement took on greater and greater strength, and its scope grew broader and broader. To support the lead of Peking, students in the major cities rose up and organized student councils, issued circular telegrams and declarations, staged demonstrations, and made public speeches. Most newspapers throughout the country gave prominent coverage to reporting the Movement and dealt editorially with it. They gave it credit for being a purely patriotic movement that truly reflected public opinion. Industrial and commerial circles, nonofficial organizations, prominent persons both at home and abroad, and Chinese studying in foreign countries all responded to the Movement. They all supported the students. The demand that the government dismiss pro-Japan officials mounted, while increasing popular antagonism was voiced against the suppression of the student movement.

On May 7, 1919, the thirty-two students that had been arrested were released. At the time Tuan Ch'i-jui, the leader of the pro-Japan clique, was not directly holding the reins of state power; and while he did not want to let these student antagonists off lightly, he was in no position to have everything his own way. For one thing, national public opinion was behind the students. The pro-Japan elements were isolated, and popular outrage focused on Ts'ao Ju-lin, Lu Tsung-yü, and Chang Tsung-hsiang. Then, too, a majority of bureaucrats and politicians in Peking, because they were caught up in the patriotism of the moment or because it suited their political ends, sympathized with the students to varying degrees, and they held influence with President Hsu Shih-ch'ang and Premier Ch'ien Neng-hsun. Tuan Ch'i-jui could not fully manipulate either of those men. As a result of all these factors, it became impossible for the Anfu and New Communications cliques to stifle the schools as they had planned. Nor did the government have any choice but to release the arrested students in an effort to appease the public.

The pro-Japan clique, nevertheless, was still strong. It still had Japanese support, too, and it did not rest content with defeat. Its members hated Peita. Centering their attack on Chancellor Ts'ai Yuan-p'ei, nothing would satisfy them but his removal. Although Ts'ai had tried to stop the demonstration, he gave us his unqualified support once it was launched; and he had withstood all attempts to put pressure on the students. Furthermore, he had thrown a great deal of effort into getting the arrested students released. Now, however, he feared that his presence would aggravate the situation. He sought to mollify the pro-Japan clique for the sake of Peita. On May 9 he silently resigned the chancellorship and departed from Peking, leaving behind a farewell note to Peita.[60]

The fact that Ts'ai had been forced to leave Peking raised the students' indignation to a new pitch. Most of them accepted his departure as clear proof of the government's oppression of education. Unless students fought the case against the government, they believed, the pro-Japan elements would grow increasingly arrogant, while both the schools and the patriotic movement would suffer. Therefore, when the Peking Student Federation accomplished nothing through various appeals and other efforts, it felt compelled to call a general student strike on May 19. The strike was intended to put pressure on the government to accept the students' patriotic demands; to punish Ts'ao, Lu, and Chang; and to induce Chancellor Ts'ai to return to Peita. Peking students refused to attend classes; and in response, students all over China did the same.

The May Fourth Movement also had its effect on a peace conference being held at the time at Shanghai between the Northern and Southern Chinese governments. On May 13 T'ang Shao-yi, the senior delegate from the South, introduced the famous Eight Conditions.[61] Their main points were that China not accept Japanese succession to German rights in Shantung, that the secret agreements between China and Japan be renounced, that those responsible for signing such agreements be punished, and that the Japanese-dominated "War Participation Army" be dissolved. The Eight Conditions were quite agreeable to the patriotic student movement, and they received broad support from people throughout the country. While they brought the peace conference to a standstill, they caused the patriotic movement to soar higher.

The Department of Public Speaking under my directorship may be said to have been the rallying point for activists from all Peking schools, and its influence on Student Federation policies was considerable. There were a great number of students working in the department. About eight hundred of them came from Peita alone. It was they who formed the speaking teams that worked in the streets throughout the Peking area, at stops along the railways, and in market towns. They delivered open-air speeches, promoted the boycott of Japanese goods, distributed printed matter, and stuck up posters. They also tried to organize the public for unified mass action. Indeed, these public speaking teams were the most significant student activity. It was they who explained the principles of this patriotic anti-Japanese movement to the general public, to the troops, and to the police. They fearlessly attacked the Peking government and its pro-Japan clique. The storm that threatened to break out all over the city at any moment was of their making.

Sometimes ineffective or misdirected at first, our techniques of public speaking improved with the passage of time. I particularly remember one occasion on which I led a team. Holding our banners high, we addressed a crowd of more than one hundred people that had gathered on a street corner to hear us. The scorching summer sun did not discourage them from listening. In fact, they brought us tea and water, and they clapped frequently in approval. Drenched with perspiration, our throats getting sore, my companions and I went right on haranguing them. When we had finished, an elderly Christian pastor in the audience, moved by our patriotic fervor, took us to his home, where he lectured us on the subject of public speaking. Our speeches were not colloquial enough, he pointed out, nor did they deal with matters that directly concerned the people. We had, moreover, failed to link the source of the people's suffering to the patriotic movement. Although we were working as hard as we could, he said, the average man simply could not grasp the full import of what we were trying to say. This ebullient man seemed to be trying to pass along to us in one conversation the knowledge that he had gained in a lifetime of preaching. Touched, we took to heart his suggestions for improving our work.

A major effort of the May Fourth Movement was a boycott of Japanese goods, as was the case in earlier anti-Japanese movements. It was a practical step that could hurt Japan economically; and the Student Federation and the Peking Chamber of Commerce worked together to implement it in the Peking area. In this work the Department of Public Speaking was especially active. It launched a movement known as National Salvation Units of Ten, which it hoped would spread nationwide.[62] This newly organized movement did play a considerable role in the boycott of Japanese goods. Each member of a unit pledged to the other nine members that he would neither buy nor sell Japanese goods and that he would urge stores not to sell them and the general public not to buy them. There were also incidents of Japanese goods being destroyed or damaged. This profoundly disturbed the government authorities. Intimidated by Japanese protests against the boycott, the authorities feared that an armed conflict with Japan might develop. And so they moved to halt the student speeches and the boycott. Still hopeful that the government would refuse to sign the Treaty of Versailles, students at first sought to prevent an irreparable break with the government. When troops and the police dispersed our speakers, we stopped public speaking for a few days. And we changed the slogan "Boycott Japanese Goods" into "Use Native Goods." Carrying sacks with the words "Use Native Goods" painted on them, we went from house to house pushing the sale of native products and carrying out the other tasks of the Department of Public Speaking in this way.

But the military and the police interfered even with this moderate kind of activity. On June 1, furthermore, Hsu Shih-ch'ang issued two pronouncements. One defended Ts'ao, Lu, and Chang; the other reiterated the ban on student strikes and disturbances. This convinced most students that the government intended to utterly destroy the patriotic movement. Their indignation promptly increased.

On June 2 a staff meeting of the Department of Public Speaking, which I presided over, decided to defy the official ban by resuming a large-scale program of public speaking. The Senate Council of the Peking Student Federation immediately gave its approval. The Department of Public Speaking then agreed to set an example by implementing the decision, whereupon I promptly led more than ten prominent department members on a mission to accomplish this. We marched through the central district, through Tun An market, along Wang-fu-ching (Royal Well) Street, and then toward the Gate of Heavenly Peace. With our banners flying, we began making speeches. Soldiers and policemen ordered us to stop, but we ignored them to harangue at the top of our lungs the masses that had gathered. This led to a fight with the soldiers and policemen which ended about six o'clock that afternoon, with the police overpowering six others and myself and dragging us into a jail. It was my first taste of prison life.

The news of our arrest spread with the speed of an electric current, outraging students in all of the schools. The public speaking campaign was greatly intensified. On the morning of June 3 groups of students from the different schools blanketed Peking. The banners of the Department of Public Speaking flew everywhere. The slogan they proclaimed to the masses this time was "The time has come for us to sacrifice freedom and life to save the nation." On June 4 the public speaking program grew still more. During those two days the military and police, acting according to plan, arrested nearly one thousand students, thus overcrowding the jails so badly that the third campus of Peita was taken over as a detention place for the students that had been arrested. It was this mass arrest of students that became known as the May Fourth Movement's "June Third Incident."

The measures taken to suppress student activities alarmed and disgruntled the citizenry of Peking. Some stores closed their doors and suspended business as an expression of sympathy. Girl students joined the speaking teams. Some soldiers that were barracked in the suburbs were sympathetic to the student cause, and the authorities had to shut the city gates to prevent them from entering and creating even greater chaos.

The June Third Incident alarmed the entire country. Students, merchants, and workers in such large cities as Shanghai and Tientsin were the first to voice support for the Peking students. They staged strikes in schools, stores, and factories. These were followed by similar incidents in other areas. The public seethed with indignation. There was nationwide alarm, and the Peking government truly felt the pressure of the people. They had no choice but to issue orders on June 5 releasing all of the students that had been arrested. On June 10 they capitulated further to student demands by dismissing the traitorous Ts'ao Ju-lin, Lu Tsung-yü, and Chang Tsung-hsiang. The fact that the Peking government had been forced to make these concessions encouraged the students not to let matters rest there. The Peking Student Federation released a message calling upon the entire country to keep up the struggle until Japanese succession to the German interests in Shantung had been officially rejected.

With the same zealousness Chinese students in Paris prevented Lu Cheng-hsiang and other Chinese delegates from attending the Peace Conference session at which the Treaty of Versailles was signed. The Chinese delegation eventually bowed before the pressure of the masses and on June 29 officially refused to sign the Treaty. It was then that the May Fourth Movement—a movement of historical significance—can be said to have achieved victory.

The European war and Japanese aggression precipitated the May Fourth Movement, while the New Culture Movement nourished it. But its importance is best realized if we understand thoroughly the humiliations to which China had been subjected for decades as well as the oppressive situation at the time. For decades the people of China had watched their country crumble around them without having any say in the matter. The May Fourth Movement, however, came as a rousing demonstration of the fact that the people could influence the internal affairs of their country as well as its foreign affairs. Indeed the May Fourth Movement startled the world, which began to realize that public opinion in China could not be totally ignored after all. Furthermore, it was a movement led by young people, and it was successful because it was able to shake off the political and intellectual evils that had shackled China in the past. Assuming a new way of doing things, applying a new method of thinking, using colloquial, easily understood language to communicate with the masses, and using effective organizational techniques, it wielded a tremendous influence. It embodied the progress of the age. It was the most important landmark in China's awakening. It was a great stride of the New Culture Movement and the patriotic movement, and even of the Chinese society as a whole. Moreover, the roots of the Chinese Communist Party, which was to be formed a few years later, go directly back to it. The May Fourth Movement was indeed epoch-making.

The Struggle to Defend Peita

Although circumstances forced the Peking government to accept the patriotic student demands, the government did not abandon its attempts to suppress student activities. Peita, the center of the May Fourth Movement, continued to be its chief target; and this made it impossible for students to resume peaceful classroom work. They had no choice but to continue their resistance activities.

Early in June, 1919, representatives of student federations in Peking, Tientsin, Nanking, and Hangchow assembled at Shanghai. This came shortly after the Peking government made the sweeping student arrests on June 3 which provoked merchants, workers, and students in Shanghai to stage large-scale strikes. Together with the Shanghai Student Federation, the representatives convened a National Student Congress in order to organize a National Student Federation. And on June 16, 1919, the National Student Federation was formally established at Shanghai. It was a great event in the Chinese student movement. For while the National Student Federation did not develop a dynamic program immediately, it did furnish an organization that integrated the activities of student federations throughout the country and that spoke with one voice on their behalf.

The Peking Student Federation sent groups of delegates to a number of areas to do the spadework of organizing the National Student Federation. Hsü Te-heng and Huang Jih-k'uei were among the first of these to arrive at Shanghai. Tuan Hsi-p'eng and several others rushed into Shanghai just in time for the inauguration of the National Student Federation, while a few other Peking delegates, including myself, managed to arrive only after the Congress had opened. By then the Congress was meeting in Nanyang Commercial Institute on Bubbling Well Road, where most of the delegates stayed. It spent several days discussing a constitution for the National Student Federation, pecking at words and phrases. Of the more than twenty delegates from Peking, only four were official delegates with voting power; and since I was not one of the four, I took little part in the official proceedings, but was assigned to work in the General Affairs Department of the Congress.

As I had no interest in the work of the General Affairs Department, I never officially assumed my post. Instead I conducted an inquiry into the progress of the student movement in various areas and found that the public speaking activities of student unions in Shanghai and elsewhere lagged behind our work in Peking. "Go into the masses" was not yet widely practiced. In order to set an example, I personally went to work in the streets of Shanghai. I wanted to move my fellow students to sell patriotic publications and to carry out the work done by the speaking teams of the Peking Student Federation. I made several news-vendor's sacks, filled them with copies of *Weekly Review, Sunday Review,* and other patriotic publications, and sallied forth into the streets, selling my publications and speaking to the passers-by.

Each evening when I returned to the school, some delegates, looking surprised, would grin and ask, "How was business, you great social reformer?"

Brimming with self-confidence, I would assure them, as if making a speech, "Not bad, naturally. All of us should have the spirit of going into the masses."

I was at this for only a few days, however. Then, in front of Wing On department store on Nanking Road, a foreign policeman roughly interfered with my activities. Without warning, he gave me a fierce shove from behind that nearly knocked me flat. When by standing my ground I showed that I would not give in to him, he acted as if he would arrest me. I did not want to create any trouble that might obstruct the organization of the National Student Federation, so I decided to leave without further show of resistance. Nor did I mention the unpleasant incident afterward. Nevertheless it left a deep impression in my heart, as it was the first time that I had tasted bitterness from a concession controlled by alien forces. It made me realize definitely that in addition to resisting Japan we must also resist the foreign concessions.

Early in July in Peking, Ch'en Tu-hsiu and eleven important members of the Peking Student Federation, including Lu Shih-i and Chiang Shao-yüan, were arrested one after another. We immediately received detailed reports. The Peking student delegation in Shanghai regarded it as a planned action by the Peking government to get control of Peita; and we realized that with the large delegation engaged in Shanghai, for the time being the Peking Student Federation was without capable, experienced leadership. It was decided, therefore, that I should immediately return to Peking and rally student resistance. We were determined that this center of the student movement should not be harmed. I caught the first train for the capital.

At that time the National Student Congress was arguing about its attitude toward the Peking government. Some delegates from Shanghai and the southern provinces expressed the view that the Peking government should not be recognized and that exclusive support should be given the Southern government at Canton. Delegates from Peking and other northern areas sympathized with the Southern government and particularly disliked the Peking government for its oppression of students, yet they did not wish to openly express this attitude. They feared that it would involve them in the whirlpool of practical politics—giving the Peking government a pretext for further oppression—and that more students would suffer as a consequence.

When we received news of the arrest of Ch'en Tu-hsiu and the eleven students, however, delegates began to insist that we adopt the Shanghai attitude and openly oppose the Peking government. Indeed, a few days after I left Shanghai the Congress invited Sun Yat-sen to address it. This was the first overt act showing that the country's students inclined toward Dr. Sun.

On returning to Peking, I learned from fellow students that the eleven students had been arrested under Peking District Court warrants. Due process of law would apply in their cases. Ch'en Tu-hsiu, however, had been kidnapped from his home by plain-clothes men; and no one knew where he was held. Some students were pessimistic. The government had been forced to bow its head the last time because the demands that the peace treaty not be signed and that the traitors be punished were supported by a roaring nationwide patriotic movement. But the situation was different now. During summer vacation most students had left their schools. Moreover, only one teacher and a few students had been arrested, and all of them came from just one school—Peita. It was doubtful that a thunderous movement against the persecution of Peita could be built up. Nevertheless, at a meeting of the Standing Committee of the Peita Student Union, I urged that our struggle continue. We would, I assured them, have the support of the whole country. I was then appointed its representative to the Peking Student Federation; and the Senate Council of Peking Student Federation promptly elected me chairman of the Federation. Thus, I spearheaded a new struggle against the Peking government.

During summer vacation neither the Peking Student Federation nor the Peita Student Union was as active as it had been in May and June. About two-thirds of the students had left Peking on vacation. Some important Student Federation members had gone to Shanghai and elsewhere, and others had been arrested. Moreover, some former activists, fearing arrest, either remained inactive or stayed away from Peking. That left only a few reuglar workers at the Student Federation, most of whom were new hands; and this increased my own responsibility. I was so busy that for at least one month I did not return to my dormitory. Resting briefly on a chair in the Federation office when I was too tired to go on, I ate in the office and worked an average of sixteen hours a day. I presided at various meetings, directed the work of the secretariat and the departments, maintained liaison and correspondence with numerous organizations and prominent people, worked vigorously for the release of the students that had been arrested, and mobilized the students in many different schools. The work went well. The Federation soon regained its strength while I experienced another lesson in leadership.

In order to stand up to the authorities the presidents, teachers, and staff members of most educational institutions adopted the Student Federation's stand. The presidents of eight national colleges and universities organized a School Presidents' Committee, with T'ang Erh-ho, the president of Peking Medical College, as its spokesman. And teachers and staff members at various specialized institutions also formed a federation. Ma Hsü-lun and Shen Chih-yuan were its spokesmen. They had frequent contact with the Student Federation, and I saw a good deal of them. Together we advocated "saving education from oppression," "retaining Chancellor Ts'ai Yuan-p'ei," and "opposing government persecution of Mr. Ch'en Tu-hsiu and the patriotic students."

Li Ta-chao was an active member of the Federation of Teachers and Staff Members. Even though it was summer vacation, he regularly went to his office in the library, and I saw him more often than anyone else. Not only did he give me many valuable suggestions, but he often drafted important documents for me. He also did his best to coordinate the views of teachers and students while maintaining constant contact with the press. From that time on, Li Ta-chao and I became comrades-in-arms despite the fact that he was a teacher and I a student.

Towards the end of August the Peking District Court, after having detained Lu Shih-i and ten other students for two months, finally declared its investigation at an end. It opened their trial.

On the day of the trial the Student Federation organized a demonstration of more than a thousand students in front of the courthouse. We all clamored for entry to the trial. We also protested the students' illegal arrest and detention and called for their immediate release. A large body of police was stationed in front of the courthouse, all set to move against us, but we managed to occupy all of the forty-odd spectator

seats in the courtroom. The remaining student demonstrators surrounded the courthouse.

Our lawyer, Liu Tsung-yu, a noted jurist and well-known leader of
the Research clique, volunteered his services and did everything possible to defend the students. The prosecutor was hard pressed to cope
with Liu's defense. Furthermore, those of us that were watching the
trial glared angrily at the prosecutor when he charged the accused with
assaulting officials, resisting the government, and disturbing public order.
And when Liu took up the defense—which, briefly, was that the accused
were prompted by patriotism and were innocent of any crime—we all
nodded our approval. The students, without disturbing the order of the
court, managed to clearly express their views; and this encouraged the
defense counsel to declare that if the accused were found guilty, thousands and tens of thousands of students throughout the country would
ask to be arrested. This strongly smacked of a threat. In any event,
under such pressure from both inside and outside the court, the presiding
judge ruled against the wishes of the government authorities. He declared the accused to be innocent and ordered their release on the spot.

We escorted the eleven released students back to the university,
cheering all the way; and on the campus we staged a welcoming rally.
It was a scene of unforgettable enthusiasm.

Because of our redoubled efforts, about two weeks later the government authorities quietly released Ch'en Tu-hsiu without trial. We
held a rally at the Peita third campus to welcome him back. As chairman of the rally, I delivered the welcoming address, pouring my heart
into it. I praised Ch'en as the pillar of Peita, the vanguard of the New
Culture Movement, the ideological leader of the May Fourth Movement,
and our respected mentor. I protested his illegal arrest by the Peking
government. I expressed sympathy for the persecution he had suffered,
and I fervently welcomed him back. In his reply Ch'en expressed the
respect and love that he felt for Peita, its teachers and students, and his
appreciation for what they had done. He declared that he would not
bend under persecution, that whether he remained at Peita or not, he
would continue his struggle. Soon afterward Ch'en Tu-hsiu, on the
advice of his colleagues, left Peking for the South. He never returned
to Peita.

These events unfolded in act after act; and the time approached
when Peita would reopen its classes. The government had appointed
Hu Jen-yuan to be the new Peita chancellor, but he had not dared to

assume his duties. For it was the unanimous view of the students and faculty of the university that the movement to defend Peita could not be considered successful until Chancellor Ts'ai Yuan-p'ei was reinstated. To accept a lesser solution would merely encourage the government to further action against the university. Because I had had much contact with Chancellor Ts'ai and because I knew well the development of events since May 4, my schoolmates elected me as their representative to visit Chancellor Ts'ai at his home in Chekiang Province and to urge him to return. So I made another trip to the South.

When I reached Shanghai, however, I learned from Tuan Hsi-p'eng and a number of other Peita students there that they had already seen Chancellor Ts'ai. He had assured them that he definitely would not return to Peita at that time. He had suggested, moreover, that Chiang Meng-lin act as provisional chancellor under the title of General Affairs Director of the University. Peita faculty and staff members and students who were then in Shanghai had all accepted Chancellor Ts'ai's opinion, they told me, and there was no need for me to visit him. Furthermore, they believed that the Ministry of Education in Peking would accept Chiang Meng-lin as acting chancellor.

Tuan Hsi-p'eng and I and a few others called on Chiang, who was staying at the Kiangsu Provincial Education Association. In the name of the Peita student body we assured him that he would be welcomed as acting chancellor. Very soon afterward he came to Peita and acted for Chancellor Ts'ai. He took up a most difficult task.

Thus, the movement to defend Peita came to an end. University classes began in October. I resigned from the Peita Student Union and the Peking Student Federation and returned to my studies.

My First Meeting with Sun Yat-sen

The Peking government placed my name high on its blacklist because of my part in the May Fourth Movement. When it tried to arrest me, I went again to Shanghai, and there I continued to be active in the resistance movement against the Peking government and in the patriotic movement against Japan. There, too, I had frequent contact with important people of the time. And I had the dramatic experience of meeting Dr. Sun Yat-sen.

As mentioned in the last section, when classes reopened at Peita in

October, 1919, I resigned all duties on the Student Union and the Student Federation. Later on I joined the Morning Garden Society (Hsi Yuan), which Teng Chung-hsia and some other schoolmates organized. Morning Garden was inspired by the New Life Movement then popular among Peking students. Promoted chiefly by the anarchists, the New Life Movement encouraged students to live communally, to assist one another in their studies, and to dirty their hands with manual labor.[63] A group would band together and rent a house, in which they did all the housework themselves, including the cooking. These houses were usually called "New Villages" (Hsin Ch'eng), and we named our new village "Morning Garden."

There were sixteen members of Morning Garden, most of them from Hunan Province and many of them quite notable persons. There was, for example, I K'e-i, who has already been mentioned. An eloquent political critic, he delighted in ridiculing the ugliness of practical politics and of prominent people belonging to either the old or modern schools of thought. Another member was Lo Chang-lung, who was then studying in the German Department. A youthful scholar doing personal research in Marxism, he always thought things out very carefully before acting on anything, and he was fascinated by the revolution in Russia. Lo's knowledge of German gave him direct access to Marxist literature, which was still closed to most of us because so little had been translated into Chinese. It was Lo who led our frequent, earnest discussions of Marx, Hegel, and the Russian Revolution. Teng Chung-hsia, the New Life advocate who looked just like an old-style scholar, perpetually harangued for the cause of social reform. In him the qualities of a traditional scholar and a missionary preacher were combined. Most other members had given good accounts of themselves in the May Fourth Movement. Each had outstanding qualities of one sort or another.

Of the members of the Morning Garden group, I had worked hardest in the student movement; so the others regarded me as a practical revolutionist of marked ability. Teng Chung-hsia jokingly called me the "student V.I.P."

But this "student V.I.P." was only a young man, twenty-two years of age, and he did not want to be submerged in the whirlpool of politics. The only movement that I felt I had to participate in was the May Fourth Movement, since it was an emergency patriotic movement. I did not want to involve myself deeply in other movements. Chiefly, I wanted to lay the foundations for my future by finishing my course at the university.

The Peking Student Federation, however, continued to be active, promoting the boycott of Japanese goods with special vigor. It also supported the Tientsin Student Federation and the All-Circles National Salvation Federation when those bodies were persecuted by local authorities in October, 1919.[64] In November it supported the Foochow students, many of whom were killed by Japanese hoodlums for boycotting Japanese goods.[65] Yet students in many Peking schools took to heart the slogan of Ts'ai Yuan-p'ei: "Save the country, but do not throw away your books; study, but do not forget to save your country." Most of them returned to class; and I also resumed my studies with great determination.

At this time two famous scholars, John Dewey and Bertrand Russell, lectured in Peking; and they further aroused my interest in study. I was an engrossed listener at most of their lectures. Except for the weekly speeches that were connected with mass education, I politely declined all invitations to take part in the student movement. My fellow students extended many invitations because they regarded me as an experienced hand.

At noon on one December day in 1919 a detachment of police suddenly graced Morning Garden with their presence. They dashed to my room to arrest me. But that day it was my turn to cook, and I was in the kitchen. Fellow students managed to warn me that trouble once more hung over my head. Immediately I smeared soot on my face and, pretending that nothing was amiss, went ahead with my work. After searching for a while, the police left, disappointed, for my improvised disguise had fooled them. They thought I was a professional cook.

After five o'clock that afternoon my housemates made sure that the police stationed around Morning Garden and the detectives hiding nearby had left. They then escorted me to the Peita first campus at Sha-t'an. I took refuge there, since the police were still hesitant to break into a school to make arrests.

At the university I met with Acting Chancellor Chiang Meng-lin and some responsible members of the Peita Student Union, and we discussed measures to cope with the situation. We believed that this police action was another move by the Anfu Clique government, acting under Japanese pressure, to retaliate against the students. Many names were reportedly on a government blacklist of students marked for arrest. Obviously, a new wave of oppression against the schools was beginning; and to ward off the blow, we decided that all students threatened with arrest should go into hiding for the time being. Some of them could go to other cities, where they could stir up support for the students in Peking. It was decided that Lo Chia-lun—another student who had slipped through the net—and I would go to Shanghai as representatives of the Peking Student Federation. And at dawn the next morning Lo Chia-lun and I, afraid to board the train in the East Station at Ch'ien Men, went a roundabout way through Yung-ting Men and slipped out of Peking as soon as that gate was opened. We got on the train at a small station and, feeling depressed, proceeded southward.

Shanghai, with the foreign concessions as its core, seemed to be comparatively free. The concession authorities appeared unwilling to meddle in the internal political affairs of China, which were perhaps too complex for them to know what to do. Within the Peking government the struggle between the Chihli and Anhwei cliques was growing more and more acute. Tuan Ch'i-jui and his Anfu Club controlled the government, to be sure; but President Hsu Shih-ch'ang had secretly aligned himself with the Chihli militarists against Tuan. North of the Great Wall, Chang Tso-lin, disgruntled about Hsu Shu-cheng—the Northeast Frontier Commissioner and right-hand man of Tuan Ch'i-jui—also began to join hands with the Chihli clique. Among Tuan's own people, moreover, there was antagonism between Chin Yun-p'eng, the premier, and Hsu Shu-cheng.[66]

At the same time in the Southern government at Canton there was the conflict between Sun Yat-sen, who was then living in Shanghai, and Ch'en Ch'un-hsuan, one of the seven directors-general of that government. In addition, there were open and hidden conflicts among the so-called Kwangsi clique, the Kwangtung clique, and the Yunnan clique.

But North and South were able to meet in Shanghai for their peace conference. Indeed, Shanghai was the center at which politicians, bureaucrats, and warlords constantly made political deals of all sorts. It was also the molder of the nation's public opinion; and national organizations, including the National Student Federation, all had their headquarters there. Thus, student representatives and delegates from organizations of all parts of the country converged in a steady flow upon Shanghai.

At the time three important groups opposed the Peking government and sympathized with the student movement. The first of these was Sun Yat-sen's group. It would have nothing at all to do with the Peking government. It was attempting to regain control of the government in the South, and so it adopted a more radical attitude in cooperating with the student movement than did the other two. The second group was the Research clique, which might be considered the Peking government's opposition party. The Anfu Club had ousted the Research clique from the Peking government, while during the active period of the May Fourth Movement the Anfu Club attacked Lin Ch'ang-min, Wang Ta-hsieh, and other members of the Research clique because of the leading roles they played in the anti-Japanese National Foreign Affairs Institute. All of the members of the Research clique sympathized with the student movement and the New Culture Movement. The third group included militarists and politicians of the Chihli clique. Wu P'ei-fu, who had recently risen to prominence in that clique, was then a division commander at Hengyang, a strategic position between the North and the South. He established a southern alliance aimed at overthrowing Tuan and sent out circular telegrams sympathizing with the popular anti-Japanese movement.[67] Advocating peace betwen the North and the South, opposing any negotiations between the Peking government and Japan on the Shantung issue, and demanding that a national assembly be called, Wu made himself out to be a truly patriotic, anti-Japanese soldier. At that time the liaison man for this clique in Shanghai was Sun Hung-i, who had been Minister of the Interior in the cabinet of Tuan Ch'i-jui but had been forced out of the cabinet by Hsu Shu-cheng.

The National Federation of All Circles of the People, which was located in Shanghai, was a federation of organizations from all over the country, of which there were a good many. There was the Tientsin All-Circles National Salvation Association, formed at Tientsin a few days after the May Fourth Movement by students, merchants, and Chinese missionaries. Another was the Joint Committee of Industrial and Commercial Interests, Schools, and Newspapers, organized in Shanghai at the time of the June Third Incident. The Shantung Provincial National Salvation Association, formed by various organizations in Shantung Province, was established even earlier, probably when the Conference of Paris first took up the Shantung question. After the National Student Federation was founded, in any event, these groups, along with others, jointly sponsored the National Federation of All Circles of the People. The National Student Federation was one of its pillars. The leading business organization to join—since none of the various provincial and municipal general chambers of commerce took part—was the Shanghai Shopkeepers Federation of Industry and Commerce. Provincial and municipal federations of all organizations, however, were ex-officio members of the National Federation. Although the National Federation did not include all of the organizations in the country, it nevertheless constituted a formidable force.

When Lo Chia-lun and I arrived at Shanghai in December, 1919, the policy of the National Federation of All Circles of the People was to oppose the Peking government; but there were very marked political differences within its ranks. The influence of KMT members was relatively strong, and they steered the Federation. They could not, however, see eye to eye with the Research clique and the Chihli clique. As the KMT saw it, members of the Research clique were merely remnants of the monarchical party who might compromise with Peking at any time. Wu P'ei-fu was viewed as an opportunist who catered to public opinion and exploited both the masses and the anti-Japanese patriotic movement in order to gain prestige for his own clique. The KMT took particular exception to the collusion between Wu P'ei-fu and the Kwangsi clique in the Southern government, because it threatened to make it more difficult for the KMT to gain control of that government.[68] Under these circumstances it was difficult for us to muster Federation support for the student movement in Peking; for while we tended to favor the KMT, we also sought to rally as many other groups as possible to form a united front against the Peking government. To accomplish this we had to ignore the doubts and suspicions of the KMT. We worked determinedly, reinforced by the unreserved assistance of two other Peita students then in Shanghai, K'ang Pai-ch'ing and Hsü Te-heng.

Lo Chia-lun and I addressed a meeting of the National Federation of All Circles of the People, discussing the Peking government's persecution of students and its prohibiting of the movement to boycott Japanese goods. There was a danger, we said, that Peking would negotiate with Japan on the Shantung question. We proposed that all organizations in the country join forces in a unanimous protest against the activities of the Peking government. But this drew the immediate opposition of KMT members.

Shao Li-tzu, who represented the KMT newspaper *Min-kuo Jih-pao* (Republican Daily News), and some other delegates to the Federation who were KMT members repeatedly insisted that they would not recognize the Peking government in any way. They contended that any demands made upon the Peking government would be tantamount to a disguised form of recognition.[69] We tried to effect a compromise between our views as student representatives and theirs. It was possible to attack the Peking government while at the same time not recognizing it, we pointed out. By voicing opposition to the Peking government on various issues, we would be taking the steps that were necessary to mobilize the masses to overthrow it. However, they persisted in their stand, suspecting that we still had illusions of getting along with Peking. They stressed the importance of severing all connections with the Peking government and of nationwide popular resistance to its taxation. To say the least, these radical policies were difficult to implement in the areas controlled by Peking.

As representatives of the students, we also had to maintain numerous contacts with the political bigwigs living in the foreign concessions. Naturally we came to establish relationships of varying depths with them. Our task was to effect liaison with different organizations in order to resist the oppression that the Peking government had practiced on the students and to stop the betrayal of Shantung. This was the continuation of the May Fourth Movement; and it still upheld the principles of "Resist the Foreign Aggressors," which called for restoration of the Shantung rights, and "Destroy the National Traitors," which called for resistance to the Peking government and the overthrow of the rule of the pro-Japan group. Needless to say, this newborn force of the students was an object to be won over by the different political groups. These factors mutually influenced one another, promoting the development of certain situations at the time, and also indicated certain trends for the future.

Wu P'ei-fu was one person that we could not afford to overlook. He had emerged as the favorite son of the time. His views, endorsing those of the popular organizations, were backed by military strength; and this had considerable effect on the political situation in Peking. For this reason Sun Hung-i, with Wu P'ei-fu behind him, became one of the prominent residents of Shanghai. There were references to the Major Sun (Sun Yat-sen) and the Minor Sun (Sun Hung-i). We saw the latter often, although we were fully aware that he was a person of the old bureaucratic type. He held no personal attraction for young people like us. Nevertheless, Wu P'ei-fu had proposed the convocation of a national assembly to settle all national issues peacefully; he had opposed negotiations with Japan over her claims in Shantung Province; and he had advocated that the people themselves raise money to redeem the Chiao-chi Railway. These ideas had won extensive support from popular organizations. The popular organizations in Shanghai held a large mass rally at the Public Stadium, and the rally addressed an open message of support to Wu P'ei-fu. Lo Chia-lun and I helped to push the message through. In Peking, however, in January, 1920, the Government dissolved both the Peking Student Federation and a national assembly formed in response to the views of Wu P'ei-fu, and it sealed their offices. Nothing came of the national assembly idea at that time because the different organizations and political groups could not agree upon the purposes it should serve.

Another man we saw frequently was Chang Tung-sun, chief editor of *Shih-shih Hsin-pao* (Current Events Daily) and Shanghai representative of the Research clique. Liang Ch'i-ch'ao, a prominent figure in the 1898 coup d'état and leader of the Research clique, returned to Shanghai from Europe early in 1920; and Chang made an appointment for Lo Chia-lun, Hsü Te-heng, K'ang Pai-ch'ing, and me to see Liang in Chang's newspaper office. Liang told us of the impressions that he had formed during his European tour, and then he talked about the special importance of carrying on academic research. He expressed regret that his political movement, after more than two decades, had not been successful; and he declared that he had no more interest in politics. Bringing up his Great Plan for Fifty Years of Cultural Work, he said that he hoped it would have the support of the youth. We explained that we had been forced out of our classrooms and into the present situation, that we could not very well carry on academic research, and that we had to engage in the anti-Japanese patriotic movement. Naturally, we also assured him of our respect for his plan to devote the whole of his energy to cultural work.

After leaving Liang Ch'i-ch'ao, we discussed him among ourselves. We concluded that Liang's words typified the passive stand of the Research clique, which, having lost its political foundation, was immersed in the dilemma of not knowing whether to advance or retreat. Liang, we agreed, had made important contributions to the movement for Chinese cultural enlightenment, but this reformism or ameliorationism had not found its way in China. Liang had gained nothing by joining the retinue of Yuan Shih-k'ai or by being, for a time, a member of Tuan Ch'i-jui's staff. Indeed, his illusion that his ends could be served by relying on the elements in power and by assuming the role of a Cavour

—the ninteenth-century Italian reformist premier of Piedmont whom he admired so much—must have been shattered by this time.[70] Now, moving toward a sort of neo-traditionalism, he sought to return to academic research. Perhaps his achievements would be greater in that field, we mused. In any event, this was the age of the New Culture Movement; and we believed that perhaps he was a little out of date.

Our contacts with the KMT people were closer than with the others and were many-sided. Such active cadres of Sun Yat-sen as Hu Hanmin, Wang Ching-wei, Chu Chih-hsin, Liao Chung-k'ai, Tai Chi-t'ao, Yeh Ch'u-ts'ang, and Shao Li-tzu were in constant touch with us. Hu Han-min and Wang Ching-wei, the two revolutionary leaders that ranked next below Sun Yat-sen, lived in seclusion; only when there were important matters for discussion would they be called on. Tai Chi-t'ao, Chu Chih-hsin, and Liao Chung-k'ai were more closely associated with us, and we frequently got together for talks and discussions. The major topic was often the promotion of the New Culture Movement. Tai Chi-t'ao liked to discuss socialism and smacked somewhat of the scholar. Chu Chih-hsin liked to discuss current affairs and showed himself to be a man of extensive knowledge. Liao Chung-k'ai was the ascetic monk of the revolution, silent and speaking little, but ever smilingly enjoying the views of other people. Yeh Ch'u-ts'ang and Shao Li-tzu represented the *Republican Daily News* at the meetings of various people's organizations, and they were virtually the public representatives of the KMT; so they seemed to be our co-workers. Shao Li-tzu, the general manager of the *Republican Daily News,* had to surmount the various difficulties met with by the paper and to raise funds to meet expenses; and so he was forever running hither and thither, never at rest. Yeh Ch'u-ts'ang, chief editor of the paper, regularly lived a night life. In his very small editorial room he would lean over his desk, busy writing and correcting manuscripts and, in addition, drinking wine and composing poetry. At the time, the National Federation of All Circles of the People adopted a resolution protesting levies on industrial and commercial organizations in the whole country. It was a masterpiece of literary composition by Yeh and Shao. We had actively supported it with enthusiasm.

One noon during the spring of 1920 Hsü Te-heng, K'ang Pai-ch'ing, Liu Ch'ing-yang (a representative of Tientsin student girls), and I lunched together at a restaurant in the French Concession. When we had finished, we strolled toward the French Park. K'ang Pai-ch'ing pointed to 29 Rue Molière and said, "That is the residence of Dr. Sun Yat-sen."

"We have never called on him," Hsü Te-heng promptly declared, "and we might as well take this opportunity to drop in now."

"Very good idea," I joined in. "As a matter of fact, Lo Chia-lun and I had decided to call on him within the next few days. It's too bad the great literary figure isn't with us today."

"It doesn't matter," they agreed. "We can just have an informal talk today. The next time we will bring Lo Chia-lun along and make an official call."

So we crossed the road, went up to Dr. Sun's house, and told the gateman of our intention. "People that wish to call upon the Generalissimo must first make an appointment," he told us. "You cannot see him without an appointment."

This so infuriated Hsü Te-heng that he bellowed in protest, "We want nothing from the Generalissimo. We only came to pay our respects. You mean you can't transmit our message without an appointment?"

Liao Chung-k'ai, who was downstairs in the house at the time, heard Hsü's resounding voice. He came out immediately, took us into the living room, and went upstairs to inform Dr. Sun. Dr. Sun promptly came down to the living room. After a polite exchange of greetings the young, spirited Hsü Te-heng began by saying, "We have always held you in great respect, Dr. Sun, because you are the leader of the common people. We did not realize that your door was so closely guarded and that you normally had no contact with the common people."

Sun Yat-sen, looking unruffled, made no reply. An awkward silence followed; so I tried to break the ice with an explanation of the point of our visit. "As the nation is in such disorder," I said, "we have come to pay our respects and to seek your guidance."

To this remark Sun Yat-sen replied, "I shall be glad to hear your views first."

That took the lid off the box of talk. One after another, the four of us spoke up. Some of us gave an enthusiastic account of the student movement and the mass movement in general. Some criticized the KMT's attitude toward the mass movement. Some pointed out that there was chaos in both the North and the South and asked if Dr. Sun had any plans and policies to cope with the situation. Some even expressed the belief that Dr. Sun paid attention only to high-level practical political activities and that he sought support from abroad, from warlord armies, and from bandits, while failing to rally the various mass movements and the New Culture Movement to his cause.

After hearing such frank talk from these youths, Dr. Sun apparently decided to treat us seriously, not just to send us away with a few platitudinous remarks. He spoke his mind with a frankness equal to ours. Briefly, he said that it was fine for us students to resist the Peking government and that our revolutionary spirit was to be commended. He added, however, that we did nothing but write articles, hold meetings, stage parades and protest, run about making appeals, and call strikes that lasted for a few days. All that the Peking government needed to put down thousands, or tens of thousands, of demonstrating students, he declared, was a few machine guns. If he gave us five hundred rifles, he asked, could we find five hundred students willing to brave death by taking them up and attacking the blackguards in Peking? If so, he said, we would truly be revolutionists.

After listening to him, the four of us grew all the more impulsive. We protested that Dr. Sun greatly underrated the youth of the day. The students would take up five thousand or fifty thousand rifles, not to mention five hundred. "The questions today are what the revolution should be for and how we should carry out the revolution," I said.

The other three, taking Dr. Sun to task, brought up the following points: Dr. Sun himself had commanded armed forces that were tens of thousands of men strong. How was it, then, that the revolution still failed? The New Culture Movement opposed the old ideology and the old influences; and in its difficult struggle, the students, barefisted, had braved death by antagonizing the Peking government. Merely because they did not arm themselves with rifles, were they to be excluded from the ranks of the revolutionaries? If that was Dr. Sun's attitude, it was no wonder that KMT followers kept saying that we harbored illusions about endorsing the Peking government every time we made demands of it. Furthermore, it seemed as though Dr. Sun not only slighted the student movement and the New Culture Movement, but also ignored the workers, the merchants in the cities, and the common people in the countryside. Apparently Dr. Sun attached importance only to guns, not to the masses.

And one of us added, "It is not easy for one to see the emergence of new situations and new forces. But if a revolutionary leader fails to see a new age clearly, if he ignores the trend of the masses, he just might be left behind."

"Dr. Sun is the man who holds our greatest respect," I said. "But I should like to ask the causes of defeat in the past. Shouldn't we change our methods today? Do you really mean to say that all you expect of the youth of today is that they take up five hundred rifles?"

We talked so long and so rapidly that Sun Yat-sen was not able to get in a word. Occasionally he appeared to be agitated, sometimes he showed disapproval, and at other times he nodded his head in agreement. In any event, he listened attentively and thoughtfully, as though giving us a chance to get everything off our minds. More than three hours passed in this way, and then one of us said, "It is after five o'clock, time we left."

Liao Chung-k'ai, who had been standing to one side all the time, interposed, "Stay a little longer. The discussion has just reached its crucial stage."

Then Sun Yat-sen calmly and in measured tones replied to the many questions we had raised. It was comparable to a parliamentary scene in which the government spokesman, after being questioned by the opposition, makes his reply. Sun Yat-sen spoke for a long time, chiefly making the following points:

1. He wanted the students to take up arms in the hope of further raising their revolutionary spirit, but he had never underestimated such student activities as holding meetings and demonstrations and mobilizing the masses against the Peking government. He believed, in fact, that these activities had an important effect.

2. Our charges that he had not attached adequate importance to the student movement and the New Culture Movement, he admitted, were not groundless. He declared, however, that he had paid great attention to propaganda and that he had always insisted that propaganda and military activities were of equal importance. The reason that the youth and the people in general did not understand his principles and purposes was that his propaganda work had not been adequately executed in actuality.

3. He reiterated his Three Principles of the People and the fact that he stood for the unconditional overthrow of the Peking government. He asked us to have faith in his Three Principles of the People and to cooperate for the sake of the future.

Sun Yat-sen's graciousness entirely transformed the atmosphere, which until then had been charged with antagonism. Everyone now wore a smile.

"We students always sound as if we are quarreling when we speak," I said lightly. "Actually, though, we were sincerely seeking your advice. Our talk today has been very thorough, and we fully support Dr. Sun's views. Next time we shall seek even more penetrating advice from you."

Dr. Sun, also looking very pleased, replied, "I have very much enjoyed this very candid interview."

And so we took leave of him.

On our way to a dinner being given by a publisher, we talked about the meeting. The stubborn Generalissimo had proved quite amenable to our views, we agreed, and it would be possible to lay the foundations of future cooperation on our interview.

The place was already packed with guests when we arrived at the dinner. Hsü Te-heng and Liu Ch'ing-yang, the two "big guns," began bragging about how we had just subdued Sun Yat-sen. K'ang Pai-ch'ing, the poet, promptly sketched a humorous word picture of the interview. Guests from the various cliques that were disgruntled about the KMT listened elatedly, while the KMT members that were present kept silent and looked rather depressed. But when we finally announced that the interview had been most satisfactory and that Dr. Sun was a truly great statesman who merited our respect, it was the KMT members' turn to feel elated, while those at odds with the KMT started talking of other matters.

Many people at that time were critical of Sun Yat-sen and the KMT. The chief charge against them was that they were given to empty talk. This charge referred to the formless organizational structure of the KMT, to the fact that it controlled no geographical area, to its lack of military backing, and to its fondness for advocating radical measures that were almost impossible to put into practice. The charge also arose from the fact that Sun Yat-sen had suffered defeat in the 1911 Revolution, in the 1913 campaign against Yuan Shih-k'ai, and in the period of the Chung-kuo Ko-ming Tang that followed. These were facts known to all. On September 1, 1917, he assumed the post of Generalissimo of the Military Government for the Protection of the Constitution, at Canton; but subsequent events only showed how little actual power he had. The two powerful marshals that Sun Yat-sen appointed to posts directly under him—T'ang Chi-yao of Yunnan and Lu Jung-t'ing of Kwangsi—adopted a position of sitting on the fence and never assumed their posts. Moreover, the rump parliament at Canton never achieved a quorum, and it was divided against itself into numerous cliques. There was no way of controlling the militarists that actually held power—such men as Lu Jung-t'ing, Ch'en Ping-kun, and Mo Jung-hsin. They protected opium-smoking and gambling concessions; and this brought trouble to the area. In May, 1918, the rump parliament, as a result of the efforts of the Kwangsi warlords and the Political Study clique, decided to reorganize the Military government. It abolished the generalissimo system and adopted instead a system with seven directors-general at the head of the government. The seven directors-general were elected on May 20.[71] Although Sun Yat-sen was one of the seven, it was clear that he was no longer in command; and so he left Canton on May 21 for Shanghai, traveling by way of Taiwan and Japan. On August 7 he formally resigned as a director of the Southern government. From that time until 1920, while he planned his return to power, he stayed in Shanghai and engaged principally in writing. It was during this period that he wrote his *Industrial Development of China* and his *Theory of Sun Yat-sen* (*Sun Wen Hsueh Hsueh*). The articles published by his followers during the same period in *Construction Magazine* and *Weekly Review,* some of which dealt favorably with Marxism, showed a resurgence of the revolutionary spirit of the old *Min Pao* of T'ung-meng Hui days. The KMT obviously was undergoing a rebirth.

Sun Yat-sen had his worst run of luck during the time of the so-called Government for the Protection of the Constitution. The Kwangsi warlords and the Political Study clique were responsible for the confusion in the ranks of the Southern government, but nominally Sun Yat-sen was in the position of leadership. As most people saw it, Sun Yat-sen was not only powerless to influence the Southern situation but was made to bear the blame for the political chaos there as well. Yet the views that he and his followers expressed in Shanghai began to attract the sympathy of most young people. At the same time, the KMT veterans, although separated from the youth of the May Fourth Movement in age, were still very close to them in their belief that revolution was necessary. We may see, indeed, that the May Fourth Movement was one factor that roused the KMT. And this rejuvenation of the Party marked the point at which youths that were baptized in the May Fourth Movement began to incline toward Sun Yat-sen and the revolutionary forces he represented.

My personal contact with Sun Yat-sen may be taken as a concrete example of this inclination. About ten days after our first meeting, Dr. Sun invited me to see him alone, and I accepted. After we had chatted a bit about the current situation and the student movement, a man named Chu Chuo-wen arrived. I learned that he was in charge of Sun Yat-sen's labor activities. Apparently he also had come by appointment. After the introductions, he joined in the conversation. Changing the subject, Sun Yat-sen asked me, "Is it true, as I hear, that you are interested in Marxism?" When I said that I was, he launched into a long discourse which amounted essentially to this: There were many schools of Socialist thought, of which Marxism was only one. In Europe, he had had contact with the leaders of all Socialist schools and had studied all of their theories. By absorbing the best in these theories and weighing them against the actual conditions in China, he had created his Three Principles of the People.

Then he pointed to a full bookcase and said, "All these books of mine are on socialism. You may take any of them to read." Apparently familiar with my work in the student movement, he went on to say, "I hear that during the student movement you paid special attention to the mass movement and the labor movement. Is that true?" I told him that the only thing we had done about mass organization during the May Fourth Movement was the drive to form National Salvation Units of Ten and that I had started looking into the conditions of existing trade unions only since coming to Shanghai. He talked about the theoretical and practical work he had done in connection with the labor movement. Then he pointed to Chu Chuo-wen. "Comrade Chu Chuo-wen is a labor movement specialist," he said. "Why don't you talk about it?"

Chu talked for a bit about his many years of experience in the labor movement. His main point seemed to be that the workers must be made to believe in the Three Principles of the People, and especially in the Principle of the People's Livelihood, if the labor movement were to have any significance.

I raised two points which I thought the KMT had not fully appreciated. The first was that the workers should be organized in trade unions according to industry, types of work, and factories. The second was that they should be helped to struggle for higher pay and better working and living conditions.

Sun Yat-sen indicated that all of these objectives should be pursued simultaneously, and that brought our conversation to an end. Our first two interviews apparently made a deep impression on Sun Yat-sen. On the many occasions when I met with him in subsequent years, he more than once referred to the first times I met him, when I was still a representative of Peking students.

I had contact with all trade-union organizations in Shanghai, for I tried to win them over to the cause of the Peking student movement. One of them was the All-China Federation of Industries, which Sun Yat-sen dominated. I knew almost everyone on its staff. Its resident director, Huang Chieh-min, was in immediate charge of the Federation. He enjoyed discussing socialism, and we often talked about the subject during my frequent contacts with him. The chairman was Ts'ao Ya-po, an old T'ung-meng Hui member. He was too preoccupied with his own political activities to pay much attention to the Federation. In any event, a few days after my second interview with Sun Yat-sen, the two of them asked me to participate in their work. Huang Chieh-min formally proposed that I serve as general secretary of the organization, with full power to reorganize and develop it so as to make it in fact, as well as in name, a truly national trade-union federation. This was a task, he explained, in which Sun Yat-sen was especially interested.

I was only a refugee student representative, but after due consideration I agreed to take the job on a trial basis. The board of directors of the organization then officially appointed me general secretary. Early in March, 1920, the Federation held a general membership meeting on the French Church commons in the French Concession. More than three hundred people attended, and I delivered my inaugural address to them.

The All-China Federation of Industries claimed more than ten thousand members. Upon investigation, however, I found that the membership consisted of nothing more than a list of names. Actually there were handfuls of members in this factory or that. There was no way of even knowing to which factories most of the people on the list were supposed to belong. Besides, some of the members were not workers at all. They had probably been recruited through the secret-society connections that some members had. The main task of the Federation merely consisted of issuing circular messages in the name of organized labor in Shanghai to support KMT political activities. At first I went about eagerly gaining an understanding of the organization; but the more I learned about it, the more difficult it seemed to be to reorganize it. Nor did the staff have an real interest in its reorganization. So my initial enthusiasm slowly dampened, and I gave up trying to reorganize the Federation. I retained my official title, but I seldom went to the office.

In April, 1920, fellow students in Peking wrote several letters informing us that the situation there had eased considerably. If I returned, I would not be in danger of arrest. As a matter of fact, however, anti-Peking organizations and the anti-Japanese movement throughout the country still suffered from oppression by the Peking government. On April 14 the National Student Federation called a brief national student strike in protest; and on May 6 the premises of both the National Student Federation and the National Federation of All Circles of the People, in Shanghai's French Concession, were closed by the authorities. It was clear that popular opposition to the Peking government was mounting. In mid-March, moreover, Wu P'ei-fu had moved his troops northward from Hengyang; and this action brought a conflict between warlords of the Chihli and Anhwei cliques closer and closer. Perhaps this impending conflict between the Chihli and Anhwei cliques drew the full attention of Peking political circles, so that they had no time to deal with student troublemakers. This must have been the reason for my friends writing as they did.

I reviewed the events that had occurred since I had come south and decided that I had discharged most of the duties that the Peking Student Federation had entrusted to me. While Lo Chia-lun and I had not fulfilled our mission as we had hoped for, we had mustered as much backing as could be expected under the circumstances. In the process, I had run about for four months in this activists' center which was Shanghai, and I had naturally grown a little attached to it. Yet I felt that my studies, which would influence my whole future, had been neglected too long. I began to consider returning to the North.

Most of the schoolmates that I had worked with in the May Fourth Movement had left Peita. The Peita student leaders then in Shanghai had all graduated and were preparing to go abroad for further study. All of them were planning their futures. Lo Chia-lun, my fellow delegate, had finished with his student representative duties. He was busy getting in touch with all kinds of prominent people in preparation for an early departure for the United States. Another important figure in the May Fourth Movement, K'ang Pai-ch'ing, while not an official Peking student representative, had been working with us. He was a tempestuous rebel against tradition and was given to light-hearted activities. Young men and women were traditionally forbidden free social intercourse, and so K'ang threw a steady stream of parties at which unmarried young people mingled as freely as they wished. He scandalized Shanghai by having a garden party at Ziccawei, which more than two hundred boys and girls attended. It was a feat that few people were capable of at that time. But he gave himself up so enthusiastically to these problems of social intercourse that he nearly abandoned plans to go to the United States for further study. Hsü Te-heng, though he had long been relieved of his duty as representative of the Peking Student Federation, had worked eagerly with us right along. He was busy visiting a number of places prior to leaving to study in France, and pretty soon we saw him off on a French mail boat sailing to Marseilles. Such other prominent figures in the May Fourth Movement as Tuan Hsi-p'eng and Chou P'ing-lin had also come to Shanghai on their way to the United States. We were together day and night for a time. I was the only one who still had two years of study to be finished at Peita, and it seemed logical that I return to the North immediately.

But these schoolmates in Shanghai all insisted that I would not be able to settle down and study if I returned to Peking. They said that I would eventually be in trouble because my name was still on the government blacklist. They urged me to go abroad with them, and every one of them offered to share his government scholarship money with me. I decided to go back to Peking, however. Even though I knew that things would be difficult for me, I believed that I could finish up my studies there. And even though many of the teachers and friends I had come to know during the previous few years had scattered, most of them still lived in Peking. Furthermore, I could not forsake the foundations of the student movement and of the work among the masses that my teachers and friends and I had built together. Therefore, early in May I asked for a leave of absence from the All-China Federation of Industries, turning my duties over to Huang Chieh-min. Then I quietly returned to my university.

In the Peita Library

After the May Fourth Movement the younger generation, oppressed inside China and finding it impossible to raise China's international status, witnessed the successful Russian Revolution and experienced an accelerated ideological change. They began to look up to the various schools of socialism. By then Li Ta-chao was a well-known key figure in Peking, who advocated Marxism, and the Peita library, which he was in charge of, was the cradle of this ideological trend toward the Left. My contact with Li Ta-chao appears to have been a significant factor in the subsequent development of the Marxist movement in China.

It can be said that from the time of my return to Peking I started to march forward with rapid strides on the road of Marxism. In the very beginning I was a passionate patriot; and like the ambitious youths of the time, I looked forward wholeheartedly to China's becoming rich and powerful. Then I became more radical by supporting the New Culture Movement, opposing the old influences, and advocating social reform and national salvation through revolution. Finally I became enthusiastic about the Communist movement, studied Marxism, and looked up to the example of the Russian Revolution, believing it to be the panacea for national salvation and the guide to revolution. The majority of the radical youths of the time were generally similar to me in pursuing such a course of development.

I respected Li Ta-chao. In the beginning our friendship was not connected with the study of Marxism. Although he was often my mentor, both of us seemed to have grown up together. With regard to the New Culture Movement and the Social Reform Movement, we always saw eye to eye. Especially during the May Fourth Movement, under the banner of "resisting the foreign aggressors and destroying the national traitors," we had consistently fought shoulder to shoulder.

Just after the end of the European war an atmosphere of jubilant celebration enveloped Peking, and Li Ta-chao was very optimistic, feeling that Versailles could bring good fortune to China. We had held ardent respect for President Woodrow Wilson, believing that his proposals could improve world affairs and could also save China from extinction or even help her achieve salvation. The depth of our understanding of things might not have been identical, since he was older and more experienced than I, but we shared the same hopes. Our meetings became more and more frequent, and we generally planned things together.

Soon, at the Conference of Paris, Woodrow Wilson suffered his defeat. China was humiliated; and thus the May Fourth Movement broke out. Just at this time the newly risen Soviet Union was loudly proclaiming such policies as "peace without cession of territory and without indemnity" and "national self-determination." These proposals were even more advanced than those of Woodrow Wilson. It was true that the Russian Revolution had led to a great amount of suffering, and therefore anti-Communist propaganda was being disseminated all over the world. Nevertheless, the reports that were issued by the Russians were like the tolling of bells deep in the night, ringing in the ears of the people. Li Ta-chao, who often had greater access to news, frequently made these reports the topic of discussion; and so we often studied the development of the Russian situation.

Li Ta-chao was not the kind of person who urged his ideas upon others, and he had never preached Marxism to me. He paid special attention to comparative studies, and previously our meetings had always seemed to be prompted by some matters awaiting urgent decision. It was not until my return to the library this time that our attention was focused on socialism, especially Marxism. The point of departure for our discussions was that if China was to be saved, there seemed to be no other road for her than that of the Russians. We fully recognized that it was due to the leadership of the Russian Communist Party that the revolution in Russia was able to register all of its achievements, overthrow the formidable conservative forces of the Tsar, and resist alien pressure, which came from all sides. In short, Marxism had shed its brilliant rays. Under the influence of Li's view that one must start with the study of Marxism, I started to study it systematically.

Early in May, 1920, I returned to Peking after a brief absence. It was only one or two days after Peita students had commemorated May Day at a ceremony in the auditorium of the third campus of the university. Friends that took part in the event told me that all of the more than five hundred persons attending the meeting were intellectual youths. Li Ta-chao presided over the gathering. He delivered an address advocating the eight-hour workday and praising highly the achievements of the Russian Revolution. For the first time *New Youth* issued a special number commemorating May Day. And the anarchists, who had in previous years commemorated May 1 as Labor Day, also put out a special issue of their *Weekly People's Voice*. These unprecedented observances of May Day in Peking were clear indications of the trend to the Left. But at the time nobody seemed to have noticed the absence of workers in the celebration of May Day. Everything indicated that anarchists and Socialists of all varieties were warming themselves up, attempting to enter the world of action. The intellectuals felt that it was their unshirkable duty to play a leading role in keeping with the times.

On the second day after my return to Peking I went to see Li

Ta-chao and described to him my exciting experiences in Shanghai. I sighed, "This vagrant life of more than four months has almost transformed me into a student politician." Thoroughly enjoying the account of my rather unusual experiences, he burst into laughter at the climaxes of some of them. He attached importance to my contacts with Sun Yat-sen and felt that I had done a good thing in serving as the general secretary of the labor union. We discussed the extent to which we could work with Sun. Both of us felt that the KMT had an old-fashioned organizational system with a very complex personnel set-up; and so it seemed to us that it was impossible for the Party to transform itself quickly in response to the influences of the new age.

Li Ta-chao was especially eager to learn about Ch'en Tu-hsiu's activities in Shanghai and also about activities connected with socialism there. I told him that while I was in Shanghai I had met Ch'en Tu-hsiu many times. He was living temporarily at the Ya Tung Bookshop, while looking for a house as a permanent home for himself and his family, who had stayed behind in Peking. He also planned to move New Youth to Shanghai for publication. He was in close touch with Tai Chi-t'ao of the KMT and with other Socialists. He abhorred the Peking government and felt that youth must carry out a thorough revolution and overthrow the rule of the warlords. He also talked expansively about Marxism and frequently expressed the view that China must follow the road of the Russian Revolution. Li Ta-chao told me that he had received letters from Ch'en containing similar sentiments.

I told Li that the ideological tide of socialism was surging up in Shanghai even more than in Peking. In the first place, Tai Chi-t'ao, Shen Hsuen-lu, and Li Han-chün wrote frequent articles propounding Marxism for Sunday Critic. I had come to know them in Shanghai. Shen, a former chairman of the Chekiang Provincial Council, impressed me as someone that had broken with typical bureaucratic ways to delve into progressive ideas. Li was a young Marxist who had just returned from study in Japan. In the second place, some Korean political refugees had organized a Korean provisional government at Shanghai.[72] Kim Kyu-sik, its premier, and Yo Un-hyong,* its foreign minister, had told me that they thought they could establish contact with Moscow and that they were hoping to join forces with the Russian Bolsheviks to overthrow Japanese rule in Korea. Furthermore, Huang Chieh-min, resident direc-

---

* The Chinese pronounce his name Lyuh Woon Hyung.

tor of the All-China Federation of Industries, was trying to organize a Ta-tung (Utopian) party, on the platform that all Socialists in China should unite, cooperate with the Korean revolutionaries, and establish connections with Russia.[73] All of these things were brewing, but they had not yet led to any concrete action.

Li Ta-chao did not, in any case, think that the time was right for concrete Socialist action, especially the formation of a party. It did not seem to him that he or his friend Ch'en Tu-hsiu or anyone else had yet carried out a sufficiently penetrating study of Marxism. Nor did he think that they knew enough about the Russian Revolution. It was his position that we should work hard at the study of Marxism. Huang Chieh-min and the people in the Korean Provisional government, he believed, were probably even less well trained Marxists. But socialism was in vogue now, and as practical politicians they had to take this into account.

During this period Li Ta-chao, myself, and other students that were preoccupied with socialism dropped the anti-Japanese patriotic movement and the New Culture Movement as the chief topics of our discussions. Socialism now concerned us more than anything else. Among the teachers and students at Peita imbibing Socialist ideas there were believers in anarchism, syndicalism, guild socialism, and Marxism.[74] Generally speaking, however, their activities were confined to studying doctrine and to popularizing it by such means as publishing articles and translating relevant works. At the same time their sympathy for the Russian Revolution, on the whole, was mounting.

Li Ta-chao was the one person in Peking who could have brought these various Socialist leaders together in a unified movement. He was mild-tempered, adept at social intercourse, patient, and tolerant of those whose beliefs differed from his own. While studying at the Tientsin School of Legal Administration around the time of the 1911 Revolution, and later as a student in Japan, he was consistently a leader of student political activities. He understood the mentality of youths during the May Fourth period. Since he himself was filled with the enthusiasm of youth, he got along well with students and teachers in the May Fourth Movement and played an important role in it. He had studied socialism before;[75] and by the time of the May Fourth Movement, furthermore, he had become a Marxist convert and sympathized with the Russian Revolution. Yet he never denounced anarchism or any of the other Socialist schools of thought. On the contrary, he maintained very friendly relations with all Socialists, supplied them with books they needed, and often exchanged ideas with them.

The Peita library at the time was still very poorly equipped, the accommodations were not spacious, and books were not very numerous. But it had already become a center of attraction, and at times it was extremely crowded. Among the large number of readers deeply interested in research, the majority were generally leftists seeking new ideas. Often every Socialist publication was out on loan. Also, in the lounge, groups of three to five would generally be discussing new ideas. Marxism and anarchism were often the common topics of discussion. The office of the library director consisted of two rooms, one used as Li's office and the other a reception room. This reception room of Li Ta-chao's was at that time the gathering place for Socialists and radicals, and I played the role of Li's principal supporting actor. I regularly read there and sometimes talked with people there. Also on many occasions forums were held in that room, with quite a few people participating. The debates were taken up very earnestly. When Li was absent, I would represent him in caring for the guests. Thus in 1920 the Marxist atmosphere of the librarian's office gradually grew.

The *Manifesto on China,* issued at that time by the Soviet government, had far-reaching repercussions; it was a major factor in promoting the development of the Marxist movement in China. The *Manifesto,* dated July 25, 1919, renounced all special privileges that the Tsarist regime had enjoyed in China and the Boxer indemnity payments. It also offered to return the Chinese Eastern Railway to China. The Chinese press did not publish the *Manifesto* until early in 1920. The students and cultural circles in Peking were the first to enthusiastically welcome it. The National Federation of All Circles, which had its headquarters in Shanghai, and members of all parties and organizations were also exuberant about it. Statements of approval had been issued jointly by these various organizations, and I had participated in this action. In the eyes of youths in general, Japan and the other Powers were all bullying China. The Soviet Union was the only exception. They felt that the Soviet move to abrogate the unequal treaties was praiseworthy, no matter what the situation of the Soviet Union itself was, or what the motive for its *Manifesto* might be.

By that time the Peking Student Federation and other people's organizations had long been sealed up. Although the students still carried out activities in secret, in comparison with the time around May 4 the tides had clearly receded. It seemed that the students generally had felt that use of the mass movement to express public opinion had become inadequate, and they were groping after new techniques. The Shantung question had become an outstanding issue that could not be resolved all at once. The war between the Chihli and Anhwei cliques was continuing to brew, and everyone looked forward to the early collapse of Tuan Ch'i-jui and his pro-Japan group. But the men that would rise to replace them would be Ts'ao K'un and Chang Tso-lin; and they would be birds of the same feather as Tuan. Though Wu P'ei-fu had expressed patriotic and anti-Japanese sentiments, he was only a commander under Ts'ao K'un, and he could not be expected to do much even after Tuan was defeated. All this made the situation look gloomy, and there was no cause for optimism. What threw a ray of hope at the time was the victory of the Russian Revolution and the Soviet Union's friendly gesture toward China. So, for people who would not stay melancholy and wanted to grope for a way out, the road of Marxist victory offered a strong attraction.

At the time, people studying the course of the Russian Revolution were to be found everywhere, from the South up to the North. Such newspapers and publications as the Peking *Chen Pao* and the Shanghai *Shih-shih Hsin-pao* of the Research clique, the Shanghai *Min-kuo Jih-pao, Construction Monthly,* and *Sunday Critic* of the KMT, as well as others operated by youths in different localities, all to a greater or lesser degree sympathized with and propagated socialism. They also printed documents and factual reports about the Russian Revolution. The people that had set foot inside the Socialist circle or were standing by its brink not only carried out propaganda in the press but also started to take action, such as going into the midst of the workers and commemorating May Day. All this was heading in the direction of a Communist organization, which was in the offing.

Most of the schoolmates close to me seemed to have undergone a marked ideological change. Some of them became even more radical than Li Ta-chao. When Liu Jen-ching, the bookworm, was arrested on June 3, his patriotic zeal had led him into a serious fracas with the military and the police. Now he buried his head in the study of Marx's *Das Kapital.* Whenever he saw me, he would tell me that the general student movement was no longer of any use and that what was needed now was the organization of a Communist party on the basis of Marxist theory. Lo Chang-lung had also greatly increased his knowledge of the Russian

Revolution. He pointed out to me that according to his studies, the Russian Revolution owed its success to the leadership of the Russian Communist Party. Chinese Marxists must also grasp this point in their march forward. There were also many other students (possibly including Mao Tse-tung) that had similar radical views.

Meanwhile, I seemed to have become a special student. I had abandoned my classes for a whole semester, and now there was no chance that I could catch up. But the teachers knew the reason for my lapse, and somehow they gave me passing marks. So I proceeded to spend most of my time in the library, reading books on socialism. It was at this time that I read in Chinese or English-language translations such works as *Introduction to Marx's "Das Kapital," Critique of Political Economy,* and *The Origin of the Family, Private Property, and the State,* by Friedrich Engels. I also dipped into the history of the German Socialist movement and the history of the British labor movement.

On account of the defeat of Atamen Gregory Semenov, the White Russian leader, in Siberia and the establishment of the Far Eastern Republic with its capital at Chita, communications between China and Russia had been restored. At the same time among the Russians residing in China there were those who sympathized with the Soviet Union. Pai-lieh-wei,* a Russian who taught in the Russian-language Department at Peita, was one of them. He was a close friend of Li Ta-chao's, and he often supplied Li with pamphlets that he got from Moscow. At that time he also gave the Peita library an English-language edition of *The ABC of Communism,* by Nikolai Bukharin and Eugenii Preobrazhenskii. This pamphlet was the first Moscow-published work that I read.

About the same time—in April or May of 1920—the Far Eastern Bureau of the Comintern at Irkutsk sent to China a special representative, Gregory Voitinsky, and his assistant, Yang Ming-chai, an overseas Chinese from Russia who belonged to the Soviet Communist Party. They passed through Peking, where Voitinsky contacted Li Ta-chao. This contact apparently was arranged by Pai-lieh-wei. For, according to *Polevoy* what Yang Ming-chai later told me, he and Voitinsky were not at all familiar with conditions in China when they first arrived. Their mission was to establish contact with leaders of the Marxist movement in China; but they had no idea who these men might be, and they did not know whom to approach. From a few resident Russians they learned a little

---

* Romanization of his Chinese name. *Polevoy*

about the New Culture Movement, that Ch'en Tu-hsiu was its leader, and that he was in Shanghai—a center of the Socialist movement. So Yang suggested to Voitinsky that they go to Shanghai and look up Ch'en before doing anything else. Though he knew little about Ch'en Tu-hsiu, it was his opinion that the Communist movement in China must be led by a person with academic qualifications. Voitinsky accepted this recommendation and looked up a Russian teacher at Peita who arranged for them to contact Li Ta-chao. Li gave Voitinsky and Yang a letter of introduction to Ch'en, which they took to Shanghai.[76] Later Yang boasted to me that his bold proposal had been proven entirely correct by subsequent developments.

Li Ta-chao and I frequently discussed Marxism now. Sometimes we even talked about the possibility of taking concrete steps to publicize the doctrine and to start a labor movement, which I was eager to do. But neither of us had decided that we ought to organize a Communist party and then join the Comintern.

This was not the first time that Li had considered forming a Marxist group. Before the May Fourth Movement, he told me, he had thought about organizing a Socialist Research Society to study Marxism and a Russian Research Society to study the Russian Revolution. But he had never actually done anything about organizing them. He and some interested friends and acquaintances, however, had formed the Young China Society, which published the magazine *Young China*. He had hoped that this group would shoulder the responsibility for publicizing Marxism. But because some of its members would not support Marxism, his hope was not realized.

Toward the end of June or early in July of 1920, during one of our long, searching conversations, Li declared his belief that a Marxist Study Society should now be formed.[77] For the moment it should be divorced from practical politics, he said. In addition to studying, translating, and publicizing Marxism, it should organize a labor movement along Western European trade-union lines. I supported his idea with enthusiasm and suggested that we get in touch with likely friends to launch the plan; and this we started to do.

Just when we reached this decision, however, the situation in Peking grew more tense. War between the Chihli and Anhwei cliques was expected to break out at any moment. We were kept busy following developments. And with war imminent, the people that we wanted to approach about the Marxist Study Society took advantage of the holidays to leave Peking along with most other Peita teachers and students.

About July 12 Li Ta-chao said to me solemnly, "It would be best if you left Peking as soon as possible." He believed that when war broke out, the pro-Japanese clique of Tuan Ch'i-jui would suppress students that had opposed it, and I would be in danger of arrest.

"But your danger is greater than mine," I replied. Li indicated that there was no reason why he should not remain in Peking. He was a Northerner, and it would be easier for him to hide.

Soon afterward, however, he announced that he was prepared to leave Peking after all. He wanted me to go with him to his home town in Loting County of Hopeh Province, where we could spend the summer on the seashore, studying Marxism.

I favored the idea of his returning to his village, but I did not want to join him. I thought that I should go to Shanghai to discuss our plans for a Marxist study group and a labor movement with Ch'en Tu-hsiu; and I explained my reasons for this to Li Ta-chao. I said that under the situation at that time, for the sake of the revolution, national salvation, Marxism, and the direction of my personal efforts in the future, I had to plan carefully and draw up a long-range plan. I was too young to take the lead in forming a Communist party. But I assured Li Ta-chao that if Ch'en Tu-hsiu and he should launch such a party, I would be glad to follow them.

Li Ta-chao gave my plan to visit Shanghai his immediate, enthusiastic support and expressed regret at not being able to go himself. He told me that Ch'en Tu-hsiu's latest letters had reflected an increasingly radical attitude and that they had advocated, in a vague sort of way, taking practical action of some kind. But Ch'en had not revealed the course of action he had in mind, perhaps because he thought it indiscreet to put too much in letters. By going to Shanghai, I could take the matter up with him in person. Li also asked me to transmit his own views to Ch'en. Chiefly he wanted Ch'en to know that while he advocated studying Marxism as the first step toward action, he would nevertheless support any more advanced plans which Ch'en might have in mind.

"The war will break out soon," he said as we parted. "Don't delay any longer. Communications may soon be disrupted."

BIRTH OF THE
CHINESE COMMUNIST PARTY

CHAPTER

Ch'en Tu-hsiu's Earliest Plans

As everybody knows, Ch'en Tu-hsiu was the founder of the Chinese Communist Party (CCP). This is true because he was the first person to plan and call for the organization of the CCP and also because his prestige at the time enhanced his call. He had the necessary determination and faith. He drew up the preliminary blueprints for organizing the CCP, and then he implemented them. As a result of his efforts the Chinese Communist movement grew from scattered activities by Marxists in various parts of the country to the formally organized CCP.

On the afternoon of July 13, 1920, I took a train for Tientsin from Peking. It was the eve of the Chihli-Anhwei War. There was an extraordinary congestion of passengers, and it was obvious that these were not normal times. The speed of the train was also erratic. It was dusk when we reached Langfang, a station halfway between Peking and Tientsin. The train waited there interminably. From outside the station came sounds of sporadic gunfire. This increased the passengers' restlessness, yet nobody dared leave the train. When other passengers and I looked out of the windows, we could see man-high sorghum covering the plains, and some fully armed soldiers filtering through it. An army officer among the passengers loudly declared for our benefit that he

96

believed two opposing advance units had made contact. If gunfire had not yet cut the railway, he said, we could still reach Tientsin that night. And soon the train did resume its journey. There were further interruptions en route, however, and we did not arrive at Tientsin until late that night.

The next day, July 14, the Chihli-Anhwei War reached large-scale proportions. Tuan Ch'i-jui of the Anhwei clique called himself Commander-in-Chief of the Army for the Stabilization of the Nation, which had as its backbone the Frontier Army which the Japanese had equipped. His men were stationed in the Peking area and they marched on Paoting and Tientsin. Ts'ao K'un and Wu P'ei-fu of the Chihli clique had organized an "Army for the Suppression of Traitors." They had the support of Chang Tso-lin north of the Great Wall and of Ch'en Ch'un-hsuan of the Kwangsi clique, which was part of the Southern government. From their central headquarters at Paoting they attacked the armies of the Anhwei clique. The war lasted five days and ended in victory for the Chihli clique.

This was the first major conflict within the ranks of the Northern warlords since Yuan Shih-k'ai had built up their mighty force after the establishment of a military training program at Hsiao Chan.[1] It was also a clear indication that the Northern warlords were beginning to disintegrate.

After staying one night at Tientsin, I caught a south-bound train in the Tientsin-Pukow Railway. On July 15 I reached Nanking, the strategic spot that had been the capital of the Six Dynasties. But summer vacation had started, and the war had made itself felt; so most of my friends attending school there had left the city. Furthermore, business was very depressed, and the scene within the city walls was desolate. Nevertheless, like most young people of the time who were eager to visit all the famous mountains and rivers, I had a sightseeing mania; and whenever possible I took time out on my journeys to visit the scenic spots. So this time in Nanking, disregarding the martial law imposed by the Chihli-Anhwei War, I visited the various scenic spots by myself. These included Yu Hua Terrace, Ching Liang Temple, Mo Chou Lake, Hsuan Wu Lake, and the Palace of the Heavenly Emperor.

When I reached Shanghai, the papers already carried news of the defeat of the Anhwei clique.[2] I immediately called on Ch'en Tu-hsiu, who then lived at 2 Yu Yang Lane, off Avenue Joffre in the French Concession. He was jubilant over the defeat of the Anhwei warlords and talked profusely of the effect it might have on the national situation. Then he asked whether or not I had come with a mission as a representative of the students, which, of course, I had not. I told him of my conversations with Li Ta-chao on the eve of my departure from Peking. He was elated and announced that he was eager to discuss the Communist movement with me. He fervently urged me to move into his home, where we could discuss our plans at leisure. There were three rooms on the upper floor, two of which were used by the family and the other by Miss Wang Hui-wu, a young radical. There were also three rooms on the ground floor. One was kept as a guest room, another was occupied by a young writer named Li Ta, and the third was vacant and, Ch'en said, all ready for my use.

Although I had enthusiasm and intended to take up the Communist movement, nevertheless my thinking was rather hazy—it was still a matter of interest, not of resolution. I had not yet decided to make this movement my lifetime work and to make revolution my profession. Accordingly, during the first few days that I lived in the Ch'en home, I was busy running around outside. I formally resigned the post of general secretary of the All-China Federation of Industries. I took time out to renew my acquaintance with Huang Chieh-min and other friends. This made Ch'en Tu-hsiu rather impatient. Mrs. Ch'en even made fun of me by remarking that I was a student representative with a large social circle and perhaps my time was taken up mainly with attention to girl friends. This was of course only a joke that did not tally with the facts.

It was nearly the end of July when I again seriously took up Li Ta-chao's views with Ch'en. He went straight to the heart of the problem by saying to me, "Studying Marxism is only part of the task. What is needed now is the immediate organization of a Chinese Communist party."

This resolute decision was the first I had ever seen in Ch'en. He went on to explain exhaustively the various reasons for his decision, and I concentrated hard on listening, sometimes agreeing with, and sometimes questioning, his views. This theme formed the main topic of many subsequent talks between us.

At one time the leader of the New Culture Movement and now founder of the CCP, Ch'en Tu-hsiu was a man of many talents. He was a great thinker. Studious and given to profound contemplation, he had extraordinary energy. Usually he read and wrote in the mornings and evenings, and in the afternoons he talked with his friends. He was a great conversationalist. While I lived in his home, he would open his box of conversation for me after lunch if there were no visitors to disturb him. Often we talked for hours on end. Far from being pedantic, his talk was enthralling. Frequently he would pose innumerable questions to a statement that he had made himself, subjecting it to the most minute scrutiny in seeking what he considered the most appropriate answer. As he grew excited in a discussion, his eyes would shine brightly and he would roar with laughter. He tended to persist in his own views and did not easily bow to the opinions of others. He refused to be ambiguous even with regard to small differences of opinion, and he insisted upon getting to the bottom of things. Yet when he was corrected on a point to which he had not given full thought, he would immediately and frankly admit his mistake. Generally speaking, he was a tenacious arguer and a searching conversationalist, a serious man with a fiery character, which was in great contrast to the moderate character of Li Ta-chao.

Although he had been greatly influenced by Western culture, basically he was a scholar thoroughly grounded in Chinese literature. Here, the spirit of skepticism and criticism filled him. He had been engaged in cultural work for many years, and his writing was both moving and sharp. He severely criticized the Confucian ideas of propriety, the worship of Confucius by K'ang Yu-wei and others, and the whole body of accepted Chinese thought and tradition. He also fostered the development of a literary revolution, the spirit of science, and democracy, all of which showed the influence of Western culture on him. He was able to understand people and to make use of Western culture to expose the backward side of China's traditions. And in this way he became the standard-bearer of the New Culture Movement.

His interest in Marxism came at a later date, and it was not until 1919 that he first published articles sympathetic to the Russian Revolution.[3] Toward the end of 1919 he was forced to leave Peking, and only then did he affirm the belief that Marxism was the best prescription for curing China's ills. His belief in Marxism perhaps initially resulted from the influence of such friends as Li Ta-chao and Tai Chi-t'ao. But when it came to organizing the CCP, he was unquestionably the man responsible. At the same time he apparently did not accept Marxism without reservations. Often he stressed the need to use it only as a guide, to be applied suitably to actual conditions in China.

Although Ch'en Tu-hsiu became famous for launching the publication *Hsin Ch'ing-nien* (New Youth), which was first issued on September 15, 1915, and was dedicated to the New Culture Movement, he had been an instigator of the Chinese revolution long before that. During the 1911 Revolution, he was chief secretary to P'o Wen-wei, the governor of Anhwei Province.[4] Apparently he did not join the T'ung-meng Hui, but he was always connected with the revolutionists and leftist literary figures of the day. He had to take refuge in Japan after the revolution failed.

Although he was perhaps not an outstanding statesman, Ch'en Tu-hsiu was definitely a rare political commentator. His belief in Marxism and his organization of the CCP had stemmed principally from his views on practical politics. In other words, China's semi-colonial status, the dark side of her internal political situation, and his own unpleasant political experiences led him—a radical democrat—into the camp of international communism.

At the time we talked at great length about the reasons for organizing a Chinese Communist party, and we touched upon a vast number of problems. As best I can remember, the following were the main points discussed: First, the social revolution in China was motivated by the desire for liberation on the part of the proletariat and the broad masses of the poor people. In order to achieve freedom under the conditions actually prevailing in China, the proletariat had no course other than class struggle and the seizure of political power, as advocated by Marxism. The experiences of the Russian Revolution also bore this out.

Second, we felt that the revolutionary movement led by Sun Yat-sen and his Three Principles of the People were not comprehensive enough, that anarchism was too idealistic and lacked means of practical implementation, and that the parliamentary system advocated by other Socialist schools could not be instituted in China in the forseeable future.

Third, the CCP that we were planning to form should continue to take part in the New Culture Movement, the antiwarlord movement, and the patriotic movement against Japan. So long as we stuck to the viewpoint of the Communist Party and acted in the proper manner, there would be no reason for opposition.

Fourth, we should not harbor any misgivings over the possibility that the high ideals of communism would not attract many supporters. On the revolutionary stand we should hold up in front of us the ultimate goal "from each according to his capacity and to each according to his need" and exert long-term efforts to seek its realization. Anyone advocating the revolution, whether he was a radical or a moderate, would invariably be looked upon with the same horror that wild animals and floods inspired and would be liable to cruel oppression. So, in the eyes of the old established order, by taking the positive step of organizing a Communist party, we could only add another to the list of "ten big crimes" with which we had already been charged—that of believing in "common property and common wives."

Fifth, China was not highly developed industrially, and her workers were too few in number and culturally backward. Therefore the workers in general could not talk about class awakening, and they could not be made the backbone of the Communist movement. On the other hand, since the May Fourth Movement there had been a steady increase in the number of intellectual youths that had cultivated a belief in Marxism. If they could be brought together, they would provide the vanguard for the movement. Though the proposed CCP could not hope to seize political power all at once, it was still necessary to launch the movement immediately and in earnest.

We discussed the platform and political program of the CCP. The Party platform that we had in mind would include the fundamental Communist beliefs and basic ways of implementing them. There were books to consult on these matters, and so the problem seemed easy to solve. The principal contents of the political program, however, had to stipulate important policies and immediate demands as well as measures for their implementation. We agreed that there should be a maximum program and a minimum program.

At the time Ch'en Tu-hsiu pointed out, "If the members of the CCP do not participate in movements similar to the 1911 Revolution and the anti-Japanese patriotic movement, then the Party should be considered a farce and certainly should have no claim to being called a Communist party." We rejected Li Ta-chao's suggestion calling for temporary abstinence from practical politics. After approaching the problem from various angles, we found it difficult to decide on a minimum program; but we agreed that it must contain our practical suggestions for dealing with the various aspects of practical politics. We had difficulty in working these things out, because we failed to understand clearly Marx's statement "the worker has no fatherland" and the relationship between the proletarian revolution and the national democratic revolution.

In the midst of this dilemma, Ch'en Tu-hsiu suggested that we did not have to try to be the Marx and Engels of China, issuing a "Communist Manifesto" at the very outset. We were only some students of Marxism who would simultaneously put into practice what we were studying. We could start by organizing the CCP, and the Party platform and political program could be decided upon after the official inauguration of the Party. Our self-imposed limitations did not include isolation from practical politics, but did include nonparticipation in government, so that Party members were not to serve as government officials. And so the Party platform and political program were temporarily shelved without drawing up the articles.

We also talked about a Party constitution and about the practical organization of the Party. Ch'en Tu-hsiu proposed that the CCP not adopt a system having a party chief, such as the KMT had when Sun Yat-sen assumed the post of *Tsung-li* (Director General). He used many examples to prove that the party-chief system had brought with it many abuses to the various political parties that had been formed in China. He advocated adoption of the more democratic committee system by the CCP, with a secretary elected from the committee members to serve as coordinator. In addition to the secretary, there should be members holding responsibility for such tasks as propaganda, organization, etc. He contended that he recommended this organizational structure not only because the Russian Communist Party used it, but also because it was suited to conditions in China. He stressed the need to limit the secretary's authority and called for all matters to be decided in common. In this way democracy could be promoted and the abuses of the party-chief system and the evils of bureaucracy could be prevented.

On the question of what qualifications would be required of people joining the Communist Party, our views at the time were primarily based on current conditions and tended to be exacting. We felt that a participant in the Party must not only sympathize with and believe in Marxism but also be prepared to work actively for the Communist cause. We agreed that members should be drawn from the ranks of workers and young intellectuals. Neither of us was willing to have people with opportunistic political backgrounds or questionable personal integrity in the Party. However, we did feel that former Socialists of any persuasion and even anarchists should be invited to join, so long as they now believed in Marxism and would participate in actual Party work. Generally speaking, we regarded the Communist Party as something sacred;

and its participants had to be of the purest quality. We preferred to sacrifice quantity for quality.

Ch'en Tu-hsiu attached the greatest importance to how we should implement various practical tasks. He was never one for empty talk, and he would take action once a decision was made. He held that we should first organize some Communist nuclei in the major cities and elsewhere, and that such programs as propaganda and organization should be launched immediately. Although we were simultaneously taking concrete action and studying, we did not want the CCP to become a Marxist political party without a foundation of Marxism. So our first tasks had to be the speeding up of our studies of the theory and practice of Marxism and the translation and introduction of Marxist literature.

Next, since the Communist Party was to be the party of the workers, it could not be without workers. And since the trade union was basic to the Communist Party organization, the Party could not afford to lack supporting trade unions. The trade unions that had already been formed at the time were either organizationally backward or were basically not unions of workers. So we had to begin all over in organizing trade unions to propagate communism among the workers, and we had to admit some outstanding workers to membership in the CCP.

Furthermore, we attached considerable importance to the youth. We not only wanted to attract the small number of radicals among them into the Party, but we also needed to use various forms of organization to draw more extensively on young people for participation in all kinds of work. We also felt that if awakened women intellectuals could undertake the task of mobilization, the broad masses of women could then be organized also. We had not talked of the peasants, perhaps because we felt that the time had not yet arrived for attention to these people; furthermore, the distance separating the peasants and communism was truly too great.

Ch'en Tu-hsiu also told me that he had already discussed his intention of organizing the CCP with such people in Shanghai as Li Hanchün, Li Ta, Ch'en Wang-tao, Shen Ting-i, Tai Chi-t'ao, Shao Li-tzu, and Shih Ts'un-t'ung; and all of them had endorsed the idea. He particularly referred to Tai Chi-t'ao as one who truly believed in Marxism and had undertaken a thorough study of the subject. But since Tai's personal relationship with Sun Yat-sen was deep-rooted, Ch'en doubted that Tai would join the CCP. Shao Li-tzu was also a KMT member of long standing, and so he had to deliberate about whether or not he should join the new organization. As to the others mentioned above, Ch'en felt there was no problem about their participation in the Shanghai nucleus. He also anticipated that such people as Shen Yen-ping (Mao Tun) and Yü Hsiu-sung would join the Party very soon.

In the view of Ch'en Tu-hsiu, the Shanghai nucleus should immediately carry out certain tasks. The first would be publication of a theoretical journal called *Kung-chan-tang Yueh-k'an* (Communist Party Monthly).[5] It was to be edited by Li Chi, a young man who had studied in Germany and was well known for his study of Marxism. Ch'en felt that Li Chi, who inclined toward being a scholar, might not want to join the Chinese Communist organization but that he would do his best to edit such an important publication. He also planned to publish a popular magazine[6] and to look for some youths to carry out activities among the workers.

Ch'en also proposed to organize a Socialist youth corps, which would serve as a reserve force of the CCP, or a Communist preparatory school. It was estimated that the Shanghai nucleus of such an organization would have more than thirty members at its inception. He explained that in the Soviet Union this organization was known as the Young Communist League, but he felt that in China the name Socialist Youth Corps would be better. The qualifications for admission should not be too exacting, so that more youths could be recruited. Simultaneously the Marxist Study Society should be organized, but its organization should be even looser than that of the youth corps. While every member of the youth corps would be required to take an active part in some work, those who joined the study society would not have to do so; and the membership in the society would be open to anyone interested in the study of Marxism. To promote greater depth in research and study, Ch'en and the co-sponsors of the Party in Shanghai planned to send students to Moscow and to enter into correspondence with Chinese students in Germany and France, such as Ts'ai Ho-sen[7] in France, calling on them to undertake independently the study and introduction of Marxism and to start Communist organizations.

Ch'en was also busy planning and sponsoring the organization of Chinese Communist nuclei in different parts of the country. He told me that the Shanghai nucleus would assume responsibility for the development of the organization in the provinces of Kiangsu, Anhwei, and Chekiang. Three people were undertaking the development of organizations in the Hangchow area in Chekiang. They were Shen Ting-i—

a well-known member of the gentry and former chairman of the Che-kiang Provincial Council who had voluntarily reduced the rents of his tenant farmers—and Shih Ts'un-t'ung and Yü Hsiu-sung—elite members of the student body who were operating the radical weekly *Chekiang Tide* (Che-chiang Ch'ao). Ch'en himself undertook to find some youths in Nanking, Anking, and Wuhu to launch the SYC in these places. His old friend Kao Yü-han, the great scholar who was then teaching in Anhwei, was the first to respond to his call.

Ch'en hoped that Li Ta-chao and I would rapidly develop the campaign in the North, starting with the organization of the Peking nucleus, and that we would promote it in such cities as Tientsin and Tangshan and such provinces as Shantung, Shansi, and Honan. If possible, attention should also be given to the development of the organization in Manchuria, Inner Mongolia, and the Northwest region. Ch'en had already established contact with Mao Tse-tung and others who operated the *Hsiang-chiang P'ing-lun* (Hsiang River Critic) in Changsha, Hunan. Ch'en was greatly impressed by Mao's talent; and he was going to write to Mao to explain his plans, seek his endorsement, and ask him to organize a nucleus in Hunan. Li Han-chün, the noted Marxist from Hupeh Province who was teaching in Shanghai at that time, assumed responsibility for contacting radicals in Wuhan, and he thought that it would be possible to get as sponsors of the movement Tung Pi-wu, a veteran KMT member then teaching in Wuchang, and Yun Tai-ying, a youth who had already gained a name as a writer and orator. Furthermore, Ch'en said that since Shih Ts'un-t'ung was about to leave for Japan, Shih could contact Japanese Socialists as well as Chinese students there, and lay the groundwork for a Chinese Communist organization in Japan.

During the time I lived in Ch'en Tu-hsiu's home I never happened upon any meeting there of Ch'en and the other co-sponsors of the Shanghai nucleus whom he had mentioned. Although I met and talked with these various people, it did not seem to me that they possessed the same devoted zeal and concentrated attention as Ch'en did towards organizing the Party; and so they had not made any impression on me. Even Li Ta, with whom I lived under the same roof, could not be considered overly enthusiastic about this matter of forming a party. He was a student of sociology who hated to leave his books, and each day he was busy at writing. He usually did not join Ch'en and me in our talks, although he was always invited to do so.

My interview with Tai Chi-t'ao, however, left a deep impression on me. He and his wife were then living in a rather large room in the front part of the second floor of 6 New Yu Yang Lane and were close neighbors of Ch'en's. The place was crudely furnished. Besides books there were only a few pieces of wooden furniture, so Tai appeared to be a single person living in a small cubicle.

In talking to me, Tai Chi-t'ao was extravagant in his praise of Ch'en Chiung-ming, whom he called a Socialist general. At the time Ch'en Chiung-ming was commander-in-chief of the Kwangtung Army, which was stationed in the Changchow and Changting areas in southern Fukien. This army general was interested in the New Culture and was fond of talking about socialism, and so he regularly corresponded and exchanged views with Tai Chi-t'ao and Ch'en Tu-hsiu in Shanghai. Accordingly, Tai had stressed that in the areas garrisoned by General Ch'en, experiments in socialism could be carried out, such as socialist education, new modes of daily living, and various social reforms. He felt that a Marxist college could be set up there and that theoretical publications such as *Communist Monthly* could also be published there. He asked me to take time out for a visit to southern Fukien and to take the opportunity to cultivate the friendship of General Ch'en. Ch'en Tu-hsiu, however, did not seem to attach special importance to Ch'en Chiung-ming, perhaps because he did not pin the same hopes on him that Tai did, or else because he believed that the area was in Sun Yat-sen's sphere of influence. I was in a hurry to return north, and so I could only thank Tai for his invitation, postponing a trip to Changchow to a later date.

My talks with Ch'en Tu-hsiu continued for more than two weeks. We arrived at a complete mutual understanding, though we did not put any documents into writing. During our talks we would sometimes be carried away by our enthusiasm and stray far from the subject at hand. But generally the conversations were carried out in a systematic manner. Our views were similar, and there was no misunderstanding; so we shared a pleasant experience. We did not put the results of our discussions into writing, primarily because we were only thinking along the broadest lines and our discussions were not precise or thorough with regard to details. Then again, we felt that we should consult more people, that it would be lacking in democracy if we should proceed directly to draw up such things as a party platform, political program, major points of the constitution, and work plans.

I enthusiastically supported Ch'en's views and plans, and I promised him that I would return north and start things moving. This was most pleasant to his ears. I also stressed to Ch'en my opinion that pending the formal holding of the inaugural meeting of the CCP, the Shanghai nucleus should assume responsibility for correspondence and liaison with the nuclei of the various areas. I added that although we did not adopt the party-chief system and would have no title similar to party chief for anybody, it did not mean abandoning the responsibility for leadership. I insisted that Ch'en assume this leadership responsibility and that he undertake matters of planning. He gladly agreed to my proposal.

One evening about August 20, when our talks were about to be concluded, I was returning to the Ch'en home when I heard Ch'en engaged in conversation in his study with a foreign guest and a Chinese with a Shantung accent. Perhaps the visitors did not leave until I was sound asleep. It was later that I found out that the two were Gregory Voitinsky and Yang Ming-chai. This was the only time that I was aware of them being in Ch'en's home.

The next day Ch'en, who was very elated, told me that a representative of the Comintern had contacted him. The Comintern would support a Chinese Communist party, if one were organized. But he did not give me the details of their conversation, nor did he tell me how many meetings they had already held, perhaps because they had agreed to maintain secrecy. It was very possible that during earlier meetings they had only touched upon general problems of the Communist movement in China, and Voitinsky naturally must have expressed the hope for early organization of the CCP.

Given such an impetus, Ch'en probably decided to step up his activities and to organize the CCP immediately. The period of his talks with me could be one of active planning. When he thought that he could start to organize Communist nuclei in Shanghai and other areas, he would officially inform Voitinsky that he had the assurance of being able to organize the CCP. Then Voitinsky would immediately express the Comintern's support. This may have been the major topic of their conversation that evening.

At the time, Ch'en explained to me why he considered it important for us to establish relations with the Comintern. He pointed out regretfully that the Chinese Communist movement was built on weak foundations. By then there was not even a Chinese translation of Marx's *Das*

Kapital. He felt that the tasks before us were truly staggering. If we could establish contact with the Comintern, we would receive valuable help both in the realm of Marxist theory and in the practical organization of the movement. He also said that we would benefit immensely if the Comintern would send a capable and influential representative as our adviser.

To sum up, before my arrival in Shanghai, talks had taken place concerning the organization of the CCP and the formation of its Shanghai nucleus; but the official inauguration of the first nucleus of the CCP —the Shanghai nucleus—probably took place toward the end of August, after I had left Shanghai. Everything was as Ch'en Tu-hsiu had told me. The founders of the CCP, who were also the constituents of the Shanghai nucleus, were Ch'en Tu-hsiu, Li Ta, Li Han-chün, Ch'en Wang-tao, Shen Ting-i, Shao Li-tzu, and Shih Ts'un-t'ung—seven persons in all. Because of his connections with the KMT, Tai Chi-t'ao did not officially join the organization.[8] It was after the first official meeting that Yang Ming-chai transferred his membership from the Russian Communist Party to the CCP, and so became a member of the Shanghai nucleus. Shen Yen-ping and Yü Hsiu-sung also joined it after the first meeting.

This was the general course of events surrounding the birth of the CCP, starting with the earliest planning by Ch'en Tu-hsiu which resulted in the official organization of the CCP Shanghai nucleus in the latter part of August, 1920, following preparations that began with meetings and discussions in May and June of that year.

Just at the time when I made my decision, my former chancellor, Ts'ai Yuan-pei, arrived in Shanghai. I immediately went to see him at the I P'ing Hsiang Hotel on Tibet Road. I told him frankly that I was living with Ch'en Tu-hsiu and that I was going to follow Ch'en in starting a Communist movement. I asked what he thought of the idea.

Ts'ai, who had always been an anarchist, replied, "It seems that socialism is the only way for China. From beginning to end, the anarchists have never organized themselves, and that is their weakness. If the Marxists are to achieve anything, they must organize quickly." Ts'ai always treated everyone with politeness and was reluctant to pour cold water on anybody's ideas; but this attitude did not apply to students that he was especially fond of. In my previous contacts with him I had recognized his great frankness toward his students. So his approval now of my proposed course of action did not seem to be mere courtesy.

All of these happenings marked the beginning of an important period in Chinese history. At that time nobody could foresee the shape that future developments would take. It is certain that Ch'en Tu-hsiu, who served as the midwife who brought the CCP into the world, could never dream that his Moscow comrades and some of his disciples would one day brand him a betrayer of communism and even castigate him as a "Trotskyite bandit," a "Chinese traitor," and a "Japanese spy." Ts'ai Yuan-pei, the respected scholar and mature-minded man who endorsed my plan to take up the Communist movement, also could not have anticipated that he himself would go over to the anti-Communist camp in 1927. And I, so enthusiastic then about the Communist ideal and one of the founders of the movement, who for eighteen years was to labor as a coolie in its service under terrible difficulties, could never have believed that I would have no choice but to leave this CCP after it had been poisoned by Stalin and Mao Tse-tung.

How could there have been such fantastic developments? Readers will find the answer in the narrative that follows. Generally speaking, when a small number of people launch an armed insurrection, a revolution of force that leads to the establishment of this or that brand of revolutionary state power and practices dictatorial rule, they must eventually abandon their idealistic principles and righteous beliefs of their early period and replace them with concepts of power, treachery and plotting, terror and cruelty, etc. The Communist movement is inseparably linked with the proletarian dictatorship; and so the Communist system of dictatorship must produce such despots as Stalin and Mao Tse-tung. Saying that they poisoned the CCP is tantamount to saying that the ugly realities of dictatorship have buried the beautiful future perspective of communism. The major inherent lesson is that the CCP has suffered from the incurable disease of dictatorship.

Forming the Peking Nucleus

After some sightseeing on the way back from Shanghai, I arrived in Peking during the last week of August, 1920, and excitedly recounted to Li Ta-chao my conversations with Ch'en Tu-hsiu. After thinking it over, Li gave Ch'en's plan his unreserved approval.

The main point for consideration, he said, was whether or not the time was ripe for organizing a Communist party. Ch'en's judgment on that was naturally sounder than ours, because he had a better grasp of the situation in the South. Since Ch'en had in effect begun his activities, it was up to us to go ahead and work with him, Li said. Li did not feel that the Communist Party would start as a tiger and end as a snake, which was the case with the Chinese Socialist Party that Chiang K'ang-hu had formed during the 1911 Revolution;[9] for Li believed that we were better equipped both ideologically and practically. He accepted as eminently feasible the organizational plan that Ch'en Tu-hsiu and I had formulated at Shanghai. On the basis of it, he declared that we in Peking could launch our drive. On hearing this affirmative reaction, I said to Li, "Then let's put your views into a letter to Mr. Ch'en."

Li had the letter ready the next day. In straightforward, earnest language it pledged our support for Ch'en's plan. Both of us signed this first important document connected with the Peking nucleus, and it was mailed immediately. All of the numerous subsequent letters that we sent to Ch'en Tu-hsiu were also cosigned by Li Ta-chao and me. Chiefly they concerned the concrete measures by which our work progressed.

We wasted no time and immediately started to work. We first invited Chang Shen-fu, a lecturer at Peita, to be one of the sponsors. Chang was a student of the philosophy of Bertrand Russell and had openly voiced approval of Marxism. He was about to leave for England in a week or two to carry on his academic work, and so the three of us as founders met twice in Li Ta-chao's office at the Peita library to discuss preliminary arrangements. We first planned for Chang Shen-fu to make use of his visit to develop activities among Chinese students in Western Europe. Unexpectedly, scholar that he was, he did not prove to be bold in carrying out decisions; and so after his arrival in England, he simply abandoned his responsibility as a founder. Later he even lost his Party membership.

Li Ta-chao and I were rather exacting in our demands in recruiting participants in the movement in Peking. We thought that my school-mates Lo Chang-lung and Liu Jen-ching were reasonably well versed in the doctrine, and they responded enthusiastically to an invitation to join. As a result of talks that Li Ta-chao had with the anarchists, moreover, five promised to join, including Huang Ling-shuang, Ch'en Te-jung, and Chang Po-ken.[10]

At that time more Peita students were followers of anarchism than of communism, and the five young men recruited by Li Ta-chao were prominent anarchists in the Peita student body. The anarchists were also very active, publishing the magazine *Min Sheng Weekly,* as well as some pamphlets. Apparently they did not realize that during the Russian Revolution the anarchists were suppressed, for they consistently voiced sympathy for Marxism and the Russian Revolution. When Li Ta-chao invited them to join the nucleus, they declared their belief that Marxists and anarchists ought to join forces in organizing a Communist party. Some were totally opposed to a dictatorship of the proletariat, and some differed from the Marxists concerning its nature; but both groups agreed that there should be a proletarian revolution, and they were prepared to work with us toward achieving it. Both Li Ta-chao and I felt that it would be possible for anarchists and Communists to cooperate within a single organization at that time, because a dictatorship of the proletariat was still such a remote goal for the Chinese revolutionary movement that the issue could lie dormant.

In mid-September, 1920, the Peking nucleus of the CCP held its founding meeting in the office of Li Ta-chao. Nine members attended. In addition to Li Ta-chao and myself there were Lo Chang-lung, Liu Jen-ching, Huang Ling-shuang, Ch'en Te-jung, Chang Po-ken, and the other two anarchists. Out of deference to the anarchist majority, who objected to all forms and symbols of organization, the meeting had no chairman, nor was any record of it kept. First we declared the nucleus formally established. Then Li Ta-chao explained the significance of its formation, and briefly outlined the plans that had emerged from my conversations with Ch'en Tu-hsiu at Shanghai. Those present endorsed the idea of forming the Party and declared themselves members. The first issue of *Lao-tung-che* (The Laborer), the weekly published by the Shanghai nucleus, had just arrived, and we passed out copies to those present. That livened up the meeting.

Then we discussed the concrete problems of organization and methods of proceeding with nucleus work. Huang Ling-shuang and the other anarchists, sticking to their doctrine, proposed that the nucleus have no officers. They also proposed that members be allowed to work without any kind of supervision at any tasks they might choose from those the group had agreed to undertake. So we decided that instead of having a nucleus secretary, for example, we would have Li Ta-chao act as coordinator. I was to be responsible for starting the trade-union movement. Huang Ling-shuang and Ch'en Te-jung were to publish the nucleus organ, a weekly magazine to be called *Lao-tung Yin* (The Voice of Labor). Full editorial responsibility went to Huang, while sales and distribution were placed in the hands of Ch'en Te-jung. Lo Chang-lung,

Liu Jen-ching, and I were to organize a SYC unit. To Li Ta-chao went the responsibility of sponsoring a Marxist study society. Li said that he personally could manage to donate eighty silver dollars a month out of his salary to support nucleus projects.

At the end of September a unit of the SYC was formed. Its first meeting took place in the office of the Peita Student Council, and I gave the inaugural address. About forty people attended, of whom I now remember Kao Shang-te, Teng Chung-hsia, Lo Chang-lung, Liu Jen-ching, Ho Meng-hsiung, Miao Po-ying, Li Shih, Lo Han, Chu Wu-shan, Huang Shao-ku, Huang Jih-k'uei, Li Chun, Yang Jen-chi, Fan Hung-chieh, Wang Yu-te, Kao Tsung-huan, We Ju-ming, Chou Ta-wen, and Liu Wei-han. They were all students from Peking schools, most of them from Peita. There was not a single anarchist among them, nor was there one of them who did not believe in Marxism. The meeting elected as secretary Kao Shang-te, a responsible officer of the Peita Student Council. The main task of the Youth Corps in its initial stages was to keep in touch with the various student councils and to recruit student members. Before long, however, most of these early participants in the Corps joined the Communist Party and formed the backbone of its early labor-movement efforts in the North.

The first meeting of the Marxist Study Group took place a few days after the SYC was started. More than fifty people were there. Li Ta-chao gave the inaugural address, and I spoke, too. Most of those who had attended the Youth Corps meeting were present, along with a number of well-known persons who believed in various schools of socialism. It was resolved at the meeting that books on socialism should be collected to facilitate research on the subject and that people should report on their research when it was especially fruitful. Later this organization held a few meetings, then its operations were suspended.[11]

In October, while we were going ahead with our work, the leader of China's first Socialist party, Chiang K'ang-hu, came to Peking, and our Communist nucleus gave him a reception in the office of Li Ta-chao. There he made a rather vague speech. Essentially he said only that he wanted to make an inspection tour of Soviet Russia and Europe before mapping out any plan of action. We raised such issues as the urgent need for a labor movement and the desirability of united action by all Socialists. But these problems did not seem to interest him. His hopes for the development of socialism in China, moreover, still lay with parliamentary activities, which we considered utterly impracticable. The meeting, as a result, was fruitless. We abandoned the intention that we had had of inviting him to join forces with us. When Chiang had left the reception, we all ridiculed this old Socialist for knowing little about socialism and for being so far behind the times in his thinking and outlook. Li Ta-chao said that indeed we all hoped that China's Socialists could unite under the banner of Marxism, but that if people like Chiang K'ang-hu were not interested in this unity, it was clearly up to us late-comers to forge ahead with courage.

In November the anarchists withdrew from our nucleus, which was another blow to Li Ta-chao's hope that all Socialists could unite. The anarchists and the Marxists then differed on two major points. One was the problem of organization. Because of their belief in absolutely unregimented organizations, the anarchists did not approve of national and regional leadership, of officials of any kind, or of any form of discipline. This created great inconvenience in actual nucleus work and gave even the mild-mannered Li Ta-chao a headache. The second point at issue was the doctrine of the proletarian dictatorship, which the anarchists opposed. At a nucleus meeting held to thrash out differences between the anarchists and the Marxists, Liu Jen-ching contended that a dictatorship of the proletariat was the essence of Marxism and that unless this was recognized there could be no uniformity in our propaganda. The result was that the five anarchists withdrew amicably from our nucleus. They handed over *Voice of Labor*, which they had edited, to Lo Chang-lung. Although we continued to maintain friendly relations with the anarchists, this must be called a serious split.

The nucleus went ahead with its work energetically, but there were now only four persons left in it. It looked so weak and isolated that we decided to invite key members of the SYC to join. Nine of them immediately came into the nucleus, including Teng Chung-hsia, Kao Shang-te, Ho Meng-hsiung, Liao Po-ying, and Wu Nu-ming. At about the same time a member of parliament named Li Shao-chiu and a Hopeh provincial councilor named Chiang Hao joined us.

The expansion of our nucleus to fifteen people was quite a shot in the arm. And at a formal meeting held about the end of November, 1920, we renamed it the Peking Branch of the Communist Party of China. Li Ta-chao was elected secretary. I was put in charge of organization, which chiefly involved directing the labor movement. The main responsibility of Lo Chang-lung, who was put in charge of propaganda, was publishing *Voice of Labor*; and the other comrades were all assigned specific duties. Thus our work began to progress along regular lines.

The work in Shanghai seemed to be even more striking. Copies of the *Communist Manifesto* translated by Ch'en Wang-tao, the first issue of *Kung-chan-tang Yüeh-kan* (Communist Monthly), and other publications were being mailed to us in Peking one after another. Ch'en Tu-hsiu indicated approval of everything we did, although, for security reasons, we could not open our hearts in correspondence with him.

In letters to Ch'en we had formally proposed that all nuclei be made provisional Party branches, pending a Party Congress. We also proposed that the Shanghai branch coordinate the activities of all branches. All the other nuclei approved our proposals. As a result of this the Peking nucleus and all the other nuclei declared themselves Party branches.

Thus, the Communist organization took on an embryonic form.

Starting the Labor Movement

The founders of the CCP considered one of its most important tasks to be activities among the workers. These activities began in the Peking-Hankow Railway shops at Ch'anghsintien, and I was the first to undertake them.

I had previously been in Ch'anghsintien, which was only twenty-one kilometers from Peking. The shops of the northern section of the Peking-Hankow Railway, which were located there, employed more than one thousand workers. When I had charge of public speaking work in the May Fourth Movement, I had led a group of students that addressed the workers on the importance of patriotism and the need to organize into "units of ten." The workers of Ch'anghsintien had received our group of patriotic youths warmly and respectfully. They had treated us to hot water, pickled vegetables, and steamed bread, which was the best they could offer. Some students, seeing flies swarming over the food and believing the steamed bread to be stale, excused themselves from accepting this hospitality. I was the only one who gulped the food down noisily, like the workers, while talking patriotism with them. Perhaps because of my conduct the workers did not create a mental division between me as a student and themselves as workers. I was able to establish an intimate relationship with some of them as a result.

The next year, in September of 1920, two or three days after the

Peking Communist nucleus was formed, I again went to Ch'anghsintien. First, I got in touch with a devout Catholic named Wu, a native of the place who had once worked in the railway shops. I cannot remember his full name. There were Catholics among the shops' staff members and workers, and occasionally Mr. Wu went to the shops and preached. In this way he had built up a large number of acquaintances among the workers. He accompanied me on a visit to them where they worked.

The workers I had met before flocked around during their rest period and talked with me. Most of them thought I had returned to propagandize for patriotism.

"This time I have come just to visit you," I told them frankly, "and to ask if there is anything I can do for you. What do you need most urgently here?" They consulted one another and then declared as if in one voice that they wanted a school for workers' children. Their children had no place to study. "If we can find a house for it," I replied, "we can have a school for workers' children."

This news thrilled them. It was not easy to find a house then; but they were very enthusiastic, and a few days later Mr. Wu came to Peking and excitedly told me that they had found a suitable place. Several workers and their families were living in the house, but they were willing to vacate it and let it be turned into a schoolhouse.

Delighted by the workers' zeal and by their confidence in me. I was determined to establish the school immediately, no matter what financial difficulties stood in the way. I promptly called on my friend Li Shih, whom I believed could run such a school. A hard worker who joined the SYC as soon as it was formed, he was interested in promoting mass education. He had organized a mutual-aid group with more than ten of his young friends, and they financed their education through spare-time work. He gladly promised to teach at the school when I broached the subject to him. I suggested that he go to Ch'anghsintien with Wu to look over the house.

As we planned it, there would be a day school for the workers' children and an evening school for the workers themselves. But about one hundred silver dollars* were needed just to get the school started. Monthly expenses would run to at least eighty dollars. I dug into my own pocket, and preparations for the school got under way.

The Ch'anghsintien school for workers' children opened in October.[12]

---

* References to dollars are to Chinese silver dollars. The average value of a Chinese silver dollar was about 50¢ U.S. during the 1920's.

Its small classroom could hold only about forty persons, and it was so full from the moment the school opened that many workers' children could not be admitted. The evening workers' class was also crowded. For several months Li Shih taught both daytime and evening classes single-handed, while Wu looked after the business end.

Once a week I spent an evening at the school, speaking to the workers. There always were so many people at these lectures that we had to move out the desks and benches, and the audience stood, packed together. Sometimes I managed to bring comrades from Peking to speak to the workers. Our lectures usually concerned the workers' lives and how to improve them, the need for trade unions and ways of organizing them.

By the end of November, 1920, about the time that the five anarchists withdrew from the Communist Peking nucleus, the circulation of *Voice of Labor* rose from one thousand to four thousand copies, which increased our expenses. Figuring in the costs of the Ch'anghsintien school and *Voice of Labor*, the nucleus needed about 250 dollars a month. My financial situation worsened rapidly under these conditions. When I ran out of money, I had to quietly pawn my clothes to meet the emergency.

There was a geographer named Su Chia-jung living in the room next to mine who was not a Socialist and never even talked politics. As the cold weather approached, he was shocked to see me pawning my winter clothing. Because he was concerned about me, he quietly told several of my good friends about it. The result of this was that one day, as I worked on an article for *Voice of Labor*, Teng Chung-hsia, who as yet knew very little about the workings of the Communist nucleus that he had just joined, walked into my room and admonished me sternly. His point was that study should be my chief concern and that I should carry on trade-union work only in my spare time. As he saw it, I was wrong to disregard the amenities of life and live by pawning things.

His tone enraged me, because I believed that he had no insight into my problems. I pounded the desk, waved a finger at him, and roared, "Get out. Who wants to listen to such trite platitudes."

He suddenly smiled and said, "Several friends are waiting for you in Central Park. Let's continue our conversation there." Disregarding my anger, he took me by the hand and forced me to leave with him.

Several of my best friends, all of them members of the SYC, were waiting in one of Central Park's cedar groves, seated around a tea table, talking. I launched into a long speech. At the start of the Communist movement, I said, there were a thousand jobs to be done. Before there could be any hope of accomplishment, somebody had to make sacrifices, to work with unswerving determination. Furthermore, I told them of our straitened financial situation. Li Ta-chao was donating about one hundred dollars a month from his own pocket, and I did not want to increase his financial burdens, because it was known that he already lived in rather reduced circumstances. I told them that I had met most of the cost of starting the Ch'anghsintien school and had made up our monthly deficit of 150 dollars. In addition, I traveled a good deal, and the three hundred dollar allowance that my family sent me each year had been spent. Now, aside from borrowing, the only thing I could do was patronize the pawn shops.

I also told them that we did not want to accept money from just anybody. For example, Liang Shan-chi[13] had made a definite offer of three thousand dollars to meet the expenses of the Ch'anghsintien school and other expenses. There was nothing but good will in his motives. Yet he was a leader of the Research clique; and to insure the purity of the labor movement, we politely declined his offer of help. This was known to Kao Shang-te, who was among those at Central Park that day. "I am pawning things because it is necessary to our work," I declared. "Now, what's surprising about that?"

Moved by my speech, they all wanted to know why I had not brought my problems up for discussion. I told them that both Li Ta-chao and I felt it best to talk about fund-raising only after our work had made some progress. Everyone there expressed a desire to share the nucleus's expenses and promptly donated some money. Some gave five dollars and others ten dollars, and I collected something less than one hundred dollars on the spot.

Soon afterward, the problem of fund-raising was brought up at a combined meeting of the Communist nucleus and the SYC. It was decided that every month every comrade would donate an amount of money in keeping with his personal financial situation. Fund-raising was placed in the hands of Li Ta-chao, and from then on we remained on a relatively stable financial footing. There was the money that Li and the other comrades donated, and in addition Li solicited contributions from acceptable sympathizers. Li Hsin-pai, of Peita, for example, donated twenty dollars a month. A teacher of Russian language, Pai-lieh-wei, donated a lump sum of one hundred dollars. As a result I no longer had to worry about our finances. I was able to concentrate on the work I was doing in a number of different places. The labor movements in Tientsin, Tangshan, and Nank'ou were all launched under my direction; and it was through my influence that more comrades specialized in the activities of the labor movement.

The labor movement at Ch'anghsintien, however, was more spectacular than the others. The school for workers' children became a regular haunt of the workers. After work, in groups of threes or fives, sometimes accompanied by their children, they would drift over to the school to hear a lecture on current events, to read the newspapers, to sing Peking opera, or merely to chat. The unrestricted recreation they enjoyed there seemed to dissipate the fatigue of a long day's work.

The school for workers' children kept Comrade Li Shih extremely busy. He was amiable and patient, and the workers would ask him all kinds of questions. They would also want him to write letters home for them and to write other things, and they sought him out as a medical adviser and as a mediator of family and other troubles. When a dispute arose between workers, it was often argued out at the school, with their friends as arbiters. The workers grouped themselves according to the different places from which they had come, and these groups frequently discriminated against one another. There were the Tientsin group, the Techou group, and the local group. Then, too, there were engineers and stokers, mechanics and their apprentices, semiskilled and manual workers; and rivalry among these occupations led to frequent quarrels. For the most part, however, their troubles stemmed from debts. By and large, Li Shih managed to solve the workers' problems equitably. For that reason he won their confidence, and the school became a place of utmost importance to them.

This school was first called the School for Workers' Children, and there was attached to it an evening class for workers. Later, the number of workers wanting to study increased, and the school was renamed Ch'anghsintien Adult Education Labor School. An inaugural meeting was held on January 1, 1921, to celebrate the occasion. Wu Nu-ming, a member of the CCP, joined the school as a teacher to assist Li Shih. Later, Li Shih left the area, and Wu took over from Li Shih the work of running the school.

During my weekly visits to Ch'anghsintien, I often called at the homes of the workers and questioned them about how they were getting along. From them I learned that they worked from six o'clock in the morning until six o'clock at night. Not counting a short rest period and time off for meals, they worked at least ten hours a day. On top of that, they occasionally had to put in two or three hours overtime at night. They received only one day off every two weeks. Utterly victimized by the shops' management, they literally worked themselves dizzy. It was as if they had sold themselves to the shops.

More important was their feeling that their wages were too low. A low-class, semiskilled worker earned nine dollars a month, while an apprentice got even less. Only the old mechanics, men who had worked in the shops for many years, received thirty dollars a month. Engineers and a handful of mechanics were paid sixty dollars, which was very special treatment. The workers' average wage was fifteen or sixteen dollars a month. This was not enough to supply their minimum requirements.

But they suffered most from exploitation by the small stores, all of which were owned by foremen or overseers from the shops. They had to buy their daily necessities from these stores. Since they were not paid until the end of the month, most workers had to make their purchases on credit. The larger their incomes, the more credit they were granted. After a while every cent of a worker's monthly salary was paid to the foremen and overseers to settle his debt, which was usually larger than his salary. Moreover, all workers had to pay ten per cent interest, compounded monthly, on these debts. As principal and interest mounted, the workers became hopelessly in debt to the stores. Those who owed several tens of dollars were considered small debtors. Usually they owed at least one hundred dollars. One worker named Chang Te-hui, who had worked in the shops for several years, owed more than a thousand dollars. It was impossible for the workers to shake off the grip of the foremen and overseers, who could pronounce what amounted to a death sentence on them by refusing further credit for their daily necessities. This was what the workers dreaded most. The only way to solve the problem was to organize a trade union to struggle against such things.

Since I was profoundly sympathetic with their lot, I asked why they had not formed a trade union and a workmen's cooperative to protect their interests. But most of them were skeptical of such things. They had no true idea of what a trade union was. Some of them declared that they were decent workers and would have nothing to do with political party affairs. Others announced suspiciously that they had never heard of a union that tried to further the interests of the workers; they only knew that in the first year of the Republic of China something called a labor union had been involved in carrying out elections. You received a union membership card after paying one dollar, you cast your vote at polling time, and that was all. Yet even that kind of "labor union" was later banned by Yuan Shih-k'ai, as a result of which some of them suffered acutely. Would not even worse trouble be stirred up if we tried to organize a union for the workers' benefit? they wanted to know. A few relatively progressive workers saw the necessity for a trade union but did not think the time was right for organizing one. Their way of thinking, which was conditioned by a fear of the traditional management and government policy of suppressing labor organizations, could not be changed overnight.

So I proposed to them that we first organize a workers' club. They accepted this idea only after much discussion and persuasion. But at the end of a long fermentation period, the club was finally organized in May of 1921. More than a thousand workers joined it. They adopted club regulations and elected officers, and an old mechanic named Wang Chun was elected chairman. In celebration he led the enthusiastic members in a parade through the shop premises and beyond. The railway officials were dumbfounded. Furthermore, a trade union was eventually organized. The club paved the way for the impoverished, disorganized workers of Ch'anghsintien to unite in a common struggle; and their struggle became the Communists' first beachhead among the working masses of China.

My First Contact with Voitinsky

Such modern Chinese revolutionary movements as the Taiping Rebellion and the 1911 Revolution were obviously caused in part by Western influence. Principally, however, they were brought about by the internal needs of China. This was also true of the Chinese Communist movement, although it was subject to more profound foreign influence through the Comintern. The Comintern's earliest efforts to establish contact with Chinese Marxists and to assist in organizing the CCP and in promoting that Party's relationship with the Comintern were made by Gregory Voitinsky.

In discussing these things, I would first like to touch upon the influence of the October Russian Revolution on the Chinese revolutionary movement. In many ways, it changed the Chinese people's conception of Russia. They came to feel that Tsarist Russia and Soviet Russia were two opposite extremes.

For the average Chinese intellectual versed in international affairs, Tsarist Russia was filled with corruption, darkness, despotism, and backwardness. It had eaten into the northern borders of China and aggressed against the Northeast (Manchuria). The Russians were looked upon as curious Arctic creatures, covered with long hair, dressed in heavy furs, and given to drinking and arrogance. They were called "Old Hairy People" (Lao Mao-tzu).

But the October Revolution gradually changed these ideas of the Chinese intellectuals. The *Manifesto on China* issued by Leo Karakhan, Deputy People's Commissar of Foreign Affairs, on July 25, 1919, was the turning point.[14] After years of Japanese aggression and the insults of Versailles, it made them feel that the Soviet Union was the only country that would treat China as an equal. The favorable impression made by the Soviet Union was quite universal at the time. Especially the radical intellectuals believed that the Soviet government, which followed Marxism, was not merely assuming a hypocritical pose in issuing this Manifesto.

Chinese intellectuals, however, knew very little about the development of the Russian revolutionary movement. What they did know consisted merely of heroic stories of nihilists who had attempted to assassinate the royal family by throwing bombs. On the whole, they had never heard about the activities of the Russian Social-Democratic Workers' Party. Nor did they know the names of Plekhanov and Lenin. But after the October Revolution, the Chinese began to learn a little about the conditions that spawned the Russian Revolution and to feel that while China and Russia were two different countries, they had certain things in common. The aristocrats and militarists that had ruled Russia were quite similar to the bureaucrats and militarists that ruled China. Moreover, because the 1911 Revolution had adopted a compromising attitude when it was only half completed, the militarists had created chaos in China. The May Fourth Movement and the New Culture Movement were only a start in the right direction; their main weakness was that neither was as complete and thorough as the Russian Revolution. So it was that most radical Chinese intellectuals tended to look for direction to the Russian Revolution.

Chinese intellectuals in general, seeing that the Russian Revolution was succeeding in spite of enormous difficulties, began to think that it must have been founded on a potent revolutionary theory or at least that it had employed Marxism very adeptly. Furthermore, such Soviet slogans as "National Liberation" and "Land, Peace, and Bread" were as attractive as the great French Revolution slogan, "Liberty, Equality, and Fraternity." Their actual influence may have been greater.

Because public opinion was in sympathy with the Soviet Union and because White Russian influence in Siberia had been eliminated and communications between China and Russia gradually had resumed, the Peking government finally received Ignatius Yurin, a Soviet Russian that came to Peking in August, 1920, as a representative of the Far Eastern Republic. On September 23 the Peking government withdrew recognition from the Tsarist Russian minister and consular representatives. In addition to negotiating with the government, Yurin was active in establishing contact with intellectuals. As a result of his efforts, a number of Chinese, including Ch'ü Ch'iu-pai,[15] who was a newspaper reporter, and a relief group dispatched to help the Russian famine victims, left Peking for Russia in November, 1920. Relations between China and Soviet Russia thus began to develop.

It was a major Comintern policy to watch the East closely and to foster national-liberation struggles in colonial and semicolonial countries. It did so partly because Russia bordered not only on Europe but on Asia as well and had interests in both directions. Yet when it took over the government of Russia, the Party did not have enough personnel, and most of the people it did have were rough-hewn workers and peasants who knew nothing about China or the Far East. Nevertheless, both the Comintern and the Russian Communist Party were determined to march eastward; and after the resumption of communications between China and Russia in 1920, they started sending people on exploratory expeditions to the East.

Voitinsky and Yang Ming-chai were not the only people the Comintern sent. I know of a Korean named Kim who was also sent by the Comintern. His activities were apparently not related to those of Voitinsky. At the time I heard that Kim made contact with people in the Korean Provisional government at Shanghai, with Huang Chieh-min, who was then organizing his short-lived Utopia party, and with other Chinese. In December, 1920, they held a meeting. Apparently it was this meeting that the Moscow newspaper *Izvestia* in February, 1921, mentioned briefly as a "joint conference of Socialists of the Eastern countries."[16] Kim declared that he had come with 400,000 gold rubles and orders to organize Communist parties in the various Far Eastern countries. Apparently he also said that since communism had come to the Soviet Union, money was no longer needed within that country. The large amount of gold that had been confiscated there could thus be used to finance Communist parties in other countries, to pay for arms, and to carry out revolutions. This approach might have appealed to the Korean political refugees, who were eagerly seeking foreign help to liberate their country from Japan; some of the old-type Chinese revolutionists might have supported it, also; but the Chinese Marxists scoffed at the idea. It would be laughable indeed, Ch'en Tu-hsiu said to me at the time, if without studying Marxism and without establishing the Communist Party's foundations among the masses of workers, one relied solely upon rubles to build a Communist party and to start a revolution. So far as I know, these activities of Kim were not authorized by the Comintern, though it may have authorized him to establish contact with the Korean revolutionaries in Shanghai.

I first met Gregory Voitinsky in January of 1921. He came to Peking then with a letter of introduction written by Ch'en Tu-hsiu just before Ch'en left for Canton. He also had a letter from Li Han-chün, who had just taken over responsibility for the Shanghai branch of the Party from Ch'en. Both letters said that Voitinsky was a comrade with whom we could talk frankly. He looked up Li Ta-chao and me at the Peita library.

This Soviet Communist was about thirty years old, of medium height, well built, with penetrating dark eyes. He spoke fairly fluent English with a clipped accent, and we communicated in that language. Before the October Revolution he fled Russia for the United States, where he worked as a laborer. When the Revolution came, he returned home and became one of the earliest participants in the Irkutsk Bureau of the Comintern. When he talked with us, he never claimed to be a representative of the Comintern, probably because he was sent from the Irkutsk Bureau, not from Comintern headquarters.

I talked a good many times with Voitinsky in the office of Li Ta-chao. Usually Li Ta-chao was also present, but sometimes I saw him alone when Li Ta-chao was busy. On one occasion the entire Peking branch of the Party was there. We touched on a wide variety of subjects, such as basic Communist beliefs, principles of organization, the founding of the Comintern, what happened in the Russian Revolution, and the

Chinese revolution. We were principally interested in exchanging views and did not attempt to arrive at any conclusions.

Voitinsky established close ties with the Chinese Communists. There are many reasons why he was able to do this. Filled with youthful enthusiasm, he very easily fell in with people that held the new attitudes of the generation of the May Fourth Movement. And he drew no distinction between Chinese and foreigners, between the yellow and white races. People found in him a companion with whom they could cooperate. He still did not know much about conditions in China, and so he did not voice opinions about Chinese political problems. This humbleness was further indicated by the respect he showed for Ch'en Tu-hsiu and the other Chinese revolutionary figures that he met in Shanghai. Generally he would say that each of them had his own special talent. His behavior showed him to be truly a new kind of Russian emerging from the Revolution, which was perhaps the main reason for his getting along so well with Ch'en Tu-hsiu and others.

In addition to meeting Communists at Shanghai before coming to Peking, he also met Sun Yat-sen. He succeeded in becoming the first bridge between the Russian and Chinese revolutions because he made the right connections from the start, with such key figures as Ch'en Tu-hsiu and Sun Yat-sen. A more important reason for his success was his ability to mix well with Chinese revolutionists. Like other Russian revolutionists, he was fond of talking and would sometimes argue endlessly. But he was basically modest.

He talked to us in detail about the relationship between the Comintern and the Soviet government. The Soviet government, he said, could not do otherwise than establish relations—diplomatic as well as trade—with other governments. The Comintern functioned differently. The headquarters of world revolution, it was an organization of Communist parties from many countries. Its seat was in Moscow, to be sure, but it must not be confused with the Soviet government. Take Sino-Soviet relations, for example. The Soviet government had to deal with the Peking government and establish diplomatic relations with it. This was no indication, however, that the Soviet Union sympathized with a government that the Chinese people disliked, or that it supported it. The Comintern, on the other hand, sought relations not with the Peking government, but with the CCP. Naturally the Soviet government could not involve itself in the Chinese revolution, since that was a matter for the CCP and the Chinese people themselves. But the Comintern, because of its fundamentally international nature, was obliged to give the Chinese revolution support. Voitinsky expressed the hope that it would be possible for the Soviet government and the Comintern to pursue harmonious policies. For this to be true in China, however, he said that there would first have to be a Chinese revolutionary government. Without it, the Soviet government and the Comintern, because of their different positions, would have to proceed along different policy lines.

Voitinsky also discussed with us at length the relationship between the Russian Communist Party and the Comintern. He explained the origins of the Comintern and pointed out that the Russian Communist Party was but one member of it. In the spirit of internationalism, the Russian Communist Party did no more than discharge the obligations of a member and enjoy membership rights. It could not control the Comintern, for all Comintern decisions were arrived at by a majority. Yet the Russian Communist Party was, after all, the only one of the fraternal parties that had led a successful revolution—the October Revolution; and its leaders—Lenin and Trotsky—enjoyed enormous international prestige. In fact, therefore, the Russian Party held a position of leadership in the Comintern. It would not abuse this leadership position, however. It would not, in other words, demand that the Comintern align itself with the foreign policy of the Soviet Union, nor would it force the Communist parties of other countries to adopt policies unsuited to the revolutionary needs of those countries. Action of that sort would merely obstruct the development of other Communist parties. He added that these interpretations were not merely his own, that they were well grounded.

These two problems—the relationship between the Soviet government and the Comintern and the relationship between the Russian Communist Party and the Comintern—were a matter of concern to the Chinese Communists then. Voitinsky's interpretation of them won our support. Possibly that actually was the policy of the Comintern during its early days. It is also possible that Voitinsky was only giving his own naive views. In any event, we certainly did not anticipate then the problems that would arise from our acceptance of Voitinsky's views. The future was to reveal that the issues were not as simple as we imagined.

Another thing we discussed in detail was the Chinese trade-union movement. I told Voitinsky about the trade-union situation and about my experiences in the movement at Ch'anghsintien and elsewhere. The current aim of the movement in China, I said, must be first of all to organize true industrial trade unions. These must struggle to further the workers' interests, to reduce working time from the twelve hours that prevailed to ten or even eight hours and to raise wages so that workers could maintain at least a minimal standard of living. Workers should be free to organize trade unions, I said, and the unions should be allowed to represent them in bargaining collectively.

Voitinsky did not think that these ideas went far enough. He believed that before all else, Chinese workers should engage in political struggle in order to lead the peasants and the rest of the impoverished masses along the road to seizure of state power as quickly as possible. Strikes and other activities by which the workers might struggle to improve their living conditions, he felt, must not be considered ends in themselves. They were merely the means to an end, rather like military exercises. The aim of the trade-union movement, he insisted, was to seize state power. Only then would it be possible to guarantee better living conditions.

I did not agree with him, however. I did not believe that the workers' economic struggle could be called a means to an end. That would dampen their enthusiasm in struggling to improve their standard of living. It should at least be considered the most immediate end. The struggle involved, after all, was a real one and not merely a military exercise. In China, it would take a fierce revolution just to achieve an eight-hour day. So why not push this economic struggle as hard as possible to begin with, I asked, so that workers could gain experience that they would then use to seize state power.

Voitinsky promptly launched into a long discourse on the need for Communists to link the workers' economic struggle to the political struggle. From the very beginning, he declared, emphasis must be placed on propagandizing the ultimate objective of the political struggle.

I thought of my own experience at Ch'anghsintien. If I had started by telling the Ch'anghsintien workers that they must overthrow the Peking government and set up a dictatorship of the workers, they would have been frightened away. It would have been impossible even to establish the school for workers' children. Indeed, the Russian Communists after the Revolution were guilty of applying a few set formulae to all situations. Actually, however, any attempt to solve a problem without reference to practical experience is like trying to scratch an itching foot through a boot. In any event, linking up the economic with the political struggle later became a problem that the CCP discussed frequently without reaching consensus.

Generally speaking, Voitinsky expressed satisfaction with the early activities of the Chinese Communists. The average Russian considered China very backward and had no knowledge of modern developments there. And Voitinsky, finding himself in contact with a great many progressive people, seemed to find that China exceeded his early expectations. He had full confidence in the organization of the CCP and in its future. On this occasion he had stopped off in Peking on his way back to Russia, where he was to report the results of his activities to the Comintern. Before leaving, he expressed the earnest hope that the Chinese that believed in communism would soon be united and that the rudimentary organs throughout the country would quickly unite so that a congress could be called to officially inaugurate the CCP. He hoped that it would then join the Comintern, becoming one of its branches as soon as possible.

We all wanted to convene a CCP congress. After the Peking nucleus was formed, Ch'en Tu-hsiu mentioned it several times in correspondence. So we naturally agreed with Voitinsky, but we had not worked out any preparatory plans for the congress. Nor did Voitinsky make any suggestions about how it should be conducted, perhaps because he preferred to get instructions from Moscow on a constitution and platform for the CCP rather than to give his own views. Preparatory work for the official inauguration of the CCP, in any case, went ahead after Voitinsky left China.

The Communist Movement Sprouts Everywhere

Sprouts of the Communist movement, one after another, began to pop up in the important cities. In a country as vast as China and with such a huge population, these nuclei were rather like drops in the ocean. It was easy to dismiss them lightly, and the general public overlooked them at the time. Yet they grew and spread very rapidly over the entire country, and they had a profound effect on modern Chinese history.

Shanghai was the cradle of the CCP and the center for propagation of Communist theory. Led by Ch'en Tu-hsiu personally, the Shanghai nucleus began active operations toward the end of August, 1920. In September a Shanghai unit of the SYC was formed, with an initial membership of more than thirty youths. At the same time, Ch'en established the Foreign Language School, to prepare people for study in Russia, and placed it under the direction of Yang Ming-chai. The first batch of students was sent to Moscow during the winter of 1920-21 to study at the University of the Toilers of the Far East, which was generally known in Chinese simply as Tung-fang Ta-hsüeh. There were eight of them, all SYC members: Liu Shao-ch'i, P'eng Shu-chih, Lo Chüeh, Jen Pi-shih, Pu Shih-ch'i, Yüan Ta-shih, Pao P'u, and Liao Hua-p'ing. This Shanghai school sent additional students to Russia later. Of even greater importance was the publication in Shanghai of *Communist Monthly*, *The Laborer*, and a variety of pamphlets, among them the *Manifesto of the Communist Party*. These publications were widely circulated in all parts of the country and produced immense repercussions.

Shanghai's activities overflowed in all directions. They were most notable at Hangchow in Chekiang Province. With Shen Ting-i, Shih Ts'un-t'ung, and Yü Hsiu-sung as prime movers, a unit of the SYC was organized there about October, 1920, with more than twenty members. Among them were Hsüan Chung-hua and Hsü Mei-k'un. Hsü Mei-k'un, a printer, began trade-union activities among the print-shop workers of Hangchow. Units of the SYC were established in such places as Nanking, Wuhu, and Anking shortly thereafter. The size of these units varied from several people to more than ten, and most participants were students. In the main their activities consisted in disseminating Communist ideas among students.

The Peking nucleus, which was more active than the others, was especially noted for its trade-union activities. In addition to its previously mentioned work in and around Peking, toward the end of the year it organized both a unit of the SYC and a Communist nucleus at Tsinan, the capital of Shantung Province. Initially there were eight members of this nucleus, two of whom were Wang Chin-mei and Teng En-ming. The Youth Corps unit was larger. Together they developed a trade-union movement in Tsinan and Tsingtao and along the Tsingtao-Tsinan and the Tientsin-Pukow railways.

A Tientsin unit of the SYC, which the Peking nucleus was responsible for, started early the next year with more than ten members, Li Chen-ying, Han Lin-fu, Yü Fang-chou, and Ch'en Hsiao-ts'en among them. They began trade-union activities among workers in Tientsin and elsewhere.

Two railway workers at Tangshan, furthermore, became Communists by joining the Peking nucleus. They were Teng P'ei and Liang P'eng-wan.

More than thirty people—two of whom were Ho Ch'ang and Wang Chen-i—joined a unit of the SYC that the Peking nucleus formed in Shansi. Units of the SYC were also organized in Inner Mongolia by Han Lin-fu, who made the Mongols his personal project; and about thirty Inner Mongolian youths were formed into a pro-Communist revolutionary organization. In the Northeast, however, there was no official organization. It was a seemingly backward region in which only a few scattered Russian, Korean, and Chinese individuals joined the Youth Corps and carried on spasmodic activities.

Mao Tse-tung started the Communist nucleus at Changsha in Hunan Province in November, 1920. In addition to Mao, its earliest participants included Hsia Hsi, I Li-jung, Ho Shu-heng, and Kuo Liang. At about the same time, an SYC unit was formed there with a large membership of more than thirty. This nucleus was always very active.

Mao Tse-tung himself had been a very active youth during the period of the May Fourth Movement. First he had formed a small organization called the New People's Study Society (Hsin Min Hsüeh Hui), and in 1919 he had edited the *Hsiang River Critic* (Hsiang-chiang P'ing-lun), a weekly publication.[17] This paper, which advocated the precepts of the New Culture Movement, ranked high in prestige among the various little provincial publications. It stood second only to *New Chekiang Tide*, published at Hangchow by Shih Ts'un-t'ung.[18] Mao Tse-tung came to believe in Marxism in Hunan under the influence of certain Peita students from Hunan, one of whom was Lo Chang-lung. Later in Peking he fell under the influence of Li Ta-chao and others, while he was working in the Peita library. He became a main founder of the Hunan CCP nucleus as a result of the encouragement Ch'en Tu-hsiu gave him in letters.[19]

It was not by accident that Chinese Communist nuclei in Hunan and Shantung were among the first to develop. Because Shantung was a target of Japanese aggression, Shantung youths generally inclined farther to the Left than those in the other northern provinces. And in the South it was always on Hunan that North-South wars converged. The Hunanese had suffered from war for a very long time, and, generally speaking, their young people inclined to the Left ideologically and were politically highly sensitive. Indeed, to each modern Chinese revolutionary movement, Hunan contributed a number of outstanding figures. Historical traditions tended to produce a people there in whom stubborn persistence during a struggle was a characteristic. The adage "There can be no army without Hunanese" is well known. This was the province that in 1920 and 1921 first sponsored the idea of a federation of autonomous provinces.[20] Influential people in various cliques that were dissatisfied with the Peking government quickly rallied around the standard of a federation of autonomous provinces in an attempt to keep Hunan out of the civil war. Mao Tse-tung and his group of leftist youths gave their support to this autonomy movement, establishing extensive contacts with KMT elements and other political groups in Hunan.

Not long before Mao Tse-tung and his colleagues organized the Hunan Communist nucleus, another group of leftists in Changsha formed the Hunan Labor Society (Hu-nan Lao-kung Hui). Chief among them were Huang Ai and P'ang Jen-ch'uan. They believed vaguely in anarchism and socialism and had only a superficial understanding of the trade-union movement; nevertheless they were hard workers. They had not established ties with Ch'en Tu-hsiu. During the period of the May Fourth Movement, young people all over the country vied with one another in forming small leftist organizations, and rivalry between them was unavoidable. This state of affairs was most marked in Hunan. However, influenced by the call for unity among fellow travelers in areas outside Hunan, Huang, P'ang, and their colleagues ultimately joined the SYC. Nevertheless, the mutual antagonism that existed between them and Mao Tse-tung quietly grew instead of being settled. Then in January, 1922, Huang and P'ang were executed for inciting a labor strike.[21] This led to a split between the Hunan committee of the CCP and the Hunan Labor Society; and this had a very detrimental effect on the Chinese labor movement.

The split in the Hunan labor movement was quite different from the separation of the anarchists from the Marxists in Peking. After the execution of Huang Ai and P'ang Jen-ch'uan, Mao Tse-tung and others condemned them as anarchists. But this accusation was not just, for the two did not oppose basic Communist beliefs. Furthermore they actively involved themselves in the workers' movement, making important contributions to the Hunan trade-union movement, whose first martyrs they became. That Mao Tse-tung was unable to cooperate with Huang and P'ang was the result, among other things, of the fact that the Hunan Communists were too radical in their attitude. It was also a result of the fact that Mao Tse-tung did not have enough prestige to attract a first-rate following.

Like the Hunan nucleus, the Wuhan nucleus was organized in November, 1920. Its first participants included Tung Pi-wu, Ch'en T'an-ch'iu, Pao Hui-seng, Lin Yü-nan, and Hsiang Ying. Some of the first participants were closely connected with the KMT, which was outlawed in Wuhan then, and were engaged in education work while lying low. A larger portion of them, however, were leftist youths of the May Fourth Movement. And May Fourth Movement activists organized a Wuhan unit of the SYC about the same time. Among these were Yun Tai-ying, Hsiao Ch'u-nü, Li Shu-ch'u, Liu Ch'ang-ch'un, and Li Ch'iu-shih. Earlier they had formed a small group called the Mutual Aid Society, whose publication, *Wu-han P'ing-lun* (Wuhan Critic), advocated the New Culture Movement.

Toward the end of 1920, Yun Tai-ying and Hsiao Ch'u-nü took up teaching jobs in Chungking. Working with Yang An-kung and others there, they brought together about thirty youths and formed the Chung-king unit of the SYC.

It so happened, however, that a man named Wu Yu-chang had already organized a Young Communist party at Chengtu. A veteran T'ung-meng Hui member, Wu had fled to France; and without contacting Ch'en Tu-hsiu, he had started his own organization after returning. In the name of the Young Communist Party, he had united scores of young people in the Chengtu region.

Disputes arose from having two similar organizations in Szechwan Province, chiefly because they both sought to contact the same type of people and to engage in the same activities. Since each considered itself the official organization, there was rivalry between them. The SYC looked upon itself as a national organization, and upon the Young Communist Party as a small local organization formed by a few people in Chengtu that wanted to be different. The Young Communist Party, on the other hand, regarded the SYC as a subsidiary of the Communist organization.

Not until 1921, when a central committee of the CCP was formed, were the two called upon to consolidate. The merger actually took place in 1922. Wu Yu-chang and Yang An-kung joined the CCP, while most of the others became members of a unified SYC in Szechwan. Differences were buried in time, and members of what had been two organizations truly worked together in one.

The Communist nucleus at Canton was formed later than the others. It was not organized until Ch'en Tu-hsiu went there in December, 1920. Although Canton, the metropolis of South China, was the cradle of China's modern revolutions, until a month or so earlier it had been controlled by the Kwangsi wardlords who had overrun the Southern government. The people there traditionally opposed the Peking government, but they had suffered such exorbitant taxation under the Southern government that they opposed it, too. A dilemma faced them. Most of the revolutionary figures of Sun Yat-sen's group, meanwhile, had been edged out of office, and the revolutionary atmosphere thinned to the point of evaporation. The activities of the anarchists, who were active in the area very early, had been divorced from practical politics. And while Canton remained the nominal revolutionary center, it was precisely there that Communist activities had been backward. The May Fourth Movement had not made itself felt extensively in this extreme southern province of Kwangtung. The small leftist organizations and their publications, as well as publications that flourished in the other provinces, had seldom appeared around Canton; and we had regretted not being able to find suitable people there to establish a Communist nucleus.

When troops led by Ch'en Chiung-ming took Canton toward the end of October, 1920, however, the atmosphere changed. This was the only military force that still supported Sun Yat-sen. The Kwangsi warlords had ousted it from Kwangtung two years earlier, and it had spent the intervening period in southern Fukien, during which time KMT people traveled frequently between Shanghai and Fukien, laying plans to return to Kwangtung. This force was regarded more or less as a good sample of KMT revolutionary wares. On my two visits to Shanghai in 1920, revolutionary friends there talked of Ch'en Chiung-ming's region as the place in China where "new" thoughts, "new" publications, and "new" people would get the best reception. At a time when Tai Chi-t'ao was keenly interested in Communist activities, he assured me that Ch'en Chiung-ming was one general who supported socialism and that initial experiments in socialism could be conducted in his territory. It was with an introduction from Tai Chi-t'ao that Yü Hsiu-sung, a member of the Shanghai nucleus, went to southern Fukien and worked as adviser to a young KMT military figure named Chiang Kai-shek. In planning the Communist movement, Ch'en Tu-hsiu often corresponded with Ch'en Chiung-ming. They discussed academic and ideological matters.

Ch'en Chiung-ming began his march on Canton in August, 1920, and occupied it on October 28. The forces of the Kwangsi militarists, who specialized in plunder and who had, in any case, already enriched themselves, could not withstand the attack. Most of them were driven back to Kwangsi. This victory enabled Sun Yat-sen to return to Canton in November and to rebuild a military government. Ch'en Chiung-ming was made governor of Kwangtung and, concurrently, Minister of the Interior, Minister of the Army of the Military Government, and Commander-in-Chief of the Kwangtung Army. He ranked second only to Sun Yat-sen, and it was he who held real power. An important step he took was to invite Ch'en Tu-hsiu to Canton to become chairman of the Education Committee of the Kwangtung provincial government.

Ch'en Tu-hsiu solicited the reactions of the various Communist nuclei to this invitation. Li Ta-chao and I wrote saying that we thought he should go to Canton. We felt that there were two important reasons why he should do this. In the first place, he would be able to spread the ideas of the New Culture Movement and Socialist thought extensively in Kwangtung. In the second place, he could launch a Communist organization there. We said that for the time being he ought not to feel bound by the understanding that Communists must not hold official posts. Education work was very important in disseminating Communist ideology. Ch'en Tu-hsiu accepted our views, and in December he turned over the duties of what was by then the Shanghai branch of the Party to Li Han-chün, Li Ta, and others. He took no comrades with him, for he did not want to slow things up by removing people from Party work that was already under way. He went to Canton alone.

In general, the young people of Canton welcomed the arrival of Ch'en Tu-hsiu. Ch'en Chiung-ming treated him with deference, accepting their relationship as a sign of his own ability to get along with the "new" people. Wang Ching-wei, the president of the Education Association, also got along well with him. The numerous speeches that Ch'en Tu-hsiu gave and the numerous articles that he wrote while he was in Canton were charged with a magnetic force that immensely stimulated the intellectuals there.

About January of 1921, Ch'en Tu-hsiu invited T'an P'ing-shan, Ch'en Kung-po, T'an Chih-t'ang, and the anarchist Ou Sheng-pai to cooperate in forming a Kwangtung nucleus. It began to publish a weekly, Voice of Labor, and to preach communism to students in the schools. It also became interested in rural activities. Past revolutionary movements in Kwangtung had risen in the countryside, and it was appropriate that the

Communists at Canton should be the first Chinese Communists to become interested in the peasant movement. The founders of the Canton unit of the SYC included P'eng P'ai, Lo Yi-yüan, and Juan Hsiao-hsien, all of whom worked in the peasant movement later. This unit was formed at about the same time as the nucleus.

Like the Peking nucleus, the Kwangtung Communist nucleus had anarchist members for a short time. In a month or two, however, the few anarchists that had joined it left the nucleus as a result of differences with the Marxists. The anarchists in Canton strongly opposed the KMT; and since they believed that Ch'en Tu-hsiu and other Communists had some sort of relationship with the KMT, they frequently complained about it. In addition to leaving this nucleus for the same reasons that the anarchists left the Peking nucleus, they had this additional fancied complaint.

As a matter of fact, however, the Kwangtung Communist nucleus did not enjoy good relations with Sun Yat-sen's group. The most loyal supporters of Sun Yat-sen, such as Hu Han-min, had already begun to differ secretly with Ch'en Chiung-ming. The mouthpiece of Ch'en Chiung-ming, *Chun Pao*, was at the time edited by two Communists, Ch'en Kung-po and T'an Chih-t'ang. Naturally, it sided with Ch'en Chiung-ming, and this alienated a portion of the KMT. As they saw it, Ch'en Tu-hsiu and his Communists were supporting Ch'en Chiung-ming in order to make trouble for Sun Yat-sen. This same issue later became a matter of great controversy within the CCP.

The activities of Communists in various parts of the country, which I have briefly described above, constituted in truth the major developments during the stage prior to the official inauguration of the CCP. Generally speaking, all of the Communist nuclei were composed of intellectuals. In the eyes of the orthodox Communists, this was not quite in keeping with their formula that defines the Communist Party as the political party of the proletariat. When they talk of the historical development of the CCP, they often go to a great deal of trouble to seek traces of the Chinese working class in its origins and its development, in order to add glamor to their narrative. Such efforts are really unnecessary.

In a backward country the intellectuals constitute the small number of outstanding individuals, and they also serve as the barometer of the political climate. The Taiping Rebellion, the reformist movement led by K'ang and Liang, and the revolutionary movement of Sun Yat-sen had all been sponsored by intellectuals that saw the light earlier. It is true that during the European war China's industry and commerce for a time registered considerable development. The May Fourth Movement likewise raised the national consciousness of China. But these incidents had not basically changed the backward status of China. Workers in general did not know what communism was. Many had not even heard of the term. Even among the intellectuals that sympathized with communism at the time, the great majority had little or no understanding of Marxism, and they possessed even less experience in organizing political parties. Accordingly, a Communist nucleus could not at its inception belong to the workers, nor could it have a large membership in the beginning.

There can be no doubt that the formation of the CCP had been influenced by the May Fourth Movement. This movement pushed China's youths toward the Left, until it became a fad for them to cultivate socialism. This was also a major factor that enabled the birth and rapid development of the Communist nuclei. For the most part the founders of the CCP were activists in the May Fourth Movement, and thus they could utilize the experience of that movement to build the first foundations of the CCP. We had cultivated the spirit of working hard and realistically for the new ideal, and we also inherited the organizational spirit of unity and mutual aid of the students in the May Fourth Movement. So we did not perpetuate the folly established by the old scholar-gentry, who tempestuously fought one another over many little issues, thus setting a pattern for the old political parties in China. From the very beginning we came up with a new attitude that was distinguished by our capacity for unity.

In the work of building the party, we rid ourselves of the historically lengthy influence exerted by the KMT and constructed our own independent organization. We gradually parted ways with the anarchists, established our front, and rapidly marched to the fore. We did not permit the infiltration of opportunists; but we brought together in our organization all of the Communists that we could unite with. The development of our organization led to the termination of activities of another "Communist party" organized by Hu O-kung, a member of Parliament from Hupeh, and of the Utopia party organized by the trade-union leader Huang Chieh-min. At the time, the Chinese Communists also seemed to have surpassed the revolutionary veterans of an older generation in taking risks and embarking on new adventures, and they also developed new areas of activity among the masses of workers. All of these were important factors in the development of the Chinese Communist movement.

We were enthralled by the Russian Revolution, but we lacked Marxist training and had even less experience in applying it to the actual conditions in China. Later, most of the major policies of the CCP were decided for it by Moscow. Even if everything had been done with China's interests at heart, handling of the China situation from Moscow could not have been completely free from the defect of impracticability. As a result, the Chinese revolution suffered indescribable damage. The facts were not as beautiful as the ideals. This could not be covered up by propaganda. A small mistake in decision often leads to incalculable harm. This is a lesson that should be comprehended by China's revolutionists.

The First Congress of the Communist Party of China

By April of 1921, those of us who had been the major promoters of the CCP concluded that work in the various areas had got off to a satisfactory start and that the time was opportune to formally organize the Party. Consultations were carried on by letters between Shanghai, Peking, and Canton, as a result of which it was decided to convene the First Congress of the CCP in mid-June at Shanghai.

The Peking branch was to send two delegates to this Congress. All of the comrades from Peking and some comrades from the other cities eagerly hoped that Li Ta-chao would be able to attend the meeting himself. Since it was the end of the academic year at Peita, however, he was too busy to make the trip. Liu Jen-ching and I were elected to be the delegates.

Because I had to take part in preparations for the Congress, I arrived at Shanghai about the middle of May, before Liu Jen-ching. I went immediately from the train to see Li Ta. He told me a great deal about the situation in Shanghai, pointing out that work there was not as intensive as it had been and that some things were stalemated. The reason for this was the Li Han-chün and other comrades were busy with their teaching and writing. They were unable to devote full energy to Party work, as they had done while Ch'en Tu-hsiu was there. Li Ta also talked about the two Comintern representatives who had recently arrived. One, who was an assistant to the other, was named Nicolaevsky,[22] a laconic, plain-looking man. The other, the man in charge, was named Maring. (Maring's real name was Hendricus Sneevliet.) This foreign devil was aggressive and hard to deal with; his manner was very different indeed from that of Voitinsky. His first meeting with Li Ta and Li Han-chün had been characterized, in fact, by a marked lack of cordiality. Li Ta said that Maring knew I was coming to Shanghai and that he was eager to meet me.

Li Ta attributed great importance to our relationship with the Comintern. While, he said, he was not eager to become better acquainted with Maring, he hoped that I would cultivate the man. Li Ta was an outspoken man. He was deep-dyed with the colors of the traditional scholar and he had his Hunanese pride, and when a conversation displeased him he would often open his eyes very wide and glare at the other person, as though unable to suppress his rage. His simple, short sentences could be as cutting as steel. I formed an amusing picture in my mind of Li Ta and Maring, both of them pigheaded, clashing head-on.

Next I called on Li Han-chün, another person of the traditional scholar type. Considered the Marxist theorist among us, he was especially interested in the economic theories of Marx. It was not easy for him to accept the views of others, and he delighted in bluntly throwing out his own dissenting views. But he maintained a calm facade, so that his appearance never betrayed his inner feelings. Especially pleased that I had managed to arrive early, he enthusiastically welcomed me and announced that we would now be able to talk about the many things which could not be discussed in any detail in letters. It would be easy to solve practical problems such as where meetings of the Congress should be held, he said, and we could defer preparation of the agenda and various draft resolutions until all the delegates had arrived. The most pressing problem, he declared, was our relationship with the Comintern. And then he told me a great deal about the situation in Shanghai and the difficulties that had been encountered.

He described the meeting that he and Li Ta had had with Maring. Maring had announced that he was the official representative of the Comintern and had unceremoniously demanded that Li Han-chün give him a work report. Li had refused on the grounds that the organization was still in its infancy and that there was nothing to report. Maring then had asked for a program of activities and a budget. He had said that the Comintern would give financial support. But Li Han-chün had decided that Maring's approach was much too peremptory. And so Li had bluntly announced that the CCP had not yet been officially formed and that it had not yet been decided whether the Party would join the Comintern. Even if the Party had been established and had decided to join the Comintern, Li Han-chün had told Maring, its relationship with the Comintern representative would have to be looked into further. Thus, it was premature to talk about work reports, plans, and budgets. If the Comintern wanted to support us, Li had said, we would certainly accept its help, but we must be free to use the money as we thought best. In this way the three of them had fallen into an unpleasant deadlock.

As Li Han-chün saw it, the CCP alone should assume the responsibility of carrying on the Communist movement in China, with the Comintern doing nothing but helping. For the sake of internationalism, he felt, we could accept theoretical guidance from the Comintern and act in accordance with it. But the Comintern should not help us financially unless we were unable to raise enough money ourselves. In other words, we should not depend upon Comintern subsidies to carry on our work. Moreover, Li Han-chün felt that the representative sent to China by the Comintern must not be considered anything more than an adviser; certainly he should not assume the role of a director. After explaining these views of his to me, Li added that Maring had encountered such a rebuff that he was eager to see Ch'en Tu-hsiu, Li Ta-chao, and me just as soon as possible. Li suggested that I have a talk with Maring and try to reach some sort of understanding with him.

Chang T'ai-lei, who had seen more of Maring, reacted to him somewhat differently. Chang was then a member of the SYC. After the Corps was organized, he had been sent to Moscow as a delegate to the International Congress of Communist Youth held there late in 1920. In fact, he was the first Chinese Communist to appear in Moscow in the role of a delegate to any meeting. Since Chang's English was fairly fluent, Li Han-chün had assigned him to be the assistant to Maring, who, though a Dutchman, spoke good English. Chang had been the interpreter when Maring met Li Han-chün and Li Ta. In Chang's opinion, Maring's chief defects were an inadequate knowledge of China and a rather unpleasant manner. Chang insisted, however, that Maring was an important figure in the Comintern and a Marxist who commanded respect, and so Chang was fervent in urging that our relations with him be improved.

Two days later Chang T'ai-lei accompanied me as I called on Maring. Maring was staying at the home of a German on Avenue Road, and that was where we had our first interview. He did not mention his unpleasant meeting with Li Han-chün and Li Ta, nor did he raise the subject of work reports and that sort of thing. There was an obvious improvement in his attitude. We touched lightly on conditions in the North, and he said that the workers' movement in the North greatly interested him. We also talked briefly about preparations for the Congress. There was an appreciable harmony in our views. As a result, I was credited with having accomplished the task of improving relations with Maring, and I was elected to be the official contact man with him.

Maring struck me as an extraordinary man. At first glance this Dutchman with a powerful physique looked like a Prussian officer. But his speech often revealed the talents of a parliamentary debater. At times he would assume a very severe posture, his eyes burning into you. And he would persist in his views with such stubbornness that you would think he was prepared to challenge his opponent to a duel. A Socialist of long standing, he had worked for many years in what were then called the Dutch East Indies, now Indonesia, and his sympathy was with the oppressed nations of the East. One time on the streets of Shanghai, for example, he encountered a foreigner insulting a Chinese coolie. He rushed forward to fight the foreigner. Yet he often dwelt too much upon the backwardness of Asian people, and he joked about the infantile simplicity of Oriental Socialists. Indeed, he left the impression with some people that he had acquired the habits and attitudes of the Dutchmen that lived as colonial masters in the East Indies. He was, he believed, the foremost authority on the East in the Comintern, and this was a source of great pride to him. He would sometimes refer to the Second Comintern Congress, at which, he said, Lenin and he together formulated the resolutions on the colonial problem. He saw himself coming as an angel of liberation to the Asian people. But in the eyes of those of us who maintained our self-respect and who were seeking our own liberation, he seemed endowed with the social superiority complex of the white man.

Apparently Maring did not take into consideration the activities that Voitinsky had already carried out in China. From the start he relied on his own subjective impressions and did what he pleased. And it was not Li Han-chün alone who felt that he was too abrupt in his ways, for later during his stay in China, he was the cause of several major upheavals within the Party. These seemed to be closely related to his personal character.

By early June, delegates to the Congress were arriving in Shanghai one after the other. Liu Jen-ching arrived only a few days after I did. A youth who buried himself in books, he had read a relatively large number of Comintern publications. He advocated that the Congress assert its belief in the dictatorship of the proletariat, and he would talk about this idea endlessly with everyone he met.

Wang Chin-mei and Teng En-ming, the delegates from Shangtung, also arrived early. They had just completed their middle school studies, but they had made a reputation for themselves during the May Fourth Movement. On this trip to Shanghai, I had passed through Tsinan, the capital of Shantung, and had stopped over a day there. They had gathered the eight Party members in Tsinan together, and we had spent the day in a boat on Ta Ming Lake. They regarded me as both their senior and their old friend, and so they laid their many problems before me and asked for detailed advice. Listening to me attentively, they took notes on the more important points and discussed ways and means of implementing our policies. We were oblivious to the beauties of Ta Ming Lake. In Shanghai, maintaining the spirit of earnest study, they read extensively and occasionally sought the advice of other delegates.

There were three delegates from Wuhan—Tung Pi-wu, Ch'en T'an-ch'iu, and Pao Hui-seng. Tung Pi-wu, honest-looking and mustachioed, resembled an old-style scholar. Only his speech revealed the strong character of a veteran revolutionary. Ch'en T'an-ch'iu wore a perpetually serious look about him and seemed to be the stereotype of a school-teacher. Pao Hui-seng, a newspaperman who had only recently stepped out into the world, loved to crack jokes. None of these delegates from Wuhan had much to say about theory. They showed greater interest in practical issues.

The delegates from Hunan were Mao Tse-tung and Ho Shu-heng. Ho, an amiable elderly man who delighted in browsing among old Chinese books, his mouth always wide open, seemed to find it difficult to speak and to express himself. Although he was lovable for his sincerity and enthusiasm, he knew practically nothing about Marxism. He was a confirmed Confucian, eager to do what was ethically right. Mao Tse-tung, who had not yet shaken off his rough Hunanese ways, was the pale-faced scholar, a youth of rather lively temperament, who in his long gown of native cloth looked rather like a Taoist priest out of some village. His fund of general knowledge was considerable, but he did not seem to understand much more about Marxism than Wang Chin-mei and

Teng En-ming. A good talker, Mao loved an argument, and while conversing, he delighted in laying verbal traps into which his opponents would unwittingly fall by seeming to contradict themselves. Then, obviously happy, he would burst into laughter. The way he carried himself when he walked and the way he shrugged his shoulders and sneered when he talked made him seem like the stock stage character of the classic strategist.

The delegate for students in Japan was Chou Fo-hai. He was a very energetic young man who seemed to have rid himself of the rough ways of the Hunanese. Looking like a worldly, veteran Shanghai resident, he presented a very smart appearance. He was well versed in the Socialist movement in Japan and took an active part in the preparations for the Congress.

The date scheduled for the Congress approach, but Ch'en Tu-hsiu had not arrived. We sent letters and telegrams, urging him and the delegates from Canton to come to Shanghai at once. A few days later Ch'en Kung-po, the delegate from Canton, arrived with a letter from Ch'en Tu-hsiu. It was addressed to all the delegates. In it Ch'en explained that his resignation from his Canton post had not yet been accepted and that he could not get away for the Congress. He set down four points on organization and policy and asked that the Congress consider them when it discussed the Party platform and Party constitution.[23]

Ch'en Kung-po had nothing to say about Ch'en Tu-hsiu's opinions. He was accompanied by his beautiful wife. They stayed at the expensive Great Eastern Hotel, and he busied himself attending to personal affairs which had very little to do with anything connected with the Congress. Most delegates regarded him merely as a smart young politician from the Canton government. He talked with us mostly about practical matters connected with the political situation in Canton.

Toward the end of June all the expected delegates had arrived, and we got ready to open the Congress. The delegates from Shanghai were Li Han-chün and Li Ta, representing nine Party members in Shanghai. Liu Jen-ching and I represented the fifteen members of the Peking branch. Tung Pi-wu, Ch'en T'an-ch'iu, and Pao Hui-seng represented the eight Party members in Wuhan. Mao Tse-tung and Ho Shu-heng represented about ten members from Hunan. Wang Chin-mei and Teng En-ming represented the eight members in Shantung. Ch'en Kung-po represented about seven members in Kwangtung, while Chou Fo-hai represented the two members among the students in Japan. Before the

Congress opened, there were in all thirteen delegates representing fifty-nine Party members. The SYC had about three hundred and fifty members throughout the country. These two organizations represented the entire Chinese Communist front on the eve of the First Congress.

After there had been a preliminary exchange of views, it was decided to open the Congress officially on July 1. We selected as the location for it a classroom in the Po Wen Girls' School on Rue Bourgeat in the French Concession. The school was vacant for the summer, and most of the delegates were staying there. A four-point agenda was agreed upon: (1) Party Platform and Political Program, (2) Party Constitution, (3) Central Tasks and Work Policy, and (4) Election of a Central Committee. Before the Congress actually opened, a few of us who were the leading delegates also discussed the delegates' qualifications. With the exception of Tung Pi-wu, we were all quite young and we had looked rather askance at the elderly Ho Shu-heng, who was almost totally ignorant of Marxism and who had not shown any ability to carry out the practical tasks of the Party. It was decided that he ought not to be permitted to attend the Congress, and I was elected to transmit this decision to Mao Tse-tung. As a pretext for getting Ho to leave, Mao promptly told him of some job in Hunan that required urgent attention and asked him to hurry back and look after it. Ho, happy to feel himself useful, scurried off to Hunan. Thus, only twelve delegates actually attended the Congress.

Formulation of a "Party Platform and Political Program" was a difficult task, but we felt that we should produce such a document. At the same time we did not feel any need for an elaborate Party constitution, since a simple one would take care of our needs at that time. I was elected to draft both documents. After collecting the views of Ch'en Tu-hsiu and of the various delegates, I prepared a draft of each and handed them over to Li Han-chün, Liu Jen-ching, and Chou Fo-hai for their scrutiny.

First I prepared a draft of the Party platform and political program, which I called "Manifesto on the Formation of the Chinese Communist Party." Its main points consisted of the basic beliefs of a Communist, the organization of the CCP, the basic policy of the Party, and the Party's intention of achieving communism through a dictatorship of the proletariat. While Li Han-chün and others did not entirely agree with the ideas expressed in my draft, they accepted it as a basis for discussion. Maring, upon seeing an English-language translation of it that Chang

T'ai-lei had made, was more severely critical. He said that the draft was quite well written so far as theoretical principles were concerned. Its chief defect was that it did not clearly specify the immediate political program of the CCP. He considered it correct in expressing support for a democratic and nationalistic revolution aimed at establishing a truly democratic republic in China. But he said that there was no indication of what concrete measures would be taken to achieve this. I thought that these criticisms were very valuable. I asked him to suggest some concrete solutions to the problems he had raised so that we could discuss them at the Congress. But he did not do so, perhaps because he had not yet arrived at any definite policy himself.

We had not yet received the text of the Resolutions on the Colonial Problem passed by the Second Comintern Congress. Only a few delegates had obtained from Maring or from Western European Communist publications some rough idea of what they contained. Nor did we have access to the Party platforms and Party constitutions of the Communist parties in other countries. Generally speaking, therefore, the work of the Congress was carried out through our own efforts as we groped in the dark.

At three o'clock on the afternoon of July 1, 1921, the First Congress of the CCP was opened. I was elected chairman. First, I formally declared the establishment of the CCP. This was followed by adoption of the four-item agenda as proposed. After deciding that there would be both morning and afternoon sessions, we proceeded immediately to the discussion of item one on the agenda, the Party platform and political program.

I explained to the Congress the background for the drafting of the Party platform and political program. I said that at first the comrades responsible for drafting and examining these items had decided to present to the Congress a draft entitled "Manifesto on the Establishment of the Chinese Communist Party" as a basis for discussion. Later, however, after careful discussion, we had decided that this draft was not well enough developed, chiefly because it lacked a clear-cut political program. And so it was thought best that everyone freely express his views on the subject and that some delegates be elected to draft a manifesto based on that discussion. Thereupon, I moved that the delegates to the Congress report on the status of their work in the various areas and express themselves on item one of the agenda. The Congress immediately voted approval of this proposal.

Li Han-chün, Liu Jen-ching, Chou Fo-hai, and I had held many preliminary discussions on the Party platform and political program. There were differences among us and these had become clearly defined. Li Han-chün now presented his dissenting views. In the contemporary world, he said, there had been both the Russian October Revolution and the revolution of the Socialist Party of Germany. Before deciding upon a Party platform and political program for the CCP, we should first send people to Russia and to Germany to study the situations there, he said. He also proposed that a research organization be established in China— perhaps a Marxist university—to carry on advanced studies. After that we could reach a final decision about a Party platform and political program. He thought that China was not yet ready for a Communist revolution and that Chinese Communists should for the time being employ the practical measures of stressing study and propaganda while supporting the revolutionary movement of Sun Yat-sen. When Dr. Sun's revolution had succeeded, he said, the Communists could participate in the parliament that would be established.

Liu Jen-ching developed an argument aimed directly at the views of Li Han-chün. He advocated a Communist party that accepted Marxism, that would use armed insurrection as the means for seizing state power and establishing a dictatorship of the proletariat, and that would have as its highest objective the realization of communism. He opposed the parliamentary policy of the Western European Social Democrats and the thinking of all reformists. The CCP must not be content merely with studying Marxism, he believed, nor must it entertain many illusions about what could be accomplished by the KMT and the parliamentary system. It must, he insisted, engage independently in its own workers' movement, so as to prepare for a Communist revolution.

The views of Li Han-chün became the focus for discussion by the Congress. With the exception of Ch'en Kung-po, who at times expressed a vague sympathy for them, all of the delegates criticized them in varying degrees. An overwhelming majority insisted that the CCP affirm the basic principle of a dictatorship of the proletariat. As to the question of practical politics, some advocated that the CCP not engage in practical political activities for the time being. Others believed that the CCP, while standing firm on its Communist position, should support the revolutionary movement led by Sun Yat-sen.

After a few days of such discussion, I summed up the views of those present and brought out several conclusions. These amounted essentially to: (1) the CCP was the revolutionary political party of the proletariat, and its basic principle was realization of a dictatorship of the proletariat; (2) for the time being, stress should be laid upon studying Marxist theory and upon the practical development of a workers' movement; (3) the CCP would not shun parliamentary and other legal procedures, but it would consider them only as means to the end of expanding the influence of the working class; and (4) while standing firm on its Communist position, the CCP could support the revolution of Sun Yat-sen, but its primary objective would remain the realization of a Communist revolution, and the social revolution led by the Communist Party must not be confused with the KMT's revolution. These four points were formally adopted by the Congress as the main points of the platform and political program of the CCP.

The discussion of this item on the agenda touched upon many other questions in an extensive way. As most delegates saw it, China would undergo two revolutions—a national democratic revolution first and then a social revolution. It was somewhat doubtful whether the KMT could shoulder responsibility for the first revolution. But it was accepted that if China were made into a truly democratic republic, the working class would have greater freedom. But we Communists had no intention of being satisfied with a democratic republic; we would follow it with a social revolution aimed at realizing a soviet type of state structure. However, at that time it did not occur to any one of us that the CCP and KMT might cooperate in the national revolution, and then advance into the social revolution.

The delegates also touched upon such matters as the nationalization of land, the peasant problem, an eight-hour working day, opposition to aggression by the Powers against China, and opposition to warlord politics. In general, the delegates accepted the fact that the Communist revolution lay somewhere in the distant future and that, for the moment, even the national democratic revolution was beyond China's grasp.

Thus, the Congress, in addition to rejecting the reformist approach of Li Han-chün, arrived at the general points mentioned above in deciding on a practical platform.

In discussing the Party constitution that I had drafted, Li Han-chün suggested two revisions. He said that the proposed central committee of the CCP ought to serve merely as a liaison organ, that it should not be able to issue orders at its own discretion. He thought that agreement of comrades in all local branches should be obtained on all matters, and that the policy should prevail of having general discussion of everything and of making all issues public. Furthermore, he believed that there should not be undue restrictions upon the admission of members, and that there should be no provision requiring all members to take part in the practical work of the Party. So long as a person believed in Marxism, Li felt, he should be sufficiently qualified for membership.

A majority of delegates, however, opposed these views of Li Han-chün. They supported the original draft, criticizing Li for wanting merely a liberal association.

The Party Constitution adopted by the Congress, then, included the following major points:

1. To join the Communist Party, a person must believe in communism, abide by all resolutions of the Party, and take part in the practical work of the Party. His application must be sponsored by two members and approved by a local committee before he is admitted to membership in the Party.

2. The CC of the CCP is to be located at Shanghai. Local committees are to be organized in the different provinces. Under each local committee, Party branches are to be established in factories, schools, and neighborhoods.

3. The committee system is to be used by units at all levels, with a minimum personnel of one secretary, one person in charge of organization, and one person in charge of propaganda in each committee.

4. All decisions must be adopted only after democratic discussion by the membership; but once a decision is reached, the minority must remain subservient to the majority and the lower echelons subservient to the higher echelons.

5. Members must observe discipline and maintain secrecy.

6. A Congress is to be held annually. When two or more local organizations express a lack of confidence in the CC, the CC shall convene an extraordinary Congress to discuss the issue.

These were the main points of the Constitution. Although the Congress, in discussing the relationship between the CCP and the Comintern, agreed that the CCP should be a branch of the Comintern, this was not written into the Constitution.

The discussion of these issues was most enthusiastic; and this fact revealed the seriousness of the delegates. Yet no personal grudges were held. While most delegates severely criticized the views of Li Han-chün, nobody labeled him a reformist or an opportunist. The Chinese Communists in those early days attached much importance to mutual friendship. They were not given to making wild charges against those who differed with them. And Li Han-chün, while persisting in his views, never quarreled with the others. When his views were rejected, he usually would declare that he intended to abide by the decision of the majority.

Nevertheless, these differences of opinion did cast some shadows over the Congress. I was a major speaker in criticizing Li Han-chün, as well as being the author of the proposals up for discussion. This caused some delegates to believe there was a feud between Li Han-chün and me. Moreover, most of them believed that Ch'en Tu-hsiu and Li Ta-chao would have supported my views, which were, in any case, held by a majority of Party members. Yet Li Han-chün also was an important Party founder, and very few people supported his views. To be sure, the Party was being brought into being smoothly, but the emergence of these differences nevertheless created a feeling that there was still something to be desired.

Neither Maring nor Nicolaevsky had attended any meetings of the Congress, although they were notified of its progress. They were very interested in the debates of the Congress, and expressed satisfaction that the majority view had won out. But Li Han-chün and Li Ta, who disliked Maring, did not want him to have much of a hand in the Congress, and even I, although I kept in touch with him, treated him strictly as an adviser. I did not go to him for instructions on anything. As a result, he felt rather neglected. When the Party Constitution came up for discussion, he asked rather impatiently to be allowed to attend a meeting of the Congress and to deliver a speech.

The Congress approved Maring's request. We decided to invite him to address us at the conclusion of the discussion on the Constitution. For the convenience of Maring and Nicolaevsky, the Congress decided to meet in the evening at the home of Li Han-chün. It was about the eighth of July, at about 7:00 P.M. When we were all seated around a large dining table in the first floor library of Li's home and the meeting was about to be called to order, a stranger suddenly pulled open the curtains at the door to the library and peeped in. "I've come to the wrong house," he said; and then he left hurriedly.

The intrusion of this stranger seemed so suspicious that we immediately alerted ourselves to the possibility that he might be a French Concession detective. I immediately told everyone to get his papers in order and to be ready to evacuate the place at once, and I explained the situation to Maring and Nicolaevsky. Exhibiting great presence of mind, Maring leaped from his seat, banged the table with his fist, and said, "I propose that the meeting adjourn immediately and that everyone leave by separate ways." Then he and Nicolaevsky departed in a hurry. Li Han-chün decided that as the occupant of the house he should stay, and Ch'en Kung-po decided to keep Li company. The rest of the delegates scattered; I was the last to leave.

As it turned out, ten minutes later a number of police detectives and other men led by a French police officer surrounded the Li home. They asked Li what sort of a meeting was being held, where the participants had gone, and who the two foreigners were. Li's perpetually calm exterior enabled him to cope with the situation successfully, although Ch'en Kung-po was rather frightened.[24] The police conducted an extensive search of the premises, but they could find nothing suspicious or incriminating, and so, disappointed, they left.

In those days we had not been very conscious about maintaining secrecy, and quite possibly the attention of the police had already been attracted to our meetings in the Po Wen Girls' School. Our move to the Li home apparently did not escape their notice, and they may have wanted to get all of us at one time. They seemed especially interested in the two foreigners.

Because of this police interference, Maring did not deliver his speech to the Congress after all. His hurried words in the Li home—"I propose that the meeting adjourn immediately and that everyone leave by separate ways"—were the only words he addressed to the First Congress of the CCP. He at no time suggested any concrete proposals for the agenda of the Congress, because, of course, his relationship with the delegates was not sufficiently friendly to allow him to do so. Nor did Maring comment on the fact that the Congress did not formally decide that the CCP would participate in the Comintern. The CCP did not formally resolve to participate in the Comintern and to become one of its branches until the Second Congress of the Party.

After this incident the Congress adjourned in order to escape police surveillance. It was to be resumed as soon as a suitable meeting place could be found and the delegates could be notified. It was not safe for me to contact Li Han-chün directly, since he was still under surveillance. Early the next morning, however, I visited Ch'en Kung-po in the Great Eastern Hotel and got from him an account of what had happened at Li's home. I told him that since the Po Wen Girls' School was very near the Li home, and since the police must be watching it, too, we would have to find a new place to meet. Then Li Ta and his wife arrived. Li was in charge of routine matters for the Congress, and his wife, Wang Hui-wu, a member of the SYC, was helping her husband in this work. Mrs. Li very enthusiastically suggested that if we could not find a suitable place in Shanghai, we could all meet in her home village. Her home, she told us, was on the shore of South Lake in Chiahsing, Che-kiang. It was only a little more than an hour by train from Shanghai. She talked of the scenic beauties of South Lake and said that she could hire a houseboat on which we could meet while enjoying the lovely scenery. And it would not matter even if our meeting should extend over several days. We agreed that it sounded perfectly safe, and so we accepted her proposal with thanks. She went off to get things ready, and I notified the delegates to take the train to Chiahsing the next morning.

On the morning of July 10 we boarded the morning train on the Shanghai-Hangchow Railway individually.[25] A little after nine o'clock that morning we arrived at South Lake in Chiahsing. The houseboat that Mrs. Li had hired was anchored by the shore. The only delegate who did not turn up was Ch'en Kung-po. He had frankly told Li Ta and me the previous day that he wanted to be excused from further meetings, because his wife was still suffering from the fear aroused by the incident in Li's home. None of the other delegates, including Li Han-chün, who was most seriously involved, had been greatly disturbed by the incident, however. We went ahead with our work in high spirits, deriding Ch'en Kung-po, whom we considered to be a weakling playboy from an aristocratic family.

We boarded the houseboat and looked about us at the scenic beauties of South Lake. There was an expanse of calm water, and, half-hidden among the reeds and tall grasses along the shore, stood a number of graceful buildings. Those of us who were seeing it for the first time decided that it was even more beautiful than West Lake at Hangchow. After the boat had made one circle around the lake, we let it drift, sometimes keeping it stationary and sometimes letting it glide slowly along.

Then we resumed the business that had not been finished in Shanghai. The agenda item before us was "Central Tasks and Work Policies."

All of us speeded up our discussions, so that few of them were long. We concentrated on the practical problems that had to be solved.

Originally there had been many things to take up under "Central Tasks and Work Policies." There were, for example, such things as a Party newspaper to carry on propaganda work, the Party's working relationship with the SYC, administration of the SYC, and the women's movement. We touched upon these things only in a general way and decided to hand them over to the projected CC for attention. The discussion of the workers' movement was more detailed, however; it involved chiefly the organization of trade unions and the admission of workers to the Party.

The Congress reached several decisions on the organization of trade unions. The first was a program for the workers' struggle. It included demands for an eight-hour day, increased wages, and the protection of working women and children. The Congress realized that conditions varied in different areas, but it felt that the masses of the workers must present collective demands for shorter working hours and higher pay, so as to attain gradually the goals of an eight-hour day and reasonable wage standards.

The second decision reached by the Congress dealt with the organization of trade unions. The Communists must not, the Congress pointed out, follow the methods of the old trade guilds and merely establish "pasteboard" unions. It was important to organize modern industrial unions. All of the workers in each industry—irrespective of their jobs or their places of birth—should be organized into a single trade union. Local trade unions of the same industry, furthermore, should be joined in a trade-union federation for that industry.

The third decision of the Congress concerned the creation of the general machinery for directing the labor movement. A centralized leadership for the labor movement would be furnished from its headquarters, which would be located near those of the CC and would have branches in all important regions. Comrades in all areas were to mingle with the lower social strata in factories and were to organize the masses of the workers in those factories into workers' clubs or trade unions.

In regard to the admission of workers into the Communist Party, the Congress pointed out that it was the task of Party organs to propagate Marxism among the masses of workers through such means as publication of popular reading material. The Congress decided, however, that membership standards would be lowered for workers who wished to join the Party. A worker who expressed a desire to join the Party would be admitted as long as he definitely wanted to participate in trade-union activities and to struggle for the workers' interests. He would not be questioned on his understanding of Marxist theory. The Congress placed the responsibility for the Marxist education of worker-members on the local Party organizations.

The sun was setting when we finished discussing this issue, and so we proceeded hastily to the fourth item on the agenda—elections. After some discussion we agreed unanimously that since the Party was so small, there was no need to organize the large CC that the Constitution called for. It was necessary to elect only three members to take charge of secretarial, organizational, and propaganda work. As a result of this decision, the Congress unanimously elected Ch'en Tu-hsiu, secretary; Li Ta, in charge of propaganda; and myself, in charge of organization. Chou Fo-hai was to act on behalf of Ch'en Tu-hsiu until Ch'en returned to Shanghai. The Congress decided that these three men would immediately assume their duties and function as the CC and that they should take the various resolutions of the Congress, put on the finishing editorial touches, and turn them into official Party documents. The CC also was empowered to deal with all matters on which no final decision had been reached by the Congress.

As everything on the agenda had now been discussed, the Congress was declared closed. We held a simple closing ceremony, and I delivered a closing address. I was in high spirits. I congratulated the Congress on its success and appealed to the delegates to return to their posts and to develop our programs and organizations on the basis of the decisions of the Congress. And so, the CCP was officially born.

Darkness had begun to settle over the lake when we left the houseboat. Lights from the fishing boats came on. We took the night train and arrived at Shanghai at midnight.

From the historical standpoint, the formation of the CCP developed more smoothly and more rapidly than any previous Chinese political organization. From the start it hoisted a banner that was clearly defined; it stipulated the direction in which it intended to exert its efforts; and it demonstrated itself to be a body that was truly outstanding. In the field of international relations, it became, after the Second Congress of the Comintern, an important Asian Communist Party organization. For it provided a testing ground for Comintern policies toward colonial areas.

A specter of communism began to haunt China—to paraphrase the first sentence of the Marx-Engels *Communist Manifesto*—and the people who produced that specter brimmed with the courage to march forward and with a spirit of determination. Their accomplishments, even when viewed by the present generation, seem somewhat mysterious.

When he was discussing the organization of the Party with me in August of 1920, Ch'en Tu-hsiu said: "The militarists and politicians of Japan are unbearably arrogant. They look down on China, with her history of five thousand years and her four hundred million descendants of Huang Ti. They think only of scheming with her old warlords, her corrupt bureaucrats, her smugglers, her drug peddlers, her gangsters, and the scum of China. They see only the queues and the bound feet of people in China, and everything that is corrupt. Consciously or unconsciously, they belittle the new thoughts and the new influences that are rising in China. But there will come a day when they will crush their own heads against the wall of their misconceptions."

Ch'en, of course, was not referring to Japan alone. He merely singled Japan out as an example. But his words prophesied the formation and development of the CCP and the influence it later wielded. The spirit that his words embodied was shared by the group of Communists who met at this time.

THE CENTRAL COMMITTEE OF THE CHINESE COMMUNIST PARTY FIRST SHOWS ITS METTLE

CHAPTER

Making a Start Is the Most Difficult Part

Although the First Congress of the CCP determined the direction of Party development, many practical problems were left to the newly elected CC. And because it was not easy to solve these problems, complicated and serious controversies arose within the CC and between the CC and Maring. Not until Ch'en Tu-hsiu and six others were arrested and subsequently released did we feel the compelling need to close ranks for a struggle, and then the disputes within the CC subsided.

As soon as the Congress ended, Chou Fo-hai, acting as secretary for Ch'en Tu-hsiu, Li Ta, in charge of propaganda, and myself, in charge of organization, held the first meeting of the CC of the CCP. The first difficulty confronting us was a lack of funds. Ch'en Tu-hsiu had heretofore raised most of the money. But very little of that was left because of the expenses of the Congress. Furthermore, as most delegates to the Congress had mentioned their own fund-raising problems, the CC could not very well ask the branches to contribute to its expenses. The CC could not afford a staff. There were only the three of us; and apart from the rented rooms in which each of us lived, there was no place where we

153

could gather to attend to official work. Moreover there were no established precedents for us to follow, and in all our work we seemed to be groping in the dark and experimenting.

At our meetings the three of us discussed ways of implementing the decisions of the Congress and of launching the work of the CC. We also wrote letters to Ch'en Tu-hsiu in which we reported the proceedings of the Congress and the problems that the CC now faced, and we urged him to come at once to Shanghai to assume his post. We thought that the work of the CC should not be held up by Ch'en's absence. Chou Fo-hai was able to devote his time to CC activities for a while, but he had to leave Shanghai to resume his studies in Japan at the end of summer vacation; and writing kept Li Ta busy. During this period, as a result, the work of the CC centered around me.

Maring was very satisfied with the achievements of the Congress. After hastily separating at Li Han-chün's home, we did not meet again until several days after the Congress ended. Then I officially informed him of the proceedings of the Congress, all of which he took down, probably for an official report to the Comintern. The ability of this newly formed CCP to shake off police surveillance and swiftly transact the business of the Congress pleased him most. It had demonstrated a zest for braving danger. It was his opinion, moreover, that the Party platform and conclusions on the Constitution generally showed a firm Communist stand and that the decisions on the labor movement were practical. He regarded these things as the most important accomplishments of the Congress.

When we discussed how the CC should carry out the decisions of the Congress, he urged that a central machinery for the labor movement be established and asked what we proposed to name it. The name was still under consideration, I told him. We could not call it the Federation of Trade Unions, since it would not be an organization of assorted trade unions in different areas. I countered by asking what name was best in the experience of labor movements in other countries. He suggested calling it the Secretariat of Trade Unions in China, which, he explained, suited Communist trade-union organization work. I agreed to it in principle, but decided to call it in Chinese Chung-kuo Lao-tung Tsu-ho Shu-chi-pu, which means the Secretariat of Labor Organizations in China, deliberately avoiding the use of the word *Kung-hui* (trade unions). The suggestion of that name apparently was the first concrete contribution that Maring made to the CCP.

Having agreed upon the name, we talked of the problem of funds. I told him that we had written Ch'en Tu-hsiu asking him to raise money for the CC. The branches could generally take care of their own financial needs. He pointed out, however, that as our work developed, more and more money would be needed. How would we carry on then? Thus, he brought up the question that had antagonized Li Han-chün. He explained to me that from the standpoint of internationalism, the Comintern was obliged to assist the various national Communist parties, and the CCP ought to freely accept such help. When I expressed agreement with this for the first time, he went on to stress the importance of drawing up work plans and budgets. He asked me to call a CC meeting to discuss these matters. I reported my talks with Maring to the CC and offered an explanation of Comintern assistance in support of his stand.

After hearing my report, Li Ta remained dissatisfied with the cunning, unruly Maring. He was of the opinion that Maring's request for work plans and budgets should receive fuller consideration and that, in fact, it would be best to postpone any decision on the matter until Ch'en Tu-hsiu arrived. Chou Fo-hai, however, supported my views. In order to speed up our work, he said, we should not postpone the decision, but should accept Comintern leadership in keeping with the wishes of the Congress; and in that case, to provide Maring with work plans and budgets would be in order. Li Ta did not press his point further. It was decided at the meeting that I should draft a work plan and budget for the Secretariat of Labor Organizations in China that would be discussed and finalized at the following meeting. Copies would then go to Maring, and we would seek his approval of them.

I finished the draft a few days later. It provided that a headquarters located at Shanghai would provide guidance to the labor movement throughout the country and give directions to the labor movement in the Shanghai area and would publish an organ entitled *Lao-tung Chou-kan* (Labor Weekly). There were to be Secretariat branches at Peking, Wuhan, Canton, and Changsha, each of which was to put out a workers' publication of its own. As many CCP and SYC members as possible were to take part in the labor movement. It was estimated that about thirty people, working full time in the movement, would need from twenty to thirty-five dollars a month each as a subsistence allowance. The entire cost, including publication expenditures, would be a little more than one thousand dollars a month.

At the CC meeting that discussed the plan, Li Ta raised fresh doubts. Paying some workers a monthly salary, he said, would create in them a mercenary's mentality. Yet the discussion ended with the decision that the plan be adopted and that work should start at once. Even so, the meeting adopted it only on a trial basis, putting off the final decision until Ch'en Tu-hsiu returned to Shanghai. We decided to submit a copy of the draft plan to Maring.

In discussing it with Maring, I mentioned the decisions of our meeting. I pointed out that the Secretariat's name had been ratified, that certain minor issues remained unsettled, and that we were waiting for Ch'en Tu-hsiu to return so that we might take up the matter together. As to funds for the program, I said that the Comintern could grant any subsidy it wished and that we would raise money to cover the deficit ourselves. Maring had probably misunderstood what Li Han-chün had said about the Comintern giving money to the CCP to employ as it wished. Apparently he had expected us to ask for a very large sum, for when he saw the small amount listed and the very frugal way it was to be used, he could not help laughing. He told me to go ahead with the plan; that the Comintern would finance the whole project. What funds we raised ourselves could be put to other uses.

The three CC members then met with Maring to talk about our work as a whole. At this meeting Maring asked Li Ta what his propaganda plans were and how he intended to carry out the decision of the Congress to publish a Party organ. Stubbornly, Li Ta replied, "There are no plans. Let's wait until Mr. Ch'en Tu-hsiu returns." Maring's face registered immediate displeasure. He could do nothing but drop the subject and turn to other matters, however. The dark cloud which hovered between the CC and Maring had not yet dissipated.

One morning late in July, Liu Jen-ching, who had not yet gone back to Peking, brought a stranger to my room. He introduced him as Chief Secretary Yang of the Shanghai General Chamber of Commerce. Abruptly interrupting Liu, Mr. Yang announced, "I want to sue Chou Fo-hai. He has committed a serious crime—seducing an innocent girl." Pointing to a copy of the *Shanghai Shih-shih Hsin-pao* (Shanghai Eastern Times), which he had with him, he said to me, "Please read this story."

I read it. The story said that a young man from Hunan Province, who claimed to be the most progressive disciple of socialism in China, was having a love affair with the daughter of a prominent figure in Shanghai commercial circles who happened to be from the same province. The young man already had a wife in his home village and was said to be a father. But it looked as though this progressive young man were going to be a bridegroom again, it said.

Yang waited until I had finished reading the story and then told me that at first he had not believed that it concerned him. But when he looked into it, it turned out to be the true love story of Chou Fo-hai and his own daughter, Yang Shu-hui. He felt that his honor had suffered and that he must sue Chou Fo-hai.

Liu Jen-ching, who shared a room with Chou Fo-hai, took this opportunity to explain matters. "Mr. Yang came to our place early this morning," he said "Chou Fo-hai was out. Mr. Yang told me about the case, and I've brought him here to see what you think."

I could see how furious Yang was, and I tried to calm him. If Chou Fo-hai were really married, I said, and had hidden the fact while carrying on a love affair with another girl, then that, of course, was not right. But, I added, there were many young men these days with old-fashioned wives at home, whose marriages were arranged by their parents. Even though they loathed their wives, the old moral code enslaved them and they could not get a divorce. So, many of them sought love away from home and perhaps even married again. It was difficult for the parents involved in such cases to deal with them fairly. I suggested that it might be best to call the couple together to discuss the matter frankly and that legal action was not necessary. "Very well," Yang declared. "I'll get Yang Shu-hui, Chou Fo-hai, and a few friends and relatives together for lunch at my home. You, Mr. Chang, and Mr. Liu must come along, too."

Yang seemed as angry as ever at lunch, but Mrs. Yang did not seem to agree with her husband. Perhaps she sympathized with her daughter's position. Under these circumstances, the guests found it difficult to say much of anything, while Chou Fo-hai and Miss Yang kept their heads bowed and remained absolutely silent. Finally, Mrs. Yang could bear the situation no longer. "Don't be angry any more," she said to her husband. "Let me speak to my daughter privately."

She took her daughter into another room, and after a while she came out and asked Chou Fo-hai to join them. Presently all three came out together. "I love Chou Fo-hai," Yang Shu-hui bluntly said to her father and the rest of us there. "He has a wife. I know it. But I have not told my parents. He loves me very much, and he is taking steps to get a divorce. We shall be married." She asked her parents' pardon.

When we heard this from Miss Yang, all of us guests agreed that since that was the way things were, the matter could easily be settled within the family. Our presence was unnecessary.

The case of Chou Fo-hai is only one of many examples of the marital problems young men and women had in those days. But it was quite a blow to Chou Fo-hai, the acting secretary of the CCP. Most of his comrades believed that it was most undesirable, both from his own standpoint and from that of the Party, for a person in his weighty position to be involved in such a love affair. Miss Yang seemed very much the pampered daughter of a rich man's family and did not seem to fit into a Socialist youth's way of life. So far as the Party was concerned, we generally agreed that a union of that kind would affect not only Chou Fo-hai's way of living, but his way of thinking as well. His friends outside the Party used the incident as material for idle gossip. All of this rather embarrassed Chou.

Under these circumstances Chou Fo-hai drew closer and closer to the rich merchant's daughter and her family. His way of life began to change. Eager to leave for Japan with Yang Shu-hui and busy with wedding preparations, he was no longer active in Party affairs. Although he attended the several CC meetings that followed, I saw no more of his bubbling energy and heard no more of his enthusiastic talk. He seemed to feel that other comrades and I had taken too stern an attitude toward his love affair.

Later he became a changed man altogether. He went from losing enthusiasm for the CCP to leaving it, and he finally ended up, during the War of Resistance against Japan, as a most senior member of the Wang Ching-wei regime at Nanking. His love affair seemed a small matter at the time, but in retrospect it may have been a turning point in his life.

Toward the middle of August of that year Ch'en Tu-hsiu resigned as chairman of the Education Committee at Canton and returned to Shanghai to assume the post of secretary of the CC. His arrival was enormously stimulating. When he first saw me, he expressed profound satisfaction with the accomplishments of the Congress. He was prepared to take up the duties of secretary at once, he said, and to work energetically at them. Yet when I saw him the very next day, his attitude had grown very much cooler. He now found it necessary to spend some time attending to private affairs, he declared. He was not yet ready to hold a CC meeting, nor did he wish to meet Maring.

It was the influence of Li Ta and Chou Fo-hai that made Ch'en Tu-hsiu hesitant and uncertain. Li Ta must have spoken to him about Maring's work style. Perhaps Li also mentioned the dissatisfaction that he felt with my conciliatory approach to Maring. These things deeply distressed Ch'en. Furthermore, Chou Fo-hai, who had originally supported me, changed his stand, apparently because I was critical of his love affair. Whatever his reason, he did not give me the support I needed when he talked to Ch'en.

And there were other factors that may have contributed to Ch'en's change of attitude. About ten days before Ch'en returned, Li Han-chün left Shanghai to teach at Wuhan. He felt that the CC had neglected him after the Congress, and he was very unhappy. Li Ta, however, had expected him to remain in Shanghai to undertake certain editorial duties; and when he decided to leave, we asked him to wait at least until Ch'en Tu-hsiu arrived so that we all might meet together. He rejected our proposal and departed without notifying us. This incident gave rise to speculation among the comrades. Because he had had differences with Ch'en in the past, some believed that he purposely advanced his departure date. Some thought that he left in anger because I had criticized him during the Congress and had not consulted him about anything after the Congress. Li Ta, who had himself been a critic of Li Han-chün's views, felt that I had been rather tactless in dealing with Li Han-chün. These things may have caused Ch'en to feel that I was inept at uniting the comrades, with the result that many problems had cropped up in a very short time.

An incident that brought about a more important controversy was Chang T'ai-lei's departure for Japan on Maring's orders without CC approval. Apparently Moscow had for some time considered convening a congress of Far Eastern revolutionary groups, which was eventually called the Congress of Toilers of the Far East.[1] In August, 1921, when the American government issued formal invitations to the relevant powers to attend the Washington Conference, Maring received an emergency directive from Moscow about convening a rival conference.[2] He busied himself recruiting representatives to it from the various Far Eastern countries. That was why he had promptly sent Chang T'ai-lei to Japan. Chang was supposed to muster support for the conference from the Japanese Socialists and get them to elect delegates to it. Following Maring's order to maintain secrecy, Chang T'ai-lei decided to go without obtaining official approval from the CC. He asked the acting secretary, Chou Fo-hai, to give him a letter of introduction to some comrades in Japan. Chou complied with this request. He and Li Ta together signed a letter of introduction to Shih Ts'un-t'ung, a Party member studying in Tokyo; and Chang T'ai-lei went to Japan with it.

Maring's behavior in this matter thoroughly enraged Ch'en Tu-hsiu. Maring had truly exceeded his authority, Ch'en told me. Chang T'ai-lei was a CCP member; and although he was assigned to Maring as interpreter, he was responsible directly to the CC of the CCP. Yet, without bothering to get CC approval, Maring had arbitrarily sent Chang T'ai-lei off on a mission. Furthermore, this was an important conference, and the Comintern, Ch'en said, had not consulted with us before calling it. All of this, Ch'en declared, amounted to belittling the CCP; therefore he absolutely refused to meet Maring, and he intended to demand that the Comintern recall him as its representative.

Then I reminded Ch'en Tu-hsiu that Maring had officially informed me that the Comintern was convening a Congress of Oppressed Peoples of the Far East (Yuan-tung Pei-ya-po Min-tzu Ta-hui) to rival the Washington Conference. (The name was later changed to Congress of the Toilers of the Far East.) It was scheduled to open at Irkutsk on November 11, 1921, one day before the Washington Conference opened. Invitations were being extended to revolutionary organizations throughout the Far East in the names of prominent Comintern figures such as Sen Katayama, the Japanese Socialist. In China the CC of the CCP had been asked to help by secretly relaying this invitation to other Chinese revolutionary groups, while Maring, in the name of the Comintern itself, formally invited the KMT to send representatives. I also reminded Ch'en that we had expressed support for the Congress and had agreed to send a representative; but I added that Maring had never spoken to me about Chang T'ai-lei's trip to Japan. I suggested that Ch'en thoroughly investigate the situation before finally deciding on our stand with regard to it.

I immediately questioned Maring about the Chang T'ai-lei issue. As Maring saw it, it was of vital importance that somebody be sent to establish contacts in Japan. Since the CC had endorsed the proposed Congress, he felt that it should provide practical support for it. His failure to obtain approval from the CC for sending Chang T'ai-lei to Japan was merely a question of formality. He felt that he had acted correctly, considering the need for secrecy and promptness. His reply did not mollify

Ch'en, however. Ch'en regarded it as clear proof that the CC of the CCP was being disparaged. So the relationship between the CC and Maring fell to another low ebb.

Time after time Ch'en refused Maring's requests that they meet. He began planning an independent work program without consulting Maring, and he kept berating the fact that Chang T'ai-lei had taken orders directly from Maring. Yet he did not call a CC meeting at which we could thrash things out in detail. He indicated, instead, that after a period of preparation, we could carefully consider the situation at a meeting. Faced with the extreme positions both parties had taken, I thought it best to say nothing more, and I contented myself with working in the labor movement. This state of affairs dragged on for more than two weeks.

Toward the end of August, Chang T'ai-lei returned from Japan. He saw me first. He came in shouting, "What strange things! What strange things! Li Ta and Chou Fo-hai gave me a letter of introduction to Shih Ts'un-t'ung in Tokyo, but they secretly wrote another letter telling him to ignore me."

If Shih, who was a stranger to Chang, had really refused to help him, Chang believed that he would have failed in his mission to Tokyo and that he might well have been in personal danger. Fortunately, he told me, after listening to a detailed explanation of Chang's mission, Shih Ts'un-t'ung showed him the letter Li and Chou had mailed directly and took him to call on Yamakawa Hitoshi and Sakai Toshihiko, leading Japanese Socialists. To them he delivered the clandestine Comintern letters inviting them to send representatives to the Congress, and they agreed to do so. His mission was accomplished.

I listened to his account with mounting annoyance. "What is all this nonsense?" I blurted out, when he had finished. "I know nothing about this. You wait here for a while, please. I must take the matter up with Li and Chou."

I started out to find Li Ta and Chou Fo-hai, and eventually found both of them at Ch'en Tu-hsiu's home. I very angrily asked, "Why did you write Shih Ts'un-t'ung to ignore Chang T'ai-lei? Do you realize the possible consequences of your action?"

Ch'en Tu-hsiu interrupted to say, "I asked them to write the letter. What do you want to do about it?"

"If it was your idea," I said bluntly, "that makes it even worse." I said that just because Maring and Chang T'ai-lei had been wrong in acting arbitrarily, there was no reason for us to jeopardize Chang's safety in Tokyo. How could we explain ourselves if because of our interference no Japanese delegates attended the projected Congress of the Toilers of the Far East? What would we say if Chang T'ai-lei, without Shih to help him, aroused the suspicion of the Japanese police and the secret were exposed?

"You are even more wrong," Ch'en retorted gruffly. "Why did you submit to Maring the work plan and budget of the Secretariat of Labor Organizations in China and provide for paying a salary to people working under the plan? That amounts to a revolution of mercenaries. Everything concerning the Chinese revolution must be our own responsibility. Every member of the Party must serve the Party without compensation. We must insist upon this stand."

"I see that while you do not support anarchism, you are not free from the influence of anarchism," I said with a cold smile.

Ch'en grew more irate. "How do I come under the influence of anarchism?" he demanded.

In reply, I launched into a lengthy discourse. Our views were not free from contradictions, I said. We supported the Comintern and were prepared to accept its help, but we would not submit our work plans to it. We acknowledged the Comintern representative as our adviser, yet we did not want him to guide us in any way or to give us any concrete assistance. We ourselves had no money. We could raise some today, to be sure, but what of tomorrow? As our work expanded, our need for money would increase; and without the necessary funds, all planning would be nothing but empty talk. The minimum subsistence needs of Party workers would have to be met if they were to work wholeheartedly, free from anxiety about a livelihood. How could a Party member develop into a mercenary by merely drawing a very small sum of money from the Party to cover his subsistence needs?

The three of them grew silent and thoughtful when they heard this. I had been responsible for a number of things since the Congress, I continued, and at times I had acted hastily, without considering all factors. But after thinking it over carefully, I had decided that I had not dealt unjustly with Li Han-chün. And even though I differed with Li Ta and Chou Fo-hai at times, I did so in the best interests of our common cause; for without bringing in personal feelings, we discussed things from the standpoint of the issues involved. Although, being a proud person myself, I resented Maring's arrogant attitude, nevertheless

I accepted the fact that he was a veteran Communist and that he could be of help to our cause. If we did not exaggerate the problem of his personality, I believed we could work with him. I said that I could see no good reason for notifying the Comintern that he was unfit for the job of representative.

The issues I raised had all along been buried in all of our hearts, but never aired. Ch'en seemed somewhat impressed by my frank statements. "Well," he said to me, vaguely, "it looks as though I shall have to think things over more carefully."

I, too, put these problems aside for the moment, indicating that they could be raised later. But Chang T'ai-lei was still waiting at my place, I said, and he would soon go to see Maring. How were we going to explain things to Chang?

At this point Ch'en turned to ask Li and Chou, "Well, just what was it you said in your letter to Shih Ts'un-t'ung?" Finding it an awkward question to answer, the two of them tried to laugh it off and stood up to get ready to leave. "Let me tell T'ai-lei to make sure not to mention the letter to Maring under any circumstances," I was compelled to say, "and it would be best if Mr. Ch'en asked T'ai-lei over for a talk." The three of them agreed to my suggestion.

This was the first important argument within our CC, and comrades in Shanghai learned about it and grew worried. Chang T'ai-lei, knowing only that we had argued, failed to understand that it actually contributed to a greater harmony in our views. He obeyed my injunction to say nothing about the letter to Maring. Yet in his talk with Maring he may have mentioned the fact that I had argued with the other responsible members of the CC, for the next day Maring asked me what the argument was about. I could not very well deny that it had occurred, but I said nothing definite in reply, which made him rather impatient.

Then, deadly serious, he proceeded to lecture me. He reminded me that comrade Ch'en Tu-hsiu, who had been back for more than two weeks, refused to see him. Furthermore, Ch'en's views did not even sound like those of a Communist. How was it possible, then, for him to shoulder the secretary's responsibilities? Why didn't I abandon him and take over the leadership myself? He pointed out that I had received considerable support at the Congress, and it was I who started the labor movement; therefore the perquisites of leadership were mine. In the past, Lenin himself had turned against his teacher Plekhanov, etc.

These words of his rather alarmed me; at the same time I laughed at him. I said that he had greatly magnified a slight matter because of his ignorance of Chinese behavior and of the close relationship between Ch'en and me. "This is utterly preposterous," I declared forthrightly. I told Maring that Ch'en was a man of remarkable ability and the only possible leader of the Chinese Communist movement. We might have differences at times, but we would reach an understanding immediately afterwards. I said that I also thought Ch'en would meet him very soon and cooperate smoothly with him. I insisted that Maring never raise such ideas again, for should other comrades learn of them, there would be endless complications. Maring merely shrugged his shoulders and said, "Well, let's wait and see."

After dinner two days later, on a rather warm evening, I put on a suit of Chinese clothes and, looking very like a shop assistant, strolled to Ch'en's home. Normally I used the back door, going straight in without bothering to announce my arrival. When I knocked at the back door this evening, however, a husky stranger opened it and demanded to know whom I wanted to see. I immediately realized that something was wrong. "I want to see Mrs. Ch'en," I said, staying outside.

"What do you want to see her for?"

"I've come to collect some tailoring charges," I said.

He scrutinized me and then asked, "Why can't you speak Shanghai dialect?"

"My shop is at such-and-such," I replied, using a tailoring shop I knew about. "Such-and-such is its name. The proprietor is so-and-so. He is a Hunanese, and I also am a Hunanese. I haven't mastered Shanghai dialect yet."

The man accepted the story that I was a tailor, said that Mrs. Ch'en was out, and closed the door. As I walked out of the lane I was convinced that something very bad had happened. After satisfying myself that no detectives were following me, I notified several comrades to keep away from the Ch'en home for the time being. The French Concession police, I learned upon investigation, had arrested Mr. and Mrs. Ch'en along with several visitors in their home about six o'clock that evening.

All of them—Mr. and Mrs. Ch'en, Li Ta, Chou Fo-hai, Pao Hui-seng, and two others—were released from the French police station the next morning. Many of his friends promptly called on Ch'en; I was among them. When most of the guests had left and only a few comrades remained, Ch'en told us, "Fortunately, they didn't find any important documents. We would have been in serious trouble if they had. We must not feel discouraged. We must go ahead all the more resolutely. We must, however, pay greater attention to maintaining secrecy. They are forcing us up Liang Mountain [the lair of the robbers in *All Men Are Brothers*], and we have no choice but to play it that way."

Chou Fo-hai, he said, was about to return to Japan, and he—Ch'en—would officially assume the secretary's duties and call a formal meeting of the CC to discuss a number of things. In the midst of this heartening conversation, Chang T'ai-lei arrived. He gave Ch'en solicitous regards from Maring and said that Maring would have come in person had he not feared that this might be unwise. "I shall arrange for us to meet in a day or so," Ch'en replied in a very friendly tone. Thus the mishap seemed to wipe out all the arguments and controversies of the past.

Pao Hui-seng asked me to leave the Ch'en home with him. Growing very excited as we walked along side by side, he said, "Mr. Ch'en is truly great. You don't yet know the details of last night." His enthusiasm mounted uncontrollably. "From the spirit Mr. Ch'en and the others revealed in that prison cell, we can expect an unlimited future for our Party. There was no misunderstanding among the comrades—only zeal." He advised me against making further reference to past disagreements. I could feel reassured and throw myself into my work, he said.

We walked to my place, where we had lunch, continuing the animated conversation the whole time. As Pao Hui-seng told me about them, the events of the previous evening were something like this: A group of policemen appeared at the Ch'en home about four o'clock in the afternoon. They charged in boisterously, posted guards at both front and back doors, and herded everyone in the house into a small room where they were closely watched. Conversation was prohibited. Meanwhile, the police searched every part of the house and carried away a large bundle of books and letters. Visitors to the house were arrested one after the other as they arrived, until a total of seven people were held inside. Fiercely Ch'en protested, "You came here to seize me. Why do you also arrest my guests?" But the police paid no attention, and at about six o'clock took them all to the police station. Mrs. Ch'en was sent to the women's detention house, while the six men were imprisoned together in one cell.

It looked bad, Ch'en told them in the cell. The police could at least prove from his letters that he was organizing a Communist movement, and as a result he expected to be imprisoned for some time. He instructed them not to tell the truth to the police. They were to focus all blame on him alone. That way, they would be freed and would be able to carry on the work, even though he had to remain in prison. Ch'en absolutely insisted upon having his way in this, and so they fell to talking about how they would handle themselves when the police questioned them. They got no sleep at all that night.

There in the cell they also worried about the chance that other comrades would be arrested. Ch'en was especially concerned. Each time a new prisoner arrived, he got up and strained to see whether or not the newcomer was a comrade. He knew that I planned to visit his home that evening, and this particularly disturbed him. More than once he said, "Kuo-t'ao often carries some documents with him, and he is hotheaded. It would be so easy for him to get into a fight with the police. His arrest would make the situation more grave."

He fretted in this way deep into the night. When no more comrades were brought in, however, he semed to feel somewhat relieved. He told the others, as though making a will, "Apparently Kuo-t'ao has not been arrested. He may not be infallible, but he is very loyal and straightforward and unselfish. He has ideas, he knows how to carry them out, and he always does what he says he will do. These are not trifling accomplishments. In our recent argument his opinions were generally sound. There is no resentment at all between the two of us. He was outspoken simply because we are close to one another. With the authorities so relentlessly harassing us, we have no choice but to establish closer relations with the Comintern. About that there should no longer be room for doubt."

He admonished them to work harmoniously with me when they were released, to combine efforts in a common cause. He suggested that I act as secretary, if no one had any objection, for then it would be easier for him to face even a year or two in prison. Ch'en's words profoundly moved them. I had always had their respect, they said. They would make me assume the leadership. Urging Ch'en to stop worrying, they assured him that they would attack their work with greater vigor than ever before.

Fortunately the police had conducted a haphazard search. They had not found such things as lists of names or copies of the Party Constitution. The letters they had seized were not regarded as incriminating, nor did they bear directly on the French Concession; so the police dropped the case for lack of evidence. After a perfunctory examination all of the comrades were released. This was the second time the French Concession police had hounded us—the first time being their search of Li Han-chün's home.

Pao Hui-seng's account intensely moved and stimulated me. A delegate from Hupeh, Pao had lingered in Shanghai after the Congress, whereas Tung Pi-wu and Ch'en T'an-ch'iu had gone back as soon as it had ended. Now, he told me, he would return at once to join in the work, and he would tell the comrades in Hupeh the good news.

It was about the second day after his release that Ch'en, for the first time as secretary, called a CC meeting. At this meeting, Chou Fo-hai seemed to be feeling the effects of his arrest and perhaps the influence of Miss Yang, too. For he did nothing more noteworthy than to formally hand over his duties. He left for Japan soon afterward and never again took part in the work of the CC of the CCP. Ch'en, on the other hand, brimmed with energy at the meeting. He suggested ways of dividing up CC work among ourselves and a schedule for our meetings. He proposed that leadership machinery for the labor movement should be discussed on the basis of my draft plan and that a decision should be reached quickly. Regarding propaganda plans, he suggested that we continue publishing *Communist Monthly* and that publication of *New Youth* be resumed. But he wanted to raise other matters, such as the SYC, at later meetings, after he had had a chance to discuss them with the people responsible for them.

A specific issue discussed at the meeting was the draft plan for the Secretariat of Labor Organizations in China. Official adoption of the plan resolved the controversies that it had produced. On the whole, my original proposals were accepted. They were merely revised to state that payments to labor-movement cadres would be called "living allowances" rather than "salaries" or "wages"; and the payment scale was reduced from the original twenty-to-thirty-five dollars a month to a maximum of twenty-five dollars.

The question of a living allowance for Party members caused this meeting to draw up a lengthy document. Communist Party members should work for the Party without compensation as a matter of principle, we believed. So a living allowance was to go only to those comrades that could not survive without it. Since the thirty-five-dollar maximum fixed in my original plan was sufficient only to maintain a rather low standard of living at that time, we decided to reduce it further to twenty-five dollars or less, so that it would equal a poor worker's income. For we considered it vital to cultivate to the fullest a working spirit that expected no financial reward. And to accomplish this, in our living allowance we set a payment scale lower than any other in the international Communist movement since the Paris Commune. It was, of course, very much less than a Party member could make in a regular job then—about fifteen per cent of what he could normally expect to earn. Party members, we contended, should live close to the toiling masses, and with less money spent on living expenses, more money would be available for the work of the Party. Allowances were not fixed according to rank, but according to the individual's actual needs. We wanted comrades receiving the smallest allowances to feel proud of the fact and to be able in this way to demonstrate the spirit of a worthy Communist. But the Party would take care of the emergency needs of all comrades, whether they drew an allowance or not. They would receive active help in cases of sickness, injury, or arrest.

This ponderous document is apparently a rare example of its kind in the history of the international Communist movement. Certainly there was no precedent for it in the history of Chinese political parties. Springing as an extraordinary achievement from our arguments, it was an important contribution made by Ch'en Tu-hsiu with the help of both Li Ta and myself. The CC disseminated the decision along with an explanatory note, both in writing and verbally, to the entire body of comrades, and it received their unanimous endorsement. After that, there were no more such questions as "Why should there be a living allowance?" and "Why should some receive an allowance and others not receive one?" No longer did comrades mention the charge of a "revolution by mercenaries." Although later we were often sarcastically called the "Ruble Party," the truth of the matter was as I have presented it, and comrades simply laughed at the accusation. From then on, moreover, a fixed, unshakable principle governed the CC's disposition of funds. It was that the funds were used where they were most needed to advance projects and that a considerable sum was held in reserve for unexpected activities and emergency situations. This differed from the traditional way of doing things that was used by other Chinese parties and government organs, which dissipated most of their money on administrative expenses. This principle explains why the CCP never afterward had any serious arguments about the use of funds. It also was one reason for the CCP being able to progress and expand so rapidly.

Ch'en Tu-hsiu and Maring met for the first time within two days after Ch'en's formal CC meeting. The tribulations they both had faced recently seemed to have made them wiser men. Like the "good fellows of Liang Mountain," who would not cultivate one another without first fighting one another, they began a very cordial exchange of views. Maring indicated that he understood that the CC would conduct all operations, while he, as the Comintern representative, would do nothing but maintain regular contact with the highest responsible CCP members in order to discuss general policy. Ch'en indicated that the CCP supported the Comintern and would, naturally, respect the policy recommendations of its representative. The understanding they achieved obliterated all traces of past disagreements. I was present and found the meeting very gratifying.

After that, Ch'en and Maring met regularly and discussed all sorts of problems harmoniously. Copies of the work plans of the CC of the CCP were thereafter sent to Maring, and Maring never disagreed with them. So far as policy was concerned, Ch'en regularly reported Maring's views to the CC meetings. The two of them also arranged for a Comintern subsidy, and it was only then that the CCP began to receive regular financial support from the Comintern.[3]

Maring and I still saw each other often, although I had been relieved of the duty of maintaining liaison with him. Only at meetings called by Ch'en did we discuss policy. At other times we usually talked about specific problems connected with the labor movement. By then the organizational structure of the CC was established, with Ch'en in charge of administrative affairs, so I no longer concerned myself with them.

So it was that in two months all of the difficulties that the CCP encountered in establishing its CC were overcome one after the other. The CC now took to the road of normal work.

The Secretariat of Labor Organizations in China

Early in September, 1921, its work plan having been ratified, the Secretariat of Labor Organizations in China was formally inaugurated. I was elected director, and Li Ch'i-han secretary, of its general headquarters at Shanghai; and Tung Ch'u-p'ing was elected editor of *Labor Weekly*. In charge of the North China branch were Teng Chung-hsia and Lo Chang-lung; of the Wuhan branch, Lin Yü-nan and Hsiang Ying;

of the Hunan branch, Mao Tse-tung; and of the Canton branch, T'an P'ing-shan. This organization was the most active project of the CC. Most Communist Party and SYC members took part in its actual work. It may be regarded as the forerunner of the All-China Federation of Labor Unions (Chung-hua Ch'uan-kuo Tsung Kung-hui), and it strongly influenced the labor movement in China.

Actual work began, however, before the Secretariat was formally inaugurated. The Chinese Communist nuclei established in 1920 had promptly grown active among the working masses, as I have mentioned. Li Ch'i-han had looked after the labor movement in Shanghai right along.

In the Putung section of Shanghai in August, 1921, workers of the British-American Tobacco Company went out on strike, demanding better treatment. We decided to try our hand in the affair as soon as we read about it in the newspapers. Work plans of the Secretariat were still under debate then, and no decision had yet been reached. Nevertheless we wanted to support the strike, and so we quickly set up temporary Secretariat headquarters in an office used by Li Ch'i-han and made preparations to get the reins of the strike into our own hands.

Utilizing his connections as a member of the upper stratum of the Ch'ing Pang,[4] Li Ch'i-han—a young man in his twenties—went to Putung to find the strike leaders. He had infiltrated this secret society because of its stranglehold on Shanghai workers. So artful and energetic was he that within a matter of hours he brought more than ten leading figures of the strike into our temporary office. We had nothing then, not even a signboard or regulations, and Li Ch'i-han had no choice but to be vague in introducing me to them. "This is Mr. Chang," he said, "an important labor-movement leader who has just arrived from Peking. Feel free to discuss whatever you like with him."

"Why did you go on strike?" I asked them. "Are you organized? What are your demands?"

They told me that they wanted a raise in wages. They had no definite demands in mind, however, nor were they organized. So I questioned them about the hopes of workers throughout the factory, and then I wrote down a set of demands that embodied those hopes. I also worked out with them a few brief instructions for organizing a trade union in the factory. Essentially they provided for a union to be formed by delegates elected from the various factory sections. The delegates were to proffer our demands as a basis for negotiating with the management. Should the management harm the delegates, it was vital that the entire body of workers back them up. All of this seemed satisfactory to the leading strikers, who departed after announcing that they would put our discussion into action.

The next day, two of them returned to our office. "You are very eager to help the workers, Mr. Chang," one of them said suspiciously. "What is your motive?" I countered by asking what they thought it was. "We've decided that Dr. Sun Yat-sen did not send you. Have you any connections with the Manchu dynasty?" he asked.

They had recalled that in discussing regulations the previous day I had not used the "tenth year of the Republic" as a date. I had referred instead to the "year 1921." They had concluded that I would surely have used the Republican dating system if Sun Yat-sen had sent me. I was clearly not Dr. Sun's man, and I came from Peking. Who in Peking could possibly be interested in the workers unless it was the Manchu dynasty, which would no doubt like to utilize the workers to overthrow the "Republic." In questioning me they gave a fine demonstration of the "good fellow" spirit that permeated Shanghai's secret societies.

I could not keep myself from bursting out in laughter at their words. Without stopping to ask where they had heard things so obviously intended to create dissension, I gave them a straightforward account of myself. I had been an active student representative in the May Fourth Movement, I told them. I had participated in mass education work; I had organized railway workers in the North; and I believed in Marxism. Marxism, I carefully pointed out, was truly a workers' doctrine, and Marxists were the workers' real friends. The word "Marxism" seemed unfamiliar to them. But they did know about the May Fourth Movement in Peking, and they believed that the students sympathized with the workers. They appeared to be satisfied when they left.

About an hour later the two workers that had questioned me came back with fourteen others that had been waiting for them in a nearby teahouse. They all looked pleased. "Mr. Chang, we are sorry," one of the men that had questioned me said. "We hope you will not mind the mistaken ideas we had about you earlier. I have told them what you said. All of us believe you now. We have come for your guidance. How shall we carry on the strike?" I assured them that they were welcome and invited them to sit down so that we could talk things over thoroughly.

They told me that their greatest problem was the chief inspector of the factory. He was against the strike, and he was trying to force the men back to work. The chief inspector, I guessed, was an "old man" in the Ch'ing Pang, a person of senior position in its abundant ranks, and they must be his secret society disciples. When I bluntly asked if this was the case, they conceded that it was by nodding. They could not get a job in the factory unless they became his disciples, they said. And each year at festivals, and whenever there was a celebration day or a day of mourning at his home, they had to give him presents.

I asked if it was not true that this "old man" was supposed to be bound by certain fraternal responsibilities and if his opposition to the strike was a demonstration of them. For a long time there was a grave silence. Finally, one man jumped up and said, "This 'old man' pays no attention to fraternal responsibilities. Not only does he constantly exploit us, but he even takes advantage of our wives and sisters if they are the least bit attractive; and since we started the strike, all of us will unquestionably be dismissed. How can we possibly stay in the factory?"

The others spontaneously nodded their heads and repeated, "It is true. It is true."

Now, at the very beginning, CCP comrades in general had thought that the target of the workers' struggles was the capitalist. In the various factories and business enterprises, the staff workers and foremen that controlled the workers, although serving their masters, were nevertheless similarly subjected to the exploitation and oppression of the capitalists, and so they could be friendly with the workers generally. So in dealing with these middlemen, the policy had been adopted of contacting them, establishing relations with them, and winning them over. At the same time most of these middlemen were leaders at various ranks of the Ch'ing Pang, and the workers under them were their disciples or grand disciples. This situation was universal in Shanghai. When Li Ch'i-han first took up the labor movement in Shanghai, he had exerted great effort to have himself admitted as a disciple of a big leader of the Ch'ing Pang, and thus he himself became a senior figure in the sect. His intention was to facilitate liaison with the large number of middlemen in the factories and business enterprises in order to reduce obstructions to the labor movement.

By the time of the First Congress, some delegates had already brought forward different views. The main point was that the authorities of the foreign concessions and the capitalists had all along utilized the influences of the secret societies in exercising their rule. The police of the Municipal Council of the Settlement and its subsidiary land- and water-inspection organs, as well as the various factories, enterprises, wharves, and warehouses, all had leaders of the Ch'ing Pang occupying important positions, including detectives, inspectors, investigators, superintendents of work, squad leaders, and foremen. These leaders of the Ch'ing Pang earned a lot of extra income, a major source of which was the exploitation of the workers. Making money by offering protection seemed a straightforward undertaking. It had become an open secret that the leaders engaged in drug trafficking, smuggling, and giving shelter to criminals—activities that yielded huge incomes.

These elements often colluded with certain foreign ruffians and shared in the fabulous ill-gotten gains. The conclusion was naturally that the leaders of the Ch'ing Pang were tools long since bought over by the capitalists, and they would no longer talk about righteous principles with their disciples and grand disciples or treat them as brethren. The CCP had not had the opportunity to go into the problem in detail, but our general concept of the problem had already undergone a change. It consisted of the continued desire to win over the large number of low-ranking foremen to the side of the workers, but to develop a direct struggle against those stooges kept by the capitalists.

I had always believed that the labor movement would never progress in Shanghai if we did not break the "old men's" control over the workers. For invariably the foremen and inspectors at factories were "old men" in the Ch'ing Pang. They did the hiring, firing, and labor contracting; and it was through them that management tacitly worked to keep the workers subdued. Management and the "old men" collaborated to victimize the helpless workers. And so, I asked provocatively, "Since you have already launched the strike, what good does it do to be afraid of the 'old men'?"

They discussed this among themselves and decided to call a meeting of all workers in the factory the following day. At the meeting they planned to propose adoption of the strike demands as well as to elect workers' delegates, who would organize the trade union. If workers turned out in force for the meeting and enthusiastically endorsed the proposals—if, in other words, the situation looked favorable—they agreed that they would take appropriate steps to shatter the pomposity of the "old man."

Dressed in workman's clothes, I watched the meeting the next day. About four hundred workers assembled in a vacant lot near the factory; but after a brief announcement of the strike demands and of the planned formation of the trade union, the meeting quickly dispersed. There was no sign of enthusiasm, which worried me. Still, the few workers who accompanied me were thrilled. Although the chief inspector was exerting all the pressure he could, they explained, nobody had returned to work. Furthermore, important people from all sections of the factory attended the meeting in spite of a police threat to break it up. They felt that the situation, therefore, had to be considered very favorable.

And indeed, after the meeting, while the chief inspector was still making a show of himself by the main gate of the factory, one of his disciples, a leader of the factory workers, silently approached him from behind, carrying a huge watermelon. The melon was filled with night soil. Suddenly, as if putting a hat on him, the worker tipped it upside down on the "old man's" head. As night soil covered the face and body of the overbearing great man, the watching workers, all of them his disciples, burst out laughing. Voices, sneering at him and reviling him, filled the open area in front of the factory. The chief inspector, who had always had his own way, had irreparably lost face. And he had also lost all power over the workers, just as a religious idol cast into a dung pit loses its potency. He no longer had the stature to interfere with the strike.

After this comedy the workers elected their delegates, and the trade union was formed. The management, accustomed to negotiating exclusively with the chief inspector, now found itself able to negotiate only with the union delegates. The strike dragged on for more than two weeks, until finally it ended in success when the management accepted some of the workers' demands.

Enormously stimulating to Communist Party members, the victorious strike of the Putung tobacco workers was an important factor contributing to the rapid passage of the work plan for the Secretariat. It excited Li Ch'i-han especially. He kept telling his comrades that he had accomplished very little during nearly a year of participating in the Shanghai labor movement. This, he said, was because he had thought of the movement as being directed only against the capitalists. He had thought it necessary to be conciliatory in dealing with the "old men." It was for this reason, in fact, that he had joined the secret society by taking as his mentor an important "old man" with the high Ch'ing Pang generation of *tung*.[5] He had always tried to keep up good relations with the "old men," in the hope that they would not obstruct the labor movement. But his efforts had not accomplished anything. Using a new policy of struggling against the "old men," however, we had hit our mark with the first shot we fired. In the future, therefore, Li announced that we should stick to this new policy.

Maring read about the strike from the English-language *North China Daily News*. He said that the paper had pointed to the strike demands and the organization of a trade union as new elements in the labor situation, as something that was different from the past and that would bear watching. Maring regarded the labor movement as very important, and this real evidence of its progress strengthened his belief in us. He urged that the work be intensified. On this issue his views differed from those of Voitinsky, for Maring was a product of the Western labor movement, and he knew something about the Asian labor movement. He never talked to me about that empty formula of linking the economic and political struggles. Once an Eastern labor movement was launched, he believed it could be counted on to pursue a revolutionary path.

The general headquarters of the Secretariat and its various branches were formally established after the strike ended. On the door of a newly rented, unattached house in Shanghai was placed the sign: Secretariat of Labor Organizations in China. Most of my time went into its work. I was kept busy directing the policies and methods of the branches in different parts of the country and recruiting talented young people who could be assigned to workers' districts in Shanghai and elsewhere. At the same time, people were being selected from among the ranks of the workers themselves to augment our forces. The office grew busier day by day. By the time I left Shanghai around the middle of October, 1921, considerable headway had been made in all areas. Furthermore, *Labor Weekly*, which started publication in September, had reached its sixth issue, and its circulation among workers had greatly increased. Ch'en Tu-hsiu, Maring, and I regularly wrote articles for this publication.

While I was making headway in Shanghai in the labor movement, I was elected the CCP delegate to the Congress of the Toilers of the Far East. Comrades in Shanghai and the CC agreed that since this was the first international conference attended by the CCP, a person of some standing should be sent. Ch'en Tu-hsiu was thoroughly embroiled in launching the activities of the CC, and he could not be spared. So this task fell to me. In addition, the CC placed me in charge of recruiting delegates to the Congress from other organizations throughout the country. The comrades knew how terribly busy I was. Because we were shorthanded, however, and because the Secretariat could carry on according to plan within the framework that had already been built, it was agreed that I was the only one who could be shifted temporarily to this mission. From then on, in fact, I was always the one in the CC who dashed here and there as a troubleshooter in all emergencies.

THE CONGRESS OF THE TOILERS
OF THE FAR EAST

CHAPTER

Toward the middle of October, 1921, I had everything ready for my trip to Irkutsk, where I was to attend the Congress of the Toilers of the Far East. The CC of the CCP assigned me the tasks of reporting CCP conditions to the Comintern, of finding out what the Comintern expected of us, and of studying the revolutionary experience of the Soviet Union and other countries. At the time we did not fully understand the nature of the Congress of the Toilers of the Far East, and so we had no proposals to make before it. Ch'en Tu-hsiu gave me money for the trip. He told me to contact Nicolaevsky and to settle the technical details of the journey with him.

Following the directions that Ch'en gave me, I went to a lane off North Szechwan Road in search of Nicolaevsky. Numerous White Russian families lived there. Nicolaevsky and his wife lived in their midst in a private, two-storied, simply furnished house that differed little from most of the White Russian dwellings. After taking me into his study, he began talking to me in his faulty English. He described the situation around Manchouli and the Sino-Soviet border. He also asked if I had enough warm clothing. When I told him that I had completed preparations and was ready to leave immediately, he took the business card of some commercial house from a drawer in his desk. It looked very ordinary. Showing it to me, he said, "This card is your passport. On it is a hole made by a pin. It is a secret mark." He told me in detail how to deliver the card surreptitiously to the proprietor of a certain Manchouli barbershop. The proprietor would escort me over the border.

This normally laconic Russian created the impression that he was only Maring's quiet and obedient assistant. But from the way he handled this affair, I must say he was a capable, careful, and experienced operator.

The next day I took a train to Manchouli, passing through Nanking, Tientsin, Fengtien (Mukden), and Harbin. It was my first trip north of the Great Wall. The farther we went, the colder it got. The double-paned windows of the houses we passed were all tightly closed. I paid close attention to the conditions in the unfamiliar areas through which we passed, and it struck me that Japanese influence was evident everywhere in southern Manchuria. When I stepped for a moment into a hotel at Fengtien, a Japanese plain-clothes detective struck up a conversation with me that amounted to an interrogation. I had dressed as a merchant, but perhaps I did not look like one.

Beyond Harbin everything was different. That area was in the Russian sphere of influence. Most of the buildings were Russian style. Even the train was Russian, as were the majority of railway personnel. Imperial Russian aggression against China had left an odor there that anyone could readily detect. That rich, beautiful land contrasted to the dreary bleakness of Siberia as heaven to hell, and this has always generated temptation in our Northern neighbors, irrespective of their political beliefs.

Except for a luggage inspection which was carried out on the train by the Fengtien Army after we left Harbin, the trip was without incident.

Manchouli lay on the Chinese side of the Sino-Russian border; but it was a typical Russian town, and almost all of its shops and hotels were operated by Russians. I registered at a Russian hotel; and then, following the directions Nicolaevsky had given me, I went to a certain barbershop for a haircut. I wrapped up in newspaper a shirt that needed laundering, and in its pocket I put the mysterious card. After having a haircut, I deliberately left the parcel behind. When I returned later to claim it, the proprietor ushered me into a back room, where he returned the shirt but kept the card. I told him the name of my hotel and my room number. He asked me to be waiting for him at the hotel after eight o'clock that evening.

It was nearly nine o'clock when the man arrived. Without a word, he put my luggage into a sleigh that was waiting in front of the hotel. The sleigh was drawn by two horses. The three of us—the barbershop proprietor, the driver, and myself—climbed aboard; the proprietor wrapped a very thick blanket round the lower half of my body; and the sleigh shot ahead toward the border.

We passed through desolate country. There were no buildings at all. Nor did I see any sentries or the barricades that usually mark borders. White Russian guerrillas and smugglers, it was said, were very active in the area; and so my two Russian companions held pistols under their coverlets, ready for any possible attack. The sleigh, shaking violently, careened forward over the meandering, rutted, snow-covered road.

About midnight we reached a railway station eighteen miles from Manchouli. It was in Soviet territory. In the cold night, with the temperature thirty degrees below zero, a thick mist gushed from the two Russians' mouths. "Feel cold?" one of them asked me. "We've arrived." I thanked them. Then, taking my luggage, they escorted me to the coach of a train standing beside the station.

More than ten delegates to the Congress from various Chinese organizations were inside the coach, along with a few Japanese and Korean delegates. Almost all of them were asleep when I entered, bundled in thick quilts and blankets. The rest sat around a candle, talking softly. They stood up and greeted me, and as we chatted I learned that they all had arrived during the previous few days.

Looking around, I noted that we were in a dilapidated third-class coach. Most of its window panes had vanished. Thick planks had been nailed up in their stead, and icicles hung from the crevices between them. The air inside the coach was both stifling and terribly cold. Other than one or two guards pacing up and down outside the station, the only Russian in evidence was a thick-bearded car attendant wearing a fur cap, fur gloves, and layer upon layer of tattered cloth wrapped around his feet and calves. He entered the coach with a flask of hot water for me. He seemed to want to strike up a conversation, but since we had no common language, we could do nothing but nod and smile at each other. Before long the other delegates helped me lay out my bedding on a hard wooden berth; we said goodnight to each other; and I dropped quickly into a contented sleep, at last getting rid of the accumulated weariness of the journey.

Early the next morning we got up one after the other, and without anyone suggesting it, we dashed into the station and did setting-up exercises to ward off the cold. The station was a simple affair. It consisted only of a stationmaster's room and a telegraph room. The troops stationed there were quartered, as we were, in third-class coaches. It was to this station that our activities were restricted, for all around us was nothing but a glaring expanse of whiteness. There was not a single tree or building—not to mention vendors—and the troops supplied our meals. These Russian soldiers wore caps with red star insignia on them and khaki wool overcoats, and they carried rifles. All were neatly dressed. Their food was better than that of the railway personnel. They had enough bread and some vegetable soup. We were looked after here exclusively by a Russian who could not speak any of our languages. No one else ever contacted us. Yet I know that our names were cabled to Irkutsk, which promptly cabled back clearance for us.

That evening a locomotive arrived from Chita. Our battered old coach was coupled to it, and we started off in a northwesterly direction, stopping here and there to pick up an additional railway car or two. We occasionally stopped at stations; and when we could see through the ice on the surviving windows, there was nothing to look at except for two or three travelers, boarding or leaving the train, and the utterly barren countryside. Nothing attracted our interest. We simply wrapped ourselves in quilts and slept.

The railroad was poorly constructed. Riding it was rather like being tossed about in a sampan by the waves. And the bridges along the way, which were made of wood, emitted disquieting creaky noises as the train crawled over them. In fact, according to some Russians on the train, repairs to the railroad were barely finished. The repairs had been hastily done and were faulty, and the line was not yet open to regular traffic. They said that travel on it was really quite dangerous.

After what seemed to be quite a hazardous trip, we reached Chita at lunchtime of the second day. We were put up in a large building that from the outside appeared to be an imposing mansion. But inside, most of the rooms had no floors, and of course they contained no furniture. Some iron beds in the few rooms that did have floors were placed at our disposal. There had been a drastic shortage of all supplies during the Revolution, a Russian told us, and during the bitterly cold weather no fuel had been available. Residents had used their furniture for fire wood. When that had been consumed, they had started tearing up the floors for fuel. Many buildings in Chita looked beautiful from the outside. Inside, however, most of them had been wrecked, although the building that we stayed in was regarded as rather more fortunate than most. The very few buildings that were in better condition had been taken over as government offices. The Russian said that they had done their best, and that our building had been assigned to us because we were foreign guests.

Chita was then capital of the Far Eastern Republic. Seen from its streets, it did not seem to have been very seriously damaged in the war. Along its boulevards stood numerous churches, their gold domes reaching high into the sky, although their bells hung silent and nobody could be seen entering or leaving them. Other large buildings on the boulevards were used as government offices. On the unpaved back streets, in row after row of huts, the Russian common people lived. All stores seemed to be closed, and no factories were to be seen. On the streets there were only an occasional pedestrian and a very limited number of horse-drawn sleighs in search of customers. Once in a while a peddler or two selling black-market bread might appear. The inflated Soviet paper currency, issued in astronomical quantities and used throughout Russia, was absent here. Here they still used the rubles and kopecks of Tsarist days.

The Russians who acted as our hosts kept telling us that the Chita situation was very confused and that there were numerous Chinese and Japanese agents around. They cautioned us against roaming the streets too much and against talking to anyone. So we only caught a glimpse of the exterior appearance of Chita. There was no way to penetrate beneath its surface and truly understand the city.

The Far Eastern Republic was established in April, 1920, with its capital at Chita. The Soviet Union set it up as a buffer zone in an effort to cope with the difficulties that beset her remote, inaccessible Far Eastern territories, especially the complicated situation arising from the refusal of Japanese troops to evacuate the area following the end of Allied intervention. It had other uses, too. For it was from the Far Eastern Republic that the Yurin mission came to China in August, 1920, ostensibly to conclude a commercial agreement. In fact, however, Moscow sent this quasi-official mission to explore the possibilities of Sino-Soviet diplomatic recognition. The Republic claimed to pursue a democratic domestic policy and a foreign policy that was independent of the Soviet government. But actually, as Stalin later conceded in a Pravda interview,[1] it was merely a special province of the Soviet Union. When the Japanese troops finally withdrew from Vladivostok in October, 1922, it had served its purpose. The Far Eastern Republic was formally abolished in November of that year.

When another group of delegates arrived from Manchouli a few days after we reached Chita, all of us boarded a train for Irkutsk, which traveled more smoothly over this roadbed. The two coaches that the forty or fifty of us delegates occupied were as dilapidated as the last one; but a dining car was attached to this train. We were able to stretch a bit by walking to it, and there we could eat the special meals provided for foreign guests. The dining car was barred to Russians. They all ate the bread they had brought with them, for they could buy nothing on the train. We noticed that they also carried a great many travel documents. These had to be produced from time to time for inspection. Most of the Russians seemed to be traveling on official assignments. Apparently the number of private travelers was quite small. A few girls were on their way to study in western Siberia.

We seemed to enjoy greater liberty on this leg of the journey. We could move freely about the stations at which our train stopped, and while the train was in motion it was possible to see out from the dining car. What attracted our attention most was the terrible destruction inflicted upon Russia by the civil war. All along the way, but especially in the vicinity of stations, we saw wrecked railway coaches and locomotives lying beside the tracks. A thick blanket of snow covered some of them. On others that were not so heavily covered, we saw the scars that both large and small guns had left or evidence of deliberate destruction. Station warehouses were not just empty, they were usually demolished. Most station office buildings were damaged. Completely gone were the huge mounds of coal usually found beside railway stations, and water towers generally had not yet been put back into working order.

Our train, which used green timber for part of its fuel, moved very slowly; and every stop was prolonged, particularly at stations whose water towers had not been repaired. There, the locomotive's water tanks had to be refilled by manual labor, and we often waited for hours on end.

When the train passed over bridges, which were usually guarded at both ends by soldiers, passengers were forbidden to look out. Some delegates did not know about this restriction. Occasionally they stuck their heads out for a look. The soldiers thereupon conveyed the idea that they were breaking the rules by taking aim and pretending to open fire on them.

The things we saw surprised and disturbed our group of uninitiated guests. Not one of the several tens of delegates could speak Russian, while none of the Russians we encountered could speak Chinese, Japanese, or Korean. We had to rely on the extremely simple, broken English that our Russian escort used, with great effort, to explain things to us. According to him, the shattered railway coaches and locomotives along the way were evidence of the fierceness of the civil war. Fighting between the Red and White armies had seesawed back and forth over that region many times, and when retreating, neither side wanted the locomotives, the coaches, or the station facilities to fall into enemy hands in usable condition. So both sides did their best to destroy those things, and we had seen the results. Although the civil war had ended, the government still faced numerous difficulties. There was a shortage of everything—a shortage of locomotives, of railway cars, of coal and charcoal. Furthermore, very little equipment could be put back into working condition. As a result, travel had become extremely difficult. Our Russian escort told us that we must not under any circumstances look out of the train while it was passing over a bridge. The reason for this was that White Russians had tried every conceivable device to sabotage the bridges. No matter who he was, a person that looked out while going over a bridge was in danger of being shot and killed by the soldiers guarding it.

Often during long stops at the bigger stations great numbers of Russians crowded around us on the platforms and tried to talk to us. "Are you Communists?" we frequently inquired, using any internationally recognized tongue we could speak. Invariably the same response came back—a sad smile and a "yes." Neither side could make itself understood beyond that, however, and so we would lapse into silence. Yet even this bothered our Russian escort. "Don't talk with these common people," he kept telling us. Sometimes he even grew irritated and drove away the people surrounding us.

All sorts of Russians, upon seeing our yellow skins, would assume looks of contempt and ask, "Do you want salt?" From men and women, youngsters and oldsters, we heard it. It was a common saying with them, but none of us had any idea of what it meant until finally one delegate encountered an overseas Chinese from Shangtung at one of the stations.

He explained the phrase to us clearly. His account went something like this: Once upon a time the father of an overseas Chinese who lived in Siberia died, and the man wanted to send his father's body back to his birthplace for burial. But the only coffins available in Russia were made of very thin wood. Fearing that the corpse would decompose, the man embalmed it with salt in order to send it back. The story may or may not have been true. The fact was, in any case, that "Do you want salt?" had become a phrase connoting barbarism with which the Russian people reviled and insulted the Chinese people.

"Do you want salt?" rapidly became the topic of conversation among the delegates. They all regarded it as a symbol of the contempt in which Chinese were held in the days of Tsarist Russia. For in those days, when Russia was bent upon aggression against China, Russian authors had been encouraged to write a good many derogatory stories about the Chinese people. The trend caught on among the Russian masses, and in this way "Do you want salt?" became a common saying.

What we saw everywhere in traveling from Harbin through Manchouli to the spot where we were at the time were the vestiges of Tsarist Russia's aggression against China. The whole area from Manchouli to Chita had originally been Chinese territory. It became Russian land after the Treaty of Nerchinsk in 1689. Nor was this all. Russia pushed on into China's Northeast and ravaged that area. We still could see evidence of this in Harbin. Those were the days when Tsarist Russia built the railroad on which we traveled in order to further her aggressive designs on China and the Far East as a whole. And since she had carried out that aggression physically, it was not surprising that on a non-corporeal level she had tried to foster in her people a contemptuous attitude toward the Chinese. Could the Communist government now in power completely wipe out this ingrained way of thinking? By what methods could they change the contemptuous attitude toward the Chinese that was held by these "old hairy beasts" (lao mao-tze) who flogged their women and drank too much? This was a question that we delegates, who had all along admired the Soviet revolution, wanted to investigate on the spot.

The first thing we noticed was that the Russians, whatever their beliefs, still seemed to be hampered by many of their old ways. Their poverty—which was revealed by the rags they wore—their unsanitary habits, and their rude speech and manners made them little different from backward Eastern peoples. Apparently no improvement had followed the revolution. Those who proclaimed that they were civilized Russians also often made fun of the Chinese inclination to "do things slowly." As a matter of fact the Russians had the same inclination. "Do things slowly" was the attitude with which they tended to approach things. We had not had much contact with Russians, yet from our escorts and from such people as the dining car waiters we kept hearing the word "seichas," which meant "right away." Although they said "right away," however, they often took hours to get anything done. And so we reciprocated with a nickname for the Russians—we called them "seichas."

One Russian habit was a respect for order. They queued up for hot water, for example. In this they were very different from the Chinese, who generally created a state of chaos on such occasions. But in their greed for tips and in their abuse of authority, they were certainly not far behind petty Chinese officials. The term seichas took on something of this meaning for us. Our use of seichas as an epithet for Russians was both just and mocking.

We spent about three days on the train and then reached Verkhne-Udinsk. Our train stopped there for a full day while a strict inspection was carried out. The documents and luggage of everyone from passengers to train crew were examined, and every corner of the train was searched. When Russian passengers underwent inspection, they first had to produce travel documents and then certificates attesting to their occupations over the past few years. Some of them gave the inspectors huge piles of documents crammed with written comments. If doubts nevertheless arose, a detailed interrogation followed. And if the interrogation left the inspectors unsatisfied, but the case was minor, the passenger's documents were endorsed to that effect before he was free to go. In more serious cases, the passenger was removed from the train. Our Russian escort explained that this rigid inspection was unavoidable, because we were about to enter Soviet territory.

No exception was made for us delegates. We had no documents for them to look at, but otherwise we were treated like the Russians. Our luggage received very careful scrutiny. While the inspectors were relatively polite to us, some of us grew restive and took this opportunity to poke fun at the inspecting officials by calling them seichas several times.

We reached the banks of the Selenga River soon after leaving Verkhne-Udinsk. There we underwent another inspection on the train before proceeding westward. The farther west we traveled after that, the more serious the food situation became. It was the primary problem that we encountered. Probably the Far Eastern Republic had been able to ease its own situation by importing food from the Northeast, in China. But in the Soviet territory that we then entered, an Allied blockade had prevented the importation of food from abroad at the same time that there was a famine in the country. The hungry people were thus bedeviled from two directions, and understandably the people on the train talked of little but the "bread problem."

Unable to understand the language, we had no way of taking part in their conversation. All that we could do was to watch the Siberian scenery and to talk among ourselves about the stories of past Sino-Russian relations. Our train, moving slowly, began to approach the shores of Lake Baikal. We passed through heavy forests and some long tunnels; then we came upon Lake Baikal, its silvery waves stretching out endlessly. It made us think of the heroic exploits of Su Wu, who tended sheep there and maintained his loyalty to his government;[2] and our minds were irresistibly drawn back to thoughts of the ancient days.

Before World War I the trip from Chita to Irkutsk took less than two days. It was nearly a week before we finally reached our destination.

What I Saw and Heard in Irkutsk

Irkutsk was an important Siberian city. The Comintern had established the Far Eastern Bureau there, called the Irkutsk Bureau for short. A branch organ of the Comintern, its purpose was to investigate Far Eastern conditions, to establish liaison with Communists all over the Far East, and to advance revolutionary movements in the various Far Eastern countries. To the east of Irkutsk lay the still unstable area governed by the Far Eastern Republic. Irkutsk was the only important town that was truly a work center of the Soviet Union in Siberia. That was why it was chosen as the site for what was originally called the Congress of Oppressed Peoples of the Far East, a name subsequently changed to the Congress of the Toilers of the Far East.

We reached Irkutsk early in November, 1921, and began to learn something of the workings of the Far Eastern Bureau. Its offices were in a building that was not very large on one of the main streets of the city. A man named Shumyatsky was its director.

Shumyatsky was virtually the king of Siberia then, for in him were concentrated the powers of the Party, the government, and the Army.

He was plenipotentiary of the Russian Communist Party in Siberia, plenipotentiary of the Soviet government in Siberia, and chairman of the Siberian Military District. Originally a Siberian railway worker, he was an old-guard Bolshevik from the period before 1905. In 1922 he became Soviet ambassador to Iran. Voitinsky, whom I had met in Peking in the spring of 1921, was his chief secretary while Shumyatsky was in charge of the Irkutsk Bureau. Because Shumyatsky held too many posts to be able to attend to everything personally, it was actually Voitinsky who handled the Bureau's routine affairs.

Under the Far Eastern Bureau were a China section, a Mongolia section, a Japan section, and a Korea section. The director of the China section was a man named Mamaev, who knew a little Chinese and who later came to China as an adviser in the military advisory group headed by General Galen. In addition to the different sections, there was an information bureau, which was the busiest organ of all, with dozens of industrious workers. By comparison, the sections operated at a leisurely pace, with only two or three workers in each section. At that time the Far Eastern Bureau had not yet actually begun practical work. It was still doing research on the data that it was gathering from the different parts of the Far East.

The Far Eastern Bureau had arranged for us to stay in a two-storied reception building. It was not very elegant, but it had all of the necessary facilities. In addition to a bed, a desk, a wardrobe, and chairs, each room contained a fireplace, which furnished warmth twice a day, in the morning and at night, when it was lighted. There was also a dining hall. For lunch we ate black bread, soup, and meat. We went without the soup at dinner, but there was enough to eat. Indeed, our lives contrasted to the average, hunger-haunted Russian's life as heaven to hell. Several maids made up our rooms regularly. The old man who built the fires in our fireplaces had been a millionaire nobleman in Tsarist days. His genteel demeanor and his difficulty in lighting fires evoked both pity and amusement in us. While starting our fires he often asked for cigarette butts, and when he received a few cigarettes or a piece of bread from one of the delegates, he overflowed with gratitude and expressions of thanks.

When he met me this time, Voitinsky, whom I already knew well, asked solicitously about my trip. When I told him about it briefly, he reiterated what he had said before. "Idealists generally think that if the revolution succeeds today, we should be in paradise tomorrow," he said.

"As a matter of fact, revolution is very brutal. Revolution damages everything, and it isn't easy to bring about social stability afterward. Waves of famine and widespread epidemics are inevitable. It takes time to restore order."

"We in China have also gone through revolutions and wars," I told him, "but I have never before seen anything like the tragic destruction in Russia. We are eager to know why the destruction suffered by Russia was so serious. Will you explain it to us when you have a chance?"

At the same time he told me, "Even though most of the delegates have arrived, we can't open the Congress on the eleventh of November as scheduled. We still don't know where it will be held." He said that he would do his best to satisfy the requests of the delegates until the Congress opened.

Living at our reception center were four Japanese delegates, one of them a student and the other three workers. They all used assumed names. Leaders of the Korean delegation of about ten members were Premier Kim Kyu-sik* and Foreign Minister Lü Yun Hong* of the Korean Provisional government at Shanghai. A delegate was there from Java, also, a youth named Semaun, who was secretary of the Communist Party of Indonesia. Maring, after coming to Shanghai, had recruited Semaun from the Dutch East Indies. However, no delegates came from the Philippines, French Indochina, Siam, or Malaya.

The Chinese delegation, with more than thirty members, was the largest. It included many outstanding figures. Among them was Chang Ch'iu-pai, a KMT member from Anhwei who had recently risen to prominence. Sun Yat-sen sent him to the Congress as the KMT representative. One of the anarchist delegates was the noted writer Huang Ling-shuang, one of the five anarchists that had joined the Peking Communist nucleus. His very close friend, a short-statured woman anarchist named Wang Li-huen, represented the Women's Patriotic League (Fu-nu Ai-kuo Hui), a Kwangtung organization. Wang Le-p'ing represented a federation of Shantung organizations. He was a former chairman of the Shantung Provincial Assembly. I had worked with him on the National Federation of All Circles of the People at Shanghai. He later became a well-known KMT member. The leader of the railway workers' delegation was Teng P'ei, the veteran Cantonese mechanic at Tangshan who later joined the CCP. Wang Kuang-hui represented the Hunan Labor Society. There was also Ho Chung-han, who later became

---

* Chinese renderings of Korean names.

prominent in the Whampoa Academy. On this occasion, however, he attended the Congress as a news correspondent from Wuhan. I was the only representative of the CCP. Others in the Chinese delegation were chiefly representatives of student councils and of professional groups in various parts of the country.

The delegates naturally worked in the interests of the organizations they represented and in accordance with their own viewpoints. But in order to handle matters concerning us all, we decided, after talking it over, to form a single delegation of Chinese delegates. I was elected chairman of it. Since, however, no one had brought along any data from which studies might have been prepared and since no interpreters were available, this delegation did nothing noteworthy.

More than anything else the Russian famine preoccupied us, and we discussed it endlessly. Under the food-rationing system in Russia, each soldier received two pounds of black bread daily; factory and railway workers received one and one-half pounds; employees of government organs received one pound; while Communist Party members received three-quarters of a pound. The bread was of extremely low quality. It usually contained only fifty or sixty per cent flour, but sometimes as little as twenty per cent. Twice each month employees of government agencies who had families were entitled to get an additional fifteen pounds of wheat, fifteen pounds of potatoes, and sometimes a little sugar and tea. More often than not, however, part of the wheat and potatoes were rotten.

Because of these conditions everyone was constantly complaining about hunger. Take as an example the employees of government agencies. They arose in the morning, had nothing but a drink of hot water, and then went to work. At the office, only when they could bear the hunger no longer, they munched a small piece of bread, taken from their daily one pound ration. The remaining bread had to be divided between lunch and dinner. Always oppressed by hunger, the Russians seemed to think solely of getting more bread. They worked day after day just for a meager allotment of it. They pleaded and plotted with the rationing office to get wheat and potatoes that were not rotten. They could do nothing but hope, however, that their daily ration of black bread would not smell of mud and grass and that its wheat content would be high. Generally they hoped in vain; but even the fulfillment of their hopes left them only half fed.

This was true unless they somehow managed to get money with

which to buy bread on the black market, where it cost a phenomenal price. But money was difficult to earn. Mamaev, director of the China Section of the Far Eastern Bureau, is a good example of this. I frequently visited his home to chat, since he spoke some Chinese. While he and his wife always behaved cordially, they never offered food to their guests, for they did not get enough to meet their own needs. His wife, who worked during the day, had an additional night job dancing at an opera house. For this she was well paid. She used the money to secretly buy blackmarket bread, which she brought home very late every night. It was only by doing this that they contrived to have a bare minimum to eat the following day.

After observing this state of affairs, I raised the question of *xleb* (bread) with Voitinsky. "The bread problem is truly serious," he said wearily. "More than twenty million people in Russia are hungry, and millions of them may starve to death. Public resentment has reached the boiling point. Incidents are reported every day. All levels of government are devoting every bit of their strength to tackling the problem. A constant flow of people is sent to scour the countryside for food. We have to send troops to forcibly collect food from the peasants, and when they manage to get some, it takes troops to guard it. Yet even with a military escort, food that passes through the stricken areas is often seized by famine victims. Even the horses hauling the food have been slaughtered and eaten in some areas. Circumstances such as these have made it even more difficult to solve the bread problem, and the famine has grown worse. Innumerable strange and tragic incidents have been reported. But the Siberian food situation cannot be regarded as the worst. Far more terrible conditions prevail in more seriously affected areas."

After a pause he added that the government fortunately had handled rationing well. Soldiers and workers were fed. And an example was made of Communist Party members by giving them the smallest ration of all. From Lenin on down, Party members received only three-quarters of a pound of bread daily, so they were not open to criticism on that score. Had this system not been enforced, he said, there might have been serious trouble.

Shumyatsky, the "king" of Siberia, finally found time to invite me to dinner at his home after I had been in Irkutsk about two weeks. At the table, in addition to his wife and himself, was Voitinsky, who said that I had been invited because Shumyatsky wanted to talk with me about conditions in China. The man was so busy, however, that not even Voitinsky was able to see much of him. As a result, a good many matters that required Shumyatsky's attention at the Far Eastern Bureau were raised on this occasion, and he devoted most of his time to Voitinsky, going over matters that were obviously of importance.

As a guest ignorant of the Russian language, I could do nothing but sit quietly. I watched them gesticulate as they talked, and then I turned my attention to the appointments of the house. It was a very nice house, set in a garden and heavily guarded. The furnishings were lavish and varied. They included expensive silk window draperies of the type found in the homes of important Shanghai capitalists. At dinner, moreover, we had not only a high-grade black bread, but a little white bread as well. The meal consisted chiefly of a soup and a meat course, which were rich and ample and tasted very good. In addition we had milk, a dessert, and fruit. The meal lacked nothing that would have been served in an elegant Shanghai restaurant. It was the first sumptuous meal I had eaten since stepping into Soviet territory.

After dinner Voitinsky and I walked back to the reception center together over the snow-covered road in the bitter cold. Sensing that I was wondering about the dinner, he explained, "Shumyatsky prepared that extravagant dinner to demonstrate how sincerely pleased he was to entertain a foreign guest. He did not have a long talk with you. Nevertheless, he is a man of great earnestness."

"You are too polite," I replied. "We are comrades. I should not be treated as a foreign guest."

Apparently feeling that his explanation had not satisfied me, he continued, "It is useless to enforce egalitarianism in a revolution. Ideas of egalitarianism were rampant during the first stages of the October Revolution. The revolutionists in general objected to better housing and food for comrades in responsible positions. They went so far as to destroy first- and second-class railway cars. They wanted everybody to travel third class. But for every car destroyed, the people had one less car. Wasn't that conception of equality harmful to the revolution? Now, take Shumyatsky. His responsibilities are enormous. By living better, it is easier for him to accomplish much more work."

I had come to know Voitinsky quite well, and I could speak frankly to him. "Didn't you tell me that Lenin himself gets three-quarters of a pound of bread and lives as frugally as the rest?" I asked. "Why should Shumyatsky enjoy so many more privileges than Lenin? It looks as though the important thing is still power, no matter what the conditions. No wonder people that oppose you claim that you are imposing a dictatorship over the proletariat."

Voitinsky patted me on the shoulder and said with a smile, "You shouldn't put it that way. You shouldn't put it that way."

Throughout this period I came into contact with many new things that made a deep impression on me and left me with mixed feelings. These feelings could not help but occasionally creep out in my conversation. Nevertheless, I approached the Soviet Union with good intentions, and I tried to see the good side of everything.

Irkutsk was an important Siberian city, yet it was inert and silent. There were few footprints in the deep snow that covered its streets. It was more like a desolate piece of countryside than a city. All shops along the streets were barred and shuttered, and, naturally, no business was carried on. The buildings emitted no smoke from their rooftop chimneys, as if they were uninhabited. Almost the only human activity on any of the deserted streets was around the railway station and in the vicinity of factories, where a few workers moved about. At certain hours groups of office workers in worn-out or greasy overcoats would go to, or return from, work. The rest of the time the city lapsed into silence.

The Irkutsk region had not yet settled back into normalcy, and the conditions of the time of the Revolution and civil war still prevailed. I saw rifles, pistols, and ammunition belts hanging in the homes of all the government workers I visited. They were often oiling and polishing their weapons. At night, loaded guns lay within easy reach beside the bed or under the pillow while they slept in their clothes. It was virtually a life of "awaiting the dawn while sleeping on your spear." Military drills were frequent. When the alarm sounded, everyone that had a gun or that had been given some special duty would rush to an assigned spot and place himself at the disposal of the army authorities there for all sorts of military exercises. The Outer Mongolia border was just south of us, and I was told that remnants of bandit gangs still hid in the outlying areas of the city. Communist Party members had to be ready to fight at all times.

Far Eastern Bureau personnel kept extremely busy. Only on Saturday nights did they take time off for parties. Held in the main room of their office building, these were very simple affairs. A piano was the sole musical instrument. There were no radios over which to get music, for these were confined to the streets, where a few loudspeakers transmitted orders and the public speeches of important people. Russian men came to the parties dressed in garments somewhat cleaner than the tattered clothes in which they worked. The women had no party frocks, but they wrapped bright-colored scarves around their heads. Highlights of the programs they put on were revolutionary songs sung in chorus and Caucasian dances. Some solo acts would follow, and then we would begin ballroom dancing, which everyone thoroughly enjoyed. The lusty Russian revolutionary songs, which were profoundly stirring, and the fierce fighting spirit of the Caucasian dances indicated a transition from the sensuous decadence of Tsarist days to a new, unvarnished spirit of virility.

We delegates from the Far East relished these evening parties and attended them regularly. No better entertainment was available. At the parties the Japanese delegates always stood out from the rest of us. Either together or individually they sang numerous folk songs and workers' songs, and they did trick wrestling. They were always loudly applauded. The Korean delegates ranked not far behind them. They sang pensive revolutionary songs and moving folk songs. We Chinese delegates were the only ones who could not do anything. We knew nothing about dancing, nor had we ever done any group singing. The only thing a few of us could do was sing some Peking opera solos. Yet the Chinese formed the largest and most conspicuous delegation there. To our considerable embarrassment the others kept enthusiastically applauding for us to do some kind of an act. The KMT delegate, Chang Ch'iu-pai, was fond of singing Peking opera, and so we asked him to sing some KMT revolutionary songs on behalf of the whole group. He told us that the KMT had no revolutionary songs; so in desperation we asked him to sing just any Peking opera aria instead. He agreed to sing, and then he thought for a bit about what to start with. The first notes deeply shocked us. The piece he had chosen turned out to be a lewd song, popular at the time, entitled "My Little Darling Is Playing Dominoes."

Because our first appearance at a party placed us in such a predicament, we all made up our minds to foster communal entertainment when we returned to China. The gradual rise in popularity over the years of China's many excellent folk and revolutionary songs has as one of its causes our experience at Irkutsk and similar experiences that many others like us had elsewhere.

The Russians, who lived in a state of perpetual hunger, had sharply curtailed the outdoor sports they normally loved. Formerly they had taken to skiing and skating, but they could no longer get equipment for those sports. Instead, some of them had picked up a game common in rural Russia called "Wooden City." A number of posts were stood on the ground, and a heavy staff was thrown at them. The person who knocked down the most posts was the winner. It was a strenuous game, and an excellent way to get warm. When played too long, however, it increased the players' hunger.

Sanitation in Russia then was bad also. Medical supplies were scarce, and there was a shortage of both public and private facilities for maintaining personal cleanliness. The average man seldom washed his clothes, and often he gave off a distinctive odor as a result. Irkutsk had only one public bath house. Government workers had to queue up and register for a bath. Their only opportunity to really wash themselves was when their turns came up. I stayed there for approximately two months, and during that time I had only one chance to take a bath.

In the past the Russians, men and women alike, had enjoyed their pleasures and the finer things of life. They had loved to drink; but they had also loved to attend the opera, dressed in evening clothes and carrying their opera glasses. Thus, Irkutsk had several large opera houses. While not as elaborate as those in Moscow, they were nevertheless quite well appointed. Classical dramas as well as ballets and modern revolutionary plays were frequently being staged in them. There were, of course, no cinemas yet. For the average Russian civilian, theater tickets cost a sizable amount of money. Government personnel received a special discount, although they had to wait their turns to go here also. This did not dampen their jubilance when the time came. Once or twice a week we delegates were able to attend a performance. We understood no Russian, and interpreters were not provided; so we could only guess at the plots by following the gestures of the actors. Still, most delegates eagerly attended, for the shows helped us to understand Russian traditions and customs.

The Irkutsk Labor Union had built a Workers' Cultural Palace in the working-class district. All delegates were invited to attend its opening ceremonies. With considerable difficulty the Far Eastern Bureau managed to borrow two trucks to get us there, and we arrived tightly packed in them along with the Bureau personnel. The Workers' Cultural Palace was the largest and best building in the working-class district. It truly was a palace for the workers, and an extraordinary number of them had turned out for the occasion. First we inspected its facilities for reading newspapers and books, playing chess, drinking tea, listening to music, dancing, staging plays, and singing. It was a tremendous achievement for those days of crippling shortages. Yet there were very few newspapers and books, and the equipment was all very simple. Furthermore, no provision at all had been made either for heating or ventilating this gigantic building. In the extreme cold the carbon dioxide given off by the huge throng mingled with the peculiar Russian body stench to nauseate people and make them dizzy. Meanwhile, muddy snow, tracked in on the workers' leather and fur boots, melted. It turned into a thick paste which spread over every part of the building. The place seemed to become a typical Chinese food market. We delegates did not feel exactly comfortable in these surroundings, but we were so carried away by the new spirit that we stayed until late at night without losing interest.

When we were ready to leave, we telephoned the Far Eastern Bureau for the trucks they had promised would take us back. By one o'clock in the morning, nothing had happened. There was nothing to do but agree with the Russians' suggestion that we walk. We tucked our trouser legs into our boots, wrapped scarves tightly around our coat collars, and jammed our hats down to our eyelashes. Then, in groups of about ten, holding each other's hands, we marched off through the snow. The temperature had dropped to between forty and fifty degrees below zero. An icy, snow-laden wind, driving with wild roars, tore at our faces like knives. We plowed through snow that in some places had drifted to waist height. If we had not firmly held on to one another, some of us would doubtless have stumbled and found it very difficult indeed to get up again. As it was, our youthful group, mustering its courage, marched boldly ahead as though into battle. We walked for more than an hour before reaching our quarters, which were four or five kilometers away. As soon as we arrived, we counted heads and were delighted to find that nobody had been left behind or lost on the way. Then we followed the Russian way of doing things: Standing just outside the door, we vigorously rubbed our hands together, jumped up and down a few times to shake the snow from our hats and clothes, got rid of the icicles hanging from our nostrils, and lightly rubbed our faces, noses, and ears. We went directly to our bedrooms after this ritual. There we had the good fortune of being able to confirm the fact that our faces really had not been frozen.

Soviet Russia at that time was vigorously promoting the "Working Sunday" system. Under it, personnel in all government agencies worked at special tasks on Saturday afternoons and Sundays. As delegates we did not have to participate in this movement; but we enthusiastically joined in to lend it our support. We of the Chinese delegation especially wanted to demonstrate that we were not weaklings. We sought to surpass the general run of Japanese and Russians in hard manual labor. On the first two Saturday afternoons we were sent to a forest to haul timber. Each short log, which weighed about one hundred pounds, was supposed to be carried by one person. The longer logs were heavier, and two people handled them. The logs had to be carried over rough snow-covered woodland ground to a roadside or to a wharf by a river. This had to be done without the use of tools. It was harder than the work of coolies in China; and after doing it on two occasions, almost every delegate had been injured, some more seriously than others. While carrying a log, I had slipped on a snow-coated wooden bridge and fallen. The log had landed on me, causing a number of separate bruises. The Russians undoubtedly realized that we were straining ourselves to make a show of physical strength. On subsequent occasions we were not assigned to the timber detail. We were given such light work as cleaning the snow away from the railway station instead.

The longer we stayed in Irkutsk, the more boring life there became. So when we learned that the local soviet was meeting, we hurried over to watch it. More than eight hundred delegates to the soviet, many of them women, were assembled in a large theater. They came chiefly from the country, and they wore ragged clothing. Even the chairman of the meeting, who looked like a laborer from some rural village, was dressed shabbily. He was making a speech when we arrived. I asked Voitinsky, who was accompanying us, about the man. "He gives a fine speech," I said. "Is he a worker?"

"Yes," Voitinsky replied. "Not long ago this worker could read and write only a few words." I asked how he had made such progress, and Voitinsky said, "Naturally, someone had to guide him. Shumyatsky guided this worker. Shumyatsky works out everything that the worker says and does."

From this I formed a better understanding of the situation. Workers and peasants, it was true, were filling many important jobs in the Soviet Union. Yet those workers and peasants were controlled by Communist

Party members; this explained the relationship between the Party and the government.

Almost two months passed in Irkutsk without a date being fixed for the Congress. We did not understand Russian and so had very little association with the Russians. Apart from preparing reports for the Congress, we usually had nothing to do. The report I prepared was a long one. It emphasized Chinese social history, giving the background for current conditions, which I analyzed. I started with the Chou, Chin, and Han dynasties and came down to the present. My report ran to more than one hundred pages and still was not finished. I had no reference materials to consult and no one to translate it into Russian, and I realized that it was probably wasted effort. Yet by working on it day after day, I kept myself occupied. Because the other delegates wrote shorter reports, they had more idle time to cope with. Feeling bored, they would wander aimlessly about, looking for Russians or overseas Chinese with whom to talk.

Overseas Chinese lived in many different sections of Irkutsk. A few of them held jobs in government offices. Some were in the army. Most of them, however, were in business or were workers; and numerous basement laundries were operated by Chinese. A majority of these overseas Chinese were dissatisfied with the Soviet government. We delegates had come to the Soviet Union as open-minded observers, but the facts we gathered from overseas Chinese there did not give us a favorable impression of it.

Essentially, the dissatisfaction of overseas Chinese with the Soviet government stemmed from economic problems. After four years of the European war, the government had adopted War communism to support its three-year civil war. War communism put the factories under semi-military control and paid the peasants for requisitioned farm products in inflated, largely worthless currency. Even if the currency had been hard, the peasants could have bought nothing with it, as there was nothing to buy. So the farmers organized themselves against the requisitioning. Troops were sent into the countryside to requisition food in a way that amounted to robbery. According to the announced theory, they were supposed to requisition only the peasants' surplus grain. In fact, however, Lenin admitted that they often took grain that the peasants needed in order to survive.[3] This naturally aroused universal anger among the peasants. As Lenin pointed out, the whole system of War communism collided directly with the interests of the peasants.[4] Workers were destitute, the peasants were destitute, and revolts broke out in Siberia, the Ukraine, and Tambov Province.[5] When the Kronstadt Mutiny broke out in March of 1921, the Soviet authorities finally grew really alarmed. The New Economic Policy was announced at the Tenth Party Congress, also held in March, 1921.[6] On April 21 of the same year, Lenin issued his treatise *The Tax in Kind,* in which he set forth the provisions of the New Economic Policy and explained their significance.[7] A main feature of this policy was that peasants were allowed to pay the grain tax in money instead of in grain. This left them free to sell what grain they did not need for themselves. At the same time, free trading was allowed for a certain number of commodities in order to give peasants and owners of small industries a production incentive.

Yet few people in Irkutsk had any confidence in the New Economic Policy. Stores remained closed even though the New Economic Policy allowed merchants to do business. Not even the barber shops opened. A few peddlers sold bread and secondhand goods, but most of the merchants were afraid to venture back into business. Nor did the peasants want to increase their grain production in spite of assurances that only a twenty per cent agricultural tax would be collected in currency. They did not trust the paper currency of the government, so barter was the general rule among the people.

Some of us delegates asked Chinese residents of Irkutsk why the Russians so deeply distrusted their government. The reply we usually got was that such a government could not be trusted. It had confiscated people's property and requisitioned their food in the past, and it would do the same thing in the future. Furthermore, the paper currency that the government issued in vast quantities was depreciating by the day. Wasn't this a case of cheating the people? they wanted to know. What, they asked, was the government good at except killing people? Compared to these things, frequent government corruption and victimization were matters of secondary importance.

For the delegates, who had originally brimmed with enthusiasm for the Soviet Union, the two months of personal experience raised more and more questions. Generally, the first question was: Where was the Soviet Union going and how could socialism develop in this backward Russia, especially in this desolate Siberia? The second question was: In what direction would the New Economic Policy lead the Russian economic system? The third question was: What difference was there between War communism and the robbing and plundering of Chinese bandits who took from the rich to help the poor? The fourth question was: Since there was such a vast difference between the conditions in China and those in Russia, could the experience of the Russian Revolution be applied to China? To these questions no answers were forthcoming. I, for one, could not answer them. The absence of answers greatly disturbed the delegates; and later on, some of them put the blame for this on me. They said that I was inept at explaining things. In fact, however, I was bewildered myself.

The delegates discussed their questions with the cleverest man at Irkutsk—Voitinsky—and he told them, "The New Economic Policy represents a concession to the peasants. Socialism can be built only on a foundation of advancing production," and so forth. Generalizations of that kind were no answer to the many specific questions in the delegates' minds. Soon afterward, we left for Moscow, still unsatisfied but determined to keep looking for the answers there.

Moscow and Leningrad

Toward the end of 1921 the Far Eastern Bureau received a telegram from Moscow directing that the Congress of the Toilers of the Far East be held there instead of at Irkutsk. This news delighted the delegates. It meant that they could leave this city, which they had tired of, and have a look at the Red capital. Early in 1922 we all bid farewell to Irkutsk and headed west by special train.

Although the same ordinary old coaches made up the special train, it was considerably glamorized by Shumyatsky's private car, which was coupled to the end. A delegation from Mongolia made its first appearance on the train. It consisted of scarlet-gowned revolutionary nobles and lamas and "now" women wearing the traditional multicolored dress of the Mongol people. They had stepped from a nomadic existence onto the train; and in order to survive in this strange new world, they were utterly dependent upon guidance from the Russians. Because we spoke no common language, we did not mix well. Our special train, gliding through the wastes of Siberia, was rather like a miniature exhibition hall of Eastern nationalities.

As we went along, we felt the difference between conditions here and those east of Irkutsk. Although we still saw civil-war damage all along the route, some rehabilitation had been accomplished. Most chimneys on the station workshops remained smokeless, to be sure, yet at Krasnoyarsk there were huge mounds of coal, and it was reported that the coal mines there had resumed production. The effects of the New Economic Policy seemed more evident the farther west we went. The number of peddlers at the stations steadily increased. The prices of bread, milk, and other foods still ran to astronomical figures, however, and one could produce a great roll of paper currency without interesting them in a sale. What they wanted was to barter.

As we passed west through the Urals and into European Russia, where the famine was even more serious, the stations were jammed with emaciated victims of the famine—men, women, old people, and youngsters—all of them begging for food from the train passengers. A scrap of bread was the most precious thing in the world to them. The peddlers wanted more than anything else to barter their goods for salt or matches. When they succeeded, they acted as though something miraculous had happened, so overjoyed did they become. Traveling thus through conditions of famine and chaos, we were the objects of surprised and envious glances from the Russian people, and of respectful salutes from honor guards and bands playing at stations along the way. After nine days of traveling, we arrived at Moscow, the headquarters of world revolution.

We received a grand welcome at the magnificent Moscow station. While the huge crowd that was there to welcome us sang the "International" at its lusty best, we were ushered to a large waiting truck. We had no time to find out what organizations were there to greet us, but they were numerous. Nor could we understand a word of what they said. By the way they acted, however, we could feel their enthusiasm. One thing does stand out in my memory: Sen Katayama, leader of the old Japanese Socialist party, was in the welcoming crowd, and he addressed us in English. I had heard of him for a long time, and finally I had an opportunity to see him.

When we reached the reception center, we found ourselves much better provided for than in Irkutsk. In addition to the three daily meals, which were far better, we delegates received cigarettes, sugar, underwear, towels, and soap. With such special treatment it was easy to forget that Moscow was struggling through an extremely critical shortage of materials, especially food.

Our primary concern was with the details of our Congress. Our chief immediate aim, however, was to take advantage of the opportunity to see and learn more. But our greatest difficulty remained our inability to find suitable interpreters. Ch'ü Ch'iu-pai, a fellow student delegate of mine during the May Fourth Movement and a graduate of the Peking Russian Language Institute, had been in Russia for more than a year as correspondent for the *Ch'en Pao*. Although the Russian he spoke was still mediocre, it was the best spoken by any of the Chinese we knew in Moscow. However, he was suffering from an advanced case of tuberculosis and was in a hospital, which he was seldom able to leave. In Moscow there were also eight young Chinese men, SYC members from the Shanghai Foreign Language School, including Liu Shao-ch'i and P'eng Shu-chih, who were studying at the Eastern University. Although they had been in Moscow for about a year, they still did not have an adequate command of Russian. The few Bolsheviks among the overseas Chinese in Moscow spoke only "pidgin" Russian. There was not a single Russian in the entire Comintern, moreover, who was expert in the Chinese language. Under these circumstances it was impossible for us to get a broad, deep understanding of Russia, which I, for one, very much regretted. The resolutions on the national and colonial questions that were passed by the Second Comintern Congress furnish an example of our predicament. A translation of them into Chinese by Ch'ü Ch'iu-pai had been mimeographed. The translation not only read badly, but also contained unreliable and unintelligible passages. While I read it along with an English-language translation, I believe that I still did not fully understand that vital document.

We delegates were rather like a group of half-deaf, half-dumb students. Russian escorts took us here and there. But rather than to say that we were taken to look at the various sites, it would be more accurate to say that we were taken to the various sites so that the Russians there could look at us. For we seemed to be the most fresh and stimulating propaganda objects available. The appearance of this distinctive and colorful group before the Moscow public tended to substantiate claims that the Comintern was making headway in the Far East and that its future there looked promising. This was at a time when the eagerly anticipated Communist revolutions in Europe were farther from realization than ever, while Moscow was making little apparent diplomatic progress in that area. Revolutionary activities in the Far East were like a shot in the arm. In any case, we saw in the Kremlin the imprint of a succession of emperors. We visited museums of the Revolution, as well as other museums and a variety of places memorable for their role in the underground days of the Revolution. Most factories had not yet resumed operations, and the schools were still disorganized, so naturally we were not shown them. At times we were honored with seats in the imperial box at the opera house, where we saw arresting operatic performances. We also went to all kinds of welcoming receptions, at which enthusiastic acclaim always followed the speeches we made. But the most stirring experience for me—the thing that touched me most deeply and left the most unforgettable impression—was a reception given by our eight young friends at Eastern University for a few other Chinese delegates and myself. They treated us with potatoes, which they had saved from their rations for a very long time. In that extremely trying city of hunger—as Ch'ü Ch'iu-pai described it at the time—the small dish of potatoes was a gesture of compatriotic and comradely affection that I would not have traded for the most valuable thing in the world.

On January 21, 1922, the Congress of the Toilers of the Far East finally opened in a rather small conference room.[8] With the addition of delegates that were already in Moscow when we arrived, and of people that were studying there or staying there for other reasons, there were altogether 119 delegates from China, Japan, Korea, Java, Mongolia, and India. Far Eastern observers brought the number to more than 160. Grigori Zinoviev, executive secretary of the ECCI, declared the Congress open.

A presidium of seventeen was elected. Among its members were Georgi I. Safarov, director of the Eastern Department of the Comintern; Shumyatsky; an American; M. N. Roy, the Indian Communist; Bela Kun, the Hungarian Communist leader; Kim Kyu-sik, the Korean revolutionist;[9] Semaun, the general secretary of the Communist Party of Indonesia; Sen Katayama; at least one Mongol; and at least one Japanese. The three Chinese elected to the presidium were Chang Ch'iu-pai, the KMT delegate; Miss Wang Li-huen, of the Women's Patriotic League; and myself, the CCP delegate. Lenin, Trotsky, Zinoviev, Katayama, and Stalin were elected honorary chairmen; and they sat on the rostrum during several sessions. At least I remember seeing all of them there except Stalin. If Stalin joined the others, it was on only one occasion. At the second session of the Congress on the next day, the following four-point agenda was adopted: (1) a report by Zinoviev on the "International Situation and the Results of the Washington Conference," (2) reports from each country, (3) a report by Safarov on the "National

and Colonial Questions and the Communist Attitude Thereto," and
(4) the *Manifesto*.

The Congress held twelve sessions between January 21 and February 2. In addition to the agenda items, the first session was devoted to greetings and the presentation of banners to the Congress. The atmosphere was spirited. Zinoviev spoke for the pulsing heart of world revolution, the ECCI. M. I. Kalinin spoke on behalf of the first triumphant Marxist government—the All-Russian Central Executive Committee of the Council of Workers' and Peasants' Deputies. Abraham Lozovsky spoke for the Red International of Trade Unions—the Profintern—of which he was executive secretary. There were speeches by two prominent Comintern figures from the Far East—Katayama, who spoke on behalf of the presidium of the Congress and of the Comintern as a whole, and Roy. A self-assured youth named Schiller, who looked scarcely twenty years old, addressed us on behalf of the Communist Youth International, of which I think he was executive secretary.

This first session of the Congress also heard representatives from each of the Far Eastern delegations. It was then that I spoke briefly on behalf of the "Communist and Revolutionary Parties of China,"[10] one of the few occasions on which I addressed the Congress. I stressed the need for a sound program of action. In conclusion, I said that as soon as a strong union of Far Eastern revolutionary forces sprang into action, the hour of doom would strike for capitalism and imperialism.

The dominant theme of the Congress was "Unite the Proletariat with the Oppressed Peoples of the World." It was a call to the toiling masses in colonial and semicolonial countries of the Far East to carry out anti-imperialist revolutions for national independence under the leadership of the Comintern. Capitalist nations were portrayed as the implacable foes of independence. Little was said about communism being an eventual revolutionary goal, however. Of greater immediate importance were national revolutions instigated by an alliance of all revolutionary forces in each country. Both Zinoviev and Safarov, in the major speeches of the Congress, made specific suggestions for conducting these national revolutionary movements. They stressed the need for both Communist and non-Communist revolutionists to work together in China, an approach echoed in numerous minor speeches by the delegates.

It was at the second session of the Congress that Zinoviev gave his lengthy report.[11] The Marxist movement had always been oriented toward Europe, with little thinking or writing about the Far East, and

this frame of mind still permeated the Comintern. Its leaders had no
real background for thinking about the China problem. This was
especially true of Zinoviev, whose background was almost exclusively
European. He probably knew a great deal more about Europe than
about Russia, not to mention China, and he readily admitted in his
speech to being "very poorly and casually informed" about China. However, lack of information did not keep him from theorizing on the subject.
It had been decided at the Second Comintern Congress that a national
revolution was called for in China. What had not been firmly decided
was how this revolution was to be carried out. Lenin had said that it
would be carried out by an alliance of anti-imperialist forces, including
the native bourgeoisie. Nevertheless, while in his speech Zinoviev insisted upon an alliance of Communist and "nonproletarian" Chinese
revolutionists, he clearly did not include the Chinese bourgeoisie among
those nonproletarians. He did not, to be sure, delve into the class structure of China at the Congress. But his sketchy treatment of the revolutionary forces in China was a good example of the confusion within
the Comintern in regard to China that was to last for years and that was
to cost China dearly. To the Chinese delegates, however, these were
insignificant fine points at the time, if they were noticed at all, particularly since the Russian-language speeches were very badly translated.
What did strike home was Zinoviev's insistence that an anti-imperialist
alliance between Communist and nonproletarian revolutionists in China
was essential. Zinoviev began his speech by discussing the vital role that
the Far East was beginning to play in world politics as the capitalist
nations carried their power struggle into that area. As an example of
expanding capitalist-imperialist greed, he cited the Washington Conference, which he called the "Alliance of the Four Bloodsuckers." Then
he declared, "And it would have been the saddest mistake imaginable
if, among the representatives of South China, there could be found any
simpleton who would accept the catchword 'open door' as the pure gold
of real democracy. . . . Yet it must be regretfully observed that, according
to our information . . . there are some people among the active workers
of the Southern Chinese revolutionary movement, among the adherents
of Sun Yat-sen, among the important workers of his Party, who at times
are looking not unhopefully towards America, that is, towards American
capitalism, expecting that just from there the benefits of democracy and
progress will be showered upon revolutionary China."

This rebuke was mild compared to the way Safarov castigated the

KMT along similar lines in his report a few days later. Galled by such charges, and no doubt with an eye to courting Soviet assistance for the KMT, Chang Ch'iu-pai huffily denied them. Otherwise, he endorsed the reports of Zinoviev and Safarov.

Emphasizing that the "present revolutionary movement in the Far East is for national freedom and independence," Zinoviev went on to say, "We know perfectly well that the protest which is growing in China against the imperialists is not a Communist protest, it is the elemental national desire of the people to be masters of their own fate."

He claimed that the success of this revolutionary movement depended largely upon what happened in Japan, and that it was with the Japanese proletariat in particular that the oppressed peoples of the Far East must align themselves. He stated flatly, "The victory of the Japanese labor movement is the key which will unlock the door of emancipation for the entire Far East."

He advised the Chinese Communists, along with the small group of Communists in Japan and Korea, to shed their feelings of intellectual superiority and aloofness. "Go right in among the tens of millions of people who are fighting in China," he urged, "and become their leaders." To the leaders of the "nationalist movement," he proposed that they give up their faith in Versailles and Washington.

"This is what the Communist International says in addressing itself to both sections of the Congress," Zinoviev declared, "to that section which is composed of conscious Communists and whose function is to organize the working class for victory over the bourgeoisie, as well as to that section which is composed of nonproletarian elements, of the leaders of those toiling masses which are fighting against aggression. An alliance between these two groups is essential, and we will be playing the game of the bourgeoisie if we by any means weaken this alliance."

That Zinoviev envisaged a well-defined, individual role for the Communists as part of this alliance is noteworthy in view of the nature of the Communist-KMT association that the Comintern representative to China more or less forced the CCP to accept later. In his addresses to the eighth and tenth sessions of the Congress, Safarov made even plainer what the special role of the Communists should be in such an alliance.

At the end of the discussion from the floor that followed his report, Zinoviev added a strikingly radical departure. He said that the Comintern felt that Far Eastern countries were ready for the Soviet system of government in their revolutionary movement even where peasants were the preponderant component of the population.

"You may boldly state," he told the delegates, "that we advocate the soviet system . . . even where these soviets will be preeminently peasant soviets."

Safarov's report, "The National and Colonial Questions and the Communist Attitude Thereto," was essentially an elaboration of what Zinoviev had said.[12] He warned the Chinese "democrats" not to rest content in working with intellectuals, but to organize the peasant masses. Then he said, "The first task confronting the Chinese laboring masses and their advanced elements—the Chinese Communists—consists of liberating China from the foreign yoke, in nationalizing the land, in overthrowing the Dutsiun [tu-chun], in establishing a single federative, democratic republic, in introducing a uniform income tax."

He said that this could only be done with support from "the great peasant masses and that these peasant masses had to be won over to the side of revolution." He added, still referring to China, "We support any national revolutionary movement so far as it is not directed against the proletarian movement." And he amplified Zinoviev's call for soviets, saying that he thought they offered the best means of combatting imperialism and capitalism.

At the tenth session of the Congress, over which I presided, Safarov, in replying to the discussion that followed his report, went a step farther in insisting that the Chinese Communists maintain their own specific identity in any alliance with other Chinese revolutionists. "Chinese workers must go independently on their own way," he said, "not linking their fate with any democratic party or with any bourgeois element. . . . We know perfectly well that in the immediate future there can be no sharp conflict between us and those bourgeois democratic organizations . . . but if they should limit the development of proletarian class consciousness, we shall oppose them completely."

The Far Eastern delegates also addressed the Congress, explaining the political situations in their countries, reporting on revolutionary problems, summarizing revolutionary progress, commenting on the reports of others, and so forth.

One evening a few days after the Congress opened, Shumyatsky and an English-language interpreter named Ivan, who later became secretary to Stalin, came to the reception center. They invited three Chinese delegates—Chang Ch'iu-pai, Teng P'ei, and myself—and one

Korean delegate—Kim Kyu-sik—to the Kremlin. We were stopped at two sentry posts along the way, where Shumyatsky presented passes and talked to the sentries, before our car pulled up at a large office building. At about nine o'clock we were led into a small reception room just big enough to accommodate us. Only then did Shumyatsky explain that Lenin wanted to see us.

Soon Lenin strode in from an adjacent office and greeted us. He was unobtrusive and completely without affectation; there was nothing extraordinary about his appearance. In fact, he looked rather like the school teacher of a Chinese village. One could not tell by looking at him that here stood the leading revolutionist of them all—a man who held massive power. Of course we did not know that his health was failing. Five months later he had his first stroke.

After Shumyatsky had taken care of the introductions, we settled down to an easy conversation. Lenin spoke in Russian, which Ivan translated into English for our benefit; while we spoke in English, which Ivan translated into Russian for Lenin. Chang Ch'iu-pai started off by asking Lenin for guidance in carrying out the Chinese revolution. To this request, Lenin, speaking frankly and precisely, replied that he knew very little about conditions in China, apart from the fact that Dr. Sun Yat-sen was the leader of the Chinese revolution. However, since he did not know what Dr. Sun had been doing in recent years, he did not think it proper for him to express an opinion. He, in turn, asked Chang Ch'iu-pai if the Chinese KMT and CCP could cooperate. Without elaborating in his statement in any way, Chang Ch'iu-pai promptly declared that the two parties would definitely be able to cooperate well. Lenin thereupon addressed the same question to me, asking me, in addition, to tell him something about the situation in China. I answered succinctly that the KMT and the CCP should cooperate closely in China's national democratic revolution, and that this was also possible. Certain difficulties might lie along the path of that cooperation, I said, although I believed these could be overcome. I pointed out that the CCP had only recently been formed and that it was still learning how to carry out its functions. But the CCP, for its part, would work to promote unity among all revolutionary forces fighting imperialism, I said. My answer seemed to leave Lenin well satisfied. He asked nothing further about the matter.

Turning to Kim Kyu-sik, Lenin asked about the revolutionary movement in Korea. Kim, who spoke better English than we did, talked in greater detail than we had. Lenin gave him some encouragement.

Then, speaking in Russian, Lenin fell into conversation with Shumyatsky. They seemed to be on very cordial terms. Shumyatsky had last seen Lenin some time before 1905, as I understood it. They had had no opportunity to meet subsequently, and so the present encounter gave them a chance to talk about events of the intervening years as well as the Siberian and Far Eastern situations and the many important issues of the Congress. Shumyatsky, who held himself in high regard, treated Lenin with great respect. He remained very much at ease, nevertheless. At the same time, Lenin radiated affectionate friendship for Shumyatsky. Close, comradely relationships of this kind vanished from Russia with the death of Lenin.

Lenin appeared to be somewhat hard-of-hearing. But perhaps it was our halting English that made it difficult for him to understand us. Throughout most of the conversation he inclined his head toward the speaker, his eyes brilliant with self-assurance, and listened intently, as though determined not to let a single word escape him. Whenever a word in Ivan's translation struck him as inappropriate, he immediately, yet very benignly, corrected it. And when we failed to make a point clear to him, he questioned us until he fully understood. He seemed to know more English than any of us there.

When we took our departure, Lenin heartily shook our hands. With a particular show of warmth, but quite sincerely, he held the hand of Teng P'ei, leader of the railway workers' delegation, in both of his hands and said to me in English, "The railway workers' movement is very important. The railway workers played a very important role in the Revolution in Russia. They will play a similar or an even more important role in China's future revolution. Please tell him what I think about this."

When I had translated it, Teng P'ei, who was a straightforward workers' leader, bobbed his head up and down and responded to Lenin's interest with a loud, pleased laugh. Lenin beamed with joy. The rest of us, watching them, burst into pleased laughter, too.

Our conversation took more than two hours, despite its simplicity, because of the time consumed by translating. It deeply impressed all of us who saw Lenin. We particularly admired the atmosphere of friendliness and sincerity in which it was conducted. I am the only member of the CC of the CCP ever to meet Lenin. To me he symbolized the Russian Revolution, and I looked upon him as one might regard the pure and incorruptible head of a religious order. Never did I find among the other leaders of Soviet Russia a character the equal of Lenin's. The others seemed flawed by traits that he did not possess, such as bureaucratism or Russian nationalism.

Lenin had launched our conversation by raising the issue of possible KMT-CCP cooperation. It was obviously one of the key issues on his mind. Furthermore, at the Congress of the Toilers of the Far East, the core of the China problem was considered to be the matter of unifying all revolutionary forces, and of course KMT-CCP cooperation was the principal aspect of this. Both Chang Ch'iu-pai and I felt that Lenin's questions indicated his hope that cooperation between the two parties would be possible. We also agreed that this cooperation was essential to the current stage of the Chinese revolution. Chang Ch'iu-pai complained to me, however, that my statement to Lenin about probable difficulties in KMT-CCP cooperation might easily lead to misunderstanding. There would be absolutely no difficulties in the way of cooperation, he declared, and to suggest that there were, or that there might be, indicated lack of confidence in the KMT. In fact, he said, by bluntly mentioning it to Lenin, I might well have influenced him against the KMT.

I explained that lack of confidence in the KMT had never crossed my mind. What I had said was merely that harmonious cooperation between two political parties could not be achieved without the efforts of both of them to overcome difficulties that would probably arise. Still, this explanation did not lessen his agitation. He later reported this incident to Sun Yat-sen to substantiate his charge that I had criticized the KMT to Lenin. As a matter of fact, subsequent events were to bear me out, for Chang Ch'iu-pai mistook for ill-intentioned criticism an observation arrived at by very elementary reasoning.

The closing session of our Congress took place at Leningrad. Zinoviev, in addition to being executive secretary of the ECCI, was the secretary of the Russian Communist Party for the Leningrad area, and he was eager to bring delegates of the Congress into contact with the people there. Our special train, which burned green timber as fuel, took a full day and night to reach Leningrad from Moscow. We arrived on February 2. We went straight from the train to the Leningrad Opera House for the closing ceremonies of the Congress. About two thousand people packed it. First, Zinoviev delivered an address for the closing session, and representatives of various Leningrad organizations offered congratulations. Then delegates from the different Far Eastern countries spoke, adding their congratulations for a successful meeting and expressing admiration for the people of Leningrad, who had started the Revolution. Finally the resoundingly anti-imperialist *Manifesto* of the Congress was read, after which the Congress was formally declared at an end amidst thunderous applause.

We returned to Moscow on the train that had brought us. Although we did not stay long in Leningrad, we did manage quick visits to several noteworthy spots in the spare time we had. It seemed to us that the food situation in Leningrad was even worse than in Moscow. The city seemed more modern than Moscow, but this very modernity made its desolation more apparent. Most factories had still not resumed operations. Most shops were closed. There were very few people on the streets. It was evident that the New Economic Policy had not yet produced any marked results. We visited the Winter Palace of the tsars, which had been the seat of the Kerensky government, and the Smolny mansion, which the Russian Communists had made their headquarters in directing the October Revolution and which now housed the general offices of the Leningrad Soviet and the Communist Party.

Upon getting back to Moscow, we delegates began planning secret return trips to our home countries. It would not be safe to bring documents of the Congress, which had not been translated into Chinese anyway, back to our own country, and so they were left behind in the Moscow archives. We started back in separate groups. I saw colleagues off on the train almost every day. But I had to remain in Moscow for a short while, and I stayed at the Hotel Lux, waiting for a suitable opportunity to return home.

During my Moscow stay I came into contact with figures that were important at that time in the Soviet Union and the Comintern, and I learned something of the conditions under which they worked. There seemed to be a scarcity of qualified workers in the Russian Communist Party, so that a tremendous work load fell to a few ranking people. They were kept excessively busy. Meetings often had to be delayed for an hour or two, because one or two of these ranking people had not arrived. On one occasion the ECCI met in a hall of the Hotel Lux. I was invited to attend as an observer. The veteran German Communist woman Klara Zetkin, the German Communist theorist A. Thalheimer, the so-called Lenin of Hungary—Bela Kun—and the Japanese Katayama arrived on time, one after the other. People filled the hall. But because the executive secretary, Zinoviev, failed to arrive, the meeting could not start. Everyone grew impatient and increasingly irritated. Even the more experienced people began to insist that latecomers would have to be punished. Not until we had waited for more than two hours did Zinoviev, Nikolai Bukharin, and Karl Radek—the Russian notables— dash in, clutching brief cases. Nobody mentioned punishing latecomers, however, and the meeting got under way. So far as I was concerned, meetings of that kind got the participants tired out before they started. And when the finally did start, it was only possible to rush them through to a hasty conclusion.

At that time pictures of Trotsky hung everywhere, along with pictures of Lenin. People generally linked the two together in conversation. Every Russian I met held Lenin in unique admiration. They revered him. But for Trotsky they merely had praise for specific attributes—his oratorical genius, his meritorious contributions to the revolution, his heroic endurance, etc.

I encountered Trotsky on several occasions without having an opportunity to really talk with him. Once was when he passed by in a car and saw Katayama walking along. He stopped, hopped out of the car, shook hands, and in the midst of the throng that quickly surrounded them, had a long talk with the Japanese. By this action he demonstrated that he had a basic style of democracy and that he was not a fearful man. He did not take part in the sessions of the Congress of the Toilers of the Far East; but more than once I heard him speak publicly, and on one occasion, on the rostrum of a mass meeting, I shook hands and exchanged greetings with him. His speeches were evidently very moving. In those days it was customary in Soviet Russia when a prominent person made a speech, for anyone in the audience to step forward and question him. And on one occasion when I heard him, a youth mounted the platform and spoke after Trotsky had finished his address. He was only seventeen years old, he said. He had been in the Red Army for three years and had been wounded five times during the civil war. Now he was a beggar, suffering cold and hunger on the streets, with nobody to look after him. What, he asked, was Trotsky, the chairman of the Council of War, doing about such things? What solution could he offer? Trotsky could offer him nothing but words of comfort. He did not outline any comprehensive program for alleviating such grave postwar problems.

Stalin was then Commissar of Nationalities in the Soviet government, but very few people mentioned his name. Although he was an honorary chairman of the Congress of the Toilers of the Far East, he did not appear at its sessions, and so I had no chance to meet him. During the course of the meetings, however, he did have contact with the Japanese delegates. It was reported that he spoke animatedly to them at some length. An important Comintern figure described Stalin to me as a man of mystery and a man with a great store of knowledge, but one who never concerned himself with international activities. The fact that he talked with the Japanese delegates indicated that he believed Japan was the decisive factor in the Far Eastern problem, the Comintern figure said.

Meetings in Moscow were of all kinds and endless. Formidable amounts of time went into them. Lozovsky, executive secretary of the Profintern, was an especially long-winded orator, and it was not uncommon for him to speak for three or four hours on end. Schiller, the executive secretary of the Communist Youth International, although a young fellow in his twenties, swaggered like a very important person when making a long address to delegates of the Congress. All of this speechmaking may have demonstrated zeal for propaganda on the part of the Russian leaders; but it seemed unlikely that anything practical could come of it so far as the Far Eastern delegates were concerned, since we understood little or nothing of what was said.

Safarov, with whom I had rather frequent contacts, was a scholarly type of man. Voitinsky told me that he had distinguished himself as a Russian expert on the East. He had, Voitinsky said, simultaneously been plenipotentiary of the Communist Party, the Soviet government, and the Red Army in Central Asia—a post comparable to that held by Shumyatsky in Siberia. He was free of the bureaucratic traits of Shumyatsky, however. To me he looked like an eccentric school teacher. In spite of his position as director of the Eastern Department of the Comintern, he often displayed considerable impatience in dealing with us delegates from the Far East who knew very little Marxism. He could speak very sarcastically to us.

Ranking Soviet officials in those days looked like a motley gang of riffraff. Most of them dressed poorly, their hair was disheveled, and even the young ones grew long whiskers. It was not only in their personal lives that they were disorderly. There was no sign of any order at all in the way they carried out their various official duties. Their revolutionary victory had made them conceited, blandly self-confident that having been triumphant in the Revolution, they could easily overcome all post-Revolution difficulties. This vitality and revolutionary spirit which filled the young people enabled the newly risen regime to relentlessly fight hunger and innumerable other obstacles and to progress at a speed that was truly astonishing.

Toward the latter part of February, I bought a third-class train ticket and, in order to be inconspicuous, boarded the train for Chita as an ordinary traveler. Like the other passengers, I had obtained at Moscow nine pounds of very bad black bread, a little sugar, and some tea as food for the nine-day journey. This ration not only left me hungry every day of the trip, but gave me intestinal trouble. I began to worry that the train would not reach Chita in nine days and that I would face the prospect of starvation. Fortunately, we arrived on schedule, thanks to the improved rail communications system. I could not help but wonder at and admire the rapid progress the Russians were making.

At Chita, I went into hiding in a house that quartered a small group of Red Army men who also were waiting for the right opportunity to board a train safely for Manchouli. The rationing system in Chita seemed different from the one that applied elsewhere. A soldier received only one pound of bread daily, not two. But in addition he was allowed soup once a day and some meat every ten days—a treatment far better than that accorded the average man. A few days after arriving, I managed to get a train for Manchouli. I crossed the Sino-Russian border without hindrance and changed to a train bound for Shanghai, thus ending my four-month visit to Russia.

My Impressions of the Congress of the Toilers of the Far East

The Congress of the Toilers of the Far East apparently was held essentially for propaganda purposes. It had its failings, but it also had its successful points.

I have already mentioned that the Chinese delegates expressed varying degrees of dissatisfaction with conditions they witnessed in post-Revolution Russia. Yet every one of the thirty-odd delegates had believed wholeheartedly in the Russian Revolution. We had clung to a naively beautiful vision of it before actually getting to Russia. Observations on the spot, however, led us all to feel that the realities of the situation fell far short of our expectations. Nor were the questions we asked easily answered by the Russians. Other than claiming victory for their Revolution, they really had nothing to boast about.

The anarchists in our delegation, people like Huang Ling-shuang, were the most disgruntled about conditions in Russia. They looked closely into the oppression of anarchists during the Revolution. Anarchist publications were still appearing in Moscow, yet many anarchists had been imprisoned or killed. In February, 1921, when Kropotkin died, for example, Lenin permitted the temporary release of anarchists that were in jail so that they could attend the funeral; but they had to return to jail afterward.

Although the new Russian aristocrats, the Bolsheviks, had high hopes for the revolution led by the KMT and Sun Yat-sen, they nevertheless regarded Chang Ch'iu-pai as a representative of the bourgeoisie. In Russia, so far as the Bolsheviks were concerned, the term "bourgeoisie" was applied to every conceivable crime. KMT people, as a result, were most eager to avoid the designation. But then, since most of us Chinese delegates were intellectuals, the Russian Bolsheviks regarded us all as petty bourgeoisie that were unworthy of their confidence. Take me, for example. While I was one of the founders of the CCP, in their eyes I was probably merely an intellectual patriot from the ranks of the petty bourgeoisie who could at best be called only a half-Communist. A large number of Russian Bolsheviks, of course, had risen from the petty-bourgeois ranks. Yet they believed that they had been proletarianized through baptism in the October Revolution. Their conception of the term "proletariat" and of the various "classes" was rather mysterious. Out of this mystic conception evolved the conceit of the Russian Communists, and it led to numerous differences between them and us.

Most of us Chinese delegates supported the principle of revolution by force. We appreciated the value of the Russian Communist Party and of some of the post-Revolution measures it had taken. Still, we felt that the Russian Revolution had relied too much on force and that in that way it was somewhat similar to the French Revolution. It was an approach rather alien to the revolutionary tradition of China, where historically revolutions had been carried out under such slogans as "Deliver the People from Turmoil and Distress," "Practice Benevolent Rule," and "Spread the Kingly Way." To Chinese revolutionists the purpose of revolution was usually to overthrow an oppressive regime, to make it possible for the people to start life anew, to bring about tax reductions and exemptions, and to give the country a respite from current difficulties so that it might lay the foundations for a prosperous era to follow. The idea of class struggle in the Russian Revolution, however, tended to call for an endless process of overthrowing one thing after another, an endless opposition to first one thing and then another. Before one struggle and civil war had ended, another struggle and civil war would develop. These things raised some doubts in our minds about the value of such extensive and penetrating destructiveness.

At the time I had no answers to these questions. Although I retained my sympathy for the Russian Revolution and wanted to serve as a champion for the faith in it, I did not feel able to produce strong arguments in its defense. It was for this reason that I made no speeches and wrote no articles on the subject after returning to China. Most of the other delegates said nothing good about Russia after their return, while some expressed views antagonistic to Russia. The fragmentation of revolutionary influence in China and of the Chinese labor movement in later years were intimately related to the bad impression that post-Revolution conditions in Russia made upon Chinese delegates to this Congress.

Be that as it may, the Congress of the Toilers of the Far East may be credited with outstanding achievements. Because of it, delegates from several Far Eastern countries made numerous contacts with leading Comintern figures, and Asian revolutionary idealism was enriched considerably. To the Russian people and to the various national Communist parties, moreover, the Congress meant that the Comintern had actually established its programs in the Far East. This certainly acted as a stimulant, especially since it came at a time when the Communist movement in postwar Europe was suffering serious setbacks, when the immediate advance in activities there was impossible, and when the Soviet Union was being dangerously isolated. It would be a blow to the capitalist world if the more than one billion people of Asia could be mobilized to rise up against colonialism, and this prospect in turn furnished new hope that the unfavorable situation facing the Communist revolution could be reversed.

While I am not able to give details of the effect of the Congress of the Toilers of the Far East upon the revolutionary movements in other Far Eastern countries, the Congress had considerable influence so far as the revolutionary movement in China is concerned. Most important was the fact that the anti-imperialist nature of the Chinese revolution was affirmed in formal and informal discussions at the Congress. Anti-imperialism now came to be looked upon as the major task of the Chinese revolution.

The movement against alien aggression runs continuously through the history of modern China. It was the natural result of China's suffering under foreign oppression. But at the time, neither the government nor the people, neither the higher nor the lower levels of the country, held a common view on the issue of patriotism. Besides there was a blind, stubborn resistance against all foreigners. Leading patriots and revolutionists consciously opposed specific acts of aggression or specific aggressive countries. In carrying out their opposition, however, they relied upon the spirit of the masses merely to achieve diplomatic successes. Never had the people of the country been mobilized for opposition to imperialist aggression as a whole or for opposition to imperialism itself, which would have been the thorough thing to do.

The Congress was held to counter the Washington Conference. The term "imperialism" was freely used, which was understood, following in the main the treatise on imperialism by Lenin, as a logical development of modern capitalism. Historical facts about the aggression that China had suffered for many years were given to substantiate the theories expounded. The views expressed could not be regarded as baseless. In any event most of us delegates were filled with indignation at the various lawless acts of the Powers in China. But we had been also among those who welcomed Western civilization, and some of us looked upon missionary activities and certain charitable cultural enterprises operated by foreign nationals in China as having played an active role in the dissemination of Western culture. After this fresh examination of the situation, however, it was felt that numerous faults accompanied these foreign activities. To deny that they also affected China harmfully seemed pointless. This conception of imperialism did not conflict with Lenin's interpretation, which the oppressed people readily accepted. There was unanimous agreement that the theories on imperialism propounded at the Congress were completely correct.

A revolution in China was usually prompted by an urgent need for national strength, and from start to finish it was directed at the domestic situation and not directly at the outside world. Care was always taken not to offend foreign interests. Most revolutionists believed that if a domestic revolution succeeded, foreign aggression would be checked; and from the 1911 Revolution to the May Fourth Movement, all efforts were directed against targets within the country. At this Congress the view was introduced that imperialism was aligned with the reactionary forces in China, a relationship which had a widespread foundation in fact. As a result of our discussions, we unanimously agreed that the reactionary forces within China were merely the tools of foreign imperialism and that opposition to imperialism must be the starting point of the Chinese revolutionary movement if it were to succeed. The KMT representative, Chang Ch'iu-pai, conceded that this was an important result of the Congress.

The CCP had consistently held that the achievement of a social revolution was its major task. Opposition to imperialism—a patriotic movement—was regarded only as a subsidiary function. After this Congress, however, the CCP accepted anti-imperialism as an important movement which needed to be developed immediately. It accepted anti-imperialism as the necessary revolutionary road to the attainment of socialism. I myself declared that once this new idea was established, it would be easy for the CCP to put together a political program.

In the beginning we did not clearly understand the theory that "the Chinese revolution is a part of the world revolution." It was only after anti-imperialism was affirmed as a major posture that we truly became supporters of the slogan "Unite, Proletariat and Oppressed Nations of the World." With this as a starting point, most delegates came to feel the need for Comintern leadership. For if the Comintern could mobilize the workers of the imperialist countries to oppose their rulers from within, then the anti-imperialist movement in China would not be isolated. At the same time, on this basis the Soviet Union would benefit, not harm, China.

It was also at this Congress that the new idea of an "anti-imperialist united front" was evolved. In the past, different Chinese political organizations had formed temporary alliances in order to promote some specific movement or to further common political interests, but they had not found it possible to establish a united front that lasted until a common revolutionary goal had been attained. Since anti-imperialism was not a cause that was common to the different political groups in China and since the success of an anti-imperialist movement called for a long-term struggle, the joint acceptance of anti-imperialism virtually laid the foundations for KMT-CCP cooperation, although at the time no discussion was carried on about the form that this cooperation would take.

The understandings described above were not given concrete form as resolutions, and in some cases the issues were left vague and confused. Nor did the various delegates accept them without reservations, chiefly because some delegates did not have plenipotentiary powers. Chang Ch'iu-pai, for example, indicated that he was not in a position to bind Sun Yat-sen to the decisions of the Congress.

The conclusions reached by the Congress, nevertheless, were transmitted to China in one way or another. When I returned to China, I reported them to the CC of the CCP, which readily accepted them. The *First Manifesto on the Current Situation*, issued on June 10, 1922, by the CC of the CCP, and the *Manifesto of the Second Congress of the CCP*, issued in July of the same year, were both based on the conclusions of the Congress of the Toilers of the Far East. And from then on, the CCP moved steadily from being an organization for the academic study of communism to an organization engaging in political activities. For the first time KMT-CCP cooperation was now formally included by the CC of the CCP in its program for the Chinese revolution.

In the main the KMT delegate, Chang Ch'iu-pai, expressed dissatisfaction with the conditions in the Soviet Union when he returned to China; and this led KMT people to feel that there was not much difference between the new regime in the Soviet Union and the Canton government led by the KMT. Chang Ch'iu-pai did, however, make a suitable presentation of the theory that the KMT and CCP should cooperate in opposing imperialism. This led Dr. Sun and his followers to pay greater attention to the question of KMT-CCP cooperation.

Most other delegates praised the issue of anti-imperialism when they returned to China.

In those days the Chinese people did not know what was meant by imperialism. But within a short time, as a result of CCP propaganda and of the various presentations of the subject by the many delegates to the Moscow congress, the term "anti-imperialism" represented for everybody a new and immutable goal. No matter what changes later took place in the Chinese revolution, the spark touched off by this term "anti-imperialism" grew into a serious conflagration which spread over the length and breadth of China and which subsequently spread over the entire East.

THE BEGINNINGS OF COOPERATION BETWEEN THE KUOMINTANG AND THE CHINESE COMMUNIST PARTY

CHAPTER

The Chinese Communist Party Launches into Practical Politics

On more than one occasion I have stated that no decision had yet been made about the political program of the CCP. At the time there was some general confusion and lack of understanding, and all the people concerned with the issue were groping for a satisfactory answer to the question of what the major contents of this political program should be. Generalizing now, I would say that this situation may have resulted from the basic questions of what China urgently needed and of which kind of revolution she could produce at the time. Clearly it was not a Communist revolution. But what was to be its nature, its purpose, and even its name? What role could the CCP play in this revolution? To put it more exactly, how was the CCP to participate in it, to influence it, and to sway its course so that it would not be abandoned mid-way or change its nature and become anti-Communist, and how should this revolution be further guided over a very long and complex course so that finally it could be turned into the Communist revolution? Such complex problems could not be solved by the method of studying. The only course was to go ahead courageously and to face the situation as it developed.

Previously our efforts had been devoted to establishing the CCP and to experiments in organizing workers and youths and to leading them in carrying on this or that struggle. By the spring of 1922, this young Communist organization, small in size, had begun attempting to make itself a revolutionary political party in name and in fact. At the time, the key problem of the CCP's entry into political activities was KMT-CCP cooperation. How were the KMT and the CCP to cooperate? Was this cooperation to be pursued outside both parties or within the KMT? Were the two parties to establish a united front, or were they to be merged into a single entity? These problems were subjects of incessant argument between the Comintern and the inner ranks of the CCP.

In March, 1922, after I had returned to Shanghai from Moscow, I naturally had to report on my trip to the CC of the CCP and to certain comrades. I also had several talks with Ch'en Tu-hsiu. Generally speaking, my report included the following major points. First, the Comintern, the headquarters of world revolution, was exerting efforts to launch or abet the revolution in different countries and to establish liaison with the revolutionary leaders, paying especial attention to the fostering of revolutionary forces in different countries. The holding of the Congress of the Toilers of the Far East was an attempt to abet the revolutions in the various countries in the Far East.

Second, within the Soviet Union there were many difficulties. The change to the New Economic Policy was an attempt to start restoring the bankrupt economy and improving the financial situation. At the same time Russia urgently needed foreign revolutions to bolster her position in the world.

Third, the main object of the two major slogans "World Revolution" and "Unite, Proletariat and Oppressed Nations of the World" was to oppose capitalist imperialism.

Fourth, most leaders in Moscow thought that the Chinese revolution was opposed to imperialism and to the domestic warlords and reactionary influences that were in collusion with it. The goal of the Chinese revolution should be to establish an independent and free democratic republic.

Fifth, this Chinese revolution must unite the efforts of all the different groups of revolutionary forces in all China. In the final analysis there must be cooperation between the KMT and the CCP. Lenin himself had emphatically brought out this point.

Among us Communists, Ch'en Tu-hsiu was certainly the most

sensitive to politics. He was the first to recognize clearly that these should be the principal points of the CCP political program and that political activities could be started on the basis of them. Ch'en's views in support of these points were generally as follows. The Comintern, the world revolution, and the Soviet Union were inseparable and had to rely on one another for existence, mutually supporting one another to seek common development. There could not be any stereotyped formula or standardized plan for the world revolution; there was only the common goal of opposition to imperialism. At the moment, the nature of the Chinese revolution was by no means the opposition of the working class against the bourgeoisie, but rather opposition to alien aggression and opposition to reactionary warlords. Looking over the country, except for the KMT, which could more or less be considered revolutionary, one could not detect any other revolutionary force. However, when he touched on this point, Ch'en felt that the KMT had many defects, most important of which were its attaching importance to the upper levels of society rather than to the common people, its utilization of bandits, its opportunistic, crafty nature which was readily given to making compromises, and the heterogeneity of its membership, which was permeated by open and concealed internal struggles.

Maring left China to return to Moscow about two weeks before I reached Shanghai. Ch'en Tu-hsiu told me that Maring, accompanied by Chang T'ai-lei, had gone to Kweilin toward the end of 1921[1] with an introduction from Ch'en's old friend Chang Chi to talk with Sun Yat-sen. Maring was quite satisfied with the interview. When he returned from Kweilin to Canton, the Hong Kong seamen's strike was under way. He saw for himself that the KMT supported the strikers and that the workers generally supported the KMT. This impressed him all the more favorably with the KMT. So he felt that it would be possible for Sun Yat-sen to establish friendly relations with the Soviet Union and for the KMT and the CCP to cooperate closely. Then Maring hurried to Moscow, apparently to discuss the concrete measures involved in implementing KMT-CCP cooperation. Ch'en Tu-hsiu, who had had contacts with KMT personalities for many years, felt that Maring's views were much too optimistic, and he seemed to imply a sarcastic comment on Maring's limited experience.

At that time, it had not occurred to the CC or to the CCP members to have Communist Party members actually become members of the KMT. I had not heard such a proposal made in Moscow, nor had

Maring made any such suggestion to Ch'en Tu-hsiu before leaving for Moscow. In our discussions Maring had stressed the possibility of establishing a united front with the revolutionary forces and various Socialist groups in China, and he had proposed methods for carrying this out. Since the KMT was the party holding the position of seniority in such a united front, we were prepared to elect to leadership the veteran Sun Yat-sen and the revolutionary group that he led in the KMT, so that cooperation would be effective and lasting. Also, we assumed that Maring would raise the subject in Moscow, without making any significant changes in our approach. So, concluding that there was no need to wait for Maring's return, we decided to go ahead with our plans.

First, we decided to convene the First National Labor Congress at Canton on May 1, 1922. We believed that the time was right for such a gathering and that it would prove to be highly significant. Early in 1922 trade-union organizations throughout the country had supported the Hong Kong seamen's strike, so that the relations among workers in all areas of both the North and the South were forged closer and their interests were increasingly interrelated. The Secretariat of Labor Organizations in China, moreover, had called upon trade unions all over the country to support the strike, and this had raised its own leadership status. As an experiment, initial KMT-CCP cooperation in the trade-union movement seemed easy to bring about. More important still, the CC of the CCP felt that if a democratic united front of all revolutionary parties and groups was to be established, the CCP must first gain the status of spokesman for the workers.

Next, we decided to hold the First Congress of the SYC at Canton at the same time. The Communist Party's second pillar of strength, the SYC, had a larger membership than the CCP. Up to that time the SYC had not yet established a central leadership organ. We felt that the affirmation of the platform of the SYC and the building of its central leadership organ to carry out the wishes and activities of its members could not be delayed, and this task had to be completed before the Second Congress of the CCP.

We further decided that the Second Congress of the CCP would be held immediately after these two meetings in order to affirm the political tasks of the Party at that stage in its development. But the site of the Congress presented a problem. If Shanghai were chosen, it was evident that we would have to take precautions against interference by the foreign-concession authorities. Holding the Congress at Canton would present no safety problem; still the political situation there had grown complex. Rumors were already circulating within the city that Sun Yat-sen and Ch'en Chiung-ming would come into conflict; and if dissension developed within the KMT, Canton would hardly be a convenient place to hold our Second Congress. So the CC decided that Ch'en Tu-hsiu and I should go to Canton to direct the National Labor Congress and the SYC Congress and that after looking into the political situation there, we should decide whether or not our Party's Second Congress should be held at Canton.

In this way the CC of the CCP planned to march ahead with bold strides. The objective was to see to it that the whole body of CC members, together with the workers and youths led by the Party, develop their activities on the basis of a unified and firmly established political platform. For the CCP, which had been formed less than a year earlier, this was truly a bold venture.

From the very outset the CCP, a small, infantile organization, in its attempt to step on the political stage took rapid strides, leapt forward quickly, shouldered heavy responsibilities, and faced gigantic struggles. Under the circumstances, how could it escape making numerous mistakes that resulted in delays and failures? Here I can only briefly describe some of them.

Most of my comrades were scholars who had just stepped out of their humble abodes, and their minds were filled with utopian ideas and anarchist viewpoints. They held practical politics in contempt and even went so far as to think that politics was unclean or infested with crime. They also had a dislike for such things as discipline, training, close-knit organization, and unity of thought and action. When for the first time I reported to the meeting of all CCP members of the Shanghai district on my visit to Moscow and such problems as KMT-CCP cooperation and the formation of a united front, although no serious argument was provoked, nevertheless surprise and doubt were certainly revealed.

At the same meeting, in accordance with the wishes of the CC, I made a second report, explaining that the Second Congress of the Party would soon be held, principally to affirm the political program; and I called upon my comrades to intensify their understanding of the contents of such a program and to abide by it unanimously, adding that ideological training and the strict enforcement of discipline would be carried out. Ch'en Wang-tao, a scholar who had a very high opinion of himself, thereupon indignantly withdrew from the meeting (eventually he left the CCP altogether). He expressed the view that a CCP member need only believe in Marxism and proceed on the basis of his belief to write articles and carry out work—that would be enough. Basically, he insisted, there was no need for a unanimity of views or for ideological training. Both Shih Ts'un-t'ung and Shen Yen-ping supported his views to a greater or lesser degree. Accordingly, the meeting adjourned without a decision being reached.

No one among us imagined that communism would be achieved in China at an early date. Many believed that if the CCP could have a few more years of preparation to strengthen itself in theory and in organization, then the revolution it took up would be easier to achieve quickly. They often declared that the method of seeking quick results arose out of ignorance of Marxist dialectical materialism. They would even add some stock phrases like "the desire for speed may lead to the failure to achieve the objective" and "the weeds must be plucked to help the growth of the tree." As a result of such viewpoints it was easy to feel that Moscow was overanxious and impatient in always seeking to add the weight of the Chinese revolution to the scale of anti-imperialism. Some people even criticized CCP members who were seeking membership in the KMT of being motivated by the desire to get an official post quickly. It was for reasons closely related to these viewpoints that Li Ta, who opposed the participation of CCP members in the KMT as members, finally withdrew from the CCP.

On the other hand, a small number among our activists had already participated in some political activities. There were rights and wrongs that needed urgent adjustment. For example, Li Ta-chao in Peking was constantly in contact with Hu Shih and other members of the New Culture Movement and even with some Chihli Clique militarists and Research Clique members. He kept up friendly relations with them all and went so far as to join in political activities that they launched—the Movement for a Government by Good Men, for example. In Canton, such CCP members as T'an P'ing-shan, Ch'en Kung-po, and T'an Chih-t'ang were politically very close to Ch'en Chiung-ming, while Lin Po-ch'ü supported Sun Yat-sen and opposed Ch'en Chiung-ming's tendency to create cliques. In Hunan, Mao Tse-tung enthusiastically supported the Federation of Autonomous Provinces Movement. It required great effort to bring about unanimity in our political steps. And it was because of this that T'an P'ing-shan, Ch'en Kung-po, and T'an Chih-t'ang were severely reprimanded by the CC of the CCP.

With regard to the stratagem of having CCP members join the KMT, it was in effect the source of disputes that developed to heaven-rending and earth-shaking proportions. Reviewing the issue now from the traces of history, I find that there was nothing to commend the measure. Maring adopted oppressive measures, relied on the "imperial edict" of the Comintern, and took the opportunity to plan the West Lake Conference which revised and actually overthrew the resolutions of the Second Congress of the CCP, which had only been held a short time earlier, and imposed this stratagem on the CCP rather arbitararily. Unfortunately, in the midst of his jubilant enthusiasm, the clown Maring vanished, and I had no means of knowing what additional schemes he might have cooked up in his head.

The historical drama which thus developed, with the CCP playing the major role, may generally be divided into four acts: first, KMT-CCP Cooperation; second, the Soviet Period; third, the War Against Japan, the Reunification of the KMT and the CCP, and Their Eventual Greater Split; and fourth, Mao Tse-tung's Oppressive Rule of China. The fourth act is not yet concluded. People can only feel that in this historical drama Mao Tse-tung is the sole victor. It is true that from the very beginning of this play Mao Tse-tung has been an important actor. He absorbed the experiences of many sides, completely abandoned the idea of KMT-CCP cooperation, and picked up the treasure of the united front as planned at the Second Congress of the CCP. He added to all this the work styles he had cultivated in his political career, including acridity, gangster tactics, disregard of the means employed, and his versatile guerrilla theory. He is there, riding roughshod in all directions, dancing with his hands and feet. It is still uncertain if he will end up with a broken head. At least, final judgment cannot be passed on him until he is entombed.

In the very opening scene of this play, I myself turned a large "somersault." From the above account, readers will know that I was an important founder of the CCP and also that I carried the responsibility of the CC of the CCP, my position being only second to that of Ch'en Tu-hsiu. At the West Lake Conference I opposed the stratagem of CCP members joining the KMT; and it was because of this that I was attacked. From that time I dropped from my position as an important member of the orthodox group to head of the opposition group. Over my head were placed such labels as opportunist, anti-Comintern element, and rightist. This incident was truly a turning point in my political career. After that I continued to do my best in implementing the policy of KMT-CCP cooperation in the interests of victory for the Chinese revolution and in fostering unity within the CCP, making my obeisance to the majority. But often I could not suppress my sense of righteousness in opposing this policy. Sometimes I faced the contradiction, and sometimes I became depressed. In the process my outlook on life and my revolutionary outlook gradually underwent changes. As I describe these events of the past now, I am still greatly agitated at heart and cannot easily think dispassionately. But I always apply self-restraint. I feel that only by refraining from agitation will I be able to reach a greater understanding. There is no need to complain to other people, there is no call for self-acclaim, and there is no room for regret and repentance; much less should I confuse right and wrong. I only want to use facts to provide some clues that will enable people to study this period of history. If people can absorb some useful lessons from this book, I shall be very satisfied.

The Canton Meetings

The convocation of a National Labor Congress was unprecedented in the history of the Chinese labor movement. The Congress was convened under the aegis of the Secretariat of Labor Organizations in China, and as director of the Secretariat I became busy making preparations for the meeting. Early in April, 1922, the CC of the CCP notified all its local branches of the significance of this Congress. It called upon the local committees of the CCP to assist trade unions in sending delegates. At the same time, under its own name the Secretariat corresponded directly with trade unions throughout the country, soliciting their endorsement of the Congress.

When some important trade unions responded favorably, the Secretariat formally notified labor organizations throughout the country that the Congress would be convened. The text of this notification gave the following information about the Congress:

1. Objects of the Congress:
   a. Commemoration of May Day.
   b. Promotion of friendly relations among the labor organizations of the entire country.

c. Discussion of the improvement of living conditions.

d. Proposals from the delegates.

2. Each labor organization is to send one delegate to the Congress.

3. Time: The Congress will be held for five days, starting on May 1.

4. Place: Canton.

5. Travel expenses are to be provided by the labor organizations themselves. Board and lodging at Canton will be provided by the Secretariat of Labor Organizations in China. The Shanghai reception office is at 19 North Chengtu Road, British Concession (the address of the Shanghai headquarters of the Secretariat).

The Secretariat carefully refrained from putting out propaganda that might make the Congress sound seditious, and it purposely couched the notification in general terms. This was done chiefly to keep the Peking government from curbing trade unions in its area.

An extensive development of the labor movement formed the background against which the Congress was held. The Chinese labor movement reached a high tide in 1922, and the working class was making progress on all sides. The outlook of workers generally tended toward the Left. Trade unions popped up like mushrooms after a rain. The number of strikes increased. Prior to the Congress, the famous Hong Kong seamen's strike occurred; while after the Congress, strikes became even more numerous. This continued until the Peking-Hangkow Railway strike of February 7, 1923, failed because of armed persecution, whereupon the first wave of strikes in the Chinese labor movement ebbed.

The Hong Kong seamen's strike early in 1922 was a major landmark in the labor movement in those days. Indeed, among the struggles waged by Chinese workers, this strike was noteworthy for being large-scale, independent, and organized. It brought closer together the labor movements led by the KMT and the CCP, and it led workers throughout the country toward the road of unity.

Seamen, in fact, were leaders of the modern trade-union movement in China. This was no accident. Seamen constantly traveled to the ports of the world and were the first to be influenced by labor movements abroad, a logical development.

A group of seamen joined the revolutionary movement of Sun Yat-sen at an early date, and this was directly responsible for the early organization of seamen's unions. In 1913, when Dr. Sun failed in his attempt to defeat Yuan Shih-k'ai, he fled to Japan. Under his leadership there, some Chinese seamen at Yokohama organized the Overseas Chinese United Seamen's Society (Chiao Hai Lien-i-she) and, in 1914, the Society for the Welfare of Seamen (Hai-yüan Kung-i-she). The latter subsequently moved its headquarters to Hong Kong, where it was renamed the Seamen's Welfare Society (Hai-yüan Tz'u-shan-she). At that time Dr. Sun regarded the organization of seamen as important chiefly because it could carry out such tasks as transporting arms and transmitting news for the revolutionary movement; and these organizations were the forerunners of the seamen's unions.

In 1920 Hong Kong seamen, in a move against the contract labor system and the threat of unemployment, demanded to be allowed to organize a union. It was the practice of the seamen to live in special seamen's boardinghouses which were frequented by members of their own cliques or by people from their own native districts. These boardinghouses were brought together to form the Seamen's Union Preparatory Committee. Complying with legal requirements, the Committee registered itself with both the Canton and Hong Kong governments. When approval was duly received from them, the Chinese Seamen's Industrial Union Federation (Chung-hua Hai-yüan Kung-yeh Lien-ho Tsung-hui) was formally inaugurated on February 18, 1921. Sun Yat-sen named the union, and it was he who wrote with his own hand the characters used for its official signboard.

On January 12, 1922, the Hong Kong seamen launched their strike. The Chinese Seamen's Industrial Union Federation issued the strike order and led the strike. The objective of the strike, which started among seamen employed on British vessels, was better treatment and higher wages. Gradually the strike spread until eventually every vessel in Hong Kong, irrespective of its nationality, was involved in the strike. By the middle of February, 166 vessels were affected. Wharf and transport workers walked out on strike in sympathy with the seamen, so that all together about 30,000 workers were involved.

The Hong Kong government resorted to highly arbitrary measures in dealing with the strike. It closed down the headquarters of the Chinese Seamen's Industrial Union Federation on February 1 and took steps to make life difficult for the seamen. It also tried to recruit men from India, the Philippines, and Shanghai to take over the jobs of the strikers. The Hong Kong authorities not only failed to achieve the results they desired by these measures, but instead they provoked expressions of sympathy for the strikers from the entire Chinese people.

This was a natural result of mounting patriotism against British colonialism.

Once the strike started, a good many seamen gradually began going to Canton as a gesture of defiance. In this they had support from both the KMT and the CCP. The Kwangtung Federation of Labor Unions (Kuang-tung Tsung-kung Hui), led by the KMT, and the Kwangtung branch headquarters of the Secretariat led by the CCP, both gave the returning strikers an enthusiastic reception and economic aid. Economic support for them also came from the Kwangtung provincial government, while expressions of sympathy poured in from all manner of organizations. As a result the atmosphere of a high tide of revolution surged into Canton, and this greatly excited Maring when he passed through the area.

The CC of the CCP at Shanghai was among the first to express support for the seamen's strike. Moreover, the Secretariat, under CC leadership, gave the strike considerable practical help. Chinese seamen were divided into two principal cliques—the Cantonese clique and the Ningpo clique. On this occasion most strikers were from the Cantonese clique. So the Secretariat worked actively with the seamen of the Ningpo clique, urging them to act in concert with the Cantonese clique. As a result the Hong Kong shipping companies failed to recruit any seamen at Shanghai to replace the strikers. Furthermore, a large sum of money was raised among workers throughout the country to support the strikers. Workers on the Peking-Hangkow Railway displayed on the trains large banners saying "Support the Hong Kong Seamen's Strike," which had a considerable propaganda impact. At the same time various trade unions telegraphed messages and sent money to comfort the strikers, and the movement assumed large proportions. Such things as these greatly stimulated the strikers, who sent back letters of thanks. Thus a tendency toward unity among workers of the whole country was created.

When on March 4 a large number of strikers were marching from Hong Kong to Canton, they were attacked at Shatin by British troops. The result was the Shatin tragedy.[2] It added fuel to the fire and aroused the strikers to flaming indignation, while the nationalistic feelings of the Chinese people mounted against the British. Realizing the seriousness of the situation, the Hong Kong authorities indicated a readiness to make concessions. They revoked the order that had closed the headquarters of the Chinese Seamen's Industrial Union Federation. They also released workers that had been arrested, and they agreed to increase wages by twenty per cent and to pay compensation to the families of workers killed at Shatin. Thus the strike ended on March 8. This victorious struggle of the workers themselves naturally provided a stimulant to the development of the labor movement.

KMT leaders had been interested in the labor movement from an early date. The centers of their activities were Canton—the seat of the Southern government—and Hong Kong, which was just a stone's throw away, and they led most of the trade unions in these two places. The KMT labor movement, however, was on the whole colored by trade-guild influences. In some cases both management and labor were lumped together in the same organization, and very few links existed between the unions. But when the Canton unions started turning toward the Left in support of the Hong Kong seamen's strike, a need was felt to form the Kwangtung Federation of Labor Unions and to cooperate with trade unions in other areas.

Quite different in character was the Hunan Labor Society (Hunan Lao-kung Hui). Anarchism had influenced its leaders, and they worked under the slogan "an independent economic struggle by the workers." For a time it established relatively close connections with the CCP in carrying out its efforts. At the time of the Washington Conference in November, 1921, for example, the Society organized a demonstration of the laboring masses at which it introduced such slogans as "Oppose the Washington Conference," "Oppose International Capitalist Imperialism," and "Oppose Domestic Warlords and Their Running Dogs." These activities obviously were coordinated with those of the Communists. They also were related to the fact that the Society sent Wang Kuang-hui as its representative to the Congress of the Toilers of the Far East. Then on January 7, 1922, workers in the Hua Shih cotton mill at Changsha went out on strike, demanding higher pay. The Society led this strike. Chao Heng-t'i, the governor of Hunan, thereupon used force to disband the Hunan Labor Society, and he arrested and executed its leaders, Huang Ai and P'ang Jen-ch'uan. The incident set off a torrent of indignation among labor organizations throughout the country. It also caused the Hunan Labor Society to change its way of doing things. Thereafter it acted independently.

In North China, the CCP had really had its origins in activities of the railway workers' movement. From the time I started work at Ch'anghsintien to the eve of May 1, 1922, clubs, workers' schools, and trade-union branches were organized at twenty-six major railway stations. They composed the movement's leading organizations. In fact the organization spread through all railways in the North, though not in the Northeast. Local strikes were declared on the Peking-Hankow Railway, the Peking-Suiyuan Railway, the Lunghai Railway, and on the Wuchang-Changsha section of the Canton-Hankow Railway. Organizationally and from the standpoint of their struggles, these railway unions were relatively up-to-date.

At Shanghai—that important Chinese industrial city—the CCP had also worked hard to expand its front in the labor movement. Abandoning the old practice of organizing mere "pasteboard" unions, the Party penetrated directly into the factories and expanded its activities everywhere. Trade unions were organized in cotton mills, machine factories, printing shops, and tobacco factories. Furthermore, the CCP led some rather large-scale cotton-mill strikes and a strike of Yangtze River seamen, which followed the Hong Kong seamen's strike.

At Wuhan and other cities, and at such important mining areas as Kailuan and Anyuan, the Secretariat grew active among the workers, launching unions organized according to trade. Even among workers at Canton and Hong Kong its prestige rose rapidly because it actively supported the seamen's strike.

While the labor movement throughout the country moved toward unity, the KMT failed to take timely, energetic steps to gain leadership. Its influence was restricted to the corner of China at Canton. Meanwhile, anarchists and the anarchist labor unionists utterly ignored organizational measures. They led workers in isolated economic struggles, but their efforts were obviously out of step with the high tide of the movement. Seeing the situation objectively, however, the CCP and the Secretariat of Labor Organizations in China, which was led by the CCP, acted realistically in organizing the First National Labor Congress. As a result the CCP established a position of leadership among the masses of workers, and this was of crucial significance in the subsequent development of the CCP.

The First National Labor Congress was called chiefly to found a united, national trade-union organization. This called not only for KMT-CCP cooperation, but also for the solution of many practical problems regarding the trade unions themselves. When Ch'en Tu-hsiu and I reached Canton toward the end of April, we began working along those lines.

Upon arriving, we called a meeting of the Canton branch of the CCP. To this meeting, Ch'en Tu-hsiu reported the great importance of the Labor Congress and the SYC Congress. He also explained KMT-CCP relations. Lin Po-ch'ü, a former T'ung-meng Hui member whom Ch'en Tu-hsiu invited to join the CCP in 1921,[3] spoke in support of Sun Yat-sen. The "Three Principles of the People" of Sun Yat-sen were most admirable, he said, as was Dr. Sun's proposal to launch a northern expedition; and he contended that KMT-CCP cooperation should center upon cooperation with Dr. Sun. Such comrades as T'an P'ing-shan, Ch'en Kung-po, and T'an Chih-t'ang made speeches somewhat critical of Dr. Sun. In general, they supported Ch'en Chiung-ming. It was their opinion that the disagreement between Sun and Ch'en had been caused by people close to Sun who had alienated Ch'en. They lauded Ch'en Chiung-ming for his sympathetic attitude toward socialism and for the wholehearted support that he gave to the Hong Kong seamen's strike in the name of the Kwangtung provincial government.

Because of the divergent views of comrades toward the KMT, the meeting in question reached no final decision on KMT-CCP cooperation. This naturally left Ch'en Tu-hsiu in an embarrassing position, for while he was chairman of the Education Committee of the Kwangtung provincial government, he got on very well with Ch'en Chiung-ming. In winding up the discussion, he declared that the CCP must cooperate with all KMT revolutionary elements, and that since there was strife within the KMT, we must carefully look into the situation before finally deciding what to do. The National Labor Congress, he pointed out, should avoid involving itself in the KMT's internal problems. It should work for unity, for cooperation among trade unions in all areas irrespective of their party affiliations or sympathies. It should work, in other words, to create a truly national labor organization. The meeting accepted his proposal, and so at that time we did not exhaustively discuss with KMT leaders the question of KMT-CCP cooperation.

A conflict between Ch'en Chiung-ming and Sun Yat-sen had been fermenting for quite some time; now it began to come to a climax. In November, 1920, Dr. Sun returned to Canton from Shanghai; and in April, 1921, Parliament, in extraordinary session at Canton, elected him president. He assumed office on May 5, formally establishing a new government of the Republic of China. In June, after pacifying Kwangsi

Province, he managed to create a situation unfavorable to the Peking government in the Southwest. The military leaders of Yunnan, Kweichow, Szechwan, and Hunan declared that they would not accept orders from Peking. At the same time, however, they put forward as their platform a federation of provincial governments with autonomy for each. They did not, furthermore, support Dr. Sun's proposal of a punitive northern expedition. It was at this time that a divergence of opinion between Sun Yat-sen and Ch'en Chiung-ming began to appear. Dr. Sun advocated using Kwangtung as a revolutionary base from which to launch a northern expedition. Ch'en Chiung-ming thereupon moved in to protect Canton by occupying it. He upbraided Sun Yat-sen for using Kwangtung as a capital for outside adventures that were not in the interest of the people of Kwangtung. Presently, Ch'en Chiung-ming went a step further in advocating a federation of autonomous provinces, each of which would undertake the work of its own reconstruction, a program quite contrary to the views of Sun Yat-sen.

In November, 1921, Sun Yat-sen established headquarters at Kweilin in Kwangsi Province, and he went there from Canton. All troops that were not under Ch'en Chiung-ming were transferred out of Kwangtung and assembled for a march from Kwangsi to Hunan as part of the Northern Expedition. The measure was an obvious concession to Ch'en Chiung-ming, who was given full sway over Kwangtung on the condition that he would furnish money to finance the military campaign. But in February and March, 1922, declaring that he could not raise the money, Ch'en stopped the flow of military funds to Sun Yat-sen. Then General Teng Chien, whose responsibility it was to raise expeditionary funds at Canton, was assassinated in the Canton railway station on March 21, 1922. Teng, a close follower of Sun Yat-sen, was at the time serving as chief-of-staff to Ch'en Chiung-ming, and Ch'en was naturally suspected of being responsible for the murder.

Relations between Sun and Ch'en deteriorated rapidly as a result of these incidents. At the end of March, 1922, Dr. Sun ordered his Northern Expeditionary forces in Kwangsi to return to Kwangtung. A reason for this move was given out for public consumption. It was that to launch the Northern Expedition through Hunan, which was advocating a federation of autonomous provinces, would provoke opposition from the Hunanese military leaders. The army was returning to Kwangtung in order to resume the Northern Expedition by way of Kiangsi instead. Actually, however, Dr. Sun wanted to go back to Canton in order to deal personally with Ch'en Chiung-ming. Sun wanted to stabilize the Kwangtung situation before making his next move. So he led his men to Wuchow and, in mid-April, summoned Ch'en Chiung-ming to see him there. Making excuses, Ch'en stayed where he was. On April 19, Sun retaliated by dismissing Ch'en Chiung-ming from the posts of commander-in-chief of the Cantonese army and governor of Kwangtung. Ch'en then took a part of his army from Canton to Waichow. Sun moved his army to Canton.

Ranking KMT members busied themselves trying to mediate between Sun and Ch'en. It was proposed that Sun send his expeditionary forces to Shiukwan immediately and that from there they move to Tayuling and southern Kiangsi. Ch'en Chiung-ming was to remain as army minister, while Sun was to personally live at the presidential headquarters on Kuan Yin Hill to demonstrate that he had no intention of using force against Ch'en. Outwardly, Ch'en pretended to accept these terms; actually, however, he maneuvered his forces in an attempt to put pressure on Dr. Sun. The attention of everyone, in any event, was focused on the developments of the Sun-Ch'en conflict, and it was not possible for the time being to discuss the question of KMT-CCP cooperation.

The First National Labor Congress opened on schedule the afternoon of May 1, after a large May Day demonstration by masses of Canton workers. Attending the Congress were 162 delegates, representing more than 110 trade unions with a total membership of about 200,000. A majority of the delegates came from Kwangtung and Hong Kong. Among the more prominent figures present were Huang Huan-t'ing, president of the Kwangtung Machine Workers General Union (Kuangtung Chi-ch'i Tsung-kung-hui); Teng Chung-hsia, director of the Peking branch of the Secretariat of Labor Organizations in China; T'an P'ingshan, director of the Canton branch of the Secretariat; Ch'en Ping-sheng and Lin Wei-min, chairman and vice-chairman respectively of the Hong Kong Seamen's Union (Hiang-chiang Hai-yüan Kung-hui); Chu Pao-t'ing, chairman of the Shanghai Seamen's Union (Shang-hai Hai-yüan Kunghui); Teng P'ei, chairman of the Peking-Fengtien Railway Workers Union; and Shih Wen-pin, delegate from the Peking-Hankow Railway Workers Union. As to party affiliations, most delegates were KMT members; CCP members formed the next largest group; and there were also some anarchists.

As director of the Secretariat, I declared the Congress open and summarized the events that led to calling it. Then I proposed that a presidium be elected. The CCP nominated a five-man presidium consisting of Huang Huan-t'ing, Lin Wei-min, T'an P'ing-shan, Teng P'ei, and Hsieh Ying-puo.[4] Because a dialect barrier came between the Kwangtung people and people from the other provinces, T'an P'ing-shan, who spoke both Mandarin and Cantonese, served as chairman throughout the Congress. It was at this Congress that T'an first rose to prominence.

The National Labor Congress took place on the premises of the Kwangtung Machine Workers General Union, which occupied a stately mansion on the south bank of the Pearl River, opposite the islet of Haichu. The Kwangtung Machine Workers General Union, which put up the building itself, had a long history. It was founded in 1907, when it was known as the Kwangtung Machine Workers Study Society (Kwang-tung Chi-ch'i Yen-chiu Kung-hui). In the beginning, it devoted itself mainly to engineering study and research. Membership then was open to factory owners, engineers, technicians, and workers in engineering trades; and its leadership was not in the hands of workers. By 1918 the research body had disintegrated, the factory owners had gradually withdrawn, and it was renamed the Kwangtung Machine Workers General Union. It had become a workers' organization. Then, together with the Hong Kong Chinese Machine Workers Association (Hiang-chiang Hua-jen Chi-ch'i Hui), the union organized the China Machine Workers General Union (Chung-kuo Chi-ch'i Tsung-hui). On its premises hung two signboards—one for the Kwangtung Union, which was a regional organization of Kwangtung machine workers, and one for the China General Union, which used the Kwangtung body to carry on activities among machine workers throughout the country. On February 27, 1922, at the crest of the high tide of support for the Hong Kong seamen's strike, the Kwangtung Machine Workers General Union proposed the organization of a Kwangtung Federation of Labor Unions, preparations for which were to be made by fifty-six trade unions. On October 23 of the same year—after the National Labor Congress—the Kwangtung Federation of Labor Unions was formally established, with more than 120 trade unions participating.

The Kwangtung Machine Workers General Union was a major base for KMT activities in the labor movement. The achievements described above were largely ascribable to KMT labor-movement leaders. A special characteristic of the organization, however, was that certain skilled workers were selected for activities in which a majority of the workers could not participate. It was the majority of workers in the Canton arsenal and in the Canton public utilities who were the organization's mainstay, yet it was from the skilled technicians, who were better off than the majority, that the leaders came. And so the union was to a large extent conservative in nature.

The Kwangtung Machine Workers General Union supported the First National Labor Congress but did not assume a leadership position in it. As a result, leadership of the Congress fell into CCP hands. T'an P'ing-shan, as chairman, conducted the open proceedings and became a conspicuous figure.

Generally speaking, the Congress went along smoothly, and its achievements were noteworthy. It adopted a basic policy, proposed by the Communists, of worker participation in the democratic revolution. The slogans "Down with Imperialism" and "Down with Warlords" embodied this policy. Workers' interests were looked after by the adoption of such proposals as those calling for an "Eight-hour Day," "Support for Strikes," and "Labor Legislation to Protect the Workers' Interests." Moreover, a "Formula for the Organization of Trade Unions" was also passed. It condemned the influence of the old guilds and secret societies on labor organizations. And it called for all workers to be organized according to the factories in which they worked or the trades to which they belonged as a preliminary step toward organizing industrial and vocational trade unions throughout the country. At the same time it urged trade unions in every province and important city to join together in forming provincial and municipal trade-union councils. National industrial trade unions were to join with the various regional trade-union councils to form a National Labor Union Federation.

Since, however, labor throughout the country was still far from completely organized, the Congress agreed that a National Labor Union Federation at that time would be premature. Pending formation of the national organization, it was therefore decided that the Secretariat would act as the center for correspondence between trade unions throughout the country. The Secretariat was also made responsible for calling a Second National Labor Congress. This decision marked the point at which the CCP acquired leadership of the national labor movement.

Meanwhile, the various trade-union delegates were busy outside the sessions of the Congress, for the KMT at Canton, and the organizations it led, welcomed the Labor Congress expansively and held numerous social functions for its delegates. Often I was among the chief speakers at these fraternizing gatherings. Invariably I stressed the need for improving workers' social conditions, the need for a guarantee of freedom for trade-union organization, the need for an alliance of all revolutionary forces in the country, the need to overthrow imperialism and the warlords, and the need to support a revolutionary government that would protect the workers' interests and respect their freedom. The leading KMT speakers, on the other hand, stressed only that a government led by Sun Yat-sen could give freedom to the workers. They gave as proof of this the fact that the Labor Congress could be held only at Canton, and they asked that workers throughout the country support the revolutionary government of Sun Yat-sen. These were among the major topics that workers' delegates and revolutionary figures loudly discussed with one another. The newspapers gave them prominence. An atmosphere of harmony among the different revolutionary groups advanced so noticeably that a call for KMT-CCP cooperation was also raised.

Shortly before the Congress ended, I led a group of delegates from trade unions that were not in Kwangtung to call upon Sun Yat-sen at his presidential headquarters on Kuan Yin Hill. Dr. Sun had politely declined an invitation to address the Labor Congress. He expressed gratification for what we told him of the progress of the Congress, but he gave only perfunctory praise to the achievements of the Congress and declared his hope that its decisions would be energetically carried out. He had nothing further to say. From what I knew of his disposition, I guessed that something urgent needed his immediate attention, and as it turned out, he left for Shiukwan the next day (May 6) to deal with military matters.

Although the KMT led them both, the Hong Kong Seamen's Union, which had been nurtured by the recent seamen's strike, was markedly different from the Kwangtung Machine Workers General Union. At the Congress the former revealed itself to be young, vital, and progressive, and its delegates got on harmoniously with delegates from other areas. Nor did the delegates of other Hong Kong unions often indulge in the pomposity and showing off that characterized Canton union delegates. In fact, the Hong Kong delegates, led by the Seamen's Union, joined in inviting all delegates from unions outside Kwangtung to visit Hong Kong in order to become acquainted with unions there.

And so, more than thirty delegates from various provinces and I visited Hong Kong after the Congress ended. We were welcomed at a grand banquet given by the Seamen's Union that was attended by more than 500 representatives of assorted Hong Kong unions. The banquet hall was elaborately decorated with arches. After a long string of firecrackers was shot off, representatives of the unions delivered addresses of welcome and we thanked them suitably. Su Chao-cheng, who later became a well-known Communist, was then director of general affairs for the Seamen's Union. He was most active and gracious in looking after us. Later, on a similar, equally ebullient occasion, the various Hong Kong unions jointly entertained us at another banquet.

The slogan "Unite, Proletariat of the World" was loudly voiced at these fraternal gatherings, and in fact Hong Kong workers and workers in China proper were brought much, much closer together. Previously, most Hong Kong trade unions were under KMT influence. There was not at the time a single CCP member among the Hong Kong workers. Our visit, however, brought CCP influence to Hong Kong for the first time, and from there it began to spread overseas. In time the Seamen's Union gradually fell into CCP hands, so that the great Canton and Hong Kong strike of 1925 was controlled from start to finish by CCP members.

When the First National Labor Congress ended according to plan, another gathering led by the CCP was under way. This was the First Congress of the SYC, which convened about May 5, the birthday of Karl Marx. By May 3 the first Chihli-Fengtien War, which broke out on April 26 of that year, had resulted in defeat of the Fengtien Army on the western front and its withdrawal north of the Great Wall. News of the Chihli Clique victory was in the newspapers. To be on hand for changes in the Peking political scene, I returned directly to Shanghai with the trade-union delegates after staying three days in Hong Kong. Ch'en Tu-hsiu remained in Canton to direct the work of the SYC Congress.

According to the organizational principles of the Comintern, the SYC was supposed to be a mass organization that acted as a reserve force for the CCP. The CCP was eager that the SYC not develop into a second party similar in nature to itself. It wanted the SYC to carry on entirely under CCP leadership. After the First CCP Congress, steps were taken to regulate the work of the SYC. Some unstable elements were weeded out, while leadership organs, known as secretariats, were established for the various units. The secretariats for such major areas as Shanghai, Peking, and Canton started youth publications in 1922. Meanwhile, the World Christian Student Alliance (Shih-chia Chi-tu-chiao Hsueh-sheng T'ung-meng) scheduled its Eleventh World Congress at Tsinghua University in Peking for April 4. In opposition to this Congress, the Peking Secretariat of the SYC mobilized Peking students to form the Anti-Christian Student Alliance (Fei Chi-tu-chiao Hsueh-sheng T'ung-meng) in March, 1922, and it issued a manifesto. Presently, the Anti-Christian Alliance expanded into the Antireligion Alliance (Fan-tsung-chiao Tai-t'ung-meng), with branches all over the country. During this antireligion movement, some students in Christian schools were expelled, which gave the SYC such a fine chance to stir up the students that for a time the movement was carried along on a high tide.[5]

Prior to its First Congress, the SYC expanded to seventeen units located at Peking, Tientsin, Tsinan, Taiyuan, Sian, Kaifeng, Shanghai, Hangchow, Nanking, Wuhu, Nanchang, Wuhan, Changsha, Chengtu, Chungking, Canton, and Foochow. Membership in these units varied from something over ten to more than 200, while overall SYC membership was about 2,000. Delegates from fifteen units attended the Congress. Prominent among them were Shih Ts'un-t'ung, Kao Shang-te, Yun Tai-ying, and Liu Ch'ang-ch'un.

The major items on the agenda were proposals for the SYC platform and constitution. Included in the platform proposals were the following:

1. Political: Oppose capitalist-imperialist aggression and the armed dictatorship of warlords. Attempt to win suffrage for workers and peasants, along with the freedoms of assembly, organization, speech, publication, and strike.

2. Economic struggle: Protect the interests of young workers, improve the living conditions of children and women workers, limit the working hours of workers under the age of eighteen to not more than six hours a day, give everyone equal pay for equal work, prohibit the employment of children under the age of twelve, strive for a weekly holiday of thirty-six hours, abolish the apprentice system, prohibit the employment of workers younger than sixteen for heavy and dangerous tasks, grant a two-month childbirth leave with pay for women workers, and improve the sanitary facilities of factories.

3. Cultural and educational work: Establish young-workers' clubs everywhere, call meetings to hear lectures, publish popular periodicals that will propagate communism among the youth, and

establish activities that will provide education—including political education—for young peasants and other youths that are normally deprived of schooling.

The major points in the SYC constitution were:

1. Young people between the ages of fifteen and twenty-eight who accept the SYC platform and constitution and are prepared to serve the SYC may be admitted as members in accordance with established procedure.

2. The basic unit of the SYC is the cell, for which a secretary assumes the responsibility. Regional committees are to be formed in the different areas, with a Central Executive Committee the highest organ in the country.

3. A secretariat, an economic section, and a propaganda section are to be established under the Central Executive Committee.

4. The principle of democratic centralism is affirmed, according to which the minority is subservient to the majority and the lower echelons are subservient to the higher echelons.

5. All members are required to abide by SYC discipline. Unjustified absence from cell meetings or failure to pay dues for three months will be punished by dismissal from the SYC.

The Congress elected a Central Executive Committee, with Shih Ts'un-t'ung as secretary. This newly elected Central Executive Committee presently returned to Shanghai and there established the machinery of the SYC center. Relations between the CCP and the SYC were also clearly defined by the Congress. The SYC formally accepted CCP leadership. Thereafter a representative of the CC of the CCP took part in meetings of the Central Executive Committee of the SYC and, from time to time, furnished guidance in policy matters. The Central Executive Committee of the SYC, at the same time, regularly sent a representative to meetings of the CC of the CCP to state the views of the SYC. Local SYC committees likewise accepted guidance from CCP committees on the same organizational level.

Most comrades then regarded the SYC merely as a rather widespread youth organization that should keep the name Socialist, rather than Communist, Youth Corps. In 1925, however, when the SYC held its Third Congress, it was agreed that it had advanced in Communist education sufficiently to be renamed. It was then officially renamed the Communist Youth Corps of China.

The First Congress of the SYC is significant in that it established a national organization for the Youth Corps, clarified its political program, provided aims for its youth activities, and defined the scope of those activities. From then on, the cultural and educational activities of the SYC had far-reaching effects. Indeed the work style of giving careful attention to study, which characterizes the CCP today, was started at that time by the SYC. Yet it was frequently impossible to separate the tasks of the SYC from those of the CCP. CCP members and SYC members often duplicated each other's work, so that the SYC could not escape the appearance of competing with the CCP and of tending to become a second party. Two opposing viewpoints, as a result, very often became the focal point of discussion at SYC meetings—one believed in preserving the independent nature of the SYC, while the other opposed its tendency to evolve into a second party.

Ch'en Tu-hsiu regularly attended the sessions of this SYC Congress, and most of its regulations came from his hand. We were aware of the seriousness of the situation in Canton before I left and realized that it was not an appropriate place to hold the Second Congress of the CCP. It was decided to convene the Congress at Shanghai instead.

When the SYC Congress ended, Ch'en Tu-hsiu, accompanied by Ch'en Kung-po and others, visited Waichow at the invitation of Ch'en Chiung-ming. Apparently Ch'en Tu-hsiu tried to make Sun Yat-sen and Ch'en Chiung-ming realize that an internecine struggle between them should be avoided,[6] but it was already too late for such a move. Ch'en Tu-hsiu felt that the situation was out of control, and so he took the other delegates to the SYC Congress promptly back to Shanghai.

From the Idea of a United Front to Actually Joining the Kuomintang

On June 10, 1922, the CC of the CCP issued its first manifesto on the current situation. This maiden document attacked the movement for a "government by good men" and the current tendency toward political compromise. Against the double oppression of the Great Powers and the warlords, it advocated an alliance of all revolutionary forces. This outcry startled the country. The manifesto injected some new ideas into the Chinese revolution. At the same time it shattered the illusion held by certain celebrated figures and scholars that their plans for improving the China situation were realistic.

Both Ch'en Tu-hsiu and I had returned to Shanghai by the middle of May, 1922. Changes in the political situation in the North promptly confronted us. The Fengtien clique had been driven north of the Great Wall, the Chihli clique completely controlled the Peking government, and Chihli militarists and their advocates began proposing new policies. They proposed that President Hsu Shih-ch'ang in the North and President Sun Yat-sen in the South retire simultaneously, that the old parliament be recalled, that Li Yuan-hung be restored to the presidency, and that a constitution be fashioned. Ts'ao K'un was already trying to exploit Li Yuan-hung as part of a plot to make himself president, but this was not as yet known; so for a time the proposals sparked a favorable popular reaction.

Since the war between the Anhwei and Chihli cliques in July of 1920, the Fengtien and Chihli cliques had been struggling, both openly and secretly, to expand their own respective spheres of influence. At the time of the Washington Conference, Chang Tso-lin installed Liang Shih-i, head of the Communications clique, as premier of the Peking government. The Liang cabinet assumed office on December 24, 1921. This upset the balance of power between the Chihli and Fengtien cliques. Immediately, Wu P'ei-fu began attacking Liang Shih-i. He charged Liang with being pro-Japanese and with negotiating the Shantung question directly with Japan instead of through the Washington Conference.[7] Liang was forced to resign; and this thoroughly enraged Chang Tso-lin.[8] As these incidents assumed greater and greater importance, the First Fengtien-Chihli War broke out. It lasted from April 26 to May 5, 1922, and the Chihli clique emerged the victor.

At that time, there actually were indications in the China situation that gave cause for optimism. The Washington Conference was chiefly called to resolve conflicts among such powers as Britain, the United States, and Japan in the Pacific and to reduce armaments. But its decisions also covered the territorial sovereignty and integrity of China and provided for consultations to improve the customs and tariff arrangements in China and to explore the question of extraterritoriality. Furthermore, the Fengtien-Chihli War, which was related to the Washington Conference, reflected a decline of foreign influence in China. Most people grew optimistic. They believed that the Washington Conference had opened the way for curbing foreign aggression. For the defeat of the Fengtien clique was regarded as a blow to Japanese influence in China, and the Fengtien clique was replaced by the anti-Japanese patriotic military leader Wu P'ei-fu. These developments gave hope that the trend toward the extermination of China by Japan, which had been noticeable since World War I, had reached a turning point.

And so, many prominent figures and scholars, people like Hu Shih, looked upon Wu P'ei-fu as a man who would try to build a good government. It was these people who published in the weekly journal *Endeavor* (Nu-li chou-pao) the proposal for a "government by good men." They advocated that everyone whom the nation regarded as a good man, irrespective of party affiliation, should step forward and organize a "government by good men." The "good men" would see to it that the *tu-chun* (military governor) system was abolished and that the armed forces of the warlords were reduced. They would publicize government financial statements, carry out the wishes of Parliament, formulate a constitution, see to the establishment of a federation of autonomous provinces, and stop all civil war in order to achieve national unification by peaceful means.

Early in June of 1922 the political situation in Peking began to clarify itself. On June 2 Hsu Shih-ch'ang announced his retirement. Li Yuan-hung agreed to resume office only if the tu-chun system were done away with and warlord armies reduced. Propaganda about a "government by good men" created especially widespread public support, and Li Ta-chao wrote to us saying that while the current tangled political situation continued, the idea must be accepted as a measure that, to a degree, was saisfactory to the people. Some New Culture Movement friends, who were not also members of our Party, directly or indirectly expressed the hope that the CCP would support the proposed "government by good men." As a result the CC realized that there was an urgent need for it to issue a statement of its own ideas about the current situation—a statement based on policies formed at the Congress of the Toilers of the Far East and linked to current Chinese developments.

It was the unanimous view of the CC in discussing this question that the Washington Conference could not possibly pave the way for an improvement in China's international status; that foreign influence would, from start to finish, obstruct progress in China; that while Japanese influence had suffered a setback, the Powers together would continue to carve up China; that it was impossible to wipe out the tu-chun system or to reduce the warlords' armies, and that the warlords would continue to fight each other and to rule the country; that the "government by good men" proposal merely obstructed the development of revolutionary thought and that it led the people as a whole down the wrong and illusory path of revisionism.

Most comrades in Shanghai ridiculed the theory of "government by good men," perhaps because the atmosphere in Shanghai encouraged people to see the dark side of Peking. In any event, when we raised the issue at a meeting of all comrades in Shanghai, most of them took an aggressive stand on it. There was no need to wait for the Second CCP Congress, they insisted, nor did we need to worry about keeping good relations with such "government by good men" figures as Ts'ai Yuan-p'ei and Hu Shih; we should immediately make our own views public. Ch'en Tu-hsiu was elected to draft a manifesto. The CCP had not yet adopted the practice of having a number of people work together in drawing up its official documents. This time, however, Ch'en Tu-hsiu declared at the meeting that he wanted all comrades to frankly revise the draft he would produce so that it would be a collective product.

As it turned out, Ch'en's draft passed without much revision when it was brought up for discussion. It pointed out various KMT failures that had resulted from compromise, it opposed the proposal for a "government by good men," and it criticized all tendencies toward revisionism and compromise. As the goal of the revolution, it propounded a democratic political program. Looking at the document now, it becomes obvious that Chinese attitudes permeated it.

The document, which was regarded as the first CCP pronouncement on the situation in China, listed concrete measures for establishing a revolutionary united front: "The CCP takes the initiative in calling a conference, to be participated in by the revolutionary elements of the KMT and revolutionary Socialists, to discuss the question of creating a united front to struggle against warlords of the feudal type and against all relics of feudalism. This struggle against a broad united front is a war to liberate the Chinese people from a dual yoke—the yoke of foreigners and the yoke of powerful militarists in our country—a war which is just as urgently needed as it is inevitable."

The manifesto was adopted about June 10, 1922.[9] Afterward, in mid-June, I was sent to Peking to bring about the political agreement of Li Shou-ch'ang (Li Ta-chao) and others. I took with me a number of printed copies of the CCP's "Manifesto on the Current Situation," which I gave to Li. I explained the situation to him, and then we discussed it. Without hesitation he declared his agreement. He added that for a time he thought the "government by good men" proposal to be practical, but that as the situation developed, he saw less cause for optimism in it. The people around Ts'ao K'un wanted to make him president, but the man himself had ulterior motives. Even Wu P'ei-fu was losing favor with Li Ta-chao, and Li was even less hopeful that the tu-chun system would be abolished or that armed forces would be reduced. He therefore regarded the manifesto of the CC at Shanghai as appropriate.

When Li got together with those of his friends who supported the "government by good men" proposal, he gave them the printed copies of the manifesto that I had turned over to him. Some of his friends dismissed the manifesto by observing that Chung-fu (the courtesy name of Ch'en Tu-hsiu) was always fond of bringing up new issues and that this was merely another example of his raising his voice in opposition. After consideration, however, others agreed that no good would come from the "government by good men" and that the views of Chung-fu were not without foundation. It was with a good deal of gratification that Li transmitted these reactions to me.

Li Ta-chao pointed out to his friends that the ideas in the manifesto did not belong exclusively to Ch'en Tu-hsiu, that they were the carefully considered opinions of a newly risen group to which he belonged. He had distributed the document among them for that reason. In this way the proposal of the CCP began to impress these people. Some began to express sympathy for the Party. For others it marked the point at which they began to take their leave of the Party.

To a meeting of the whole body of CCP members in Peking I reported on the great care that the CC had taken in issuing this manifesto. All of them declared their support for it. The younger comrades, who inclined especially to the Left, saw no hope in the "government by good men," and some of them believed that the CC had not take a sufficiently strong stand. In their view it was not possible for the Chinese bourgeoisie to be revolutionary. They thought that the CC should make itself the backbone of the revolution. Nevertheless, in order to destroy the revisionist illusions then current and to explain the realities of the situation, the meeting unanimously passed a resolution supporting the stand of the CC and calling for the development of propaganda among the northern masses. At the same time, the meeting decided to take advantage of the relatively greater freedom that obtained then in Peking to demand labor legislation, abolition of security police measures, organization of an anti-imperialist alliance, and opposition to imperialist activities. In time these activities carried out by the comrades in the North brought suitable results.

After about a week in Peking, I returned to Shanghai where I reported the Peking events to the CC. In keeping with the constitution, which called for an annual congress, the CC actively began to prepare for the Second Congress.

It was at that time that comrades Ts'ai Ho-sen and Hsiang Ching-yu were deported from France and returned to China. Influenced by the European Communist movement, the two of them—husband and wife—showed themselves to be sincere and enthusiastic Marxists. While in France, they had been harassed by the French government. They had also been involved there in disputes with Li Shih-tseng and Wu Chih-hui, who were then in charge of "working student" activities. In any event, they were outraged by what had happened to them and eager to return to their country to do something worthwhile. Liu Shao-ch'i, Yüan Ta-shih, and Ch'en Wei-jen, who had been studying in Russia, returned to Shanghai from Moscow. They had received considerable Comintern training, and all of them now were ready to demonstrate their abilities in practical work in China.

These new arrivals unanimously endorsed the "First Manifesto on the Current Situation," but they were not satisfied with various portions of it. Ts'ai Ho-sen pointed out that the document did not fully explain the role of the Chinese proletariat and its vanguard, the CCP. It was his view that the Chinese bourgeoisie could not play the positive role that the bourgeoisie of France played in the French Revolution. For China, he said, was a semi-colony, and Chinese workers ought to join forces with the broad masses of the peasantry and the petty bourgeoisie to form an anti-imperialist revolutionary alliance.

While they were abroad the newcomers had thought that CCP activities were well organized and dynamic. But upon returning to China they discovered that laxity characterized everything the Party did. The absence of unanimity of political views among Party members greatly distressed them, and they began stressing my proposal to bring about a unification of views and to introduce ideological training. Moreover they regarded the labor movement under my leadership to be, relatively speaking, exemplary; and they insisted that all Party tasks, especially political activities, emulate the labor movement.

Ch'en Tu-hsiu gave great weight to the views of these comrades who had returned from abroad. They would add new blood to the Party, he declared, while correcting the outlook of comrades in China that were too much the products of their environment. Much encouraged, he agreed that the Second Congress should produce another manifesto that would include material absent from the first document.

The time arrived for the Second Congress of the CCP to convene; but Li Ta-chao, Mao Tse-tung, and the delegates from Canton, all of whom were scheduled to attend the Congress, failed to arrive.[10] We waited a few days and then formally opened it about July 10, 1922, in a house on Chengtu Road, Shanghai, which the CC rented.

There were about 123 members of the CCP at that time, and only nine official delegates actually attended the Congress. Ch'en Tu-hsiu, Li Ta, and I, as members of the first CC, were ex officio delegates. Ts'ai Ho-sen represented the CCP group in France, Kao Shang-te represented Peking, Pao Hui-seng represented Wuhan, and there was one delegate from Shanghai and one from Hangchow whose names I do not remember. Shih Ts'un-t'ung represented the CC of the SYC. In addition to these nine official delegates, observers, including Chang T'ai-lei and Hsiang Ching-yu, also attended.

First, the Congress heard reports from the CC. In his report, Ch'en Tu-hsiu discussed the general status of CC work and the political proposal it had issued. I reported on the Congress of the Toilers of the Far East, the status of the labor movement, and the First National Labor Congress. Shih Ts'un-t'ung reported on the First Congress of the SYC. The Congress devoted one whole day to listening to and discussing these reports. It decided to ratify the work of the CC, the "Manifesto on the Current Situation," and the resolutions of the Labor and SYC congresses. Because of security problems imposed by the situation in Shanghai at that time, we decided not to hold regular plenary sessions, which involved too many people, in order to avoid detection. Then the Congress elected a committee composed of Ch'en Tu-hsiu, Ts'ai Ho-sen, and myself to draft a manifesto. When our draft was finished, it was agreed that another plenary session would be called to discuss and act on it and to elect a new CC at the same time.

The drafting of a political manifesto was, in fact, the one important task of the Congress. Ts'ai Ho-sen and I elected Ch'en Tu-hsiu to actually draft it. After two days he produced a first draft and laid it before the drafting committee for discussion. The committee met several times. Ts'ai Ho-sen made many revisions and inserted numerous supplementary ideas, and I put in some suggestions.

After having been suspended for about one week, the Congress again met in plenary session and ratified the draft of the manifesto that we had produced. Then we elected a new CC, which everyone agreed should consist of only three members. Li Ta announced that in his one year of CC work he had come to realize that he was more suited to the work of writing. Since, in any case, he was preparing to go to Hunan to take up a teaching job, he asked that he not be placed in charge of propaganda again. As a result of the election, Ch'en Tu-hsiu, Ts'ai Ho-sen, and I became the members of the second CC, and we were placed in charge of secretariat, propaganda, and organization affairs respectively.

The "Manifesto of the Second Congress of the CCP"[11] obviously consisted of the "First Manifesto on the Current Situation" of June 10 with important additions and revisions. In dealing with China's international relations, the document actually listed examples of alien aggression against China while intensifying the anti-imperialist aspects of the "First Manifesto." In dealing with the domestic situation in China, the new document retained references to opposing feudalism, but it did not repeat the call to oppose the feudalistic system of the bourgeoisie. Instead, it vaguely referred to the neutral nature of the Chinese bourgeoisie, while emphasizing the need to establish a democratic united front of Chinese workers, poor peasants, and petty bourgeoisie.

This manifesto formally declared that "the Chinese Communist Party is a branch of the Communist International" and stressed that "in assisting the national revolution, the proletariat is not capitulating to the bourgeoisie, but is, rather, taking a necessary step toward shortening the life of feudalism and toward cementing the proletariat into a real force." It reiterated as the major political goal the establishment of a democratic united front to consist principally of the democratic forces of the Sun Yat-sen group, which it interpreted as coming from the petty bourgeoisie and the enlightened segment of the bourgeoisie. It also introduced the theory of a democratic revolution to be followed by the second revolutionary stage of the Soviet Union.

The CC of the CCP truly worked hard throughout this period to bring about a unanimous political outlook among Party members, and this gave rise to an inner-Party struggle. About June 10, when the CC issued its "Manifesto on the Current Situation," we distributed printed copies of it to Sun Yat-sen and certain other important KMT people. We expressed to them the hope that a united front with our two parties as its mainstay might be realized at an early date. Then, on June 16, Ch'en Chiung-ming surrounded the presidential headquarters of Dr. Sun. This caused Ch'en Tu-hsiu to inform Chang Chi and other prominent KMT members then in Shanghai that Ch'en Chiung-ming, with whom they had once cooperated, had betrayed the revolution. Ch'en Tu-hsiu assured them that the CCP would sever connections with Ch'en Chiung-ming and join in the attack against him. The CC wrote to T'an P'ing-shan and other responsible members of the Canton branch of the CCP, demanding that they immediately sever all connections with Ch'en Chiung-ming and declare their support for Sun Yat-sen. Party members at Canton, however, did not submit to this CC directive. Ch'en Kung-po and T'an Chih-t'ang continued to work for the Canton newspaper *Ch'un Pao* and to write articles supporting Ch'en Chiung-ming. The CCP thus demonstrated that it harbored two diametrically opposed political stands.

To cope with this embarrassing situation, the CC stepped up its overtures to the KMT. It asked Sun Yat-sen to take the initiative in calling a conference of the revolutionary forces of all organizations, and declared that the CCP would not, because of his temporary setback, alter its stand of cooperating with him. The CC said that it would actively oppose all reactionary views and actions that lent support to Ch'en Chiung-ming and that it was, moreover, taking steps to rectify the mistaken attitude of individual Party comrades in Kwangtung who supported Ch'en Chiung-ming.

After the Second Congress of the Party, the CC again wrote to the committee of the Canton branch of the Party, sternly taking it to task for its incongruous attitude toward Ch'en Chiung-ming. A harsh warning was given Ch'en Kung-po and T'an Chih-t'ang. They were told that if they did not change their attitude, they would be expelled from the Party. T'an P'ing-shan, who was secretary of the Canton branch, was told that if he continued to tolerate the defiant actions of the others, he too would incur severe disciplinary action. Even then these comrades did not fully comply with the CC directive. As a result, T'an Chih-t'ang was expelled from the Party, Ch'en Kung-po received a scathing warning and withdrew from the Party, while T'an P'ing-shan, who received a reprimand, was temporarily relieved of his duties as secretary of the Canton branch.

This incident was a significant illustration of the CC's determination to thoroughly implement its political proposals and to maintain political discipline. At the same time it left Ch'en Tu-hsiu terribly dejected. He could not help feeling that he was the patriarch of a family. The fact that such an unpleasant incident had arisen within his Communist Party family depressed him. T'an P'ing-shan, Ch'en Kung-po, and T'an Chih-t'ang, long before they began cooperating directly with Ch'en Chiung-ming, had come under the influence of Ch'en Tu-hsiu when he was chairman of the Kwangtung Provincial Education Committee. When Ch'en Chiung-ming openly revolted, however, they were unable to distinguish right from wrong as Ch'en Tu-hsiu could, and Ch'en Tu-hsiu had been forced to invoke Party discipline to restrain them. In his innermost heart, he could not avoid feeling like Chu-Ko Liang, who, with tears in his eyes, ordered the execution of his favorite general, Ma Su, who had committed a grave blunder by disobeying orders.

A few days after the Second Congress ended, Maring returned to Shanghai. He promptly dashed cold water on the efforts the CCP had made to build up its political program. He castigated the united front as an impractical leftist idea. It was like having a robber suddenly loom up in the middle of the road down which you were walking.

At one of our meetings with Maring, he explained that Sun Yat-sen would not agree to a united front. The only thing that Sun would agree to, he said, was inviting CCP members to join the KMT. Furthermore, he stated that the Comintern endorsed the idea of having CCP members join the KMT and considered it a new route to pursue in achieving a united front. Maring proposed that the CC call another meeting to discuss the question; but we disregarded his proposal. Some of us treated it with the utmost sarcasm, suggesting that we call another congress to revise our resolution. Maring was left feeling that he could do nothing about the situation.

Needless to say, however, Maring stopped at nothing to see his proposal carried out. The so-called problem of factions within the Party provided him with exactly the opportunity he sought. It enabled him to realize his desire to call a special plenum of the CC.

At the time of the Second Congress the CC divided Party members in Shanghai into several small groups in order to make it easier to hold meetings in secret. These groups discussed general political issues and introduced ideas that were referred to the Congress for discussion in connection with its manifesto. The small group that I headed was the largest and was made up of workers in the Secretariat of Labor Organizations in China. After the Congress closed, this group continued to hold meetings, chiefly to discuss labor problems, although most participants were interested in political questions, too.

While our debate with Maring over the question of having CCP members join the KMT was still under way, the issue came up at one of our small group meetings. Chang T'ai-lei, who called to see me on business, joined in the group discussion. When we finished dealing with Secretariat affairs, Liu Shao-ch'i and Yüan Ta-shih aired their feeling that there was too little discussion of political questions within the Party. The membership, they said, tended to be uninformed about these things. They requested that the practice initiated during the Second Congress be continued and that at each group meeting there be some discussion of political questions. They were followed by other comrades, who declared their opposition to the proposal that CCP members join the KMT. The effect of this on Chang T'ai-lei was to make him uneasy. Chang T'ai-lei's practice of saying yes to all of Maring's whims had already somewhat irritated the comrades that had recently returned from Russia and France, and they could not resist this chance to intensify their opposition, intentionally making a show of it before Chang.

Chang T'ai-lei immediately reported the happenings at the small group meeting to Ch'en Tu-hsiu. He pointed out that the question of CCP members joining the KMT was still under secret negotiation between a small number of CC members and Maring. How was it that comrades in general knew all about it? According to Chang, the fact that a small group meeting was discussing a policy not yet passed by the CC might be misinterpreted to mean that there was more than one Party center; people might say that it was producing a tendency to form factions within the Party. At first this report by Chang T'ai-lei rather annoyed Ch'en Tu-hsiu. No group of members, he declared, should discuss a question that was still secret and undecided.

I went to see Ch'en Tu-hsiu about the matter. Without allowing me to explain, he announced that we had done nothing wrong and that there was no need to mention it again. In great good humor, he told me it was he who had talked about joining the KMT to the comrades taking part in our small group discussion. He had told them that one must be fingerprinted and swear allegiance to Sun Yat-sen in order to join the KMT and that CCP members would have to comply with this procedure if they were to join it. What possible relationship was there between this, he had asked them, and our strategy of forming a united front? So, he thought that I was not the one who had raised the issue that moved the comrades to oppose Maring. Rather, he thought that perhaps they had learned of the problem from his own conversation, had felt concerned about it, and so had begun discussing it. Ch'en added that he had not really considered this possibility when Chang T'ai-lei mentioned the incident to him. Now, however, to avoid further misunderstanding, he said that he would explain everything to Chang T'ai-lei.

As soon as Maring heard about the incident, he quickly made capital of it. He made an appointment to see me alone. He took pains to remind me that after the First Congress of the CCP I had done my best to persuade him to respect Ch'en Tu-hsiu. My advice had proved to be altogether correct, and he was very grateful to me. Yet the things I was now doing consciously or unconsciously, he said, tended to oppose Ch'en Tu-hsiu. He therefore wanted to give me the same advice I once gave him. When I objected to his viewpoint, he went on to say that the Party had carried out a direct struggle against Ch'en Kung-po and the others in order to affirm its political stand; but that did not solve everything. For apart from the Canton affair, Party members were being relegated to two categories—those who were active and those who were passive. And it seemed, according to Maring, that somehow I was regarded as the representative of the active group, whereas Ch'en Tu-hsiu was in certain respects looked upon as less active. These matters had already created a feeling that differences of opinion existed, he said. True, Ch'en had repudiated his initial statement to Chang T'ai-lei; nevertheless, Maring said that the minute Chang had mentioned the problem of factions within the Party, Ch'en had reacted with a great deal of emotion. This, he claimed, clearly proved that divergent opinions really did exist. Maring said that the opposition to joining the KMT expressed in the small group discussion did not worry him; he merely hoped that I would not oppose the calling of a special plenum of the CC, which he considered essential for reaching a decision on Party policy and for eliminating differences within the Party.

Li Ta-chao arrived at Shanghai about this time. The responsible members of the CC realized that if we had postponed the Second Congress a little bit longer, both he and Maring would have been able to attend it. And now that Maring had raised views different from those which had emerged from the Congress, perhaps this was a good time for all of us to get together and talk things over. Furthermore, Li Ta-chao, with his more realistic approach to things, concluded after contacting Maring that Maring's ideas were worth considering. So the CC decided to hold a special plenum at West Lake.

Early in August, 1922, about three weeks after the Second Congress, a conference even more important than the Congress convened at West Lake. Its participants included Ch'en Tu-hsiu, Li Ta-chao, Maring, Ts'ai Ho-sen, Chang T'ai-lei, Kao Shang-te, and myself. Li Ta-chao and Maring were attending their first formal CC meeting. They both played very positive roles in it. The two-day Plenum particularly discussed the question of CCP members participating in the KMT. Although the "Manifesto of the Second Congress" was not formally revised, this meeting affirmed the famous policy of CCP cooperation with the KMT by actually operating within the KMT, which in effect did revise the original policy decided upon at the Second Congress of the CCP.

Maring was the chief speaker. He persisted in his view that CCP members must join the KMT. Apparently to placate the opposition, however, he did not say that what ailed the "Manifesto of the Second Congress" was infantilism. His argument was that the only practical concrete measure for bringing about a KMT-CCP united front was for CCP members to participate in the KMT. The major reasons he gave for this position were as follows:

1. For a very long time to come, we in China would be faced not by a Socialist revolution, but by a national democratic revolution. At the moment, the proletariat had very limited strength and influence.

2. The KMT of Sun Yat-sen was currently a strong, democratic, national revolutionary political party. It must not be regarded as the political party of the bourgeoisie, but rather as an alliance of the revolutionary elements in all social strata.

3. Since Dr. Sun was prepared to go no farther than to accept CCP members into the KMT, he obviously was not prepared to establish a united front with the CCP by placing the CCP on an equal footing with the KMT.

4. The CCP must learn from the trade-union movement in Western Europe, where the Comintern had gained experience by promoting the practice of having Communists join united fronts of Social Democratic parties and trade unions. The CCP must respect the wishes of the Comintern.

5. By joining the KMT, CCP members could work to unite all revolutionary influences and make the KMT more revolutionary. At the

same time, a large portion of the working masses led by the KMT could be influenced to come over to the side of the Communists.

Ts'ai Ho-sen and I spoke out against Maring's ideas. So far as we were concerned, the case of CCP members joining the KMT could not be compared with Western European Communists and workers joining Social Democratic parties and trade unions. The KMT was the political party of the bourgeoisie. By joining it, CCP members would be merged with the bourgeoisie, and in this way the CCP would lose its independent identity. This did not conform with the theses propounded by the Second Comintern Congress. We pointed out that it was possible to remain outside the KMT and still establish a united front with it; this had been done before in alliances between the KMT and other parties and groups. If we organized a united-front committee, Sun could be elected its chairman, and the KMT members on the committee could be about twice the number of CCP members. What we tried to explain was that the CCP was not asking for a united front in which the CCP would hold a position parallel to that of the KMT, but that the CCP only desired to retain its independent status. We also pointed out emphatically that the CCP had tasks in addition to establishing a united front with the KMT and cooperating with it. We also had to pay attention to the broad masses of workers and peasants that did not fall under the KMT in order to build up our own ranks. On the basis of these arguments, we insisted that Maring's ideas be rejected and that the Comintern be asked to reconsider the question.

Ch'en Tu-hsiu was the chief spokesman against Maring's views. He stressed that the KMT was principally the political party of the bourgeoisie. Simply because there were some nonbourgeois elements within its ranks did not mean that we could overlook the fact that its basic character was bourgeois. He also explained in detail that numerous complicated problems, which would be difficult to solve, would arise once CCP members joined the KMT and that in the end these would be detrimental to the unity of revolutionary forces. Nevertheless, Ch'en said that if this were an unalterable Comintern decision, we would have to abide by it. The most we could do was to voice our dissenting opinions.

Ch'en set conditions for obeying the decision, even though Maring declared it to be a firm Comintern policy. Ch'en stipulated that if Dr. Sun revoked the rule forcing people joining the KMT to take an oath of allegiance to him personally and to sign the oath with their fingerprints and if he reorganized the KMT so that it was based on democratic principles, CCP members would join it. If these conditions were not met, Ch'en said he would oppose joining the KMT even though the Comintern ordered it.

Li Ta-chao assumed a conciliatory position. While he sympathized with some of our ideas and praised the conditions which Ch'en set, basically he supported Maring. He observed that the KMT was very lax organizationally. Anarchists, he said, had been joining the KMT for years and, as KMT members, had continued to carry on anarchist propaganda. They were not restrained in any way. Even the strictly KMT members held an assortment of political views, and there were many examples of their independent political activities. He felt that the easiest method of achieving unity was to join the KMT.

It was on the basis of views such as these that Li Ta-chao undertook to mediate between the two sides. He explained that by participating in the KMT under set conditions and by having a few CCP leaders join the KMT to serve as a bridge for cooperation between the two parties, we would eventually carry out the policy fixed by the Second Congress while avoiding a serious clash with Maring and possibly with the Comintern as well. And so Ch'en Tu-hsiu proposed that when the KMT dropped the requirement of taking an oath and signing it with fingerprints and when it agreed to reorganize itself along democratic lines, a small number of responsible CCP comrades, who would be named by the Party, could become members of the KMT. This proposal was passed, although it was not put into writing. It was accepted as a mutual understanding. The decision clearly included appropriate revisions of Maring's original proposal, which called for unconditional and unrestricted participation by CCP members in the KMT.

Then Maring took from his pocket the prepared text of a resolution on the problem of the establishment of factions. It briefly stated that no factions existed within the Party at the time, but that there was a tendency toward their establishment. While this tendency had sprung from an innocent love for the Party, it should not have existed in the first place, much less should it be permitted to exist in the future. The unexpected appearance of such a resolution brought the meeting to a state of tension. Everybody lapsed into silence for a time. Ch'en Tu-hsiu looked surprised and embarrassed. Evidently he had never seen the document before and did not expect Maring to by-pass him and lay things directly before the meeting.

Finally, Ts'ai Ho-sen stood up to declare that there was absolutely no need for such a resolution. No tendency toward the establishment of factions was indicated, he said, when an officially sanctioned group discussion raised current political issues, even when opposition was expressed to policies on which the CC had not reached a decision. To pass such a resolution would be to suppress democratic freedom of discussion within the Party, he said. Kao Shang-te, who shared our opposition views on the united-front issue, indignantly berated Maring for trying to suppress opposition views.

Unable to contain himself any longer, Maring began to bear down on me. He proclaimed sternly that the statements of comrades Ts'ai and Kao proved that some young comrades from the CC actually were tending toward becoming a leftist opposition faction and that I must be held responsible for this. At the very least, he said, I had done nothing to correct the tendency. He hoped that I would allow the resolution to pass without incident and that no further mention would be made of the matter.

With considerable effort, I managed to remain calm. I got to my feet to say that I stood against any tendency toward the establishment of factions within the Party, that I did not believe such a tendency existed, and that I therefore would not support the resolution. I started to accuse Maring of being rude and ridiculous, but Li Ta-chao leapt up and interrupted.

Li praised everybody for frankly exchanging ideas, for reaching agreement on the problem of joining the KMT, and for the fine spirit of harmony that had made mutual concessions possible. It would be best, he said, to let Maring's resolution lie where it was as a reminder in the future. He declared that I was not tending toward factionalism and that he felt sure the other comrades had this same confidence in me. Ch'en Tu'hsiu made a point of saying that he, too, believed there was no tendency in me to establish a faction. Nevertheless, it was his opinion that since the generalized resolution had been brought up, it ought to be left to lie where it was. Because the CCP did not wish to aggravate the disagreement and because it is traditional with the Chinese to consider the face of each person in a dispute, the resolution was not voted down as I proposed. Instead, it was placed on the record under an ambiguous ruling to "let it lie where it was." Seeing that I had the confidence of Ch'en Tu-hsiu and Li Ta-chao and that he lacked the support of the other comrades, Maring decided to drop the argument.

The mingling of the so-called problem of factions with the policy of joining the KMT subsequently led to many disagreements within the CCP. It was the first occasion on which the Comintern method of suppressing the opposition through inner-Party struggle was introduced to China. Actually, although neither Ch'en Tu-hsiu nor I ever again mentioned the episode, the fact that the resolution was not voted down caused uneasiness in both of us. A dark shadow passed over our normally open friendship. Here was a valid example of the fact that when unanimity was forced upon Communist Party members, pain and anguish followed.

Maring had brought into play literally all the power at his command, yet his proposal had barely been carried. The result was both his victory and his defeat. Afterward, while we kept in touch in connection with our work, he grew cautious in speaking to me. I had reacted vehemently to the whole affair, but I could not help laughing at his foolishness. When he presented his resolution, he quite possibly believed that his power was sufficient to arbitrate all matters within the ranks of the CCP. He had not attracted the support he anticipated, however. Instead, he had made people feel that he was abusing his authority and inciting dissension. I lost the respect that I had felt for him as a veteran. I began to see him as a man who regarded me as an opponent and who would stop at nothing in order to strike out at me. I even suspected that his policy of making us join the KMT was designed to dissolve the CCP in the KMT and that he would opportunistically use such points as the resolution on factions to attack his opponents in a distorted report to Moscow. All these things laid the foundations for a final break between us.

Ch'en Tu-hsiu seemed to have the same reactions at the meeting. When discussion of the so-called problem of factions ended, he arose and proposed that Li Ta-chao remain in Shanghai for a little while in order to establish relations with the KMT. He also proposed that I be appointed representative of the CC to visit Peking, Wuhan, and Changsha. My mission was to transmit the decisions of the various CC meetings, to win unanimous support for them, and to steer the development of Party affairs and the labor movement in these areas. Ch'en said that this demonstrated complete confidence in me. Everyone present supported his proposals, for they thought that the move would, to a certain extent, heal the disagreements.

The policy of joining the KMT could not, of course, be carried out merely because the CCP had decided upon it. It was the needs of Sun Yat-sen and the KMT that presently led to early implementation of the policy.

The ever-changing political fortunes of modern China left Sun Yat-sen a disillusioned man. Moreover, the Powers never adopted a friendly attitude toward him. After World War I he wrote *The International Development of China,* in which he proposed to use the organizational, managerial, and skilled technical personnel that the Powers had employed in the War to develop China's rich natural resources. The Powers received the idea coldly. Nor did the Powers accept his proposal to send his own delegation to the Washington Conference, which caused Wu Ch'ao-shu, then deputy foreign minister of the Southern government, to refuse an appointment by the Peking government to the Chinese delegation. The Southern government declared that it would not accept as binding any decisions of the Washington Conference with regard to China. Meanwhile, Sun Yat-sen sent Chang Ch'iu-pai as his delegate to the Congress of the Toilers of the Far East at Moscow.

Especially in domestic affairs it was necessary for Dr. Sun to constantly fight political enemies around him, both militarists and nonmilitarists. He repeatedly suffered reverses. And while he steadfastly attempted to win understanding and sympathy from the Powers, they generally lent their support to his enemies. Incidents exemplifying this are too numerous to mention and caused him endless trouble. Thus, although his revolutionary ideas formed a background for his pro-Russian policy, that policy was nevertheless forced upon him by the course of events.

Toward the end of 1921, when Maring interviewed Dr. Sun at Kweilin, the two very quickly found common interests. They explored the field of Sino-Soviet relations, and Dr. Sun came to better understand the Soviet Union. On the question of KMT-CCP relations, an understanding seems to have been reached about members of the CCP joining the KMT as members. For at the West Lake Plenum, it was with great confidence that Maring claimed that Sun Yat-sen favored the idea of CCP members joining the KMT. Yet Maring never told me or any other responsible member of the CCP the details of his interview with Dr. Sun. It was on the basis of our own experiences with Sun Yat-sen that we believed Maring's statements were founded on fact. We also envisaged the possibility that it was on Sun Yat-sen's initiative that Maring had introduced the issue.

Sun Yat-sen had always looked upon himself as the one and only leader of the Chinese revolution. He had always believed that he could encompass all revolutionary elements under his revolutionary standard. So long as people supported his revolution, Dr. Sun did not much care what personal revolutionary beliefs they held. Before we organized the CCP, knowing quite well that we believed in Marxism, Sun Yat-sen said to me and to friends of mine who were to become important figures in the CCP that if we wanted to take part in the revolution, we ought to join the KMT. His later explanation for acquiring Communist members in the KMT was the same. Apparently he pictured himself as a large circle—the large circle of the revolution—into which he wanted to place the then small circle of Communists, which he sought to prevent from wandering beyond the circumference of the large circle.

Quite apart from Maring's lengthy harangue on the subject, considerations such as these gave us reason to suspect that Sun Yat-sen might well have taken the initiative in proposing that we join the KMT. In any event, if the proposal actually did originate with Dr. Sun, it suited Maring perfectly. While in Java, Maring had directed the left-wing Social Democrats there in their move to join the Saraket Islam, a movement that merged religion and politics in the fight against Dutch colonial rule.[12] But Maring did not dare make the proposal in China without permission from the Comintern, and so he hurried to Moscow for orders after finding out what Sun Yat-sen's intentions were. In time I learned from Voitinsky and others that on this trip to Moscow Maring had recommended that we join the KMT and that the Comintern had accepted his recommendation. Details of the steps to be taken in this move, however, and the full implications of it were not worked out explicitly at that time, these sources said.

Soon thereafter the revolt of Ch'en Chiung-ming appeared to divest Sun Yat-sen of everything, for the time being at least. The effect of this was a general advance in KMT-CCP cooperation and in Dr. Sun's policy of alignment with the Soviet Union. Had Sun Yat-sen remained as President at Canton, his full attention might have remained on the military operations of the Northern Expedition, and he might not have noticed the "small question." It must be remembered that both Zinoviev and Safarov openly found fault with the KMT at the Congress of the Toilers of the Far East, while CCP members at Canton seemed to have very improper connections with Ch'en Chiung-ming. Dr. Sun naturally required an explanation of these matters.

At dawn on June 16, 1922, the troops of Yeh Chü, under Ch'en Chiung-ming, massed near Canton and shelled Kuan Yin Hill. Sun Yat-sen was forced to take refuge on the warship *Yung Feng*. The Northern Expeditionary Forces, then marching calmly on Kiangsi, came under attack both from the front and rear and suffered crippling losses. They withdrew to eastern Kwangtung, but did not have enough power to reach Canton and suppress the revolt. The government of Sun Yat-sen collapsed.

The position of Sun Yat-sen at that time was utterly untenable. Not only was Ch'en Chiung-ming militarily victorious, but Ch'en also had a certain amount of popular support. Many people believed that the enforced retirement of Sun Yat-sen would promote the cause of national unification, and effective support also reached Ch'en Chiung-ming from Hong Kong. While Peking loudly cried for the simultaneous retirement of Sun Yat-sen and Hsu Shih-ch'ang, the leader in North China who truly had power—Wu P'ei-fu—and the advocates of a federation of autonomous provinces in the Southwest supported Ch'en Chiung-ming both openly and in secret. At the same time, many KMT people defected. Among them were the forty-nine KMT veterans led by Li Shih-tseng, Ts'ai Yuan-p'ei, Wu Chih-hui, and Wang Ch'ung-hui who jointly issued a call for Sun Yat-sen to retire. This was a terrible blow to Sun.

In fact, it could almost be said that only the Chinese Communists sympathized with Sun Yat-sen at that time. Denouncing Ch'en Chiung-ming as a reactionary, the CCP openly declared its wish to cooperate with Dr. Sun, while without hesitation it punished the handful of Party members at Canton that sided with Ch'en. These things deeply moved Sun Yat-sen, who came to feel that the CCP sincerely wanted to cooperate with him.

On August 9, 1922, Sun left his warship in the Macao passage and reached Shanghai on August 15, just five days after the West Lake Plenum. Ch'en Tu-hsiu, Li Ta-chao, and Maring each called on him separately. Dr. Sun readily agreed to let CCP members join the KMT, and he dispensed with the standard procedures for entering his Party— the oath of allegiance and the fingerprinting. He also consented to reorganize the KMT into a party based upon democratic principles. A few days later, with Chang Chi as their sponsor, Ch'en Tu-hsiu, Li Ta-chao, Ts'ai Ho-sen, and Chang T'ai-lei formally joined the KMT in a ceremony at which Sun Yat-sen officiated personally.

I left Shanghai on my mission to Peking, Wuhan, and Changsha several days before Dr. Sun arrived. At the West Lake Plenum, to be sure, the controversy over joining the KMT had been serious. Once the resolution was adopted, however, every one of us meticulously carried it out. To meetings of the local CCP committees at the important cities of Peking, Wuhan, and Changsha, I reported on the "Manifesto of the Second Congress" and the understanding reached at the West Lake Plenum, carefully avoiding controversial issues. In this way I easily won support for the CC decisions from the comrades there. In keeping with the special conditions that applied in each place, a start was made in establishing a cooperative relationship with KMT people.

I returned to Shanghai early in September. Ch'en Tu-hsiu told me at once that he and the others had become members of the KMT, and he explained how it had happened. He said that they had told Dr. Sun that as one of the responsible members of the CC of the CCP, I should have joined the KMT with them, but that I was away on business. Arrangements were made for me to go through the formalities later. Dr. Sun had told Ch'en that as soon as I returned to Shanghai he would welcome me into the Party.

Ch'en took me to see Chang Chi, because Chang had assumed the role of our sponsor in the KMT. We explained the purpose of our visit, and Chang Chi announced that Sun Yat-sen especially welcomed me into the KMT. He would report to Dr. Sun and ask him for a date on which he could personally officiate at the ceremony. I said that it was very fitting indeed that Sun Yat-sen had officiated at the first ceremony at which CCP members joined the KMT, but that since I was joining at a later date, I thought that P'u Ch'üan (courtesy name of Chang Chi) might just as well officiate, with Ch'en Tu-hsiu acting as my sponsor. If Dr. Sun wanted to talk things over, I would later make a special call on him. Ch'en Tu-hsiu favored this idea, too. Chang Chi offered a few polite objections, but in the end he cheerfully acceded to my request, and we held the simple ceremony in the drawing room of his home. We raised our right hands and read a statement about joining the Party. There was no mention in it of obedience to Sun Yat-sen, but only a pledge of allegiance to his Three Principles of the People. When we had finished reading the statement, all of us signed a certificate. There was no fingerprinting.

Chang Chi was radiant with smiles. He said that he would immediately take my membership papers to Sun Yat-sen. We chatted at length about the Chinese revolution, about relations with the Soviet Union, and about KMT-CCP relations. He seemed particularly pleased to be the sponsor of the important Communists that joined the KMT. He seemed to look upon this as an outstanding contribution to his Party. While this gentleman subsequently became well known as an opponent of communism, nevertheless that occasion symbolized the broad harmony of the early stages of KMT-CCP cooperation.

Sun Yat-sen and Joffe

Most members of both parties seemed to feel that the launching of KMT-CCP cooperation set the revolutionary movement on a new course. Alliance with Russia and Soviet support for the Chinese revolution, however, became the key questions in the revolutionary movement. For Sun Yat-sen apparently did not think that reorganization of the KMT and the entry of a few CCP members into it would bring about a miracle. First of all he sought to restore his stronghold in Kwangtung; and perhaps with concrete assistance from the Soviet Union, he hoped to avoid the serious reverses that had plagued him in the past. In any event, it could be said that KMT-CCP cooperation resolved the contradiction that had existed in Soviet support for the Chinese revolution. Sun Yat-sen established a relationship with the Soviet Union through Adolf A. Joffe, which in turn vastly stimulated KMT-CCP cooperation. Thus the second half of 1922 was a period of generation and development in the three simultaneous movements—KMT reorganization, KMT-CCP cooperation, and the alliance with Russia.

Joffe, a deputy commissar of foreign affairs in the Soviet government, arrived in Peking as a diplomatic envoy on August 12, 1922. After the West Lake Plenum, I went north on the instruction of the CC and arrived at Peking a day or two before Joffe. After the Yurin mission returned to Russia, a chargé d'affaires at the Soviet Mission had maintained regular contact with Li Ta-chao. But since Soviet diplomatic representatives seemed reluctant at that time to stick their hands into the affairs of the Comintern or the CCP, the contacts between this chargé d'affaires and Li Ta-chao were superficially of a social nature. The man was an acquaintance of mine. He was eager to hand these duties over to someone else, and since Li Ta-chao was in Shanghai, he arranged for a meeting between Joffe and me.

On Joffe's second day in Peking, I called at the Soviet Mission to see him. The chargé d'affaires mentioned above acted as our interpreter. Joffe did not appear to know much about the situation in China. Referring to a list of Chinese dignitaries, which he had not mastered, he kept asking if I knew such people as Wu P'ei-fu, Ts'ao K'un, Chang Tso-lin, and some former Peking premiers and foreign ministers. I kept replying, "I do not know him" or "I have no contact with him." Finally, I frankly told him, "I'm sorry. I am a young man, and I simply don't know those big people."

Both of us realized that our conversation left a lot to be desired. Joffe naturally was most concerned about this mission to establish diplomatic relations with Peking, and his questions chiefly concerned this issue. He seemed unwilling to discuss the CCP or the KMT. Instead of treating me as a representative of the CCP, he tried to treat me as just another celebrity. This revealed the diplomat in him. At the same time it revealed something of his egotism and arrogance. As for me, I demonstrated something of the proud attitude of the leftist youth. I did not have much respect for the Peking government and did not like the idea of diplomatic relations between Peking and Moscow. The most important issue so far as I was concerned was Soviet support for the Chinese revolution, which was in keeping with the decisions of the CC of the CCP.

The chargé d'affaires, who was doing the interpreting, presently sensed what was happening and gave Joffe a voluble explanation in Russian. Apparently he introduced me all over again, pointing out that my knowledge of politics was excellent, for Joffe switched to asking what I thought of the China situation. I said that the list of names he had mentioned to me was not worth thinking about. As a matter of fact, I declared that I took pride in having nothing whatsoever to do with such corrupt, backward warlords and politicians. What I did know quite a bit about was the common, reasonable Chinese people, and I said that the people would discard the warlords and politicians who were headed for destruction. The hope of China lay in the broad masses of the people and in their revolution.

Joffe next asked who was able to lead the Chinese revolution. Sun Yat-sen, I replied. He pointed out that Dr. Sun had been forced out of Canton. Could he speedily return to Canton and reestablish a revolutionary regime there? Joffe wanted to know. Absolutely, I said; in the near future Sun Yat-sen would most certainly return to Canton. I added that Sun Yat-sen was a figure of hope, that he could unify China, and that he could lead the country down the right road.

Although I was not able to say whether or not the Northern warlords would collapse soon, Joffe seemed interested in my long-range views. Eagerly he asked me, "Do you think that as an envoy of the Soviet government whose mission is to establish diplomatic relations with the Peking government I would be able to meet Dr. Sun?"

"Not only would you be able to," I bluntly assured him, "but you must not miss the chance to meet him. If you do, the envoy of the revolutionary Soviet Union will regret it."

Joffe politely thanked me for my "enlightened views," and then we separated.

While this talk with Joffe was exploratory, it was by no means merely a polite gesture. I had raised the question of relations between the Soviet government and the Chinese revolution, and this was a key issue. For Soviet diplomacy had two faces: on the one hand it sought normal relations with existing governments, while on the other hand it sought to support the revolutionary forces that would overthrow those governments. It was Joffe's personal responsibility to carry out such a dual policy, and he soon carried it out in China. Subsequent events were to show that one concrete achievement of Joffe in China was his establishment of relations with Sun Yat-sen.

Important members of both the KMT and the CCP were at this time developing activities favorable to the revolution that were numerous and many-sided. Some of them led to disagreements.

Maring was the chief matchmaker in these developments. He not only promoted the entry of CCP leaders into the KMT, but he worked out the relationship between Dr. Sun and Joffe as well. The Sun–Joffe interview was largely the result of his efforts. Yet Maring assumed the role of a man of mystery in his political activities. His work style was quite different from that of Voitinsky. Just as he never showed the CC any Comintern decisions, so he never discussed with us his efforts to draw Sun and Joffe together. We merely observed that he kept endlessly dashing between Peking and Shanghai, and to this we reacted with amusement. Apparently he tended to forget his liaison mission between the Comintern and the CCP in order to engage in top-level political activities. In truth, he did seem to pay less attention to routine CCP affairs than formerly.

Maring apparently saw himself sitting on top of the world with the main strings of the Chinese revolution held in his hands. He was very friendly with Joffe. Occasionally he hinted that Joffe fully supported his views. Sometimes he even declared that Joffe attached greater importance to the KMT than he did, that Joffe believed the full strength of the Chinese revolution resided in the KMT. Sun Yat-sen also was very close to him. It seemed as though they consulted each other on everything. This underground Comintern representative did not enjoy the formal diplomatic status of Joffe and so could operate with greater freedom, unencumbered by the restrictions of diplomatic custom. Yet Maring was not, after all, a citizen of the Soviet Union, nor did he serve the Soviet government in any capacity; so his ability to influence Soviet foreign policy was very limited. The policy of the Soviet government remained primarily centered upon establishing diplomatic relations with the Peking government, and this made it impossible for Maring to fulfill certain demands made by Sun Yat-sen. Moreover, he could not carry out all of his wishes even in the field of KMT-CCP cooperation. Often he encountered opposition from both the Comintern and the CC of the CCP. Eventually he found himself so enmeshed in difficulties that it was necessary to turn the role he had played over to Michael Borodin.

Li Ta-chao was an important figure in CCP political activities despite the fact that he was not a member of the CC. Particularly during this period he represented sizable political capital. His moderate nature made him better equipped than other CCP leaders to cultivate friends, and arguments and disagreements never arose between him and the KMT people. Thus, at the start of KMT-CCP cooperation, his efforts were especially welcomed; and he played a very positive role. Furthermore, his relations with progressive elements of the Chihli clique were long established. Through a good friend of his, Pai Chien-wu, director of the political department of Wu P'ei-fu, he could indirectly influence some of the things that Wu P'ei-fu did.

At the time of the West Lake Plenum, Li Ta-chao told me that the Chihli clique had split into two groups, the Loyang group and the Paoting group. He believed it was possible to say that the Loyang group, led by Wu P'ei-fu, was composed of patriotic militarists. Acting on this assumption, he suggested that the practical political situation in China would advance along more progressive lines if Sun Yat-sen and Wu P'ei-fu could be made to cooperate. The idea attracted attention in several different quarters. The CC of the CCP doubted that anything would come of it, but thought it was worth trying. Joffe also thought the idea was important, and the contact that was established thereupon between Soviet representatives and Wu P'ei-fu was the result of the background efforts of Li Ta-chao.

Sun Yat-sen, who had had early contacts with Chang Tso-lin and the Anhwei clique of Tuan Ch'i-jui, was highly indignant over Wu P'ei-fu's collusion with Ch'en Chiung-ming. But when Li Ta-chao suggested to him the possibility of cooperating with Wu P'ei-fu, he showed no outward sign of resistance to the idea. Possibly the reason for this was that in a sense Dr. Sun was marooned in Shanghai. At such a time, it was not undesirable for someone to unsnarl his relations with Wu P'ei-fu for him.

The capacity of Li Ta-chao to influence Wu P'ei-fu was not great, however, and his suggestion ended in notable failure. For one thing, Joffe's talks with Peking encountered numerous obstacles, and Wu P'ei-fu did not help him to overcome the obstacles. Eventually Joffe could do little but come to the South, where, without fear of the consequences, he and Sun Yat-sen issued their joint declaration. Actually the idea of cooperation between Sun Yat-sen and Wu P'ei-fu was too idealistic. Gradually a triangular alliance involving Sun Yat-sen, Chang Tso-lin, and Tuan Ch'i-jui assumed concrete form, whereupon the KMT resoundingly attacked the efforts by the CCP to bring about cooperation between Sun and Wu. As to relations between the CCP and Wu P'ei-fu, they were irreparably severed when Wu suppressed the strike of the Peking-Hankow Railway workers on February 7, 1923, killing many workers at Hankow. Indeed, Li Ta-chao himself had to flee Peking for temporary refuge at Shanghai.

Ch'en Tu-hsiu, who had little confidence in the idea of CCP members participating in the KMT, adopted a passive attitude as the work of participation progressed. On September 4, 1922, Sun Yat-sen called a meeting of fifty-three senior KMT cadres to discuss KMT reorganization. He explained to them the new policy of alliance with Russia and toleration of Communists, and he won their unanimous backing. On September 6 he named nine people to a committee to draft a plan for reorganizing the KMT. Ch'en Tu-hsiu was one of them. Dr. Sun called another meeting of his senior cadres on November 15 to discuss the plan that the nine-man committee produced, and it was at this meeting that Hu Han-min and Wang Ching-wei were elected to draft a manifesto announcing reorganization of the Party. On January 1, 1923, the KMT issued its reorganization manifesto.

Ch'en Tu-hsiu had often faced KMT people in the past and had frequently disagreed with them. The fact that Sun Yat-sen appointed him one of the nine men to draft the reorganization program, therefore, obviously was of great significance in promoting good KMT-CCP relations. Still, Ch'en Tu-hsiu consistently placed himself in the position of a guest that did not wish to express too many opinions on the internal affairs of the KMT. And he had no hand in the final stages of the reorganization plan because the CC of the CCP sent him to Moscow to attend the Fourth Congress of the Comintern.

Within the KMT, Sun Yat-sen always occupied the position of a person whose vision and knowledge outdistanced all others. He stood more resolutely than the others in favor of alliance with Russia and toleration of Communists. He showed the greatest interest in all matters connected with these questions. Most of his followers, however, did not think in the same vein. While outward statements of support rolled in from Sun's followers, these same people harbored serious reservations in their innermost minds. Both leftist and rightist ideological trends existed simultaneously within the KMT. Some people feared that alliance with Russia and toleration of Communists would antagonize the Powers and that this would have an unfavorable effect on the political development of the KMT. Others felt that since the Soviet Union was prepared to cooperate with Sun Yat-sen, it ought to break off its talks with the Peking government regarding diplomatic relations. Still others found an alliance with Russia acceptable, but regarded the toleration of Communists as dangerous. Reservations were numerous as well as varied.

On November 5, 1922, Chang Chi, then an active supporter of the policy of alliance with Russia and toleration of Communists, traveled from Shanghai to Peking to interview Joffe. He carried with him a personal letter to Joffe from Sun Yat-sen. His primary objective was to induce the Soviet Union to help the KMT launch military operations against the Peking government in the North. But when Joffe made it clear to him that there was not the remotest possibility of carrying out this plan, his enthusiasm for an alliance with Russia and the toleration of Communists began to cool.

As a result of these various developments, when Joffe passed through Shanghai on his way to Japan and then home early in 1923, he several times met with Dr. Sun. Their meetings led to the publication on January 26, 1923, of the famous Sun–Joffe Declaration.

The Declaration chiefly established the relationship between the KMT regime and the Soviet government. It was a victory for Sun Yat-sen. Joffe agreed that neither communism nor the Soviet system were suited to China, and he expressed unqualified support for the revolution led by Dr. Sun. Naturally Sun Yat-sen quite sincerely welcomed the Declaration. The situation in Kwangtung had changed. Ch'en Chiung-ming withdrew to Waichow on January 15 and announced his retirement. KMT circles were enthusiastically making plans to return to Canton when the Sun–Joffe Declaration further added to their prestige.

The CC of the CCP, which meanwhile had moved to Peking, was at the time busily directing the labor movement. Not only did it not participate in the Sun–Joffe talks, but it had absolutely no advance knowledge of them. We read the Declaration in the press and decided that the phrase "the Communistic order or even the Soviet system cannot actually be introduced into China" involved a denial of the role of the CCP. In addition, it was quite inappropriate for Joffe and Maring to make such a public statement without obtaining our concurrence. Nevertheless, we wanted friendly relations between the KMT and the Soviet Union to be established quickly, and we regarded the Declaration as just so much diplomatic verbiage which placed no restraints upon the CCP; and so we did not express any opposition to it.

The effect of this Declaration was truly extraordinary. Since a Soviet envoy to Peking and the leader of the Party that opposed the Peking government had issued it jointly, it landed almost like a bomb on the Chinese political scene. It was, of course, a threat to the Peking government. More importantly, however, it heralded a new turn in the tide of modern Chinese history. For it meant that Sun Yat-sen and the Southern government, which he was soon to return to Canton to lead, would carry out a policy of alliance with Russia, while it affirmed Dr. Sun's intention to reorganize the KMT and to tolerate the Communists.

Yet it was on the basis of this extraordinarily significant Declaration that the KMT later expelled the Communists and turned on them, an action that brought disaster to the cause of the Chinese revolution. Perhaps this was the result of Joffe making more promises than he could fulfill. In any case, it revealed what was behind the two faces of Soviet diplomacy—principally an absence of unanimity between the Soviet foreign ministry and the Comintern. Generally speaking, enthusiastic revolutionists tended to be subjective, to expect achievements too quickly, to forcefully seek unity in spite of complex contradictions, until finally all attempts at lucidity ended in utter foolishness. So it was that the triangular relationship between the Soviet Union, the KMT, and the CCP started out in such a spirited and pleasant way and ended in a disastrous breakdown.

COOPERATION DEVELOPS BETWEEN THE KUOMINTANG AND THE CHINESE COMMUNIST PARTY

CHAPTER

The Failure of the February Seventh Strike

Subsequent to the West Lake Plenum, the Third Congress of the CCP, in June, 1923, ratified a policy whereby large numbers of CCP members could join the KMT. For its part, the First Congress of the KMT ratified the Party reorganization plan and agreed that members of the CCP could become KMT members if they joined as individuals rather than as Communists. These two congresses marked an extension of KMT-CCP relations from limited cooperation to overall cooperation within the KMT. After this policy of cooperation between the two parties had been established, the Chinese revolution took large strides forward. But because the two parties were mingled, many disputes sprang up between them, and since the disputes could not be settled easily, they ultimately led to a split.

The labor movement that was led by the CCP in the northern provinces was suppressed by Wu P'ei-fu prior to the Third Congress of the CCP, and the well-known February Seventh Strike ended in tragedy. This deprived the Chinese Communists of the major front of their public activities. They were forced to switch their attention to Canton, and so a majority of delegates to the Third Congress accepted the policy of widespread CCP membership in the KMT. The CCP thus began working with the KMT in the armed revolution against the Peking government, and therefore I propose to begin the account of this period with the February Seventh Strike.

There can be no doubt that the CCP continued to mature as a result of oppression and resistance to oppression. The CC of the CCP, although it waved high the banner of anti-imperialism, was located in the foreign concession of Shanghai. Naturally the foreign-concession authorities had no intention of allowing this sprout to grow large while they looked the other way. They were forever landing damaging blows on the CCP. Their methods were rather shrewd; and the harder the Communist Party worked, the harder they pressed down upon it.

In June, 1922, the French Concession police closed the New Youth Book Store, the organization that issued Communist publications. By September of the same year, however, *Guide Weekly* (Hsiang-tao Chou-pao), the organ of the CC, was being secretly published in Shanghai. In accordance with the decision of the Second Congress, it called for the overthrow of imperialism and the warlords; and the International Settlement police banned its publication and distribution. It was widely circulated, nevertheless, and sales mounted. But to accomplish this, the CC had to wade through countless difficulties and to suffer near-crippling financial losses.[1]

At the same time, the Shanghai headquarters of the Secretariat of Labor Organizations in China was closed down.[2] This made it virtually impossible for the CCP to carry on public activities in Shanghai. The Secretariat had all along carefully preserved the superficial appearance of a normal trade union; it displayed no Communist colors, and its existence in Shanghai was perfectly legal. The enmity of the Settlement authorities was roused, however, because it had supported the Hong Kong seamen's strike in the spring of 1921, because the First National Labor Congress was called on its initiative, and because it acted as the liaison agency for the National Labor-Union Federation. Since I had long been aware of this enmity, I had made the necessary preparations to meet any possible emergency. The Secretariat office, for example, kept no secret documents, and *Labor Weekly* did its best to keep inflammatory articles out of its pages. Members of the Secretariat were kept widely scattered, working in secret and staying underground. As extra protection, an English lawyer was employed as adviser to the Secretariat. All of these steps were taken in the hope that the Secretariat might continue to operate legally.

In September, 1922, however, a secretary at the Secretariat, Li Ch'i-han, was suddenly arrested by plain clothes detectives. The Mixed Court, over which the British consul-general presided, decided, on the basis of a Chinese law banning strikes, that Li Ch'i-han was guilty of attempting to incite workers to strike. The Court sentenced him to three months in prison to be followed by expulsion from the Settlement. It was then that both the Secretariat and its publication, *Labor Weekly*, were closed down. The only thing our British lawyer did was to request a reduction in Li Ch'i-han's sentence. Although by established Settlement practice, trade unions were permitted to exist openly and workers to strike, our lawyer did not even try to exonerate the defendant. It did not seem to me that he fully discharged his responsibilities to us. Several other trade-union leaders and I were spectators at the trial. We saw for ourselves the way foreigners ran roughshod over us in territory that really belonged to China, and we saw the threatening arrogance of the police toward us when the judgment was handed down. I was livid with rage.

Whether the verdict was excessive or reasonable, the case went down on the record of atrocious imperialist behavior. It added fuel to the angry fire burning in us Chinese Communists and certain radical workers. In the opinion of the Secretariat, the implication was clear that it would be impossible for the CCP to find legal outlets for its activities in Shanghai. Li Ch'i-han had been given a nominal sentence of only three months in prison, but when he was released at the expiration of his sentence, the Settlement prison authorities turned him over to Ho Feng-lin, the Shanghai garrison commander. It was reported that the Settlement authorities had reached an agreement with Ho Feng-lin by which he was to court-martial Li Ch'i-han. This meant that Li's life was in danger. This was the usual ruse employed by the Settlement authorities—using barbarous Chinese militarists to see to it that people were executed. As things turned out, Li spent two years in a military prison after being expelled from the Settlement. Then, luckily, he was released.[3]

Circumstances made it impossible at that time for the CC to resist the forces at work to destroy the Secretariat. In our estimation, we could not launch a strike in the Settlement as a protest demonstration. Even if we had been able to overcome the difficulties that stood in the way of such a strike, we did not feel that enough would be achieved by doing so; and so we swallowed our pride. In order to minimize the effect of this unfortunate affair upon the labor movement and upon the rising wave of strikes, we treated it gingerly. We announced the removal of Secretariat headquarters to Peking, while giving no publicity to the fact that the headquarters at Shanghai had been closed down by the authorities.

The movement of the Secretariat's headquarters to Peking, however, was not prompted solely by the persecution it suffered from the Settlement authorities. Conditions then differed widely in various parts of China, and this was an additional reason for the move. The Shanghai Settlement authorities had hounded the Secretariat on the basis of the laws of Yuan Shih-k'ai's regime.[4] Wu P'ei-fu, on the other hand, was at that very moment loudly proclaiming a policy of protecting labor. The effect of this policy throughout North China and in Hupeh and Hunan provinces was to spur on the open organization of trade unions. It was also possible to organize strikes openly, so that the labor movement in these areas was developing well. Indeed, the work of the CCP at Peking, Wuhan, and Changsha made notable progress. Contrasting the conditions in these areas to those in Shanghai, we felt, for the moment at least, that the conservative old warlords of China were actually a grade better than the foreign officials of the Shanghai Settlement, who so prided themselves on being civilized. So it was that the CC of the CCP, indignant at being persecuted by the Shanghai Settlement authorities, decided to move the Secretariat north. It decided at the same time to move all organs of the CC to Peking also.

The decision to move the CC to Peking was, in fact, reached chiefly to take advantage of the enlightened actions of Wu P'ei-fu. We wanted to expand and consolidate the labor movement in the North and in Hupeh and Hunan. Meanwhile, Sun Yat-sen had lost his base in Kwangtung, and KMT activities were at low ebb everywhere. From our point of view the moment was not auspicious for KMT-CCP cooperation to accomplish much in the practical political field. The removal of the CC to Peking would cause numerous inconveniences in our contact with the KMT, for the KMT had then established its center at Shanghai. That this would affect party cooperation was obvious. Yet the idea was approved by the Comintern, and so we moved to Peking.

The movement of the various CC organs to Peking had been accomplished by October, 1922. By then it was necessary for Ch'en Tu-hsiu and Liu Jen-ching, who were being sent as delegates to the Fourth Congress of the Comintern, to hurry off to Moscow;[5] and the division of work in the CC had to be accommodated to their absence. The CC decided that CC leadership work would be my special responsibility. I was to act as secretary of the CC while Ch'en Tu-hsiu was out of the country. My duties as director of the Labor Secretariat headquarters were taken over by Teng Chung-hsia, while Lo Chang-lung became assistant to Teng and editor of *Labor Weekly*. From then on, my main preoccupation was with the political policies of the CC, and I was no longer directly in charge of the labor movement.

The plans of the CCP to expand the labor movement in areas controlled by the Peking government were short-lived. Those plans promptly encountered the persecution of Wu P'ei-fu. For Wu, in a rather intricate transition, switched from a policy of protecting labor to actually massacring workers. There is only space here to describe this transition briefly.

When I visited Peking after the West Lake Plenum in mid-August, 1922, Teng Chung-hsia, the responsible CCP member in North China, was actively working for the adoption of labor legislation. He believed that the labor movement could achieve legal status under Wu P'ei-fu, and he had returned from the National Labor Congress at Canton to take charge of the labor movement in the North. While Li Ta-chao was in Shanghai, Teng also was in charge of CCP affairs in North China. At the time of my visit he was taking advantage of the fact that students were away on summer vacation to live in a Peita dormitory. He had a large room to himself, which he used as an office, and he kept very busy. From his office he quite openly and freely carried out the activities of the CCP—such as those of the Labor Secretariat, Party affairs, the distribution of Party publications, the Anti-Imperialist Alliance Movement, and a movement for labor legislation. After working underground in Shanghai, I was most impressed by the way Teng was able to do things.

He had prepared a draft labor law,[6] and he had mobilized workers from all parts of the country in order to launch with the greatest possible effect a movement for parliamentary abolition of the Security Police Law and adoption of labor legislation. He and the workers' representatives in Peking held a reception for members of Parliament and the press in order to attract their attention to the Draft Labor Law. As a result, some members of Parliament did place a token law for the protection of labor before the legislative body. But the law was never passed. Even its sponsors treated it as nothing more than a gesture in keeping with the fact that Wu P'ei-fu had advocated the protection of labor.

But Wu P'ei-fu and the CCP had worked out one concrete project for cooperation in the labor movement. The minister of communications, Kao En-hung, while a trusted supporter of Wu P'ei-fu, knew nothing at all about railway matters. He was eager to get rid of the influence that the Communications clique of Liang Shih-i had over the railroads in order to take over financial control of the railroads and increase the revenue that would come to Wu P'ei-fu; so he turned to Li Ta-chao for help with this problem. The Communications clique had consistently suppressed the railway workers' movement, and for this reason Li Ta-chao agreed to help Kao rid the railroads of its influence. Li recommended that six CCP members secretly serve as inspectors on the six major railroads—the Peking-Hankow, the Tientsin-Pukow, the Peking-Mukden, the Peking-Suiyuan, the Lunghai, and the Cheng-tai. These secret inspectors were to directly encourage the development of railwaymen's unions. They were at the same time to investigate corruption on the lines, giving Kao an opportunity to dismiss members of the Communications clique and to replace them with people through whom he would control the railroads. Kao accepted the idea.

This was the only case of CCP cooperation with Wu P'ei-fu, and it led to a rift between the two. The six young CCP members who were appointed special secret investigators received passes to travel free on the railroads. They promptly became active all along every one of the lines, organizing the railwaymen, relentlessly mobilizing workers to demand improved conditions from the railway authorities, and devoting full time to the labor movement. They entirely forgot that Kao En-hung had entrusted them with the task of ousting the members of Liang Shih-i's Communications clique. Instead of being a help to Wu P'ei-fu and Kao En-hung, these investigators were the source of a good deal of trouble; so the relationship rapidly deteriorated.

But the CCP did not see the approaching change in Wu P'ei-fu's attitude. Party members in the North felt elated over their achievements. At the major stations and large cities along the railways the workers' movement was experiencing such a golden age as had never before been witnessed. Trade unions were increasing at a startling rate, as was the number of union members. The organizational structure of unions was growing stronger. They compared favorably with unions in Western countries. What was more, the strike movement especially was growing, and most striking workers finally won victories. It was in this atmosphere of general jubilation that blood was shed in the suppression of the strike of Kailuan Mine workers—the first falling leaf of autumn, as it were.

The Kailuan Coal Mine was the oldest and largest modern mining enterprise in China. At first it was operated by Chinese capital, but gradually British merchants intruded upon it.[7] By 1922 it was almost completely British-owned. It employed as many as 50,000 workers, including temporary hands. This coal mine was notorious for being a world of darkness, where workers were maltreated, where the chief labor contractors carried out the extremes of exploitation, and where opium-smoking and gambling were alarmingly prevalent. It was generally acknowledged in the mine that "human beings fare worse than animals"; for the mine paid sixty dollars when a horse died, but when a miner died in the course of his work, only twenty dollars was paid in compensation. Furthermore, accidents were frequent. Such were the conditions when a strike was called in that area before the unions involved were well organized and before the necessary preparations had been made.

On October 23, 1922, the miners went out on strike to demand higher wages. A demonstration of workers on October 25 was put down by Indian troops, which landed from British gunboats, and by security-police troops sent from Tientsin by the director of police for Chihli. Both the Indians and the Chinese police opened fire. Several workers were killed on the spot, and about fifty of them were wounded. The mine union and unions in the railway, textile mill, and cement factory at Tangshan all were closed down. A ban was placed on workers' meetings, and all strike leaders that did not manage to escape were arrested. Because of student sympathy for the strike, the Tangshan College of Engineering was forced to suspend classes. The strike hung on until November 16. On the one hand the union did not have the strength to resist oppression, while on the other hand the mine made some small concessions;[8] so the strike was called off.

This strike was a bad shock to the CC, which had just moved to Peking. We had not yet seriously reviewed the future of the labor movement in North China. But Ts'ai Ho-sen and I regarded the episode as the first move by the northern warlords, including Wu P'ei-fu, to abuse the workers. Li Ta-chao, on the basis of his own inside information about the political scene, believed that the incident resulted from British pressure and from the fact that the Tientsin-Paoting portion of the Chihli clique had fallen under foreign influence. For that reason he treated the incident as a special case on the basis of which one could not conclude that Wu P'ei-fu had changed his much-publicized policy of protecting labor. Teng Chung-hsia and others at the head of the Labor Secretariat felt that the Kailuan strike was defeated chiefly because of a weak union organization, lack of proper preparation, and inadequate leadership by the Secretariat. Had it not been for these factors, they believed the outside pressure could have been withstood and victory won. And so we decided that under our leadership the workers should redouble their efforts to withstand the pressures put upon them, to strive for the freedom of union organization, and to strive for the freedom to strike.

Except at Tientsin and Tangshan, where reactionary authorities interfered, the labor movement was able to go on developing freely. Wu P'ei-fu gave no indication that he would block trade-union activities. We went ahead with our original plans, energetically promoting a railwaymen's union federation and various regional trade-union councils.

Of all the unions, the Peking-Hankow Railway Workers' Union was the best organized. Its leaders, with support from the Secretariat, called a congress of workers from the entire length of the Peking-Hankow Railway for February 1, 1923, to formally establish a Peking-Hankow Railway General Union. But when this Congress opened, Wu P'ei-fu ordered the Chengchow Police Bureau to stop it, and this led to a strike and to the famous February Seventh Incident.

The CC attached great importance to this Congress. For as soon as the Peking-Hankow workers were organized into a general union, we planned to form general unions in the other railways and then a national union of all railway workers. Until the incident actually occurred, we did not anticipate any interference from Wu P'ei-fu. The interference, when it came, caught us unprepared to cope with it. I was sent to direct the Congress, because the CC felt that I was the first to bring railwaymen into the labor movement and that the railwaymen trusted me. Furthermore, Ch'en Tu-hsiu had returned to Peking from Moscow a month before the Congress opened, relieving me of the duties of acting secretary, and so I had time to make the trip to Chengchow.

Preparations for the Congress were thorough. Great propaganda blasts preceded it. I arrived at Chengchow on the eve of February 1. According to its size, each of the sixteen branch unions on the Peking-Hankow Railway sent delegates to the Congress. The total of these delegates was sixty-five, while 130-odd delegates came from other railroads and from trade unions in Wuhan. A total of more than two hundred delegates, therefore, attended the Congress. Because of the large number of delegates and because they represented so many different labor units, in effect the gathering was a small-scale labor congress for the northern provinces. For that reason, the agenda was not restricted to discussion of the Peking-Hankow Railway General Union.

The Congress was ready to open on February 1 in a large Chengchow theater, the Pu Lo Yuan. All delegates reached the theater on time, and Chengchow railway workers were to stage a parade to celebrate the formation of the Peking-Hankow Railway General Union. When some delegates entered the theater, however, they found the stage occupied by a number of armed policemen under the leadership of Huang Tien-ch'en, chief of the Chengchow Police Bureau. Large numbers of soldiers and policemen appeared outside, too, and the workers were forbidden to parade. Both the theater and the offices of the General Union were surrounded. Then Huang Tien-ch'en publicly announced that he had orders to ban the meeting. A few union leaders and I rushed onto the stage to reason with him. Normally, Huang maintained good relations with those union leaders. On this occasion, however, his attitude was severe. He indicated that he intended to carry out his orders strictly and that there was no room for discussion.

The gathering had been planned quite openly. The union had inserted announcements in newspapers at Peking, Tientsin, Shanghai, and Hankow; while official notification had been given to the railway authorities as well as the local military and police. On January 28 Wu P'ei-fu had ordered Chin Yun-o, the Chengchow garrison commander, to ban the meeting. When the union received this information, it had sent five representatives to Loyang to see Wu P'ei-fu about it. Wu P'ei-fu had told them that although the General Union could be formed, no meeting should take place because Chengchow was a military zone. The representatives had taken this to mean that nobody would interfere with a simple ceremony inaugurating the General Union.

When Police Chief Huang Tien-ch'en intruded, the major union leaders strongly pressed him on this issue. First they argued that the provisional constitution guaranteed the people the freedoms of assembly and organization and that no official could revoke these freedoms. Huang retorted that no matter what the provisional constitution said, he had his orders as a military man. Then the union leaders assured him that Wu P'ei-fu personally had said it was all right to inaugurate the General Union, even though he had not agreed to the holding of the congress. The leaders offered not to hold an official congress if Huang would save the situation by allowing the workers to conduct a simple inauguration ceremony. Huang, however, remained adamant. He declared threateningly that if the meeting were not disbanded in five minutes, there would be bloodshed.

When I saw how critical the situation was, I quietly urged the union leaders to avoid bloodshed. The inauguration ceremony and the congress could be held elsewhere at another time, I said, but nothing should be insisted upon at the moment. Accepting this suggestion, they shouted to the delegates in the theater that the meeting was suspended for the time being. The crowd grew boisterous and refused to disband. Li Chen-ying, a secretary in the General Union and an enthusiastic CCP member, stood up in wrath and cried, "Long live the inauguration of the Peking-Hankow Railway General Union." Furious, Huang Tien-ch'en rushed forward and clamped his hand over Li's mouth to stop him from saying anything more. Huang declared that Li had by his action violated the ban on the meeting, whereupon the crowd went out of control. Shouting "Long live the inauguration of the Peking-Hankow Railway General Union," they left the theater in a wildly demonstrative mood.

Insofar as this incident was concerned, the union had made concessions; but that did not satisfy Huang Tien-ch'en. He feared that he had failed in his assignment because there had been a verbal declaration of the inauguration of the General Union. He ordered the soldiers and police to disperse the parading workers, to seize a large placard bearing the name of the union, which the workers were carrying, and to destroy the many presents that had been sent to the meeting. Police also occupied the union's premises, and nobody was allowed to enter or leave it. All of this goaded the workers to new heights of anger.

The irate union leaders left the theater and reassembled in the large room I had at the Wu Chou Hotel to discuss the situation. Some of them wanted me to telephone Loyang to find out what really was happening. I said that from the way Huang Tien-ch'en acted, it looked as though Wu P'ei-fu had lied when he had said that he would not interfere with the inauguration of the General Union. To inquire would therefore be pointless. In any case, I said that I had no direct contact with Loyang and so was not in a position to inquire. Any such inquiry would have to go through Li Ta-chao in Peking, and there was not enough time for that. So they agreed to drop the idea.

Then the union delegates met in small groups to secretly discuss the possibility of calling a protest strike immediately. They unanimously supported the idea of a strike on behalf of the freedom to organize. A majority of the delegates came from Wuhan, and it was these delegates who most fervently insisted upon the strike. They demanded, furthermore, that the Peking-Hankow Railway General Union move to Wuhan, and that a strike be called there immediately. They assured us that other Wuhan unions would rise to its support. The attitude of these Wuhan delegates strongly influenced the decision that was reached.

The trade unions at Wuhan were at that time the strongest in Central China. There were twenty-eight of them, and they were, on the whole, well organized. Over them was a highly respected provincial trade-union council. Both KMT and CCP leaders in the labor movement at Wuhan were active, and they worked harmoniously together. As a result, the trade-union movement had developed smoothly, and the KMT and CCP leaders there enjoyed the support of student bodies, cultural organizations, newspapermen, and lawyers. Ch'en Tien, a KMT member and an old member of the Kwangtung Machine Workers' General Union, was then chairman of the executive committee of the Hupeh Provincial Council of Trade Unions. A short man, active and capable, he had worked for years in the Yangtze Machine Works, had been an early participant in trade-union work, and was trusted by the Wuhan workers. Ch'en was among the people attending the meeting at Chengchow, and his views were even more radical than the views of CCP members.

This radicalism among Wuhan trade-union leaders was a matter of long standing. After the West Lake Plenum in August, 1922, I visited Wuhan to inspect our work in the area and took part in several open meetings of these leaders. The development of trade unions there was already outstanding. All activities were carried out openly, and tens of union delegates would meet together in the teahouses. They would not only discuss union affairs, but they would also often call for the overthrow of the warlords, or they would criticize Wu P'ei-fu. Sometimes they would disseminate propaganda concerning the Three Principles of the People and communism.

When I saw what was going on, I asked them a number of questions, such as: Wouldn't their radical statements arouse Wu P'ei-fu to retaliate? Since Wuhan was one of Wu P'ei-fu's major bases, why was Wu so foolhardy as to allow KMT and CCP revolutionists to carry out their work without interference, even to oppose him openly? Had they thought of the possibility that Wu P'ei-fu might one day turn against them? And so forth. To my questions they generally replied that the local authorities would not interfere with trade-union activities for the time being out of respect for the announced policy of Wu P'ei-fu to protect labor. Even if Wu P'ei-fu did turn against them, they said they would not hesitate to resist. The KMT people seemed even more resolute than the Communists in their opposition to Wu P'ei-fu. They declared that their objective was precisely to oppose Wu P'ei-fu, and that they would make no concessions to him even if this meant shortening the period in which they could openly carry out their work.

This background of general feeling against Wu P'ei-fu, added to his sudden interference in the Chengchow meeting and to the brutality of the Chengchow soldiers and police, incensed the workers all the more. Demand for a strike rose high. I, too, believed that we might gain a little freedom through a large-scale strike. It seemed to me that if the strike failed, the worst thing that could happen would be that the unions would lose their legal status. I did not anticipate the sweeping massacre that was to come. So I supported the strike proposal, and focused my attention solely upon ways and means of insuring its success. We decided upon the following measures:

1. The strike would be launched on the Peking-Hankow Railway on February 4, 1922, with other railways and trade unions going out on sympathy strikes as soon as they received word that the Peking-Hankow Railway workers had taken action. The duration of the strike would be determined later, in keeping with developments.

2. The Peking-Hankow Railway General Union would immediately move to Kiangan Station, Hankow. There, working with the Hupeh Provincial Council of Trade Unions, it would establish the headquarters from which the strike would be directed.

3. The demands of the striking Peking-Hankow Railway workers would be:

a. Recall of Chao Chi-hsien, the director of Peking-Hankow Railway administration, and Feng Yün, head of the southern section of the railway, and punishment of Huang Tien-ch'en.
b. Payment to the workers of $6,000 in compensation by the railway administration.
c. Withdrawal of troops stationed in the Chengchow union, return of the General Union's placard, and tendering of an apology.
d. A day of rest with full pay on Sundays.
e. A one-week holiday with full pay at the time of the Lunar New Year.[9]

On the whole, the workers' delegates did not believe there was any agreement between the Chihli clique and the Communications clique, which largely controlled the railway, nor between individual members of the two cliques. Furthermore, there was proof that Chao Chi-hsien, Feng Yün, and Huang Tien-ch'en had attempted to persecute the union. Other ranking railway administration officials, however, did not necessarily share the views of these three. (The head of the Traffic Department at Chengchow, for example, sympathized with the workers and provided special railway cars to take delegates to Hankow.) The delegates believed that by singling out only three people for recall or punishment, they were giving Wu P'ei-fu an opportunity to save face. Yet this was what outraged Wu. That egocentric, stubborn militarist felt that a demand that his subordinates be punished was tantamount to a demand that he himself be punished.

Early on the morning of February 2, I accompanied the union delegates southward in the two special cars provided by the railway administration. At Hsinyang, Kuangshui, and other major stops along the way, the responsible members of local unions all declared support for the strike. Everyone at a meeting of CCP members and trade-union leaders, which was held after we reached Hankow, believed the strike would succeed. Meanwhile, the CCP in Peking said that it supported the strike, and so did unions in other railways. Neither the communications authorities in Peking nor Wu P'ei-fu showed any indication of bargaining with the workers in order to settle our differences, and so the strike had to be called.

The strike began along the entire length of the Peking-Hankow Railway at noon on February 4. I became its over-all director. Needless to say, many of the important labor leaders and I lacked experience in directing a strike of such great scope. It was the first experiment of its kind among railway workers. I laid down two guiding principles before the union leaders. The first was that we would try to bring success to the strike through negotiation. The General Union would promptly respond to any indication from the Peking communications authorities that they wanted to negotiate. We would base our negotiations on the five demands we had listed, while striving to the utmost to achieve the freedom to organize. It would be permissible to make appropriate concessions in the demand that Chao Chi-hsien and the others be recalled. The second principle was that the trade unions must be tightly organized as a precaution against military action so as to forestall possible attempts at sabotaging the strike. The labor leaders unanimously adopted these two principles.

The headquarters of the Peking-Hankow Railway General Union was established at Kiangan Station, Hankow. It was the site of the rolling-stock repair shops for the southern section of the line. Thousands of railway workers lived around the station, virtually forming a workers' village. In this village the Kiangan branch of the General Union had its headquarters. In front of the branch's office was an open area, in the center of which stood a large bamboo platform. All contact with the outside world originated there, meetings were held there, and it was from it that the strike was freely directed. This was a secret closely guarded from the world beyond.

After the strike began, Hsiao Yao-nan, the *tupan* (military commissioner) of Hupeh, occupied Kiangan Station with his troops in an attempt to sabotage the strike. A body of soldiers sent by his chief-of-staff, Chang Hou-sheng, seized four locomotive engineers, who were to be forced to drive locomotives. However, representatives of the General Union parleyed with the soldiers, insisting that only by the decision of the General Union could the locomotives be operated. The soldiers were asked to invite the communications authorities in Peking and Hsiao Yao-nan to jointly send representatives to open negotiations with the General Union, which was the proper channel for reaching a settlement. Because of this resistance from the workers, Hsiao released the four engineers that had been arrested and abandoned force as a means for getting the trains started. He declared that he would ask for instructions from his superiors before taking further action.

On February 6 the Hupeh Provincial Council of Trade Unions held a demonstration in Hankow. The demonstrators marched to Kiangan

Station to comfort the railwaymen. More than 10,000 workers gathered in the square in front of the station, all of them shouting, "Strive for the freedom to organize trade unions." At this rally a spokesman for the Hupeh Provincial Council of Trade Unions publicly announced that if the government did not promptly accept the railway workers' demands, every worker in Wuhan would go out on strike.

The impressive front presented by the workers made the militarists realize that the strike could not easily be sabotaged. Quite possibly the obstinate, conservative militarist Wu P'ei-fu never thought of compromising with the workers. He could think only of the prestige he would lose if his orders were not obeyed. How could he possibly condescend to send representatives to negotiate with the workers on a basis of equality? Since the workers had resisted his orders, the only thing to do was to confront them with guns. At the time we did not realize this, of course. We still held the illusion that in one way or another, Wu P'ei-fu would honor the talking he had done about protecting labor.

At dusk on February 6, Chang Hou-sheng, who was responsible for suppressing the strike, sent a subordinate to the Kiangan union's branch office. The man identified himself as an adviser in the governor's office and told union representatives that were there that the government had decided to negotiate with the workers in order to settle the strike. Fixing the time for a meeting at five o'clock the following afternoon and the Kiangan union as the place, he asked them to give him a list of union delegates and to assemble there the next day. He said that someone from the office of the governor of Hupeh would act as mediator and that people from that office would accompany communications representatives to the spot to conduct the negotiations. The labor delegates told the man that they welcomed the proposed negotiations and that they hoped for an early end to the strike. But they explained that the General Union would have to decide about the list of workers' delegates to attend the talks; it would be produced at the following day's meeting. The adviser spoke in a casual, friendly way and did not betray any treacherous intentions.

As soon as it received the news, the Peking-Hankow Railway General Union called a meeting to deal with this development. Some people at the meeting were optimistic. They contended that the strike was too well organized for the opposition to sabotage it. Furthermore, all the industrial workers of Wuhan stood ready to walk out in a general strike, while workers on other railways probably were waiting to go into action even though news of the strike had been suppressed in the North. They believed that the threat confronting the government was so real that it simply had to make concessions. For that reason, the General Union was prepared to name representatives to negotiate the case.

Still, I felt suspicious. I pointed out that the Kiangan union office was such an unlikely site to choose for the negotiations that some trickery must be involved. I suggested that we select the delegates to the talks at once, but that these delegates, along with the other union leaders, remain hidden in the village until after the government delegates had arrived. I urged that our list of names be produced only when we had satisfied ourselves that nothing was amiss and that only then should our delegates appear. My suggestions were adopted, and we went ahead with our arrangements accordingly.

At five o'clock on the afternoon of February 7 our delegates to the negotiations were secretly assembled in the offices of the General Union. Other union leaders were hiding in various workers' homes. The offices of the Kiangan union were gaily decorated, and Hsiang Ying, the secretary of this branch of the General Union, stood at the head of a group of workers comprising the reception committee that was awaiting the arrival of the government delegates. At about 5:30 P.M. sporadic gunfire was heard in the distance.

As those of us at the General Union headquarters listened to the first shots, two or three workers, whose job it was to gather information about what was going on, dashed up to us. They announced that a large military force was on its way from Kiangan Station and was encircling the village. Advanced units of the force had opened fire on the Kiangan union office, and people there had fallen. Other troops were making a house-to-house search, they said. I immediately gave the order to disperse, saying that the proposed talks were a ruse by Wu P'ei-fu and Hsiao Yao-nan to catch us all. To avoid any unnecessary sacrifice, all people responsible for the strike were to leave the village. I ordered the chief leaders of the workers to rendezvous immediately at a certain teahouse in the French Concession of Hankow.

The gunfire grew louder as union leaders began to leave the village by different lanes. After seeing to all arrangements, I followed Yang Te-fu, the chairman of the Peking-Hankow Railway General Union, out of the office. We were the last to leave this secret location. Yang knew the area well, so he led the way. Carrying a basket, which helped to disguise me as a peanut vendor, I followed at a safe distance. Armed sentries blocked the intersection of our lane with the main road. Yang easily passed through them after answering some questions; but when I reached the soldiers, two of them lowered their bayonetted rifles at me and demanded to know if I were a railway worker. I said that I was a peanut vendor, and they released me.

Leaving the terror-stricken village behind, we hurried toward Hankow. I was torn by mixed feelings. On the one hand, I was outraged by the brutality of Wu P'ei-fu. I wondered how many of our worker-comrades had been killed. On the other hand, I realized how fortunate we were that most of the leaders of the workers had escaped. A majority of them must have been out of danger by then.

Subsequent investigations were to show that thirty-seven workers were killed that day, the best known of whom was Lin Hsiang-ch'ien, chairman of the Kiangan union. While the soldiers killed and arrested workers, Lin hid in his own house. Perhaps he felt that it was his responsibility to lead the Kiangan workers personally and that he must not leave his house. Perhaps that was why he was arrested there. More than eighty workers were arrested, four of whom, including Lin Hsiang-ch'ien, were leaders of unions. Chang Hou-sheng tried to force those four to order the workers back to their jobs, but they refused, and so they were executed. Their severed heads were hung from telegraph poles at the railway station.

It was dark by the time Yang Te-fu and I had walked the approximately ten li which brought us to Great Wisdom Gate, the entrance to the French Concession of Hankow. The friends we had arranged to meet had all arrived before we did. They were pacing back and forth in front of the teahouse. As we exchanged information we learned that Hsiao Yao-nan had imposed a curfew, that he had cordoned off the foreign settlements, and that a search for the strike leaders had been ordered. All of us who had managed to escape to the French Concession decided to seek shelter for the time being in the home of Hsiung Ping-k'un, where we would be relatively safe. Few of us had ever met Hsiung; but he was known for his sense of righteousness and for his hospitality, and he received every one of us.

More than ten of us crowded into the small sitting room of the Hsiung home. There were not enough chairs, so some of us squatted on the floor. The place truly was crammed to capacity. The owner of this house was none other than Company Leader Hsiung, of the Engineering Regiment, who had fired the first shot at the Ch'u Wing T'ai arsenal at

Wuchang in the 1911 Revolution. He occupied the ground floor of the small French Concession house at 103 Ch'ang Ch'ing Lane. Most refugee revolutionists knew it well, for it often provided temporary shelter for them. Because Hsiung enjoyed the prestige of a revolutionary veteran, the French Concession authorities treated him with a certain amount of respect; and this enabled him to offer asylum to such refugees. This virile revolutionist was not afraid of being involved in our venture. Rather, he encouraged us. He said politely that everything had happened so suddenly that he and his family could not accommodate us any better, but he assured us that we could rest safely in his home.

We temporarily turned the tiny sitting room into a meeting hall. There was no time to lose. We had to discuss what steps to take next. The room looked toward the road and was separated from it only by a thin plank fence. We could hear distinctly the footsteps of policemen on patrol. Throughout the entire night French Concession police were on patrol outside the Hsiung home, as though they were acting in concert with Hsiao Yao-nan and were threatening us.

We were too preoccupied by the emergency to bother about such things, however. We threw ourselves into a discussion of what lay ahead, and this led to a heated argument. First, I brought up the need for issuing a back-to-work order immediately. My chief argument was that when the time came to draw back, it was important to draw back quickly. Our peaceful strike could not stand up to the armed oppression of Wu P'ei-fu. I reminded everyone of what had happened to the union in Kiangan, where the warlords had resorted to trickery and massacred the workers. We could anticipate more massacres and suppression in the future. Therefore, to prevent needless sacrifices and to preserve our forces for future action, we had no choice but to endure our pain and return to work. Almost everyone there was against my proposal. The opposition of Hsiang Ying, the secretary of the Kiangan union was especially spirited. He insisted that the strike continue until it was victorious. He contended that there was no such thing as retreat in revolutions or strikes and that the workers would suffer increasingly terrible persecution and slaughter rather than surrender at the slightest setback. He berated me for improper leadership, demanding to know why if I believed the strike could not resist armed opposition, I had called it in the first place. He asked how we could possibly surrender at this point simply because we had encountered armed opposition. Hsiang Ying seemed to be possessed by uncontrollable wrath, yet he could not suggest a concrete course of action. I asked him many questions. Since we were cordoned off and Kiangan had suffered a horrible massacre, was it not reasonable to expect similar occurrences in other places? If the strike were not called off, would Wu P'ei-fu continue these massacres? And if he did continue them, could the workers endure the suffering? Wouldn't the workers, after making even greater sacrifices and being beaten to the ground, still be forced to return to work?

Our argument dragged on for a time, but we could not reach agreement. Our host, Mr. Hsiung, listened intently. He added fuel to the fire with his occasional remarks. The actions of revolutionists must be revolutionary, he said; there was no such thing as a temporary retreat; it was better to be totally defeated than to surrender, and so forth. The pronouncements of this veteran revolutionist only increased the stubbornness of Hsiang Ying and his supporters. It was almost three o'clock in the morning. I decided that nothing was going to be accomplished through the normal channel of discussion, and so I produced my trump card.

I demanded that the discussion stop. As the plenipotentiary of the CC of the CCP and of the Labor Secretariat, I ordered work to be resumed immediately, and I called upon everyone present to abide by the order. Then I made the following explanation: The current struggle for the right to organize trade unions was both correct and necessary, but we had committed the error of failing to accurately evaluate the situation. We had not fully appreciated either the brutality of the militarist Wu P'ei-fu or the great influence that domestic and foreign reactionary forces had on him; and so we had not worked out in detail methods for coping with armed oppression before calling the strike. Now it was necessary for all unions to take effective steps promptly by notifying all strikers to return to work. I once again called upon everyone there to carry out my order thoroughly. I assumed full responsibility for the consequences, and said that opposition views might be held in reserve and charges brought against me at a higher level in the future.

My announcement was immediately supported by some of them, nevertheless Hsiang Ying and the rest of the majority declared that they would accept my order; so our discussion turned to ways of implementing it. I drafted a return-to-work order. One section of it read: "Our enemies have brought such overwhelming pressure to bear on us that if we are to preserve our vitality for future retaliation, the entire body of workers has no choice but to endure the situation for the moment and return to work. . . . We must realize that it is only by enduring our pain now and by returning to work today that an opportunity will come for us to avenge ourselves. We must struggle for the freedom to speak, publish, assemble, organize, and strike. Warlords, bureaucrats, and both Chinese and foreign capitalists must be overthrown, but in order to do this, we must endure our pain for the moment and return to work, so that in the future we may once again take action."[10]

At that time it was no easy matter to transmit the order to the workers. Our links with the trade unions and factories had been cut. We knew that the authorities had closed the Hupeh Provincial Council of Trade Unions and that its offices were being watched. But we did not know about the other unions. The only course open to us was to brave the danger of arrest and execution, visit the various trade unions to see for ourselves what was happening, and personally transmit the order. I volunteered to undertake the most difficult task of going to Hanyang, which was the farthest away, to look into conditions at the Hanyang Ironworks and at the Arsenal and to establish contact with the unions there. Yang Te-fu and Hsiang Ying decided to transmit the order to the railway workers. Ch'en Tien and some others undertook to transmit the order to the various Wuhan unions. The Wuhan unions planned to go out on strike on the eighth or ninth of February, whereas some factories already were in a semistrike state. Ch'en Tien had to visit them in order to revoke the original strike order and to urge the workers to go to work as usual. Lin Yü-nan, secretary of the Provincial Council of Trade Unions, was to go to our secret headquarters and stay there, supervising things and seeing to it that our decision reached the North and the various railway lines as quickly as possible.

In the weak light of dawn I hurried to the Dragon King Ferry and crossed the Han River on it. I reached my destination about seven o'clock that morning. The offices of the unions in the Hanyang Arsenal and the Hanyang Ironworks were both located in a large temple at the foot of Turtle Hill in Hanyang. Everything there was quiet and tranquil. There was nothing unusual about the place. More than ten union officials lived there, and some of them were still asleep. I quickly roused them and asked if they knew about the Kiangan tragedy. They said they had heard about it, but they were nevertheless preparing to abide by the order of the Council of Trade Unions to walk out in a sympathy strike. For the past two days their workers had either actually taken part in demonstrations or at least had not worked.

I immediately announced: "Soldiers and the police may be here at any moment to close your union and massacre you the way they did the Kiangan workers. Last night the Hupeh Provincial Council of Trade Unions decided to order you to go to work as usual in order to minimize sacrifices so that we may rise up again later. Now, you should do the following things: (1) Immediately notify all workers to go to work as usual at the arsenal, the ironworks, and other factories in the vicinity; (2) immediately hide or destroy all union documents, especially those listing members or officials; do not let them fall into enemy hands; (3) immediately get all officials out of here; (4) notify the small number of union officials that have operated in the open to hide themselves and return to their factory jobs only when they are certain there is no danger of arrest; (5) immediately set up a secret office for liaison purposes and wait for the Council of Trade Unions to contact you." I impressed upon them the great urgency of acting right away, and they did what I urged them to do.

When these matters had been pretty well attended to and most union officials had left, the workers that had been posted as sentries rushed in. They told us that troops had crossed over from Wuchang and were marching on the union office. It soon would be surrounded. The union's chairman and I went out a back door, turned down a narrow lane, and climbed a rise in the land to have a look. We saw approaching us a company of armed soldiers led by a soldier carrying a sign that declared martial law. Most of the soldiers carried lengths of rope and broad-bladed swords. They surrounded the union office, tore down its signboard, and swarmed into the building. Fortunately the building was empty. Their mission had proved fruitless. The union chairman standing beside me told me to get out of the danger zone at once. He grasped my hand tightly, as though expressing endless gratitude to me for warning them in time; then we parted.

Having completed this emergency mission, I went to our secret hideaway in Wuhan, where Lin Yü-nan was taking care of the affairs of this new office and preparing relevant documents. The other friends, who had assumed responsibility for transmitting the back-to-work order, arrived one after the other to report on their missions. All of the unions they had visited had experienced military and police oppression in circumstances similar to those at Hanyang, but because we had taken action one step ahead of the soldiers, further sacrifices had been averted. These facts made us realize that the decision reached the previous night was a necessary one. The stubborn, overbearing attitude of Hsiang Ying apparently had changed. It was fortunate, he told me, that Kiangan workers were spared a repetition of the previous day's tragedy because our return-to-work order reached them in time, for the order reached Kiangan quickly. The workers there, holding in their emotions, went to their factories at 7:00 A.M. and resumed work in accordance with the order. Nevertheless, troops at the Kiangan station and at the union's headquarters fanned out in large numbers to arrest workers and force them back to work. They announced that those who resisted or tried to escape would be summarily executed. In time, however, senior members of the railway administration explained that the union had issued an order to resume work and thus persuaded the troops not to interfere. Only then did the barbaric activities of the soldiers stop. With assistance from the staff of the railway administration, the back-to-work order was transmitted northward along the railway, station by station.

Even though the unions hastily withdrew, Hsiao Yao-nan kept up his persecution. His troops occupied all the trade unions in Wuhan, closed the Hankow *Chen Pao*, a newspaper run by KMT members which was consistently sympathetic to striking workers, and ordered the arrest of the newspaper's staff. Hsiao did not believe that the unions actually were helping to restore order in the factories. He continued to order the arrest of labor leaders and others connected with trade unions.

Best known among the people arrested was Shih Yang, the lawyer. A KMT member who joined the CCP after its initial organization, he never took part in the secret work of the CCP. Instead he used his position as a lawyer to defend the poor. It was a work to which he devoted himself happily and tirelessly. In 1922 he began serving as honorary legal adviser to various trade unions, and he was active and capable in this position. But as his prestige grew, officialdom came to hate him. The afternoon of February 7, when the troops began their massacre of Kiangan workers, Shih Yang was arrested in his office. He was shot on February 15 without even the formality of a trial. His death filled us with a profound sorrow. It recalled the many contacts we had had with him since 1920.

It was difficult and dangerous for the CCP organization at Wuhan to meet during the state of emergency caused by Hsiao Yao-nan's bloody rampage. I could not get in touch with comrades Tung Pi-wu, Ch'en T'an-ch'iu, and others living in Wuchang. The only CCP members I could bring together to discuss our next moves were Hsiang Ying, Lin Yü-nan, and Hsü Pai-hao, secretary of the Hanyang Ironworks Trade Union. We decided in our discussions that while the strike had ended, the struggle against Wu P'ei-fu had just begun. We decided that we must expose the crimes of Wu P'ei-fu and the other warlords to as large an audience as possible in order to arouse the sympathy of everyone in the country. Moreover, we laid detailed plans to strengthen secret CCP activities whereby underground unions and Party fractions *(tang-t'uan)* would be organized in the factories. It was our estimate that most of the leading trade unionists would escape arrest because of the course we had taken. Still, we thought that those who headed unions would lose their factory jobs. They would be unemployed, and providing help for them was an urgent matter. Having looked after these arrangements, I decided to return to Peking to report to the CC.

I could not very well travel by way of the Peking-Hankow Railway; that was too dangerous. So on the evening of February 8 I took a river boat to Nanking, and there I boarded a train on the Tientsin-Pukow Railway. I made use of a stopover at Pukow to discuss with Wang Ho-po, chairman of the Pukow branch of the Tientsin-Pukow Railway Union, and others what to do to maintain the union underground. The union at Pukow, it turned out, was the only one of the railway unions that escaped molestation. Perhaps this was due to the fact that Wu P'ei-fu could not directly exert his influence in Pukow. In any event, I caught a train for the North and reached Peking on February 12.

An atmosphere of terror also enveloped Peking and its environs at the time. The authorities closed the railway union at Ch'anghsintien late on the evening of February 6 and arrested eleven of its officials. Then, early the next morning, February 7, soldiers and police opened fire on the working masses there, killing more than ten workers and a few residents and seriously wounding more than thirty others. Trade unions also were closed in other places, and most of their officials were arrested. When the authorities commanded Hu Chuan-tao, a member of the executive committee of the Hsinyang branch of the union, to run a locomotive, he refused; so they cut off one of his arms. At railway stops where they had been established, most of the schools for workers' children, part-time schools for workers, and workers' clubhouses were closed. *Labor Weekly* and other publications of the Secretariat of Labor Organizations in China were banned. In Peking itself it was quite possible that CCP members would be arrested. All of these facts went together to demonstrate conclusively that the warlords were suppressing the labor movement throughout the North.

In the face of this staggering blow, the CC of the CCP launched a propaganda campaign against Wu P'ei-fu's persecution of trade unions and his massacre of workers. Some members of Parliament laid questions about the situation before that body.[11] But these resistance forces were negligible, and they could not influence the attitude of Wu P'ei-fu and the other warlords. Thus the CC came to realize that workers' strikes could not withstand the armed strength of the warlords. In this way it came to place greater hope in the KMT plan to build up its armed forces and expand the revolutionary base at Canton.

Most of the capital that the CCP had at the time, figuratively speaking, was invested in the labor movement. Taking a hard look at the labor movement following the defeat of the February Seventh Strike, we discovered that we had lost ninety percent of that capital. Only in Hunan Province did the trade unions escape strenuous persecution. And Hunan was strategically located between North and South. There, the allegiance of Chao Heng-t'i, who advocated a federation of autonomous provinces, still wavered between North and South. Furthermore, Chao had lost ground because he had executed the two labor leaders Huang Ai and P'ang Jen-ch'uan, and so it was necessary for him to be careful about what he did. On the whole it was possible for the unions in Hunan to stay in existence. We directed comrades in Hunan to take strict precautions even though severe persecution had not descended on the unions there. In all other places, however, we had no choice but to organize underground trade unions.

At the same time we concluded that the center of our work no longer was in the North and that we should strengthen our work at Shanghai and Canton. If the CC of the CCP remained in Peking, it might easily fall prey to the machinations of the warlords. We therefore decided to immediately and secretly move the machinery of the Party center back to Shanghai, which would strengthen our leadership in the South and further KMT-CCP cooperation.

On the basis of my report on the February Seventh Strike, the CC studied the achievements and failures of our leadership. Ch'en Tu-hsiu mentioned his profound regret at the failure of the strike, and then went on to express, among other things, his misgivings by asking, "Could we have taken steps ahead of time to avoid the massacre?" Maring, however, fully backed my leadership of the strike. He said that strikes for greater freedom could not be stopped and that we should have promoted the strike at the time we did. He thought that after the February 7 massacre had occurred, rapid withdrawal had been the correct step to take. After hearing this praise from Maring, the CC decided that my leadership of the strike had been correct.

Maring, moreover, proposed that I go to Moscow to report on the February Seventh Strike, while the CC secretly moved to Shanghai and made its new arrangements there. He said that the CCP was growing rapidly and was able to organize large numbers of workers into unions, to launch strikes for greater freedom, and to draw back at the appropriate time in order to avoid excessive losses. Such things, he declared, proved that the leadership of the CCP was maturing. The Chinese labor movement had a great future, and the Comintern should be made fully aware of this. The CC adopted Maring's proposal.

About February 20, 1923, a few days after the Lunar New Year, taking the route through Manchouli that I had taken before, I braved the severe winter cold and again crossed the Sino-Russian border without incident. The New Economic Policy was then in force in the Soviet Union. It was making some progress in restoring economic order. Lenin was in high spirits and reported to the Comintern that currency inflation was a thing of the past in the Soviet Union and that the government held a reserve of two million rubles. As I passed through Siberia, I saw things that substantiated his claim. The trains left on schedule, and even though supplies were still scarce, prices were generally stable and production was being restored.

My chief task upon reaching Moscow was to report what actually had happened in the February Seventh Strike to Safarov, the head of the Eastern Department of the Comintern; Voitinsky, the head of the Comintern's Far Eastern Section; and Lozovsky, the chairman of the Profintern. The report did not seem to receive the attention Maring expected it to receive. News of defeat does not inspire people. This is a normal human reaction, and the Comintern acted in accordance with it.

Not long before my appearance, Ch'en Tu-hsiu had attended the Fourth Congress of the Comintern, at which he had not attracted much attention either. A part of the reason for this, apparently, was Chen's tendency to speak frankly. He refused to indulge in exaggeration. I spoke in the same vein as Ch'en Tu-hsiu. I did not want to make wildly optimistic predictions about the distant future, since nobody in the Comintern expected the Chinese revolution to develop spectacularly in the near future. It was generally thought that the only thing that could be said for the CCP was that it had begun to work in earnest and that it had some accomplishments to show for its struggle.

At the time more important issues kept the Comintern busy. A few days after I arrived in Moscow an Enlarged Plenum of the ECCI met. The major items on the agenda were the united front of the labor movement in Western Europe and problems within the Soviet Union. Social-Democratic parties influenced a majority of workers in Western Europe, and the Comintern strategy of forming a so-called United Front of the Lower Strata with the workers of these parties had not met the success that it had hoped for. This problem generated enthusiastic discussion.

As to the so-called problems within the Soviet Union, at that time thirty-two ranking senior members of the Russian Communist Party had formed an opposition group. In front of the Comintern they had accused the CC of the Russian Party of errors in leadership. Karl Radek spoke on behalf of the CC in making its defense. He declared before the Enlarged Plenum that the Russian Communist Party had committed about a thousand mistakes but that the nature of these mistakes was not basic. The Party had led the Revolution to victory, he pointed out, and conditions were improving daily. This proved that the opposition's charges were not relevant. These remarks by Radek described the situation in Russia at that time more or less accurately.

I spoke about the China question to a session of this Plenum, reporting chiefly on the February Seventh Incident. My report did not spark a discussion. It merely provided an interlude in the agenda.

I stayed in Moscow for about three weeks. Responsible members of the Comintern and Profintern worked with me in drafting a set of measures to be taken in organizing underground trade unions in different parts of China. We had already carried out most of them. The Comintern and Profintern promised to raise some money for the relief of families of workers that had been killed and to help workers that had been dismissed from their jobs. They said they would send the money to China in installments. Because Sun Yat-sen had just returned to Canton and conditions there did not yet look stable, KMT-CCP cooperation was not discussed. Thus, my mission to Moscow ended, I hurried back to China.

The Third Congress of the Chinese Communist Party

When I returned to Shanghai toward the end of March, 1923, the CC of the CCP was still passing through the tragic aftermath of the February Seventh Strike. We were all exploring new avenues of Party development, and serious differences arose among us. This state of affairs was reflected in the discussions of the issue of KMT-CCP cooperation at the Third Congress of the CCP.

The machinery of Party headquarters then operated underground at Shanghai in utmost secrecy. Even I did not know the residential address of Ch'en Tu-hsiu, which was kept secret. His secretary arranged the time and place of our first meeting. Maring had returned to Moscow two weeks earlier, Ch'en told me. Ch'en said that because of defeat in the February Seventh Incident, Maring thought it would not be easy to resume the Chinese labor movement. Also, knowing that Joffe was returning to Moscow from Japan, Maring had hurried back to participate in discussions of the China question and to help determine future work policy.

Ch'en Tu-hsiu said that the most important issue at the present, of course, was strengthening KMT-CCP cooperation. He noted that the directive on the labor movement that I had brought back from Moscow was in keeping with decisions already reached by the CC. It was necessary for the moment to use them as a basis for rebuilding the losses suffered in the February Seventh Incident. Such questions as KMT-CCP cooperation, he said, could await further discussion at the Third Congress of the CCP, which would be held when Maring returned.

Li Ta-chao also arrived in Shanghai from Peking at this time to avoid the danger of being arrested in Peking. He was in hiding at the home of Sun Hung-i. The two men came from the same province. Sun Hung-i, a member of Parliament who had been Minister of Internal Affairs around 1917, was known to maintain relations with Wu P'ei-fu and the Chihli clique in general. He also was known as a KMT member who probably served in a liaison capacity between the Chihli clique and the KMT. I called on Li Ta-chao at Sun's home and told Li about my trip to Moscow. When we had finished our talk, Li asked me to have a chat with Sun Hung-i, whom I already knew. It was intended to be just a friendly meeting, but unexpectedly it led us to sever all relations with the Chihli clique warlords.

When the formalities of greeting were over, Sun began to explain to me that the events of February 7 at Hankow were all the result of a misunderstanding. People had provoked Wu P'ei-fu, he said. In the first place, he pointed out that labor unions in various parts of the country were connected with Sun Yat-sen's Southern government and that the First National Labor Congress was held at Canton. In the second place, the CCP openly publicized its alliance with Sun Yat-sen to overthrow Wu P'ei-fu. Furthermore, Liang Shih-i and other members of the Communications clique had exploited the situation to sow dissension. For these reasons Wu P'ei-fu, who had not originally intended to do so, turned to persecuting the unions.

Sun Hung-i's explanation roused my ire. "The warlords rely on their rifles to slaughter people indiscriminately and without cause," I protested. "This has become their regular habit. Furthermore, the February Seventh Incident occurred without any warning at all. It was undeniably a crime and cannot hide behind the word 'misunderstanding.'"

My blunt reply promptly ended our conversation. As a result of this unpleasant exchange between Sun Hung-i and me, Li Ta-chao decided that if he stayed on in Sun's home, people might easily begin to wonder why he continued to maintain contact with the Chihli clique. Two days later he moved out to demonstrate that he was finished with the clique. A few days after that he received word from friends in Peking that he was no longer in danger of arrest there, and so he quietly returned to the Peita library. From then on, Li Ta-chao unequivocally demonstrated that he opposed Wu P'ei-fu. More resolutely than ever he insisted that the CCP cooperate closely with the KMT.

Meanwhile, in January, 1923, Ch'ü Ch'iu-pai returned to China from Moscow. He came from Peking to Shanghai, where he was the only ranking person in the CCP able to operate in the open, for he appeared in the guise of a newspaper correspondent. He had not yet displayed his Communist colors. Apparently his lung trouble had been arrested, and he was energetic and extremely eager to show what he could do. A lover of literature, he managed to make his quarters in Chapei look like an author's study. His most frequent visitors there were young writers. He also maintained an intimate friendship with the veteran KMT writer Yü Yu-jen, with whom he planned to establish Shanghai University. Yü was to be its president and Ch'ü the dean of studies. The university soon was founded and became a place for training young revolutionaries. Because of reverses in the labor movement, the CCP gave Ch'ü Ch'iu-pai every assistance in these activities, which it regarded as novel cultural ventures that could forge closer ties with well-known KMT figures.

The labor movement, to which the CCP attached the greatest possible importance, continued to suffer reverses. In this period of retreat for the movement, jobs or relief were needed for the families of nearly one hundred workers that had been killed and for nearly one thousand workers that had lost their jobs because of the strike. The CCP simply could not handle this burden. Every day I busied myself with the problem; but even after investing endless effort in it, I could not cope with the needs of a majority of the needy people.

The taste of defeat is difficult to describe adequately. Some KMT elements laughed and attacked us. They laughed at us for having illusions about Wu P'ei-fu, and they berated our policy toward Wu as the cause of the workers' suffering. KMT members even tried to take advantage of this opportunity to seize the initiative from the Communists in the labor movement. They used Shanghai as the center of their activities against the Secretariat of Labor Organizations in China.

Wang Hsien-hui and others in the Hunan Labor Society, along with certain anarchist elements, supported some of the KMT people in these activities. Primarily because they were disgruntled about the vainglorious attitude that the Chinese Communists assumed in the labor movement, they organized a united front against the CCP's labor movement. It was their position that unions should fight for the workers' economic interests, that they should have nothing to do with political parties, and especially that they should not be used by the CCP. A slogan they used was "CCP members are from the long-gown class; let them get out of the unions." They also publicized the contention that the February Seventh Strike failure was the result of mistaken Communist leadership. They called upon the workers to demand compensation from the Communists.

Some workers were influenced by this anti-Communist propaganda and changed their attitude towards the CCP. Even some of the labor leaders that had always sympathized with the CCP, but had lost their jobs because of the strike, began to have doubts. "Because of your leadership we took part in the strike," a few of them told me. "You are responsible for the fact that we are unemployed." A very small number of them went so far as to say, "We hear that you went to Moscow to raise a large number of rubles for our relief. Well, why don't you distribute them among us?" Fortunately, a majority of union leaders saw the truth and retained their confidence in us. In spite of the agitation against us, no serious difficulties arose.

The whole affair had its effect upon the ranks of the CCP. More than once Ch'en Tu-hsiu referred to the infantile nature of the Chinese proletariat and to its tendency to be a *Lumpenproletariat*. He said that when the labor movement was progressing smoothly, the workers were lovable heroes; but once reverses set in, they revealed their true natures. The attitude of Ch'en Tu-hsiu irritated Teng Chung-hsia. In *A Brief History of the Chinese Labor Movement* Teng later called Ch'en's attitude a tendency toward liquidationism and said, "From the defeat on February seventh, Ch'en concluded that the working class had no strength, and his whole opportunist theory was completely evolved at that time."[12]

Ts'ai Ho-sen, who was then fully engaged in editing *Guide Weekly*, also disagreed with the attitude of Ch'en Tu-hsiu. The CC was holding so few meetings at the time, however, that not everything could be discussed at them. Articles by Ch'en Tu-hsiu, to which Ts'ai took particular exception, were not discussed and had to be published as they were. While I had tasted the bitterness of the strike's defeat, I could not accept the views of Ch'en Tu-hsiu either. Frequently I reminded him that we must not lose confidence in the working class merely because we had discovered that the workers had their weaknesses, but we never found an opportunity to explore these differences of opinion. Not until the Third Congress of the CCP did the disagreements finally break into the open.

Maring returned to Shanghai from Moscow in May, 1923, carrying with him a special instruction from the Comintern to the CCP. On the basis of this instruction he demanded that the CCP immediately intensify its program of cooperation with the KMT, and he proposed an early convocation of the Third Congress at Canton. The CC accepted his proposal and promptly got ready to hold the Third Congress.

I had left for Peking at the time to settle certain urgent trade-union problems in several areas. When I returned to Shanghai, Maring had already left for Canton, while members of the CC were in the process of leaving, one after the other. I got to Canton early in June, apparently one of the last to arrive. On the whole, preparations for the Congress had been complete by then.

As a meeting place for the Congress, the CC rented a rather

inexpensive house in the Tungshan residential area of Canton. CC members and the delegates all lived there, and it was there that the Congress was held. Maring lived nearby in a more ostentatiously appointed house. With him lived Ch'ü Ch'iu-pai and Chang T'ai-lei, who worked as his assistants. It looked as though Maring were prepared to live in Canton for a long time. His rooms were so well furnished that he could have been taken for an ambassador from the Comintern.

This congress was unlike the previous two congresses, which had been held secretly in Shanghai, in that nobody tried to interfere with this Congress. I went straight to Maring's house when I reached Canton to have a look at the famous Comintern instruction. Ch'ü Ch'iu-pai had already translated it into Chinese. It included the following points:

1. The national revolution is currently the central task of the Chinese revolution.

2. The KMT is the leadership core of the national revolution. Members of the CCP should join the KMT and actively work within the KMT in order to overthrow the rule of the imperialists and their lackeys, the wardlords, in China.

3. In the national revolution, the CCP should preserve its independent organization and the freedom of political criticism.

4. The labor movement is still an independent movement, development of which the CCP should actively promote.

When I had read the brief document, Maring immediately explained that after he reached Moscow, the Comintern had formed a committee, headed by Bukharin, to discuss the China question. He said that the committee had drafted the important document I had just read on the basis of his report. The principal significance of the instruction, he said, was its call for all CCP members, without exception, to join the KMT and to actively work within the KMT. All work would be done by the KMT, he said, in keeping with the fact that the national revolution was the central task. He declared that this was the most important point. Furthermore, Maring explained that the independent organization of the CCP and its freedom of political criticism should not be overemphasized, for these were subsidiary issues in the instruction; to act otherwise would be to undermine KMT-CCP cooperation. As to the labor movement, while it was an independent movement, it was nevertheless a part of the national revolution. For that reason, Maring said that the CCP should recruit large numbers of workers for the KMT so that they would accept KMT leadership in the national revolution. The CCP should do no more than carry on class education among workers, he said.

At once I expressed doubts about the directive. I pointed to the phrase "preserve its independent organization and the freedom of political criticism." I insisted that the word "preserve" readily lent itself to misinterpretation. I did not agree with Maring's interpretation, for I believed that it would completely dissolve the CCP in the KMT.

Maring reacted quickly and strongly to my opposition. He mentioned nothing, however, about what had been said in the Moscow discussions. Neither did he mention the disputes that were already emerging in Moscow, nor what the disputes were about. He had worked in China for two years, and he felt that he enjoyed sufficient prestige and authority to use high-pressure methods. So far as he was concerned, any opposition to his interpretation amounted to opposition to the Comintern instruction itself. He told me that I was fundamentally opposed to making the national revolution the central task and to the basic policy of joining the KMT. An argument of unprecedented heat thus erupted between Maring and me.

The argument clearly was a continuation and development of the dispute, now carried to its peak, that had gone on since the special West Lake Plenum. The national revolution was the central task, and there must be cooperation between the KMT and the CCP. This was the fundamental policy affirmed by the Second Congress of the CCP and accepted by all. The argument focused on the form of KMT-CCP cooperation, that is, on whether all CCP members, or only a limited number of them, should join the KMT. Maring and I had become antagonists, and the situation might be likened to "a meeting of enemies who kept their eyes especially wide open."

Maring wholeheartedly held to the theory that once the KMT and the CCP were merged into one body, miracles would occur in the development of the national revolution. His indignation was immediately aroused when he heard such theories as those of building a KMT-CCP united front, of maintaining a revolutionary camp of various parties and groups, of the independent development of the CCP, and of limited CCP participation in the KMT. But his theory, after all, lacked persuasive power. He had to resort to such measures as relying on the Comintern instruction to exert pressure, accusing his opponents of basic opposition to KMT-CCP cooperation, and attempting to sabotage relations between Ch'en Tu-hsiu and myself. But his strength was not equal to his desire. He grew outwardly strong but inwardly weak, so that as time went by, he had to rely increasingly on the support of Ch'en Tu-hsiu.

I myself basically abhorred the policy of joining the KMT. I felt that the result of the merger of the KMT and the CCP into one body would damage both KMT-CCP cooperation and the revolution. Nevertheless, the first step in the policy of participating in the KMT had already been taken at the special West Lake Plenum, and I could not openly resist the Comintern instruction, for to do so would cast me into an unfavorable position. In resisting the attack launched by Maring, therefore, I could only resolutely persist in making a last-ditch stand on the need for independent CCP development and for limited participation in the KMT.

The argument thus started before the Congress opened. In the hope that some sort of mutual understanding would be reached, the Congress was postponed for one week. Maring and I were the chief disputants, and the major points of the argument were as follows: To begin with, I declared that I supported the idea that the national revolution currently was our central task. In point of fact, when the February Seventh Strike set the labor movement back, an anti-imperialist wave was rising in China. An anti-Japanese movement had started in March, 1923, demanding the restoration of the leased territory of Dairen and Port Arthur. In April some foreigners traveling on the Tientsin-Pukow Railway had been kidnapped, and the foreigners had strongly advocated international control over Chinese railways. This had led to a movement against imperialist aggression. Early in June, Japanese marines had killed some Chinese at Changsha, as a result of which a boycott of Japanese goods sprang up in various parts of the country. All of these incidents clearly demonstrated a rising wave of anti-imperialist sentiment. I said that I believed a national revolution was an urgent necessity and that I thought the anti-imperialist wave could be turned into a broad revolutionary force.

After thus answering Maring's slanderous accusations against me, I went on to say that although the national revolution was the central task of the CCP, it was not its only task. There was the class struggle in addition to the national revolution; and while the national revolution was currently the central task of the Party, the class struggle still remained.

Maring refused to agree with me. Since the national revolution was the central task, he said everything ought to be included in it, as in fact everything was. What was left over was merely the class education of the CCP. He insisted that if both the national revolution and the class struggle were stressed, the national revolution would suffer.

As his second point, Maring said that no matter how you looked at it, the Chinese proletariat was weak. "Where is your labor movement?" he asked, laughing at me. "It was long ago crushed by the few rifles of Wu P'ei-fu." Without qualification, he said that it would be impossible for a CCP of any real strength to appear for at least five years. He scoffed at the CCP membership as being merely a small number of zealous, well-intentioned students of Marxism. He said that if they did not do some practical work in the national revolution, there would be no meaning to the CCP; it would furnish a few high-thinking saboteurs of the national revolution and nothing more.

Maring's ideas infuriated me, and I contended that what he was saying violated Comintern decisions.[13] I said that the birth and growth of the CCP ought to be a matter of pride and satisfaction. While it had suffered a terrible blow, it would recover quickly and play a noteworthy role in the national revolution. Indeed, I insisted that after a prolonged period of difficult struggle, the CCP would finally lead the Chinese revolution to complete victory.

At that point Maring said that he considered the KMT to be much closer to an ideal national revolutionary political party with real strength than the Saraket Islam of Indonesia. Giving fulsome praise to Sun Yat-sen and his aides, he observed that they had a strong national consciousness, while at the same time some of them were well versed in Marxism. The Three Principles of the People were acceptable in their entirety. Moreover, he said that the KMT was not the political party of the bourgeoisie. Most of the elite of China's revolutionary ranks were members of the KMT, as were most of the elite of the working class. Maring contended, therefore, that the CCP should not insist upon certain conditions before its members could join the KMT. It should not, for example, insist that the KMT reorganize itself along democratic lines. In fact, CCP members should frankly enter the KMT in order to develop a national consciousness.

Maring's overly optimistic evaluation of the KMT also encountered opposition from Ch'en Tu-hsiu. It was the most serious difference between them. In addition, I emphasized that Maring saw only the bright side of the KMT; he did not see its dark side. On the basis of my experience in 1920 in the All-China Federation of Industries, I pointed out that the KMT was made up of widely disparate elements, and that it was lacking both in organization and discipline. I added that if the KMT did not forthrightly reorganize itself, it would not be able to accomplish much even with the large-scale participation of CCP members.

It was Maring's fourth point that produced the fiercest argument. This was the practical question of having the entire CCP membership join the KMT and actively participate in its work. To have all CCP members join the KMT and actively work for it, I held, meant that Ch'en Tu-hsiu would have to undertake the concrete tasks of the KMT. He would have to accept KMT leadership, become immersed in that Party's work, and speak to the world at large as a KMT member. Where, then, would be the independent existence of the CCP? Furthermore, if CCP members rushed into their midst, all asking for a share in the practical work, wouldn't questions be raised by KMT people, such as: Why are these people with hazy family backgrounds coming into our midst? Do they want to help us, are they petty thieves, or are they highway robbers? At the very least, I said, it would be thought that CCP members intended to usurp the positions held by old KMT members. Nominal KMT-CCP cooperation would in this way develop into KMT-CCP hostility.

I insisted that the Comintern instruction calling upon CCP members to join the KMT and to work actively within it could not possibly be interpreted in the way Maring was interpreting it. My understanding of the instruction was as follows: The KMT and the CCP, two dissimilar political parties, should be more closely linked together for the sake of one national revolution, and more CCP members than originally was planned should join the ranks of active KMT workers. But Communists that held positions of leadership in the various levels of their Party and those engaged in labor-movement activities unrelated to the KMT need not join the KMT. If, however, they did join the KMT, they should not be required to work actively within it. If this were not the meaning of the instruction, I said, it would not have included the words "preserve its independent organization." These words would be meaningless if the instruction were interpreted otherwise. Nevertheless, my interpretation was unacceptable to Maring.

As his fifth point, Maring referred to preserving the CCP's freedom to make political criticisms of the KMT. In the capacity of KMT members, he stated, members of the CCP should offer necessary criticisms of KMT activities, although it was essential that these criticisms be constructive if they were made in the name of the CC of the CCP. Naturally it was my view that we could not afford to throw out criticisms at random if we hoped to foster a satisfactory cooperation between the KMT and the CCP. I felt that we would have to avoid unnecessary criticisms and attacks. At the same time, however, it was essential that CCP members maintain their true Communist natures. This, of course, applied to Party members operating outside the KMT. But it also was important that members working within the KMT not lose their true Communist identities by being mere yes men. As to making political criticisms, the CC and the leadership organs at different levels of the CCP should not be bound by needless restrictions, nor should they be afraid to criticize. Actually, the differences between us on this point were not great, although Maring was dissatisfied with my stand.

The sixth point related to the labor movement. I persisted in my view that the CCP must lead an independent movement. To be sure, I said, the CC of the CCP must lead trade unions everywhere into active participation in the national revolution. To lead them into the KMT labor movement, however, was unthinkable. I stated that the CCP would develop by a sweeping recruitment of members from among the working masses. Some workers that joined the CCP might also join the KMT, but the CCP certainly was not obliged to recruit KMT members from among the working masses. If it did so, the independent labor movement would be transformed into a KMT-led labor movement. Maring strongly objected to this idea. While he regarded the working class as an integral part of the revolution—its Left Wing, in fact—he insisted that the working class must first develop a national consciousness. He berated me for treating the national revolution and the KMT as two separate issues instead of as a single issue. He insisted upon turning the CCP-led labor movement over to the KMT, which was not really willing to accept it.

Maring and I took diametrically opposed political stands on the above disputed points. He castigated me for retaining what he called the leftist ideology prevalent at the time of the Second Congress of the CCP, by which he meant the idea of building a KMT-CCP united front. He contended that I disparaged the national revolution and opposed the basic policy of joining the KMT. I, in turn, flayed Maring for committing the rightist mistake of liquidationism. I held that he was trying to destroy the independent existence of the CCP, trying to convert it into the Left Wing of the KMT. I insisted that this not only belittled the role of the Chinese working class, but also undermined the unity of national revolutionary forces.

Apparently deciding that he could not obtain my concurrence with his views, Maring began to apply pressure. He insisted that his interpretation was the original intention of the Comintern instruction, and he asked if I was prepared to disobey the instruction. I replied that if the Third Congress of the CCP did not fully agree with the instruction, it had the right to raise opposition views. In fact, I told Maring that I hoped he would report my views to the Comintern. But I added that what was more important at the moment was the fact that all of us were prepared to accept the Comintern instruction; the only opposition was to Maring's distorted interpretation of it. That I drew a distinction between him and the Comintern profoundly annoyed Maring. So visible did his anger become that he seemed on the verge of challenging me to a duel.

Throughout the argument both Ch'ü Ch'iu-pai and Chang T'ai-lei supported Maring. They moved energetically among the delegates, promoting the idea that the interpretation Maring gave to the Comintern instruction was its original intention and urging that the Third Congress of the CCP not go against the instruction. At the same time, Ch'ü Ch'iu-pai stressed the theory that China was a patriarchal society ruled by a feudal system. For that reason he believed that the current stage of the Chinese revolution called for a revolt of the bourgeoisie against feudalism and that therein lay the major component of the national revolution. I did not agree with Ch'ü Ch'iu-pai in this, and I argued with him about it. The chief problem in China, I believed, was that it suffered from imperialist rule. A feudal system no longer existed, while marked class divisions had emerged increasingly. Thus opposition to imperialism was the major component of the national revolution. I said that in addition to the antagonistic feudal remnant, there was within China the important revolutionary component of the working class fighting the bourgeoisie, both domestic and foreign.

The arguments gave Ch'en Tu-hsiu a headache. He could not side with either faction. In general, he adopted the compromising attitude that Li Ta-chao had used at the West Lake Plenum, although he retained his patriarchal position of final arbiter. Starting out realistically, he stated that no immediate development could be expected in the labor movement after the February Seventh Strike, which had proved that the

Chinese working class was weak. Therefore, the stronger bourgeois force should lead the national revolution, of which the working class was merely the Left Wing. He said that he did not wish to go against the Comintern instruction, nor did he believe that Maring would distort its meaning. Furthermore, he endorsed the view of Ch'ü Ch'iu-pai that bourgeois opposition to the feudal system was the major component of the national revolution. He also declared, however, that the national revolution must not be confused with the KMT and that he did not agree with Maring's overestimate of the KMT. He expressed the fear that numerous disputes would arise between the two parties as soon as large numbers of CCP members had joined the KMT and taken part in its work. Finally he proposed acceptance of the Comintern instruction, after making some slight revisions in the interpretation Maring had given it.

Mutual consultations and concessions did not shorten the distance between our views by much. Our main differences remained unreconciled. So Ch'en Tu-hsiu suggested that since the West Lake Plenum had decided that only a few CCP members picked by the CC should join the KMT, the Third Congress ought to go further and decide that all CCP members should join the KMT as individuals. Nevertheless, he said that a portion of CCP members should be free from having to carry out the practical work of the KMT. So as not to obscure the independent nature of the CCP, cadres in positions of leadership at all levels of the Party organization, in particular, should not hold KMT posts concurrently. Ch'en Tu-hsiu declared that at the same time, in order to strengthen working-class influence in the national revolution, the CCP should help the KMT get more worker and peasant members and spread its organization in these two classes. Maring announced his agreement with Ch'en Tu-hsiu. I agreed only with the first part of Ch'en's proposal; not with the second part. Thus, the matter had to be turned over to the Third Congress for final settlement.

The argument became the major theme for discussion at the Third Congress of the CCP. The Congress was held in mid-June of 1923, with seventeen voting delegates in attendance.[14] They represented more than four hundred Party members.[15] After the Congress opened, Ch'en Tu-hsiu first made a report that concentrated on the work of the CC of the CCP during the past year and on changes in the policy of participation in the KMT. Ch'en emphatically told about the defeat of the February

Seventh Strike and its repercussions, which proved the weakness of the forces of the proletariat. He stressed the importance of the national revolution, accepted the KMT as the leadership core of the national revolution, and advocated that in principle all CCP members join and work actively in the KMT. The CCP should lead the masses of workers and peasants, he said, and constitute itself the powerful Left Wing of the national revolution.

A ferocious debate developed when Ch'en's report came up for discussion. All of the dissenting views that I have described above were brought up one by one. Ch'ü Ch'iu-pai was the main supporter of Ch'en Tu-hsiu. Ch'ü Ch'iu-pai did not accept the idea that clear class demarcations existed in China. He held that in China the chief movements were anti-imperialist and antifeudal in character and that they were movements of all the people, the proletariat being merely an insignificant portion of the people. Ch'ü's belittlement of the strength of the proletariat roused dissatisfaction in quite a few delegates.

Ts'ai Ho-sen, Mao Tse-tung, and I were the principal speakers in opposition to these views of Ch'ü Ch'iu-pai. My statement was general in nature. I explained that the strength of the Chinese proletariat was growing rapidly. Although the working class was numerically small, it nevertheless was spirited and united; and if it allied itself with the broad masses of the poor peasants, it would inevitably become the major strength of the national revolution. I stressed that the CCP was an independent political party and that the labor movement was an independent movement led by the CCP. The fact that the CCP believed the national revolution to be the goal of its struggle at the present stage must not lead the working class and its political party, the CCP, into becoming the Left Wing of the KMT.

In his statement Ts'ai Ho-sen described the importance of maintaining the organizational independence of the CCP and its freedom of political criticism, and he quoted the Comintern instruction to support his position. He said that this position concerned a principle that should not be violated by participation in the KMT. Mao Tse-tung stressed the importance of the peasant revolution. He went on to point out that the forces of the KMT lay only in a corner of Kwangtung Province and that the CCP should concern itself with the broad masses of peasants throughout the country.

Most of the above points had been argued repeatedly before the Congress opened. Only the peasant movement seemed a new factor.

Indeed, the Third Congress was the first of the meetings of the CCP at which this issue was drawn to everybody's attention, and on this occasion especially, Mao Tse-tung paid attention to the peasant question. The first Chinese Communist leader of the peasant movement, P'eng P'ai, had established the first peasant associations in the Hai-feng–Lu-feng area of Kwangtung in September, 1922. By the time of the Second CCP Congress, his work had already achieved considerable success. But Hai-feng and Lu-feng were controlled by Ch'en Chiung-ming, and information about them did not easily leak out; so P'eng P'ai's work had not attracted much attention. Ch'en Tu-hsiu and the CCP Kwangtung Regional Committee had encouraged P'eng P'ai in his activities. But in his report to the Third CCP Congress, Ch'en Tu-hsiu did not mention this peasant movement. Instead, he lamented the fact that the peasants, although numerous, were backward and could not be mobilized all at once.

At the time of the Third CCP Congress, Mao Tse-tung knew nothing of P'eng P'ai's activities. Thus, like the other delegates, he could merely dabble vaguely in the peasant question. He did point out to the Congress that in Hunan there were few workers and even fewer KMT and CCP members, whereas the peasants there filled the mountains and fields. Thus he reached the conclusion that in any revolution the peasant problem was the most important problem. He substantiated his thesis by pointing out that throughout the successive ages of Chinese history all rebellions and revolutions had peasant insurrections as their mainstay. The KMT had built something of a foundation in Kwangtung, and this too was due to its possession of armies composed of peasants. If the CCP would concern itself with the peasant movement and mobilize the peasants, it would not be difficult for the Party to build a situation similar to that in Kwangtung. This was the greatest contribution that this son of a peasant family made to the Third CCP Congress. I will not discuss here where Mao's ideas took him. In any event, at this time the peasant question was an important one.

The debate continued for nearly a week, until Maring finally intervened personally. He addressed the Congress, expressing support for Ch'en Tu-hsiu's report. He stressed his initial proposal that all CCP members join the KMT and that all work be carried out in the name of the KMT. He condemned as empty leftist talk any views that underestimated the KMT and exaggerated the strength of the working class. Maring had always held the peasants in contempt, and he did not mention a word about the peasant problem. In conclusion, in a threatening tone he said, "Whether or not Mr. Ch'en's report is passed will demonstrate whether the Congress accepts the Comintern instruction or is prepared to violate it."

Ch'en Tu-hsiu and I tried to reach an understanding by talking things over, but eventually these efforts failed. Finally, at the conclusion of the debate, a revised version of my proposal was put to a vote. This revised proposal was based on our unsuccessful attempt to reach an understanding. Its main points were as follows: First, in the national revolutionary movement the CCP must strengthen its leadership of the labor movement and develop CCP organization among workers. Second, in the labor movement the CCP must cooperate closely with KMT-led labor unions and with KMT members in those unions. Not all CCP members among the workers should join the KMT, however, but only those for whom such a move was necessary. Third, since the labor movement was an independent movement led by the CCP, the CCP should not adopt a policy of actively encouraging large numbers of workers to join the KMT, although neither should the CCP obstruct KMT activities among workers or keep workers from joining the KMT.

When this revised proposal was put to a vote, there were eight votes for it and eight against it. Ch'en Tu-hsiu as chairman cast the deciding vote. In other words, my proposal was defeated by a majority of one. This rejection of my proposal was tantamount to passage of Ch'en Tu-hsiu's original proposal, the general provisions of which were that the CCP should develop the authority and influence of the KMT among the masses of workers and peasants (especially among the peasants). So far as those of us who stood in opposition were concerned, the provision about developing KMT authority and influence among the peasants was immaterial, since the CCP did not yet have any power among the peasants. But the provision for the unlimited development of KMT authority and influence among the workers was tantamount to abandoning the major front of the CCP; it virtually meant abandoning the foundation of the independent existence of the CCP.

And so Maring scored a victory for his proposal. Knowing that he owed it mainly to the support of Ch'en Tu-hsiu, however, he felt that this victory was insecure; so he stepped up his pressure against me. He openly claimed that I opposed Ch'en Tu-hsiu's leadership and that I was thereby violating the Comintern instruction and undermining Party unity. Feeling that I should be severely punished, he attempted to defeat me, his opponent, once and for all.

Meanwhile, according to established Comintern practice, people holding opposition views had to state their positions before the Congress. Those of us in opposition did not express unanimous views. Mao Tse-tung, who had been the first one to support my revised proposal, light-heartedly announced his acceptance of the decision of the majority. Following him, Ts'ai Ho-sen, in one solemnly spoken sentence, announced that he would obey the majority decision. In my statement before the Congress, I made it obvious that I would obey the majority decision, but I reserved my original views. Such variation in our statements and my emphasis on reserving my original views concentrated the attacks on me all the more. Maring declared that the implication of reserving my views was that I would continue to take opposing positions, and this would lead to disputes within the Party. He said that consequently I must perforce be put under restraint.

At that juncture a delegate from Harbin, Ch'en Wei-jen, who represented the CCP organization in Northeast China, rose and spoke. He said that he had voted in support of Ch'en Tu-hsiu's original proposal as an expression of confidence in the CC led by Ch'en Tu-hsiu. He said, however, that he did not support the policy of joining the KMT or the position of sacrificing the independence of the CCP and that he did not believe Ch'en Tu-hsiu really did either. With all sincerity he called for Party unity and asked Ch'en Tu-hsiu to respect the views of the opposition. He especially stressed that rather than being punished, I should continue in the future to assume responsibility in the Party leadership.

Ch'en Wei-jen, who had not been drawn into the argument very much, said this most sincerely. His action changed the atmosphere of the meeting, causing Ch'en Tu-hsiu to decide that it was time to call a halt to the dispute. And so Maring was unable to make use of his overbearing policy.

After this initial storm of disagreement within the CCP had receded, calm returned to the Congress, which went on to other items on the agenda. Special mention should be made of another proposal Ch'en Tu-hsiu brought forward—the question of Party fractions.* Essentially he proposed that CCP members undertaking KMT work should organize Party fractions, which would insure a uniformity of views among CCP members in the KMT and would further their influence on the KMT. In making this proposal, Ch'en Tu-hsiu seemed to be trying to give some

---

* *tan t'uan:* A unit made up of CCP members within an organization other than the CCP to which those particular CCP members belonged.

comfort to those of us who had opposed him by demonstrating his disinclination to sacrifice CCP independence. By then, all the arguing had induced something of a state of shock among the delegates, most of whom felt restless, and a let-down atmosphere prevailed in the Congress. As a result, Ch'en's proposal passed unanimously and without discussion. But later this issue was to become a major one in the KMT-CCP dispute.

The manifesto[16] that the Congress finally adopted accepted the leadership position of the KMT in the national revolution and expressed the hope that all revolutionary elements in the society would rally round the KMT. However, it did not mention any of Maring's high-sounding phrases, such as "All work through the KMT" and "All revolutionary tasks are part of the tasks of the KMT." This, too, was undertaken out of consideration for Party unity.

At the election of the CC of the CCP, I was not reelected and so was dropped from the CC. The five members of the new CC were Ch'en Tu-hsiu, Li Ta-chao, Ts'ai Ho-sen, Mao Tse-tung, and Ch'ü Ch'iu-pai. Ch'en remained as secretary, Ts'ai remained as head of propaganda, and Mao Tse-tung replaced me as director of the Organization Department.

Subsequent CCP accounts generally state that the Third Congress of the CCP dismissed me from the CC either because of my basic opposition to KMT-CCP cooperation or because of my basic opposition to the policy of participating in the KMT. These accounts are on the whole rather imprecise.[17] I believe that the account I have given above tallies with what actually happened at the time. Apart from myself, Mao Tse-tung appears to be the only surviving participant in the Third Congress. If he is prepared to uphold historical truth, he will not repudiate the account I have given above.

This decision of the Third Congress authorized a new undertaking in the historical development of the CCP. The resolution of the West Lake Plenum merely stated that a minority of CCP members would join the KMT. It was the Third Congress that went further in adopting the policy of all-inclusive KMT-CCP cooperation within the framework of the KMT. Comintern and CCP historians, as a result, often dwell upon this Congress in an attempt to prove, from various angles, that Comintern leadership was correct.

Viewed from any angle, however, this policy of joining the KMT cannot be regarded as having been proper. To be sure, its implementation did lead to appreciable achievements in furthering the Chinese national revolution, but it cannot be demonstrated that the same, or even greater, things could not have been achieved had KMT-CCP cooperation been pursued within the framework of a united front. And it is an incontrovertible fact that the KMT-CCP merger eventually led to the drastic splitting of revolutionary forces that plunged China into the double tragedy of civil war and alien aggression. In carrying out this policy, the KMT and the CCP fell into an abyss of contention that ultimately transformed them from friends into irreconcilable enemies.

Later, after the KMT-CCP split in 1927, the Comintern maintained its posture of "the king can do no wrong"; it stressed the validity of the policy of joining the KMT and falsely attributed all mistakes to improper CCP implementation of the policy. Many accounts state that the Comintern was absolutely correct in proposing that the CCP adopt the policy of joining the KMT in order to seize the leadership of the national revolution and thereby win final victory. The Chinese revolution ended in defeat, they say, because in carrying out the policy of joining the KMT the rightist opportunist Ch'en Tu-hsiu abandoned efforts to seize the leadership. At the same time, for my early opposition to this policy, I have been criticized for committing the leftist mistake, which was later called a rightist mistake, of refusing to seize the leadership of the national revolution. But in fact what was discussed at the Third Congress was the question of whether or not the CCP should preserve its independence, and there was essentially no discussion of the question of the proletariat striving to win the leadership of the national revolution.

Perhaps I may be pardoned here for making a small criticism of Ch'ü Ch'iu-pai. He had an ingrained habit of playing with words and phrases. At the Third Congress, in doing his best to find a theoretical basis for Maring's proposal, he stressed that China was a clan society, that class demarcations were not yet marked, that the goal of the revolution was to overthrow feudalism, etc. If such ideas of Ch'ü's had been developed further, he might possibly have been even more rightist than Maring, for he would have removed the theoretical foundation for the existence of the CCP. But later, when he had succeeded Ch'en Tu-hsiu as CCP leader, he never again mentioned that he had taken this position at the Third Congress. Instead, quoting things out of context, he proceeded to claim that everybody else was wrong and opportunistic, while he alone was correct, meaning that he had advocated KMT-CCP cooperation within the framework of the KMT in order to seize the leadership. As a matter of fact, however, the national revolution and the KMT were two different things. It is a morally tenable approach for two political parties (such as the KMT and the CCP) to compete with one another for leadership of the national revolution; but for the CCP as a political party to join the KMT in an attempt to seize its leadership as a prelude to seizing the leadership of the national revolution is a morally untenable method of dealing with an ally. No wonder Wang Ching-wei said at that time, "This is the method used by the Monkey King in dealing with the Pig," referring to the story in the novel *Hsi-yiu-chi* (The Westward Journey) that the Monkey King, Sun Wu-kung, subdued the monstrous Pig, Chu Pa-chieh, by getting himself into the latter's belly.

The policy of joining the KMT was the source of all the troubles that followed. At the time of the Third Congress, Moscow's direction of the CCP was very confused. More than anything else, Moscow did not fully understand the China situation. Comintern leaders knew only about the importance of the national revolution and the need to concentrate revolutionary forces—two empty principles. They ignored the actual conditions of the two parties—the KMT and the CCP—and sought to forcibly merge them. In January, 1923, the resolution of the Enlarged Plenum of the ECCI still stressed the independence of the CCP.[18] However, in April, 1923, apparently under the influence of such people as Joffe and Maring, its instruction clearly marked a change in direction. For this instruction considered CCP participation in the KMT to be of primary importance, making the preservation of the CCP's independence a secondary issue. In other words, the Comintern's April instruction was the starting point of the CCP's turn toward the Right.

Maring's personal views were even farther to the Right than the Comintern instruction. He not only introduced the proposals I have described above, but he attempted to carry them out. He sought to play the part of the important person who had arranged KMT-CCP cooperation. He wanted to take up residence in Canton to await the Third Congress resolution that he thought would enable him to put his proposal into effect immediately. Unfortunately, he had the bad luck to encounter obstacle after obstacle. His proposal apparently did not interest the KMT. The KMT people seemed most interested in having practical help from the Soviet Union made available to them—especially military aid. So far as the entire CCP membership joining the KMT was concerned, it did not seem to strike the KMT as the urgent need of the day. Nor did Ch'en Tu-hsiu wholly agree with Maring. Ch'en insisted that the CC of the CCP immediately return to Shanghai to carry on its work. Apparently he did not relish the idea of staying in Canton to become a vassal of the KMT. This, too, was something Maring could not influence at will.

Although most of Maring's proposals were accepted by the Third Congress, they were never implemented. From my point of view, nothing good would have resulted even if they had been carried out. For the KMT veterans generally were quite cliquish, and they frequently looked down upon the younger members of their own Party. Even if CCP members in joining the KMT had completely shed their Communist coloration and worked wholly for the KMT, they could not have escaped being stigmatized as heretics of questionable lineage. How, then, could they have been free to carry out KMT activities? Furthermore, most CCP members regarded themselves as youths of better-than-average accomplishments, and some of them had originally been KMT members, but had left that Party to join the CCP. While they had still been in the KMT they had made known their dissatisfaction with its conventions. If these CCP members now returned to the KMT, is it likely that they would remain content in the role of secondary wives? We had good reason to say that the policy was essentially a flight of fancy.

Ch'en Tu-hsiu not only remained a considerable distance from Maring in his stand, but from start to finish he had reservations about our primary policy being that of the CCP joining the KMT. It was unfair of the Comintern to condemn him as a rightist. Indeed, at the time, the Comintern policy for China was more to the Right than the proposals of Ch'en Tu-hsiu. Ch'en's position stemmed from a more realistic viewpoint than that of the Comintern. He thought that China's proletariat was weak and that the CCP could not for a time readily play the role of leader of the national revolution. This was a fact. But he did not ever hold that in joining the KMT, the CCP should increase its strength and expand the scope of its activities within the KMT. On the contrary, he believed that the CCP was making some sort of a sacrifice, and he frequently worried about the possibility that disputes would arise between the KMT and the CCP. It was chiefly out of deference to the leadership of the Comintern that he accepted this policy of the CCP joining the KMT.

After arguing about it at the West Lake Plenum, Ts'ai Ho-sen, myself, and others had accepted a conditional and limited policy of

CCP members joining the KMT. We held that this was a structure for bringing about a united front. But we stood firm from beginning to end on the basic stand that a united front should be formed by the KMT and CCP. At the Third Congress we agreed to an increase in the number of CCP members who would join the KMT. Nevertheless, we stuck to the positions that the CCP should maintain organizational independence, put forward its own political proposals from time to time, maintain independent leadership of the labor movement, and develop activities among the broad masses of the peasants. These positions indicated our belief that the CCP should assert independence equal to that of the KMT.

But the policy that the CCP actually carried out was one of a "merging of KMT and CCP" rather than of an "alliance of KMT and CCP." Our views were shelved. Had the CC at the time persisted in seeking an alliance of the KMT and the CCP, Sun Yat-sen would have agreed to it. And in my opinion, had KMT-CCP alliance been achieved, we might have averted many needless disputes between the two. The alliance could have taken the form either of an equal partnership or of the KMT being the senior partner and the CCP being the junior partner. Either of these forms could have prevented the development of a situation in which both parties vied for position and power within the KMT. If the scheme had developed well, it could have led to a normal multi-party democracy. And if that had happened, it is possible that China's contemporary history would have to be written quite differently from the way in which it has been written.

I Attend the First Congress of the Kuomintang

The dissension in the Third Congress of the CCP over KMT-CCP relations quickly spread to local CCP organizations in various areas. Perhaps in the proposal to create such abnormal relations between the KMT and the CCP by intermingling them in a single body there were too many loopholes, for both within the CCP and outside it the issue became a focal point for endless disputes. Meanwhile, the responsible members of the CC of the CCP and I hurriedly returned to Shanghai after the Third Congress. Very soon thereafter Maring arrived at Shanghai from Canton, and so disputes over the KMT issue once more developed within our Party at Shanghai.

Our Party attached great importance to harmony then. While there were serious disagreements among us, we did not want the Party that we had built up with such difficulty to disintegrate. Nor did we want this group of good friends to split to a point beyond reconciliation. Accordingly, all of us, consciously or unconsciously, sought agreement. I know that such feelings motivated me. At first I kept silent, not wishing to be involved in further arguments. Then I undertook the task of mediation. And finally I attended the First Congress of the KMT to demonstrate that basically I had no thought of opposing KMT-CCP cooperation.

Maring proceeded differently, however. To the end he disregarded all else in attempting to carry out his proposals. When he returned to Shanghai, he did his best to suppress opposition views, and he continued to use high-pressure methods against me. He objected to the CC assigning me any work, and he declared that I would be placed under disciplinary restraint if I continued to oppose the policy decided upon by the Third Congress. He did all this quite pointedly, against the background of harmony within the CCP, to prevent the CC from making any concessions to me.

However, Maring very soon left China to return to Moscow. It seemed that because he had instigated such a serious incident in the CCP, the Comintern began to lose confidence in him, relieved him of his original duties, and transferred him back. The stand he took at the Third CCP Congress clearly did not have Comintern support. He did not visit China again, and I saw no more of him.

When the CC of the CCP returned to Shanghai, it faced many trying problems connected with KMT-CCP cooperation. At the Third Congress, Ch'en Tu-hsiu and the majority of delegates had the support of most members of the Party in Kwangtung Province, which made it seem as though they had strong backing. But upon returning to Shanghai, they found the situation clearly different. In such major areas as Shanghai, Peking, Hunan, and Hupeh, a majority of Party members expressed doubts about the resolution of the Third Congress and denounced it. Many members criticized the Comintern for its ignorance of conditions in China and for its arbitrary decision to dissolve the CCP in the KMT. They also criticized Maring for his foolhardiness. Demands that the Comintern recall him increased.

The CC worked very hard to put down such opposition views. Yang Ming-chai, for example, who had always been known for worshiping Ch'en Tu-hsiu, excoriated the policy of joining the KMT. He called it a virtual betrayal of the CCP to the KMT. He had such a violent quarrel with Ch'en over this issue that he declared he would never see Ch'en again, which was quite painful for Ch'en. This forthright son of Shantung volunteered for service in Kansu Province, for neither the KMT nor the CCP had established organizations there and so the question of cooperation did not arise. Since the CC could not persuade him to change his mind, it had to accede to his request. I had no inkling that the quarrel with Ch'en was brewing, but after the incident Yang gave me a very spirited account of it. I tried to dissuade him from his decision by calling upon him to uphold Party unity before all else, but I could not change his mind. After that I heard nothing further of him.

I lived idly in Shanghai for more than a month, maintaining my silence. Not since joining the CCP had I experienced an idle period. At the Third Congress I had declared that I reserved my original views because I had strong confidence in my own stand and did not want to make a show of supporting the aspirations of the CC. At the same time, keeping my promise to obey the majority, I stopped expressing opposition views. Although rumors were current that I opposed the Comintern, the KMT, and KMT-CCP cooperation, I made no reply to them. I did not want my relations with the CC to deteriorate further. Also, I did not believe that Maring's ideas could be carried through to their conclusion. I was waiting for Ch'en Tu-hsiu and the others to change their minds.

Toward the end of August, Ts'ai Ho-sen came to see me on behalf of the CC of the CCP. He officially informed me that Maring had returned to Moscow, that Ch'en Tu-hsiu had consistently rejected Maring's attitude toward thwarting oppositionists, and that Ch'en, under the pressure of opposition views within the Party, was gradually altering his original ideas. He added that the CC and many comrades were anxious about the question of inner-Party unity. They hoped that the CC would give me an important assignment and that I would accept it with good will, he said, so as to prove that there were no differences between the CC and me that could not be patched up. I assured him that I would gladly abide by CC decisions and would accept whatever job it assigned me; but I said that I still reserved my original views and that when an opportunity presented itself, I would again bring them up for discussion.

As a result of this conversation with Ts'ai Ho-sen, I was invited to attend a meeting of the CC a few days later. The reception Ch'en Tu-hsiu gave me was earnest and sincere. He expressed the hope that I would go to Peking to take charge of railway-union work and that I would immediately establish a national railwaymen's union. I accepted the assignment. And so the harmony we had formerly enjoyed began to return.

Early in September, 1923, I again returned to work in Peking. Most of the more than forty comrades in that area had supported the views I expressed at the Third Congress and sympathized with my position. While Li Ta-chao held ideas on political issues that differed from mine, he was extremely cordial and placed no restraint on exchanging views with me. He told me that both the KMT and the CCP wanted him to develop KMT organization in the North. He had accepted the task and was laying his plans. I supported his stand, for I regarded him as eminently suited for the role of promoting KMT-CCP cooperation. We agreed that I was to throw myself into activities of the railway-workers' union. Everything went smoothly.

Each regular meeting of CCP members in Peking was given over to endless arguments about KMT-CCP relations. Some members present insisted that the participation of all CCP members in the KMT was a mistake in principle. Others stressed the need to maintain CCP independence. They did not want the Party to be a vassal of the KMT. Still others were critical of the CC for disparaging the labor movement. On every occasion Li Ta-chao, as chairman, explained and defended the policy and strategy of the CC of the CCP. The divergent views were generally recorded and reported to the CC for review. It was not easy for me to remain aloof from these disputes. Yet I could do no more than announce at the meetings that all comrades were already thoroughly familiar with my thinking, that I had to abide by the majority decision, and that I could not therefore very well continue to express opposition views by participating in their discussions.

Since it was well known that I led the opposition within the CCP and that I represented the views of a strong group, Soviet personnel in Peking seemed to grow eager to learn about my ideas and activities. Sileipak (sp.?), chief of the Peking bureau of the Sino-Russian News Agency, maintained constant contact with me. Since he had once worked in the Comintern as an assistant to Gregory Voitinsky, we already knew each other. Now, as we renewed our acquaintance, he and his wife grew especially close to me, and I frequently visited their home to chat.

Although they never expressed an opinion on current CCP policies, I gathered from their attitude that they sympathized with my ideas. Some of the views I expressed seemed to pass on to the Comintern through him.

Toward the end of September, the famous Michael Borodin arrived in China, passing through Peking on his way to Canton. At Sileipak's invitation, I had a talk with him. I did not then know who Borodin was or what his mission might be. He began by indicating that he was in Peking for only a few days and that he had had no contact with Chinese friends there. He said he was unacquainted with conditions in China and that he wanted to go immediately to Canton to look over conditions in the South. He hoped I would tell him something about China.

We talked in a general way about conditions in China. From what I had to say he could see that I did not fundamentally oppose KMT-CCP cooperation, and this seemed to please him particularly. But when I declared that Chinese warlords were a self-seeking lot that had no conception of patriotism, he disagreed. Without offering any substantiation for the statement, he announced that there were many patriots among the Chinese warlords. This sort of thinking was typical of the attitude of some Soviet diplomats of the time, and Borodin impressed me as being just an ordinary diplomat.

As it turned out, of course, this man who made no special impression on me at the time—Borodin—was subsequently to play an extraordinary role in China. We maintained cordial relations after that initial contact. He had been sent to work in Kwangtung Province by Karakhan, who had reached Peking in August of that year and had received from Sun Yat-sen a request for Borodin's services. When Borodin first arrived at Canton, however, he seemed to have no official status. But because he got on well with Sun Yat-sen, he became the representative at Canton of both the Soviet Communist Party and the Soviet government, and he was at the same time political adviser to Sun Yat-sen and the KMT.

Early in November, Voitinsky came back to China. He passed through Peking on his way to Shanghai, and made an appointment to see me alone at the home of Sileipak, as had Borodin. First, he announced that he was replacing Maring as Comintern representative in China. He was familiar with my statements at the Third Congress of the CCP and declared that the Comintern disagreed with Maring's action and had instructed him to heed my views.

Voitinsky was delighted to learn that while political differences

remained within the CCP after the Third Congress, unity had nevertheless been maintained. But he frankly assured me that the Comintern
insisted upon the policy of the CCP joining the KMT. Some people in
the Comintern suspected me of tending to oppose this basic policy, he
said, and he spoke at great length in an effort to persuade me not to do
so. He added that the Comintern disagreed with Maring's disparage-
ment of the CCP; it wanted the CCP to join the KMT in order to revolutionize the KMT, and there was decided opposition to sacrificing CCP
independence. He also stated that my contention at the Third Congress
that responsible CCP members should not hold concurrent KMT posts
and my call for active leadership of the workers' and peasants' movements had received praise from the Comintern, which considered that
Maring was wrong in attacking such views.

I was enormously relieved upon hearing what Voitinsky had to say.
Still, I asked him why the Comintern did not adopt a KMT-CCP united
front instead of intermingling KMT and CCP in one organization, which
could not but lead to differences within the CCP. He said participation
in the KMT was precisely the method for realizing a united front. In
joining the KMT, the CCP was not expected to take orders from that
party in all matters, nor was it to constitute the Left Wing of the KMT,
rather it was to support and unite with revolutionary KMT elements to
oppose compromise trends within the KMT and to expel nonrevolution-
ary elements.

Finally, he said that certain deviations in the policy of the CC were
unavoidable because of the influence of Maring. At least, its interpretation of the basic policy was improper. It was fortunate, he said, that
after the Third Congress the CC had not pursued an erroneous path of
development and that I had avoided doing anything to aggravate inner-
Party dissension. He announced that he would immediately go to
Shanghai, where he would quietly correct deviations in the CC. He said
that he hoped I would not make statements in opposition to the CC, so
that future work could be carried out smoothly.

And so, on this basis, Voitinsky and I reached a mutual understanding. I told him that my future attitude would be decided by the actions
of the CC. If its deviation was corrected, inner-Party differences would
be eliminated.

Strictly speaking, Voitinsky should have spoken of these matters
directly to the CC of the CCP, not to any individual member of the
Party. He made a special point of bringing them up with me because

at the time a wave of opposition to CC policy was running high. He went out of his way to disclose the fact that he represented the Comintern in an attempt to remedy the situation and avert trouble.

That the Comintern had changed its attitude was unknown to other comrades, and so at a meeting of Party members in Peking one more horrendous argument broke out over the question of KMT-CCP relations. At this November meeting in Peking, Li Ta-chao reported that the KMT had decided to hold its First Congress on January 15, 1924. It was stipulated that six delegates from Peking would attend it, of whom three would be named by Sun Yat-sen and three elected by KMT members. He (Li Ta-chao) had been named one of the delegates and was preparing to attend the Congress. Headquarters of the KMT in Peking would undoubtedly hold an election of delegates, he said, and he hoped that comrades would take a positive attitude toward this important matter.

Li Ta-chao's report promptly raised a din of questions and denunciations. "You are a well-known CCP leader; now that you are attending the KMT Congress, what stand will you adopt?" some members wanted to know. Others demanded of him, "If the KMT calls on you to declare allegiance to the Three Principles of the People and to declare obedience to KMT decisions and orders, what are you going to do?" Li had no ready answers to these questions. As a result, many comrades refused to support the idea of CCP members serving as KMT delegates. Some of them went so far as to suggest, "Mr. Li had best attend the KMT Congress in a private capacity and not as a CCP member." This was far from being polite talk. Even Li Ta-chao, who seldom lost his temper, grew furious.

"How can I do that?" he demanded, bursting with rage. "Even though I am attending the Congress as a KMT member, I am well known to everybody as a member of the CCP. How can I renounce my status as a CCP member? Actually, you are fundamentally opposed to my participation, you are opposing the present CC policy, and you are not treating me as a comrade." After saying that, Li began to stalk out of the meeting in protest.

As a witness to this scene, I felt that I had no choice but to get up and try to dissuade Li Ta-chao from leaving. So I climbed up on the platform and made a speech. It was the first public statement I had made on the issue since the Third Congress, and it consisted of the following main points: First of all, I described the happenings at the West Lake Plenum and the Third Congress and the views to which I had persistently adhered. I pointed out that more than anything else I opposed Maring's inclination to liquidate the CCP. I expressed the belief that the Comintern would reject Maring's approach. The Comintern, I said, had emphasized the importance of the national revolution only in the hope that the CCP would become an active element in this imminent national revolution and assume a role that would further its development.

Next I conceded that the policy of participation in the KMT had given CCP members dual party membership, which was awkward. From the start I had had doubts about this business, and it was not in the least strange that comrades still refused to support it. However, it could not be said that participation in the KMT, or being a delegate to its Congress, would disassociate a Communist from the stand of his Party. A member of the CCP could still persist in his stand at the KMT Congress. The KMT would not demand that members of the CCP renounce their CCP membership. Clear substantiation of this was provided by the case of T'an P'ing-shan at Canton. He was a member of the Provisional Central Committee of the KMT, yet he remained a member of the Kwangtung District Committee of the CCP.

Then I pointed out that the policy of participating in the KMT was firmly held by the Comintern, and that it was passed by a majority at the Third Congress. I said that in the interest of Party unity, we should not basically oppose it. Since CCP members had joined the KMT, it was natural that some of them would take part in the KMT Congress, to demonstrate the sincerity of their cooperation as well as to influence others by their Communist views. Furthermore, the CCP ought to preserve its independence and develop its own organization and its own work among laborers and peasants. More than ever before, it must not sacrifice its position of leadership in the labor movement.

Finally, I declared that Li Ta-chao was a leader in whom we all had confidence and that he was an ideal person through whom to realize KMT-CCP cooperation. It was our duty to support his participation in the Congress in the hope that he would reveal there the enormous vitality of CCP members. In the election of KMT delegates, moreover, our comrades should adopt an equally positive attitude. I said they should consult with KMT elements and nominate candidates along with them.

My speech, aimed at mediating differences and promoting unity, moved the audience. They gave me their full attention. Nobody raised any questions. In fact, the information and opinions I presented seemed to give them new insights.

Then Li Ta-chao spoke up again. He expressed gratification at my speech. Judging from what I had said, he thought that there should be no irreconcilable differences within the Party. He explained that the CCP had taken the initiative in advocating KMT-CCP cooperation and in suggesting that the KMT convene a Congress to reorganize itself. He said that if after the Congress was called, we did not attend it, our behavior would be inexplicable. He also said that the Third Congress had been wrong in failing to adopt my proposals and that this mistake had led comrades to misinterpret the goals of the policy of joining the KMT. He hoped that this situation would be corrected as soon as possible. Finally, he stated that he bore no ill will toward the comrades that had put questions to him and that his only desire was for inner-Party differences to be resolved and unity achieved. He was quite prepared, as a Communist Party member, to work hard and bear criticism. Even if the work grew harder and criticisms more severe, he would not desert his comrades.

Next to take the floor was Ho Meng-hsiung, the member of the CCP Peking District Committee who had been most critical of Li Ta-chao's views. He said that my speech had given him information that he had not been aware of. He proposed that the question be discussed by the District Committee and then be placed before a meeting of members for decision. There was no opposition to this proposal, so the scene closed peacefully.

Another meeting of Party members was held a few days later. The Peking District Committee presented a carefully prepared draft proposal on the participation by CCP members in the work of the KMT, which was discussed. After much debate and explanation, the proposal was adopted. It was based chiefly on the speech I had made. The effect of this action was not merely to do away with most of the friction among comrades in the Peking area, but also to launch all of us into active participation in KMT work. The decision influenced CCP members in other areas, too. Their attitude toward KMT-CCP cooperation, which had been one of watching and waiting, changed.

On the surface the progress of the KMT organization at Peking gave cause for optimism. This state of affairs was closely related to developments in the over-all situation there. The Peking government, controlled by Ts'ao K'un and Wu P'ei-fu, of the Chihli clique, was faring badly, and its prospects were even worse. On June 13, 1923, they had driven out President Li Yuan-hung;[19] and on October 5 Ts'ao K'un had bribed the members of Parliament, and they had elected him president.[20] Ts'ao assumed the presidential office and promulgated a constitution. This debacle put an end to all the delightful proposals the Chihli clique had been making for years—proposals for the abolition of military governors, for the reduction of warlord armies, and the establishment of a "government by good men." Now the Chihli clique became notorious, and people throughout the country despaired of it. On the other hand, Sun Yat-sen had organized his Headquarters of the Generalissimo at Canton on March 1 of that year. While his position was at first precarious, it had gradually improved. He was advocating a reorganization of the KMT, seriously trying to build up a good government, and successfully repulsing the attacks that Ch'en Chiung-ming made on Canton. People that were disgruntled with the realities of the day began to pin great hopes on him.

In September, 1923, Li Ta-chao, Wang Fa-chin, Ting Wei-fen, and Li Shih-tseng began forming a KMT organization at Peking. The KMT members of Parliament that had accepted bribes from Ts'ao K'un had cut themselves off from the Party, and the new members admitted to the KMT were mostly young people with radical ideas. By November of 1923, after CCP members began to support the KMT actively, KMT membership in Peking increased to more than one thousand. Most of these members were the cream of Peking young people. About one-third of them were members of either the CCP or the SYC.

There was a good deal of enthusiasm among young people at that time for rallying around the KMT. They did not thoroughly understand the situation in Kwangtung or the objectives of the KMT reorganization, but they were utterly fed up with the Peking regime. My friends, whether or not they had joined the KMT, generally assured me that Ts'ao K'un had gone too far and that at least the KMT and Sun Yat-sen must be a little better than the crowd in the North. This was levelheaded public opinion, and it stimulated people.

At this point a report by Borodin gave me a greater insight into what was really going on in Kwangtung. Upon arriving at Canton, Borodin apparently proceeded very cautiously. He prepared a report on conditions there, which was apparently intended for Moscow and for

Karakhan, and asked Sileipak to send me a copy of its English-language translation. I read it carefully and learned about cooperation between members of the CCP and KMT at Canton—how they had thoroughly mobilized the masses to support Sun Yat-sen and repulse the attacks launched by Ch'en Chiung-ming on October 23 and November 19, thereby delivering Canton from danger. I felt that Borodin's report was a piece of objective reporting rather than a propaganda effort.

The first stage of KMT-CCP cooperation might truthfully be compared to a state in which two parties, confronted by a common enemy and acting in their common interests, shared both the good and the bad, bore hardships together, and struggled hand-in-hand to march forward against all odds. Numerous epic incidents were recorded in this period. Friction between the two parties had not yet emerged, or was very slight if it existed. As I saw for myself how the KMT was developing in Peking and then looked into the situation in Canton, I felt that for the time being no disunity would arise from CCP members taking dual party membership.

These developments made me more optimistic about the future of KMT-CCP cooperation. On the basis of the data supplied by Borodin, I published an article entitled "The New Atmosphere at Canton" in the magazine New Republic (Hsin Min-kuo). It touched upon KMT-CCP relations, but it chiefly aimed at calling for cooperation from all revolutionary elements. Citing Canton as an example, I contended that it was possible for revolutionaries in all parties and positions to cooperate publicly and unselfishly in a common revolutionary cause and that, in fact, such cooperation was essential. New Republic was the organ of the recently established KMT organization in Peking and was edited by Fan Ti-jen, a non-Communist. I wrote the article at his request.

My article had considerable influence. With it I demonstrated my support of KMT-CCP cooperation and cleared up any misunderstanding about my opposing such cooperation. Comrades and friends in Peking who read it considered my approach sound. Later, at the First Congress of the KMT, Liao Chung-k'ai praised the article, saying that it was the best explanation of the real significance of KMT-CCP cooperation.

The opening of the First Congress of the KMT was approaching. The KMT organization at Peking got ready to elect three delegates to it, and I was one of the candidates. While I was the only CCP member among the candidates, I received the greatest show of support. Li Ta-chao favored my participation in the Congress. He believed that it would reveal to the world at large the unity that existed within the CCP; and with both of us at the Congress, we would be able to discuss any questions that might arise. Supporting Li Ta-chao's proposal that I be a candidate were other CCP members, who regarded me as the best representative of their views. Most KMT members indicated approval of my candidacy, too. So far as they were concerned, it showed that the CCP was choosing delegates to the Congress carefully.

My first reaction was to decline the job, and I explained to the comrades why I could not go. My main job was with the railway workers. Railway union groups were developing secretly and were planning to secretly convene a National Congress of Railway Workers on February 7, 1929, the first anniversary of the February Seventh Strike. If I went to Canton, this congress would be delayed. Furthermore, I did not want to accept any duties in the KMT. I suggested that the CCP organization in Peking send a delegate that was in a position to take up KMT work. But my reasons for declining were not accepted. My comrades unanimously nominated me as a candidate.

The KMT election was held in the auditorium of the Third Building at Peita in December. With more than two thousand people in attendance, the place was crowded to capacity. I was elected a delegate, receiving the largest number of votes cast for any candidate.

Early in 1924 I accompanied Li Ta-chao to Canton, going by way of Shanghai. During our stay in Shanghai, the CC of the CCP invited us to a CC meeting to discuss the positions we were to take at Canton. The CC then felt optimistic about the development of KMT-CCP cooperation throughout the country. Li Ta-chao reported on KMT organizational progress in the North. He also declared that there were no differences of opinion among CCP comrades in Peking, and he praised my participation in the Canton Congress as a good sign of Party unanimity. Ch'en Tu-hsiu expressed gratification at the report. He suggested that the two of us join with T'an P'ing-shan and Ch'ü Ch'iu-pai, who were already in Canton, to organize a steering committee that would coordinate the steps taken by CCP members attending the KMT Congress.

I quickly declined this assignment. Repeating what I had said in Peking when I was nominated as a candidate, I pointed out that I could not wait for the conclusion of the KMT Congress, that I would have to return to Peking before that. I also pointed out that I was not a suitable representative of the CC, since I still did not support the idea of most CCP members holding KMT posts. Ch'en Tu-hsiu had nothing definite to say against the points that I raised. We went on to other things in what was a convivial conversation. As a result the responsibility for organizing the steering committee fell to Li Ta-chao.

We reached Canton about January 10, 1924. There did not seem to be any marked change in its atmosphere. Some multicolored slogans were in evidence in the streets. Scattered along the Bund in goodly numbers were the usual "conversation houses."[21] People were busy with preparations for the Congress, and there were even more banquets than usual. The situation was somewhat like that in a large family when some great festive occasion is about to be celebrated.

The day after we got there, Sun Yat-sen received us along with ten other delegates at his Generalissimo's headquarters in the Canton Cement Works. Dr. Sun distributed to us a draft of his *Outline for National Construction,* which he had written personally, and asked for our opinions of it.

"The very first article in this *Outline*," I said quickly, "states that the National government is to build the Chinese Republic in accordance with the revolutionary Three Principles of the People and the Five-Power Constitution. Under such an arbitrary provision, is the existence of other political parties permitted?"

Instead of answering me, Dr. Sun referred the question to the others there. One of these delegates, Yeh Ch'u-ts'ang, declared that the *Outline* had been written by Dr. Sun after long research and that adequate provision had been made for the solution of all questions. He said we would understand everything better after a more thorough study of the work. Then Li Ta-chao announced that he would submit his opinions after carefully studying the *Outline*. Our conversation turned to exchanging information and to other lighter subjects.

But the question I had raised certainly was basic. It was aimed at the position of Sun Yat-sen, which called for Party rule of the country, construction of the country by the Party, and the exercise of political tutelage by the Party. It was also immensely relevant to KMT-CCP cooperation. Neither Sun Yat-sen nor the KMT leaders ever subsequently tackled this question directly. Indirectly, however, they all indicated that they were against a multiparty system; the CCP was looked upon merely as a small circle within the large circle. Some of my comrades wanted to know whether or not I intended to speak out on the subject. I told them that I did not like to raise issues on the spur of the moment, but that I was preparing to make an official statement at the

Congress. For to accept intolerance in the matter of a multiparty system tacitly was tantamount to losing the identity of the CCP in the national revolution, which would tend to abet the tendency within the KMT to demand the abolition of the CCP.

Borodin then lived in the Tungshan district of Canton. He was busy drafting various documents for the Congress. Living in his house, too, was Ch'ü Ch'iu-pai, who served as his assistant and translator. Often Borodin invited Li Ta-chao and me and a few of the leading CCP delegates to his house to talk. Each time I was there he showed me some documents. Borodin, Wang Ching-wei, and Ch'ü Ch'iu-pai together had prepared the draft of the "Manifesto of the Congress"; and they had devoted a great deal of time to the work of translating and retranslating it.

The Borodin of that time was cautious in his relations with people, assuming a serene, friendly attitude and never involving himself in arguments. He singled me out for the political platform that was to be submitted to the Congress. Under "Nationalism" was to be opposition to imperialism, the abrogation of unequal treaties, and equality of treatment for the national minorities. Under "Democracy" was to be a denial of the theory of heaven-bestowed rights and the assertion of revolutionary people's rights—granting democratic freedom to the majority but denying it to counterrevolutionists. Under "People's Livelihood" were to be listed the specific terms by which the interests of workers and peasants were to be protected. All of this indicated notable progress.

On the question of whether or not several revolutionary parties would be allowed to coexist in the national revolution, Borodin agreed with me in principle, but he did not consider it a suitable issue for debate. It was, rather, a matter of practical work, he said. If the CCP had the strength to survive, nobody could wipe it out. Most of my comrades agreed with Borodin. They viewed the Congress as a felicitous occasion for the KMT and urged me not to mar it by bringing up such a difficult issue. Li Ta-chao, as head of the steering committee for CCP delegates, declared that my idea was correct, but since it had already been raised once and its significance demonstrated, there was no need to bring it up again. So I could do nothing but keep silent on the subject.

After we had gotten over that problem, another arose that sparked differences of opinion. The "Constitution of the Kuomintang" that Borodin had drafted was virtually a translation of the constitutions of Communist parties the world over. The provisions for the duties and responsibilities of the Central Committee and of Party organs at different levels

—the system of democratic centralism—and the code of discipline for Party members were identical to the principles upheld by Communist parties. I suggested that these principles were not necessarily applicable to the KMT, the constitution of which should provide for a greater degree of democracy. The KMT had heretofore operated under great laxity, and the abrupt imposition of such rigid restrictions might hamper its wide development and lead to other complications. CCP members with dual party membership, for example, might not be able to abide fully by the KMT restrictions under which they would be placed. I thought, therefore, that the KMT constitution ought to provide for a considerable degree of democracy. While KMT members should abide by the political platform of the national revolution, divergent views should be permitted. Only then, I said, would CCP members be able to remain within the KMT.

Borodin saw the difficulty in dealing with my ideas, but he did not say much as we talked, sometimes merely shrugging his shoulders. One thing he did say to me, in a light vein, was, "Your opinions are very reasonable. But people do feel that a revolutionary political party must have a rigid organizational structure if it is to shoulder its historical mission."

These disagreements placed me in an embarrassing position. I seemed to be throwing cold water on comrades who were elated over the good relationship that had grown up between the KMT and the CCP. Although T'an P'ing-shan held dual party membership, he had been designated director of the Organization Department of the KMT, and I asked him how he could possibly apply rigid discipline to such a large number of Party members and Party organizations. But he brimmed with optimism. He said that he had already shouldered the job for more than two months without running into difficulties. As long as the KMT constitution made clear-cut provision for rigid organization and discipline, he believed that there would be no question of his being able to implement it.

From all of this I concluded that I would have to choose one of two possible courses. I could disregard everything else and assert my views, which would bring down upon me the opposition of most of my comrades and the displeasure of the KMT people. Or I could preserve CCP unanimity by making an early departure from Canton to take charge of the Congress of Railway Workers. The latter course would lay me open to charges of being evasive, but it would allow me to retain my views and wait for a suitable opportunity to air them in the future. My comrades seemed to see through my feelings. Directly or indirectly they expressed the hope that I would follow the second course, and so before the Congress had formally opened, I began to prepare for my return to the North.

Even though I felt depressed, I attended the various receptions. At most of the daily dinner parties before the Congress opened, Sun Yat-sen made two-hour speeches. In them, speaking slowly and deliberately, he explained his hopes for the Congress. As best I can remember, I have given the main points that he made below.

He said that the 1911 Revolution had failed because the role of the Revolutionary party had been disparaged. He stressed that the mistake at that time was the idea "When revolutionaries arise, a revolutionary party is no longer needed." From then on, it was vital to have a rigidly organized KMT to fulfill the tasks of revolution and national construction on the basis of the revolutionary Three Principles of the People. This deeply moved his listeners.

In these speeches Dr. Sun did his best to explain his own stand. In comparing the Russian Revolution to the Chinese Revolution, he said that the Russian victory was attributable to the strongly organized Russian Communist Party, but that the communism that that Party advocated had failed. The New Economic Policy then in force in Russia, he said, resembled the land system carried out by the Taiping Rebellion. With that as a basis, he reasoned that since communism could not be implemented even in Russia, the most appropriate course for China would be to put into effect the Three Principles of the People. When he touched upon the relationship between the Three Principles of the People and communism, he invariably stated that the Principle of the People's Livelihood was socialism, which was also called communism, and that the ideals embraced by the two were identical. Communism was, accordingly, only a small portion of the whole Three Principles of the People. But at the same time he denied the theory of class struggle, contending that in China there were only the very poor and the slightly poor and that there were no marked class distinctions.

Obviously his object in emphasizing the above points was to rally all revolutionists around the banner of the KMT. But so far as I could see, his powers of persuasion here were rather limited. It seemed to me that some KMT figures there doubted that CCP members were able to sincerely accept the Three Principles of the People. His criticisms of the Russian Revolution and his various interpretations of communism, at the same time, left the CCP members that were present feeling rather uneasy. When members of the KMT applauded specific points that Dr. Sun made in his speeches, I saw no CCP member join in the hand-clapping. I personally thought that his insistence on revolutionaries of all creeds and colors being dissolved in the same melting pot was too subjective.

The First Congress of the KMT was originally scheduled to convene on January 15, 1924; but because preparations were not completed in time, the opening date was postponed to January 20. Dr. Sun, who delivered the inaugural address at the opening session, promptly formed a five-man presidium, to which he named Hu Han-min, Wang Ching-wei, Lin Shen, Li Ta-chao, and Hsieh Ch'ih.

Hu Han-min chaired the next day's session, when procedural matters were taken up. At this session two young CCP members, who had just joined the KMT, Mao Tse-tung and Li Li-san, had the most to say. I sat there without opening my mouth. Many veteran KMT members looked askance at the two youngsters, as if to ask, "Where did those two young unknowns come from? How is it that they have so much to say?" A few of the old KMT members, however, seemed to enjoy the youthful spirit of the two. When the session ended, Wang Ching-wei came over to me and said, "The young people of the May Fourth Movement are something to be reckoned with, after all. Look at the enthusiasm with which they speak and at their energetic attitude." In reply, I could only smile.

This was the only formal session I attended, and so I had no chance to hear the other views expressed by Mao Tse-tung and Li Li-san at the Congress. Later, comrades told me that throughout the Congress the two had more to say than anyone else and that they were often at variance with one another. Li Li-san, who had just returned from France, where he had been a working student, was a delegate from the Hankow municipality, and he singlehandedly leveled frequent criticisms at the KMT. Mao Tse-tung took a different stand. He repeatedly quoted Sun Yat-sen to illustrate his own views. This may have been the first encounter between Mao and Li.

At a meeting in Borodin's home on the evening of January 21, we discussed the need for unanimity of views among CCP members. When that discussion ended, I took the opportunity to inform Li Ta-chao, T'an P'ing-shan, Ch'ü Ch'iu-pai, and Borodin, all of whom were there, of my desire to return to the North. The KMT Congress would not end for some time, and I had to return to take charge of the National Congress of Railway Workers, which was about to convene. They agreed to my proposal. Since I had certain things to attend to before leaving, I asked T'an P'ing-shan and Li Ta-chao to request that Sun Yat-sen and the presidium of the Congress grant me leave.

When Dr. Sun heard that I was leaving Canton early, he summoned me to an interview. We met to talk at 11:00 P.M. on January 22 in a dining hall of the West Bund Hotel, after a dinner there. I began by telling him of my work in building up the Railway Workers' Union, of the events surrounding the February Seventh Strike, and of the railway-men's organizations that had been secretly revived after that reverse in spite of great difficulties. I told him that I had decided to hold a National Congress of Railway Workers secretly in Peking on February 7, the first anniversary of the strike. With that date approaching, I said that as the person principally responsible for the Congress, I had to return to take part in it. A man of experience, Dr. Sun did not inquire into my opinion of the KMT Congress. He cheerfully approved my plan. He said that taking charge of the National Congress of Railway Workers was even more important than attending the KMT Congress; it was a matter of more urgent necessity. He urged me to hurry off, for he said we would have many opportunities to exchange ideas in the future. So we shook hands and took leave of one another. This turned out to be the last time that I was to meet with Dr. Sun Yat-sen.

Dr. Sun knew quite well that I differed with him on the question of KMT-CCP relations, but he did his best to smooth over the differences. Late that night he sent a trusted aide to me with a letter that contained his best wishes for the success of the Congress and for the unhampered development of my work, as well as two thousand silver dollars, which were his donation to the Federation of Railway Workers' Unions.

I left Canton on January 23. I had arrived in haste and I departed in haste—a reflection of the situation in which I found myself, of my thinking, and of the depression within the ranks of the CCP. Reflected here, too, may perhaps be a general summary of the development of KMT-CCP relations.

Disputes During the Initial Stage of Kuomintang-Communist Cooperation

The First Congress of the KMT was able to produce a new political platform in an effort to rally all revolutionary forces around it, and this certainly was encouraging. But to actually fulfill this effort was difficult. The abnormal relationship between the KMT and the CCP was in itself an enormous stumbling block to putting theory into practice; it was the focal point of all disputes between the two parties.

I left Canton on January 23, 1924. I passed through Shanghai, and there I gave Ch'en Tu-hsiu a realistic picture of the problems I had discovered while in Canton. I pointed out that as far as I was concerned, no good would come of mingling KMT and CCP in a single organization, with some CCP members holding important KMT posts. I wanted the relationship between the parties placed on a democratic foundation, with some distance between the two. While I was in Canton, I could find no way to carry out this idea, and I hoped that the CC of the CCP would give the matter its attention. Ch'en did not commit himself by replying to my statements. It seemed as though he had adopted an attitude of waiting to see what would develop.

Toward the end of January, I reached Peking. I explained my views to the comrades there and told them why I had left Canton early. Since I did not want to precipitate an argument, however, I spoke in moderate tones. The KMT Congress would not reach an early conclusion, I said, especially since it had recessed for three days because of the death of Lenin; and so I had left early, chiefly in order to attend the Congress of Railway Workers. On the whole, the Peking comrades still supported my ideas, and they endorsed my action in leaving the Congress.

The Congress of Railway Workers secretly opened in Peking on February 7, as scheduled. Present were about twenty delegates from the underground labor unions of the major railway lines. I made a report to the Congress entitled "The National Revolution and the Task of the Railway Unions," in which I called upon the workers to support the national revolution and to strive for the freedom of labor to organize and for the improvement of workers' living conditions. The Congress adopted my report and issued a manifesto based on it. The Congress also sent letters to the CC of the CCP and to Sun Yat-sen, thanking them for supporting the railway workers. And finally, the Congress elected an executive committee of the National General Union of Railway Workers and formally proclaimed the birth of the General Union. Teng P'ei was elected chairman, and I was elected general secretary. The office of the General Union was located at Peking.

The formation of the National General Union of Railway Workers indicated that the railway workers had recovered from the wounds of the February Seventh Incident. Membership in the secret units of the union, which were spread over all the railways, had increased, as had the work of the units. At that time the KMT had not yet organized railway workers anywhere. Nevertheless, the First KMT Congress greatly stimulated them. "Now that the Kuomintang and the Chinese Communist Party have joined forces as one family to carry out the revolution," many railwaymen were saying, "Wu P'ei-fu will soon fall." A clamor to avenge the martyrs of the February Seventh Incident also mounted with the organization of the General Union. Very soon, however, the railway workers' union was subjected to oppression in a series of incidents.

Following the failure of the February Seventh Strike, railway workers in all areas were consistently persecuted. They struggled heroically against this oppression. Those of us who worked in the union, furthermore, encountered numerous dangers as we threw ourselves unsparingly into the tasks involved. Still, the railway workers' movement at the time, and indeed the labor movement as a whole, seemed to be relegated to an insignificant place in the total revolutionary movement. The eyes of all revolutionaries were focused on Canton. Even within the CCP, except for the few that had been active in the labor movement right along, members were chiefly stimulated by KMT-CCP cooperation. And shortly after the National General Union of Railway Workers was formed, when Li Ta-chao and the other delegates to the KMT Congress returned to Peking with all sorts of news, revolutionary circles there were considerably stirred by it for a time.

For Li Ta-chao was highly optimistic when he got back to Peking. He gave unstinting praise to the Canton congress. He said that the manifesto it had issued and the Party constitution and resolutions it had adopted were epochmaking. He lavishly praised Sun Yat-sen and the ranking KMT leaders for their determination and sincerity in carrying out KMT reorganization. He believed that the development of KMT-CCP cooperation would be smooth; he anticipated a most satisfactory future for it.

Li Ta-chao, always a kindhearted man, felt strongly about the need for a unity of revolutionary forces. Earlier he had sincerely hoped that Socialists of all persuasions and anarchists would be united with the Marxists. Now, in the same vein, it was his hope that the KMT and the CCP would be organized truly as a single family, with no distinction made between them. Starting from such a position, he seemed to easily grow expansive about the bright side of things while neglecting the dark side. He told us that such people as Teng Tse-ju and Feng Tzu-yu within the KMT opposed KMT-CCP cooperation, but he considered this opposition unimportant. He urged his comrades to participate actively in KMT work; but his comrades lacked the breadth of enthusiasm that he himself exhibited.

Li Ta-chao told me that the CC of the KMT would be located at Canton, with executive departments of the CC at Shanghai, Peking, and Wuhan. An executive department had extensive powers. As a branch of the CC, it had full authority to direct Party affairs in its area. Dr. Sun wanted veteran KMT leaders to assume nominal leadership of the different executive departments while new comrades were elevated to do the actual work. Hu Han-min and Wang Ching-wei were to be in charge of the Shanghai Executive Department, with Mao Tse-tung, its secretary, as the administrator. Chü Cheng and T'an Chen were to be in charge of the Wuhan Executive Department. Dr. Sun had expressed the wish that I go there to serve as administrator. The Peking Executive Department was to be led by Ting Wei-fen, Wang Fa-chin, and Li Ta-chao; the three of them were to select the administrator there.

Li Ta-chao, speaking in greater detail about the issue, asked if I would go to Wuhan. He said that when Sun Yat-sen stressed the idea of pumping new blood into the Party, he had cited me as an example. Some people had charged me before Sun Yat-sen with opposing KMT-CCP cooperation. They had said that I should not be listed as a member of the CC. They contended that my withdrawal halfway through the Congress indicated that I still held dissident views. But Li Ta-chao said that Sun Yat-sen had firmly rejected such ideas. Dr. Sun had pointed out that the fact that I had attended the Congress proved that basically I had no thought of opposing the two-party cooperation. He had said that I left early for Peking because it was necessary for me to attend to important matters there and that he knew all about it. He said that even if I had criticized the KMT formerly, I no longer harbored grievances against it. This indicated that I was not biased in the matter. Li Ta-chao said that I had deeply impressed Sun Yat-sen, who had on several occasions referred to me as "a capable students' representative during the May Fourth Movement," and that he had all along wanted to give me some sort of assignment.

But Li Ta-chao also told me very frankly that while Chü Cheng and

T'an Chen had asked him to welcome me on their behalf to the Wuhan job, he had heard from another source that these two KMT leaders had expressed the fear that I would not be easy to control. He said that both he and the CC of the CCP regarded the development of KMT-CCP cooperation as an immediate, urgent task and that they naturally hoped I would go to Wuhan. He said that they believed that I would manage to surmount any difficulties that arose. He added, however, that both the CC of the CCP and he wanted me to consider the matter and reach my own decision.

I told him that I was unwilling to go to Wuhan to work for the KMT. This was not because I could not cooperate with Chü and T'an, I explained, nor was it, as the CC of the CCP feared, because I was a "major criminal of the February Seventh Incident" in the eyes of Wu P'ei-fu and would inevitably be in great danger in Wuhan. I said that I was unwilling to go because basically I did not favor the course of action itself. By occupying key posts in KMT organs, I suggested, CCP members could accomplish very little good, but they could easily arouse the enmity of the veteran KMT members. In any event, as a result of my tacit refusal, the plan was shelved.

Li Ta-chao at the same time sought to bring some of our comrades into the practical work of the Peking Executive Department. He met an unfavorable reaction, for most of our comrades in Peking then did not equate taking jobs within the KMT with participation in the practical tasks of the revolution. They felt that CCP members should naturally vie for priority in leading or participating in the revolutionary movement, but as Communists. To enter a KMT organ merely to help build up somebody else's show struck them as a thankless exertion of effort. In the face of such attitudes, Li Ta-chao, who was a man of wisdom, very soon apparently experienced what the Buddhists would call enlightenment.

The Peking Executive Department of the KMT was organized rapidly. An office, which no CCP organ could begin to approach in ostentation, was established in a fairly large building. Ting Wei-fen regularly looked after office affairs. The CCP members that frequently visited the office to attend meetings or sometimes to do official work were Li Ta-chao and Yü Shu-te, who were concurrently members of the CC of the KMT, and Yü Fang-tan, Han Lin-fu, and myself, who were concurrently alternate members of the CC of the KMT. Of those holding dual party membership, Li Ta-chao took up leadership duties, Yü Shu-te and Yü Fang-tan were responsible for organizational and other work in the Tientsin area, and Han Lin-fu was responsible for work in three special administrative areas and Inner Mongolia. No CCP members, apart from these, undertook any regular work in this department.

Whenever Ting Wei-fen, who kept office hours, brought up the question of finding persons to fill various jobs, Li Ta-chao would ask him to look for people himself and bring them up for approval at a meeting. Ting Wei-fen and I shared the same office, with my desk opposite his. On the rare occasions when I was in the office, Ting invariably launched into discussion of one question or another with me, and I always politely suggested that he make the decisions. Because of our behavior, the CCP organization in Peking clearly did not come under suspicion for trying to monopolize control of the KMT organization there.

After the First KMT Congress, the KMT and the CCP began to come into conflict everywhere—especially at Shanghai and Canton—with the single exception of Peking. In fact, we were not fully acquainted with the details of the conflicts. That the KMT organization at Peking did develop peacefully and smoothly was perhaps not unrelated to the beneficial effect on the situation of the attitude that Li Ta-chao, I, and the other Communists had.

Moreover, most members of the KMT organization at Peking were young people of the post-May-Fourth-Movement era. Untainted by the old KMT practices, they energetically endorsed the new political platform that had come out of the First KMT Congress and the most recent interpretation of the Three Principles of the People by Sun Yat-sen.

Thus, there were no markedly divergent views among the KMT members at Peking; there was merely the general awareness that some were also members of the CCP, while the majority were members of the KMT alone.

At Canton, the old base of the KMT, the situation was very much different. There, most KMT members had a special quality to them, seen chiefly in the conceit of the veterans, who found it difficult to reconcile themselves to the newly prominent CCP members in their Party. Some KMT veterans feared, furthermore, that the policy of alliance with the Soviet Union and tolerance for the Communists might lay the KMT open to attack from powerful quarters both within the country and abroad. This would leave the KMT politically isolated. Especially because of CCP members participating in KMT activities, a struggle for rights and positions arose between old and new members. All of these things produced a rising undercurrent of opposition to those who had membership in both parties.

On October 25, 1923, Sun Yat-sen named Teng Tse-ju, T'an P'ing-shan, and seven others to the nine-man Provisional Executive Committee of the KMT, which was to carry out his program of KMT reorganization. Soon afterward—on November 9—Teng Tse-ju and ten other important KMT members addressed a secret communication to Dr. Sun.[22] This letter expressed opposition to the activities of Ch'en Tu-hsiu and T'an P'ing-shan within the KMT. Their activities, it charged, were part of a CCP plot to exploit the KMT and usurp its powers. I had no knowledge of this letter at the time, and the CC of the CCP appeared to know nothing about it either. Later we were to learn that Sun Yat-sen, in a reply, denied the validity of the charges. But these people did not abandon their position.

When Li Ta-chao returned to Peking from Canton, he informed me that some people had proposed to the Congress that the KMT constitution specifically preclude the existence of a party-within-a-party and that it forbid KMT members to hold membership in other parties concurrently. Li had there and then made a statement on the subject.[23] He pointed out that CCP members were joining the KMT as private individuals and that while it might be said that they held dual party membership, it could not be charged that one party existed within the other party. He said that CCP members who joined the KMT would abide by the constitution and discipline of the KMT in carrying out the KMT political platform. He urged veteran KMT members to put aside their suspicions and not to think of taking precautions. Li Ta-chao felt that his statement had a salutary effect; but it seems that he underestimated the seriousness of the issue.

Some veteran KMT members lost their influence because of the Congress, and as a result the cry against a party-within-a-party and dual party membership rose to new heights. In a notable example of this, Feng Tzu-yu and others raised the banner of anticommunism. The degree of opposition to, and suspicion of, the CCP on the part of KMT members varied. But from Canton the feeling spread to Shanghai and to other areas, and it began to grow everywhere. Leaders of both the KMT and the CCP were kept busy making explanations and patching up differences. In Shanghai, Ch'en Tu-hsiu seemed to have the widest experience with such problems, and from this experience he realized that the differences were not easy to explain away.

Toward the end of April, 1924, I received from the CC of the CCP a summons to take part in an enlarged plenum of the CC in mid-May at Shanghai. The Plenum was to discuss KMT-CCP cooperation. It was specified that I must attend it.

Upon reaching Shanghai and seeing Ch'en Tu-hsiu, I realized that his attitude toward KMT-CCP cooperation had undergone a marked change. He was no longer optimistic about the future of cooperation. He described the situation within the KMT to me. After the First Congress of the KMT, he said, KMT members were generally divided in their attitude toward KMT-CCP cooperation, even to the point of obstructing active development of the work of the national revolution. Some veteran KMT members fundamentally opposed reorganization of the Party; others opposed the policy of alliance with Russia and acceptance of the Communists; while still others, influenced by the reactionary propaganda of the imperialists, feared a process of bolshevization of the KMT. In any event, a majority of them expressed dissatisfaction and doubt about the existing relationship between the KMT and the CCP. From all of these various elements came a loud clamor against permitting a "party-within-a-party" and against "dual party membership elements." Ch'en Tu-hsiu said that they seemed determined not to settle for less than the dissolution of the CCP.

In speaking of the situation within the CCP, Ch'en made a special point of stressing the slogan "Members of the CCP must not monopolize the work of the KMT." This slogan was not aimed solely at reducing the suspicions and anxieties of KMT members. It also implied a modification of the resolution of the Third Congress of the CCP that laid down the rule that CCP members must "work actively within the KMT." Ch'en said that in some places CCP members had taken over the work of KMT organs, occasionally acquiring the bad habits that went with KMT departmentalization, and this he did not regard as a salutary situation. For while the CCP had no intention of "bolshevizing" the KMT, it in turn did not want to be "Kuomintangized."

Ch'en Tu-hsiu went on to say that work within the KMT constituted merely a portion of the activities of the CCP, which must continue to devote its main attention to its own development, a task that could not be relaxed for a moment. He said that a majority of our Party members should share the tasks of the labor movement and the youth movement, while furthering activities among the peasants.

Ch'en Tu-hsiu seemed to prefer not to bring up again the disputes of the Third Congress. Nevertheless, everything he said amounted to an acceptance of the views I had proffered at that Congress. Furthermore, he told me that they especially wanted me to attend the Enlarged Plenum of the CC so that all of us together might try to rectify deviations in the work that we were doing in connection with KMT-CCP cooperation.

Ch'en Tu-hsiu invited me to get together with Voitinsky. Voitinsky also held that the work policy of the CC of the CCP should concentrate on the development of its own organization and on independent leadership in such activities as the labor movement. On the question of KMT-CCP cooperation, he particularly stressed the belief that CCP members working within the KMT must actively support that party's Left Wing and oppose its Right Wing. Only in that way, he said, could we foster the process of making the KMT revolutionary.

Voitinsky had not been back in China for long. After we had talked in Peking the previous November, he had stayed in Shanghai for a time but had soon returned to Moscow. He was not in Shanghai when I went down to Canton early in the year to attend the KMT Congress. These hasty trips of his seemed to be connected with consultations with Moscow on policy toward the KMT, for at that time Moscow was not well informed about conditions within the KMT. Both Karakhan and Borodin, who had recently arrived in China, were green to the situation, and only as they went ahead with their work did they increase their understanding of what actually was going on in the KMT. Meanwhile Voitinsky moved about from one to the other, apparently serving as the coordinator between them.

If the policy of the CCP joining the KMT was not to be interpreted as Maring had interpreted it, then it could only be interpreted as meaning that the CCP would enter the KMT in order to seize the power of leadership in it. Such a course of action, however, would have been premature. And so the theory of "supporting the Left Wing and opposing the Right Wing" emerged. Voitinsky had revealed his intention of following such a course in our conversation of November, 1923. Subsequently, at the First Congress of the KMT, Borodin had also questioned KMT leaders about the existence of Left and Right wings within their Party.[24] Voitinsky definitely stated then that the CCP, operating within the KMT, must actively support the Left Wing while working against the Right Wing. His position seemed to be based on a new decision reached in Moscow.

Two days later the Enlarged Plenum of the CC convened. Ten people participated in it. They included three members of the CC—Ch'en Tu-hsiu, Ts'ai Ho-sen, and Ch'ü Ch'iu-pai. Li Ta-chao was absent, and Mao Tse-tung, who apparently was traveling between Shanghai and Changsha, busy with his work in the KMT, was not there either. Shen Ting-i and I had been specially invited to the Plenum, so we attended. Others that attended were important members of the district committees of Shanghai, Hupeh, Hunan, and Canton and leaders of the SYC.

We met in the utmost secrecy. The Plenum began with Ch'en Tu-hsiu reporting to us on KMT-CCP cooperation and the work of the CC of the CCP. He emphasized that CCP members must not monopolize KMT work. He pointed out that within the KMT there existed a Left Wing and a Right Wing. The Left Wing endorsed reorganization and supported current policy, while the Right Wing opposed them. Ch'en said that it was the task of the members of the CCP to support the Left Wing of the KMT so that the national revolution could develop unhampered. Then he emphatically stated that the CCP must energetically develop its own organization. CCP members working within the KMT must tenaciously preserve their excellent, well-established Communist work style; and a majority of members must play active leadership roles in the labor movement and in other undertakings so that such undertakings could develop independently. These activities would augment the strength of the national revolution. Ch'en criticized the tendency, which developed after the Third Congress, for members to slacken their efforts in the labor movement and in our other undertakings because they were preoccupied solely with KMT-CCP cooperation. He seemed to try to rid himself of the charge that in the past he had tended to belittle the strength of the proletariat.

In his report Ch'en Tu-hsiu assumed a position of great humility. He said that he alone had made most of the CC policy decisions, and because they were bound to contain deviations, he asked the Enlarged Plenum to review them. He proposed that Shen Ting-i chair the meeting. Some of the members there insisted that as secretary of the CC, he had to be the chairman ex officio of the meeting. But Ch'en would not budge from his proposal. He said that the Enlarged Plenum differed from a regular meeting and that with Shen in the chair it would be easier for the rest of us to treat him as a person whose work was under review. Upon completing his report, he proposed that the Plenum appoint a three-man committee, with me as one of the three, to examine it. He stressed that this was absolutely essential.

After the Third Congress, changes actually had taken place within the CC. The powers of Ch'en Tu-hsiu had increased. Numerous matters were being decided by him alone, without being considered at meetings. Mao Tse-tung, who was then in charge of organizational work in the CC, was away from his work most of the time. Ts'ai Ho-sen, who was in charge of propaganda, kept the promise that he had made at the Third Congress to abide by the decision of the majority; and so he buried himself in writing, taking very little part in matters of policy. Ch'ü Ch'iu-pai, who had no specific department under him, stayed in Canton long after the others left; and when he did return to Shanghai, he kept himself busy with work at Shanghai University. At about that time the term "patriarch" was a designation for Ch'en Tu-hsiu. All of these things must have had something to do with the humble attitude Ch'en adopted at the Plenum.

But the most important issue remained that of KMT-CCP cooperation. Everyone at the Plenum was worried about the dual party membership status of CCP members in the KMT. Because Ch'en Tu-hsiu was one of those most concerned, he was all the more depressed. But since the Comintern persisted in the policy of having CCP members join the KMT—a policy that had already been carried out in any case—and because we had profited by the lesson of the Third Congress, at which our arguments had led to intra-Party disputes, none of us felt inclined to thrash out the matter exhaustively. Thus an atmosphere of harmony prevailed.

Shen Ting-i, who became the Plenum's chairman, was one of the early founders of the CCP. Initially, he was a veteran KMT member. During the autumn of 1923, on orders from Sun Yat-sen, he accompanied Chiang Kai-shek and others on a trip to look over the Soviet Union. It was said that he was among those who opposed the policy of CCP members joining the KMT. Normally quite garrulous in expressing his views, he became extremely courteous at the Plenum and ventured scarcely any opinions from beginning to end. One opinion he did on occasion reveal, however, was "If one must be a KMT member and have dual party membership, it would be far better to proceed on the basis of one's old position and be a member of the KMT pure and simple." And that is exactly what he proceeded to do.[25]

I sincerely welcomed this meeting, because so far as I was concerned, it virtually accepted the ideas I had put before the Third Congress. I took an active part in its work, and I expressed my views in a resolution, which the Plenum accepted, that was based on an examination of the report of Ch'en Tu-hsiu. My attitude was sincere. I did not bring up the arguments of the Third Congress, and so I had the sympathy and support of a majority of those present. It might be said that the policy of the CC of the CCP was corrected to a marked degree at this gathering. Subsequently Teng Chung-hsia, in *A Brief History of the Chinese Labor Movement,* stated, "The tendency toward liquidationism in dealing with the labor movement which was held by the Central Committee of Ch'en Tu-hsiu was not corrected until the Enlarged Plenum of the Chinese Communist Party in May, 1924."[26]

While the point that CCP members within the KMT must support its Left Wing and oppose its Right Wing was included in the resolution, it was not particularly stressed. The reason for this was not only that the battle between Left and Right wings in the KMT developed only after this Plenum, but also because at the time we did not feel that CCP members should make a prominent point of opposing the Right Wing— that was the concern of the Left Wing of the KMT. The important issue that was decided upon at the Plenum was that a small number of CCP members should undertake practical work within the KMT—not the routine work of its organs, but the work of leadership of mass movements—while a majority of CCP members should throw their efforts into work among the broad masses of workers, peasants, and young intellectuals and seek to develop their own Party.

Disagreements over KMT-CCP cooperation, however, quickly broke into the open after this Enlarged Plenum. Our Plenum lasted about three days, and on the second day after it ended, just before noon, I visited Ch'en Tu-hsiu and took leave of him to return to the North.

"Wang Ching-wei and Chang Chi just called for a talk," he declared the minute he saw me. "The subject of their conversation was the organization by CCP members of Party fractions within the KMT."

Ch'en informed me that during their visit Wang Ching-wei and Chang Chi showed him publications of the SYC and an SYC resolution on the organization of CCP and SYC fractions within the KMT. They said that Hu Han-min and Hsieh Ch'ih did not endorse the practice of forming CCP and SYC fractions in the KMT. They considered this to be a violation of the statement that Li Ta-chao made at the First Congress of the KMT, which clearly stated that CCP members were joining the

KMT as private individuals and that while they held dual party membership, this did not constitute a case of creating a party-within-a-party.
But, they asked, was not the creation of CCP and SYC fractions within
the KMT clearly a case of a party-within-a-party?

Ch'en said that he openly admitted that CCP and SYC members had
formed fractions within the KMT, but he denied that this violated the
statement by Li Ta-chao and that it constituted a case of a party-within-
a-party that might endanger the KMT. He told Wang Ching-wei and
Chang Chi that the CCP and SYC fractions within the KMT were
organized to insure that comrades abided by KMT decisions and discipline and that they took an active part in the work. There was no intention to call upon members to struggle for power or to develop sectarian
movements or to do anything harmful to the KMT. But Ch'en told me
that his interpretation of the development satisfied neither Wang nor
Chang. As a result he promised them that the CC of the CCP would call
another meeting to discuss the matter and that another reply would be
given to them.

Ch'en Tu-hsiu was tremendously embarrassed and greatly agitated
by this episode. He told me that it all resulted from the policy of joining
the KMT. He pointed out that to abide by the wishes of the KMT in
abolishing the fractions within it would be tantamount to dissolving our
organization in that of the KMT. This would mean that the CCP would
no longer exist independently; this we could not permit. But the KMT
would never even tacitly approve of the existence of our fractions within
it; so he could see no way to resolve the issue. He said with feeling that
if he were a KMT member, he also would stand against the establishment of fractions by the CCP.

Ch'en thoroughly analyzed the importance of this situation. He felt
that Hu Han-min, Hsieh Ch'ih, Wang Ching-wei, and Chang Chi were
in a position to represent the whole KMT. Of the four, Hsieh Ch'ih had
been against the Communists all along. But the other three could not
be considered rightists; they supported the reorganization of the KMT.
With the four of them standing together on the issue, it could not be
treated as trivial.

He also talked to me about the feelings of other KMT leaders on
the current relationship between the KMT and the CCP. He cited Wu
Chih-hui as an example. He said that a few days earlier Wu Chih-hui
had called on him and asked in all seriousness when we expected the
great revolution led by the CCP to succeed. He told Wu that it might

take about thirty years. In alarm, Wu replied, "In that case, the KMT has only another thirty years of life." Wu said that the anarchist revolution that he advocated would not materialize for another five hundred years, so there was no real conflict of interests between the anarchists and the KMT. Ch'en quickly added that when he said the revolution led by the Communists would succeed in thirty years, he did not mean that in thirty years the KMT would go out of existence; but his explanation did not satisfy Wu.

We discussed matters such as these throughout the entire afternoon, talking calmly. So far as we were concerned, the CCP and SYC fractions could not be dissolved. Under no circumstances could we accede to what amounted to a KMT demand that we dissolve our Party. There was now only one of two courses to follow. Either the KMT tacitly recognized the existence of these fractions within its organization, or the CCP would have to undertake an early withdrawal from the KMT while seeking to establish cooperation between the two parties outside the KMT framework.

I indicated to Ch'en that the current formula for KMT-CCP cooperation could not possibly be maintained for long. The best we could hope for was that the parting of the two would not be unpleasant. Ch'en took a very serious view of the matter. Before deciding on a new policy, he wanted to ask Voitinsky to seek instructions from Moscow.

Early the next morning I boarded a train for the North. Before long I spent five months in prison, and this prevented me from knowing in detail about subsequent developments. But very soon everybody knew about them when Chang Chi, Teng Tse-ju, and Hsieh Ch'ih, three members of the KMT Supervisory Committee, presented a bill of impeachment to Sun Yat-sen.[27] Their action proved that negotiations between the two parties on this issue of CCP-KMT cooperation had not been successful.

FIVE MONTHS IN PRISON

CHAPTER

On May 21, 1924, the second day after I returned to Peking, I was arrested and thrown into prison. I nearly lost my life. Although I received advance warning of what to expect, I failed to take the necessary precautions. This led to a disaster which seemed to be a just punishment for my posing as a brave man and for my love of adventure.

On the afternoon of the day I returned to Peking—May 20—I went first to see Li Ta-chao to tell him of the proceedings of the Enlarged Plenum. Tense and preoccupied with his own affairs, he interrupted me to announce gravely that he had learned that morning from Wang Fa-chin, who had sources of information within the Chihli clique, that the Peking military and police authorities had drawn up a blacklist of more than one hundred persons that were to be arrested immediately. Li Shih-tseng was the first name on the list. The second name was his own, and mine was the third. He said that he was making necessary preparations; and he told me to go at once to my quarters and my office to put my papers in order and then to hide myself.

Li Ta-chao said that this large-scale arrest of revolutionists by the Peking authorities was inevitable. The main reason for it was the expansion of activities by both the KMT and the CCP. Li said that both organizations had opposed the election of Ts'ao K'un by bribery and the Peking regime itself and that their words and actions had long since

347

incurred the wrath of the authorities. The mass movement in the North, past strikes by railwaymen and their current activities were all blamed on us; and we were members of the KMT Central Committee, which the KMT had publicly announced. Furthermore, on May 15 a bomb had exploded at the residence of the foreign minister, Wellington Koo.[1] Although the incident was in no way connected with the KMT or the CCP, the Peking authorities, who were an incompetent lot, decided that the KMT and the CCP must have engineered the plot, since the two of them had right along opposed Koo's policy toward Russia. As a result they promptly launched their own plot to arrest members of the revolutionary parties. Li Ta-chao urged me to take precautions against the threat of arrest; although from what Wang Fa-chin had learned, Li confidently expected two or three days to pass before the military and police actually struck.

I left Li Ta-chao and went directly to the secret office of the General Union of Railway Workers, where I went about my duties as though nothing had happened. First of all, I received a number of worker-comrades from various railway lines and took care of the problems that they brought to me. I told them individually to leave that evening or the next morning for their posts. Only after attending to these things did I tell my colleagues the news of the emergency that Li Ta-chao had passed on to me. I called upon them to prepare themselves. Consequently all important union staff members went into hiding, and most membership lists and other important documents were taken away in time. Only P'eng Yung-ho and Li Pin were left behind to look after the office.

I reached my quarters in Ta-chiao Hutung at 11:00 P.M. In that apartment house, which was built around four courtyards, my wife and I had two rooms facing south. Yang Tzu-lieh and I had only recently been married—in February, 1924. She was one of the first women members of the CCP, having joined the Party at Wuhan in 1921. Now in Peking she was in charge of proofreading and circulation of *Hsin Min-kuo* (New Republic). Of the two adjoining rooms, one was our bedroom and the other was the circulation office of the magazine, where my wife worked. Stacks of issues of *New Republic* were stored in her office along with numerous documents connected with the magazine's circulation. When I told her about the blacklist, she could not decide what to do about all those papers.

Kao Shang-te lived in the south room of our courtyard, and Fan

Hung-chieh in the west room. Both of them were members of the Peking District Committee of the CCP. Immediately I consulted them about the blacklist. They knew about it and had done what they had to do to be ready for the situation. They were staying on in their rooms for the time being, however, because they had used assumed names there, thus making it difficult for the military and police to locate them. Moreover, they did not expect the arrests to start for another two or three days. They had decided to wait until then before hiding themselves, but they were worried about me. In the eyes of the military and police I was a "major culprit." They urged me to get everything in shape and leave the place by the next morning, saying that this would be the safest thing to do.

I went back to my room, where my wife and I started to burn some of the more important documents. But we had accumulated too many documents in those two rooms to take care of them all at once. Besides, it was very late at night, and we were tired. We decided that there would be time in the morning to finish the job. After burning a few documents, we went to sleep.

Little did we realize that the police were moving one step faster than we were moving. Before dawn had fully broken the next morning, my quarters and the office of the Railway Union were surrounded simultaneously. The apartment manager knocked at my door. I awoke from my dreams thinking that the railway workers that were supposed to return to their posts that morning had decided to look me up on some important business or other before leaving town. I opened the door, and the police rushed in. Without showing us any credentials, and without giving us any explanation, they arrested my wife and me.

The police busied themselves turning out the boxes and bags in our rooms, and they carried off a large number of documents. They were thoroughly rude in speech and manner. They infuriated my wife to such an extent that, shouting at the top of her lungs, she called them bandits and brigands that arrested people and searched their things without observing due process of law. To this they reacted with angry growls. I felt conscience-stricken for having been so careless as to fall into the police trap. Fearing that I might involve my comrades Kao Shang-te and Fan Hung-chieh, I got the idea across to my wife that she should stop arguing so that we could get out of the place faster. Fortunately, Kao and Fan were not affected by the incident. My wife and I were escorted to a van and taken to the Detective Office of the Police Department at Ch'ien-men.

The Detective Office was infamous in Peking as a place where people were killed. The director, a man named Kao, had come up through the ranks. He had been a bodyguard to Ts'ao K'un, and so he was able to approach Ts'ao directly. A hulking fellow with a fierce look about him and a very rough way of speaking, he did not seem able to read very well, and he knew nothing of the law. He had the face of an opium smoker. In fact, he looked like an advanced addict. Chang, the assistant to Kao, was an old man, more than sixty years of age. Compared to Kao, he had a cultured manner of speaking and a kindly face. Apparently he was an educated person. Kao treated him as if he were one of the "Shaoshing advisers" of the old imperial days. He bossed the old man around, but he seemed to respect his opinions—perhaps a consequence of the fact that Kao was extraordinarily useless and had no choice but to lean upon the knowledge of Old Chang. In any event, our case seemed to preoccupy them. Both the director and his assistant took part in our interrogation, which lasted four days, and then we were sent to the Police Department proper.

The two secretaries in the office of the General Union of Railway Workers were arrested at the same time as my wife and I. One of them, P'eng Yung-ho, who was in charge of sending messages, was a silent chap by nature. The other one, Li Pin, a railway worker from Shihchiachung, was in charge of general affairs in the Union. He normally dressed like a workman and looked somewhat like a stoker. The editor of *New Republic,* Fan Ti-jen, was also arrested as a result of the discovery of the magazine's circulation office. Among these five, my case was the most serious. When we reached the Detective Office, the first thing they did was to put on my ankles a chain weighing nine catties (about twelve pounds)—the kind used on convicts that were under the death sentence —and then I was placed in a room. The others were confined in individual cells.

The interrogation started at noon of that day. They began by concentrating on the bombing of the home of Wellington Koo. I had already left for Shanghai when the incident occurred. The wooden box involved, which was supposed to contain a gift, had been shattered by the explosion that occurred when Koo's servants opened it. But the wood splinters remained, as well as some newspaper that had been used to wrap the box and some writing on the paper. They looked for clues in the splinters and paper and writing.

In handling the case, the Detective Office assumed from the start that the bombing was the work of the CCP and the KMT. Acting on this hypothesis, their investigations showed, incorrectly as it turned out, that I had gone to Shanghai just at the time of the explosion, and so they suspected that I was behind the plot. They produced some fake evidence—splinters and paper—that they claimed they had found in my rooms. They also compared the writing on the paper in which the bomb had been wrapped with the huge quantity of documents that they had taken from the homes of the five of us whom they had arrested.

A team of twelve detectives occupied the room in which I was detained. These detectives, who were sufficiently literate to get through the newspapers and to write simple reports, seemed to be among the cultural elite of the detective force. They carried pistols and watched over me day and night. They also engaged me in conversation in the hope that through a slip of the tongue I might reveal my guilt. They specifically asked me to write one thing and another. One of them produced a white fan for me to write on, while another wanted to know how certain phrases were written; but their efforts got them nowhere. On the other hand, I learned quite a bit from them. On the first day they revealed that the writing on the bomb wrapper did not match any of the writing found in the seized documents—a fact that seemed to depress them greatly. I learned from our chats that they were so worked up about the case because Wellington Koo had offered a reward of $100,000 to the person who broke it.

When the formal interrogation began that first day, the director of the office, Kao, started off by asking me, "Are these the splinters from under your bed?"

"I've never set eyes on those splinters," I replied.

"These papers were found in the drawer of your desk. Is that right?" he asked next.

"No such papers were ever in my drawer," I insisted.

Then he took out a bunch of the seized documents and showed them to me, one after another, asking me who had written them. In each case I told him either that I did not know or that the writer had signed the document and that he could read the name himself. He continued this aimless questioning until I grew a bit impatient. "What do you have in mind in asking these pointless questions?" I asked him.

Kao, the tough erstwhile bodyguard, pounded on the desk and shouted, "You, you rebel, are destined to die no matter what happens. You committed this bombing outrage. Why don't you be quick about confessing it, and get it over with? Why waste our time? Let me tell you frankly, whether you confess or not, you will die. The sooner you confess, the less you will suffer. Think it over."

So the examination moved directly to the bombing case itself. They tried to extract from me the statements they were after. I explained that I stood in fundamental opposition to assassination, and that I never would have committed such a crime. I assured them that this did not apply to me alone, but that KMT and CCP members did not approve of assassinations. I said that the business of Huang Fu-sheng and Wang Ching-wei trying to assassinate the Prince Regent was a thing of the past. I ridiculed them for jumping to the wrong conclusion.

The situation seemed to turn in my favor as the interrogation continued. At first they suspected that I had left Peking after the bombing incident. But from the documents they seized and the evidence I produced, it was clear that I had left Peking about one week before the bombing. The Detective Office might have been able to fabricate false evidence in the form of splinters, papers, and other inconclusive items, but it could never fake the handwriting of myself and my comrades, nor could it trace the bomb to its source or find its makers. This gave the detectives the feeling that they did not, after all, have enough evidence to implicate these intellectuals, who had a reputation for social activity, and that the accused could not be declared guilty without some proof.

But Kao, the bodyguard, seemed to thirst after that $100,000 reward. He tried to force evidence out of me, even though I had none to offer. He bellowed time after time that he would apply torture. The worst occasion was when he forced me to kneel for about half an hour on a pile of iron chains, during which time I really sweated. Several members of the judicial police stood by my side. They held large wooden poles ready to crush my feet with, to give me a taste of the torture known as "foot-binding." I gritted my teeth, knelt on the chains with my body erect, and endured the terrible pain without saying a word. Kao saw that I would not yield, that he could not force from me the statements he wanted; and so he devoted himself to raving and shouting.

"You're a little puppy pretending to be a strong man," he threatened furiously. "But you'll die once you taste the 'foot-binding' treatment."

But his anger could not grow ferocious enough to prevent his nose from running. The longer the examination continued, the harder it was for him to last it out; for his craving for opium mounted with the minutes. The deputy director, Chang, who sat beside him, took the opportunity to suggest that Kao take a rest while he, Chang, continued with the examination. Although his mouth still brimmed with vile oaths, Kao discovered that his feet quickly took him away to a back room.

"You can't talk properly kneeling down," Chang said to me as soon as Kao was out of earshot. "Better stand up and say the right things." Furious at the indignity imposed on me, I clung to my silence. Old Chang could not do much more than say, "You go and rest a bit and talk later."

Each examination followed roughly the same pattern. Kao, the bodyguard, could last only about one hour before he had to retreat to his opium couch, whereupon Old Chang would take over for him. And Old Chang could never carry on a third-degree interrogation for long. After all, he was advanced in years. The examination dragged on in this way interminably. Chang never showed anger in front of me. At worst he would say, "Better speak properly to the Director so that he won't torture you." I would reply by explaining my position. He always listened in silence, without expressing an opinion one way or the other.

By the afternoon of the third day they switched the direction of their examination. They no longer wanted to know about the bombing incident. They began interrogating me about my activities in the CCP, the KMT, and the railwaymen's labor union. I did not deny taking part in these activities, but I avoided giving them any information that might be damaging to me. Moreover, I protested that by being a member of the KMT and the CCP and a labor-union official, I really was not violating any law; but they refused to answer my protest directly. After a time they seemed to lose their vigor and to want to conclude the investigation as best they could. Subsequently I learned that their behavior was motivated by a warning from Wellington Koo against using the case to trump up charges against revolutionists. He withdrew his offer of $100,000 reward to emphasize the warning, and my interrogators relaxed their efforts.

So far as examination by the Detective Office was concerned, our case ran its course on the fourth day. Old Chang arranged to have us transferred to the Police Department. I saw no more of the bodyguard Kao. Only Old Chang dealt with me, and his questions had to do chiefly with changes that had to be made in legal forms. The situation evidently had eased greatly. Unexpectedly, Old Chang seemed to sympathize with me.

At the final examination that Chang conducted, after he told me the examination had been completed, he said some things that accurately reflected the social situation at the time. He said that our case was rather serious, and it was going to be handled by another agency. If I could hold to the attitude I had demonstrated during the last few days, my situation might not worsen. But I must consider myself lucky to have escaped torture at the hands of Director Kao, he said, for Kao was very short-tempered. Chang sighed and declared that he himself was getting on in years, that he had become a Buddhist convert and so always took a compassionate stand in handling cases. He said that he had four sons studying in different universities. Two of them had taken part in the May Fourth Movement. They had praised me as a good student and as a leader in that movement. Times had truly changed, he mused; nowadays young people were thinking differently from their elders, and this was true of his sons. Finally he hinted that for me the bombing case was practically a thing of the past and that the other charges against me were less serious at least. He urged me to defend myself properly.

I had often noticed Old Chang with his rosary, and I knew that he must be a Buddhist. He spoke sincerely, and I responded by expressing my gratitude to him for protecting me consistently during the past few days and for the pains that he had taken to get me out of trouble. He sighed and said that talented people like me should not be subjected to such suffering, that it was not the fault of the young people that the affairs of state were in such a mess. And then he frankly told me of the contradiction that was tearing him apart. He said that his official duties required him to deal sternly with me, but that in the interest of the future of the younger generation, it was his responsibility to treat me with sympathy. He kept thinking, he said, of what his four sons, who held the same views that I held, had been telling him right along. As he spoke of these things, tears rolled down his cheeks.

I was moved. The relationship between us was no longer that of an examining official and a prisoner in the dock. Instead, I had to comfort him by praising his kindness and his farsightedness. He said that he had not reserved his magnanimity solely for me, but that he had treated the other prisoners in the case in a similar fashion. He said that Li Pin, who posed as my cook, had been subjected to some physical torture, but none of the others had been tortured. He also told me that none of the people involved in the case had implicated anyone else, a fact that he considered commendable. All of us were to be transferred that evening. Fortunately, he said, we had got safely over this hurdle.

When Old Chang finished his examination, the detectives watching over me were ordered to remove the chains from my ankles. I said that I did not want them removed. I insisted that I wanted to wear the shackles into court as evidence that the Detective Office maltreated prisoners. The detectives turned to placating me with honeyed words, and eventually I let them take off the chains. These detectives had originally looked upon me as some kind of rebel who played with bombs, someone similar to the brigands that plundered society. They had no idea of what was meant by "revolutionaries." In addition to my getting helpful information from them in the conversations that we held during those few days, I also gave them some suitable lessons in politics. The lessons might well have been entitled "What Is a Revolutionary Party?" and "Can One Maltreat Members of a Revolutionary Party?" The lessons seemed to have some effect on them. Many CCP members that were arrested subsequently patterned their treatment of the jailers, to varying degrees, on the experience that I had had.

At about seven o'clock that evening each of us involved in the case was moved separately to the Police Department. The police took me to the same cell that I had occupied on June 2, 1919. As I stood there thinking "Why, I've visited this place before," a guard came up and said, "You back here again?"

"You remember me?" I replied. "After all these years, haven't you been promoted?" He looked me over with apparent embarrassment, fell silent, and walked away.

At about ten o'clock that night some guards took me to a large hall in the Police Department. The officer in charge there did nothing more than check my name, and then a sizable detachment of armed policemen escorted me into a big van, which promptly drove away from the Police Department.

I began to grow alarmed. "Could it be," I wondered, "that I have just had my identity verified and that I am now being sent off in the dead of night to be executed?"

"Where are you taking me?" I asked a policeman next to me, without thinking.

"To garrison headquarters," he replied. "We'll be there almost immediately."

I was still doubting him when the van pulled up at the side door of the yamen of the Commandant of Infantry, a building I knew well. It had been the yamen of the Chief Admiral in the days of the Ch'ing dynasty. At the beginning of the Republic it was converted into the yamen of the infantry commandant, and it accommodated the garrison headquarters. Wang Huai-ch'ing, a big gun of the Chihli clique, who was noted for lusting after the blood of revolutionary party members, was both garrison commander and Commandant of Infantry at the time. All important cases that had to do with revolutionaries were referred to him by the Detective Office and the Police Department. By now I realized that I was not destined for immediate, secret execution, but fear still gnawed at me. In four days I had made the rounds of the three most dreaded organizations in the city of Peking, and I did not know what they planned to do with me. I was taken into the ancient yamen jail, over which the Commandant of Infantry presided.

In this venerable old jail, regulations used in the days of the Ch'ing dynasty were still enforced. Beneath a feeble lamp hanging high above our heads, the chief warden and some jail guards made a thorough job of searching me. They even took away my belt and the buttons on my clothes. My handkerchief was ripped into four parts and then returned to me. Naturally, this treatment put me to considerable inconvenience, but more than that, it led me to believe that they intended to imprison me for a long time. These jailers had more moderate attitudes than the detectives in the Detective Office. The chief jailers informed me that the room I occupied was their bedroom and that the fact that I was kept there indicated preferential treatment. They urged me to sleep in peace.

I awoke the next morning to find that I was indeed receiving preferential treatment. I could move about at will in the courtyard, which was surrounded by high walls, whereas other prisoners were allowed in the courtyard only for brief, stipulated periods of time. I also learned that the place in which I was held was called the "detention house" and that it was only a small part of a large jail. This jail stood behind the detention house, along with the isolation cells, the women's blocks, and the main building, which housed the offices and living quarters of the guards. My room contained a huge brick bed—a *k'ang*—on which twenty people could sleep. It occupied two-thirds of the floor space of the entire room. In the room also were one table, four long benches, and two wooden plank beds, which were used by the four jailers and the sentry that stood guard there. All of these men had been "bannermen"

—Manchus or Chinese who had sworn allegiance to, and were in the service of, the Manchu rulers. Most of them had held their jobs since the days of the Ch'ing dynasty. Two of them were past fifty years of age, and the other three were past forty. To the right of my room was the regular confinement section of the detention house, a large room that accommodated forty prisoners, most of whom had committed minor crimes. Opposite this confinement section was a smaller room where, it was said, a whole company of guards had once been stationed. Only one of them remained, an old soldier in his fifties. Right in the center of the detention house was an open courtyard, which was large enough that forty prisoners walking about and eating did not overcrowd it. The only door through the high, sturdily built walls that surrounded the detention house was so narrow that only one person at a time could pass through it. The door was kept closed, with guards on duty outside of it. A small square hole in one wall in my room opened into the jail proper and permitted communication back and forth. Through it contact was maintained with guards and officials inside the jail.

I saw Li Pin, who was held in the confinement section of the detention house; and I learned from the guards that the rest of my comrades-in-distress were here and there in the yamen. My wife was in the women's block. Fan Ti-jen and P'eng Yung-ho had apparently been placed in the isolation block at the back. Between seven o'clock in the morning and nine in the evening I could wander about the courtyard as I chose and talk freely with the guards. I tried to use this freedom to contact the others, but I managed no more than a few words in private with Li Pin.

When I did find a chance to talk with Li Pin, the frank labor leader, I tried to comfort him for the suffering that he had undergone in the Detective Office, and I examined his wounds. He said that he had steadfastly refused to admit that he was anything but a cook, or that he knew anything beyond that. He told me that he would not have changed his story even if they had intensified the torture. In the Detective Office they had confronted him with P'eng Yung-ho. P'eng had insisted that he was a student who knew nothing about the case, and he had confirmed Li's story that he really was a cook. I told Li that I had denied everything that could not actually be proved against me. I told him to stick to his story and to push all the responsibility onto me. Then the guards decided that we had talked too long and moved to break us up. Li Pin told me earnestly to take care of myself. I stuck my thumb up and assured him with "That's the boy." And then we were separated.

Although the organization that held us was now known as the garrison headquarters, it was nevertheless the direct descendant of the old Admiral's Yamen. The old practices left behind by the Manchu dynasty still held sway. Decadence and pessimism seemed to pervade all the people in the yamen. The overstuffed chief warden compared nicely with a Manchu prince. In one of his hands there were always two polished walnut shells, which he rolled endlessly, and he was never without his magnificent snuff bottle, which he now and then put to his nose. He walked with the affected stride that was used in the imperial palaces. All in all, he presented quite an awesome appearance. But except for his interest in squeezing money from the prisoners, he concerned himself scarcely at all with what went on in the jail. The guards were in their favorite element when they discussed food, drink, and clothes. They were wretchedly poor. The uniforms they wore were remodeled cotton-padded winter uniforms from which the cotton padding had been removed. Suffusing their minds, perhaps, was the belief that "only with a reigning emperor can there be peace in the world." For them such terms as "republic," "Kuomintang," "Communist Party," "warlords," "president," and "Ts'ao K'un" might just as well not have existed. I found it impossible to talk intelligently with them. At first I thought they had been trained to keep their mouths shut, but I discovered that their minds actually were vacant and that there was no common base from which we could carry on a conversation.

Normally there were something over thirty prisoners in the detention house, most of whom were petty thieves, with heroin addicts making up the next largest group. A system was used of having certain prisoners control the rest of the prisoners. Three prisoners in the detention house had committed grave crimes, and they were kept in shackles. These three were placed in control of the others—one was in charge and the other two were his assistants. The chief prisoner enjoyed greater freedom than the rest, and he would sometimes come out into the courtyard to chat and stroll on the pretext of looking after official business. He had been sentenced to three years' imprisonment. He regarded me as a person of far greater consequence than himself, for I was a "rebel" against the throne, whereas he was merely a common criminal. As a matter of fact, though, he did not really understand what a rebel was, and it would have been so difficult to instill in him propaganda about the revolution that I did not try. But I did urge him not to maltreat Li Pin, and this had the desired effect.

After I had been in the "preferential treatment" room for five days, I was taken in the evening to be examined. The office that I went to was lined with shelves, which were cluttered with documents and files. At a desk by the window sat a lanky judge advocate who was about thirty years old. He looked like a disillusioned Teddy boy. Later I learned that he was a Manchu aristocrat and an opium smoker. On his desk lay a pile of documents connected with my case. He read through them, made some marks, and then, in a half-hearted manner, asked me some questions. He did not look the least bit ferocious. While this went on, I stood in front of his desk with husky guards on either side of me. Nobody made a transcript of the examination.

The judge advocate began by announcing that he had looked through everything in my file. He did not mention the bombing incident. Then he scrutinized certain papers in the file. He pointed to them and said that according to press reports and to the seized documents and to my statements at the Detective Office, it was established that I was an alternate member of the CEC of the KMT. He asked if I denied this. I told him that I most certainly did not deny it, that on the contrary I held it to be an honor. Next he wanted me to name the KMT leaders in charge of Party operations and to tell him what the Party was doing. I dismissed all such questions with the reply that I knew nothing about them. Without paying the slightest attention to this answer, he declared that the government knew all about these things and that his question was merely a matter of routine.

The second examination also took place at night. This time the CCP was the main issue. In the manner that he had used on the previous occasion, the judge advocate mentioned various pieces of evidence establishing my participation in the CCP that was organized at Shanghai by Ch'en Tu-hsiu and proving that I was a responsible member of the Party. I did not deny these facts either, saying that I regarded it as an honor, not as a crime. His knowledge of communism seemed to be especially limited, and he kept mentioning such clichés as "sharing property and sharing wives," which made it difficult for me to keep from laughing. This examination, like the previous one, yielded him nothing.

The third examination dealt chiefly with the Railway Workers' Union. He announced that a "rebel organization" of railwaymen had been broken up the previous year at Hankow and that many of the major criminals involved in it, headed by Yang Te-fu, had been arrested. From documents seized on that occasion and from the statements of the arrested men, it had been established that their "superior officer" was one Chang T'e-li. Furthermore, from the documents taken from my quarters, it had been proven that Chang T'e-li was none other than Chang Kuo-t'ao. He asked what I had to say about that. I said that Chang T'e-li was my courtesy name and that I had indeed undertaken the highly estimable task of organizing railwaymen. He made a record of that.

A good many issues were touched upon in these examinations. On one occasion the judge advocate asked me why the KMT and the CCP had created such havoc in Peking. He wondered if it was because the Russians or Sun Yat-sen at Canton had provided large sums of money for these operations. I told him that I knew nothing about such things. I added, however, that what I did know was that ever since the establishment of the republic, the warlords had made a mess of the country. I said that anyone with a sense of righteousness, compassion, and patriotism had no choice but to rise up and save his country. He seemed to warm up to these views. Quite possibly he believed that "without the Manchu emperor, the republic can do no right," and so, from a standpoint much different from mine, sympathized with what I said.

A period of two weeks passed without an examination, and then came the final one. It was rather dramatic. The judge advocate announced that he held a document, part of which was devoted to a succinct account of my statements, which he would read to me. He told me to stand some distance away from him, and then he held up the document and read from it. It went something like this: "Chang Kuo-t'ao, alias Chang T'e-li, age _____, a native of _____, having studied at _____ and held the positions of _____, is an alternate member of the Central Committee of the rebel party of Sun Wen, is an important Communist radical element, and is general secretary of the illegal organization of railway workers. . . . On repeated occasions he has assembled the masses in order to create trouble . . . he has attempted to carry out revolts. . . . The criminal, concealing nothing, has confessed to the above facts. . . ." He wanted me to affix my fingerprint to the document, but I promptly refused to do so. I said that I had not read the document myself, and none of the parts that he had read aloud were what I had said. I offered to write a statement of my own, but I refused to be fingerprinted.

Noting the firmness of my refusal, he signaled the guards to force me to do as he wished. The guards quickly grabbed my wrists. I struggled to fight them off, and quite a lively battle scene followed. Eventually they pinned my arms behind my back and managed to maneuver me, face first, against a wall. The judge advocate thereupon left his seat at the other end of the room, put some ink on my thumbs, and by pressing the document against them, got the prints he wanted. While this was going on I was loudly protesting, "This forced finger-printing has no validity whatsoever. I will bring accusations against you in court."

The judge advocate responded by announcing that the procedure was only a matter of routine, a mere formality, and that it concluded my examination. He added that under military law it also concluded my trial and that I did not have the right of appeal. I demanded to know what crime I had committed. "Sedition!" was his angry reply. I asked just what constituted sedition. "Sedition means sedition," he bellowed, motioning the guards to take me away.

As they led me out the door, the judge advocate ordered his guards to get my wife and to let the two of us meet. Very soon thereafter, two female guards appeared with my wife firmly in their grip. She was not allowed to come near me, but had to stand at a distance. We were forbidden to talk. I looked at the tears that welled up in my wife's eyes. Sorrow and rage engulfed us both. Then all at once we were separated again, each of us returning to his confinement block.

After I had returned to the detention house, my mind churned with thoughts about the crime of sedition and forced fingerprinting and the extraordinary meeting with my wife. I assumed that they were all indications that I was to be executed. There was no doubt about the fact that sedition was punishable by death, and the encounter with my wife looked like our final meeting before my death sentence was carried out. Although I believed that my head was in danger, I hoped that my comrades might escape the same fate. I resolved to try to save myself, but to do that, I had to establish contact with the outside world. On several occasions I bribed the guards handsomely to get information out, but I never managed to get any replies.

During the period of my interrogations, Li Pin was examined once. Blows from military clubs added more scars to his back. I tried my best to comfort him and to get him medical attention. Since I knew that even under torture he had held to his story that he was a cook, I felt the chances were that his examiner believed him. That being the case, I thought that he would be released before any of the others. I worked out with him what he would have to do if he did get out first, and particularly what to do about getting help for the others and me. Indeed, in less than a month Li Pin was released. I felt indescribably happy.

By then I had lived in the preferential-treatment section for two months. Six weeks had passed since the termination of my examination, but I had not yet received any accurate information about what was to happen to me. In a state of intolerable depression, I repeatedly asked the chief warden of the detention house to give me some books to read. I made a big issue of it without having my request granted. Finally, I staged a hunger strike in protest. On the second day of my fast the chief warden appeared, asked the reason for my behavior, and then went to the judge advocate for instructions. The judge advocate had me brought before him for questioning about two o'clock that afternoon.

"Have you been badly treated in the detention house?" he asked.

I countered with a question: "Isn't the fact that I am forbidden access to books a case of maltreatment?"

"You are a criminal, suspected of attempting to carry out seditious acts," he told me, with a conscious effort to appear kindly, "and you cannot expect an early release. You must be a bit more patient. Do you want to read books? I shall order them to supply you with some Buddhist scriptures, but you will not be allowed to use pen and paper."

On this occasion my request brought results. In the first place, I knew that I was no longer guilty of sedition; I was merely suspected of attempting seditious acts. The graveness of my case seemed to have diminished. The judge advocate had plainly hinted that it was only for the time being that I could not be released. In the second place, I was now permitted to have some books to read. I wondered whether or not these developments were due to the determined efforts of my comrades on the outside. That night the chief warden brought me a copy of *Liao Chai Chih I* (Stories from a Chinese Studio), and I called off my hunger strike.

My prison situation definitely improved. About one week after I called off my hunger strike, a journalist named Liu, who was imprisoned in the jail, actually managed to carry on a conversation with me through the hole in the wall of my room. He told me that the guards on both sides of the wall had invented pretexts to be away from our vicinity and that we could discuss anything we wished. He handed me an old newspaper and told me to read it. One of its stories said that 190 members of Parliament had questioned the government about the arrest of our group and had demanded our immediate release. The news greatly heartened me.

Liu told me, with evident pleasure, that our case was exciting less commotion now. He said that the four days I had spent in the Detective Office were the most dangerous, but that even after I was sent to the detention house I stood in danger of being sentenced to death under military law. That danger had not definitely passed, although it had been rumored that the authorities intended to keep me in prison for life. Nevertheless, it was easier to deal with that situation now than it would have been earlier. Perhaps I would be released after six months or a year, he said. Liu told me that a few days earlier Wang Fa-chin had instructed him to pass this information along to me. Not until that day, however, had he managed to get tacit approval for our conversation from the guards.

After thanking him, I asked about his own situation. He told me that he was thrown into prison for writing articles against Ts'ao K'un and that he had been there for eight months. Initially he also faced the threat of execution. Subsequently his case had been straightened out as a result of the efforts of Wang Fa-chin and others. "We were comrades in the KMT," he reflected, "and Wang Fa-chin was looking after us both." The fact that Wang had connections in all quarters made it possible for him to take very effective action on our behalf.

It was not until after I was released from prison that I learned the inside story of my deliverance from danger. Then Wang Fa-chin told me that he had not carried enough weight to save me, but that my salvation had come from a single sentence unwittingly spoken by Ch'i Hsieh-yuan. It seems that Wang Huai-ch'ing went with the document on which my thumb prints had been forcibly impressed to Ts'ao K'un and asked for instructions in disposing of my case. "Shoot him," Ts'ao K'un barked. But the Kiangsu tupan, Ch'i Hsieh-yuan, happened to be there at the time. He was eager to demonstrate his artfulness in handling revolutionaries, and so he interjected, "If we shoot one of these rebels, the rest of them will clamor and shout. It would be better to lock him up for life and let him languish in jail."

Upon hearing this, Ts'ao K'un turned to Wang Huai-ch'ing and gave him new instructions. "Let us do as Brother Ch'i suggests," he said.

It was a bodyguard of Ts'ao K'un who revealed this account. In any event, it was an important reason for the judge advocate to say that I was charged with attempting to carry out sedition instead of continuing to call me a criminal guilty of sedition.

As a result of this unexpected development, our case became much less menacing. My wife became ill and was moved from the women's block to the hospital. P'eng Yung-ho was released. It became possible for my wife and me to pass novels to each other occasionally. Using the charred ends of matches to write brief messages in the books, we passed along information and inquired about how things were going. But for me the ban on communicating with the outside world was still rigidly enforced, and by now I had not a cent on me. Each of my two daily meals consisted of one large bowl of coarse, foul-smelling rice and a few salted vegetables—nothing more. My only clothing consisted of what I had on my back. What a person endured under these conditions can well be imagined. Perhaps this was what was meant by making me "languish in prison."

But I managed to achieve a certain emotional calmness, and I did what I could to overcome the difficulties of day-to-day living. I maintained friendly relations with the other prisoners in the detention house. They received two pieces of steamed corn bread for their meals. Often I exchanged my rice for their corn bread, which pleased them. The change in the monotony of my diet naturally made me feel good too. I was allowed to bathe every day, and every now and then I managed to borrow a pair of short trousers, which gave me a change of clothing.

The other prisoners were in a different position from mine. Friends and relatives were allowed to send them clothing and money. The clothing went directly to them, but the money had to be deposited with the chief warden, from whose custody it could be withdrawn as needed for the purchase of food. This procedure gave the prison functionaries their chief source of pressure. The chief warden normally deducted from thirty to fifty per cent of every withdrawal that the prisoners made from the money deposited with him. Then the food which the prisoners bought or prepared was always divided three ways—one-third of it went to the guards, another third to the head trusty, and the remainder went to the prisoner that had paid for the food. This meant that a prisoner actually received the value of only about ten cents from every dollar deposited for him. To all intents and purposes this practice had the status of an unwritten law. The guards kept a schedule among themselves to ensure that each one had the same income from this squeezing.

If several days passed without an opportunity to extract some squeeze-money, the guards would resort to beating the prisoners to induce them to spend their money. When a great many prisoners decided to buy food on the same day, so that more than ten dollars was spent, pork would be brought in by the catty and full packets of Pirate cigarettes would arrive (cigarettes were normally bought one at a time). A feeling of elation would spread through the detention house, and the keepers would take a real interest in procuring the supplies. But when the food had been consumed, the conversation would turn to criticisms of its quality, and the prisoners would talk among themselves about how to bring about a reduction in the squeeze.

Prisoners in the detention house were kept in close custody all day long. By a system of rotation, two of them would sweep the courtyard each day, but otherwise they had no work to do. Sanitary conditions were deplorable, and sickness was prevalent. The superstition still prevailed in the jail that rats could not be killed, and so these abhorrent rodents simply swarmed over the place. If when I ate my meals I dropped a few grains of rice on the floor, the rats would surge out of their holes in full force to go after the food. When I slept on the k'ang, it was commonplace for one or two of the rats that regularly fought in the rafters to fall through ceiling holes and land on me. Bedbugs and lice were also noticeably prevalent. In one ten-day period I filled a small box with the bugs I had caught, an achievement second not even to that of the well-known newspaperman Shao P'iao-p'ing.[2] Furthermore, droves of mosquitoes played their symphonies every night, accompanied by a refrain of groaning from the malaria-stricken prisoners.

The detention house was also a training center for petty thieves, which operated without interference from any quarter. Many of the prisoners were petty thieves, and often they already knew one another. Since they had nothing to do all day, they would get together to exchange experiences and study one another's techniques of stealing and picking pockets. After such training, first offenders were graduated as well-trained lawbreakers. One day a thief who was a minor was admitted. The next day his fellow prisoners beat him until he wept. When he was taking his ten-minute walk in the courtyard, I asked the boy his age, and he told me that he was seventeen years old by Chinese reckoning, meaning that sixteen years had passed since his birth. He had stolen food because he was hungry and had been sentenced to one month in the detention house. I asked why the other prisoners had beaten him.

He told me that they were trying to force him to accept a thief as a mentor; but the boy said that he would become a rickshaw puller rather than become a professional thief. The head trusty, who stood there in chains, glared angrily at me. I could not resist turning to him and saying, "What's the matter? You don't seem to like my meddling in this affair, but you have no right to beat this boy."

The detention house also was frequented by heroin addicts. Practically every day one or more of them would be admitted or released. These addicts generally received sentences of about one month. Actually, most of them were released after about three days. They were a dreadful lot. There were injection scars all over their bodies. As the craving for the drug gripped them, they sickened, and the sound of their screams was unendurable. They sounded as though each breath they took were their last. At first I thought it was for humanitarian reasons that the yamen released them ahead of schedule, but the inside story indicated another reason.

The chief warden, who slept in the room I occupied, eventually revealed to me the true reason behind the early release of heroin addicts. This fellow had all the habits of an old-style bannerman. When he had a little money, he would don civilian clothes and strut pompously to a teahouse to spend his time and money there. But most of the time he stayed inside and complained of his poverty. He told me that in the days of the Manchu dynasty the yamen of the Commandant of Infantry had been a lucrative place to work, although it was now a very poor place. Whatever income it produced was now grabbed by the garrison headquarters and the police. Thus, the only course open to the yamen was to levy a tax on heroin. He said that the Japanese and local gang leaders were the large-scale heroin smugglers. As wholesalers, they distributed the drug to numerous peddlers in Peking, and the yamen now depended on collecting a tax from these drug peddlers. Outwardly, of course, a show of prohibiting the drug had to be made. But he pointed out that by releasing the addicts three days after they had been arrested, the yamen was meticulously following its practice of both openly prohibiting the drug and secretly deriving an income from it. However, if heroin were ever truly prohibited, or if the addicts were forced to cure themselves by being held in prison, the yamen would be deprived even of this source of income.

His explanation made me shiver. I told him that the practice even ran counter to the laws of nature. "A good many other things run counter to the laws of nature, too," he grunted in reply.

When I asked him to tell me some other stories of official practices, he smiled. "One is enough, I think," he said. "It is best to keep one's head so that one may enjoy one's meals for a long time. Right now the only thing to which I look forward is having a little cash so that I can sit in the teahouse and enjoy some good tea. Let the days flow past in this trivial way."

His words vividly reflected the state of affairs that prevailed in government organizations in Peking at that time and the mentality of most of the people in those organizations.

Just during my relatively short stay in prison, I heard and saw so many things that I cannot possibly describe them all. They taught me an important lesson, and I achieved a deeper understanding of the dark side of China's society. I decided that social reform in China was a colossal undertaking that would take a very long time. I also realized that China had an urgent and vital need for a truly democratic republic that would sweep the country clean of dirt.

In prison, days were naturally apt to pass like years. I could not be considered isolated, but I was lonely. What I mean is that those with whom I came into contact every day seldom had anything in common with me, so I could not pour out my heart to them. It was not with ease that September finally arrived and then the late autumn, when Liu, the journalist who had succeeded in secretly talking with me through the wall, was finally released. We had another chat just before his departure. I was delighted that he had been freed. It made me feel that the chances of release had increased even for me, a political prisoner. But in a sense it was painful to see him go, for I was losing the one person with whom I could talk and also the one person who could supply me with any information at all. Many thoughts crowded my mind. Liu was leaving prison, but I could not do so. This must mean that it had not been easy for the people outside to render help and that I might have to be in prison for a few years. If they would only let me read what I wanted to read for a few years in prison, I might succeed in becoming a good scholar. But unfortunately I had access only to novels, and a pitifully small number of them. Trying to find new truths, I went over in my mind what I had done in the past and the books I had read.

In the courtyard of the detention house I kept strolling back and forth, freely and peacefully, regularly doing some physical exercises.

Sometimes I would test the solidarity of the walls and their height and listen to noises from outside the walls. I would also test the foundation below and wonder if it was possible to dig a tunnel. I would pay attention to all relevant matters and even think of ways of storming out of the doors of the prison, to match wits with, and to fight, my adversaries. All these were but dreams about means of escaping from prison should it become necessary. Of course in my dreams I could hardly think of any practical measures; I was merely ridding myself of some of the feelings of indignation and resistance that are natural for a prisoner. In the long hours I always thought about this and that. At first, what occupied the most important position in my thoughts was the safety of myself, my wife, and my fellow victims. Next, I would think of the effects that my arrest might have on the entire revolutionary cause of my comrades and of the progress that they might make in their work.

As time passed, my thoughts turned increasingly to ways and means of making use of the time in prison to strengthen myself. As I took my strolls I was so engrossed in thought that my head would seem to be swollen and I would feel dizzy. At some times I would shake my head, and at other times make gestures with my hands. I would even cry out a sentence or two loudly. This attracted attention and caused alarm to the people nearby that were watching me, and they must have considered me mentally deranged. When I got tired of walking, I would lie on the bed. The ceiling would turn into a silver screen, and mirages and pictures of all kinds would grow out of my illusions. When I went to bed at night, I always found it impossible to go right to sleep, and dreams would follow the pictures of my illusions. I came to realize that one cannot keep from having confused and erratic thoughts when one is deprived of discussions with teachers and friends, has no books to read, and remains alone in a small enclosure, cut off from the outside world and lacking contact with society and its experiences. It was hard to avoid emotional outbursts and impossible to consider everything at the same time, so that one's thinking could not be deep, accurate, and systematic. As to the damage that deep thinking might inflict upon the body, I was young at the time and did not give the matter much attention.

The thoughts that I had while I was in prison exerted considerable influence over my later actions. Generally speaking, they reduced the fearless spirit for driving ahead that I had as a twenty-seven-year-old youth at that time, and they polished off some of the sharp corners of the bluntness with which I had dealt with people. What I thought about constantly at that time and what left an impression on me was the fact that I—a young patriot who had originally wanted to study natural sciences—should turn out to be an important Communist. I had studied very little or not at all in the fields of political science, economics, social science, philosophy, and history; and so I lacked preparation for making outstanding achievements. Surely I could not rely on enthusiasm alone to be successful in this work. I might as well suppress my great ambition a bit, for in all the time in prison I could not think of a plan for the realization of communism in China.

On the question of the national revolution and a democratic republic, however, I had many ideas. I believed that a historical period must elapse before notable achievements could be made, a period perhaps in excess of the thirty years that Ch'en Tu-hsiu had suggested. My doubts had chiefly arisen out of my concept of "revolution." I no longer held a superstitious belief in the revolution, as I had in the past. I had come to believe that revolution was an extraordinary means, but that it could not solve all of the innumerable social problems. Furthermore, revolution could bring along with it some undesirable by-products. I recalled the Russian Revolution, which I was acquainted with, and the Chinese revolution led by Sun Yat-sen, the growth of the Chinese Communist Party, and the campaign against me that had been waged by Maring and others. I self-confidently felt that I had a deeper understanding than they of the theory and practice of such concepts as "unanimity," "organization," "power," "leadership," "political Party," and "revolution" itself. All of these concepts had their positive and negative sides. Sometimes they constituted the motive power that pushed history forward, and at other times they proved to be demons and wildfires that destroyed human achievements. I realized that there was nothing unusual about the fact that Maring's various measures against me had been taken within the Communist Party. It would be very naive of me to express surprise over these past events.

What I gave most thought to was the urgent current problem of KMT-CCP cooperation. I recalled the events of the Enlarged Plenum, which I had participated in at Shanghai, and I tried to remember as much as possible, not without some silent amusement, about the embarrassment evinced by Ch'en Tu-hsiu at the time. I also thought of the disputes between the KMT and the CCP over the Party and SYC issues and of the reintroduction of the proposal of cooperation outside the parties' organizations. I felt gratification over my previous proposals.

At the West Lake Plenum, I took a position in favor of the establishment of a united front between the KMT and the CCP and opposed Maring's proposal that members of the CCP join the KMT. At the Third Congress of the CCP, I opposed Maring's tendency to liquidate the CCP and resolutely supported the call for independent existence and development of the CCP. At the First Congress of the KMT, as soon as I saw Sun Yat-sen, I immediately brought before him the fundamental question of permitting the coexistence of various parties. I followed this up with the proposal that since the reorganized KMT would include revolutionary elements of all brands and hues, the Party constitution should not be too rigid but should embrace a wide variety of elements. The numerous incidents preceding my imprisonment had proved the correctness of my foresight.

As I went over my thoughts, I realized that in my inner self I had consistently and fundamentally opposed the policy of having CCP members join the KMT. Why, then, did I not state my position resolutely rather than compromise and mediate because of the fear that the internal unity of the CCP and its unity with the Comintern would be damaged? This showed that I was not sufficiently resolute in my stand. I realized that it had not been enough for me merely to persist in my opposition, but that I should have gone further by introducing positive proposals in the form of a clear-cut and complete counter-program.

I went on to think about why, around the time of the Second Congress of the CCP, I had not drawn up a plan for a united front, a program for its enforcement and its future development, and so forth. I also asked myself why I had not carried out more studies with comrades and published articles to explain that the united front was the only practical program. I also thought, however, of the fact that even had I done these things, I could not have convinced Maring, who put up the strong argument at the West Lake Plenum that the united front would only become empty leftist talk principally because Sun Yat-sen would not support it. He held that any proposal not supported by Sun Yat-sen, or any view that disregarded Sun's support or otherwise attempted to influence Sun to change his original stand with regard to support of the united front, would be useless.

I regretted that after the West Lake Plenum I had felt that it would be practical for a small number of CCP leaders to join the KMT in order to achieve KMT-CCP cooperation and form a united front. I had not fully realized the possibility of this policy developing into one of having all CCP members join the KMT and of merging the two parties into one. This was truly very foolhardy. So I regretted all the more that I had lost my opportunity. In September of 1922, when we held the ceremony of joining the KMT at the home of Chang Chi, I should have approached Sun Yat-sen directly and proposed that he change his stand of "I am the revolution, and all revolutionists should come under the standard of the Three Principles of the People" and permit instead the existence of many parties, forming a united front with the CCP and the various other revolutionary forces. This would have been tantamount to the reorganization, necessitated by a change in the situation, of his one-owner "revolutionary company" into a partnership having a monopoly of the enterprise, with him remaining the major stockholder, chairman of the board, and general manager. Could this not have been done?

I kept on thinking about the many occasions during that period when I should have approached Sun Yat-sen, and I speculated about how I should have discussed the matter with him. Had I succeeded, the repercussions would have been tremendous. Even if I had failed to change Sun's original stand, the venture would have been of deep historical significance. I felt by then that I had lacked foresight, and I realized that the lost opportunity could not return. By the time of the Third Congress of the CCP in June, 1923, after Maring's long-term maneuvering and the Sun-Joffe Declaration, the KMT had decided on its reorganization and the admission of Chinese Communists, and the Third International had made its April resolution. By then it was very late, but I could still have devised measures to reject Maring's proposal and to approach Sun Yat-sen directly, and it would still have been possible to save the situation a little. But when the KMT held its First Congress, it was too late. All I could do was to express some views and then withdraw.

This deep thinking over a long period included speculation and review. It finally made me realize that I had to temper my youthful boldness in forging ahead and step up my maturing sense of being discreet. I could not clearly visualize the development of the Chinese revolution, which seemed to contain many possibilities. I could only hope that it would turn out well, that is to say that the KMT and the CCP would not get involved in serious trouble that would lead to bitterness. The situation had by now developed to the stage where the only course was for both parties to tolerate each other in the interests of the country under the *fait accompli* of their cooperation within the

KMT. Or else they could quickly reach a friendly agreement to change to cooperation outside either party structure. Even after the national revolution had succeeded, the KMT and the CCP should avoid being hostile toward each other.

These thoughts of mine were reflected later in my words and actions after my release from prison. Fan Ti-jen, who was released along with me, and Chao Shih-yen and other comrades, who had argued with me, all remarked that I, who had been a fiery mass, had been transformed into a more mature person. Some people even ridiculed me for not being able to stand the hardships of imprisonment. I did not completely repudiate this theory. On one occasion I told Comrade Chao Shih-yen and others that having learned a lesson from my personal experience in the February Seventh Strike and my near-dismissal from the CCP because of my opposition to overall participation in the KMT, I had reviewed these events in detail during my prison term; and so it was that I had matured. Perhaps it was not a case of my having retrogressed or turned to the right, but rather of having progressed and reduced my mistakes.

Early in October, signs of a second war between the Chihli and Fengtien cliques became more and more evident, and so greater precautions were taken in the prison. News also reached my ears of the war between Kiangsu and Chekiang and of the alliance of Sun Yat-sen, Tuan Ch'i-jui, and Chang Tso-lin against the Chihli clique. Then fragmentary reports of the large-scale outbreak of the Second Fengtien-Chihli War were received. I conjectured about, and even prayed for, the collapse of the Chihli regime, as this would increase the possibility of escape from prison. But in order to avoid trouble I did not reveal my designs, and so I passed the days as usual.

On October 23 a guard told me in secret that the army of Feng Yü-hsiang had suddenly returned to Peking and had surrounded the presidential mansion. Soon after that I was forbidden to go into the courtyard, and the door to my room was locked. The guards began to show signs of alarm and rigidly enforced the ban on conversation among prisoners. Fully armed sentries went on duty outside the jail; and inside, we could clearly hear them marching. On October 24 a keeper told me that Wang Huai-ch'ing had been deposed. Feng Yü-hsiang had sent a man named Liu to take over the position of garrison commander. These developments led me to the conclusion that I really did have a chance of being released.

On October 25, at about four o'clock in the afternoon, I was sitting in my room, unaware of what was actually happening and turning over in my mind all sorts of conjectures. Suddenly a guard opened my door and led me off to a huge room in the garrison headquarters. The room was jammed with both high and low officials. The new garrison commander that Feng Yü-hsiang had appointed had just formally taken over. This man rose from his chair and stood beside his large conference table to receive me. My wife and Fan Ti-jen had also been brought in. In my heart there was an indescribable feeling of anticipation. Yet I felt it was beyond all expectation that Feng Yü-hsiang should treat us so nicely, and so I restrained myself, maintaining a wariness for the possibility of more unpleasant developments.

The new commander raised his voice to ask me: "What crime have you committed?"

"I have not actually committed any crime," I replied. "The judge insisted that I was guilty of attempting to carry out seditious activities, but I have never admitted it."

"Did they beat you?" he asked. "Did they maltreat you?"

"I was personally fortunate in having escaped physical violence," I told him.

Whereupon he announced, "Not guilty. To be released immediately." He added that I had been wronged and that I should take a rest and recuperate.

He asked my wife and Fan Ti-jen the same questions that he asked me.

"I have committed no crime," my wife replied. "I was illegally arrested and imprisoned."

Fan replied that he had committed no crime but patriotism, and he accused those responsible for his arrest and confinement of maltreating him.

The officer declared both of them not guilty, ordered their release, and then, smiling, he soothed them and expressed regret at the hard luck they had had.

When we, the political prisoners, got out of jail, our comrades and friends comforted us in various ways that it is not possible to go into. Fan Ti-jen blamed me for not taking the lead in lodging complaints against the Chihli warlords for their suppression of human rights. I soothed him by saying, "The political situation may still change in all manner of ways. We are very lucky to have been released the way we were. For the time being, let's forgive them. Let's devote our full attention to developing our future tasks."

SUN YAT-SEN'S TRIP NORTH

CHAPTER

The Dispute Within the Chinese Communist Party over Sun Yat-sen's Trip to the North

The entire situation seemed to have changed by the time I was released from prison. A tendency to oppose the KMT had grown unnoticed within the CCP. Not long after my release this tendency was demonstrated in the opposition to Sun Yat-sen's trip to North China. The Peking District Committee of the CCP regarded the trip as tantamount to seeking a compromise with the Northern warlords, and it threatened to split the KMT and the CCP in Peking. The danger of a split was averted as a result of my strenuous efforts to placate the parties concerned and to heal the differences.

The secretary of the CCP Peking District Committee was then Chao Shih-yen. After the Third Congress of the CCP, the CC had gradually carried out a system of appointing responsible members to the Party organs at lower levels. Chao, who was very young, had been sent to Peking by the CC. During the May Fourth Movement, he had been the representative of the student council of the middle school attached to Peking Higher Normal School. Those of us who were representatives of university student councils in those days had regarded him as a younger brother. He went to France as a working student after finishing middle school, and there he joined the CCP. He returned to China after I entered prison and immediately assumed leadership in the Peking district, where he naturally lacked prestige and experience. Because he had read some Communist works, could speak and write well, and was enthusiastic and responsible, however, he won the respect of some comrades in Peking. Meanwhile, Li Ta-chao and other ranking leaders, who were few in number, lived underground and dared not operate in the open during the final stage of Chihli Clique rule. Thus, Chao Shih-yen suddenly became the central figure of the CCP in Peking.

Since Chao Shih-yen and I were old friends, he enthusiastically invited me to stay at his home for a while when I got out of prison, and I accepted. Thus, there were several days during which we saw each other all day long. He impressed me very favorably. I decided that his years in France had been most fruitful, but I also very quickly discovered that there was an enormous gap between his views on the political situation and mine.

Chao Shih-yen believed that support of the Sun-Tuan-Chang (Sun Yat-sen, Tuan Ch'i-jui, Chang Tso-lin) triangular alliance marked a great change in KMT policy. He felt that it was tantamount to abandoning the revolutionary policy of KMT-CCP cooperation and that it represented a shift to seeking a compromise with the warlords that were in power. He also said that the current CCP policy was not one of supporting the Left Wing of the KMT and opposing the Right Wing; rather it was a policy of opposition to the current KMT policy as a whole. It could be said that at the time a majority of comrades held that view, and the view had developed from roots in the past.

As was mentioned in chapter six, during the middle part of May, 1924, Wang Ching-wei and Chang Chi had opened negotiations with Ch'en Tu-hsiu on the question of CCP and SYC fractions within the KMT. Not only did they fail to reach a compromise in those negotiations, but an additional shadow was cast upon the chances for mutually beneficial relations between the two parties. In the talks, Ch'en Tu-hsiu clung to his original stand, refusing to abolish CCP and SYC fractions within the KMT. And on June 18, 1924, Teng Tse-ju, Chang Chi, and Hsieh Ch'ih—all members of the KMT Supervisory Committee—submitted to the CC of the KMT a proposal to impeach the CCP. It stated that the existence of CCP and SYC fractions within the KMT violated the discipline of, and was a threat to, the KMT.

This impeachment proposal was rejected by the CC of the KMT. The resolution of the Second Plenum of the CC of the KMT in August, 1924, stated: "The China Kuomintang only asks of Communists who have joined the Party that their actions be in keeping with the principles and political platform of the Kuomintang, and does not enquire into their other activities. . . ."[1] Thus, on the surface, the question of Party and SYC fractions was lightly dismissed. But this offered no practical solution to the issue, which had a very detrimental effect on KMT-CCP cooperation. On the one hand, from the issue of CCP and SYC fractions, KMT members generally drew the conclusion that to greater or lesser degrees CCP members were dissidents. CCP members, on the other hand, came to the conclusion that KMT members were exploiting the issue of fractions in order to abolish the CCP. The two parties grew farther apart. From my conversations with comrades after I was released from prison, I realized full well that they all felt disgruntled about this question.

Of more concrete political significance was the divergence of opinion between the KMT and CCP that resulted from the Sun-Tuan-Chang triangular alliance. This divergence came into the open in the course of the fight against the Chihli clique. On September 3, 1924, the Kiangsu-Chekiang War broke out, with Ch'i Hsieh-yuan and Sun Ch'uan-fang of the Chihli clique fighting Lu Yung-hsiang of the Tuan Ch'i-jui clique. On September 15, Chang Tso-lin of the Fengtien clique marched on Shanhaikwan, and the Second Fengtien-Chihli War broke out. Then on September 18, Sun Yat-sen left for Shaokwan to lead an expeditionary army northward. He promulgated the "North Expedition Manifesto,"[2] which voiced support for Lu Yung-hsiang of Chekiang and Chang Tso-lin of the Fengtien clique, and opposition to Ts'ao K'un and Wu P'ei-fu of the Chihli clique. While the mutiny of the Merchant Volunteer Corps at Canton subsequently led to the failure of Sun Yat-sen's plan to march on Kiangsi, which was to have been the first stage of the Northern Expedition, KMT members all over the country were shaken by the episode.

As I got it from my comrades, KMT rightists and those who believed in gaining political power at any cost entertained highly optimistic illusions about the Sun-Tuan-Chang alliance when the Chihli-Fengtien War broke out. They did not favor opposition to all warlords at that stage. The Chihli warlords Ts'ao K'un and Wu P'ei-fu were the only ones that they felt should be attacked. Similarly, they did not favor opposition to all imperialists, but only to the imperialists that supported the Chihli clique. For them the major political theme had become one of implementing the policy of the Sun-Tuan-Chang alliance, not KMT-CCP cooperation. The CCP insisted that the established policy of the KMT was opposition to all warlords and all imperialists and the abrogation of all unequal treaties and that this could not possibly be misinterpreted. So far as the CCP was concerned, it might be all right to utilize the Tuan Ch'i-jui clique and the Fengtien clique in opposing the Chihli clique, but to really compromise with the pro-Japan Tuan Ch'i-jui and Chang Tso-lin was insupportable.

I can no longer remember the many tales that my comrades told me of the disputes between the two parties that sprang from this divergence of views. But I do recall one case which one of the participants in the dispute told me about later. According to him, early in September, 1924, after the outbreak of the Kiangsu-Chekiang War, the Shanghai Executive Department of the KMT held a mass rally in the General Chamber of Commerce building at T'ien Hou Temple. Most of the participants were university and middle-school students. Yeh Ch'u-ts'ang, director of the Youth Section of the Shanghai Executive Department, had the chair. Ho Shih-chen, who had been a representative of Shanghai students during the May Fourth Movement, delivered a report to the meeting. He explained that the KMT had to unite with the relatively progressive militarists such as Tuan Ch'i-jui, Chang Tso-lin, and Lu Yung-hsiang in order to jointly overthrow the most reactionary warlords—Ts'ao K'un, Wu P'ei-fu, and their Chihli forces. When he had finished, a young CCP member named Kuo Shou-hua stood up and spoke in opposition to him. Kuo contended that there were no progressive warlords and that it was essential for the KMT to overthrow all warlords. Kuo had hardly finished speaking when somebody at the meeting called him a spy for Ts'ao K'un and Wu P'ei-fu. This was followed by cries of "Beat him up," and Kuo was beaten in the melee that ensued. The meeting accomplished its purpose. Similar incidents were reported in other areas.

With these conditions in mind, Chao Shih-yen and other comrades pointed out to me, when I came out of prison, that the KMT had adopted a two-faced policy. On the surface it adhered to a revolutionary policy of alliance with Russia and tolerance of the Communists, but actually its policy was one of compromise with the warlords. My comrades believed that Tuan Ch'i-jui and Chang Tso-lin were notoriously pro-Japanese warlords, who had been rejected by the people of the country. "Could the CCP, then, operating through the KMT, sit at the same table with Tuan and Chang?" they demanded.

For the moment, at least, the defection of Feng Yü-hsiang from Ts'ao K'un placed him in control of the Peking situation. Feng organized the National Army with himself as its commander-in-chief. Concurrently, he placed himself in command of the First Army. He made Hu Ching-i and Sun Yüeh, one-time Chihli militarists who had fallen from grace and now held some connections with the KMT, commanders of the Second and Third armies respectively. On this occasion Feng Yü-hsiang actually did something that was a matter of considerable popular gratification. He drove P'u Yi, the Manchu emperor that had abdicated, from the Forbidden City and sent off a message stating that Sun Yat-sen would be welcome in the North. He and his Christian friend Hsu Ch'ien also established contact with KMT people in Peking and with Karakhan, the Soviet ambassador at Peking. But he was subjected to pressure from the diplomatic corps in Peking, which did not recognize the cabinet of Huang Fu which Feng supported.[3] Meanwhile the forces of Chang Tso-lin reached Tientsin, where they disarmed the Chihli forces, to which they were superior. But Feng had taken over those Chihli forces and was reorganizing them. Thus, he was threatened by the possibility of a war. Consequently Feng Yü-hsiang began to waver. He indicated that the pressures being brought to bear upon him were beyond his power to resist. Quickly he began avoiding KMT people. He was even more frightened of being suspected of turning Communist.

Faced with this state of affairs, Chao Shih-yen and others could not see that the rise of Feng Yü-hsiang's army, the Kuominchun (National Army), had made any change in the Northern situation, since the warlords still ruled there. They felt that Feng Yü-hsiang and his colleagues could not be regarded as progressive militarists sympathizing with the KMT; they were unregenerate warlords playing the game of power. But at the time it was widely rumored that Feng Yü-hsiang favored the organization of a committee to rule the country—a committee to be made up of Sun Yat-sen, Tuan Ch'i-jui, Chang Tso-lin, himself, and a few other celebrities. It was rumored that his invitation to Sun Yat-sen to come to the North had been issued in the hope that Sun would join this committee. Therefore Chao Shih-yen and his colleague advocated that Sun Yat-sen refuse the invitation and refuse to join the committee in order to avoid a compromise between the KMT and the warlords.

On November 10 Sun Yat-sen issued his "Manifesto on Proceeding to the North."[4] He left Canton on November 13. So far as Chao Shih-yen was concerned, the "convocation of a National Assembly and the abrogation of unequal treaties," which Sun advocated in his manifesto, would not be realized. Chao believed that Sun Yat-sen actually sought nothing but a compromise with the warlords, and that it was therefore essential to express opposition to his trip. This caused the danger of a split between the KMT and the CCP in Peking.

Meanwhile, the popular organizations in Peking that had come under KMT and CCP influence were making good progress. CCP members and some leftist leaders of the KMT led nearly one hundred of these organizations in raising high the banner of opposition to Sun's trip north. At the same time KMT members that were regarded by the CCP as rightists controlled about the same number of popular organizations, and these were busy rejoicing over the trip of Sun Yat-sen. The two parties were at loggerheads; each refused to give way. The predicament grew serious.

I consistently opposed this policy of the CCP District Committee, while Chao Shih-yen and the others persisted in their view. They explained away my opposition as being the result of my having spent more than five months in prison, with the result that I was not thoroughly familiar with developments on the outside during the period. They said that the CC of the CCP had changed its policy toward KMT-CCP cooperation since the Enlarged Plenum of May, 1924. After the Plenum, CCP members in Shanghai had held a meeting at which Mao Tse-tung, who was concurrently a member of the CC of the CCP and of the Shanghai Executive Department of the KMT, had expressed the position that "all work must be done in the name of the Kuomintang." Since a majority of comrades opposed him, Mao could not stay on in his job, and on the pretext of illness, he left his post in the CC of the CCP. At the same time, many comrades had returned to China from Moscow and Paris to take up important posts. They included P'eng Shu-chih, Ch'en Yen-nien, Chou En-lai, Wang I-fei, Jen Pi-shih, and Yin Kuan. Most of them were dissatisfied with the existing relationship between the KMT and the CCP. They stressed the need to maintain the independent status of the CCP. After telling me about these developments, Chao Shih-yen and his colleagues put the following question to me, "These comrades are, on the whole, supporting the views you expressed at the Third Congress. How is it that you yourself seem to have changed?"

This serious disagreement arose in many informal discussions and was taken up at a meeting of the Peking District Committee. Finally, a decision had to be reached on it at a general meeting of CCP members in Peking. Toward the end of November, as Sun Yat-sen was leaving Shanghai on his way north by way of Japan, Chao Shih-yen started off this full meeting of CCP members in Peking by presenting a long report. He maintained that opposition to the northern trip of Sun Yat-sen was a correct policy, in keeping with various directives of the CC of the CCP. He called it a farsighted and independent policy, and he quoted CC directives and articles in *Hsiang-tao* to support his views.

Then I spoke as the one opposed to the policy. First, I reviewed my consistent opposition to the policy that called upon all CCP members to join the KMT and my particular desire that the CCP not sacrifice its independent development. But I insisted that I had never opposed KMT-CCP cooperation; nor did I support any anti-KMT trend within the CCP. I contended that this so-called farsighted and independent policy was incorrect. The directives of the CC of the CCP merely opposed a compromise between the KMT and the warlords in power; they at no point clearly voiced opposition to the trip of Sun Yat-sen to the North. I explained that the Sun-Tuan-Chiang triangular alliance was a union formed against the Chihli clique and that it was only a temporary strategy. Just because certain KMT rightists tended to compromise with the warlords was no reason for jumping to the conclusion that Sun Yat-sen and the KMT as a whole were behaving similarly. I praised the recent manifesto by Sun Yat-sen, especially his call for a national assembly and for the abrogation of unequal treaties, which, I said, had touched off a favorable response from the masses in the North. I conceded that Feng Yü-hsiang and others in the National Army organization were speculators in the power market; but if they showed an inclination to come over to the national revolution, it was not our place to keep them out.

With some emphasis I went on to point out what I regarded as the mistakes involved in the policy of opposing the northern trip of Sun Yat-sen. I believed that unfavorable repercussions from that policy could already be felt. It had caused a majority of KMT members to split with both the CCP members that had joined the KMT and with KMT leftists. There was also unrest within the CCP. If when Sun Yat-sen arrived in a few days he found the CCP opposing his activities, the way it had been doing, the consequences would be unthinkable. I asked the CCP members to welcome Sun Yat-sen, to work toward implementation of his manifesto, and to oppose the tendency of the rightists to compromise with the warlords—a tendency that violated the manifesto.

Our two opposing positions were put to a vote. The vote resulted in my being severely defeated, something that had never before happened to me in Peking. Chao's position was supported by an overwhelming majority of thirty-seven votes, while I had only five supporters and ten people abstained from voting. But the decision did not subdue me; I rose and asked that the whole matter be reexamined. I said that the vote was a manifestation of the infantile disorder of leftism. It could lead to serious consequences—to a split between the KMT and the CCP as well as to a split within the CCP itself. I insisted that on the one hand, instructions be requested from the CC and that on the other, the question be reviewed. After I made this proposal, some of those who had abstained from voting supported my proposal that the issue be reexamined.

Chao Shih-yen noted that the members supporting me and those abstaining were among the most important members of the Party. Perhaps, too, my statements had a persuasive effect on him. In any event, he adopted a more moderate tone in responding to my proposal. He conceded that a majority opinion might sometimes be wrong because of political inexperience. Since the vote had been taken, however, there was no choice but to abide by it for the time being. But he accepted my proposal to seek instructions from the CC and to examine the issue further.

After that meeting the situation generally tended to swing in my favor. More than five thousand people turned out to prepare a welcome for Sun Yat-sen at a mass meeting called by the group that favored Sun's trip. This episode discredited the statement made by Chao in his report that not very many people actually welcomed the Sun Yat-sen trip. It also caused him to realize that the CCP might find itself isolated. Li Ta-chao, who had not attended the general membership meeting, also strongly supported my position. He persuaded Chao Shih-yen and his group to change their stand without waiting for a directive from the CC in view of the imminent arrival of Sun Yat-sen. Furthermore, Effin, who held an important post in the Soviet embassy, personally assured Chao that both the Soviet Union and the Comintern supported the northern trip of Sun Yat-sen.

Under these circumstances the Peking District Committee of the CCP had no choice but to change its position. But more than a few comrades could not help feeling that they had lost face, and it again fell to me to save the situation. I managed to do this at another general meeting of Party members in Peking. I told them that after the defection of Feng Yü-hsiang, the policy of developing activities among workers and students, which the District Committee quite correctly pursued, had accomplished a great deal that commanded respect. It was only in the matter of opposing the northern trip of Sun Yat-sen that the Committee was inclined to turn leftist. However, it was not too late to salvage the situation. I explained carefully that the mistake was nothing to pass off lightly, that its roots went down deep. After the Third Congress of the CCP, I said, too much optimism had developed within the Party about KMT-CCP cooperation. Then, when the KMT rightists, using unprincipled methods, struck out at us, our optimism gradually turned to despair, and we went to the other extreme. But I said that if our comrades would just remember the way Sun Yat-sen put down the mutiny staged by the volunteer corps of the Canton Chamber of Commerce, the forceful way that he dealt with attempts at interference by the British consul at Canton, and the recent manifesto on his trip to the North, they would realize that such an ally could not be lightly dismissed; they would immediately see, in other words, that opposition to his trip was less than appropriate. I pointed out that this infantile leftist disorder did not exist in Peking alone; it could be found in CCP organizations elsewhere. Even CC directives up to that point could not be regarded as entirely free of its flavor. I said that with the imminent arrival of Sun Yat-sen, time was short; comrades in Peking should muster up the courage to revise their original decision and express their welcome to him.

As a result of these efforts at persuasion, the meeting passed my proposal without dissent. It also entrusted me with the job of mediating with the popular organizations and of bringing their positions into harmony. On the basis of this resolution, I succeeded in bringing around the CCP members and some KMT leftists, who were leaders of the opposing organizations. As to the KMT members in the welcomers' group, they had no wish to see people come out against the arrival of Sun Yat-sen, and so they gave my mediation work their full support.

It was now two days before Sun Yat-sen would reach Tientsin. I invited three important representatives of each of the two opposing groups to a conference in a large room of a famous teahouse in Central Park. I began by emphatically stating that they were all from organizations led by the KMT and that it was therefore a matter of deep regret that they were divided into one faction that welcomed the northern trip of Sun Yat-sen and another that opposed the trip. Then I made the following three proposals: (1) All members of the KMT, of the CCP, and of popular organizations under their leadership should unanimously welcome Sun's trip to the North; (2) support should be voiced for the manifesto Sun Yat-sen issued on coming north, and every effort should be made to realize it, while opposition should be voiced to all violations of the manifesto and to any attempt at compromise with the warlords in power; and (3) the leadership organs of the two factions of these popular organizations should be merged into one for the purpose of promoting the first two principles.

My proposals received unanimous support; and the atmosphere of the conference, which had been solemn, immediately became gay. It was decided that the leadership organs of the two factions of these popular organizations should confer on the spot about taking steps to merge into a single leadership organ.

This great storm, which might well have caused a serious deterioration in KMT-CCP relations, thus abated for the time being. A few days later, a directive to welcome Sun Yat-sen arrived from the CC of the CCP. The policy of the CCP changed from one of suspecting that the KMT was about to compromise with the warlords and of opposition to Sun's trip north, to one of welcoming Sun's trip and of promoting the convocation of a national assembly.

The Political Council of the Kuomintang in Peking

On December 4, 1924, Sun Yat-sen, a giant of his age, arrived at Tientsin. It was an event of vast interest to revolutionaries and the masses in the North. But suddenly sickness attacked him, and the ambitious scheme behind his trip and the hopes of revolutionaries in general were dashed. While Dr. Sun lay critically ill, the KMT struggled against great difficulties. Fortunately, the senior ranks of that Party, Communists among them, did their best to preserve unity. At the same time, news came from Canton of the victory of the first expedition against Ch'en Chiung-ming, which consolidated the position of the Canton government. As a result, the death of Dr. Sun did not basically disrupt the KMT.

A provisional government at Peking was organized before Sun Yat-sen reached Tientsin. Tuan Ch'i-jui left Tientsin for Peking on November 22, and on November 24 he assumed the post of Chief Executive of the provisional government. But Tuan, the veteran of the Peiyang warlords, had no real power with which to influence the political situation in Peking. Furthermore, his direct subordinate, Lu Yung-hsiang, had been defeated in battle, thereby losing his military base in Chekiang Province and the power that went with it. Tuan Ch'i-jui was placed in power on this occasion entirely because of support from the two military leaders Chang Tso-lin and Feng Yü-hsiang, who found the move necessary because of the situation they faced.[5]

To gain recognition for his government from the diplomatic corps after he had assumed office, Tuan announced a policy of honoring all national commitments to the rest of the world and of respecting all foreign treaties. At the same time he advocated the convocation of a rehabilitation conference. According to provisions for the Rehabilitation Conference, which he drew up on December 2, warlords and bureaucrats were to be its chief participants.[6] This move was aimed directly at a proposal in the manifesto that Sun Yat-sen issued on his trip north. The manifesto proposed calling a national assembly, composed chiefly of representatives of popular organizations, which would advocate the renunciation of unequal treaties. Thus, Sun Yat-sen arrived at Tientsin to find himself in political disagreement with Chief Executive Tuan.

Sun Yat-sen felt unwell when he reached Tientsin. It was widely reported among revolutionary circles in Peking that he was merely suffering from a slight cold. Perhaps—so the word went—he had no more than a political sickness, resulting from the fact that his ally, Chief Executive Tuan, had launched into national affairs in a direction diametrically opposed to that of Dr. Sun, without even consulting Dr. Sun or giving him a chance to interject a word. This could scarcely do anything but anger Sun Yat-sen.

The venture of Tuan Ch'i-jui destroyed the triangular alliance, but it promoted unity within the KMT. Even members of the CCP believed that now there would not be a compromise between Sun Yat-sen and Tuan Ch'i-jui. To a greater or lesser extent, the revolutionaries changed their political views. They agreed that it would be unthinkable if Sun Yat-sen, who had undertaken an alliance with Russia and officially tolerated the Communists, should make concessions to Tuan Ch'i-jui. Revolutionary leaders kept themselves busy traveling between Peking and Tientsin, seeking ways to improve the situation, while representatives of numerous popular organizations formed themselves into missions of sympathy. They went to Tientsin to comfort Sun Yat-sen in his illness and to assure him of their support, in order to dispel the effects of the increasingly overbearing attitude of Tuan.

During the middle part of December, I led a ten-man delegation of railway workers to call on Sun Yat-sen. Sun was in bed asleep when we got there, and his secretary, Wang Ching-wei, received us. The railway-union leaders Teng P'ei and Sun Yung-p'eng expressed their concern for Dr. Sun and declared that all railway workers stood behind him. They also mentioned certain ideas about how Sun Yat-sen's objectives could be attained. Wang Ching-wei thanked them on behalf of Sun Yat-sen and added that as soon as Dr. Sun recovered, he would make an appointment to meet them personally.

Wang Ching-wei privately hinted to me, however, that the condition of Sun Yat-sen was far more serious than the world at large seemed to realize. "Do you think it better for Dr. Sun to go to Peking in spite of his illness," he asked, "or to leave Tientsin to seek a good place for treatment in the South?" I replied that it depended mainly on Dr. Sun's condition and upon his own wishes in the matter.

"Chief Executive Tuan does not respect the views of Dr. Sun," Wang than stated. "And Chang Tso-lin wants Dr. Sun to abandon his policy of alliance with Russia in order to make up with the Legation Quarter.[7] Because of his military weakness, moreover, Feng Yü-hsiang is growing passive. What would be the use of Dr. Sun going to Peking now?"

I replied to the effect that if Sun Yat-sen went south for medical treatment, would he not feel that he was making a political withdrawal? If, on the other hand, he received medical attention in Peking, where all the popular organizations, at least, rallied round his standard, wouldn't this have an active political effect? Wang agreed to pass my ideas along to Sun Yat-sen.

Whether or not Sun Yat-sen should go to Peking in spite of his illness was a much-debated issue at the time. Nobody yet realized that his affliction was a fatal ailment, cancer of the liver. But KMT leaders generally considered the medical facilities available in Peking as well as the political effects in studying the problem, with the result that most of them favored his going to Peking; and Sun Yat-sen agreed with them. So, on December 31, 1924, amidst an enthusiastic welcome from the masses, Sun Yat-sen reached Peking, bringing his ailment with him.

In Peking, Sun Yat-sen could not receive visitors, nor could he attend to his duties. He promptly designated a Central Political Council of the KMT, made up of the members of the CEC and CSC committees of the KMT that were then in Peking.[8] According to the announcement of its formation, which was made by Wang Ching-wei, the Council was to be temporary in nature, designed to take care of all political matters on behalf of Sun Yat-sen for the duration of his illness. Its membership, headed by Wang Ching-wei, included Li Shih-tseng, Wu Chih-hui, Yü Yu-jen, Ting Wei-fen, Wang Fa-chin, Li Ta-chao, myself, and others—a total of more than ten members. (The number was increased by several members of the CEC of the KMT and its CSC that subsequently arrived in Peking.) It might be maintained that the activities of the Council characterized the general situation of the KMT at the time.

The Political Council held two regular meetings each week in addition to extraordinary sessions. It was with a heavy heart that those of us involved in the developments of the time regularly attended the meetings. Each meeting elected its chairman. No secretariat was maintained. But all of us looked to Wang Ching-wei as the focal point of the Council because he was the sole intermediary between the Council and Sun Yat-sen. Wang Ching-wei, however, maintaining an attitude of great humbleness, refused to assume the role of Council leader.

At each meeting, Wang Ching-wei reported in detail on Dr. Sun's condition. Sometimes, too, reports from Canton and other areas were read. Then the participants would make their own reports. The agenda was never fixed, and only rarely were any proposals prepared. All of this left the members with an awareness that organization was lacking and that the system needed improving. Many members, myself included, asked Wang Ching-wei to assume chairmanship of the Council and to improve it organizationally, but Wang invariably demurred with noncommittal replies that never clearly gave his reasons.

The humility of Wang Ching-wei reflected the existence of a difficult situation. It was said that Wang Ching-wei did not want to assume the post of chairman because there was a permanent Political Council at Canton over which Hu Han-min, in the capacity of Acting Generalissimo, presided on behalf of Sun Yat-sen. Although Sun Yat-sen lay ill in Peking, the central machinery of the KMT was in Canton. The Political Council in Peking was of a temporary nature and could not act without regard for Canton.

Li Ta-chao and I were the two Communists on the Council, and we had to proceed very cautiously. All along, the CCP had made known to the outside world its unqualified support of Sun Yat-sen, while opposing any concessions to Tuan, and so it was all the more anxious that the illness of Sun Yat-sen should not cause a deterioration in KMT-CCP relations. We punctually attended meetings, sat there solemnly, speaking only occasionally and then only to support ideas that agreed with our own. For we feared that if we showed greater initiative and this led to arguments, it might be thought that we were exploiting the illness of Sun Yat-sen to instigate dissension between the two parties.

Since the Council thus lacked system, the major part of each meeting was taken up in the random expositions by Wu Chih-hui. The meetings were generally held in the mornings. About an hour would be devoted to reports. With some two hours left on our hands, Wu Chih-hui assumed the leading role in passing the time. He was a good talker, but he devoted himself principally to disconnected events, which he interlarded with blatant slanders, satirical quips, attacks, and castigations. There did, however, seem to be a law which governed the flow of his words. Whenever he disagreed with something or did not wish to discuss it, off he would go on one of his interminable, rambling monologues until finally he had led the meeting to an end without its having reached a conclusion. On the other hand, when he happened to want the question before the meeting settled, he would clear the way for it by keeping silent. The questions that he did not want discussed generally related to what might be the consequences of opposition to Tuan Ch'i-jui.

The random conversational gambits of Wu Chih-hui increasingly revealed his political ambitions. Li Ta-chao told me that one day he and Wu Chih-hui left the meeting together. Wu said to him, "I used to respect this youngster Chang Kuo-t'ao. But now I hear that actually he has loose morals, that he is given to chasing after prostitutes and to gambling."

This greatly surprised Li Ta-chao, who said that he promptly and sternly told Wu, "I can definitely guarantee that Chang Kuo-t'ao is not that kind of person. He does not go in for women and gambling. He carefully maintains his personal integrity, and he is no cynic."

I was so annoyed at hearing about this episode that I started shaking. "Don't get angry," Li Ta-chao said. "There is more to come." He told me that he regarded Wu's remarks as having been haphazardly spoken by a man who felt that his seniority entitled him to take certain liberties. But Li said that he did not believe Wu merely intended to make a personal attack on me—there was something more to it. So, Li took Wu to lunch, and they had a prolonged chat, chiefly about conditions in the North and the relations between the KMT and the CCP. Li Ta-chao told Wu about the years that I had devoted to leading the railway workers, about my struggle against Wu P'ei-fu, and about the fact that I was the first member of the CC of the KMT to be thrown into jail. He also recounted the strenuous efforts that I had made after getting out of jail to placate the leftist elements that opposed the northern trip of Sun Yat-sen. Li pointed out that at that moment some popular organizations were agitating for a demonstration against the Tuan government, and it was I, Chang Kuo-t'ao, acting in accordance with the wishes of the Political Council, who was doing his best to pacify them and stop them from taking action.

Li Ta-chao, of course, was trying to prove to Wu that I had worked for the cause of KMT-CCP cooperation. He did not want Wu to harbor any misunderstandings in the matter. He also assured Wu that while in the past I had criticized anarchism, I did not discriminate against anarchists, and that I regarded Wu Chih-hui with particular respect. Li hoped that Wu would behave calmly out of consideration for the general situation. Li told me that Wu Chih-hui had nothing more to say after that; and Li asked me not to mention the incident. He suggested that if I had time, I might heal this breach by calling upon Wu as a show of respect.

I refused to comply with Li's suggestion. I said that it would take all the self-restraint I had to keep from exposing the slanderous rumor that Wu Chih-hui had spread about me. It seemed to be a fact, I added, that Wu's attack was not aimed at me alone, but that he was exploiting the illness of Sun Yat-sen to cause trouble for the CCP. He was never discriminating about the tactics he used in attacking people he did not like. Although he brimmed over with talk about the high ideals of anarchism, he was an unprincipled worshiper of power. Already he had given in to demands by the Tuan clique in trying to persuade Sun Yat-sen to cooperate with Ch'en Chiung-ming.[9] How were we to know, I asked, that he was not again looking with reverence at those in power and seeking to induce Sun Yat-sen to break off relations with the CCP? Thus, I thought it would be useless to give him explanations or to curry his favor. The most I felt able to do was to treat his ideas with respect and to remain silent about the episode with Li Ta-chao. But I warned

Li that if Wu continued to slander me indiscriminately, I would give him a bit of leeway and then leap to the counterattack in earnest.

Li Ta-chao agreed with me; but he urged me not to attach too much importance to the ravings of Wu Chih-hui, which nobody believed anyway. Above all, he warned me not to fall into Wu's trap. He planned to play along with Wu and advised me not to make any open show of my displeasure. We agreed that this would be our technique in dealing with Wu; so Wu was never given an opportunity to attack either me or the CCP.

Wu Chih-hui finally fired off his "gas gun" at Wang Ching-wei. At one meeting of the Political Council, Wang Ching-wei tactfully explained that Sun Yat-sen was very ill, that he could not receive members of the Council, and that Madame Sun (Soong Ch'ing-ling) was especially insistent that he not have visitors because she feared they might adversely affect his health. On hearing this, Wu Chih-hui launched into one of his rambling monologues. He talked about the imperial households of successive dynasties. Wu pointed out that when an emperor lay on his deathbed, he was generally surrounded only by a small circle of imperial relatives, imperial concubines and eunuchs, and unscrupulous officials. This state of affairs often gave rise to curious developments, such as the promulgation of false orders, about which the emperor had no knowledge. Wu's discourse plainly was aimed directly at Wang Ching-wei. But he did not stop at that; he went on to make some evasive but sinister insinuations to Madame Sun and Wang Ching-wei that were unprintable. Wang Ching-wei sat there listening, speechless with outrage. The entire gathering was dumbfounded by Wu's performance; we could only pretend to have heard nothing and to demand that the meeting close.

After the meeting, the episode became the chief topic of conversation among those who had attended it. All of us felt baffled, for we all knew that Wu Chih-hui, Li Shih-tseng, and Wang Ching-wei were good friends. At the time Wu Chih-hui and Wang's wife, Ch'en Pi-chün, were both staying at the home of Li Shih-tseng. It was totally beyond belief that such insufferable things would be said at a meeting. So far as I know, this was the first evidence of ill feeling between Wu and Wang, and perhaps from that time onward they went their separate ways.

Nobody believed that Wu Chih-hui had spoken truthfully. On the contrary, a majority felt that Wang Ching-wei had been wronged, and their sympathy and respect for Wang increased. People realized that

Wang was not the only important figure in the KMT and that he had accompanied Sun Yat-sen on the northern trip merely to handle public relations. But it was felt that his patient tolerance of the ideas of others demonstrated that he was a man of greater magnanimity than was Hu Han-min. The impressions that Wang created may possibly have had great influence on his subsequent rise to authority. At the time, some people said that Wang foresaw the difficulties that lay ahead of him when he declined the chairmanship of the Political Council. Others thought that Wu Chih-hui may have had something to say to Sun Yat-sen but could neither get through to him nor get the support of Wang Ching-wei and that this led him to behave as he did. Still others contended that, after all, Wang Ching-wei had worked hard to maintain an equitable situation, and that he certainly would not try to isolate Sun Yat-sen from his comrades. And finally a small number of radicals blamed Wang Ching-wei himself, feeling that the excessively humble stand he took led to the trouble.

In spite of such curious goings on, the Political Council continued to exist and was responsible for some positive accomplishments. This was the result of pressure from the provisional government of Tuan Ch'i-jui. First of all, Tuan adopted an arrogant attitude toward Sun Yat-sen. Many people used their good offices to try to mediate between Tuan and Sun. They asked Tuan to pay a personal call on Sun at his sickbed; but Tuan steadfastly turned down such requests, thus making all KMT elements indignant. A good number of them accused Tuan of wishing for the early death of Sun Yat-sen and of hoping to hasten his demise by annoying him. In the second place, Tuan deprecated the KMT and its strength in Kwangtung. He failed to invite KMT elements to his Rehabilitation Conference, and he continually threatened to arrest KMT members in Peking or to ban their activities at least. His behavior had the effect of checking the tendency within the KMT to seek a compromise, and a majority of KMT members decided that they would have to continue to cooperate with the CCP and to maintain the alliance with Russia.

It was under these circumstances that Borodin's position gained in importance. He had preceded Sun Yat-sen to Peking, and as political adviser to the KMT, he participated in meetings of the Political Council. Cautiously keeping himself from becoming embroiled in the disputes which arose there, he seldom spoke. For the few important proposals he did introduce, he first obtained the endorsement of Sun Yat-sen and made sure that the Council would carry them before bringing them up in any detail. Consequently the Council generally adopted his proposals unanimously, and the Council members gradually came to believe that if an important issue were to stand a chance of being settled, it was best to have Adviser Borodin introduce it. In any event, several matters affecting policy were solved in the Council meetings; and these had a considerable effect upon the subsequent development of the KMT.

First, there was the issue of the Rehabilitation Conference versus the National Assembly. On January 17, 1925, Sun Yat-sen issued a statement containing a concession to Tuan,[10] in which he indicated that he would not insist upon any particular name for the conference and that he did not care whether it was called a rehabilitation conference or a national assembly. But in it he presented two demands: (1) that the Rehabilitation Conference must include representatives of industrial bodies, chambers of commerce, educational associations, universities, student federations, peasant associations, and labor unions; and (2) that in questions relating to military and financial systems, the final decisions should rest with a national assembly. He guaranteed that if these two conditions were met, he would support the Rehabilitation Conference. With the concurrence of Sun Yat-sen, Borodin presented this declaration to the Political Council, and the Council adopted it.

In the eyes of the KMT, Sun had made important concessions in the declaration. Support for Tuan's Rehabilitation Conference was offered, but no quotas were specified for representatives from the various popular organizations whose participation in it Sun demanded. Hence, the nature of the Rehabilitation Conference would not be affected by their presence. As to reserving decisions on military and financial matters until later, this simply indicated a desire to ensure that the position of the Kwangtung government would not immediately be affected. Many KMT leftists at the time, and the Communists especially, expressed anxiety over these concessions, and the KMT had to send letters and telegrams to its organizations in Kwangtung and elsewhere to explain its position. I had to explain to a meeting of CCP members in Peking that since a preliminary meeting to form a national assembly could not be held, participation in the Rehabilitation Conference would merely be conditional—similar to the participation of Communists in Western European countries in their respective parliaments. Most comrades of the KMT and CCP accepted such explanations.

But the Tuan government stubbornly and unequivocally rejected the two demands of Sun Yat-sen. On January 29 Tuan sent Sun a tele-gram.[11] In it he agreed only to invite heads of the various provincial assemblies, educational associations, general chambers of commerce, and provincial peasant associations and the heads of the chambers of com-merce of Tientsin, Shanghai, and Hankow to serve as special committee-men, who would be available to the Rehabilitation Conference for consultation. This reply from Tuan was an obvious slap in the face so far as the final concessions of Sun Yat-sen were concerned. The Political Council felt that all would be lost if further concessions were made. On January 30, therefore, the Council adopted a resolution to the effect that no KMT member would take part in the Rehabilitation Conference.

Thus, Sun Yat-sen and Tuan Ch'i-jui completely broke off relations. For the provisional government of Tuan Ch'i-jui, this meant losing its last chance to unify the country. For the KMT, it meant that only one course was left—to consolidate the Canton government and prepare for the Northern Expedition.

The Rehabilitation Conference of Tuan Ch'i-jui held its opening ceremony on February 1, 1925. On February 2 the Political Council issued an open telegram to the nation in the name of the KMT. It stated: "In deference to the wishes of the tsung-li of our Party [Sun Yat-sen], it cannot support the Rehabilitation Conference."[12] On February 10 an additional open telegram was issued, which called upon the citizens themselves to formulate an "Organic Law of the National Assembly." And so the KMT and the Peking government once more became open antagonists.

Two gatherings were held in Peking that February. One was the Rehabilitation Conference just mentioned, a gathering that had no real effect on the Peking political situation. Tuan merely used it as a tool to help make the provisional government into an official government. All political developments continued to be the result of warlord manipula-tions. The second gathering was a conference called by the KMT to promote a national assembly. Its participants were chiefly representa-tives of student councils, labor unions, and organizations of intellectuals. Its tasks were to repudiate the Rehabilitation Conference, to endorse Dr. Sun's call for a national assembly, and to provide the machinery for organizing that assembly.

The KMT and the CCP intended to turn the meeting called to promote a national assembly into a broad, effective national movement; but their objective was not realized. The CC of the CCP called the

Fourth Congress of the Party in January, 1925, at Shanghai; and there the Party decided that its major immediate task was to promote a national assembly. The KMT, oppressed by Tuan Ch'i-jui, could not do much more than promote a national assembly as its chief expression of resistance. In view of the embarrassing situation caused by the critical illness of Sun Yat-sen, however, many KMT leaders were unwilling to carry their conflict with Tuan to extremes. They wanted to avoid increasing the worries of Sun Yat-sen. As a consequence, the movement to promote a national assembly never reached sizable proportions. It merely remained a symbol of defiance.

Another question that arose was that of the relationship between the KMT and the Kuominchun. Derided by Tuan, KMT leaders felt the need for military backing; and so one of the major undertakings of our Political Council was to plan to build ties with the Kuominchun. Wang Ching-wei and others undertook numerous contacts with Feng Yü-hsiang and his representatives.[13] Meanwhile Yü Yu-jen took upon himself the responsibility of getting in touch with the Second Army of the Kuominchun, which Hu Ching-i commanded. It was the job of Wang Fa-chin to try to bring around the Third Army under Sun Yüeh. Borodin was especially enthusiastic about this venture. With the help of the Soviet embassy at Peking, he went to Kalgan, where he had a long and fairly successful talk with Feng Yü-hsiang.

At a meeting of the Political Council in February, Borodin presented a report on the Kuominchun, which stated that Feng Yü-hsiang was prepared to cooperate with the KMT, but that he was not in a favorable position to do so openly at the time. The large army of Chang Tso-lin was pressing in on him, the main forces of Wu P'ei-fu and Wu's remnant forces on the Hupeh border remained hostile to him, and Tuan Ch'i-jui was in league with Chang Tso-lin against him. Thus, he could not publicly make his stand known. Feng suggested that Yü Yu-jen replace him as commander-in-chief of the Kuominchun. It would be easier for Yü to speak out than for Feng, and Feng could meanwhile give Yü secret support. Borodin felt that this idea of Feng Yü-hsiang's was worth considering.

However, Yü Yu-jen questioned the sincerity of Feng Yü-hsiang. He did not want to become a figurehead commander-in-chief. He said that even if he did assume the post—which he would only do reluctantly —it would not help, and he himself would suffer. Most of those present sympathized with Yü; but they suggested that he might make a try at it, since the cause of the national revolution was worth one's effort even if this involved personal suffering.

I, too, talked the matter over with Yü Yu-jen. I pointed out that in view of his deep-rooted connections in the Second Army, his position might not be entirely hopeless. I suggested that he might make a trip to Kalgan and talk it over with Feng. But Yü Yu-jen was adamant in his refusal. How could anyone expect Feng Yü-hsiang to hand his army over to someone else? he asked. He said that even in the Second Army, of which he was the former chief, the situation was an intricate one that was beyond his control. And if he held the title of commander-in-chief, one person would be at him for arms, another one for a base, and he would suffer miserably. He said that if there were any chance of success, he would not refuse the job; he would bear the hardships and the blame. If that happened, however, he added that he would ask me to share some of the responsibility with him.

The matter was shelved because of Yü's opposition. No KMT leader actually undertook work in the Kuominchun, although the relationship between Kuominchun generals and the KMT grew closer. The fact that the KMT then operated in Peking, free from armed suppression from the Tuan government, was related chiefly to the attitude of the Kuominchun. For at the time the garrison forces in Peking fell within the realm of Feng Yü-hsiang. Contacts pursued at this time, however, did pave the way for the subsequent participation of Feng Yü-hsiang in the KMT.

Eventually we began to discuss arrangements that the KMT should make if Sun Yat-sen succumbed. Everyone seemed to realize by the latter part of February that Dr. Sun was destined for the worst. Each person seemed preoccupied with the future course of the KMT. The future was a matter of constant concern; and so the question of Dr. Sun's will came up for discussion.

It seemed that the members of the Political Council did not really discuss what the will should contain, but those present merely expressed some thoughts on the subject. Some of them felt that Sun Yat-sen should leave a detailed will that would spell out the organic principles of the KMT and a policy for its reorganization. Others believed that a simple will was called for, something containing no detailed directives. Some believed that if Sun Yat-sen should die, the KMT would no longer have a tsung-li; and so in both Party and governmental affairs a committee system should be adopted. Some said that the last words of Sun Yat-sen should decide his successor to the leadership of the Canton government. But the Political Council did not explore these various ideas in detail.

The Council did, however, express great anxiety over the question of a will. A majority favored its early preparation. But Wang Ching-wei explained that every mention of the will deeply pained Madame Sun and that she thought it would profoundly depress Dr. Sun. She requested that the matter be deferred. Under the circumstances, the Political Council thought about a number of ways of trying to get some final behest from Dr. Sun, but did not act upon them out of deference to the feelings of Madame Sun.

Early in March, while KMT leaders from all parts of the country were rushing to Peking to take their final leave of Sun Yat-sen, I slipped silently out of the city. I was evading the threat of immediate arrest, and it was on the advice of all my comrades that I felt compelled to leave Peking on March 8. I was at the railway workers' union in Cheng-chow on March 12 when I received the news that Sun Yat-sen had died earlier that day. With profound regret I realized that I could not attend the funeral of this revolutionary pioneer whom I respected. I immediately called a meeting of railwaymen to pay homage to Dr. Sun, and at it I described my personal feelings for this great man. At the same time I was thinking about the possible changes that might take place in the KMT now that it had lost Dr. Sun.

A few days later I returned to the CC of the CCP at Shanghai. In a letter from Li Ta-chao, I learned that Wang Ching-wei drafted the famous will of Sun Yat-sen and that Dr. Sun endorsed and signed it. Li wrote that the letter from Sun Yat-sen to the Soviet Union was drafted jointly by Borodin, Soong Ch'ing-ling, and Wang Ching-wei and was likewise signed by Dr. Sun. There was no decision on a successor to Sun Yat-sen.

Just as the leader of the KMT lay critically ill in Peking and everybody was feeling restless with uncertainty, military victories reported from Canton had a stabilizing effect. The military forces of Ch'en Chiung-ming, which held sway over the East River district of Kwangtung, were the most serious threat to the Canton government. Taking advantage of the absence of Sun Yat-sen from Canton, Ch'en Chiung-ming launched an offensive against the city. His men occupied Tungkuan and Sheklung, near Canton, early in 1925. In Canton, Acting Generalissimo Hu Han-min mobilized all the military forces of the KMT for a counterattack. Chiang Kai-shek at that time led the Party Army, which had been organized with Whampoa cadets as its backbone and had a strength of about two regiments. It was in this battle that he first showed his hand and proved the superior combat ability of his army.

On February 4, 1925, the Cantonese Army led by Hsü T'sung-chih and the Party Army directed by Chiang Kai-shek, which formed the right flank of the KMT forces, captured Tungkuan; and on February 15 they recaptured Tanshui. This had a tremendously stimulating effect on Dr. Sun, who lay in his sickbed, and on the members of our Political Council. Moreover, the military victories continued. On March 13, the day after Dr. Sun died, the Whampoa Party Army achieved a decisive victory in the battle at Mienhu. This was the famous First Eastern Expedition. It marked the initial success of Dr. Sun's policy of reorganizing the KMT, and it stabilized the foundations of the KMT in Kwangtung. It also eased the feelings of uncertainty that beset members of the KMT, who had just lost their leader. Furthermore, it was the starting point of the rise of the Whampoa Academy.

THE LABOR MOVEMENT AND ANTI-IMPERIALISM

CHAPTER

My Return to the Central Committee of the Chinese Communist Party

The movement for a national assembly began to decline with the death of Sun Yat-sen, while the national revolutionary movement grew increasingly active as the situation unfolded. It developed along two lines. One was the revival of the labor movement, which gradually took on an anti-imperialist nature, culminating in the fierce May Thirtieth Incident. The other line of development involved the founding of the National government at Canton and its mounting strength, which laid the foundations for the victory of the subsequent Northern Expedition. I took a direct part in both of these developments. Chapter nine deals with the first line of development; the second line is treated in chapter ten.

During this stage of the national revolution—a stage of rapid expansion—the CCP gradually outstripped the narrow bounds of a small organization to grow into a popular, mass political party. The overall situation was a tangle of complex events and developments. My personal experiences, however, give a general impression of the scope of what was going on.

The labor movement was revived in October, 1924, after the collapse of the rule of Ts'ao K'un and Wu P'ei-fu. This was especially true in the provinces of Chihli and Honan, where the National Army held sway and trade unions once more were permitted to exist openly. In the other areas, where the power and loyalties of the ruling forces fluctuated a good deal, every opportunity was used to promote trade-union activities.

Although I had spent some time after getting out of prison in the consultations that the northern trip of Sun Yat-sen involved, leading the railway trade unions continued to be my major task. We took advantage of the situation to press for the open existence of trade unions, and we made some progress in this respect. But at the same time, until we could strengthen our organization, we were quite serious about taking precautions against any possible attempts to crack down on the unions. Among other precautionary steps, we provided meeting places for the unions, as well as private offices.

All of this was a complicated, exacting business and I could not take time off from it to attend the Fourth Congress of the CCP, which was held at Shanghai in January, 1925. After the Congress closed, however, I received notification that I had been elected to the CC again and that I was in charge of the CC's Labor Movement Committee. In keeping with a resolution of the Congress, the CC of the CCP asked me to resign immediately from all positions that I held in the North and to go to Shanghai to assume my new duties. I wrote the CC to the effect that in view of the then critical condition of Sun Yat-sen, it would be awkward for me to abruptly leave the Political Council that the KMT had organized in Peking. At the same time, I wrote that I was busy with preparations for the Second Congress of Railway Workers, which made it difficult for me to go south at once.

On February 7, 1925, the General Union of Railway Workers convened its Second Congress in Peking. Forty-five delegates representing unions in twelve railway lines attended the Congress. Among the resolutions adopted by the Congress was one to fight for the right of trade unions to freedom of assembly, speech, and strike; another insisting upon trade-union participation in a national assembly; another calling for the restoration and consolidation of various defunct trade unions; and another to fight for the economic interests of the workers. There were ten resolutions in all. This Congress marked the resumption of activity of the railway workers' movement, which had lain dormant for two years following the tragedy of February 7, 1923.

The acclaim I received from the delegates when I addressed the Congress at the opening meeting on February 7 was clamorous. It was an expression of esteem resulting from the narrow escape that I had had in prison. When the time came for the elections, I told the meeting that I would have to go to Shanghai to assume my new post in the CC of the CCP, and would therefore have to resign as secretary general of the union. The delegates accepted the fact that there was no way for me to stay in Peking. Instead of being secretary general, I was elected to the Committee of the General Union of Railway Workers. They also did me the honor of making me honorary president of the union, a gesture that moved me deeply. The duties of secretary general were taken over by my chief assistant, Comrade Chang Kung-ti.

These activities of mine aroused the hostility of the Tuan Ch'i-jui government. In the eyes of the stooges of Tuan Ch'i-jui, I was a major figure in the KMT and it was I who incited workers to make trouble. I had led popular organizations in welcoming the northern trip of Sun Yat-sen. They believed that I had also organized the Committee for the Promotion of a National Assembly in order to defy the Rehabilitation Conference. (As a matter of fact, in order to avert warlord hostility, I did not take part in the Promotion Committee meetings; although Tuan Ch'i-jui's incompetence caused him to err in adding this to my account.) Furthermore I had only recently been released from prison, where I was suspected of being an undesirable person. As a demonstration of hostility toward revolutionary influences, they therefore set out to arrest me.

All of my friends cautioned me to take the threat of arrest seriously. Friends in the KMT, such as Wang Fa-chin, told me that the Tuan government planned to arrest a few KMT personages as a threat to Sun Yat-sen, in an attempt to hasten Sun's death. Wang said that I was one of the people chosen; and he admonished me to be careful. Comrades in the CCP—with Li Ta-chao chief among them—urged me to make an early departure for the South for the same reason. I wanted to stay on in Peking for a time, however, mainly because I did not want to leave while Dr. Sun lay critically ill. In the middle of February I handed over my duties as secretary general of the General Union of Railway Workers and went into hiding in the West City of Peking. Li Pin and his wife rented two rooms there in their own names, and I lived as their guest in one of them. Even Li Ta-chao did not know my address.

On March 7 Li Ta-chao got in touch with me through my runner. When he asked me if I lived in such-and-such a house on such-and-such a *hutung* (side street) in the West City, I admitted that I did. He explained that he had found out about it through detectives in the Tuan government. He said that since my address had been discovered, I obviously stood in imminent danger of arrest. He urged me to defer to the wishes of both KMT and CCP comrades and not to delay my departure from Peking any longer.

Early on the morning of March 8 I quietly slipped out of Peking, escorted by a few railway workers, and walked to the railway station at Lukaochiao. There I boarded a train of the Peking-Hankow Railway and went to Chengchow. Having left Peking, I felt safe, for the authority of the Tuan Ch'i-jui government was limited. The northern section of the Peking-Hankow Railway was the main communications artery of the National Army. While the train was crowded and many military men were traveling without tickets, a modicum of order still prevailed.

I stayed a few days at Chengchow, primarily to wait for my wife so that we could go on to Shanghai together. Shortly after her release from prison, my wife had gone to her home in Hupeh Province to visit her parents. We had agreed that she would stay in the village until she heard from me. When I reached Chengchow on the evening of March 8, I telegraphed her to join me there, so that we could catch a train on the Lunghai Railway and then transfer to a Shanghai train on the Tientsin-Pukow line. I could not risk going to Hupeh to pick her up because Hsiao Yao-nan of the Chihli clique still controlled that province.

I used my time at Chengchow to look over the situation in the local railway workers' union. This trade union for the mid-section of the Peking-Hankow Railway was located in the same old premises that Wu P'ei-fu had sealed two years earlier. Most responsible members of the union were my comrades-in-arms of the February Seventh period. I spent every day with them, visiting and offering my sympathy to workers or their dependents that had suffered persecution during the February Seventh Incident and looking at places connected with that tragedy. I could not help feeling outraged about the past. By that time the right to exist openly had formally been restored to the union; but most workers realized full well that the open existence of unions was precarious at best. They had not regained the heights of enthusiasm that they had attained before the February Seventh Incident.

I learned in conversations with the workers in general that they harbored a great many grievances against Hu Ching-i, the ruler of Honan Province (of which Chengchow was the capital) and against the National Army's Second Army, which Hu led. They complained that

Hu's army had absolutely no discipline, and they described some of the disorderly conduct of its soldiers on the railway. They went on to emphasize that in various counties in the countryside the lawless abandon of the soldiers was even more pronounced, and the soldiers had incurred the burning hatred of the peasants. Peasants in the Red Spear Society had grown active in a number of regions, and some incidents had occurred in which they had defended themselves against the Second Army. The workers thought the army would collapse before long. The situation made the future look anything but bright to them.

On March 13 we held a memorial service for Sun Yat-sen. In my address to the rally, I said that while the revolutionary camp had lost Dr. Sun, the revolutionary forces would remain united and would continue to develop. I said that before long the Revolutionary Army would reach the North from Kwangtung and wipe out these warlords. This message certainly roused the spirits of those present. After the meeting, Liu Wen-sung, chairman of the Chengchow Railway Workers' Union, told me enthusiastically that they hoped that after I reached the South I would lead the Revolutionary Army from Kwangtung to Honan to deliver the workers and peasants from their suffering.

My wife arrived at Chengchow that day, and early on the morning of March 14 we boarded a train on the Lunghai Railway. As soon as we stepped aboard it, everything I had heard from the workers was confirmed—the situation was chaotic. The train was jammed with military men traveling at their own discretion without paying. It was not just that they did not buy tickets for themselves. Each of them seemed to have a small group of civilians in tow. They claimed that these people were relatives, and they collected from them the fares that should have gone to the railway. Smugglers and other lawless elements had only to connive with the soldiers to have things made easy for them. Peasants, bona-fide merchants, and peddlers could scarcely board the train even though they had bought tickets. In all the stations along the line and on the train itself this resulted in a constant bedlam of disputes and quarrels. The train itself, moreover, moved by fits and starts. Our journey took twice the normal time, and it was dark by the time we finally reached Hsuchow.

At that time Hsuchow was divided up under the influence of three major groups—the National Army, the Fengtien Army, and the Chihli Army. Everything there was in a chaotic state. My wife and I had to stay overnight in order to board a southbound train the next morning, but the military occupied all of the hotel rooms. Travelers had to spend the night crammed together in the railway station. Some of them had been waiting at the station for two or three days without having been able to get on a train. With very great difficulty we found a place for ourselves in the overcrowded railway station and managed to get a little rest.

Before dawn the next morning, carrying our heavy luggage, we joined the other travelers swarming onto the train in a wild dash to grab seats. Had we been just a bit slower, we might not even have found standing room. As it was, we sat grimly in the seats we found, afraid to leave them even for a moment. The train started about nine o'clock that morning, and once we were in motion, order on the train improved a bit. All the way to Pukow and Shanghai, in fact, we were fortunate in not encountering any great difficulties, and finally we reached Shanghai.

Every single episode in this personal experience has remained vividly in my memory. I became convinced that the warlords were doing their best to sow the seeds of revolution.

I arrived at Shanghai on March 16, 1925, and immediately moved into a residence assigned to me by the CC of the CCP. This building, with two rooms on the first floor and two rooms on the floor above, became the office of the Labor Movement Committee of the CC of the CCP. Liu Shao-ch'i and his recent bride had already moved into the front portion of the second floor, and my wife and I took over the main room on that floor. The first floor served as our offices. Teng Chung-hsia and others took up temporary quarters there from time to time. This was merely one of the branch offices of the CC of the CCP at the time, but compared to what we had had before, it appeared quite imposing. It was immediately obvious to me that the CC, from which I had parted company for a while, had undergone considerable change; an infant had grown up rather rapidly.

Ch'en Tu-hsiu came to see us the day we arrived. He expressed his concern over our prison experiences in Peking and was especially solicitous of my wife, whom he was meeting for the first time. He also bestowed his blessing on the two newly married couples—the Liu Shao-ch'i's and the Chang Kuo-t'ao's. Earnest and openhearted, Ch'en abundantly showed the warm friendship that existed between us.

After the exchange of personal talk, he praised as highly appropriate my correction of the leftist mistake of Chao Shih-yen and the others who opposed the northern trip of Sun Yat-sen. The attitude toward the KMT that Li Ta-chao and I had assumed in Peking also received his praise. He felt that we had succeeded in unobtrusively implementing the policies of the CCP. He expressed anxiety about the possible repercussions of the death of Sun Yat-sen. The military victories in the East River district of Kwangtung, however, delighted him. It was his position that since the KMT had lost its leader, it should expand democratic processes within the Party and should function under a system of committee leadership. His confidence in the future of the CCP had increased. He stressed the need for independent development of the CCP, and he believed that the general situation was gradually developing in a way that would make this possible.

Ch'en Tu-hsiu based his optimistic view of the future of the CCP on the background of progress in Party activities. At the time of the Fourth Congress, Party membership approached the one thousand mark.[1] Central and local Party organizations had been established on a reasonable scale, and Party members had greatly increased their activities. Accordingly, the resolution of the Fourth Congress had raised the question of the CCP seeking to seize leadership power in the national revolution.

I promptly threw myself into the work of the CC of the CCP, quickly accepting the optimistic factors that Ch'en Tu-hsiu pointed out. After the Fourth Congress the CC of the CCP had not yet created a Political Bureau, although the rudiments of one had already been formed. Our weekly meetings were of two kinds. One kind of meeting generally took place at the home of Voitinsky. Regular attenders at these affairs included only Ch'en Tu-hsiu, Ts'ai Ho-sen, Chü Ch'iu-pai, and me—four of the members of the CC.[2] Voitinsky attended, too, as the representative of the Comintern. At these meetings we chiefly discussed policy matters. The other kind of meeting was not attended by Voitinsky. At such meetings, in addition to the four people mentioned above, were P'eng Shu-chih, the newly elected CC member in charge of propaganda; Jen Pi-shih, secretary of the CC of the SYC; Wang I-fei, secretary of the Shanghai District Committee; Liu Shao-ch'i and Li Li-san, members of the Labor Movement Committee; and Hsiang Ching-yu, chairman of the Women's Movement Committee. We generally discussed routine business matters in these meetings. Thus, the first-mentioned gatherings were somewhat similar in nature to the meetings of a Politburo, while the latter meetings carried out the practical work of the CC.

The meetings of the CC were now held in far more orderly fashion than they had formerly been. Each meeting had an agenda and produced clear resolutions. I shall mention briefly certain developments in the meetings of the group that was similar to a Politburo that had enormous bearing on the future of the CCP.

At the time, the CC of the CCP attached great importance to the strategy of the united front. We realized that the combined forces of the CCP and the working class were not adequate, so that it was essential to use a strategy of uniting with larger forces in order to achieve the national revolution. We made the vital task of achieving the national revolution the joint effort of all social strata. This approach removed the anxiety, prevalent at the time of the Third Congress, that the CCP might be turned into a part of the KMT; and so it had the unanimous support of the entire Party.

Consequently the major discussions at meetings held in Voitinsky's home fell generally into the following three categories: (1) How the working class could lead the broad masses of peasants and the petty bourgeoisie and unite with the national bourgeoisie to oppose the comprador class, the warlords, feudal influences, and imperialism; (2) how the CCP could unite with the Left Wing of the KMT to win over the Center and oppose the Right Wing; and (3) the development of the CCP itself, unification of the labor movement, and the development of peasant associations.

The three major categories mentioned above involved numerous broad issues, of which the question of KMT-CCP relations seemed to be central. We felt that the Left Wing of the KMT represented the class of the petty bourgeoisie and supported a triple policy of alliance with the Soviet Union, toleration of the CCP, and regard for the Communists as its closest comrades-in-arms. We looked upon the Right Wing as just the opposite—it represented the comprador and other conservative interests, and stood opposed to the triple policy. The Center, we believed, represented the general trends of the petty bourgeoisie and the national bourgeoisie, vacillating between Left and Right, not supporting the triple policy wholeheartedly, and yet opposing the rule of the warlords and imperialists. We also believed that the Center was numerically the strongest. We felt that establishing contact with the Center and winning it over to our side was an important step in achieving a broad united front.

But the CC of the CCP and Borodin held divergent views on these matters. After the death of Sun Yat-sen, Borodin returned to Canton and devoted himself exclusively to building up the Whampoa Academy, in an attempt to use this force to establish a so-called revolutionary dictatorship. He, therefore, presently expressed dissatisfaction with the united-front strategy of the CC of the CCP, which was aimed at establishing ties with the KMT Center.

Voitinsky, on the other hand, cooperated very well with the CC of the CCP. No disputes over policy ever emerged between us. As a matter of fact, Voitinsky exerted a very great influence over CC policy decisions; but he was extremely careful always to act in accordance with Comintern resolutions and directives and never to express opinions that represented merely his own personal whims. Still, he held limited authority, for he had no influence over Karakhan in Peking or Borodin in Canton, since these two men fell under the direct authority of the Soviet government, in which Voitinsky had no position. Thus, he had to make frequent trips between Moscow and Peking to carry on consultations.

It was the responsibility of Voitinsky to maintain liaison between the CC of the CCP and Moscow. We could not contact the Comintern without going through him. Around the time of the May Thirtieth Incident, he spent most of his time in Shanghai, where he seemed to have done a good job of organizing his work. He had several assistants, who helped him in handling the daily routine, while he devoted himself particularly to the study of policy questions. His wife, a quiet, kindly woman, frequently fell ill; but she worked hard to help her husband. Often she traveled between Moscow and China as a courier of secret documents.

At the time, Voitinsky lived on the third floor of a small house beside the Kunshan Gardens. A wealthy White Russian merchant was his landlord, and we were careful not to bother the man on our visits to Voitinsky. During one of our meetings in Voitinsky's rooms, a number of Settlement police officers suddenly appeared on the first floor. At first we felt apprehensive, but Voitinsky remained calm. He assured us that the police officers were friends of the landlord and frequently visited him. He said that we could meet there in complete safety unless detectives followed us to the house. It was apparent that it was possible then for Voitinsky to receive cover from White Russians in Shanghai, perhaps because of the growing stability of the Soviet government.

Ch'en Tu-hsiu presided over our meetings. He prepared an important policy question for discussion at each of them, and the meetings seemed to proceed with great efficiency. Those present were also able to introduce proposals during the meetings and request that they be discussed. An atmosphere of democracy was reasonably in evidence. Although Voitinsky spoke more than anyone else, he never tried to influence our decisions by applying pressure in the name of the Comintern, and he always abided by the views of the majority. There was a vast difference between him and the aggressive Maring.

The CC, and especially Ch'en Tu-hsiu, was very eager at this time to increase the leadership powers of the CC. It did not, moreover, take kindly to too much interference by Soviet people in the internal affairs of the CCP. Within the ranks of the CCP, the Peking and Kwangtung District committees were forever tending to behave as though they were sovereign, independent bodies. Sometimes, while ignoring CC directives, they would reach decisions not altogether in keeping with those directives as a matter of local expediency, or through their contacts with Karakhan in Peking or Borodin in Canton, they would obtain Comintern views direct. The Kwangtung District Committee in particular, in reports to the CC following the May Thirtieth Incident, frequently gave as the reason for failing to respect CC directives its use of Borodin's ideas. This stirred up the animosity of Ch'en Tu-hsiu. He often complained at meetings that the Kwangtung Committee did not seem to treat the CC with due respect since the views of Borodin had become available to it. In this matter Voitinsky took the same stand that the CC took. He said that any actions that undermined the central leadership of the CC were indefensible.

The CC of the CCP grew organizationally larger after the Fourth Congress, and its meetings became more frequent. All affairs had to be handled in keeping with the complicated procedures of the organizational system. The authority of Ch'en Tu-hsiu, as secretary of the CC, was expanded. The CC even designated some members of various local organizations, who were, on the whole, responsible people. Following these developments, there emerged within the ranks of the CCP a tendency to divide into the so-called practical workers' clique and the clique of returned scholars from Russia and France.

As secretary of the CC, Ch'en Tu-hsiu was in charge of the Central Secretariat. He also acted as director of the Department of Organization. The Central Secretariat, which was in charge of administrative affairs, had an administrative officer, who looked after everything under the direction of the secretary. A comrade named Jen first held the post of administrative officer, but he was replaced very soon by Wang Jo-fei, who had just returned from France. The Central Secretariat was divided into sections dealing with documents, financial matters, publication matters, and communications. It prepared all decisions of the CC as official documents and distributed them to the various local organizations for compliance. Financial matters were handled in complete secrecy. They were never discussed at CC meetings. Since member contributions made up only a small percentage of the total income, the major financial support for the CCP at that time came from the Comintern; and Ch'en Tu-hsiu personally consulted with Voitinsky about financial needs.

The Department of Organization, headed by Ch'en Tu-hsiu, also expanded greatly. Membership in the CCP had been small up to that time, and the work of the Organization Department had been simple. After the Fourth Congress, however, membership exceeded one thousand and was continuing to grow, thus increasing the work of the Organization Department. At that time, the Department maintained three sections. They dealt with investigation and registration of members, the distribution of work assignments, and the training of members. After proper motions had been passed at meetings, Ch'en Tu-hsiu, in his capacity of director of the Organization Department, made all transfers of personnel.

Similarly, the propaganda work of the CC of the CCP increased. P'eng Shu-chih, director of that department, had a three-room building for his office. He was responsible for directing general propaganda work within the Party, including popular propaganda, political propaganda, and cultural and educational activities for Party members. However, the editing of Party publications such as *Hsiang-tao Chou-pao* (Guide Weekly)—the main significance of which, the CC felt, was to provide political guidance—was entrusted to Ts'ai Ho-sen and Chü Ch'iu-pai, with editorial policy being decided by the CC. Such work was not subject to interference from the Department of Propaganda.

The Labor Movement Committee, which I led, was also staffed by notable persons. Its members included Li Li-san; Liu Shao-ch'i, who played a leading role in the Anyuan Coal Miners' Union, which had been enlarged into the Han-yeh-p'ing General Trade Union;[3] Teng Chung-hsia, who had been in charge of the labor movement in the North, but who had of necessity come to Shanghai when he no longer could stay in the North; Hsiang Ying and Lin Yü-nan, both of whom had led secret trade unions in Wuhan; Li Ch'i-han, who had been released from prison six months earlier; and Wang Ho-po, leader of the Pukow Railway Workers' Union. As chairman, I was in charge of policy decisions. Routine work of the committee was carried out with the help of Liu Shao-ch'i. Li Li-san was engaged particularly in leading the trade unions in Shanghai. Teng Chung-hsia was then teaching at Shanghai University, where he was responsible for recruiting young intellectuals for work in the trade-union movement. Other members directed the labor movement in other areas.

The Secretariat of Labor Organizations in China went out of existence following the defeat of the February Seventh Strike. The job of convoking a Second National Labor Congress thus fell on the shoulders of our Labor Movement Committee. The plan was to organize a National General Labor Union and through it to exercise unified leadership of the trade-union movement throughout the country.

The CC also planned to form a Military Department and a Peasant Movement Committee. However, plans for these additions were shelved for a time because of the lack of suitable personnel to staff them. Following the May Thirtieth Incident, we established a Military Department for the first time, with myself concurrently director of it and of the Labor Movement Committee. But the Peasant Movement Committee was not organized until the spring of 1925, and its story must come later.

Other organs of the CC, such as the Women's Movement Committee, expanded, too. Membership in the SYC, which was renamed the Communist Youth Corps at its Third Congress in February, 1925, increased to nine thousand. Thirty percent of its members were young workers, while most of the rest were progressive intellectuals, especially young students.[4] Its CC and its work naturally increased also.

All of these CCP organizations existed underground in Shanghai, and of course we had to pay attention to security measures. The CC of the CCP began to organize a "liaison" system. Contact between different organizations and their responsible members in Shanghai, contact with people coming to Shanghai on business and their reception, the handling of money, and so forth, were all taken care of by members of the liaison organization. The number of these liaison men gradually increased, first to more than ten, and eventually to more than twenty.

The CCP, while larger than before, nevertheless remained but a small sparrow dwarfed by the broad masses of the country. But the body of this small sparrow was replete with a full complement of organs, and its revolutionary spirit was mightily stirred. While Sun Yat-sen still lived, the CCP leaders always looked upon him as their senior and deferred to him. Now that Dr. Sun was dead, however, things were different. KMT rightists had become active, and Ma Chun-wu, Feng Tzu-yu, and others were organizing the KMT Comrades Club.[5] The CC of the CCP now felt that it must take the initiative in establishing a united front to carry out the revolution.

A growth in the strength of the CCP itself, however, was the first prerequisite for realizing this ambition. So the CC and local CCP organizations tirelessly studied the problems of recruiting members, of strengthening the Party's leadership power, of unifying the leadership of trade unions, and of expanding the CYC. The Kwangtung District Committee of the CCP at that time already had a Military Department and a Peasant Movement Committee. Whether or not similar organs should be created within the CC was one theme of our discussions; others were the development of activities among troops in the North and plans for transforming the Red Spear societies in Honan Province into peasant associations. Generally speaking, the goal toward which the CCP struggled at this time was to strengthen itself in order to increase its proportionate influence in the national revolution. This aim was supreme, and it propelled the CCP forward.

But in the course of its development, the CCP encountered internal difficulties. The political disagreements within the CCP had greatly diminished by that time; but serious arguments arose over the question of organization. P'eng Shu-chih and his group advocated the centralization of authority and demanded that the authority of the CC, which had already been enormously strengthened, be strengthened still further. Lacking the experience of practical work, they repeatedly quoted Marxist-Leninist doctrine to support their views and to criticize members working in the field for neglecting organizational principles, for preserving the work methods of handicraft organizations, for failing to abide rigidly by Marxist-Leninist principles, and for acting merely according to their own limited experiences.

The view of P'eng Shu-chih and his group had strong backing

within the Party. Ch'en Tu-hsiu supported P'eng's position, and so, to a greater or lesser extent, did most of the comrades that had returned from Russia and France. These comrades included Wang Jo-fei, a returnee from France, who was in the Central Secretariat of the CC; Yin Kuan, a returnee from France, who was an executive secretary in the Department of Organization; Jen Pi-shih, a returnee from Russia, who was secretary of the CYC; Wang I-fei, a returnee from Russia, who was secretary of the Shanghai District Committee; and Lo Chüeh, a returnee from Russia, who was director of the Organization Department of the Shanghai District Committee.

Most of those who disagreed with the position of P'eng Shu-chih were practical workers in the Party, and they did not favor excessive centralization of power in the CC. It was their position that within the framework of decisions made by the CC, Party members should have considerable freedom of action. They insisted that Marxist-Leninist principles be applied on the basis of the conditions that actually existed in the various areas. They took P'eng Shuh-chih and his group to task for being armchair strategists, who could do nothing more than recite Marxist-Leninist dogma and who habitually brandished the words "directive of the CC" as a threat to people.

Within the CC, Ts'ai Ho-sen, Ch'ü Ch'iu-pai, and I all supported the latter views. I, especially, frequently argued that excessive centralism would throttle the vitality of most comrades, and so I was looked upon as leader of the practical workers' group. Supporting our view to varying degrees were Li Li-san, Liu Shao-ch'i, and Teng Chung-hsia— all of whom were connected with the labor movement—Fan T'ai-ying, a member of the CC of the CYC, and large numbers of comrades in the local organizations.

Of these people, Li Li-san was the one who opposed the P'eng Shu-chih view most energetically. Completely a man of action, he looked only for results, and he was unaccustomed to restrictions from the organization. His work in leading the trade-union movement in Shanghai generally called for him to deal with problems that required immediate solutions. He could not bear to have these problems go through meetings of the Shanghai District Committee, the Labor Movement Committee of the CC, and then the CC itself and to have them discussed at each level before a solution was decided upon. He always insisted that he "had to have an immediate solution"; and he asked for a joint meeting of the three organs or for the designation of an action committee to deal with his urgent problems. Moreover, he bridled at listening to instructions from the Marxist-Leninists, whom he felt would disrupt things with their conference-table discussions. In the course of leading the Shanghai labor movement, he commonly resorted to rather forceful methods instead of depending upon persuasion. He felt that action based on the prevailing conditions was the most important thing. He insisted that all the talk about "centralization of power" and "half-baked doctrines and dogmas" was pure rubbish.

The CCP, then still in its infancy, was doing everything in order to achieve quick results, and so these differences of opinion did not at the time lead to serious disputes. They merely formed the rudiments of trouble. Yet all subsequent disputes within the CCP were related to these divergent views. Historically, within the CCP, Wang Ming, Ch'in Pang-hsien, and others of the Mif clique, to a greater or lesser extent, were heirs to the ideas of P'eng Shu-chih. The "Sinofication" of Marxism-Leninism by Mao Tse-tung descended directly from the stand of the practical workers of an earlier stage.

Revival of the Labor Movement

With the restoration of trade-union organizations, there was an increase in the number of strikes during the spring of 1925. One of the biggest strikes prior to the May Thirtieth Incident occurred in February among workers in the Japanese cotton mills at Shanghai.

Japan, as a leading world power, took advantage of the special privileges of the unequal treaties to establish more factories of various kinds on Chinese territory than any other power. There were forty-one Japanese cotton mills in China then, with twenty-seven of them in Shanghai alone. Competition in the cotton industry was fierce. The Japanese mills had more capital than the privately owned Chinese mills and were protected by the unequal treaties. They not only resorted to lowering wages to maintain, or increase, their profits, but they proceeded to buy up or outmaneuver the privately owned Chinese mills. Their behavior led to agitation among textile workers in resistance to their tactics, and it aroused the indignation of Chinese industrialists and merchants.

The most powerful of the Japanese mills was Naigai Cotton Mills, Ltd., with sixteen mills in China, eleven of them in Shanghai. For

Chinese workers, employment in the company was like working in hell. They worked day and night shifts of twelve hours each. Large numbers of women and children worked there, averaging a daily wage of a little more than ten Chinese cents—less than four U.S. cents. Their living and lodging conditions were indescribably bad. Severe discipline over the workers was rigidly maintained, and they were frequently penalized by deductions from their wages. It was commonplace to see workers being beaten. Furthermore, these mills created a special technique for enhancing their profits. Taking advantage of the unemployment and poverty so prevalent among the Chinese people, they recruited large numbers of child laborers, both male and female, who were placed in training classes that resembled concentration camps. The children were called "workers in training." These workers in training, who were trapped in their situations for a prolonged period, were exploited as substitutes for adult workers, who were more prone to resist authority and to want higher wages. As time went by, more and more adult workers were dismissed.

On February 1, 1925, word went around Naigai's Number Eight Mill that another large batch of adults had been fired. This stirred the workers into a state of intense agitation, and it was reported that some were arrested and beaten. On February 9 workers began to go out on strike. Their primary slogan was "Oppose the Beating of People by the Japanese." This strike spread to twenty-two Japanese cotton mills in Shanghai and involved more than forty thousand workers.

On this occasion the strike involved a movement against Japan, and it had the support of such popular organizations as the Federation of Students. The Shanghai General Chamber of Commerce acted as mediator on February 25, and the Japanese mills agreed to four conditions, one of which was that "people should not be beaten without reason."[6] The strike ended. While a total victory was not won, the influence of the Trade Union of Workers in Japanese Cotton Mills rapidly grew. The number of workers in Japanese mills that joined the Union increased to 9,000; and additional labor-management disputes subsequently arose in the Japanese cotton mills. The workers stepped up anti-Japanese activities, which reached a high point on May 15, when a worker named Ku Cheng-hung was killed by a Japanese staff member of the Number Seven Mill in the Naigai group. It was this incident that led to the May Thirtieth Movement.

Many comrades told me about the heroic events of the strike after

I reached Shanghai on March 16. Up to then I had always thought that most of the cotton-mill workers were women and children that did not have much of a capacity for unity and that it would be extremely difficult to organize trade unions among them or to get them out on strike. The remarkable achievements of February proved that new life had indeed come into the labor movement.

I visited cotton mills in West Shanghai to look them over, and found that our comrades there were making good use of the experience they had acquired earlier, especially those who had been active in the Changhsintien labor movement, which I had started. The Shanghai District Committee of the CCP had opened some workers' clubs and night schools in areas heavily populated by cotton-mill workers and through these had promoted a sense of unity among a large number of the workers. Most of the schools and clubs were led by young intellectuals, the most capable of whom was a Shanghai University student named Liu Hua.

By the time of the February strike, the organization of the cotton-mill workers' union had yet to be consolidated, however. The strikers, under the slogan "Oppose Japan," had adopted the technique of preventing large numbers of women and child workers from going to their jobs. This was the masterful idea of Li Li-san, drawn from his experience in strikes developed by the Anyuan Coal Miners' Union. But the workers did not yet recognize the evil consequences that could flow from such use of force.

I talked with some of the workers. Most of them indicated that it was absolutely right to oppose the Japanese for beating people, that every Chinese would endorse such action. Even the women and child workers with relatively low levels of intelligence, on hearing about "anti-Japanese" action, were roused to take a righteous position. I considered that this indicated a new direction to be taken in the labor movement in Shanghai. The economic struggle of the workers, with the added factor of nationalism, endowed the movement with incomparable vitality for development.

After a delay of two years, the Second National Labor Congress finally convened at Canton on May Day, 1925. The achievements of this Congress laid the organizational groundwork for the May Thirtieth Movement, which immediately followed it.

Nominally the Congress was sponsored by the General Union of

Railway Workers in the North, the Han-yeh-p'ing General Labor Union in Central China, the Workers' Congress of Canton,[7] and the Seamen's Union of Hong Kong; but the Labor Movement Committee of the CC of the CCP actually made the preparations for the Congress. We immersed ourselves in the business of getting in touch with different trade unions about sending delegates to the Congress. And in the names of the General Union of Railway Workers and the Han-yeh-p'ing General Trade Union, we telegraphed an invitation to the Red Workers' International to send a delegation. We also prepared the agenda for the Congress. Toward the end of April my comrades and I left for Canton to take charge of the gathering.

On May Day in Canton a Labor Day Memorial Rally was held, in which more than fifty thousand people took part. The rally was followed by a parade. Participating in this undertaking, in addition to workers in all trades, were peasants from the outlying areas of Canton and students from the schools of the city. The group in the parade that attracted the greatest attention was the delegation from the Whampoa Military Academy. These cadet officers, carrying the banner of the "Federation of Young Military Men," wore crimson ties, held themselves erect, and clearly showed themselves to be something quite different from the old type of military man. They joined the other paraders in shouting in unison such slogans as "The Great Union of Workers, Peasants, and Soldiers," "Down with the Warlords," and "Down with Imperialism." Scarcely ever before had there been such a sweeping revolutionary atmosphere.

The First Kwangtung Provincial Congress of Peasants opened on the same day. Delegates to the labor and peasant congresses decided to hold a joint opening ceremony on the afternoon of May 1 in the auditorium of Canton University. Including guests, more than one thousand people attended the ceremony. Liao Chung-k'ai represented the KMT, and I represented the CCP. We both made congratulatory addresses. Ostronovsky, a representative of the Red Workers' International, was invited to speak, and he did so. Among the other speakers was a representative of the Whampoa Military Academy. All of these events gave convincing evidence of the prevailing atmosphere, which was summed up in the slogans "Close Cooperation Between the Kuomintang and the Communist Party," "Unite, Workers and Oppressed Nations of the World," and "The Great Union of Workers, Peasants, and Soldiers."

Participating in the Labor Congress were 281 delegates representing

166 unions, with a total membership of about 540,000. This represented a great increase in strength over the First National Labor Congress in 1922.[8] KMT members, CCP members, and delegates belonging to neither party each constituted about one-third of the total number of delegates. CCP strength in the Congress showed a marked increase over the previous Congress, and most of the delegates that had no party affiliation were leftists who sympathized with the CCP. Therefore the CCP controlled the Congress.

In the course of the seven days during which the Congress was in session, the seven most important resolutions that it adopted dealt with

1. the working class and political struggle
2. the economic struggle
3. the question of organization
4. the alliance between workers and peasants
5. the elimination of traitors in the labor movement
6. the Constitution of the National General Labor Union of China
7. participation in the Red Workers' International.

These resolutions were adopted without serious argument, and they had the approval of an absolute majority of delegates.

The Congress proceeded with considerable smoothness as a consequence of the role that the CCP and the CYC played. I attended solely as the representative of the CC of the CCP, not as a delegate from any trade union, and so did not have to attend meetings regularly. I devoted myself to working within the group of Communist delegates, promoting its guiding influence on the Congress from behind the scenes. Members of the CCP-CYC committee included Su Chao-cheng, a delegate from the Hong Kong Seamen's Union; Wang Ho-po and Sun Yung-p'eng, delegates from the Railway Workers' Union; Teng Chung-hsia and Li Ch'i-han, delegates from the Shanghai Cotton Mill Trade Union; and Feng Chü-p'o and Liu Yu-sung, delegates from the Canton Labor Congress. This group unquestionably constituted the policy-making element in the Congress. We prepared all the resolutions and all the lists of candidates for election.

In this way the National General Labor Union of China was born. The Congress elected twenty-five persons to the Executive Committee of this General Labor Union. Lin Wei-min, president of the Hong Kong Seamen's Union, was elected chairman of the Executive Committee. Liu Shao-ch'i, president of the Han-yeh-p'ing General Trade Union, and Liu Wen-sung, president of the Peking-Hankow General Railway Union, were elected vice-chairmen. Teng Chung-hsia was elected secretary general of the Executive Committee as well as director of its Propaganda Department. Li Shen (Li Ch'i-han) was elected director of the Organization Department of the Executive Committee, and Sun Yung-p'eng was elected director of the committee's Economic Department. It was decided that the union would locate its headquarters at Canton and that it would immediately begin functioning.

The first meeting of the Executive Committee of the National General Labor Union of China was promptly held at Canton. Those attending the meeting felt that directing trade-union work in other areas from a headquarters at Canton would be difficult. It was decided, therefore, to open an underground office in Shanghai, and I was elected chief of the Shanghai office. This decision greatly facilitated the work of the Labor Movement Committee of the CC of the CCP. During the May Thirtieth Incident, I made use of the position to rapidly organize the Shanghai General Labor Union and to push forward the May Thirtieth Movement.

In keeping with a decision of the Congress, the National General Labor Union of China formally joined the Red Workers' International, and the Chinese labor movement established an organizational relationship with Moscow. The fact that Ostronovsky took part in the Congress facilitated the resolution on joining the Red Workers' International and settled certain practical issues involving the two organizations. At that time none of the trade unions in China had established any contact with the Workers' International at Amsterdam, and they were free from the influence of the Social-Democratic parties of Western Europe. No obstructions were encountered in having the newly organized General Labor Union participate in the Red Workers' International.

The KMT and the CCP cooperated quite harmoniously in leading the Labor Congress. Liao Chung-k'ai, director of the Workers' Department of the CC of the KMT, was preoccupied at the time with looking after finances in Kwangtung; and in a genuine spirit of cooperation with the CCP, he entrusted the job of trade-union leadership to Feng Chü-p'o, a member of his Workers' Committee who was also a member of the CCP. I always consulted Liao Chung-k'ai directly about important matters; and he never expressed disagreement with my views. His wife, Ho Hsiang-ning, also told me quite definitely that Liao was busy with political matters in Kwangtung, that in the labor-movement field he wanted to serve merely as a symbol, since he had no time to go into the practical issues involved, and that he would not oppose whatever the rest decided.

The greatest achievement of the CCP at the Congress was to increase its influence over the workers of Hong Kong. The Hong Kong Seamen's Union was the bulwark of the unions in Hong Kong, and the prestige of Su Chao-cheng was greater than that of any other Seamen's Union leader. Having worked on vessels of one kind or another for twenty years and having made Hong Kong his permanent residence, he had only rarely visited Canton and knew little about conditions in China. But in February, 1925, as a representative of the trade unions in Hong Kong, he traveled to Peking to take part in the meetings of the Committee for the Promotion of a National Assembly. There he had an opportunity to really understand what was going on in the country, and he was won over by the CCP. A veteran KMT member, he finally changed over and joined the CCP.

At the time of the Congress, Su Chao-cheng told me about the events surrounding his decision to participate in the CCP. During his trip north, he said, he had a chance to visit the trade unions in Nanking and Shanghai. The activities of these unions, which he felt were highly laudable, completely convinced him that the CCP truly worked in the interest of the workers and that the Party was in fact as well as in name the political party of the working class. He said that he had been a member of the KMT for many years, but that the KMT cared nothing for him, and he could not exercise any influence within it. He felt that he was isolated, that his only function was to look after uninspiring documents at the Seamen's Union. He found the CCP to be something different. All members of the party and all of its activities were organized; and the activities of individual members were supported by the organization. So while he was still in Peking, he indicated a desire to join the CCP. But it was in Shanghai, where in behalf of the Seamen's Union he supported the plan of the CC of the CCP to call the Second National Labor Congress, that with a good deal of pleasure he formally became a CCP member.

Su told me, furthermore, that the responsible members of the various trade unions in Hong Kong had been unfamiliar with union activities in their own country. Many of them had thought that the inland unions were mere pasteboard affairs, most of which were opportunistically manipulated by the CCP. When he got back to Hong Kong, however, he had told his colleagues there about what he personally had seen, and this had broadened their understanding of the Chinese labor movement and inclined them more favorably toward the Communist Party.

One success of the Congress was in dispelling the antagonism of the Hong Kong Trade-Union Council toward the CCP. For while this Hong Kong Council sent delegates, it expressed disgruntlement with CCP leadership in the Congress. One of the leading Council delegates pointed out to me that the Hong Kong Trade-Union Council was an organization made up of more than one hundred trade unions, of which the Seamen's Union was only one. So why, he asked me, was the Seamen's Union named one of the organizations that convened the Congress while the Trade-Union Council was ignored? He wanted to know if this was a case of belittling the Council or if it was an attempt to monopolize the Congress. He was not satisfied with any of the various explanations that I gave him.

Nevertheless, I persisted in adopting a friendly attitude toward the Council when we discussed this dissension in the Communist group at the Congress. I insisted that we must not cause a split in the labor movement by referring to the Hong Kong Council as a "yellow union." My comrades accepted my view and by electing one of the major Council delegates to the presidium of the Congress, showed that we were not discriminating against it. Meanwhile, Su Chao-cheng and others stepped in to explain matters, and so the Council took an active part in the work of the Congress. Not only did this episode heal the original breach, but it also served to remove possible obstructions to the participation of all workers in the subsequent "Great Canton and Hong Kong Strike."

There were unions, however, that adopted an attitude of opposition to the Congress from start to finish—the Kwangtung Machine Workers' Union, for example. It took part in the First National Labor Congress but adopted the passive approach of nonparticipation in the second one. And then in August, 1924, when the CCP and the KMT leftists organized the Workers' Congress of Canton, the Kwangtung Machine Workers' Union, which was a bastion of the Right Wing of the KMT, immediately refused to participate. Relying on its deep-rooted position in Kwangtung, it went on to struggle both openly and secretly against the newly formed Workers' Congress of Canton, without showing any signs of relenting. Then it refused the invitation to the Second National Labor Congress. We knew that we could not change its mind, and so we let it go.

Another organization that adopted an attitude of opposition to the Congress was the Shanghai Federation of Trade Unions, which was organized by KMT rightists in August, 1924. Participating in it were thirty-two unions that claimed to have a total of more than three hundred thousand members,[9] although this figure was rather exaggerated as a matter of fact. It always maintained an attitude of opposition to the CCP and refused to try to remove the misunderstandings that stood between its unions and those led by the CCP. In February, 1925, during the strike in the Japanese cotton mills, this Federation organized an "Anti-Communist Alliance of Male and Female Workers." It distributed pamphlets among the workers expressing its readiness to support the strike but advising the workers not to let themselves be used by the Chinese Communists. The incident outraged the CCP, which felt that the pamphlet was aimed at undermining the anti-Japanese strike. Moreover, the Federation failed to fulfill its promise to support the strike.

Because the Federation of Trade Unions did not look after the interests of the workers but devoted itself solely to opposing the CCP, it gradually lost the confidence of the workers. The CCP, meanwhile, castigated it for being a "pasteboard union" and the "union of traitors to the labor movement." It was not invited to take part in the Congress. Because of this it issued a declaration opposing the convocation of the Second National Labor Congress. The declaration had no effect at all. During the May Thirtieth Movement, this organization faded gradually into oblivion.

Generally speaking, the revolutionary forces, even though they met obstruction from the rightists, marched forward rapidly. Canton, the center of the revolution, was still occupied by Yunnan and Kwangsi armies, which protected dens for gambling and opium and generally made a mess of things. But the Whampoa Party Army was growing rapidly and was already shedding a new light on Canton. Most people felt that the future was unlimited. At the same time, convocation of the First Kwangtung Provincial Congress of Peasants and the formation of the Peasant Association with a membership of more than two hundred thousand[10] caused people to realize that the influence of the revolution had spread to the remote countryside.

Optimism permeated the atmosphere of the Second National Labor Congress. Workers' delegates from Canton stuck their thumbs up and vividly described the heroic episodes that occurred as they had helped to suppress the revolt of the Merchants' Volunteers and had joined in the First Expedition to the East River District, fighting shoulder to shoulder with the Party Army and the masses of peasants. These accounts caused the workers' delegates from the North, who were unfamiliar with conditions in Kwangtung, to feel that the "great alliance of workers, peasants, and soldiers" had already been realized in the common struggle for the national revolution. Similarly, Northern delegates recounted their struggles over the previous few years against the warlords and imperialists, telling of unnumerable experiences that gave them cause for pride. These accounts in turn stimulated the Southern workers, who now felt that they had comrades in arms all over the country.

We who were leaders of the CCP felt that the Labor Congress had achieved the hoped-for results. It brought together a majority of the organized workers that could be brought together, and it established the National General Labor Union of China, thereby attaining unified leadership of labor unions. From that point onward the CCP could call itself in fact as well as in name the political party of the working class.

On May 8, to thunderous applause, the Congress closed; and delegates from the different areas began their return trips north. Most of them were in high spirits, prepared to inform the masses of workers in all areas of the achievements of the Congress.

My orders from the CC of the CCP were to guide the work of the Kwangtung District Committee, and so I remained in Canton for some time. It was on the eve of the campaign to suppress the warlords Yang and Liu and their Yunnan and Kwangsi armies. Talk of reorganizing the National government was brewing. I had policy matters to discuss with Borodin and the members of the CCP Kwangtung District Committee. Had it not been that the worker Ku Cheng-hung was killed at Shanghai, quite possibly I would have stayed in Canton until after the National government was officially inaugurated.

Ku Cheng-hung, a worker in the Number Seven Mill of the Naigai group, was killed on May 15, shortly after the Second National Labor Congress ended. The incident roused extraordinary popular indignation. The CC of the CCP in Shanghai wrote me about the tension that prevailed in the Shanghai labor movement and asked me to return immediately to take charge. I hastily wound up my affairs in Canton and departed on May 26. I arrived at Shanghai on precisely the night of

May 30; and barely having shaken off the dust of my travels, I was thrust directly into the current of the fight against imperialism.

In the Midst of the May Thirtieth Movement

On May 30, 1925, in front of the Laocha Police Station in the Shanghai International Settlement, police opened fire on a crowd of unarmed people and killed or wounded scores of them. Superficially it looked like an accident, but actually it fully revealed the established, barbaric, and utterly senseless way in which the colonialists oppressed the Chinese people. This oppression ignited the angry fire of anti-imperialism which the Chinese had smothered for so many years. It led to the May Thirtieth Movement that is so famous in the history of modern China.

I returned to Shanghai from Canton by way of Hong Kong and landed at about six o'clock on the afternoon of May 30. I had picked up a cold on the voyage, and I felt miserable. Dragging my ailing body and my simple luggage, I debarked from the ship on the French Bund and caught a rickshaw for Chapei. Along the way both pedestrians and vehicles were noticeably scarce. Groups of three to five people clustered together at street corners, talking furtively, tense expressions on their faces. Shanghai, which I had left only a short time before, looked as if it were in the midst of a grave incident.

When I reached my house on Paohsing Lane in Chapei, my wife and Ho Pao-chen, the wife of Liu Shao-ch'i (Liu and his wife were living with us), met me at the door. My wife busied herself with looking after my things. Ho Pao-chen, who had taught at the school for Anyuan coal miners' children, brimmed with indignation as she addressed me.

"Do you know what has happened?" she demanded. "A few hours ago the police on Nanking Road opened fire on a crowd of students and residents and killed or wounded many of them." Her voice rose to a shout. "Can the Chinese people be massacred at will this way? This time I will give my life to fight the imperialists."

The outrage that Ho Pao-chen expressed seemed to be a capsule version of the prevailing popular feeling. In the previous chapter I said that the slogan "Oppose the Japanese" was a source of incomparable vitality. The foreign colonialists regarded the beating of Chinese merely as a method of sustaining themselves in power. That it was a barbaric trampling upon human rights never crossed their minds. Even though this abuse had led to a fierce wave of strikes in February, the Japanese mill owners had promised only that they would not beat people without reason. Actually they continued to use the flimsiest of pretexts to beat their Chinese employees.

Early in May of 1925 workers' representatives in the Number Eight Mill of the Naigai group in Shanghai were dismissed and some workers were injured, as had happened before. This led to a protest strike in several Japanese cotton mills on Ferry Road. Adopting a firm stand, the mill owners refused to negotiate with the workers. There was a depression, and they gave this as the reason for closing the mills and locking out the workers.

On May 15 the strikers at the Number Seven Naigai Cotton Mill assembled at its entrance and demanded that they be allowed to resume work. The owners refused, and disputes arose. Thereupon members of the Japanese staff of the mill opened fire on the workers, seriously wounding seven of them and killing Ku Cheng-hung, who was hit four times.

The Shanghai Settlement authorities took no legal action in the killing of Ku. Instead, they forbade workers to assemble and arrested some of the strikers. The Settlement police, at the same time, tried to conceal the incident from the world, and they forbade Shanghai newspapers to publish the news of the killing of Ku Cheng-hung.

A feeling of mounting outrage welled up, starting among students in the schools of Shanghai. The Shanghai Student Federation, led jointly by the KMT and the CCP, quickly spread the news, which stirred the students to public expressions of indignation. There was an anti-Japanese tradition among the students. They had long felt that heaven and earth had to be reckoned with if a single Japanese national received the slightest injury in China, while the Japanese could hide behind the unequal treaties and on Chinese territory could kill as many Chinese as they chose. The killing of Ku Cheng-hung was a flagrant example of this sort of thing, and it further clawed at their hearts.

Furthermore, the students had long been disgruntled about the rules of the Settlement authorities, and they accepted this incident as additional proof that the Settlement authorities were in criminal collusion with the Japanese. To many students all colonialists were birds of a feather, who trampled upon the Chinese as if it were their God-given right to do so. The slang phrase "tasting foreign ham"[11] was current in

Shanghai. Thus it seemed only natural, since they were all birds of a feather, that the Settlement authorities should protect the Japanese.

On the whole, the young people and intellectuals of China were quite prepared to make a show of their nation's self-respect, which had been long-established historically. At the same time they were especially aware of the difficulties in which China then found herself. They knew that China was not unified, that the warlords and the various parties and cliques were competing and squabbling with one another, that the Peking government would not champion the cause of the people, and that the people themselves were generally backward and disunited. Therefore they felt that in order to resist oppression from the outside, they must start by awakening the masses.

So the Shanghai Student Federation launched a propaganda campaign. It organized students to make street-corner speeches, to raise relief money for the injured parties, and to hold a memorial service for Ku Cheng-hung. The Settlement authorities promptly took steps to suppress these student activities. Some students were arrested on May 23 and 24 for making speeches. In an effort to help their companions that had been arrested, the students demanded that Ch'en Shih-kuang, the Shanghai Commissioner of the Ministry of Foreign Affairs, be allowed to start negotiations for their release with the Settlement authorities. The Settlement authorities disregarded the request, thus causing the students to expand their street-corner speech-making.

Chinese merchants in Shanghai normally felt nothing but distaste for the rulers of the Settlement, although they never dared to express their anger. They were sat upon by the foreign merchants, whose capital was enormous; and they had no rights at all in the Settlement, other than the right of fulfilling their obligations as taxpayers. Only foreigners were members of the Shanghai Ratepayers' Association and the Shanghai Municipal Council—a situation which had long since led to demands from the Chinese merchants that Chinese members be added to the Council. Right then the Settlement authorities were also enforcing new regulations on printing while initiating a wharfage tax and slapping a registration fee on exchanges. All of these measures increased the financial burden of the Chinese merchants and generally aroused their opposition. Furthermore, the Settlement authorities resorted to building roads that went beyond the bounds of the Settlement in order to expand their jurisdiction. And when handling Sino-foreign litigations, the Mixed Court,[12] which was controlled by foreign consular officials, invariably meted out harsher treatment to Chinese merchants. The Chinese merchants found all of these things unbearable. Therefore the Ku Cheng-hung incident moved them, just as it moved the students, to sympathize with a fellow sufferer.

The Shanghai Student Federation issued a simple document, which seemed to reflect the national feeling of the day, reading:

> Down with imperialism!
> Friends! Do you find life painful? Do you know why everything is more trying than it used to be? It is because: (1) The British, French, American, and Japanese imperialists have taken control of our Customs, making "import duties" lighter than "export duties," to prevent the development of native products. Foreigners bring in foreign goods to take away our cash and make us poorer and poorer each day. (2) The British, French, American, and Japanese imperialists commonly lend money to our warlords and take away railroad and mining rights. The warlords borrow their money and then collude with their gangsters to buy arms to carry on warfare, so that our own lives are placed in jeopardy. (3) The Japanese kill our compatriots, but instead of punishing them, the police arrest our workers. Students seek to collect subscriptions for the relief of the workers, so that they need not be forced into uprisings, but the police arrest the students, too. We seek to express our sorrow for Ku Cheng-hung, who was killed, and once again the police arrest us. Those who are under arrest are hungry and cold in their cells. Yet we are not only prevented from sending them food and clothing, we also are not even allowed to see them. But remember this: Shanghai, after all, is the Shanghai of the Chinese people. (4) Recently the Municipal Council started building roads beyond the bounds of the Settlement, roads which encroach upon our territory. They also enforce printing by-laws and a wharfage tax to carry out oppression in every possible manner. The evil of opium is known to everyone, yet the headquarters for the opium traffic is located in the foreign settlements (especially in the French Concession)! Such oppression can only kill us. Let us rise up and struggle against them in order to live. Let us all be united.
> Down with imperialism!

From this statement we can clearly see the rise and development of anti-imperialism. It started with "opposition to the Japanese for beating people"; it moved on to the protest against the killing of Ku Cheng-hung; then it developed into the fight against imperialism.

The shots fired on Nanking Road on the afternoon of May 30 brought this angry fire of anti-imperialism into official contact with the high-pressure policy of the imperialists. On that day Shanghai students again made their speeches here and there on the streets, and the police stopped them as usual. A little after three o'clock in the afternoon a foreign police officer seized two students who were speaking and took them off toward the Laocha Police Station. Behind them as they went, moved more than two hundred of the students engaged in speech-making, holding small paper flags in their hands, and a large crowd of spectators. When the crowd reached the door of the Laocha Police Station, it was met by shots fired by police. Eleven people were killed, and more than forty were wounded. This tragedy added fuel to the fire burning in a Chinese people that was waking up more and more, and it caused far-reaching repercussions in the development of the anti-imperialist movement in China and in the subsequent history of the country.

At about eight o'clock on the evening of May 30, Ch'en Tu-hsiu, Ts'ai Ho-sen, Li Li-san, Liu Shao-ch'i, Fan T'ai-ying, Wang I-min, and Lo Chüeh arrived at my home, one after the other. They did not know about my return. They had decided, however, to use my residence for a meeting to discuss the tragedy on Nanking Road. Because of the urgency of the matter at hand we could not waste much time in personal greetings, and we quickly opened an emergency meeting in my bedroom. First, each one reported on conditions in his particular field of work. Li Li-san and Liu Shao-ch'i, who spoke for the labor movement, said that the factories were in a state of great agitation. The workers were demanding a general strike. Fan T'ai-ying, who in addition to his Communist position was then serving as secretary of the Youth Department of the Shanghai Executive Department of the KMT, had just come from the KMT office at 44 Vallon Road. He said that all the KMT people were highly indignant and were discussing countermeasures. Some of them, he said, had been so moved that they beat their breasts and shed tears. Wang I-fei and Lo Chüeh, who spoke for the Shanghai District Committee of the CCP, stated that schools and popular organizations were thoroughly enraged and were holding meetings. It seemed to me that these reports indicated that the entire city of Shanghai was seething with anger.

We did not waste any time at the meeting. First we decided to launch a series of strikes to resist foreign oppression—strikes that would close business houses, factories, and classrooms. Next we drew up an outline of the demands that we would make. In the main this outline contained the following: The ruling authority in the Settlement must accept blame for the criminal massacre and be responsible for making restitution; the authority for ruling the Settlement must be transferred to the municipality of Shanghai, and the unequal treaties and consular jurisdiction rights must be abrogated; and foreign troops must be withdrawn from China.

Then we discussed the concrete measures that would have to be taken to achieve these goals and the central machinery that would have to be organized to lead the movement. It was our estimate that the big merchants might not be resolute enough, and so we advocated using the strength of the masses to force the Shanghai General Chamber of Commerce to take concerted action. We decided to organize a Shanghai General Labor Union at once. This organization, together with the National Student Federation, the Shanghai Student Federation, the Shanghai General Chamber of Commerce, and the various street federations of merchants, all were to be organized together in a Federation of Workers', Merchants', and Students' Organizations, which was to form the leadership core of the movement.

We also discussed the point that the movement, which was to be anti-imperialist, was not intended to inconvenience the citizenry as a whole, much less result in economic losses to Chinese. The main purpose of the strike of business houses, for example, was to cut off supplies to the foreigners in Shanghai. It was necessary to minimize any losses that Chinese merchants might suffer, while ensuring that citizens as a whole received their usual supplies. By the same token, the strike of workers should not spread to Chinese-owned factories. And since such public utilities as power and water affected the livelihood of everyone, no strike would be called against them for the time being.

We realized full well that the implementation of these decisions would merely constitute a peaceful movement against imperialism. The masses had no armed backing, so the movement could not develop into an armed insurrection. We also realized that the general situation in China was so chaotic that the Peking government could not stand in a common front with the masses. So we decided that in the movement there could be no retaliatory killing of foreigners, and mass disturbances would have to be avoided in order to deprive the foreigners of an excuse to apply armed pressure.

Having decided upon these policies and measures, those of us at the meeting immediately addressed ourselves to our immediate problems. I led off by saying that early the next morning I would go to the temporary office that had been found for the Shanghai General Labor Union, which was about to be organized, to take charge of things there and see to the union's organization. "That's fine," some of my comrades promptly volunteered. "It is very good indeed that you are going to work right away in spite of your illness."

As to the division of labor, Ch'en Tu-hsiu, naturally, was to take charge of the overall situation; Li Li-san was to represent the Shanghai General Labor Union in its external relations, particularly in liaison with merchants and students, to achieve unanimity of action; and others were to stick to their current posts and develop activities with the KMT and with the various popular organizations. In this way we were to see to it that our decisions were fully implemented.

The meeting lasted only two hours, during which time all important questions were settled. That very night, as soon as the meeting closed, our comrades threw themselves into their activities, and in the end all of our decisions were indeed realized. Looking back, it seems to me that the meeting was truly unprecedented in the tension that prevailed, in the smoothness with which our discussion proceeded, and in the enthusiasm felt by all the comrades, who were braced against every possible hardship. Some people may believe that the May Thirtieth Movement was merely the result of the advance blueprint which the CCP prepared. But I felt at the time that nationalism was more important than any of the other factors involved in it and that this was true even for the CCP. So far as my personal experience is concerned, people were moved by more sweeping nationalistic feelings in the May Thirtieth Movement than was the case even in the May Fourth Movement.

Early on the morning on May 31 Comrade Chang Hsueh-lan, secretary of the Labor Movement Committee of the CC of the CCP, and I arrived at the two-story building on T'ien Tung An Road in Chapei that was the temporary office of the Shanghai General Labor Union. This small, plain building had just been rented, and it was devoid of any furnishings. Comrade Chang Hsueh-lan quickly rounded up a rough table, a chair, and a few benches. On the table he placed the stationery and books that he had brought along to be used for registration. On a sheet of white paper he wrote in large characters "Temporary Offices of the Shanghai General Labor Union" and pasted it on the door. I sat in the only chair, reading the morning papers, which carried our announcement calling upon all trade unions to send representatives to register with us. Going over the comments and reports in the various papers and reading between the lines, I found that all of them inclined toward fervent opposition to foreign oppression.

At about ten o'clock that morning representatives of trade unions and factories arrived in large numbers to register with us. The information we collected in our register, in addition to information about the organization of each union, consisted principally of statements about whether they had already called a strike or, if not, whether they could call one. All of the entries were affirmative; either strikes had been called, or they were to be called at any moment. In about three hours more than one hundred persons came to register or talk things over. Only a few of them knew me, and I did not recognize all of those. Most of them I had never met. Some union representatives with whom we had had no contact seemed doubtful about what they were getting into. "How can the General Labor Union of All Shanghai be like this?" they seemed to ask themselves. Some veteran union representatives that were acquainted with the situation took it upon themselves to explain for me, "This is only a temporary office." They introduced me by saying that I was the famous Chang T'e-li, the original head of the Secretariat of Labor Organizations in China on North Chengtu Road, now director of the Shanghai office of the National General Labor Union. "The staff of the General Union is busy in different factories," they explained. "Even though the director is sick, he has come here to take charge, and he is not afraid of police intervention. What more is there to say?"

Our small room was crammed with a highly indignant crowd. From every corner came calls for a strike. "It will be easy to get things done now that there is a General Union," some declared. Others noted, "There aren't any chairs, but we don't mind standing or sitting on the floor." Some of them insisted that they be sent out to work for the union, while others offered to stay behind and protect the office.

In addition to union representatives, more than ten people came to the office to donate money to the union. I told them that we did not yet have anyone to look after the money and asked that they send in their donations the following day. I knew two of these donors, and they insisted upon leaving their contributions with me. Their fervor was truly moving. There was nothing to do but write out receipts and accept the more than two hundred dollars they donated.

In the afternoon the union representatives, who saw that I did not feel well, persuaded me to return home to rest for the time being, while they looked after things at the office. I asked that most of them return to their normal duties in their unions and that only a few stay to help out temporarily with General Union tasks and to assist Chang Hsueh-lan with the work of registration. I asked them to look for suitable quarters for the union. I also asked them to go ahead with arrangements for making the announcements and sending out notifications of the official inauguration of the General Labor Union the next day.

That afternoon I saw a doctor and rested for a while. Ch'en Tu-hsiu, Li Li-san, and some others came to my house, and we exchanged information. The principal features of the situation that day were that strikes were declared in a great majority of foreign factories as planned, most schools suspended classes, and the street federations of merchants, which supported the idea of a business strike, were beginning to take action. At about two o'clock that afternoon large numbers of students, workers, and representatives of street federations of merchants went to the Shanghai General Chamber of Commerce at Tien Hou Temple and demanded concerted action. The responsible people at the General Chamber at first held back, trying to evade the issue. In the face of indignant demands from the delegations, however, Fang Chiao-pai, the vice-president of the General Chamber, eventually gave his support to a general suspension of business.[13] This made it possible to achieve a suspension of business on the part of all Shanghai businessmen. Furthermore, the Federation of Workers', Merchants', and Students' Organizations could be formed after the three had consulted among themselves. The Shanghai General Chamber of Commerce, while it supported this organization, did not want to participate in it, so as to leave itself open to act as a mediator if that were necessary.

And so it was clear that on the whole we would be able to carry out all the decisions we had reached the previous night. Our comrades left my place about dusk to let me get some more rest. They selected another location for continuing their talks. After a night's sleep, I began to recover.

I arrived at 2 Shun Tai Lane, Paoshan Road, Chapei, about eight o'clock on the morning of June 1. The building there had been rented the previous afternoon and already had been fixed up as the head-quarters for the Shanghai General Labor Union. It had three stories, with two rooms and a large hall on each floor, and made a highly suitable office. More than one hundred workers' representatives were there when I arrived, and they did not overcrowd the hall on the first floor in which they had gathered. I looked over the whole building and found that a good job had been done in furnishing and decorating it. The ten-odd workers that had taken responsibility for doing this had obviously devoted a great deal of time and energy to it. I decided to use the first floor for meetings and receiving visitors, the second floor for general offices, and the third floor for handling financial matters.

Then I assembled the workers that had come to attend the inaugural ceremony. As director of the Shanghai Office of the National General Labor Union, I declared the formation of the Shanghai General Labor Union. Amidst such exclamations as "congratulations on the inaugura-tion of the General Labor Union," "support the Shanghai General Labor Union," "strive for victory in the strikes," and "avenge the martyrs," we put up a large, newly made sign, which proclaimed "Shanghai General Labor Union," and hoisted the union's standard, which bore its name. Using only volunteers, we assigned everyone that could stay to do union work to duties in four categories—general affairs, public relations, ac-counting, and picketing. From that day onward the building served as the center for the leaders of the strike movement in Shanghai.

At two o'clock that afternoon, in the borrowed quarters of a Can-tonese guild on Jukiang Road, the Shanghai General Labor Union con-vened its First Congress. About six hundred delegates attended it, filling the hall to capacity. After a number of spirited speeches, the Congress elected Li Li-san president of the Shanghai General Labor Union, Liu Shao-ch'i chief of General Affairs, and Yang Chien-hung, a KMT member, chief of Public Relations. I cannot remember the names of the heads of the Accounting and Picketing sections. The Congress unanimously adopted a resolution calling upon me to remain in the union to guide its work. Then the Congress adopted a resolution for-mally declaring its participation in the Shanghai Federation of Workers', Merchants', and Students' Organizations, and discussed the goals that it wanted the movement to achieve, especially goals that affected the workers. The goals were decided upon, and union representatives were authorized to present them to the Federation of Workers', Merchants', and Students' Organizations.

That same day the Shanghai Federation of Workers', Merchants', and Students' Organizations was officially formed also. It was organized with a small body of responsible representatives from each of the three bodies, and it served as the general leadership machinery for the movement. On June 8 it was the Federation that presented the famous seventeen conditions[14] as a concrete program for settling the May Thirtieth tragedy.

The anti-imperialist movement developed as the organizations that comprised its machinery were formed, one after the other. Shanghai workers began to go out on strike on June 1, and factories owned by Japanese and British interests in Shanghai were the first to be affected. Then workers in the tramways, the bus company, the power company, the telephone company, as well as domestic servants in foreign homes and sanitary coolies joined in the strike; and on June 5 some Chinese policemen joined the strikers' ranks. These moves were clearly directed against foreign rule in Shanghai. By the middle of June the number of strikers exceeded 156,000.[15]

Merchants began to close their shops in the International Settlement and to suspend business on June 1. On June 5 shops in the French Concession closed their doors for one day in a gesture of support. The strike of merchants did not extend to the French Concession, because the French Concession authorities had not taken a direct hand in the oppression. The Movement was mainly directed against the British and Japanese. Meanwhile, shops in the Chinese-controlled parts of Shanghai continued business as usual, which made the anti-imperialist character of the Movement more noticeable.

As to students, after the May Thirtieth tragedy, many schools in Shanghai suspended classes. Gradually the missionary schools operated by foreigners also were involved, and some conflicts arose between the foreign authorities that ran these schools and their students. A large number of students walked out of St. John's University, for example, because they were disgruntled about certain measures the University authorities had taken. Throughout the period of this Movement, generally speaking, foreign missionary schools in China were hard hit.

The angry wave of anti-imperialism surged rapidly over the entire country. In Peking, Tientsin, Hankow, Changsha, Tsinan, Foochow, Tsingtao, Chengchow, Kaifeng, Kiukiang, Nanchang, Chinkiang, Swatow, Canton, and Hangchow—one after the other—large-scale demonstrations by students and other citizens were held. A boycott of British and Japanese goods was initiated, and strikes and other movements against the foreigners were carried out. In various places foreigners also staged incidents in which Chinese were brutally massacred. Popular organizations in the centers of activity generally included among their demands abrogation of the unequal treaties, withdrawal of foreign naval and land forces, severance of economic ties with Britain and Japan, and reparation for the wrongs done to their compatriots that had been killed. These anti-imperialist cries, which were accompanied by a baptism in blood, were heard in every corner of the country.

The Great Canton and Hong Kong Strike was one of the prominent developments of the Movement. In Hong Kong and on the island of Shameen at Canton, workers began to go out on strike on June 19 in support of the May Thirtieth Movement in Shanghai. On June 23 British and French troops on Shameen opened fire on demonstrators across the narrow waterway separating Shameen from Canton. They killed or wounded more than five hundred Whampoa cadets and other Chinese, thereby perpetrating the famous Shakee Tragedy. Most of the workers in Hong Kong responded by going out on strike. The number of strikers there rose to more than one hundred thousand, and many of them left Hong Kong to go to Canton. The strike lasted for sixteen months. The action of the strikers not only dealt a serious blow to the economy of Hong Kong,[16] but it was an important contribution to bolstering the influence of the National government which had recently been formed at Canton.

In spite of the enthusiasm and fanfare with which the May Thirtieth Movement was launched, existing conditions both objectively and subjectively restricted its development. In the first place, it remained a movement of peaceful resistance to alien aggression, unable to advance beyond that stage. Secondly, the influence of the Powers in China was so enormous that even the entire strength of the country could do nothing against it. Thirdly, while the established policy of British imperialism was to use high-handed methods in dealing with the national movement in China, it also resorted to a fragmentation policy of using Chinese to control Chinese, a state of affairs that became especially apparent in the May Thirtieth Movement. Fourthly, it was not only because the foreign forces were strong that the May Thirtieth Movement failed to achieve its anti-imperialist goals, but also because China was disunited. Fifthly, the May Thirtieth Movement so agitated the country that the anti-imperialist movement in China moved from a general propaganda stage to the brink of concrete action. All of these factors seemed to become evident as the Movement progressed.

Soon after the May Thirtieth tragedy, the International Settlement authorities, led by the British, quickly declared a state of emergency. Marines of several foreign countries were landed to guard communications points in conjunction with the armed volunteers organized by foreigners in the Settlement. The pivotal areas in Shanghai, such as Nanking Road, were closed to Chinese, while in other areas Chinese had to submit to being searched. A special point was made of prohibiting Chinese from carrying printed matter or loitering on the street. Chinese were forbidden to go anywhere in groups of three or more, and a curfew was enforced after 8:00 P.M.

During the two weeks that the curfew was in force, terror enveloped all of Shanghai. There were daily reports of foreign troops firing at or assaulting pedestrians, many of whom were killed or wounded. The police launched a large-scale campaign of arrests throughout the city, the actual number of victims of which was never published. Troops occupied Shanghai University, Ta Hsia University, Nan Fang University, Wen Chih University, and Tung Teh Medical College and its hospital, all of which lay inside the Settlement. These institutions were dissolved, and their staffs and students were driven from their campuses. On June 12 foreign policemen traveling along North Szechwan Road entered Chinese territory to arrest students. About two hundred Japanese and American marines, with armored cars, accompanied these policemen. They were deployed against the Defense Corps in the Chinese area, and an armed clash very nearly ensued.

The use of such arbitrary methods by the Settlement authorities could not check in any way the resistance of the Chinese people. The alliance to bring about a general strike continued to make progress. At first the die-hard colonialists, disparaging the Chinese for their inability to unite, believed that all resistance would collapse under a high-pressure policy. On June 1, when shops in the International Settlement suspended business, the foreign and native banks stayed open as usual. Instead of closing, they merely sent a letter to the Shanghai Municipal Council protesting the tragedy. The Council ignored their protest, and the British-owned *North China Daily News* ridiculed the banks for their inability to unite with the other businesses. In this way the foreign and native banks were forced to close their doors, too, on June 3.

The die-hard British colonialists also tried in various ways to slander the Movement as a general antiforeign movement, for they wanted to line up all the Powers against China. But their charge, which was not in keeping with the facts, had little effect. Needless to say, all Chinese, regardless of their party affiliations, thought of the May Thirtieth Movement as a matter of upholding righteousness. Even among the foreign residents many believed that the Movement could not be treated on a level with such events as the Boxer Uprising. Russia and Germany, to varying degrees, expressed sympathy with China, while French and American diplomats in China openly indicated that their attitude was not the same as that held by Britain and Japan. And Japan itself eventually made a calculated withdrawal before the surging tide, allowing the righteous drive against imperialism to direct itself solely at the British.

The policy of trying to throttle the Chinese national movement at birth obviously did not work. Foreign forces led by the die-hard British colonialists therefore adopted a policy of trying to fragment the national movement by attacking the Communists. This fragmentation policy was extensively employed over a prolonged period. At the time it chiefly involved making tempting concessions to the Peking government, sowing dissension between the big merchants on the one hand and the workers and students on the other in order to undermine their unity, creating conditions conducive to a split between the KMT and the CCP, and undermining CCP influence over the trade unions. While this approach side-stepped the perfectly justified demands of the Chinese nation and dealt with minor issues, it did prove effective for a time, and the May Thirtieth Movement was checked for the moment. Subsequently they used the same techniques to split up the 1927 revolutionary movement. But these old debts accumulated and developed into one of the factors that led to the final success of the CCP.

The May Thirtieth Movement managed for a while to rouse the Peking government to a sense of responsibility for the nation. Faced with the indignation of the masses (even a few Northern militarists went so far as to call for a war against Britain and Japan), Tuan Ch'i-jui tried to exploit national sentiment in dealing with outside forces in an effort to stabilize his regime. Basically, however, his regime relied upon foreign support for its existence, and it could not muster enough courage to take a real stand. It did lodge protests with the Diplomatic Corps based on the demands of the Shanghai Federation of Workers', Merchants', and Students' Organizations. But the Diplomatic Corps either ignored the protests or put off dealing with them. Beset by endless difficulties, the Tuan regime had no choice but to permit the foreigners to investigate the situation. This merely delayed any settlement of the issues, an eventuality that the regime was powerless to do anything about. Eventually, when the foreigners agreed to call a tariff conference to consult on tariff revisions, the Tuan regime felt it best to pretend to be deaf and dumb.

After the death of Sun Yat-sen the KMT was busy reorganizing the National government at Canton and purging unreliable armies. Its leadership in the Movement was weak for this reason. The leaders of the KMT in Canton gave unqualified support to the Hong Kong and Canton strike, which was right at their door, but found the anti-imperialist movement in other areas beyond their reach. To be sure, KMT members in Shanghai and elsewhere took an active part in the Movement; but local KMT organizations were unable to assume fully a role of leadership. When action had to be taken, decisions were usually made in secret by a CCP caucus and then formally adopted as a resolution by the KMT organization.

The CCP that I knew so well truly played a leading role in the Movement; but at the same time, the Movement fully exposed the fact that the CCP had not yet acquired adequate leadership power. Caught up in this great tide of anti-imperialism, the CCP immediately realized that it did not have enough workers. All of its members were busy doing this or that, and it was impossible to devote proper attention to everything. This was especially true for the CC of the CCP, which was so harried that it could not devote enough time to the formulation of policy. It was constantly called upon to look after specific, concrete tasks that could not be postponed for a moment. Although, as I have mentioned, the CC of the CCP worked out thorough preliminary plans for the Movement, it was unable to produce additional policies to cope with new situations. As a result, it could only watch the leadership of the Movement being taken out of its control.

The Shanghai General Labor Union, which was the main base of the CCP, in itself used up a major portion of the manpower of the CCP organization in Shanghai. The union was hastily established, it used a staff of more than one hundred people, and its duties were complex.

Creating an orderly system within which everyone worked efficiently was a difficult job. Under the General Union, moreover, were more than one hundred member unions, most of which had either just been formed or had recently expanded. Naturally, large numbers of able cadres were needed for organizational consolidation.

The president of the General Union, Li Li-san, who represented it in external relations, came to play a leading role in the Federation of Workers', Merchants', and Students' Organizations. This left him with no time to look after the work of the union. In the beginning, furthermore, Liu Shao-ch'i was kept busy directing the work of unions in the factory areas. Thus I was responsible for guiding the work of the General Union; in fact I had to take charge of its internal affairs. Sometimes I was unable to leave it for a second, not even to take part in policy-making meetings of the CC of the CCP. This sort of thing went on for two weeks, and then Liu Shao-ch'i, who was the union's director of General Affairs, took charge, thereby relieving me.

From the day of the founding of the Shanghai General Labor Union, its office was constantly crammed with people. Every day, in an endless line, hundreds of them came to give money. While the total of these donations was a large figure, most of the donors themselves were people with small incomes. Occasionally someone would make a large donation of several thousand dollars; but most donations ranged from a few tens of dollars to a few hundred dollars. Many of the people came carrying bags of silver coins or coppers. Among the donors, too, were coolies and old women, who brought things it had taken them years to save—bits of gold or silver jewelry or long-treasured silver coins—to give to the workers. Sometimes we tactfully refused contributions from people who obviously could not afford to make them, but they persisted in trying to give away their money. They were literally overflowing with patriotism. Some old women wept when we refused to accept their contributions. The scenes we witnessed could not possibly have been more moving.

Periodically we gave money to the striking workers as donations came in. Once every three days in each area or factory we gave every striker one dollar. This undertaking had a considerable stabilizing effect on the strike.

The Settlement authorities, who seemed to realize for the first time that there was such a thing as patriotism among the people of China, regarded the General Labor Union as a mote in their eye and secretly attempted to get rid of it. The foreigners put up considerable sums of money to turn out printed material that slandered the General Union and its staff. Because of our countermeasures, however, these activities did not have their hoped-for success. So their next move was to buy over Chinese from the underworld, and these Chinese persistently tried to wreck the union. But this scheme also failed in the face of the spreading patriotic fervor of the people. Toward the end of the strike, however, the Shanghai General Labor Union did suffer from the efforts of the gangsters to wreck it. It was said that this was one of the master strokes that the foreigners accomplished from behind the scenes.

In addition to coping with the type of problem mentioned above, I had to keep a wary eye open to check excesses in the patriotic zeal of the masses. The situation at the time was so profoundly tragic that the masses might easily have let themselves go in taking destructive retaliatory action. It seemed to me that we were not strong enough to handle this problem. I felt that at any moment the people might fly out of control. And if incidents should arise in which foreigners were killed, the Chinese people would be made to pay for such deaths with a greater shedding of their own blood. I did everything I could to persuade my colleagues and the workers in general to limit their activities to an economic boycott. I pointed out that the boycott would be enough to make the foreigners feel the prowess of the Chinese nation. For the time being, they should go no further. I told them that if they went further, we would suffer from the consequences.

After the May Thirtieth tragedy, far-sighted merchants and most of the better-known Chinese believed that it was not enough merely to rely upon passive mass resistance to foreign oppression. They felt that the government would have to take up the matter. Even leftist students advocated that the government work out effective negotiations in keeping with legal procedure. Yet this apparently was too much to expect of the Peking government, the uselessness of which people began to feel with an increasing sense of depression.

The CC of the CCP thought that nothing could be expected from the Tuan government at Peking, for the foreign colonialists, with their blind belief in might, would not lightly make concessions to the people of China. The CC felt that only by strengthening popular forces through the use of revolutionary techniques would we be able to settle our basic domestic and foreign problems. For a time, however, we could not arrive at any concrete plan, although we discussed the situation over and over again. Among us there were people whose thinking followed that of Sun Yat-sen when he took his Northern trip and called for the convocation of a national assembly and the organization of a government that would stand united against the foreign powers. But we realized that the KMT, which had lost Sun Yat-sen, did not at the moment have the prestige to initiate the move. Nor would the CCP, which was still in its infancy, attract attention by issuing such a call by itself. In fact, were the CCP reluctantly to take the step, it might well only lead to disagreements that would affect the united front against the foreigners.

On June 5 the CC of the CCP issued a "Message to the People."[17] In addition to expressing wholehearted indignation at the barbarism and brutality of the imperialists, it pointed out that the "Shanghai incident is neither accidental nor legal, but altogether political" and that "we can never rely upon, or have confidence in, negotiations by the Government." It opposed mediation and compromise while calling for caution in opposing the imperialists, who would utilize anticommunism as a pretext for sowing dissension and undermining unity. It also called for persistent, long-term resistance and for the consolidation of the anti-imperialist united front. But the message did not propose any concrete plan for a political settlement of the incident or suggest what the future of such a settlement might be. Instead it hinted that we might prefer to accept a glorious defeat. The message apparently showed the limits of the CCP's ability to take action.

Nevertheless, the CCP did succeed in expanding organizationally in the course of the May Thirtieth Movement. Numerous workers and students joined either the CCP or the CYC, and it was at this time that the CCP began group recruitment. I presided over several of the ceremonies in which new members were admitted to the Party. About forty people were admitted on each occasion. Most of them were activists in the May Thirtieth Movement who had undergone a short period of ideological training before becoming full members. Most of them, when they joined, had demonstrated their respect for CCP leadership in the May Thirtieth Movement and were zealously nationalistic.

As the situation developed, Yü Cha-ching, a leading actor in the May Thirtieth Movement who represented the big merchants, gained prominence with his conciliatory policy. He was President of the General Chamber of Commerce and a powerful force among the big businessmen. The General Chamber of Commerce was a legally organized body. Making use of his position in it to carry out his conciliatory policy, Yü won the support of almost all of the big merchants in Shanghai. He happened to be in Peking when the May Thirtieth Incident occurred. Hurrying back to Shanghai, he undertook the mission of mediating the incident for the Tuan government, to a certain extent; and in doing this, he demonstrated his mettle as a politician. He employed the two-faced method: on the one hand he established good relations with the Federation of Workers', Merchants', and Students' Organizations and exploited the spirit of the masses to force the foreigners to make certain small concessions; and on the other hand, contending that the foreigners would not accept our conditions, he exploited the position of the General Chamber to revise the seventeen conditions of the Federation of Workers', Merchants', and Students' Organizations and to gradually achieve his ultimate aim, which was compromise.

On June 11 the Shanghai General Chamber of Commerce revised the seventeen conditions that the Federation had promulgated on June 8, turning them into thirteen milder conditions.[18] The Federation of Workers', Merchants', and Students' Organizations at first unanimously opposed this revision. It felt especially disgruntled about the manipulating that Yü Cha-ching was doing.

Initially the CC of the CCP, too, fiercely opposed the scheme. It had especially strong feelings about not agreeing to change the sixth of the original seventeen conditions, which stated:

> On the question of good treatment of workers, foreign-owned factories must abide by regulations for the protection of Chinese workers to be worked out by the Shanghai Municipal Council in conjunction with the Chinese Ratepayers' Association, and must not maltreat them. They must recognize the freedom of workers to organize trade unions and strikes. There must be no dismissal of workers in connection with the present strike.

As incorporated into the seventh and eighth of the Chamber's thirteen conditions, this was amended to read:

> Workers in foreign firms, seamen, and factory workers who stopped work because of their grief will be reinstated in their old positions, and no deductions will be made from their wages during the period they did not work. . . . Workers must be well treated, they must be allowed to work or not as they like, and they must not be dismissed for striking. . . .

As far as the CC of the CCP was concerned, this amendment was made to further the class interests of the big merchants themselves and to intentionally wipe out the demands of the workers.

Nevertheless, so as not to break up the united front, the CC of the CCP gave way in the end. The CC felt that it would be a miracle anyway if even the thirteen conditions worked out by the Shanghai General Chamber of Commerce were carried out. And preservation of the united front remained the most burning question for the time being—a serious matter that did not have the prior approval of a meeting of representatives. But I called upon the delegates to coolly discuss the problem itself. Fortunately, I was able to fall back upon the prestige that I normally had in order to dispel the tension that permeated the meeting. As a result of the discussion that followed, the more than six hundred delegates unanimously decided that in order not to undermine the united front of workers, merchants, and students, there was nothing we could do for the moment but protest the revisions made by the General Chamber of Commerce while expressing the hope that the General Chamber would sincerely cooperate with the Federation of Workers', Merchants', and Students' Organizations to present a united front in dealing with outside forces. As to the provisions in the sixth of the original seventeen conditions, these involved the personal interests of the workers, and it was decided that the workers themselves would have to carry out a prolonged struggle for their realization.

Yü Cha-ching in effect overruled opposition from the Federation of Workers', Merchants', and Students' Organizations by negotiating with the foreigners on the basis of the thirteen conditions of the General Chamber of Commerce. Even these conditions were rejected by the foreigners. This gave Yü a satisfactory pretext for proceeding; and it resulted in the gradual collapse of the Movement.

Yü began by calling a halt to the strike of merchants. On June 26 shops throughout Shanghai announced the end of their suspension of business. Furthermore the Shanghai General Chamber of Commerce, the Federation of Workers', Merchants', and Students' Organizations, and the Chinese Ratepayers' Association of the International Settlement jointly issued a solemn declaration.[19] It announced the resumption of business on July 26, but promulgated the following three continuing boycott measures: (1) a boycott of British goods until the May Thirtieth Incident was settled, (2) a boycott of Japanese goods until the Japanese cotton mill incident was settled, and (3) a boycott until economic aid was given to the striking workers.

The resumption of business by Shanghai merchants marked the beginning of the decline in the anti-imperialist movement in Shanghai. But, at the same time, the Shakee tragedy at Canton and the Great Hong Kong and Canton Strike provided the focal points for momentous popular excitement. Far from believing that the time was right for a withdrawal, both the KMT and the CCP felt that the movement should be expanded, and they proposed this. Their proposals, however, could not reverse the trend toward compromise launched by the big merchants. In this way the CCP learned from experience that the big merchants could not be relied upon. The CCP at the same time was profoundly aware that it was not enough to depend solely upon the Shanghai General Labor Union or even upon the working class as a whole. But the broad masses of peasants could not be mobilized immediately, and there was nothing to be done about it.

At this time, the CC of the CCP raised the priority of its work among the peasants, and it began to concern itself with propaganda in the army as well. Consequently, in keeping with a decision of the CC of the CCP, I rid myself of the routine activities of the Shanghai General Labor Union to concentrate my energies on the various issues in the CC that needed to be solved immediately.

As a result of Yü Cha-ching's policy of gradual withdrawal, the striking workers at the Japanese mills went back to work on August 25. For after repeated negotiations between the Chinese and Japanese sides, on August 12 the Japanese mill owners agreed to recall the two Japanese staff members responsible for killing Ku Cheng-hung. They also agreed to pay $10,000 in compensation to the family of Ku Cheng-hung and to forbid Japanese to carry firearms into the factories. In addition, they agreed to recognize the right of trade unions to represent the workers when the Chinese government promulgated trade-union regulations.[20] This proviso on the right of trade unions to represent the workers was, of course, a mere pretext for side-stepping the issue, which a defective Chinese legislature had provided for the Japanese. It left one feeling somewhere between laughter and tears. But since the shops had long since reopened for business, the workers had borne the brunt of the strike on their own backs too long as it was, and they were suffering severe losses. So it was that workers in the Japanese mills were persuaded by the Shanghai General Labor Union to resume work on August 25 in accordance with the conditions mentioned.

After the Japanese mills reopened, the movement became all the more marked as being solely directed against the British. But the British would not expose their weaknesses. The Power Company in the International Settlement cut off the supply of power to Chinese-owned factories, leaving them paralyzed. This carefully aimed blow hit Chinese industrial and commercial circles right below the belt. They had to accept defeat. The General Chamber of Commerce negotiated with the British firms on seven conditions for resolving the trouble. These included the resumption of power to Chinese-owned factories and the payment of partial wages, as a maintenance allowance, to striking workers, and a return to their jobs on September 30 of workers in British enterprises.[21] Thus the strike in the British-owned mills also ended.

In the course of this gradual withdrawal, the Shanghai General Labor Union was subjected to increasing, diverse forms of oppression. Early in September, gangsters wrecked its premises. The premises were sealed up on September 18 on orders from the commandant of the Shanghai curfew, Hsing Shih-lien. Subsequently Liu Hua, the vice-president of the union, was killed when Sun Ch'uan-fang ousted Feng-tien influence from the Kiangsi-Chekiang area. Thus the Shanghai General Labor Union, which carried on the movement longer and more effectively than any other organization, had to go underground.

The experienced British colonialists employed procrastination and fragmentation to resolve the gigantic episode, and it was they who sounded the drums of victory. They blithely put an end to the movement by announcing, on December 13, the resignations of McGowan and Edwardson, the two British police officers who gave the order to open fire at the Laocha Police Station on May 30. At the same time they agreed, among other things, to add two Chinese members to the Shanghai Municipal Council and to pay a compensation of $75,000 to the families of those who were killed, a compensation that was refused by the Chinese.

After that the colonialists no longer dared to underestimate the national movement in China. In fact they began to stress a policy of anticommunism, which they sought to use as an effective weapon to undermine the unity of the Chinese people in dealing with foreign countries.

As for the Chinese people, outraged and depressed by the defeat of the May Thirtieth Movement, most of them felt heavyhearted. The anti-imperialist fervor that the May Thirtieth Movement had aroused, however, remained, and it did a great deal to germinate subsequent revolutionary movements.

THE KUOMINTANG AFTER THE
DEATH OF DR. SUN YAT-SEN

CHAPTER

On the Eve of the Establishment of the National Government

I stayed in Canton during most of May, 1925, in order to participate in the Second National Labor Congress. This gave me an opportunity to understand the political situation in Canton. After the death of Dr. Sun Yat-sen, reorganization of the Canton government became a necessity. At the same time, the process of reorganizing provided the source for many subsequent disputes.

The first thing I did after arriving in Canton at the end of April, 1925, was to visit Ch'en Yen-nien, secretary of the CCP Kwangtung District Committee. He was the elder son of Ch'en Tu-hsiu. He had joined the CCP when he was a student in France, and after his return to China in the latter half of 1924, he became district secretary. He showed that he was experienced and a keen thinker. I felt that he was more worldly than Chao Shih-yen, who was working in Peking.

Ch'en Yen-nien described the situation in Canton to me. He pointed out that after the successful suppression of the revolt of the Merchant Corps and the subsequent victory in the Eastern Expedition, the general situation in Kwangtung had improved. But orders issued by the Canton government had not yet been effective over all of Kwangtung Province, primarily because of the havoc played by the system of having the different armies garrisoned in various parts of the province. Of these armies, the ones from Yunnan and Kwangsi, commanded by Yang Hsi-min and Liu Chen-huan, were of particular concern. They controlled the Canton municipal area, collected opium and gambling taxes, and were able to do whatever they pleased. Furthermore, Ch'en Yen-nien was not very optimistic about the labor and peasant movements in Kwangtung. He believed that the rightist Machine Workers' Union was still antagonistic toward the leftist Labor Congress in Canton. In the different *hsien* the influence of the landlords was far greater than the power wielded by the peasant associations. Everywhere the landlords were armed and had constructed pillboxes. Innumerable instances of oppression of peasant associations were reported.

My next visit was to Hu Han-min, who was at the time the highest authority in the Canton government. He was secretary general of KMT Headquarters, acting generalissimo, and also governor of Kwangtung. When I went to see him, he was suffering from an eye ailment. Not once during our hour-long conversation did we touch upon the political situation in Kwangtung. I gave Hu a report on the conditions of the Second Labor Congress, and he gave me a promise of help. Other than that, we talked mostly about his eye ailment. Although Hu had always been fond of high-flown political discussions, this time he seemed depressed and was not inclined to talk much about politics.

Up to this time the CC of the CCP had consistently regarded Hu Han-min as the leader of the Middle-of-the-Road clique. The CCP comrades in Canton, however, looked upon him as a rightist. Ch'en Yen-nien had pointed out to me that after the death of Dr. Sun, Hu Han-min had worked energetically to become the official successor to Sun. Hu's policies were rightist, and he gathered together a group of backward militarists like Yang Hsi-min and Liu Chen-huan to strengthen his position. At the same time his close associates, such as Wu Ch'ao-shu, Ku Ying-fen, and Fu Ping-ch'ang were secretly cultivating Hong Kong. The Cantonese comrades were not satisfied with Hu's actions. They believed that only people like Wang Ching-wei, Liao Chung-k'ai, and Chiang Kai-shek could be considered leftists that would support a policy of alliance with Russia and tolerance of the Communists.

Although Wang Ching-wei was a member of several committees, I found that he had no real responsibilities. He had expressed a position in favor of liquidating Yang Hsi-min and Liu Chen-huan and of reorganizing the National government. When I met Wang Ching-wei, he assumed the posture of having personally received Dr. Sun's will as an order, and he talked at great length about the need to continue the revolution in obedience to the will of the *Tsung-li* (Director General). On several later occasions at the home of Borodin, I met him—always carrying a brief case, always arriving and departing hurriedly. When specific issues were discussed, Wang Ching-wei would become very secretive, possibly because he could not be sure that his plans could be realized.

The person in the Canton government who held some substantial power then was Liao Chung-k'ai. He took responsibility for the finances of Canton, and he served as the KMT representative at the Whampoa Military Academy, as well as director of the Labor Department of the KMT Central Committee. He was the person that I saw most often. When we talked about the Second Labor Congress, Liao would say that his secretary, Feng Chü-p'o, knew its problems more clearly than he did. Nevertheless he promised to give financial support to the Congress. His conversation was always frank and charming. Even though at the time he was resorting to extraordinary measures to raise funds to satisfy the needs of the army, he told me that he did not want to continue doing so indefinitely.

One of the busiest among the important personages in Kwangtung then was Borodin, who was brimming with knowledge and plans. After Dr. Sun's death Borodin's power and prestige grew daily. Each day many people called on him and often had a long wait before being received. Ch'en Yen-nien often went to see him on business and would have to wait for an hour or two. Borodin's office was opposite the KMT central headquarters. When I first called on him, I also had to wait for a time in the room of his secretary, Chang T'ai-lei, before I saw him.

In our first conversation, Borodin pointed out that the greatest problem in Kwangtung at the time was inadequate finances. Borodin said that it would be necessary to unify Kwangtung in order to solve this problem and that only by unifying Kwangtung would it be possible to organize the National government. The primary tasks of this government would be to centralize control of finances, to prohibit armies and officials from collecting their own revenues, and to increase revenues by fostering integrity. It was also to be hoped that if government funds could be impartially allotted, the income would be adequate to meet the urgent needs of the revolution. In a lighter vein, Borodin also said that what he was advocating was a "government of integrity." He believed that such a government would be full of revolutionary significance, that it would clearly distinguish the revolutionary from the antirevolutionary, the leftist from the rightist. In other words, he felt that corrupt men are often antirevolutionary, whereas men of integrity are by nature admirable people whom no one would want to oppose.

Borodin was a person who would not reveal his plans until he was ready. He made no exception even in dealing with me. Chang T'ai-lei told me that a few days after our meeting, Borodin formulated his plans, which were based on his reaction to the opposition that a majority of generals expressed to the monopolizing of revenues by Yang and Liu and on his dissatisfaction with Hu Han-min's policy of procrastination. Thus, Borodin issued a call for centralized control of finances, and he secretly planned to liquidate Yang and Liu. After these things had been accomplished, the National government would be organized. The military plan for liquidating Yang and Liu was being discussed only in secret. Their armies were entrenched inside the city of Canton, and the least indiscretion that would let the secret leak out would cause Yang and Liu to liquidate us first.

Canton appeared to me at the time to be a curious city on whose backward and chaotic foundations a tinge of revolutionary color was being overlaid. Opium dens and gambling houses abounded along the Bund. They were the source of revenue for the Yunnanese and Kwangsi armies. There were only a few private automobiles, most of which were owned by the militarists. These often sped along the roads, with two or four armed soldiers riding on the outside and military personages or their families inside. The books and magazines published in the city retained the character of "old" literature, and "yellow" reading materials made up the majority of the publications. Such a backward atmosphere was rare even in the northern cities. However, multicolored signs bearing revolutionary slogans were apparent everywhere on the roads and streets. Streamers of white cloth with moving slogans in red hung at intersections. On the bustling thoroughfares one could see Whampoa military figures with their revolutionary personalities, wearing red neckties and Sun Yat-sen uniforms. They mingled with the crowds and attracted people's attention. The doors of most trade unions and other mass organizations were also decorated in a variety of colors; compared with most of the stores, they looked like stars in heaven. All this caused people to smell the heavy aroma of revolution, so rare in the northern cities. This atmosphere of both progress and backwardness was immediately apparent to any one and gave rise to a feeling of discord.

The CCP Kwangtung District Committee, which had its office on the second floor of a building on Wen-te Road, could be considered a semipublic organization. Although there was no sign on the door and there had been no official public announcement of its address, many people knew that the office was that of the Committee. Activities that were carried on from this office seemed so open that they never met with interference. It was the only branch of the CCP in all China at this time that operated publicly. Of all the revolutionary organizations in Canton city, it was also the most active.

Although the office could not be considered large, there was nevertheless a continuous stream of people visiting it. Often, several meetings were held there simultaneously. At this time there were about two hundred members of the CCP in the city of Canton, and they called regularly at the District Office to receive instructions. Workers that were not members of the CCP also visited the office frequently on matters connected with the trade unions. Occasionally some KMT leftists visited the office. The CCP Kwangtung District Committee also had a Peasant Movement Committee and a Military Affairs Department, although the CC of the CCP had not yet established such units. The Peasant Movement Committee was under the charge of P'eng P'ai, Lo Yi-yüan, and Juan Hsiao-hsien, while the Military Affairs Department was under the charge of Chou En-lai and Nieh Jung-chen. Barefooted peasants and military men with their leather breast belts often appeared at this office. These sidelights illustrate the character of the Kwangtung District Committee at the time.

The work efficiency of the CCP Kwangtung District Committee was not high, and there was even chaos at times. This was in great measure related to the small space available at the office, the lack of communications facilities, the hot weather, and the crude equipment. More important still was the fact that although the responsible members of the committee lacked experience, they had to cope with a complex situation. They had to respect both the directives issued by the CC of the CCP from Shanghai and the views of Borodin, who was with them day and night. Sometimes the views of these two higher authorities were at variance. Generally speaking, the work of the Kwangtung District Committee produced good results, although it did not have the responsibility for policy-making in the district.

The central headquarters of the KMT appeared to house an organization that was carrying on routine duties. Its outward appearance was far more imposing than that of the CCP District Committee, and it had a larger number of workers. The atmosphere there did not seem tense. I had called there several times and had had some private conversations with the staff members. I felt that most of them were energetic people with an ideal, but some were not contented with life in the office. T'an P'ing-shan told me that as director of the Organizational Department of the KMT, he was merely concerned with attention to routine matters. Important matters of policy were decided by a small number of high KMT leaders in consultation with Borodin. General personnel and work problems, including allotment of tasks for the KMT leftists, were decided in advance by the CCP Kwangtung District Committee. T'an himself only implemented such decisions.

All these facts brought me to the profound realization that Canton had lacked a leadership core since the death of Dr. Sun Yat-sen. Borodin had filled the vacuum, but this was not proper. Furthermore, such an organizational situation was abnormal. I had talked earnestly with Chang T'ai-lei about this matter. He believed that under the existing conditions, Borodin could not afford to be delicate and to avoid the charge of assuming power. After the loss of Dr. Sun, the KMT's affairs had to be administered by a foreign national who could assume actual responsibility and play the role of maintaining equilibrium. This could not be considered bad strategy.

I had also visited General Galen, who was then military adviser to the Canton government. This military man of stalwart stature and sincere attitude expressed extraordinary respect for the leadership of the CC of the CCP. He unrolled a map to explain the disposition of armies in Kwangtung, and he hinted to me that militarily the liquidation of Yang and Liu was assured. He also said that after the two were liquidated, the military system would have to be reorganized, and some army units that were capable of being improved would be given the opportunity to develop in the same manner as Whampoa. His viewpoint appeared somewhat at variance with that of Borodin, which stressed the fostering of Whampoa only.

Chou En-lai, then a member of the CCP Kwangtung District Committee and head of its Military Department, proposed that the committee should adopt the policy of making Whampoa the center of its military activity. After his return to China from France in 1924, Chou En-lai immediately became deputy director of the Political Department of Whampoa Military Academy and had continued to discharge the duties of director of that department. At the time of my visit to Canton he was working with General Chiang Kai-shek throughout the Chao-chow Swatow area. He returned to Canton to meet me, and his conversation showed that he was optimistic about the future of Whampoa. He did not mention any differences with Borodin, who encouraged and helped him. Both advocated raising the status of General Chiang Kai-shek so that the Whampoa forces could develop more rapidly.

After the reorganization of the KMT in 1924, the first important measure seemed to be the establishment of the Whampoa Military Academy,[1] which provided the cradle for the Party Army. Dr. Sun Yat-sen at once designated General Chiang Kai-shek, who had visited the Soviet Union in 1923 to study military affairs, president of this academy. As this institution was preparing for its inauguration, Chiang Kai-shek, who had been appointed president, suddenly left Canton for Shanghai and indicated that he was resigning from the post. However, Tai Chi-t'ao hurried to Shanghai to persuade Chiang to change his mind, and only then did Chiang return to Canton to take over the post.[2]

During the first stage of his presidency of Whampoa, Chiang appeared to be very pro-Communist. Of the more than 460 students of the first class,[3] there were more than eighty members of the CCP and the CYC. At the time Chiang treated them on an equal footing. Chiang relied upon the Soviet instructors and gave them real authority in the school. CCP members filled most of the political instructorships and handled most of the political work. The Young Soldiers' Alliance, which was led by students that were CCP members, also had Chiang's support.

After its inauguration, the Whampoa Academy suffered from the oppression of various army units in Kwangtung. During the suppression of the revolt of the Merchant Corps, General Fan Shih-sheng, who had real power, had spoken to Chiang Kai-shek in an attitude of condescension, asking, "Isn't a Party Army being trained in Whampoa? Why isn't it called upon to fight?" It seemed that Fan had thought the newly established Party Army was small and could not fight; it also seemed that he would have liked to see the defeat of the Party Army, which would have provided him with a source of merriment. Actually the Party Army was victorious in suppressing the revolt. In September and October, 1924, arms taken from the Merchant Corps and arms shipped from Russia were both kept at the Whampoa arsenal. The commanders of the different armies had asked for the distribution of these arms among themselves, and it was even rumored that they planned to seize the arms by force. To prevent such an eventuality, Chiang had organized all the cadres in the school to keep a close guard on the arms. Because the financial resources of Canton were controlled by the different armies, Whampoa never had a sure source of income. Fortunately, Party representative Liao Chung-k'ai resorted to all kinds of measures to raise money; and although it was difficult, the Academy was able to maintain itself. These considerations caused the teachers and students at Whampoa to disregard the boundaries between the KMT and the CCP and to unite against outside influence, thus constituting an inner force that could not be bullied.

Unfortunately, this young, emerging force soon showed signs of incipient internal discord. Nieh Jung-chen, secretary of the Political Department at Whampoa, later told me that at the time of the First Eastern Expedition in the spring of 1924, the first model regiment of Whampoa had been organized barely three months. The strength of this regiment was only a little over one thousand men with no more than eight hundred rifles, and Ho Ying-ch'in served as regimental commander. The second model regiment had just been organized with no more than eight hundred men and no combat power to speak of. When the first model regiment engaged the superior forces of eight regiments from the division of Lin Hu under Ch'en Chiung-ming in the Huai-lai area,[4] it was immediately plunged into a desperate fight lasting a whole day. The second regiment, personally led by Chiang, was about sixty li from the front line; and it stayed there without advancing. General Galen saw the critical position at the front, and he repeatedly urged Chiang to take his force forward rapidly to give support. But Chiang did not take prompt action. At this time Chiang was concurrently chief-of-staff to Hsü Ts'ung-chih and commander-in-chief of the Kwangtung Army. Apparently Chiang expected Hsü's Kwangtung Army to proceed to the front and give support, thus avoiding the sacrifice of the second model regiment. General Galen believed that Chiang's refusal to give his aid was tantamount to exposing the first model regiment to the danger of complete annihilation.

Spiritedly and with many gestures, Nieh Jung-chen described the courageous experiences of the battle. The first model regiment fought for a whole day. General Galen and other Russian advisers, as well as the political workers whom Nieh led, joined in the fighting on the front.

Finally they broke through position after position to penetrate to the center held by Lin Hu, thus forcing the enemy to retreat toward Hsing-ning and Wu-hua at dusk. The first regiment was worn out, having suffered more than three hundred casualties, including the sacrifice of many cadres of the rank of platoon leader. Those who were left were tired and hungry and could hardly stand on their feet. At this point General Galen still displayed strength and energy all over his body, and with his resounding voice he addressed the force, calling on the men to rouse what was left of their courage and to ride on in victorious pursuit of their enemy. He shouted, "Long live the first model regiment!" and "Long live Regiment Commander Ho Ying-ch'in!" As Galen was talking, President Chiang arrived with the second regiment. Seeing Galen, he appeared embarrassed. General Galen not only refrained from giving a call of "Long live President Chiang," but instead he showed signs of displeasure. Then the forces marched through the night in pursuit of the enemy. Nieh Jung-chen believed that this incident not only left a scar on the relations between Chiang and Galen, but also cast the first shadow over the internal unity of Whampoa.

At that time our idea was not only to overthrow Yang and Liu, but more especially to ensure that no new successors would arise after their demise. At the same time we wanted to create a truly new situation in the Kwangtung government. Among the small number of us that knew the inside story, some favored the proposal of Galen for the building of a perfect military and political system. They did not want to permit a certain individual or a certain clique to control the core of power. We hoped to prevent trouble before it started. Most of us among the small group in the know, however, supported Borodin's view that the Whampoa influence had already built a foundation and would not change its quality midway. Further, we believed that should Whampoa lack support, all our efforts would prove to be in vain.

I had many discussions with Borodin over this matter. These discussions involved two major issues: the first was the readjustment of the Kwangtung leadership; the second was the reorganization of the National government after the liquidation of Yang and Liu.

On the first issue, Borodin proposed that the CC of the CCP move to Canton. He had never attached importance to the mass movement in the northern provinces, and so he considered that the CC of the CCP should concentrate its forces on work in Kwangtung. Furthermore he seemed to feel that the CCP Kwangtung District Committee was not his "opposite number." Therefore he felt that the discussion of policy and all secret political issues could only be carried on with the small number of people in the Central Committee. With this in mind he had tried to convince me of the importance of the work in Kwangtung and his reasons for optimism over its future. He intended to prove that after its removal to Canton, the CC of the CCP would not have to worry about relaxing its leadership over other provinces.

I told Borodin that under no circumstances would the CC of the CCP move to Canton, because we believed that work in the provinces other than Kwangtung was also important. Even in the development of Kwangtung itself, it was necessary to have effective support from the other provinces; and the CC should strive to gain this support. Furthermore, the CCP did not want its CC to be located at the same place as the CC of the KMT, in order to avoid friction in the leadership.

On the basis of the fact that the CC of the CCP could not be moved to Canton, I recommended that Borodin establish a system of joint leadership with the CCP Kwangtung District Committee. This would take the form of regular policy-making meetings between Borodin and the principal members of the Kwangtung District Committee, namely Ch'en Yen-nien, T'an P'ing-shan, and Chou En-lai; and the Kwangtung District Committee would report the decisions of such meetings to the CC. I believed that this would enable the Kwangtung District Committee to gain experience in overall leadership and thus become a leadership core in the midst of the complex situation in Kwangtung. It would also eliminate all avoidable misunderstandings between the CC of the CCP, Borodin, and the Kwangtung District Committee.

Ch'en Yen-nien and other members of the Kwangtung District Committee supported my view. Ch'en told me that in the past he had always had to call at Borodin's residence to acquire bits of political information and also that he and his colleagues did not like to show disrespect for Borodin's directives. The members of the CC of the CCP, on the other hand, often felt that they did not immediately receive the reports of conditions in Kwangtung and that there were actually things that they themselves did not know. If there were a regular political conference, such abuses would disappear.

Borodin attached importance to personal acumen. Although he verbally agreed to act as I suggested, he actually did not live up to his promise. He continued to act in a dictatorial manner. There were also relationships of cause and effect between his work style and his peculiar position. He was truly like the *ssu-pu-hsiang* (a legendary animal with horns like a stag, neck like a camel, hooves like an ox, and tail like a horse). Although he was neither the ambassador nor the special envoy of the Soviet Union to Canton, he was nevertheless the unofficial representative of the Soviet Union and could truly speak on behalf of the Soviet government. He was not a member of the KMT, but even though he was a foreign national and only a political adviser, his statements carried decisive weight. He was an important member of the Communist Party, but he would not accept direction from the representative of the Comintern in China. He exploited his position to deal suitably with all sides and to develop his personal influence. His relations with the CCP Kwangtung District Committee remained the same as they always had been. Not only did he fail to consult it before something happened, but after the event he would not tell the committee the full story. Even though he sometimes held meetings with Ch'en Yen-nien and others, he held them only to give necessary explanations of his own views.

Lenin had now been dead for a year and a half, and disputes between Stalin and Trotsky were getting sharper. Borodin often directly accepted instructions from Stalin, and this had important consequences for the Chinese revolution. Borodin could approach the highest authority, and Karakhan and the other Russians in China could exercise no control over him. He had no respect for the Comintern or the CC of the CCP. In everything he did in Kwangtung, Borodin always acted first and explained afterward. The CC of the CCP and its subsidiary organs merely coped with situations created by his political *faits accompli*.

Borodin did not want to discuss the problem of establishing the National government, and he pointed out to me that it could not be discussed at the time because of conflicting views within the KMT over the liquidation of Yang and Liu. Borodin believed that until this had been accomplished, discussion about establishing the National government could only give rise to internal dissension. Furthermore, he did not support the idea of having the CC of the CCP make advanced recommendations on this problem, since the decision would have to be made in the light of the situation existing after the liquidation of Yang and Liu.

Borodin did reveal to me, however, a little of the best of his thinking about the organization of the National government. When we talked of Hu Han-min, he shrugged his shoulders and smilingly said, "Hu Han-min? He has some faults. If we let him know anything, his followers would know about it, then the British would know about it, and every-thing would be messed up." These few comments of his showed that he had no confidence in Hu, and when an opportunity presented itself, he would certainly suppress Hu.

When we talked of Wang Ching-wei, he said that Wang could be consulted about things. He added that Wang's work style had remained as humble as it was in Peking and that Wang would not suddenly take drastic action. If Wang could be induced to assume responsibility, he would not retreat. When we talked of Liao Chung-k'ai, he sighed and said, "It is a pity that there are so few people that are as efficient as he is who will take up concrete tasks." He also pointed out that Liao wanted to do practical work but was reluctant to assume the title of leadership.

These statements of Borodin's concerning personnel matters indi-cated the outline of his thinking about the National government, and the facts were to prove this later. Borodin and I went on to discuss a pos-sible manifesto of the government and what its major administrative policies should be. On these points Borodin seemed to be somewhat at a loss. Perhaps at the time he had adopted the attitude of dealing only with things as they came up.

He affirmed his support of the committee system for the National government, but he also pointed out that the committee system had both advantages and disadvantages. If the committee lacked a central focus and strong support, it could not accomplish anything. This indicated that Borodin did not believe in the democratic and united-front ideas being applied to a committee. He seemed to be bent on planning for a central control that he could lead and further expand. He believed that the real strength should be in Whampoa and that it could be used to establish a "revolutionary dictatorship."

I had pointed out to him that according to Dr. Sun's *Fundamentals of National Reconstruction,* the country would be ruled by the KMT and that according to Dr. Sun's "Manifesto on Proceeding to North China" and his will, a national assembly would be called. In consideration of these facts, the CC of the CCP would support the building of the National government on the foundation of the national assembly. I also reminded Borodin that the CC of the CCP considered it important to win over the Middle-of-the-Road clique within the KMT and that the committee looked upon Hu Han-min as the representative of this clique. We did want to know if Hu was sincere in opposing imperialism and in struggling for the independence and freedom of China. We did not want to be too adamant in demanding that he completely support our policy of alliance with Russia and toleration of the Communists.

Borodin also considered these problems very important, but he insisted that they should be decided after the liquidation of Yang and Liu. Borodin wanted me to stay longer in Canton so that we could consult from time to time. I agreed; but later, because of the execution of Ku Cheng-hung, I found it necessary to hurry back to Shanghai. Therefore, although I knew in advance the general outlines of Borodin's master plan for establishment of the National government, I was not able to participate in the establishment directly. The CC of the CCP was busy directing the May Thirtieth Movement and had not expressed an opinion on the important issue of the establishment of the National government; so everything was in Borodin's hands.

The Disintegration of the Revolutionary Camp

After the establishment of the National government, an important conflict occurred within the KMT. The Western Hills Conference clique, which opposed the leadership of the Canton government, had evolved by this time. In order to lessen the effect on the national revolution of this crisis which was brought about by the conflict within the KMT, the CC of the CCP proposed winning over the Middle-of-the-Road clique of the KMT in order to isolate the rightists. We also felt that the base of the National government should be broadened. This policy came into conflict with the so-called revolutionary dictatorship of Borodin.

After I returned to Shanghai from Canton, I reported to the CC of the CCP on the situation in Kwangtung as I had observed it and on my talks with Borodin. I told them that before I left Canton, Borodin had indicated that since the CC of the CCP could not be moved to Canton and since I had to return to Shanghai at once, the only thing for us to do was to have confidence in his dealing with everything and have confidence that he would consult with the Kwangtung District Committee, as occasion demanded. At this time the CC of the CCP was devoting its full energy to coping with the May Thirtieth Movement; consequently it did not discuss my report in detail, and it was shelved.

Ch'en Tu-hsiu, who was very familiar with the internal situation of the KMT, expressed some of his concerns. He thought that Hu Han-min was the representative figure of the Middle clique—the traditional line of the KMT—and that Hu's influence inside the Party was very deep-rooted. Wang Ching-wei, although he had a good reputation, was rather weak and had no real power. If Hu was forcibly dragged down from his position of acting generalissimo, there would be trouble. However, since Borodin had not clearly stated his position at the time, Ch'en refrained from publicizing his opinion.

Early in June, 1925, the Kwangtung Army, led by Hsü Ts'ung-chih, and the Whampoa Party Army, led by Chiang Kai-shek, returned to Canton. On June 13 they liquidated Yang Hsi-min and Liu Chen-huan, who constituted the most serious menace to them. It was reported that the war had been carried out very smoothly, without casualties or any serious damage being suffered. Some reports even said that this was due to the Russian adviser personally firing some volleys at the headquarters of Yang and Liu, thus routing and destroying the enemy forces.

On June 19 the workers at Hong Kong and Shameen in Canton started to strike in support of the May Thirtieth Incident in Shanghai. On June 23 the famous Shakee tragedy occurred. This incident shook the whole country and tended to turn the revolutionary spirit in Canton further to the Left. The CC of the CCP tried all the harder to mobilize the anti-imperialist forces of the whole nation in support of Kwangtung.

On July 1, 1925, in the midst of the wave of anti-imperialism over the whole country, the establishment of the National government was quietly announced. The CC of the CCP learned of this important news in the newspapers. The National Government Council[5] was organized in accordance with the decision of the KMT Central Political Council. Wang Ching-wei was chairman. Hu Han-min was demoted from acting generalissimo to minister of foreign affairs and had nothing to do. Some of us who were leaders of the CC of the CCP thought that this National government was only temporary in nature. We believed the official National government should be born out of a national assembly. In our despair we seemed to be attempting to minimize the importance of the incident.

The KMT personalities in Shanghai very rapidly pressed different views on the reorganization of the National government. At first they all declared their ignorance of the inside facts in Kwangtung. Later they found that appointments of members to the National Government Council (or State Council) had been made by the political council and had not been submitted to the CEC for ratification. News of opposition to this by such persons as Tsou Lu and Teng Tse-ju reached Shanghai, and then there were discussions at which varying views were expressed. Tai Chi-t'ao, for instance, held that the demotion of Hu Han-min was something that could and should have been avoided.

At this time, the KMT's public-relations system lacked efficiency. Most of the events in Kwangtung were not adequately reported. To add to this difficulty, the strike in Canton and Hong Kong interrupted communications between the two ports and caused a scarcity in direct shipping services from Canton to Shanghai. So news from Canton was generally disseminated through foreign news agencies, and most of the reports were naturally unfavorable to the Canton authorities. The CC of the CCP was also depressed over the lack of accurate reports on Kwangtung.

The first item of bad news that we received from Kwangtung concerned the transfer of General Galen away from the area. He was the military pillar of Kwangtung, having contributed exceptionally meritorious services. On the basis of my report, the CC of the CCP felt that the transfer of Galen must have been due to differences of opinion between him and Borodin. Chang T'ai-lei told me later that the real reason for Galen's transfer was that he was in favor of appointing Hsü Ts'ung-chih as the military head and of establishing a military council. Borodin, on the other hand, supported Chiang Kai-shek. The matter had to be arbitrated by Moscow, and Galen's view was rejected.

After these events, the Sun Wen-chu-i Hsüeh-hui (Sunyatsenist Society) was formed at the Whampoa Academy. According to the report of the Kwangtung District Committee, this society was opposed to the Young Soldiers' Alliance led by members of the CCP. Most of the members of this new society were rightist students, such as Tseng Kuang-ching and Ho Chung-han of the first class. Kan Nai-kuang and others among the instructors helped in planning the Society, which had already been approved by Wang Ching-wei and Liao Chung-k'ai.

This particular development alarmed us greatly. We believed that there were some mistakes that could not be overlooked in the work that was being done in Kwangtung. At a meeting of the CC of the CCP, some members pointed out that both Wang and Liao were noted leftists and that it was difficult to see how they could agree to the organization of the Sunyatsenist Society, which was opposed to the Chinese Communists. Perhaps the affairs of the Young Soldiers' Alliance were being monopolized by members of the CCP, who took every opportunity to show off, thus arousing the jealousy of the KMT members and causing such pro-CCP leaders as Wang and Liao to permit the formation of a new organization.

The assassination of Liao Chung-k'ai on August 20 shocked the entire revolutionary camp. The CC of the CCP believed that it was clearly a plot of the rightists to overthrow the National government and that it indicated a crisis in the Canton situation; therefore the committee advocated severe suppression of those responsible. After analyzing the situation, the CC of the CCP concluded that Liao was the really central figure of the KMT Left. He was the one who could unite with Wang, Chiang, and others. Among Party members, military men, the general public, and the various people's organizations Liao enjoyed high prestige. These reasons must have led the rightists to select Liao for assassination. His assassination would remove the thorn in their flesh and the center of support for the alliance with Russia and the tolerance of Communists. The removal of Liao would seriously undermine KMT-CCP cooperation and the National government. In considering these factors, we felt that only measures of suppression could check the continuation of sabotage efforts by the rightists and that the most fundamental need was still to unite all possible forces within the KMT. Before the revolutionary front could be consolidated, we felt that it was necessary to isolate the rightists so that they could not cause any more trouble.

At Borodin's suggestion, the National government organized a special committee, with Wang Ching-wei, Hsü Ts'ung-chih, and Chiang Kai-shek as members, to handle the Liao case. From that time on, the people that were currently the most powerful in the Kwangtung government were transferred from the Central Political Council of the KMT to this Special Committee.[6] Hu Han-min's cousin Hu I-sheng and his confidantes Lin Shih-mien and Chu Chuo-wen were all involved as suspects in the Liao case. Lin Shih-mien was arrested. Hu Han-min himself was under house arrest at Whampoa. Soon afterward, on October 2, Hu was sent to the Soviet Union on a mission of investigation; this was tantamount to exile.

In September of 1924 the troops of Ch'eng Jun-chi and Mo Hsiung, subordinates of Hsü Ts'ung-chih, were suspected of conspiring with Ch'en Chiung-ming in an attempted revolt. Therefore, on September 20 Chiang sent troops to surround their forces and disarm them. Hsü himself resigned on September 23 and left Canton. So the Special Committee became a duo composed of Wang and Chiang.

Because of the lack of reports from the Kwangtung District Committee, the CC of the CCP at first did not know in detail about the inner circumstances surrounding these important changes. We felt that a thick mist surrounded the Kwangtung situation. KMT elements in Shanghai freely circulated reports that these acts were perpetrated by the CCP to undermine the KMT. There were also rumors that the Canton and Hong Kong Strike Committee had become the second government and that communism would immediately be enforced in Canton. The CC of the CCP was depressed over its inability to put forth facts that would refute the rumors.

It was not until late September, when the decision had definitely been made to send Hu Han-min to the Soviet Union, that the CC of the CCP received a simple communication from Borodin. It explained the necessity for having Hu leave Canton so that the political situation in Kwangtung might be stabilized. It also said that he had been given the status of representative of the KMT to the congress of the Comintern in Moscow. Borodin had hoped that the Comintern would have Hu remain in Russia and not permit him to return to China. When we read this communication, we felt that Borodin's primary intention was clear: he was requesting that the CC of the CCP express to the Comintern its support of Borodin's proposal.

This matter had greatly taxed Voitinsky's mind. At a meeting of the CC of the CCP he had expressed the opinion that if Hu Han-min was truly the instigator of the plot to kill Liao, he should be punished in Canton according to law. If Hu was not punished, at least his plot should be publicized to expose his true self. Otherwise, if Hu was not responsible, he should not have been under house arrest. Borodin even agreed to send this dispatch to Moscow. This would give the Comintern a difficult problem to deal with.

The report from the Kwangtung District Committee, which described conditions in Kwangtung, agreed with Borodin in calling the "Wang-Chiang cooperation" situation a "revolutionary dictatorship." This report also mentioned that the rightist forces were still very strong. The pamphlet by Tai Chi-t'ao entitled *The Nationalist Revolution and the Chinese Nationalist Party* enjoyed wide circulation in Whampoa and among the KMT members. It wielded great influence and seemed to develop a new Right clique. The Kwangtung District Committee rejected the idea that a large Middle clique existed in the KMT and affirmed the belief that the CCP only needed to unite with the KMT leftists to promote the development of the revolution toward the Left.

These views of Borodin and the Kwangtung District Committee aroused a fierce reaction from Ch'en Tu-hsiu. He felt that the comrades in Kwangtung had underestimated the strength of the entire anti-Communist camp. They lived off in a corner in Canton and attempted to use a small part of the revolutionary military force—the more than 100,000 strikers in Canton and Hong Kong and the more than 200,000 organized peasants—to oppose the entire imperialist camp, the northern warlords, and the anti-Communist forces in general. This clearly committed the error of underestimating the strength of the enemy.

So a discussion on the Kwangtung problem developed in the CC of the CCP. Some members of our committee cynically referred to the theory of "revolutionary dictatorship" as self-deception that was divorced from the class viewpoint. Some asked how talk about "revolutionary dictatorship" could be realistic when it was not even possible to deal with Hu Han-min without seeking the help of the Comintern. Others said that if under the name of "revolutionary dictatorship," the Soviet Union's work-style of proletarian dictatorship were confused with the Chinese ideas of emperor and king and the arrogance of militarists, it would be a mess.

As a result of these discussions the CC of the CCP decided that no matter what happened in Kwangtung, it was essential that the national revolution have a broad, nationwide front. This meant that we could not discard the strategy of the united front or cooperation with the Middle clique of the KMT. The policy of the united front could not be changed because of certain setbacks in the May Thirtieth Movement or because of the incidents in Canton. In fact, the committee believed that emphasis on the revolutionary dictatorship would de-emphasize the role of the united front and that the ability of the leftists in Kwangtung to consolidate their leadership hinged on their ability to promote the united front.

In this way, there emerged a serious divergence of views between the CC of the CCP and the comrades in Kwangtung. In October the CC of the CCP held an enlarged plenum in Peking, which I was unable to attend due to pressure of duties demanding my presence in Shanghai. Party membership had reached 10,000, so the meeting emphasized the independent development of the CCP. To avoid more serious friction between the KMT and the CCP and to preserve the political individuality of the CCP, Ch'en Tu-hsiu proposed that the CCP withdraw from the KMT at the appropriate moment.[7] Although the majority of members present opposed this proposal, it was indeed like the first falling leaf, which heralds autumn. It had become inevitable that the course of KMT-CCP cooperation was to be strewn with thorns and rushes. The meeting also criticized the Kwangtung District Committee for its neglect of independent CCP development and for substituting itself for the KMT leftists, a situation that had to be rectified.

During this period the internal disintegration of the KMT had also become evident. On November 23 members of the KMT's first Central Executive and Supervisory committees—Chang Chi, Hsieh Ch'ih, Lin Shen, Chü Cheng, Tsou Lu, and others—held a meeting at Western Hills, Peking, to form the Western Hills Conference clique. Claiming support of the majority of the Central Executive and Supervisory committees, they made the following decisions: (1) to cancel KMT membership for members of the CCP; (2) to dismiss adviser Borodin; (3) to expel Wang Ching-wei from the KMT; (4) to determine the KMT's future attitude toward the Soviet Union; (5) to dismiss Communists, such as Li Ta-chao, from the CEC; (6) to abolish the Political Council; and (7) to transfer the CEC of the KMT to Shanghai.

Before the Western Hills Conference was held, the CEC of the KMT at Canton had already notified the whole country that the Second Congress would be held in January, 1926. The meeting at Western Hills, therefore, appeared to be a deliberate move in opposition to the Canton congress. The slogan "alliance with Chiang to overthrow Wang" that was circulated by these people and the views expressed by *Min-kuo Jih-pao* (Republican Daily News), the Shanghai organ of the KMT, both advocated raising Chiang and suppressing Wang. Perhaps these were aimed at breaking up the Wang-Chiang alliance.

Sensing the seriousness of the situation, the CC of the CCP immediately discussed ways of saving it. On the basis of what we knew, we felt that the activities of the Western Hills Conference clique would lead to a complete split in the KMT, and the situation in Canton might collapse as a result. We analyzed the make-up of the Western Hills clique and felt that it included certain middle-of-the-road persons who would not want to see the destruction of the Canton revolutionary structure. So we decided to adopt concrete measures to break up the Western Hills clique.

On the initiative of Ch'en Tu-hsiu and with the assistance of Voitinsky, we arranged a meeting with Sun Fo, Yeh Ch'u-ts'ang, and Shao

Yuan-ch'ung at the Russian consulate, which was beside the Bund Bridge at Shanghai. These three men were to greater or lesser degrees connected with the Western Hills clique, and we looked upon them as representative figures of the KMT Middle clique. The CCP's position was represented by Ch'en Tu-hsiu, Ts'ai Ho-sen, and myself. We planned to discuss problems of KMT-CCP relations at the meeting, which could be called a conference of parity.

At nine o'clock that morning, the six of us arrived and were seated in the reception room on the ground floor of the consulate. The staff of the consulate did not appear to pay any attention to our meeting, much less did any of them participate in it. We seemed merely to be guests using their space. When we met, we seemed our usual selves and exchanged greetings, although there was some solemnity in the atmosphere. None of us talked about what had happened in Canton, Shanghai, and Western Hills, and everyone avoided words that would cause strain and lead to disputes.

When the meeting started, Ch'en Tu-hsiu was the first to speak. He said that the CCP had no intention of monopolizing the affairs of the KMT, but that it actually opposed such an attempt. The CC of the CCP had notified its branch headquarters in various localities to elect more members of the KMT as delegates to the Second Congress. The CCP did not hope for an increase in the number of CCP members on the KMT central committees that would be elected at the Congress. The CCP advocated that KMT members should hold responsibility for the affairs of the KMT. As to the situation in Kwangtung, Ch'en said that the facts were not as rumored outside, to the effect that certain elements would be excluded from participation. The responsible authorities in Kwangtung had hoped that the various leaders would be unanimous in joining them to shoulder the numerous responsibilities of the KMT central committees and the National government. After expressing these views, Ch'en asked the KMT representatives what their intentions were.

After hearing Ch'en's words, Sun Fo, Yeh Ch'u-ts'ang, and Shao Yuan-ch'ung, one after another, issued simple statements. Principally they expressed their love and concern for everything in Kwangtung, and they said that as long as the situation permitted, they would go there to attend the Congress.

The attitude of both sides enabled us to talk earnestly and to exchange explanations. The result was a seven-point agreement. The contents were briefly these: a call for unity and, under the Three Principles of the People of Dr. Sun and the established policies of the reorganized KMT, support by all for the CEC of the KMT in Canton and the National government led by it; agreement that the CCP would make the national revolution its main task and would continue to work cooperatively with the KMT, but that it would not try to monopolize KMT affairs or exclude the faithful members of the KMT. The atmosphere of the meeting was relaxed, and the agreement on the seven points was signed by everyone on both sides. Both sides agreed that specific problems should be resolved by the Second Congress of the KMT. In order to avoid further complications, neither side wanted to discuss them in detail.

This agreement reaped beneficial results. Though some of the diehards of the Western Hills clique condemned it as a "compromise with the CCP," most KMT members changed their tune as a result of it. They no longer pressed the point that the Canton government was enforcing communism and that it was being monopolized by the Communists. Instead they asked for unity in order to preserve the Canton revolutionary situation. This change of tune appeared to check the attempts of the Western Hills clique to split the KMT.

The CC of the CCP implemented the agreement faithfully, and it repeatedly used this guideline to warn its members. The CC decided to send me to Canton as its representative to the Second KMT Congress to help guide the activities of the Party and the CYC and to make a strenuous attempt to correct past deviations. Voitinsky consistently supported this new policy of working hard for the independent development of the CCP and of interfering less in the internal affairs of the KMT. To prevent the split of the KMT, the Comintern also supported this policy.

KMT-CCP relations had always worried the CC of the CCP. At meetings of the CC of the CCP, this problem was studied from various angles, and often we felt that there was difficulty in either advance or retreat. Ch'ü Ch'iu-pai sometimes pointed out that the Comintern would not abandon the policy of the CCP joining the KMT and therefore that Borodin could not be taken to task for acting under such a guideline. Borodin himself was not optimistic about future developments. The majority of us felt that this fundamental policy of joining the KMT brought more harm than good. We felt that we should promote two-party cooperation outside the KMT; however, this was not permitted by the Comintern.

Before I was sent to Canton to transmit the views of the CC, I had explained at a meeting of the Committee that its decision could not completely convince the comrades in Kwangtung. If the policy of two-party cooperation outside the KMT were implemented, we would have to withdraw from the KMT. We had to solve this problem. On the basis of the Comintern's views, Voitinsky held that the CCP should remain within the KMT and unite with all forces possible. Naturally I did not want to have a dispute with the Comintern; and since there was not enough time for us to make a fundamental change in policy, we accepted Voitinsky's views. Thus the policy of the CC of the CCP differed from Borodin's only in degree. In the matter of KMT-CCP relations, we were put in a defensive position and could only let the power-wielding clique in the KMT solve the problem by forceful methods.

The Second National Congress of the Kuomintang

The Second National Congress of the KMT, which met in January, 1926, overflowed with leftist tendencies that gave people cause for optimism; nevertheless it neglected the solution of practical issues. This was characteristic of the leadership style of Wang Ching-wei, but it also resulted from the lack of unanimity in the views of the three sides, namely the CC of the CCP, Borodin, and Wang Ching-wei. It was impossible for these three to achieve a suitable compromise. Here I shall stress the important points of divergence in the views of the different sides at the time of the Congress.

In mid-December, 1925, I took a boat directly from Shanghai to Canton, by-passing Hong Kong (because of the Canton and Hong Kong Strike, Shanghai vessels did not stop at Hong Kong). When I reached Canton, I had an earnest talk with Borodin to get his opinions. He had been partially informed of events in Shanghai and showed signs of dissatisfaction. I told him of the decision of the CC of the CCP regarding the policy about Canton and of our talks with Sun Fo and other representatives of the KMT Middle clique. I also expressed the view of the CC of the CCP, and of myself, that we should talk things over with him first. If he supported our decisions and if he agreed that it was desirable to revise the existing policy about Canton, he could take the initiative. I myself did not want to express any opinions publicly that might cause people to think that differences existed between us.

After listening to my report, Borodin expressed his strong reaction toward the policy of the CC of the CCP. He said that during the preceding half year Kwangtung had gone through a difficult struggle. Had he and the comrades in Canton not adopted a series of emergency measures, the revolutionary movement might long since have been destroyed. Then he asked, "After expelling the KMT rightists that plotted to sabotage the revolution, why should Kwangtung now invite them back?" Borodin asked me to let him consider my proposal for a few days before having another discussion. He did show gratification over my thoughtfulness in consulting him first.

Though Borodin did not agree with the policy of the CC of the CCP and the actions based on it, he seemed to sense that they had the support of Voitinsky and possibly of the Comintern. He therefore felt that my proposals could not simply be ignored. He indicated that he would have to find out first what the intentions of Moscow and Karakhan were before he could make any definite statements. He expressed regret that he had failed in the past to report fully to the CC of the CCP about conditions in Kwangtung, thus causing misunderstanding. He also admitted that foreign propaganda and reporting procedures had not been either adequate or effective. I said that since I needed a little time to observe the actual conditions in Kwangtung, delaying our detailed discussion a few days would not matter.

Many changes were taking place in the Kwangtung situation, and it was not an easy task to get an overall picture in a few days. The accounts told to me by responsible members of the Kwangtung District Committee were mostly optimistic, but they did reveal certain inherent dangers. The main points of their information follow.

The assassination of Liao Chung-k'ai on August 20, 1925, was the signal for the bloody struggle between the revolutionaries and the counterrevolutionaries. CCP comrades in Canton felt that there were three principal factors to the Liao case: the first was the fight between the pro-Communist and the anti-Communist elements; the second was the struggle for power within the KMT; and the third was the lack of modern democratic methods. The methods used in political struggle were so backward that assassination was invariably used to deal with opponents.

To be more specific, the assassination of Liao had placed great suspicion on the Hu Han-min clique. In mid-June, Yang and Liu were liquidated; and on July 1 the National government was formed and Hu Han-min lost power. At the time, Liao Chung-k'ai played the role of Liang-shan (in the novel *All Men Are Brothers*), and was the person most responsible for the replacement of Hu Han-min by Wang Ching-wei. Liao was a bulwark in the government and had close relations with Borodin and CCP elements. In his rigid enforcement of the policy of unified finances, Liao had attacked certain rightist bureaucrats related to Hu. Many CCP comrades believed that Hu Han-min and his confidantes were still important figures in the government; and in view of the Shakee tragedy, all wanted a united stand against outside forces. It was therefore unpardonable for Hu to cause the death of an old comrade-in-arms and to shake the foundation of the Kwangtung government.

Members of the District Committee described the sudden emergence of a state of terror in Canton after the Liao incident. All of the important personages in the city except for T'an P'ing-shan and Su Chao-cheng, who continued to appear in public as usual, felt that they were in danger. Wang Ching-wei had advised T'an P'ing-shan to be careful. Borodin remained calm and proposed the organization of the three-man Special Committee.[8] Only then did the situation become stabilized. The subsequent dispatching of Hu Han-min to Russia was in keeping with the traditional face-saving policy of the KMT.

With regard to the disarming of the trooops under Hsü Ts'ung-chih, it was reported that the Hsü elements were complex in nature and that the senior officers often wavered. It was true that some had ideas of warlordism and that some were close to the Hu clique, but it was not true that they had colluded with Ch'en Chiung-ming. It was also reported that the trouble had been caused by the newly risen General Chiang Kai-shek, who wanted to expand his influence and have Hsü's subordinates transferred to his own control, thus consolidating his position of military leadership.

In October, due to military successes, the Canton situation became more stabilized. The troops of Ch'en Chiung-ming, who occupied the Hui-chou area on the East River, were marching on Canton. In southern Kwangtung the troops under Teng Pen-yin were attacking Kongmoon near Canton. Chung-shan County was occupied by native bandits under Yüan Tai. These military attacks by counterrevolutionaries attempting to overthrow the National government seemed to have the support of Hong Kong. The Hong Kong authorities were employing the tactic of "using Chinese to harass the Chinese" in dealing with the situation in Canton, which was the center of anti-British feeling. General Chiang Kai-shek took his army on another eastern expedition to wipe out the troops of Ch'en Chiung-ming. The troops under Chu P'ei-te, Li Chi-shen, and Ch'en Ming-shu wiped out the revolts started by Teng Pen-yin and Yüan Tai. The troops of Hsiung K'o-wu, who were in collusion with Ch'en Chiung-ming, were also disarmed by T'an Yen-k'ai and Chu P'ei-te. With the exception of Hainan Island, where there were remnants of the Teng Pen-yin army, Kwangtung was more or less unified by these military victories.

This was the first time that the province of Kwangtung had been unified; the people were all exhilarated. Many KMT members optimistically reported to me that the armies in Kwangtung had been organized into the six armies of the National Revolutionary Army, all under the direction of a military council. Thus there was considerable military unification, and the orders of the National government were effective throughout the province. Revenue receipts were increasing daily, and there were many gains in the field of foreign affairs. It could be said that the National government had been firmly established. The CCP comrades in Canton also praised these achievements, feeling that the worker and peasant masses led by the CCP had made great contributions to the unification of Kwangtung. Furthermore, they believed that this success was the result of Borodin's policies.

During this period of expansion in the national revolution, the path of KMT-CCP relations continued to be strewn with thorns. The most conspicuous conflict within Whampoa was between the Young Soldiers' Alliance and the Sunyatsenist Society. Most of the Whampoa students that were members of the Young Soldiers' Alliance were political workers, most of their leaders were members of the CCP, and many of their members were leftists that sympathized with the CCP.

Most of the officers of the Sunyatsenist Society were members of the KMT, and most of its leaders openly expressed their anti-Communist stand. They also developed their organization outside Whampoa. The Sunyatsenist Society in Canton University, for example, called itself the "stick party." It obviously wanted to resort to physical means in combatting Communist elements.

Ch'en Yen-nien felt that the organization and expansion of the Sunyatsenist Society was directly related to defects in the work of the Young Soldiers' Alliance. He told me that the Young Soldiers' Alliance had Chiang's support and that it wanted to include the entire Whampoa student body, so that it could deal with the old-type military men outside Whampoa. Later, under the leadership of CCP members, the Alliance committed leftist deviations, thus causing restrictions to be placed on the admission of members. Some Whampoa students did not seek membership, and some that applied for admission never obtained approval. This aroused the reaction of some students that were KMT members. Ch'en thought that the excessive arrogance of the Sunyatsenist Society showed that it had the secret support of President Chiang.

Tai Chi-t'ao's pamphlet *The Nationalist Revolution and the Chinese Nationalist Party* appeared to be the classic text for the Sunyatsenist Society. Ch'en Yen-nien told me that the pamphlet had been translated into English and sent to Borodin, who indicated that Tai Chi-t'ao's statement on the position of the KMT could not be challenged. Borodin said that he could cope with everything but the KMT-CCP disputes, which he admitted were utterly beyond him. Ch'en Yen-nien condemned Tai Chi-t'ao and the Sunyatsenist Society as the new rightists, but he did not go further and try to seek a solution to the problem.

I could not help being somewhat irked by what Ch'en Yen-nien said. I pointed out that Borodin's assertion was utter nonsense. If he had no way of resolving the KMT-CCP dispute, he had no way of dealing with any problem. I countered with a question: "By avoiding direct discussion of this issue, is Borodin indicating that he has lost confidence in the Comintern's policy of merging the KMT and the CCP into a single body?" Ch'en Yen-nien remained silent and seemed unwilling to discuss this point; but we both realized that means must be devised to untie this knotty problem.

A second problem was connected with the activities of the Canton–Hong Kong Strike Committee, led by the CCP, which caused many people to look askance. The Strike Committee was a colossal organization with an imposing front. Strikers by the tens of thousands were assembled in public buildings and in former opium dens and gambling joints that had been closed. In addition to such usual structures as the Secretary's Bureau, the Committee maintained a Trial Office. The Trial Office determined the adjustment of such cases as the sabotage of the strike, smuggling of food to supply Hong Kong, and the secret sale of enemy goods. A jail was maintained for detaining criminals, and there was even an auction room for the disposal of enemy goods. The Picket Corps, which was organized by the Committee to furnish both land and sea preventive service, had more than two thousand members, with more than four hundred rifles and twelve boats. They were distributed in different ports to implement the blockade of Hong Kong. In addition there were such structures as the Law Codification Bureau and the Road Building Committee. Such an elaborate organization naturally usurped the authority of the government in many ways.

I discussed this problem with comrades in Canton in relation to the policies decided by the CC of the CCP. The demands that the Canton and Hong Kong Strike Committee were presenting to Hong Kong were divided into two major sections. The first section consisted of support for the seventeen conditions that had been presented by the Shanghai Federation of Workers', Merchants', and Students' Organizations after the Shanghai incident. The second section dealt directly with six demands of Hong Kong, namely (1) political freedom, (2) equality before the law, (3) popular elections, (4) labor legislation, (5) reduction of house rents, and (6) freedom of residence.[9] I pointed out that it was essential to take into account the changes in the situation and to reduce these demands. I emphasized the importance of consulting with the Hong Kong authorities on a settlement that might end the strike promptly. If the strike were ended, the organization of the Strike Committee would no longer be necessary. This would automatically nullify the charge that it was "the second government."

Su Chao-cheng, chairman of the Strike Committee, and Teng Chung-hsia, along with other CCP leaders in control of the committee, supported my proposal. They said, however, that Hong Kong authorities had consistently failed to give a clear indication of their attitude toward negotiating for a settlement. If the Hong Kong authorities would demonstrate their sincerity by agreeing to a consultation, the Committee was prepared to make certain concessions regarding the conditions of settlement.

The committee members pointed out some important results of the Canton–Hong Kong Strike and the blockade of the ports by the workers' pickets. Hong Kong had suffered great economic loss, which resulted in the loss of foreign support to the rebels in Kwangtung. The strikers also participated in suppressing internal traitors and counterrevolutionaries that supported the military operations; and with their cooperation the smuggling was stopped, and the revolutionary government at Canton became more stable. For these reasons the National government felt that the strike was beneficial. Although those opposed to the strike complained about the excessive authority wielded by the Strike Committee, they did not deny that it had made a contribution to the revolution. Because they had received large donations from the government and private organizations, the strikers were able to maintain relatively stable living standards. However, the economic blockade of Hong Kong led to the lack of foreign supplies in Canton and the surrounding areas. Some localities were considerably inconvenienced, and the merchants suffered some losses. The agricultural produce of the peasants could not be marketed. These conditions caused more reactions.

Consequently, early in September, the "special license" system was enforced, stipulating that "all vessels and all cargoes that are not of British origin, are not carried on British vessels, and are not passing through Hong Kong will be permitted to sail directly to Canton."[10] Such special licenses were issued over the joint signatures of the Foreign Ministry of the National government, the Department of Commerce of the Kwangtung provincial government, and the Public Security Bureau. With the enforcement of this system, American and Japanese vessels started to request licenses for direct sailings to Canton. As a result, shipping services between Shanghai and Canton and between Canton and Siam were gradually resumed. More than forty vessels entered and left the Canton waters each day. This measure achieved great results in the "isolation of Hong Kong," the "increase of revenue," the "alliance between industry and trade," the "alliance between workers and peasants," and the "stabilization of the people's minds."

A third problem concerned disputes between the peasant associations and the local governments and landlords. In the course of their development, the peasant associations often had disputes with landlords over the reduction of rent, reduction of interest, and certain other economic problems. Most important were the armed conflicts between the peasants' self-defense corps of the peasant associations and the militia corps led by the landlords of various counties. Such conflicts were reported every day. Either the peasant self-defense corps surrounded the fortresses of the landlords, or the militia corps killed and injured the responsible persons of the peasant associations. In dealing with these disputes, the various county governments usually sided with the landlords and often castigated the peasant associations for attempting to constitute a second government and for usurping the authority of the county governments.

The Commissioner of Civil Affairs of Kwangtung Province, Ku

Ying-fen, both openly and secretly supported the landlords and militia corps of the different counties. The CCP comrades in Kwangtung looked upon him as the thorn in their flesh and felt that unless the rightist Ku Ying-fen was removed, the peasants could never stand on their own feet. But Chang T'ai-lei told me that lately Borodin had become crafty and did not interfere with Ku Ying-fen's support of the reactionaries. Chang T'ai-lei felt that if Borodin did not speak up, the rural problem could not be settled. However, Borodin, not wanting to become involved in this argument, seemed incapable of speaking up. As a result, since the National government did not have an established rural policy, the various villages became the focal points of contention between the forces of the two sides.

After learning these facts, I made an appointment with Borodin for a few days later to discuss our differences of opinion. By that time Borodin seemed to have received a reply from Moscow, and he was ready to state his views. He took the initiative and called Ch'en Yen-nien, other major responsible members of the Kwangtung District Committee, and myself to a conference.

At the conference Borodin spoke first. Optimistically he described the situation in Kwangtung as being stabilized. Touching on foreign relations, he pointed out that due to the close-knit organization of the Strike Committee, all plots of sabotage on the part of Hong Kong authorities had been unsuccessful. He anticipated that the Hong Kong authorities would very soon negotiate with the Canton authorities for the settlement of the strike. There was the immediate possibility that normal relations between the two would be restored. As for the United States and Japan, their merchant vessels had sailed directly to Canton for some time and were carrying on normal trade. Furthermore, Japan had started to talk with the National government about resuming development of the Tien-tu iron mine on Hainan Island. The National government was prepared to permit this development. On the basis of these conditions, he pointed out that the Powers could not help but recognize the fact that the National government had been stabilized.

When it came to the internal situation of Kwangtung, he held that Kwangtung was unified and that no internal revolt was pending. Wang-Chiang cooperation could not suffer from outside interference. The Kwangsi militarists were improving their relations with the National government, and there were hopes that Kwangsi would become another province under the jurisdiction of the National government. There were no military powers around Kwangtung that could endanger its safety. The revenue of Kwangtung was increasing each month, and there were hopes of even greater increases. He hoped that on this stable foundation smooth progress could be made in reorganizing civil affairs and training the different armies.

On the basis of this optimism, Borodin held that the KMT leftists and the CCP should continue to attack the rightist forces, so that the Kwangtung situation would become even more stable. There should definitely be no withdrawal, because a policy of withdrawal would only confuse our own policies and encourage the rightists. Borodin condemned the policy of the CC of the CCP of "uniting with the leftists, establishing ties with the Middle clique, and attacking the rightists." He called it a stereotyped formula, and he explained that the KMT Left clique was considered weak and that it was necessary for the Left clique and the CCP to merge into a single unit in order to constitute a strong force. Although he admitted that the wavering Middle clique constituted the majority, he opposed using the formula of "making concessions to the rightists" in order to forge ties with the Middle clique. Borodin advocated forcing the Middle clique to follow the Left clique and then forcing both into unconditional support of the National government and the KMT Middle clique. He ridiculed the CC of the CCP's agreement with Sun Fo, Yeh Ch'u-ts'ang, and Shao Yuan-ch'ung as an appeasement policy that was undesirable.

Borodin went further and called on the CCP comrades in Canton to resist the decision of the higher authority. He said that they should not obey the decisions of the CC of the CCP without questioning them. The responsible members of the Kwangtung District Committee, on the basis of their true understanding of Kwangtung conditions, could bring forward views for the revision of such decisions.

I felt that the address of Borodin had many loopholes, so I immediately stood up to answer him. I first admitted that the Kwangtung situation had been stabilized. I also said that the CC of the CCP did not disregard the contributions of Kwangtung comrades in stabilizing the situation. However, we were not as optimistic about the future as the Kwangtung comrades. Even on the basis of my own observations during the past few days, it could be proven that within Kwangtung there were many problems that urgently needed to be solved.

I pointed out that the agreement between the CC of the CCP and the Middle clique of Sun Fo and others was not only reasonable but necessary. To forge ties with the Middle clique and overthrow the organization of the Western Hills Conference was in itself a major method of attacking rightist influences. I questioned Borodin about the so-called merger. Would merging the KMT Left clique and the CCP mean that during the Second KMT Congress, the leftists and the CCP would have to monopolize the seats of the KMT central committees? And how should we force the Middle clique to follow the Left clique and to attack the Right clique?

These questions of mine were difficult for Borodin to answer. So I went on to explain that the CCP was still in its infancy and had no members participating in the National government. We also lacked experience in controlling state power, much less did we have experience in controlling military authority. The CCP had no members serving as senior military officers. Most of the members in the National Revolutionary Army were engaged in political work, which was looked upon as a subsidiary branch of activity in the army. They did not, after all, directly control the army. Therefore, I believed that if we were to occupy a few more seats on the KMT central committees, we would arouse the reaction of the KMT elements, but would still not strengthen the CCP leadership of the national revolution.

I then insisted that the comrades in Canton not treat the policy of the CC of the CCP as one of withdrawal, but rather that they treat it as necessary so that the CCP might seek its own independent development and consolidate the national revolutionary front. They should not ask for its revision but rather put it into operation. I also said that at the forthcoming Second KMT Congress, we should unanimously advocate some kind of national government system and not resort indefinitely to extraordinary measures of the revolution to handle problems. At least we should consolidate the Wang-Chiang leadership core on a systematic foundation, so that it might not suffer from outside interference.

I also brought forward three problems that urgently needed to be solved. The first was elimination of the antagonistic attitude between the Young Soldiers' Alliance and the Sunyatsenist Society. We needed either to abolish the two organizations or to merge them into one. The second was the necessity of taking the initiative in seeking an end to the Canton–Hong Kong Strike. If the Strike Committee could not be eliminated, it should at least conduct its activities within the purview of the National government. The third was our request to the National government that it adopt a clearer policy in support of the development of the peasant movement. The armed forces of the landlords in all localities needed to be reorganized as the armed forces of the local governments in order to wipe out armed conflicts in different areas and to satisfy the peasants' economic demands for rent and interest reduction.

I said to Borodin, "The dismissal of the Western Hills Conference clique (from the KMT) and the increase of the ratio of CCP members in the KMT central committees do not constitute any real revolutionary advances. If what I have said here can be achieved, particularly with the peasant forces gaining superiority in the rural areas, then it will in reality be a revolutionary advance."

Borodin listened to me, but he did not answer. Comrades of the Kwangtung District Committee seemed disinclined to get involved in the dispute between us. No one spoke up, so the meeting was adjourned. However, the facts proved that the majority of the responsible comrades of the Kwangtung District Committee were on Borodin's side. They particularly opposed the agreement that the CC of the CCP had entered into with Sun, Yeh, and Shao. They held that this was a clear example of making concessions to the rightists. Although they did not look upon me as the principal representative of the policy of withdrawal and might even feel that I had a sympathetic understanding of the Kwangtung situation, they nevertheless felt that my views smacked of withdrawal.

What Chang T'ai-lei told me seemed to draw an accurate picture of Borodin's position. He pointed out that Borodin was struggling with Wang and Chiang and that they were in uneasy harmony. Only Borodin could smooth over the controversies that might arise within the KMT and stabilize the present leadership. But lately Borodin had seemed depressed; and in the handling of various Kwangtung problems, he often met with numerous difficulties. He met opposition from the Right clique; and Moscow and certain Russian military advisers in China seemed to disagree with his methods. The present decision of the CC of the CCP worried him even more. Chang added that Borodin had worked two years before he became completely acquainted with the Kwangtung situation. If the authorities in Moscow should decide to send someone else to take over as adviser, they would have difficulty finding a suitable candidate.

I assured Chang T'ai-lei that the CC of the CCP did not want Borodin to be replaced. When I came to Canton, I consulted him first, because of our respect for him. The agreement between the CC of the CCP and the Middle clique of the KMT also stressed the need to obey

Dr. Sun's established policy of alliance with Russia and tolerance of the Communists. These things should not lead Borodin to feel that his position was insecure. But Chang T'ai-lei still wasn't satisfied. He pointed out that the Western Hills Conference clique had openly advocated dismissal of Borodin, Wang Ching-wei, and CCP members; and the Second Congress of the KMT should deal them a counterblow of a demonstrative nature. It was important to create an enthusiastic atmosphere in support of Borodin and the Wang-Chiang cooperation. He felt that it was certainly not enough for us merely to make a hollow demand that the Middle clique obey Dr. Sun's established policy unless we also made a specific demand that they support the current Canton leadership.

By this time the Second Congress of the KMT was about to open. No agreement had yet been reached by the CC of the CCP, Borodin, and the Kwangtung District Committee. The CC of the CCP had reached an agreement with the Middle clique of the KMT and so it could not change its stand midway. Borodin felt that this was a withdrawal and that the position had to be revised. Time would no longer permit repeated consultations. As the person in the middle of this situation, the best I could do was to try not to expose our divergent views to the outside world.

The problem of the Sunyatsenist Society was one that I believed could be settled quickly. Ch'en Yen-nien and his colleagues felt that having been formed earlier, the Young Soldiers' Alliance was the legal organization in Whampoa, whereas the Sunyatsenist Society was the product of the new Right clique and had not yet been officially approved. They felt that it would be too great a concession to abolish or merge the two organizations. Ch'en Yen-nien did not openly oppose my views, but he seemed to adopt the tactic of procrastination. He suggested that we wait to dispose of this matter until the return of Chou En-lai, who held responsibility at Whampoa. Chou En-lai was in Swatow where he also held the post of director of the East River Administrative Bureau. He was so busy that he could not come to Canton. Ch'en Yen-nien held that Chou enjoyed the deep trust of General Chiang Kai-shek and was respected by the responsible members of both organizations. It would be better for Chou to suggest measures for disposing of the case to Chiang.

The issue of concluding the Canton–Hong Kong Strike could not be settled by Kwangtung alone. As Borodin had said, Hong Kong sent unofficial representatives to Canton as feelers for a channel of settlement. Negotiations were drawn out over a long period of time because the views of the two sides were so widely divergent. By the time of the March Twentieth Incident, Hong Kong seemed to think that there was no need for further negotiations, and they cut off all contacts.

The matter of conflicts between peasants and landlords was later shelved because of the passage of a resolution on the peasant movement by the Second Congress of the KMT.

The Second Congress of the KMT, which opened on January 4, 1926, was supposed to be conducted under the leadership of Wang Ching-wei; but in fact he did not fulfill his mission. Before the Congress opened, I had officially informed him of the talks we had had with Sun, Yeh, and Shao and of the reasons for the CC of the CCP taking such action. Apart from formal exchanges of greetings with me, he did not express any opinion, but he discussed everything with Borodin, even the question of KMT-CCP relations. Perhaps he felt that it was better to deal with the matter through Borodin. I felt that after he became chairman of the National government, Wang Ching-wei became weighed down by the burden of heavy duties and seemed rather confused.

Borodin seemed very pleased with himself over the situation. When I tried to talk with him about the need to strengthen the leadership core of the Congress, he stated that the Congress had its legal presidium to assume leadership. He said that he would take care of important issues behind the scene; therefore there was no need to worry about further discussions of any problem.

It seemed to me that Borodin was like a ship without a rudder or compass. He did not agree with the policy of the CC of the CCP, which he believed would lead toward withdrawal from the KMT. He insisted that the CCP stay in the KMT and cooperate closely with the leftists, but he failed to consider what would happen to the CCP if such a course were pursued. He did not entertain the idea of the CCP directly seizing the leadership of the KMT. He only wanted the CCP to form the foundation of the KMT Left clique (later he even stated that the CCP was fated to play the role of the coolie). Although he found difficulties in both advance and retreat, he still thought that his political acumen was sufficient for manipulating the Canton situation to the benefit of all.

On the eve of the Congress, Moscow sent a very long telegram. Borodin translated it and found it to be a theoretical treatise against imperialism. As Borodin and I were reading this long telegram Wang Ching-wei arrived. Without explanation, Borodin handed the message over to Wang. Before he had finished it, Wang stated that the contents were very good indeed and could be used as material for the manifesto of the Congress. Later this essay was written into the first section of the manifesto of the Congress.

After Wang Ching-wei left, Borodin seemed pleased and boasted to me that everything could be settled smoothly and without much effort after he had gone over it. I felt dissatisfied and asked Borodin if Moscow had sent any specific instructions in addition to the telegram. He replied, "No." He explained that with regard to actual problems, Moscow perhaps had faith in our ability to consult and to solve our problems here. I felt that this reflected a lack of sensitive feeling for the China situation on the part of Moscow and continued to allow Borodin to handle things as he thought fit.

Under the leadership of Wang Ching-wei, the Congress issued a manifesto, passed the report on Party affairs, accepted the political testament of Sun Yat-sen, impeached the Western Hills Conference clique, and adopted resolutions on the labor movement, the peasant movement, and the merchants' movement. Everything looked impressive, and the spirit of reorganization exhibited at the First Congress seemed to reassert itself.

Wang Ching-wei, a moving orator, did a good job in displaying his abilities. His political address to the Congress, though very long, was filled with zealous phrases and won considerable applause. Wang especially impressed the people with statements emphasizing the harmony between the Communists and non-Communists on the battlefield. He said that their blood had flowed together and congealed in a single blot so that no distinction could be made between the two. Since they had died for the same goal, they could all the more live for the same goal.

Wang did not use the same enthusiastic tone when he called on KMT members outside Kwangtung to refrain from joining the Western Hills Conference clique and to unite and cooperate at the Second Congress. This seemed to be the one flaw in his address.

This was the first time that General Chiang Kai-shek attended such an impressive gathering, and he showed himself to be a man of extraordinary achievement. At the mass meeting on January 1, he put on a cloak that attracted great attention. From the platform of the presidium he accepted the ovation of the public. In every way General Chiang exhibited the pose of an important military bulwark. Wang Ching-wei and the others paled into insignificance beside him. At the reception he gave at Whampoa for the delegates attending the Congress, he again showed that he was in a class by himself. In the military report that he made before the Congress, he pointed out that the National Revolutionary Army contained nearly one hundred thousand men. He emphasized the achievements in the military field during the past year. Chiang was elected a member of the standing committee of the CEC, as well as chairman of the Military Council. His leadership in the military area was affirmed. In the eyes of the delegates in general, Chiang and Wang Ching-wei constituted a dual focus—Chiang in the military field and Wang in the political field. However, some delegates had already begun to have doubts over the continued cooperation between Wang and Chiang.

"Raising Chiang and suppressing Wang" was an important tactic used by the Western Hills Conference clique to sabotage the Kwangtung situation. They seemed to exploit this opportunity. I had discussed this question solemnly with Borodin. Borodin vaguely indicated that differences did exist in the personal characters of Wang and Chiang. Wang was adept at understanding people and would get the trend of things once he was informed of the fundamental facts. However, when he was called upon to shoulder responsibility, he often expressed humility and would retreat. Chiang, on the other hand, had limited knowledge but was brave about shouldering responsibility. At the moment there were no differences between Wang and Chiang. Chang T'ai-lei, who served as interpreter between Borodin and the two, added that only with Borodin serving as a stabilizing force could the cooperative leadership of Wang and Chiang be maintained.

About one-third of the delegates at the Congress were CCP members serving as representatives of various local headquarters of the KMT.[11] Nevertheless, they could not make a positive contribution toward consolidating the leftist leadership. The person who served as secretary of the CCP and CYC groups in the Congress was Kao Yü-han, a political instructor at Whampoa. He was the major CCP spokesman at the Congress. He was a rousing orator, a match for the melodious orator Wang Ching-wei. In his statements he made no distinction between the KMT and the CCP, and the audience felt the spirit of harmony. He knew that the basic problem within the CCP was that of CCP-KMT cooperation and that no decisive policy had been formulated, so he avoided raising issues that would lead to argument.

The existence within the KMT of another party—the CCP—made

members of the KMT very uncomfortable. The so-called leftists were no exception. During the Congress the majority of the delegates had some reaction against the CCP. Those KMT members less favorably disposed toward the CCP often took pains to express their strict KMT stand.

I attended the sessions of the Congress regularly. I was not a delegate to the Congress, but I attended in my capacity as alternate member of the first CEC of the KMT and sat in the special section reserved for CEC members. Very few people occupied seats there. As I remember, there was only one other regular occupant—Madame Sun Yat-sen (Miss Soong Ch'ing-ling). She was not a member of the CEC, but was an invited guest of the Congress. Of the remaining members of the first CEC, some had been expelled, some did not attend, and some had other duties at the Congress. All in all, members of the first CEC present at this Congress were less than half of the possible number. This caused some of us to feel depressed.

I was responsible for directing the activities of the CCP and the CYC. I adopted the democratic formula of respecting the views of the majority of the members of the Party, the CYC, and the CCP Kwangtung District Committee. Like the members of the KMT, most of the comrades of the CCP considered the Congress merely as an occasion for revelry; therefore, they felt that problems involving argument should not be brought up. I myself tended to stress the need for explanations of KMT-CCP relations. The existence of the CCP and the CYC within the KMT was the cause of most of the unrest among the KMT members. Therefore I issued a letter to all KMT members,[12] pointing out that the activities of the CCP and the CYC within the KMT did not undermine KMT unity, but quite to the contrary, promoted the unity of the KMT and the CCP.

Before the election of the central committees by the Congress, Wang Ching-wei had asked me to come to Borodin's place for a discussion. He brought forward a list, which he had drawn up in advance, of candidates for the central committees to be elected by the Second Congress and asked that we agree to it. Borodin made no comment. I read the list carefully and found that the majority on the list were either so-called leftists or people that were close to Wang. I felt that he had not respected the view of the CC of the CCP that we needed to win over the Middle clique. Of this clique, neither Yeh Ch'u-ts'ang nor Shao Yuan-ch'ung was included, although Sun Fo was.[13] The list included all CCP members that had been on the committees elected by the First

Congress as well as Wu Yu-chang, Tung Pi-wu, Fan T'ai-ying, and Yang P'ao-an, who already occupied high positions in the KMT.

It was out of place for me to interfere in the disputes of the KMT; so on the basis of the decision of the CC of the CCP, I only expressed an opinion about the nomination of CCP members to the KMT central committees. I stated that such CCP members as Ch'ü Ch'iu-pai and I no longer held posts in the KMT and therefore should not be reelected. The number of other CCP members up for election could also be reduced in keeping with the original desire of the CC of the CCP to occupy only a few seats in the KMT's central committees.

Wang Ching-wei immediately objected. He pointed out that both Chü Ch'iu-pai and I had been selected by Dr. Sun himself when he was still alive and that we should therefore be reelected. I tried patiently to explain to him that other members of the central committees elected by the First Congress had been omitted from the list, so it was fair and reasonable that some CCP members, including myself, be withdrawn. When Wang saw that Borodin still withheld comment, he went no further. Thus the candidates for the central committees elected by the Second Congress were considered to have been selected after consultation.

During the election of the central committees at the Congress, Hu Han-min, who had recently been banished, was reelected by the largest number of votes.[14] This embarrassed everyone. The election of Hu was of course prearranged, but his winning the largest number of votes proved that he had no determined opponent among the delegates. Some of my comrades used this incident to show that the leftists should never make concessions to the Middle clique. With the loss of Liao Chung-k'ai, the Left clique had weakened a great deal, and the slightest sign of making concessions could cause its dissolution. This was a reason why Wang disagreed with the policy of the CC of the CCP.

When the Congress was about to close, Borodin told me that Wang Ching-wei was rather dissatisfied with the CC of the CCP, first because he viewed the CCP's talks with Sun, Yeh, and Shao as tantamount to seeking the favor of those opposed to Canton, and second because the CCP adopted a passive attitude at the Congress, not wanting to be involved in the internal struggle of the KMT. Borodin said that Wang saw this as a tendency to withhold support from the leftists. In speaking thus, Borodin was clearly using Wang's name to attack me.

I admitted that I did not thoroughly endorse the views of the CC of the CCP, but I also said that Wang Ching-wei had never held detailed discussions with me in advance in order to evolve a more acceptable plan. In turn, I took Borodin to task, saying that he had only expressed views opposed to the policy of the CC of the CCP and had not brought forward constructive proposals. His attitude toward the Congress could only be considered passive. Finally, I stated that certain problems needed immediate solution and that I must therefore return to Shanghai immediately to ask the CC of the CCP to make its final decision.

Borodin told me that he would soon be returning to Moscow, adding that some problems had to be clarified in Moscow before they could be dealt with in Canton. I did not see why the work in Kwangtung under the Wang-Chiang leadership could not be carried out normally, so that Borodin's temporary departure would not produce any noticeable effects. Borodin thought that the Congress had achieved good results and that on the whole there were no important differences with the views of the CC of the CCP. As to the questions of the antagonism between the Young Soldiers' Alliance and the Sunyatsenist Society, the conclusion of the strike, and the peasant movement, Borodin believed that the general situation would not be affected by them for a while. He was confident that after his return from Moscow, the views in Moscow, Shanghai, and Canton would tend to become the same. It would not be too late then to take up those problems. It was impossible to foresee that changes in the situation would occur so rapidly that Borodin's expectations would be completely wrong. When he returned to Canton after the incident of March 20, everything had changed and had been taken out of his control. As a matter of fact, while the Second Congress was meeting, General Chiang Kai-shek issued an address declaring that he would not tolerate any further antagonism between the two organizations within Whampoa. Borodin and the CCP had reacted too late. The unfortunate March Twentieth Incident became a reality. Even from today's standpoint neither the CC of the CCP nor I can be blamed for improper handling of these incidents of the past. The main reason was Borodin's excessive self-confidence, which lost for all of us an opportunity to solve the outstanding problems at the Congress.

THE VEXATIONS OF THE CENTRAL COMMITTEE OF THE CHINESE COMMUNIST PARTY AROUND THE TIME OF THE MARCH TWENTIETH INCIDENT

CHAPTER

On my return to Shanghai toward the end of January, 1926, I felt deeply that the CC of the CCP faced a difficult political dilemma whether it marched forward or retreated. It was shackled by the policy of staying within the KMT. Lenin had said that a man is worse off than a chicken, for when a chicken is placed inside a circle drawn with chalk, it can go out of the circle by itself; but a man is often placed inside a circle that he has drawn himself and cannot get out of it. This description was very apt indeed for the CC of the CCP at that time.

When the CC of the CCP discussed my report on the trip to Canton, we all felt that the dispute between Shanghai and Canton was directly linked with the basic policy of the CCP remaining within the KMT. The majority, headed by Ch'en Tu-hsiu and including myself, felt that development of the so-called policy of attack on the basis of Borodin's proposal of merging the KMT leftists and Communists into one body

484

could only follow two possible future courses. The first possibility would be to implement the policy by force. This would involve seizure by the CCP of the leadership of the CEC of the KMT. The CCP would assume leadership but would lack military power to back it up. All members of the KMT, including the leftists, would rise in opposition, thus making too many enemies for the CCP and isolating it, so that if the combined party did not collapse in the internal quarrel between the CCP and the KMT, it would be destroyed by the superior forces of the imperialists and the reactionaries. The second possibility would be for the CCP to become part of the Left Wing of the KMT and to work exclusively to support the current leftist leadership in Kwangtung. This would weaken the CCP, which would no longer be assuming an independent political stand. The CCP would thus be exerting effort without making any gains, but rather losing its own identity and hurting itself.

On the other hand, if Borodin's views were rejected and the policy originally adopted by the CC of the CCP were carried out, the CCP would definitely have to withdraw from the KMT. And since the KMT had adopted the policy of having the Party rule the state, there would be no national assembly with multi-party participation or coalition government in which the CCP could cooperate with the KMT outside the Party organization.

This problem was so troublesome that differences of opinion also developed among members of the CC of the CCP. P'eng Shu-chih had criticized Borodin for urging comrades of the Kwangtung District Committee of the CCP to oppose the decision of the CC, branding this action as sabotage of the leadership of the CC. He also showed dissatisfaction with me by taking me to task for not announcing the decision of the CC and ordering the comrades of the Kwangtung District Committee to enforce that decision. Ch'ü Ch'iu-pai, however, took the opposite approach, praising me for attaching importance to the views of the Kwangtung comrades while I was in Canton, saying that while I generally carried out the decisions of the CC, I did not expose the dissident views within the CC.

At this juncture we received another document from the Kwangtung District Committee, which took the CC of the CCP to task for its policy of withdrawal at the Second Congress of the KMT and advocated changing to a policy of attack against the KMT rightists. The CC of the CCP believed that this document had been prepared after I had left Canton and that it was based on the views of Borodin. The majority of us clearly indicated that we could not accept this document.

After our discussions, we adopted a policy of waiting for a directive from the Comintern. For the time being we did not refute the document of the Kwangtung District Committee. Voitinsky had returned to Moscow before my return to Shanghai, and Borodin was to follow him there. Obviously they would undertake basic discussions in Moscow. Although the CC of the CCP did not send a representative to Moscow to participate in such discussions, it would no doubt await the directive that would result from them. We resented this procedure, feeling that it was unreasonable; but since from the beginning the CC of the CCP had followed the tradition of paying respect to Moscow, we accepted it with silent resignation.

On its own authority the CC of the CCP could not independently make a quick decision and take quick action on the basis of its understanding of the situation; instead it had to take orders from the Comintern, which was far away in Moscow and was very unfamiliar with actual conditions in China. This was the main reason for all our difficulties. Moreover, at the Fourteenth Congress of the Soviet Communist Party in December, 1925, a fierce struggle had developed between the Stalinist forces and the combined opposition of Trotsky, Zinoviev, and Kamenev, so it seemed that Moscow could not give full attention to the China problem. Moscow had never given any clear directives about certain problems in Kwangtung, which I have described above, that needed to be solved immediately. By the time Voitinsky and Borodin returned to China, the March Twentieth Incident had already taken place. By then these problems were all issues of the past.

In addition to the important political problem described above, the vexations of the CC of the CCP included the problem of strained feelings among us, the responsible members of the Committee. We had different personalities and different ways of life; some of us could even be considered weird figures. For example, the romantic life of P'eng Shu-chih at the time was really a very ordinary private affair, but it was the cause of our internal dissension being brought into the open. I shall touch on it briefly here, for it may possibly reveal some of the setbacks in the growth of the CCP.

A few days after my return to Shanghai, Ts'ai Ho-sen called a meeting of the CC of the CCP in his home, which was also the office of the Department of Propaganda of the CC, and the home of his wife

(Hsiang Ching-yu), P'eng Shu-chih, and his secretary, Ch'eng Chao-lin. At the meeting Mrs. Ts'ai first reported that while her husband was away from Shanghai (Ts'ai had left for Peking a few days before I left for Canton and had returned to Shanghai about the same time that I did), she had had a love affair with P'eng Shu-chih. She had frankly told Ts'ai about it on the very day that he returned to Shanghai. At the meeting she described the painful situation that she was in. For many years she had shared a life of suffering with Ts'ai. She still loved him and did not want to hurt him. At the same time she could not suppress her love for P'eng Shu-chih, because his manner was truly moving. She asked the CC to permit her to leave Shanghai and to send her to Moscow for advanced study.

Not all of us had known about this incident involving their private lives, and we did not all feel comfortable about expressing an opinion. After a period of silence, Ch'en Tu-hsiu started to talk. He praised the union between Ts'ai and Hsiang and said that he was loath to see them go separate ways because of the incident. Then he criticized P'eng Shu-chih for his lack of self-control, which had impaired the marital relations of comrades. But he did grant Hsiang Ching-yu's request; and she left for Russia very soon afterward.

In view of the characters of the individuals involved, it would not seem that the situation developed overnight. In the first place, Ts'ai Ho-sen did not appear to be a husband that could make his wife happy. He had worked especially hard during the early period of the CCP. I had lived with him for a short period in 1923 while Hsiang Ching-yu was working in another locality. Our bedrooms were separated only by a wooden partition. He would remain silent a whole day, burying himself in reading and writing; and when he came upon an interesting sentence, he would utter a dry laugh. He suffered seriously from asthma; and when he had an attack, he would breathe heavily and issue noises that sounded like bellows being fanned. He would never listen to people that urged him to stop work because of his ailment. His eating hours were naturally irregular, and he often skipped meals. The papers and books were thrown about in such a disorderly mess in his room that it was unclean. When he was tired, he would fall on the bed and go to sleep without taking off his clothes or his shoes. After a while he would jump up and continue his work.

Whenever I returned to the house late at night, Ts'ai would still be writing articles or reading documents. Often when he was thinking about a problem, he would pace the floor of his room, his poorly made shoes making creaking sounds that prevented me, a tired man, from getting my needed sleep. At times I would get up and help him with his work so that he could get to bed earlier. Sometimes both of us would work until dawn. There was a deep friendship between us, but I still felt that living with him was an ordeal. I felt that his living habits would be an obstacle to wedded bliss.

By nature Hsiang Ching-yu was a lively and amorous girl, but she had been inhibited by old Chinese moral concepts. She did not talk and laugh freely, but was usually reserved and solemn. She had cultivated the habit of working hard and seemed to seek spiritual comfort in her work. Though she was one of the early leaders in women's work, she was still less than thirty years old. She always had such a solemn appearance that women colleagues looked at her in awe. They nicknamed her "old grandma."

Public knowledge of her love affair caused both her personal prestige and the women's work of the CCP to suffer. Most women comrades criticized her for her inability to suppress her feelings and keep them under control. They also criticized her "old grandma" demeanor as being unnatural and feigned. After that she lost her leadership position among women.[1]

P'eng Shu-chih was a happy-go-lucky and talented scholar. In his attention to work and his daily living, he was light-hearted yet well organized. Away from home he often engaged in the serious teaching of doctrines; and so he was nicknamed "Confucius." At times he would engage in light chatter and interesting dialogue that engaged people's attention and revealed his true character. In the Communist Party the nickname of "Confucius" carried elements of satire. It generally referred to the fact that P'eng was a youth with political ambitions who took on the pose of a teacher engaged in serious preaching. His advocacy of increasing Party authority smacked a bit of the theory propounded by Confucius of "raising the position of the emperor to resist the barbarians." It seemed that he looked upon Ch'en Tu-hsiu as the "emperor" and on the other old cadres of the CCP as "dukes of the various regions," while he himself was responsible for "strengthening the trunk and weakening the branches." After the incident of the love affair, he continued to work as usual and appeared to retain his original attitude without being perturbed. The behavior of P'eng Shu-chih led to Ch'ü Ch'iu-pai's open dissatisfaction with the leadership of Ch'en Tu-hsiu.

By a coincidence my wife, who was about to have a baby, for the sake of safety and to further her studies, had left for Moscow three months previously. I became a bachelor temporarily. At the same time my office in the Chapei area was becoming unsafe and could not be used any longer. Ch'ü Ch'iu-pai was living in the French Concession. It was considered a relatively safe area, and most of the organs of the CC were also located there; so I was assigned to live with Ch'ü. This enabled me to have the opportunity to listen to his complaints and expressions of dissatisfaction.

Ch'ü Ch'iu-pai was a tireless worker who treated night as day; he was also a scholar who covered a wide range of subjects. He had suffered for a long time from tuberculosis, and he also had insomnia. Often when I went to bed about midnight, he would start to read and would not stop until eight the next morning, after the paper had been delivered. He would read the paper and then have breakfast with me. He often liked to talk about outstanding portions of a book that he had read the preceding night. It was a common thing for him to read through an entire book in one night. After breakfast I would leave for work, and it was only then that he undressed to sleep. After 2:00 P.M. he attended to his work and wrote articles. We had dinner together, and he always leisurely drank a few glasses of Chinese yellow wine (Shao-hsing). After dinner he often smilingly conversed with me, his talk seemingly endless. When he was aroused, he would spray his saliva all around and at times it would come right up to my face. I often thought that I was plunged into a thick mist of tuberculosis bacteria, and it seemed a miracle that I did not contract the disease.

His wife, Yang Chih-hua, had fully experienced the test of living, and she was kindly and animated. She attended to domestic chores in accordance with Ch'ü's way of living, doing everything in an orderly manner, so that even her maidservant felt that her home was a quiet and high-class one. She was a member of the CCP and had undertaken some leadership work in the women's movement, so she was rather busy; nevertheless, she always made it possible for Ch'ü to sleep peacefully the whole morning. In the course of my political conversations with Ch'ü, which were rather dull, she often injected a few light and interesting remarks. This made me, a temporary house guest, feel completely at home.

Ch'ü Ch'iu-pai was very dissatisfied with P'eng Shu-chih. He criticized P'eng, saying that he was inadequate both in theoretical studies and in political experience and was not qualified to undertake leadership work in the CC of the CCP. He particularly took P'eng to task for his poor leadership of propaganda work. He held that P'eng's irresponsible behavior had undermined the marital relations of comrades and had caused these two major members of the CC of the CCP—Ts'ai Ho-sen and Hsiang Ching-yu—to suffer pain. He openly expressed the view that a man like P'eng Shu-chih should not be allowed to remain in the CC of the CCP, but should be sent to a local post to undertake some difficult and practical work in order to be trained.

For the first time Ch'ü Ch'iu-pai expressed his dissatisfaction with the leadership of Ch'en Tu-hsiu also. He referred sarcastically to Ch'en Tu-hsiu's leadership as a patriarchal system rich in the aroma of the *hsiu-tsai* scholar, which was incapable of preserving its "purity of family honor" because of Ch'en's protection of P'eng Shu-chih. Though he had respect for Ch'en's experience and knowledge, he took Ch'en to task by saying that his political leadership was not sufficiently decisive. He said that while Ch'en failed to carry through his own view by insisting on withdrawal from the KMT, he was still unwilling to make concessions to Borodin's views, thereby revealing his vacillation and weakness.

Ch'ü Ch'iu-pai, who smacked even more of the scholar than Ch'en Tu-hsiu, had shown respect for Borodin's work methods all along. He held that Borodin was one of the most capable Soviet workers in China and that he could represent the views of Stalin. Ch'ü pointed out that China could not pursue the road of democracy and that a national assembly with multi-party participation could not appear in China. He firmly believed that the Comintern would not change the basic policy of having the CCP work inside the KMT. Though he did not deny that there were certain defects in Borodin's work, he nevertheless resolutely adhered to the view that the CC of the CCP should not oppose Borodin. He believed that the existing relations between the Communist Party and the KMT had reached the state where the man had mounted on the back of the tiger and could not afford to get off in midstream.

These opinions of Ch'ü Ch'iu-pai seemed to provide the basis for his later action in seeking to replace Ch'en Tu-hsiu; at the time, however, I had not observed this. There were still political differences between him and me. I held that if at the opportune moment we did not change CCP-KMT relations from cooperation within the KMT to cooperation outside the KMT, we would eventually find ourselves on the tip of the ox's horn. But I agreed with his view about improving the leadership of the CC, and I felt that this should be openly expressed so that the problem would not remain buried in the hearts of the people to constitute a source of trouble. Ch'ü would not directly discuss these problems with Ch'en, but he wanted me to transmit his views, and I agreed to do so.

When I diplomatically presented to Ch'en Tu-hsiu the views of Ch'ü Ch'iu-pai, I expressed my own support of the proposals to transfer P'eng Shu-chih out of the CC and to strengthen the collective leadership of the CC. Ch'en Tu-hsiu's reaction was not favorable, and he rejected my recommendation. He added that if the CC of the CCP wanted to raise its prestige, it could not tolerate a work style like that of Ch'ü Ch'iu-pai, who was displaying his teeth and his talons ferociously. He criticized Ch'ü Ch'iu-pai's ambiguity in speaking and writing, saying that Ch'ü was not as clear-cut and firm as P'eng Shu-chih. He denied the existence of political differences within the CC, and he was not prepared to suppress P'eng Shu-chih because of an incident in his private life. He stuck to his view that we should await the directives of the Comintern before dealing with any issue.

I did not argue with Ch'en Tu-hsiu over this matter; I only asked him to give it more consideration. But I did feel uncomfortable over the matter, and I felt that Ch'en's words implied a reprimand of myself. I felt that it was better not to transmit Ch'en's words to Ch'ü, in order to avoid aggravating the breach between the two. I believed that there should not be undue haste in solving the problem and that with time there would be an improvement in the situation.

However, P'eng Shu-chih appeared to know what had happened, and he staged a counterattack. Within the CC of the CCP the rumor circulated that I and Ch'ü Ch'iu-pai were attempting to organize an opposition bloc. The rumor seemed to compare Ch'en Tu-hsiu with Stalin, and Ch'ü Ch'iu-pai, Ts'ai Ho-sen, and me with the opposition bloc of Trotsky, Zinoviev, and Kamenev. Ts'ai Ho-sen, who did not know the content of my conversation with Ch'en Tu-hsiu, was also involved because he was unhappy with P'eng Shu-chih for undermining the relationship between himself and his wife. We were also looked upon as heads of the clique of old cadres or of the clique of practical workers.

Just as difficulties arose within the leadership of the CCP, the whole revolutionary situation also faced a drastic deterioration. First, the Kuominchun (National Army), which was close to the National Revolutionary Army, suffered reverses in the North, and on March 18, 1926, the government of Chief Executive Tuan Ch'i-jui massacred demonstrating students in Peking. Next came the March Twentieth Incident in Canton.

The Fengtien Army general Kuo Sung-ling, with the support of Feng Yü-hsiang,[2] launched the war against Chang Tso-lin on November 22, 1925. On November 23 Chang Tso-lin, with military aid from Japan, squashed the attack of Kuo Sung-ling. This led to a direct conflict between the National Army and the Fengtien Army that resulted in the encirclement of the National Army by the combined forces of Chang Tso-lin and of Wu P'ei-fu from Hupeh. While the National Army of Feng Yü-hsiang was stationed at Taku in Tientsin, building defense works to resist the attack of Chang Tso-lin from the sea, the Japanese shelled the National Army, on the basis of the Treaty of 1901, which demilitarized Taku. Together with the other signatories of the 1901 Treaty (Britain, the United States, France, Italy, the Netherlands, Belgium, and Spain), Japan presented an ultimatum to the Peking government on March 16, calling for the dismantling of defense works within forty-eight hours.

Gradually the National Army led by Feng Yü-hsiang was unable to hold its own. About March 18 its important base, Tientsin, was surrounded on three sides; and the Fengtien Army, attacking from Shanhaikwan, as well as the Chihli-Shantung Coalition Army led by Li Ching-lin and Chang Tsung-ch'ang, attacking from Shantung, were nearing Tientsin. After capturing Honan, the army of Wu P'ei-fu, which was marching northward along the Peking-Hankow Railway, had also sent its vanguards to Shihchiachuang. The National Army was also subjected to interference from the Powers; so it evacuated Tientsin and withdrew toward Peking.

On March 18 students of various schools in Peking, under the leadership of the KMT and the CCP, protesting against foreign interference with China's civil war and demanding the abrogation of the 1901 Treaty, held a demonstration to lodge an appeal. When the ranks of the students had assembled at the square in front of the office of the chief executive on Tieh-ssu-tzu Hutung, Tuan Ch'i-jui ordered his guards to open fire. More than forty persons were killed and more than one hundred more were wounded. At the time, Peking was garrisoned by the National Army. Obviously Tuan Ch'i-jui had dared to take such action because he found the withdrawing National Army had lost its day. Therefore he massacred the students to curry favor with the Fengtien Army and to meet the demands of Japan and other Powers. This incident aroused the indignation of the people in all localities.

When the CC of the CCP discussed this critical situation, it was clearly at its wits' end. Though the National Army led by Feng Yü-hsiang had the support of the Soviet Union, its opponents, including the superior military forces of Chang Tso-lin and Wu P'ei-fu, had the support of Japan and the other Powers. This reactionary coalition force was raising high the cry of "Oppose the Reds." The aim of this slogan was to isolate and annihilate the revolutionary front, so that the anti-imperialist movement could not lift its head. The KMT rightists in Peking and Shanghai labeled the anti-imperialist and anti-Peking-government movements led by the CCP and the KMT leftists as Bolshevik movements; and they slandered and sabotaged everywhere. We did not think that the situation would permit us to revive the spirit of the May Thirtieth Movement and deal direct counterblows against the reactionary forces.

The March 18 massacre was followed closely by the March Twentieth Incident in Canton. For the Chinese Communists, this incident was virtually a bolt from the blue. At the time the Shanghai newspapers carried such banner headlines as: "Gunboat *Chungshan* Attempts Revolt"; "Chiang Kai-shek Detains Soviet Advisers"; "Arrest of Communists"; "Dissolution of Canton–Hong Kong Strike Committee"; and so forth. The CC of the CCP did not believe the reports at first, thinking them to be new rumors spread by the imperialists. When the news was confirmed, we felt deeply that the occurrence of this incident at a time when the situation as a whole was deteriorating was a very serious matter.

But the CCP had matured after all. Our demand for unity to resist alien forces appeared to loom larger than all our previous troubles. We had no time to discuss further the dissension between Borodin and the CC of the CCP, and we no longer haggled over the problem of internal leadership. All of us concentrated our energy on discussing the policy to deal with this development and save the situation.

The discussions resulted in our view that whether the March Twentieth Incident was caused by the leftist mistakes of our comrades in Canton, by the scramble for internal leadership on the part of the KMT, or by Chiang Kai-shek changing his political attitude due to the influence of the rightists and the anti-Communist forces, the CC of the CCP should now adopt an attitude of concession and compromise in order to stabilize the situation in Canton. To be specific, we had to try to preserve Chiang-Wang cooperation, continuing to adopt a friendly attitude toward Chiang while rectifying the leftist mistakes of our Canton comrades mentioned in chapter ten and settling other issues. We had no choice but to adopt a delaying policy of compromise.

The CC of the CCP also decided to send me to Canton to investigate the true facts of the incident and to implement this policy of compromise. When Ch'en Tu-hsiu explained this decision, he pointed out that I was the most suitable candidate; and he vested full authority in me. It seemed that he was trying to remove the misunderstandings that had cropped up between us. P'eng Shu-chih also expressed respect for me and supported the decision to allow me to handle the affair as I thought fit. On the basis of this decision, I made another trip to Canton, carrying with me a mission even more gigantic than the one on my previous visit.

After the March Twentieth Incident

The CC of the CCP held that the incident of March 20, 1926, was the open expression of the bourgeoisie in its seizure of the leadership of the national revolution. To put it more accurately, the incident involved such important factors as nationalistic feeling, shown by resistance to Soviet control, anti-Communist feeling in seeking to suppress CCP influence, and the use of Napoleonic and Chinese warlord habits. General Chiang Kai-shek, who led this incident, adopted an unusual military move as a means of establishing a new leadership. After the second plenary session of the second CEC of the KMT on May 15, 1926, the leadership of Chiang Kai-shek was firmly established. The CCP gradually switched from supporting the KMT leadership to resisting it.

About ten days after the incident I arrived in Canton. After the tempest the city superficially appeared to have regained its calm. As a matter of fact the many problems aroused by this incident were still present and unresolved. The original chairman, Wang Ching-wei, avoided visitors, so I could not see him. General Chiang Kai-shek stayed in Whampoa and Hu-men (Bocca Tigris) and outwardly appeared to be reluctant to be publicly involved in the affair. The duties of chairman of the National government were temporarily taken care of by T'an Yen-k'ai, commander of the Second Army. People were at a loss about the future development of the situation as a whole and of the relations between the KMT and the CCP in particular.

From what I knew, the events connected with the March Twentieth Incident were generally as follows: At the very outset, Li Chih-lung, director of the Naval Bureau and commander of the gunboat *Chungshan* was arrested in his home by General Chiang Kai-shek. Li Chih-lung was a member of the CCP and a graduate of the first class of Whampoa Military Academy. He was under the direct command of Chiang. The reason for his arrest was his unauthorized move of the gunboat *Chungshan* out of Whampoa, which appeared to be an attempt at revolt. But according to Li Chih-lung's defense, his removal of the gunboat had been carried out in response to a telephonic order from the office of the President of Whampoa Academy that had been relayed to him by Ouyang K'o, deputy dean of studies of the naval school. Li said that he was acting under orders and had done no wrong. Comrades of the CCP in Canton held that it was a trap set by the Sun Wen-chu-i Hsüeh-hui (Sunyatsenist Society) and that Li Chih-lung was merely careless and fell into the trap. Many KMT personages also held that the charge of revolt against Li Chih-lung was merely a pretext for launching the incident.

After Li's arrest, at about 3 A.M. on March 20, the Second Division of the First Army, which was commanded by Chiang Kai-shek and was then garrisoning Canton city, declared martial law. Troops were sent to surround the Canton–Hong Kong Strike Committee, and members of the workers' picketing corps were disarmed. The pickets obeyed orders and surrendered their arms, so there was no conflict. In the Tungshan district the guards at the residences of the various Russian advisers were disarmed at the same time. Members of the CCP working in Whampoa Military Academy and in the First Army were ordered to leave their posts and to assemble at the Academy to await orders. Responsible members of the CCP Kwangtung District Committee pointed out that those carrying out the curfew orders were all members of the Sunyatsenist Society and that the Sixth Regiment, which was completely controlled by that society, had exhibited the greatest zeal in the work. The incident was obviously launched on the initiative of Chiang, but many people consciously or unconsciously interpreted it as an illegal act of the Sunyatsenist Society.

It was stated that Wang Ching-wei actually had no prior knowledge of the incident, that only after the incident had occurred did he get a report over the telephone. He had indignantly cut off the telephone, had uttered not a single word, and had made no public appearance since that time. According to people that were familiar with the inside facts, Wang and Chiang had several talks after March 20, but they failed to arrive at a decision on handling the incident. Wang had indicated that such action was inexcusable and that in the interests of the prestige of the KMT and the government, he could not carry on. Though Chiang formally asked for disciplinary action against himself,[3] he nevertheless contended that everything had resulted from Wang's poor leadership and that Wang should be the first to express repentance.

As to the concrete causes of the incident, the following points should be noted: First, the policies and attitudes adopted by the Soviet military advisers such as Kisanko in Canton constituted an important factor in arousing a serious reaction from Chiang. These advisers had charge of the staff, information, service of supply, and the aviation and naval affairs of the military council. In their views, their attitudes, and living habits, they easily aroused the dislike of a Chinese military leader who had great pride in his own capabilities. For example, it was a Soviet policy to attach great importance to the strength of Feng Yü-hsiang. In February, 1926, when Feng was fighting against Chang Tso-lin and Wu P'ei-fu, Kisanko and his colleagues had blatantly recommended to Chiang that he send his troops by sea to Tientsin to give Feng Yü-hsiang support. They even wanted Chiang to go north to undertake the training of cadres for Feng Yü-hsiang.[4] Such proposals clearly betrayed an ignorance of the concepts of a Chinese military leader. Chiang wanted to create a world by himself; how could he be expected to play second fiddle to Feng? One can readily understand how he would nurture the feeling that the Soviet Union was not attaching importance to the National Revolutionary Army in Kwangtung and was intentionally snubbing him personally.

It was, however, a doubtful point whether the Soviet Union really wanted to suppress Chiang. I had never met Kisanko and his colleagues; but according to my information, they had always in the past acted in accordance with Borodin's directives and had made no political contacts with the outside. On this occasion, the responsible comrades of the CCP Kwangtung District Committee informed me that Borodin and the Soviet military advisers held Chiang in higher respect than Wang and that surely they could not have any intention of suppressing Chiang. But the Soviet people had attached too much importance to Feng Yü-hsiang's "coup in the capital." They were anxious to change the status quo of the Peking government so that the Chinese revolution could achieve a phenomenal development that would benefit the foreign relations situation of the Soviet Union. And so they naively requested Chiang Kai-shek to send his armed forces to the North to make some spectacular accomplishment. After the departure of Borodin, these "village bumpkin" type Soviet militarists had had to undertake the duties of diplomacy, and their political methods apparently were so crude that they aroused Chiang's reaction.

The second point to be noted as a cause of the incident was the conflict of power between Wang and Chiang. According to the observations of Chinese Communist comrades in Canton, the positions of Wang and Chiang in the KMT were clearly distinct from each other, due to their backgrounds, places of birth, and personal relations. Since succeeding Liao Chung-k'ai as the Party representative at Whampoa, Wang at times wanted to put his finger into the affairs of Whampoa. This interfered with Chiang's monopoly of military power. Moreover, after the departure of Borodin the differences between the two in their attitudes toward the Soviet advisers, KMT-CCP relations, and the handling of military and financial affairs became increasingly aggravated. It was clear to observers on the outside that both men were right on some points and wrong on others, but the principal reason for their differences was the lack of room to accommodate the "Big Two"—one in the army and the other in the government.

The third point was the deterioration in the relations between the KMT and the CCP. I have referred earlier to the antagonism within Whampoa between the Young Soldiers' Association and the Sunyatsenist Society. Friction between these two organizations kept increasing. A review of the situation made by the CCP Kwangtung District Committee showed that while infantilism and prejudice unquestionably existed in the Sunyatsenist Society, the Young Soldiers' Association had been guilty of committing many drastic leftist acts. Chiang, however, did not believe that there had been any improper action on the part of the Chinese Communists and the Young Soldiers' Association, which had supported him all along. Nevertheless he could not help having some misgivings as he watched the daily growth in influence of the Chinese Communists in the army, in the various local KMT headquarters, and among the masses of workers and peasants. Furthermore, the CCP was an organization in itself, and its members in the army did not subject themselves absolutely to Chiang's control. This caused him great unrest. CCP comrades felt that Chiang's actions on this occasion were not directed primarily at the CCP, but that in fact all the Chinese Communists were made scapegoats and took the blame.

For the above-mentioned reasons, the March Twentieth Incident developed as it did, and the political situation in Canton was very confused. The Wang clique held that Chiang's action violated the policies laid down by Dr. Sun and undermined the discipline of the National government. They demanded that Chiang be suppressed so that Wang could continue to carry the heavy burden of the state. All of the six armies making up the National Revolutionary Army, with the exception of the First Army, felt dissatisfaction with Chiang to a greater or lesser degree. In the non-Cantonese Second, Third, and Sixth armies, some generals felt that if Wang's leadership were lost, they would have even less chance of receiving equal treatment with the First Army. The Fourth Army, which had greater actual strength, had been developed directly out of the Cantonese Army system, and in it particularly there was the reaction that the "Chekiang people from the outside were suppressing the Kwangtung people." Generally speaking, Wang, who had been attacked, got most of the sympathy at the time. But since Wang had withdrawn himself from the public, the horde of dragons were without a leader, as it were, and most of them adopted a wait-and-see attitude, giving vent to their feelings merely by airing some disgruntled views.

The Chinese Communist comrades in Canton were especially indignant over the incident in many ways. Many people demanded that contact be established with forces on various sides to deal a counterblow to Chiang. Some took the Kwangtung District Committee to task for supporting Chiang Kai-shek exclusively, for looking upon Whampoa as the center for the military, and for neglecting the balanced development of all the armies, saying that these policies had led to the current situation. Mao Tse-tung, who was then in Kwangtung, subscribed to such a view. Yun Tai-ying and others considered that this incident was further proof of the bankruptcy of the CCP policy of cooperation within the KMT, and they demanded an immediate change of that policy. However, as soon as the subject of what should be done was broached, most comrades felt that at the moment there was no one capable of assuming leadership in an anti-Chiang move. Nor was there anyone with real strength who could come forward quickly. Perhaps the CCP was expected to take the initiative in suppressing Chiang. This was not only beyond its capacity, but also was a course that was not conducive to a successful future for the national revolution.

An additional factor was that the Soviet military advisers in Canton had in fact already adopted the policy of granting concessions to Chiang; and Kisanko, who was *persona non grata* with Chiang, had left Canton. Chou En-lai and Chang T'ai-lei, who were familiar with the inside situation, told me that the Russian advisers were waiting for Borodin's return to Canton to devise measures to remedy the situation. The Soviet Union Communist Party had sent Ivan Rofoski and more than ten others to Canton to make observations, and they had departed for home on March 24. Before their departure they had expressed to Chiang their desire to continue cooperating. The Soviet advisers that remained in Canton expressed even greater deference to Chiang, and it seemed that they were pushing the boat along with the tide, helping to make Chiang into China's Napoleon.

In the midst of such a disturbing situation I could not avoid adopting the measure of wielding a sword rapidly to cut off the entangled cords of hemp and to bring forth a clear and simple policy to cope with the situation. At the emergency meeting of the CCP Kwangtung District Committee, I reported that on the basis of the national political situation, the CC of the CCP had decided on a policy of compromise and had demanded that all comrades abide by it unanimously. We were to express to Chiang our readiness to grant concessions, and comrades were not to exhibit any discrepancies in their statements or their actions involving outside parties. This recommendation of mine had their unanimous support.

After this meeting, accompanied by Chou En-lai, I called on General Chiang Kai-shek (the time was about three days after my arrival at Canton) and conducted direct negotiations with him. I had visited Whampoa several times, and I had addressed cadets there; but this was a new visit to a familiar spot, and there was the feeling that times had changed. Chiang received me very politely, and we had lunch together as we talked.

I first informed Chiang that in calling on him I was representing the CC of the CCP. I explained that the CCP was consistently supporting him and hoped that there would continue to be sincere and unrestrained cooperation between us, so that the Kwangtung situation would become more stabilized and the revolutionary aspiration of the unification of all China would thus be realized. After Chiang had expressed similar sentiments, I went on to bring up two problems with him. The first was that people outside all hoped that he would continue to cooperate with Wang, but we did not know what his view on the subject was. The second was that CCP members among Whampoa cadets had always respected and obeyed him, but that they had suffered from the disease of infantilism; and I wondered how he was to teach them. On the first question Chiang did not express a definite opinion. On the second question he said that the Whampoa cadets that were members of the CCP were all good students of his, that he had always loved and protected them, and that he would surely make good use of them. In this way our conversation was brought to an end in a light and relaxed manner.

The two problems that I brought up with Chiang had been jointly decided upon at the meeting of the CCP Kwangtung District Committee. Chiang had never been fond of talking too much; and the attitude of reserve that he generally maintained seemed to show that he was assuming responsibility. This characteristic was revealed especially during our conversation on this occasion. What he said at least showed clearly that he fundamentally had no intention of excluding the Chinese Communists. His attitude toward Wang Ching-wei was necessarily an internal affair of the KMT; nevertheless we felt that we had a moral obligation toward Wang and that we had to bring up the issue before Chiang. But we had also anticipated that he would not give a definite reply.

My friendly call on Chiang on this occasion tended to ease the tension between the two sides. After our conversation he issued an order to organize a senior training class in Whampoa to accommodate the more than fifty Chinese Communists that had been removed from their posts in the army, and he appointed Chou En-lai as director of this class. At the time, Chou En-lai was in a very embarrassing position. He had been relieved of his duties as director of the Political Department at Whampoa, and his prestige had suffered greatly. But he had to keep on working at Whampoa and dealing with Chiang every day. Furthermore, his comrades in the Communist Party were taking him to task on many counts, holding that he must bear considerable responsibility for the occurrence of the March Twentieth Incident. This tested his endurance for the first time and also revealed his genius in handling situations. He never explained or answered questions about what had happened; and on the basis of our decisions, he carried out his training duties at Whampoa nonchalantly and showed even greater respect for Chiang.

A state of vacuum existed in the leadership in Kwangtung. It seemed vaguely that all actions had to be taken with deference to Chiang's whims, but what Chiang actually wanted to do and how far he would go appeared to be questions that no one could answer. In this situation T'an Yen-k'ai, the acting chairman of the National government, played the role of an intermediary who was supposed to piece together the views of the various sides. He did not seem to be hampered by the routine duties of the National government, but he spent the greater part of his time in meetings with various important persons. His activities served to stabilize the situation.

T'an Yen-k'ai maintained regular contact with me. We used the office of Borodin as our meeting place, with Chang T'ai-lei acting as the host. T'an was a political veteran. He had an adroit way of dealing with situations, betraying no traces of his inner feelings in his statements; although he did reveal to some degree his anxiety about giving prior attention to the general situation. He often talked garrulously and at length while seated calmly; and without making a fuss, he could develop the role of arbiter in dealing with disputes.

T'an and Chiang were very close to each other then. T'an often spent hours traveling by boat to Hu-men (Bocca Tigris) to see Chiang. Once he went there very early in the morning and did not return until he had to hurry back that evening for a meeting with me. He told me that he had spent the greater part of the day at Chiang's home and that nobody else had been there to see Chiang. T'an wondered where Chiang's imagination might have led him if he had not been there to engage Chiang in conversation and to inform Chiang accurately about facts from the various sides. Coming from the mouth of a deep-thinking and trained veteran like T'an Yen-k'ai, such words naturally implied inside developments that taxed one's mind.

The many contacts I had with T'an led to conversations covering a wide range of problems. We had discussed the fundamental policy of alliance with Russia. T'an had pointed out that had Kwangtung not received Soviet aid in arms, the national revolution would have been empty talk. It was not difficult for us to see generally from these words that Chiang would not abandon the policy of alliance with Russia. T'an went on to say that Borodin was adept at dealing with the problem and that everybody was waiting for his return. T'an fully outlined the significance in different areas of the policy of alliance with Russia. I also indicated to him my belief that Borodin's friendship for Chiang would not change. Our elucidation of the problem seemed to clear up certain doubts that people had with regard to the problem.

When we discussed the problem of KMT-CCP relations, I expressed to T'an the hope that Dr. Sun's policy of alliance with the Communists would not be distorted. With a comforting expression, T'an stated that Chiang had undergone a change of heart on this point and that there were facts to prove it. He also said frankly that it was possible that the CCP and the KMT might have to suffer a little setback. For example, members of the CCP and even leftist elements of the KMT would no longer be able to work in the First Army, but they could continue to work in the other armies. He also assured me that this would be the case in the Second Army, which he himself led. In other fields, such as work in the Party organization, he felt that even if Chiang should want to bring in some new people, it would not matter, because nobody could replace the Chinese Communists and the leftists in the leadership of the mass movement.

On this question T'an seemed disinclined to assume too much responsibility. He spoke in a light vein, "Chang Ching-chiang is the only one who could make decisions for Chiang, and there is no harm in having a talk with him." However, out of respect for T'an's position, I declined to follow his suggestion. With regard to this issue, we agreed that we should insist that neither CCP nor KMT members openly air their grievances out of consideration for the overall situation. I also explained to T'an in various ways that all incidents causing upheavals in Canton city were not connected with the Chinese Communists and that all members of the CCP could abide by discipline. T'an's explanations of this issue to Chiang and to others played a considerable role in dispelling the misunderstandings of the period.

Another major theme of our discussions was the problem of the leadership of the National government and the KMT. He had pointed out that there were difficulties in the resumption of cooperation between Wang and Chiang: Wang had not wished to continue in office, and outsiders could not force him to do what he did not want to do. I also told him that we were morally obligated to support Wang, but that we had no intention of suppressing Chiang by supporting Wang. Furthermore, this was an internal affair of the KMT, and we did not want to involve ourselves in the dispute.

T'an showed very great concern over this problem. He had told me frankly that the drama in Kwangtung could not be solely a military one and that there had to be a political front. There were then six armies, and without a political standard, they would be very difficult to control. Moreover, in the Kwangtung area it would not do for everything to be controlled by people from other provinces. He went on to say specifically that in view of the news of the pending return of Hu Han-min, since Wang did not want to carry on, there were those who would support Hu. Those who had such a proposal in mind thought that since Hu was returning from Moscow, he must have acquired a deeper understanding of the policy of alliance with the Soviet Union and tolerance of the Communists.

With regard to this problem affecting the leadership personnel of the KMT, I felt that to avoid complications it would be wise for me not to express a definite opinion. I only asked T'an what his inclination in the matter was. He pointed out that this would have to be determined by Hu's attitude after his return. He anticipated that there would be many difficulties in the way if members of the Hu clique tried to restore Hu to power. He proved his point by referring to Chiang's recent act by publicly showing people letters from Dr. Sun, particularly drawing their attention to a portion that read, "The Revolutionary Council today . . . is not one for Han-min and Ching-wei to preside over suitably. . . ."[5] This implied that at the time Chiang was also dissatisfied with Hu. Perhaps these words of T'an's were spoken merely to transmit to me the views of the Hu clique as a feeler. Since I refrained from any comment, T'an also said that he was an outsider himself and was only touching on the subject.

The sensitive T'an Yen-k'ai gradually came to feel that Chiang had realized that his subordinate forces had grown up and that he wanted to achieve a monopoly of the power. In a controversial vein T'an had talked about a Chinese Napoleon; he asked exactly what such a person would do and what effect he would have on the Chinese revolution. His facial expressions showed some anxiety. The host, Chang T'ai-lei, added that when he had accompanied Chiang in 1923 on a visit to the Soviet Union, they had viewed the historical relics of Napoleon's attack on Russia, and Chiang had unconsciously revealed his thoughts by comparing himself with Napoleon. "Chiang Kai-shek and Napoleon" immediately became an interesting topic in our talks. Although he was adept at going along with the tidal movement, T'an Yen-k'ai nevertheless could not be considered pleased over this development in the situation. I thought, however, that he would never act in opposition to the developing trends.

The fact that Chiang's intentions were now transformed into a desire to climb right to the top did not seem to be detected at once by Chang Ching-chiang. Chang, a native of Chekiang, was a middle-aged, ailing person adept at scheming, and he was Chiang Kai-shek's sworn elder brother. After the March Twentieth Incident he was especially invited by Chiang to come to Canton, and he lived in a house across from that of Chiang at Tungshan. He never appeared in public, but he was known by all as the man behind the scenes. Before T'an Yen-k'ai wanted me to contact Chang Ching-chiang, I had paid a courtesy call at his home. He told me that he had come to Canton for the Second National Congress and that all of his friends there had expressed views that were entirely optimistic. As one from an outlying province, he could not make heads or tails of it all. At the time he already had some doubts, and then unexpectedly the March Twentieth Incident happened. He pointed out that this proved that the leadership in Canton had not done a good job and that we from outlying provinces would now have to readjust the situation with an objective and impartial attitude, undertaking the settlement of all disputes from the roots. These words of his clearly expressed his self-assurance; possibly he had not yet fully understood what Chiang really expected of him.

On hearing these words from Chang Ching-chiang, I expressed my respect for him and asked what the policy for settling disputes from the roots was. He assumed an air indicating that top secrets could not be revealed. Probably it was because there were still some issues that he had not yet thrashed out with Chiang, so he could not express views offhand. He used his physical disability as an excuse for evading my questions. After all, he was not really the person officially responsible for political matters, and it was not convenient for me to call on him frequently. Sometimes I only asked T'an Yen-k'ai to transmit my views to Chang, and needless to say, in most cases there was no follow-up of the issues raised. T'an had told me that Chang Ching-chiang did not completely understand the Kwangtung situation and that he was highly reserved. To some degree this criticism supported the then-current rumors that referred to Chang as an old, incapable person and one who had come under the influence of the Western Hills Conference group.

Generally speaking, KMT-CCP relations, which had been about to break down, were finally eased. This was due, of course, to the fact that the opportunity for anti-Communist action was not yet ripe; but it was also due to the fact that as the spokesman of the CCP, I resolutely adhered to the policies of compromise and unanimity of position in dealing with outsiders that had been adopted by the other comrades of the CCP and that revealed an inherent force that would not be easily subdued. In the KMT also there were elements, like T'an Yen-k'ai, that did not want to alter an established policy, and they undertook the task of mediating a compromise. The dangerous situation created by the March Twentieth Incident thus gave way to signs of a change for the better.

The address delivered by General Chiang Kai-shek at Whampoa in defense of his actions in the March Twentieth Incident[6] criticized Kao Yü-han, the chief political instructor at Whampoa, for his improper conduct in hinting that Chiang was a new warlord. Chiang also explained that the CCP was not involved in the gunboat *Chungshan* incident, that such action was not in keeping with the general policy of the CCP. He also expressed opposition to the Western Hills Conference group in order to show that his action had not been influenced by the rightists. Furthermore, both the Young Soldiers' Association and the Sunyatsenist Society were abolished at the same time, presumably to show that he had no intention of siding with either of the two organizations. Following this, on April 14, Li Chih-lung, looked upon as the main character in the incident, was released; whereas orders were circulated to arrest Ou-yang K'o, who was active on March 20 as the provisional director-general of naval operations. This seemed to absolve the CCP from responsibility. All this at least proved that Chiang was not inclined to proceed to further extremes.

The CCP comrades in Canton were not thwarted by our measures of making concessions, but continued to develop their activities. They continued to make active preparations for the Third National Labor Congress, scheduled to open in Canton on May 1, and the Second Kwangtung Provincial Peasants' Congress. The Canton–Hong Kong Strike Committee and its picket corps (whose weapons were restored to them shortly after they were disarmed) carried out their duties as usual in the blockade of the ports. T. V. Soong, who succeeded Liao Chung-k'ai as Minister of Finance, also believed that the activities of the striking workers continued to make contributions to government revenue. Active membership in peasant associations in the various counties continued to increase; but under the restraint of the CCP, there was a marked reduction in the number of armed conflicts between the peasants and the landlords.

Under such circumstances, seizure of the leadership of the KMT from within appeared to become the focal point in the development of the situation. Hu Han-min returned to Canton from Moscow toward the end of April, and his arrival at this particular moment led to many rumors. Members of the Hu clique circulated reports that Hu had reemerged from retirement to form a Hu-Chiang alliance, and they also propagated a vigorous anti-Communist campaign. But the cleavage between Chiang and Hu appeared difficult to patch up. It was stated that Hu had met Chiang at Whampoa, but the nature of their talks was not made known to the outside world. It was a fact, however, that Hu never made a public appearance. This was a great disappointment to the anti-Communist heroes of the time.

On April 29 Borodin returned to Canton (a little later than Hu Han-min).[7] He landed at Whampoa and went to see Chiang first. When I learned this, I went to his office to wait for him; and in a little while, I met with him. His mind was uneasy and he expressed regret that the situation had deteriorated so much in just three months since his departure—something he had not anticipated. He told me that General Chiang Kai-shek had just told him that Hu Han-min had asked Chiang not to trust Borodin any more and to place the latter under detention. When he said this, Borodin shrugged his shoulders. He added that while he did not believe that he would be detained, he nevertheless felt that his good friend General Chiang Kai-shek actually had used Hu's words to make a show of power in front of him, and this could not but make him feel that times had changed.

Borodin pointed out to me that he had no confidence in being able to restore the Canton situation to its previous status, that he could only act as developments allowed. But Moscow respected his views and had vested greater authority in him. He had practically been given plenipotentiary powers to deal with everything as expediency required. On the basis of Moscow's wishes, he asked me to inform the CC of the CCP and comrades in general that they should have full confidence in him as Moscow did. Particularly at such a moment, we could not afford to be the least bit out of step. For my part, I naturally told him succinctly what I knew of the situation.

After he returned, Borodin rapidly became the nerve center of political contacts. My work situation also underwent a change. I rid myself of the greater part of political activities with the outside and turned my attention to guiding the routine tasks of the CCP Kwangtung

District Committee and the two important labor and peasant congresses about to be convened.

On May 1—Labor Day—1926, the Third National Congress of Labor and the Second Kwangtung Provincial Peasants' Congress were opened. The labor congress was attended by 502 delegates, who represented about 1,240,000 members of trade unions in all areas. The primary goal of the Congress was to further consolidate the foundations of the All-China Labor Federation. The peasant congress was attended by more than two hundred delegates. In addition to the delegates from the peasant associations in sixty of the counties of Kwangtung (with a total membership of about 620,000), there were also some representatives of peasant organizations in Kwangsi, Fukien, Hunan, Hupeh, Chekiang, Kiangsu, Honan, Shantung, Shansi, and Kweichow. It was much livelier than the First Congress, and it paved the way for the later vigorous development of the peasant movement during the Wuhan period. I attended both these congresses and delivered addresses. The CC of the CCP also sent communications to these two meetings calling for great unity among workers and peasants.

The progress of these two congresses revealed the strength of the CCP among the masses of workers and peasants. They also helped to promote a leftist development in the situation. The workers of the city of Canton and the peasants of its environs held a mammoth demonstration and appealed to the National government to launch the Northern Expedition at an early date. They also demanded protection of the interests of the workers and peasants. General Chiang Kai-shek held a banquet at Whampoa to welcome the entire delegations of these two congresses. On that occasion he expressed views that were the same as those he had expressed previously and that were filled with revolutionary flavor. This appeared to make up for the noticeable absence of Whampoa cadets among participants in the two congresses. Be this as it may, memories of the March Twentieth Incident were still fresh, and the feelings of those present were naturally a little strained.

At this time, all important political problems were being discussed in private among the "big three"—Chiang Kai-shek, Chang Ching-chiang, and Borodin. Even T'an Yen-k'ai, who had always served as the middleman, seemed to be excluded from participation in meetings in the inner sanctum. Borodin's home was no longer the scene of intense activity that it once was. In the past all important personages had called on him there for advice, but now he had to take himself to the home of Chang Ching-chiang, who was semiparalyzed, to carry on detailed discussions with Chiang Kai-shek and Chang.

It was about May 2 when Borodin made a second appointment with me. He was apparently calmer in spirits. He praised my statements and acts during the critical period as appropriate and effective in helping to salvage the situation. He expressed his desire to follow the line I had taken and his hope that I would help him.

Though Borodin expressed such views, his actions showed that his attitude was somewhat different from mine. His primary concern seemed to be with healing the breach in the relations between the Soviet Union and Chiang Kai-shek. KMT-CCP relations and the position of Wang Ching-wei appeared to be secondary issues. In order to save the shaky prestige of himself and Moscow, he placed responsibility for the outbreak of the March Twentieth Incident on the shoulders of the CC of the CCP. This policy of his guided all his actions during this period.

At this meeting that I had with Borodin, he analyzed the causes of the outbreak of the March Twentieth Incident. He expressed the opinion that General Chiang Kai-shek was politically in the middle and that Dr. Sun Yat-sen was also in the middle, but that both had strong anti-Communist feelings. Had Dr. Sun been alive, he would also have taken certain measures to restrain the activities of the CCP. Such a line taken by Borodin led me into having doubts. I asked him whether he held that the March Twentieth Incident was absolutely unavoidable and whether he held that the policy of CCP cooperation within the KMT must necessarily be wrecked. When I questioned him thus, he seemed to realize that his explanation was untenable, and so he changed his tune and said, "Had Dr. Sun been alive, if he had wanted to restrain the activities of the CCP, he would not have adopted the form used on March 20."

And so Borodin abandoned the exploration of the basic causes of the incident and turned to telling me directly that the central problem of the day was whether or not the Russians would be forced to leave Canton. He quoted propaganda in Hong Kong, such reports as "Canton authorities will expel all local Russians" and "the practice of expelling the Communists." Hu Han-min actually did officially propose Borodin's detention. All this proved that the imperialists and rightists were making serious plans to undermine China-Soviet and KMT-CCP relations.

Considering these conditions, Borodin told me that if our situation were not so bad as the imperialists and rightists hoped, there was still a possibility of devising measures that would heal the breaches, at least temporarily, and that victory could still be ours. He also stated solemnly that Moscow both in theory and in practice supported the Chinese national revolution and had therefore established relations with the KMT. Should the March Twentieth Incident lead to the undermining of these relations, Moscow would find it impossible to justify its policy both to the country and to the world. Accordingly Moscow had consistently tried to play down the seriousness of this incident and hoped that we could devise measures to salvage the situation.

Borodin thus revealed that both he and Moscow were in an embarrassing situation. Except for attempting once more to make use of his artifices, there seemed no other really effective measure. Assuming a sympathetic attitude, I asked him what exalted measures he had in mind. He thought for a while and replied, "At present idle talk will not help matters. The one thing on which we can pin our hopes is that in my pocket I still have some green stuff." I asked him smilingly, "May I ask Adviser Borodin how much green stuff he has brought with him in his pocket this time? Are you not afraid that such statements of yours will rouse reaction from people?" He smiled over my question and gave no answer.

After this conversation with me, Borodin started to act. He first adopted the method of attacking the CC of the CCP in order to reestablish his personal prestige. He asked the CCP Kwangtung District Committee to hold a plenary session. At the meeting he made an address attacking the inappropriateness of the policy of withdrawal previously adopted by the CC of the CCP. He explained that at the end of 1925 the CC of the CCP at Shanghai had had a meeting with Sun, Yeh, and Shao of the KMT. This meeting led to an agreement that produced bad results. This action primarily gave the anti-Communist elements in the KMT a hint that even if they should adopt measures opposing and suppressing the CCP, the latter would accept them meekly; and so this encouraged the outbreak of the March Twentieth Incident.

This analysis of Borodin's was an attempt to place the responsibility for the March Twentieth Incident on the CC of the CCP; this was very clear. He pointed out that Moscow had already rejected such a policy of withdrawal on the part of the CC of the CCP; but the policy of withdrawal that he was about to adopt was inevitable and temporary. He further declared that he was limiting his review to the past and that he did not imply basic opposition to the leadership of the CC of the CCP. He especially requested the CCP Kwangtung District Committee to cooperate closely with me so as to present a united front in coping with the current situation.

These views of Borodin had the support of the majority of members of the Kwangtung District Committee. I, as the representative of the CC of the CCP, pointed out at the time that the CC's consistent policy of uniting with the middle group to isolate the rightists was not the real reason for the March Twentieth Incident. But the majority of the responsible comrades in Kwangtung agreed that the matter should not be discussed in detail, and thus they lightly laid aside the views that I brought up. After the meeting, Chang T'ai-lei gave me an explanation that seemed to cover the trouble that Borodin had taken to deal with this issue. Chang pointed out that since the incident of March 20 could not be explained as absolutely unavoidable, then we ourselves (meaning the Communists as a whole) should at least share some responsibility. If we said that the policy of Moscow or the acts of the Russian advisers were at fault, then it would produce a very bad effect in the international field. And if we said that Borodin was wrong, it would be impossible for him to carry on his work. So only by admitting that the CC of the CCP had made a mistake in the measures it took during a certain short period could we minimize the damage done.

Borodin's delicate approach produced results for a time and thus solved the problem of the shaky positions of Borodin and the leaders of the Kwangtung District Committee. Chou En-lai, who held an important post at Whampoa, could not shirk his responsibility, but he had been absolutely silent at the meeting. Now that Borodin had provided this explanation, which gave him a way out, he seemed to be greatly relieved. Mao Tse-tung had always been dissatisfied with the methods of Borodin and the Kwangtung District Committee. After the March Twentieth Incident he had rid himself of the propaganda duties given him by the CEC of the KMT and had devoted himself entirely to the Peasant Movement Training Institute; so he did not take part in this meeting. When he found out later about what had happened, he told me that he was surprised that the foreign devil Borodin had resorted to such political tactics. He expressed sympathy for me and the other comrades that had labored so hard and then taken the blame. But from beginning to end he himself stayed away from the dispute and remained a bystander. He seemed to have gained considerable experience from it.

At the time I felt that Borodin's reasons for castigating the CC of the CCP were untenable and contrary to the principle of righteousness; but

I appreciated the great difficulties of the moment and decided to be tolerant temporarily. Very soon the CC of the CCP came to know the facts and adopted the same attitude. This policy of disregarding right and wrong and giving concessions to authority was to cause endless trouble in the future. When the CCP later suffered defeat at Wuhan, Stalin again laid the responsibility for the failure on the CC of the CCP. This showed that the Russian leaders were consistently pursuing the policy of "laying down the law like a master." Had we, the responsible members of the CC of the CCP, been far-sighted at the time and disregarded success and failure to stick to our guns, later developments might possibly have followed a different course.

Many of the other things that Borodin told me at the time also gave me much food for thought. When we discussed the problem of the leadership of the KMT, Borodin said that he had already told me about Wang's character, and since Wang did not want to appear in public, others could not do anything about it. (It was said that Wang very much wanted to have a talk with Borodin; but Borodin never told me whether they met or what they talked about if they met.) The designs of Hu Han-min could not succeed either. From Borodin's revelation, it was possible to see that the transfer of KMT leadership had been decided upon, and it was also easy to guess who was to assume the leadership. But he did not want to make any conjectures about the future of the KMT after the transfer of leadership.

So it transpired that before the May 15 meeting of the CEC of the KMT (it has been reported as being on May 9), Wang Ching-wei and Hu Han-min both left Canton. The coincidence was that without previous appointment they found themselves on the same boat.[8] This incident immediately became a topic of conversation among the persons in high places in Kwangtung. Some said, "Enemies meet on a narrow path and actually find themselves on the same boat. We wonder what their feelings were when they met on the boat." Some said, "When the crane and the oyster hold fast to each other in a struggle, the fisherman by the side profits. These two powerful men contended for the chairmanship and are now both expelled, while a newly risen person, who would have had to knock them down one by one, assumes the post of leadership. It is truly a case of poetic justice."

The next time that Borodin described the position of the Russians in Canton, he seemed to be more optimistic. He said frankly, "China is no man's land." He followed this with the statement that all through history when foreigners had come to China to engage in activities, though they had suffered some setbacks, their spirit of adventure and capacity to handle situations had always brought them appreciable returns. So why couldn't the Russians have the same opportunities? I told Borodin sarcastically that such a view was contrary to the revolutionary stand and smacked a little of the colonialists, who held the Chinese people in contempt. He only smiled and did not defend himself. He seemed to be indulging in self-appreciation of his political acumen, saying that if it were not for the protection of Russian interests, he could not afford to bother with the future of the Chinese national revolution.

One Soviet vessel loaded with arms reached Whampoa; this was sensational news. Soviet arms had arrived; and rumors circulated everywhere that Chiang would again ally with the Communists to suppress the anti-Communist elements. The story even spread that at the meeting of the CEC of the KMT on May 15 an announcement would be made concerning the adoption of communism. The news also circulated that General Galen was returning to Canton to assume once more the post of general military adviser to Chiang Kai-shek. Needless to say, Borodin's spirits were greatly lifted, and it seemed that the "green stuff" in his pocket had produced results.

I felt deeply that under Borodin's policies the CCP would continue to be attacked. So I asked him, "What changes are going to occur in the relations between the KMT and the CCP?" He replied, "To speak frankly, the CCP appears to be fated to play the role of a coolie in the Chinese revolution." Then I asked, "Are you prepared to serve as the foreman of these coolies?" And he replied, "Some people actually entertain such a hope; but I am an old Bolshevik and will not assume such a dishonorable post." From that time, Borodin's statement—"the CCP is the coolie of the Chinese revolution"—became a classic saying known to all.

Needless to say, I could not resign myself to serving as a coolie of the Chinese revolution. I solemnly asked Borodin why if the Soviet government could supply large quantities of arms to an unreliable Chiang Kai-shek, did it not give some of them directly to the Chinese workers and peasants? If the Soviet government did so, the CCP could, by using the ports controlled by the Workers' Picket Corps and Peasants' Self-Defense Corps, help to solve transportation difficulties. Since Borodin had claimed that his current measures of concession were different from the concession policy of the CC of the CCP in that they called for

temporary withdrawal and stressed the importance of land revolution, I
aroused Borodin further by saying that if the peasants were not armed,
all this talk about temporary withdrawal and land revolution would be
idle talk. After some consideration, Borodin rejected my proposal to arm
the peasants, pointing out that it was not permissible under existing conditions and that a future opportunity would have to be awaited.

Generally speaking, Communists would not make an aimless retreat.
Even if a policy of retreat were actually being carried out, it had to be
accompanied by some explanation of attack. For stark retreat would be
considered opportunism in its worst form. What Borodin proceeded to
carry out was precisely a policy of retreat accompanied by explanation.
And he continued to put such big labels as "refusal to attack" and "no
attention to the land revolution" on the head of the CC of the CCP.
Later Stalin's criticism of the opportunism of Ch'en Tu-hsiu was a
further development of this strategy. We only need to note that at this
critical moment Borodin rejected my proposal to arm the peasants, to
prove that such criticism was at least excessive.

During this period of early May preceding the plenum of the CEC
of the KMT, all important issues were discussed in secret among the big
three of Chiang, Chang, and Borodin. Borodin seemed to abide by the
agreement of the trio and would not reveal the true facts to me. Most of
what he did tell me was ambiguous. I was dissatisfied with this and
expressed a desire to return to Shanghai, to show that I did not want to
share responsibility with Borodin. He always asked me to have confidence in him and asserted that he would not make a mess of things.

At about 5 P.M. on May 14, Borodin looked up T'an P'ing-shan and
me and asked us to call on Chiang Kai-shek and Chang Ching-chiang
immediately. He said this was absolutely necessary, because the KMT
plenum was to take place the following day and there were a lot of
rumors around, principally that the Communists would launch a demonstration to oppose the resolutions of the KMT. Chiang Kai-shek had
expressed concern over these stories. So Borodin hoped that we would
tell Chiang that since we did not know what the next day's meeting
would discuss, we naturally could not make any open signs of opposition
and that if any pamphlets, slogans, or other actions opposing the meeting
were in evidence in Canton the next day, they had nothing to do with
the CCP.

Borodin's proposal embarrassed both me and T'an P'ing-shan. T'an,
a Communist who served as the director of the KMT Organization De-

partment, had always been close to Wang Ching-wei and other leftists. After March 20 he had no contact with Chiang and consistently maintained an attitude of silence. On hearing Borodin's words, he smiled without speaking, and his attitude showed that he felt the proposal difficult to carry out. I indicated that in Canton rumors were current that undermined KMT-CCP relations. People already knew that they were not connected with the CCP. At the time we only knew that a proposal on the adjustment of Party affairs would be brought up at the KMT meeting, but we did not know its details. If we assured others that we would definitely not oppose it, we would practically destroy the status of the CCP. However, after Borodin's repeated persuasion, we finally acceded to his request.

At about eight that evening T'an P'ing-shan and I drove to Tungshan to call on General Chiang Kai-shek. In accordance with Borodin's request, we explained to Chiang the attitude of the CCP toward the meeting of the KMT. Chiang was greatly elated as if he had won a great victory and immediately accompanied us to see Chang Ching-chiang. Once more we gave our explanation, and Chang also showed signs of great elation. He indicated that this was indeed very good and since we could tolerate one another in the interests of the country, the success of the revolution was assured.

This interview of ours was concluded in the midst of an atmosphere of harmony. But both T'an P'ing-shan and I had heavy hearts. T'an P'ing-shan especially remained silent during the return journey in the car, and his facial expression revealed great displeasure. He seemed to be thinking that he might be purged in the Party Affairs Readjustment Plan to be discussed in the meeting the next day and that as one about to be purged, he had had to go first to his political foe and assume a smiling face toward him. After all, it was not an enjoyable experience.

On May 15, 1926, the Second Plenum of the second CC of the KMT opened under heavy security conditions. The main task to be accomplished at the meeting was passage of the Party Affairs Readjustment Plan under the guise of preparation for the Northern Expedition. Important changes were made in KMT-CCP relations and in the leadership of the KMT. From that time onward, Chiang Kai-shek climbed to the apex of the leadership. It was also the beginning of the ascendancy of military authority over Party authority.

The principal contents of the Party Affairs Readjustment Plan[9] were: (1) members of the CCP in the KMT must not have doubts about or criticism of the Three Principles of the People; (2) a person with dual Party membership could not serve as director of a department at KMT central headquarters, and CCP membership on an executive committee of a high-level KMT organization could not exceed one-third the total membership of the relevant committee; (3) a KMT-CCP joint conference was to be established; (4) Communist International's directives to the CCP and orders of the CC of the CCP to Communist Party members within the KMT must first be presented to the Joint Conference for approval; (5) a list of CCP members within the KMT must be given to the chairman of the CEC of the KMT for custody; (6) KMT members must not join the CCP; and so forth. In the eyes of the CCP, the measures adopted by the KMT for the readjustment of Party affairs did not constitute the so-called transition from "toleration of the Communists" to "alliance with the Communists"[10] but rather were intended to restrict the development of the CCP and abolish its independent existence.

The meeting put an end to the leadership of Wang Ching-wei. Nominally Chang Ching-chiang replaced him, though actual power fell into the hands of Chiang. On the proposal of General Chiang Kai-shek, Chang Ching-chiang, who had been a member of the CSC, was elected chairman of the CEC. T'an Yen-k'ai succeeded Wang as chairman of the KMT Central Political Council as well as chairman of the National government. Chiang himself replaced T'an P'ing-shan as director of the Department of Organization of the central headquarters of the Party. Chiang promoted all of these reforms by himself, although they might have been discussed beforehand in secret by the big three of Chiang, Chang, and Borodin.

Communist Party members present at the meeting, like T'an P'ing-shan and Lin Tsu-han, adopted an attitude of tolerance and reservation. They declared that they were not authorized to decide on certain things, which had to be dealt with by the CC of the CCP.

However, the meeting also exposed internal disputes within the KMT. At the election of the chairman of the CEC on May 19, Li Chi-shen, commander of the Fourth Army, asked, "Can someone not present at this meeting be elected?" Chang Ching-chiang, who presided over the meeting, could only reply, "Surely he can." So Li Chi-shen wrote on the voting slip the three characters "Hu Han Min," each one the size of an apple, and withdrew from the meeting. This incident led to talk among important persons in Canton. Some said, "Li Chi-shen is not satisfied with Chiang Kai-shek's arrogance and had wanted to vote Wang Ching-wei; but he feared this would lead to dispute, and so he voted for Hu Han-min instead, to show his nonsubmission." Others said, "The people of the Fourth Army, being Cantonese, have been dissatisfied with the arrogance of the Chekiang clique,[11] and the slogans against the Chekiang clique that are found in the city have all been their work. Li Chi-shen's vote for Hu Han-min proves this story." It is possible that this was the beginning of the strained relations between Li Chi-shen and Chiang Kai-shek.

When the Party Affairs Readjustment Plan was announced, CCP members in Canton were all alarmed and indignant. Some said, "Borodin was kidnapped, and Chang Kuo-t'ao and T'an P'ing-shan served as the representatives that made the surrender." Some said, "Why don't we take the initiative and suggest a change in the form of KMT-CCP cooperation, from cooperation within the KMT to cooperation outside the KMT? Why do we not withdraw from the KMT? Why do we assume a defensive position and let ourselves be readjusted by others in a way that smacks of punishment?" These reactions could not be easily suppressed.

Borodin was not happy. But he put up a calm front and made many explanations that were to his benefit. He said to me, "The Hong Kong papers are writing in a disappointing mood that with the conclusion of the May 15 meeting, the anti-Communist elements continue to be attacked, and Chiang Kai-shek continues to maintain cooperative relations with Moscow and the CCP. These reports show that we have not been expelled from Kwangtung, and this is a disappointment to them [meaning the imperialists]. Since we are not expelled, there is still a chance for victory. This point alone shows that we did not make a mistake in our handling of the situation."

Borodin also stated that on May 15 there were actually rumors of a business strike, there was a run on the central bank, and slogans such as "practice communism and share properties" and "kill the Communists" were reported. These facts proved that the counterrevolutionaries were very active. The military authority [referring to Chiang Kai-shek] was very nervous about the situation and feared a second March Twentieth Incident. We had foresight, and consistently adopting a calm attitude, reached an understanding with Chiang and Chang before the event. In the meeting we did not express opposing views. Borodin said that all of this proved that we were not foolhardy enough to voluntarily throw ourselves into the trap laid by the enemy.

He also stated that the rightists did not get the upper hand at the meeting. He himself was not detained, but Hu Han-min, who called for Borodin's detention, was himself expelled. Wu T'ieh-ch'eng, who was plotting trouble, was detained; and Wu Ch'ao-shu, who was in collusion with Hong Kong, also voluntarily left Canton. The Western Hills elements were unable to establish a foothold in Kwangtung. All this showed that we were not the party to be severely hit. He also told me that according to what he had learned, the rightists were depressed and showed their disappointment. Furthermore, the resolution of the meeting clearly stipulated that there should be cooperation among all revolutionary forces in the struggle against the reactionaries. We could surely use this as the basis to do something vigorous, to promote the KMT, and to continue marching in the direction of revolution.

Not only was the disappointment of the KMT rightists a fact at the time, but the so-called leftists also were disappointed and indignant. Among them some held that had Wang Ching-wei been able to bring up a well-thought-out plan for the readjustment of Party affairs in the spirit of promoting KMT-CCP cooperation, what happened might have been averted. The majority of them paid attention to the question of Party power. Some said, "Wang Ching-wei has been ousted, and Party power is also bankrupt. Today it is the world of the militarists." Borodin, who was the peacemaker, needed to do some comforting work among these disgruntled leftists.

When I discussed the course of future action with Borodin, he indicated that despite the majority of Communist comrades advocating withdrawal from the KMT, the Comintern would definitely not approve of it. The reason was that since the CCP members had joined the KMT, they could not now withdraw before they had achieved something. He also stated positively, "The KMT and the CCP must separate, but the later the separation, the better. When the Northern Expedition reaches Peking, it will be probably a good time for separation to be carried out. Today there must be toleration and cooperation."

On the basis of such a viewpoint, Borodin recommended to me that the CC of the CCP not attach importance to this plan for readjustment of Party affairs. The actual losses were only the stipulations that Communists could not exceed one-third of an executive committee of a high-level Party organ and that a Communist could not serve as director of a central department. As to the handing over of lists and the examination of CCP orders to its members, these were unilateral decisions of the

KMT, and the CC of the CCP could protest them in a future meeting of the Joint Conference.

Borodin knew that I was about to return to Shanghai, and he wanted me to transmit his recommendations to the CC of the CCP. He advocated procrastination in dealing with the Joint Conference demanded by the KMT. If it was not possible to procrastinate, the CC of the CCP should dispatch representatives to Canton to participate. He added, "You have personally gone through the developments in Canton. Needless to say, you will become one of the representatives. If you are, then you might come first and look into the situation. If the KMT really wants to hold the Joint Conference, there will still be time for the other CCP representatives to come here."

At this point T'an P'ing-shan injected another view. He indignantly said to me that he was a member of the old Tung-meng Hui. Since Chiang Kai-shek was so arrogant and the CCP so tolerant, he did not want to be a Communist any longer. He wanted to use his status as an old Tung-meng Hui member to fight Chiang Kai-shek and the Chekiang clique openly by uniting with Li Chi-shen, a man with actual military power, and the group of veteran KMT members who were natives of Kwangtung. At T'an's request, I accompanied him to call on Borodin for a secret discussion. During this discussion Borodin revealed another inclination of his.

Quite contrary to my expectation, Borodin not only refrained from opposing T'an P'ing-shan's view, but he even asked T'an what plans he had for forging ties with Li Chi-shen. T'an proceeded to say that if we were not against his proposal, he would make a try. Borodin no longer concealed his resentment against Chiang Kai-shek and Chang Ching-chiang. He pointed out that there were many disputes within the KMT and that in particular many people found the stubbornness of Chang Ching-chiang abhorrent. It was not strange that there should be people that opposed him.

These words indicated that although Borodin outwardly went to the extremes of toleration in dealing with Chiang and Chang, he actually attempted to exploit the internal contradictions of the KMT. He wanted to start with opposition to Chang Ching-chiang in order to change the status quo. This became the guiding principle for all his future actions and supplied the footnote to his use of temporary retreat to attempt a new attack. As to T'an P'ing-shan, he did not achieve marked success in forging ties with Li Chi-shen. Possibly this was because Li, while opposing Chiang, did not want to be pro-Communist. A short time later T'an left Kwangtung and went to Moscow to participate in the Seventh Enlarged Plenum of the ECCI, held in November, 1926. Stalin had a high regard for T'an and seemed to have the idea of letting him succeed Ch'en Tu-hsiu in the CCP leadership. Perhaps it was because his proposal of allying with A to overthrow B was appreciated by Stalin.

At the time I felt that Borodin's way of thinking was full of the character of adventure. I felt that everything that happened in Canton during the period March 20 through May 15 was on a course that weakened control of the KMT by the Soviet Union, doused the flames of the CCP, and strengthened the leadership of the bourgeoisie. It also signified the rise of warlordism. All these factors called on the CCP to change its course and seek to advance outside the KMT.

I talked to Borodin about some of his ideas, such as: "The CCP is fated to be the coolie of the Chinese revolution"; "We cannot withdraw from the KMT with empty hands"; "Unite with all revolutionary forces"; and "Exploit the internal contradictions of the KMT." I felt that these various views were contradictory. I talked to him about my view that the CCP should adopt a strategy of advancing by way of retreating. CCP members should gradually withdraw from the KMT and turn their attention to the independent development of mass work among workers and peasants, thus not involving themselves in the internal disputes of the KMT. With the projected Northern Expedition and with the rise of the influence of the militarists, the internal disputes of the KMT would increase endlessly. If the CCP would exploit the opportunity to expand its strength, there would be opportunities for advance. Borodin sarcastically referred to my views as "steps of retreat." He held that if after May 15 the CCP adopted the step of gradual withdrawal from the KMT, it would be a sign of its weakness and inability to withstand the blow.

I did not persist in my view to the point of developing a debate with Borodin. The basic reason was that I did not have sufficient self-confidence. I still believed that Borodin was an old hand with greater knowledge; and with the all-powerful Comintern behind him, he was not to be taken on the same level as Maring. So I could only return to the CC of the CCP in Shanghai to make further detailed studies. At the same time, CCP comrades in Canton were expecting me to return to Shanghai to decide on an overall policy to be followed in the future. So in the latter part of May, I hurriedly left Canton, the area of trouble.

Prelude to the Northern Expedition

The changes in the Canton situation from March 20 through May 15, 1926, were interrelated to the preparations for the Northern Expedition. Viewed from the angle of the Northern Expedition, the changes within the camp of the revolutionists were even more clearly explained. The policy of the Northern Expedition was a traditional one originally conceived by Dr. Sun Yat-sen. Using Kwangtung as the base for the revolution, an army was to be sent northward to suppress the warlords and unify China. General Chiang Kai-shek issued the call to implement the will of Dr. Sun by carrying out the Northern Expedition. He roused the revolutionary spirit of the KMT; but some people felt that he did not possess the prestige equal to that enjoyed by Dr. Sun, and this made them feel that he was exploiting the situation to establish his personal military dictatorship. It was the root of the subsequent split in the revolutionary camp.

After I returned to Shanghai at the end of May that year, I immediately found out that the CC of the CCP had received instructions from the Comintern clearly prohibiting its withdrawal from the KMT.[12] This proved that Borodin's proposal had won Stalin's support. At the time, Voitinsky obeyed orders strictly and naturally could not voice any dissent. Even in speaking to Borodin he did not express further doubts. Though at the time Ch'en Tu-hsiu and I had placed before a meeting of the CC the pros and cons—the advantages and disadvantages—of withdrawal from the KMT, the discussion resulted in the majority of us advocating obedience to the instruction from the Comintern. A considerable role was played by Borodin's statement "after May 15, the adoption of the step of withdrawal from the KMT by the CCP would be an admission of weakness due to its inability to withstand the blow given it."

We had a lengthy discussion and decided that the policy we should adopt in dealing with the KMT at that stage was to unite with the leftists, restrain Chiang Kai-shek, and attack the rightists. We held that in the March Twentieth Incident, the KMT leftist clique had exhibited its weakness, but it still possessed considerable potential. We sympathized with the leftists that hoped Wang Ching-wei could stage a comeback, and we felt that without Wang Ching-wei we would have no way of uniting with the left wing. This kind of thinking on our part—supporting Wang Ching-wei and restraining Chiang Kai-shek—was nothing more than an attempt to prevent the excessive rise of military power and to avoid having the rightists create trouble by using the militarists. There was still no fundamental desire to oppose Chiang personally.

In dealing with the KMT request for the organization of the two-party Joint Conference, we accepted the recommendation of Borodin and did not attach much importance to the matter. If the KMT presented an official invitation, we would send representatives to Canton to attend it. We advocated, however, that the Joint Conference not be exclusively given over to disputes between the two parties, but rather that it be constructive in character, having as its primary topic of discussion the future close cooperation of the two parties. The CC of the CCP elected Ch'ü Ch'iu-pai, T'an P'ing-shan, and myself as the three representatives to any such conference.

It was at this moment that we received a letter from the CCP Kwangtung District Committee, reporting that Chang Ching-chiang had verbally transmitted an invitation to representatives of the CCP to attend the Joint Conference. So the CC of the CCP sent me to Canton first, to discuss the procedure of the Joint Conference with the CEC of the KMT. On this occasion I stayed in Shanghai only about a week and once more hurriedly reappeared in Canton.

After a short absence I found Canton had undergone marked changes. Talk of the Northern Expedition filled the air, and people did not seem to be concerned with the two-party Joint Conference. According to what Ch'en Yen-nien told me, after the verbal message from Chang Ching-chiang, no further invitation had been received from the CEC of the KMT. Borodin also told me that nobody had mentioned the Joint Conference to him. When I visited T'an Yen-k'ai, I mentioned the proposal that the Joint Conference should be constructive in character. He said, "Today the center of people's attention is the Northern Expedition, and nobody now mentions the Joint Conference. If this meeting is really held, how would it further active cooperation between the two parties? It can only lead to a quarrel over some disputed issues." He also suggested that I did not need to contact Chang Ching-chiang on this subject. And so the two-party Joint Conference died an abortive death before a single session was held. I was glad not to bring up the issue any more, and for the time being I lived in a mansion at Tungshan with flowers and shrubs around it[13] and became a relatively leisurely visitor.

People had pinned great hopes on the Northern Expedition. KMT elements in general were optimistic over the Expedition and seemed to think that it would be successful in a short time. Military officers of the middle and lower ranks were very enthusiastically rubbing their hands, wanting an opportunity to display their talents in the Northern Expedition and to discharge their revolutionary obligations. The awakened masses of workers and peasants looked forward to liberation from the rule of the northern warlords, who had oppressed them for so many years. The Kwangtung merchants and citizens in general were also elated over the Northern Expedition, thinking that their burden would be lightened if the large armies massed in Kwangtung were transferred northward. All this made the Northern Expedition possess a magic power, which held sway for the time.

A small number of military leaders had different designs on the Northern Expedition. General Chiang Kai-shek, who was steadily climbing to new heights, seemed to rely on armed might to realize his ambitious personal objectives and to display his great talent. Perhaps because there was marked exclusion of outsiders by the Cantonese, heroes from other provinces generally felt that Kwangtung was not the place for them to exhibit their talents and that only by returning to their own villages and provinces on the lower reaches of the Yangtze could they build up the foundations for their life-long reign of power. Others, including generals that were natives of Kwangtung, could not but think that when these heroes from outside left the province to fight for their own empires, they themselves would be able to become the real masters of Kwangtung. The majority of generals from other provinces also felt that by seeking a foothold outside Kwangtung, they would be relieved of their present depression and would be able to develop in the future. And so another term for the Northern Expedition was "development outward." The role of this policy of outward expansion would be to further reduce internal contradictions. Furthermore, the time was most favorable for the Northern Expedition.

After the unification of Kwangtung, General Chiang Kai-shek did not concur with the proposal of Kisanko about the dispatch of troops to the North to support Feng Yü-hsiang, but he immediately issued a call for the Northern Expedition. KMT leaders started preparations for the task. In the winter of 1925 ties were forged between Wang Ching-wei and the Kwangsi military leader Li Tsung-jen, and in February, 1926, Li assumed the post of commander of the Seventh Army of the National Revolutionary Army. This not only unified the two Kwang provinces, but it also increased the capital for the Northern Expedition.

When Dr. Sun Yat-sen had launched the Northern Expedition

earlier, Hunan, which was controlled by Chao Heng-t'i, blocked his way. Now the situation had changed. A portion of the military forces in Hunan volunteered to serve as the vanguard in paving the way for the Northern Expedition. The division of T'ang Sheng-chih, the commander of Chao Heng-t'i's Fourth Division, which garrisoned southern Hunan, had from an early date colluded with the Kwangsi military leaders. In February, 1926, T'ang Sheng-chih marched on Changsha, expelled Chao Heng-t'i, who was pro–Wu P'ei-fu, and succeeded Chao as governor of Hunan. Later, over the question of the unification of the armies of the whole province, Yeh K'ai-hsin, originally commander of the Third Division under Chao, did not submit to orders and colluded with Wu P'ei-fu, who sent troops into Hunan to reinforce Yeh. T'ang was defeated in the battle, and on April 20 he withdrew to Hengyang. T'ang sent an emergency appeal to the authorities of the two Kwang provinces in the hope of getting military aid. In May portions of Li Chi-shen's Fourth Army and of Li Tsung-jen's Seventh Army entered Hunan in answer to T'ang's appeal. On June 2 T'ang himself accepted the appointment of Commander of the Eighth Army of the National Revolutionary Army. Thus the Northern Expedition actually had already started.

Another aspect of the situation was that internal disputes among the northern warlords had weakened them. Though the Kuominchun of Feng Yü-hsiang had been forced to withdraw toward Kalgan and Paotow, the Executive government at Peking under Tuan Ch'i-jui, had been overthrown by the Kuominchun on April 9.[14] Chang Tso-lin, who occupied the land north of the Great Wall, Wu P'ei-fu, who used the Peking-Hankow Railway zone as his base, and Sun Ch'uan-fang, who controlled the five southeastern provinces, were competing against one another for power. The greater portion of Wu P'ei-fu's army had been transferred north, and Hupeh Province was somewhat lacking in defenses. Wu himself stayed at Changhsintien near Peking and politically competed with Chang Tso-lin for control of the Peking government. Militarily the primary job was to deal with Feng Yü-hsiang. Wu seemed to have underestimated the Northern Expedition from the two Kwang provinces, believing that the forces of Sun Ch'uan-fang in Kiangsi and Fukien and the Yeh K'ai-hsin army in Hunan, which he supported, were capable of coping with the southern force.

Preparations for the Northern Expedition were progressing daily, and the power of Chiang Kai-shek swelled with it. On June 5 the CEC of the KMT passed a resolution to dispatch the army on the Northern

Expedition and appointed Chiang Kai-shek Commander-in-Chief of the National Revolutionary Army. The authority of the commander-in-chief was higher than everything else, and even the National government and central KMT headquarters in effect became subsidiaries of the headquarters of the commander-in-chief. On July 5 Chiang was appointed director of the Military Department of the KMT with plenipotentiary powers to represent the central headquarters of the KMT in the appointment and dismissal of Party representatives to military organizations. On July 6 the Plenum of the CC of the KMT elected Chiang chairman of the Standing Committee of the CEC. During the period of the Northern Expedition, Chang Ching-chiang and T'an Yen-k'ai were to serve as acting chairman of the Party Affairs Committee and acting chairman of the Political Committee of the Standing Committee respectively.[15] On July 7 the organizational outline for the headquarters of the commander-in-chief was promulgated, stipulating that the military, civilian, and financial organs of the National government were subject to the direction of the commander-in-chief.[16] In this way Chiang became the supreme chief in name and in fact.

General Chiang Kai-shek concentrated in himself the great powers of the KMT, the government, and the army; but since he was a military man, he employed the methods used in directing the army in directing all matters. He did not seem to realize that political, economic, foreign-relations, judicial, social, and other problems could not all be completely resolved with the issuance of orders. To satisfy the needs of the army, he relied primarily on the printing press to supply large quantities of paper money such as the military scrip. He seemed to attach little importance to the detailed planning of the political program of the Northern Expedition, thinking that everything could be solved by obedience to orders. At the time, this inclination aroused displeasure in Borodin, who thought that this undermined some of the principles that he had established. This was perhaps a major factor in the subsequent successes and failures of Chiang.

The methods that Chiang had advocated and used since the March Twentieth Incident had started qualitative changes in the KMT. The revolutionary ideals and faith of young KMT members generally seemed to be ebbing and being replaced by concepts of fame, profit, and power. Leaders in high places stressed obedience; and the requirements for obedience to an individual were unconditional. If someone had personal connections and could stand the oppressive paternalistic practice of both kindness and discipline, it did not matter whether he had made contributions to the revolution or whether he was capable of making such contributions; he could still get promotions. Where the wind blows, the grass bends, and the importance of one's own future gradually outweighed everything else.

From the very beginning, Chiang had differences of opinion with the Communists on many issues concerning preparations for the Northern Expedition. First, there was General Galen, who had returned to Canton to become chief military adviser. His view on the military situation was that more time was needed to prepare for the Northern Expedition. Judging from the relative strengths of the enemy and ourselves, he felt that if the Northern Expedition were launched immediately, we might be victorious in reaching Wuhan, but that we might be incapable of reaching Peking in a single effort. So it would be strategically appropriate to allow a period of preparation so that one's strength could be reinforced from all sides. Such an objective analysis as General Galen's could not be refuted by anyone. But what Chiang Kai-shek attached importance to was not missing the opportune moment for starting the Northern Expedition; and so he insisted on the immediate dispatch of troops northward.

Next there was Borodin, who was dissatisfied on many counts with Chiang's actions during this period. By that time Borodin was no longer a "teacher," but merely an "adviser." He was relatively relaxed, but also a bit depressed. He had said to me that in addition to his agreement with General Galen's military views, he felt that Chiang was not giving full consideration to political strategy. He advocated that the Northern Expedition pursue the Canton-Hankow and Peking-Hankow railway lines in order to form a juncture with the forces of Feng Yü-hsiang and that it build up a territorial area that would include the extensive northwest and southwest in order to be better prepared for dealing with the imperialist influences along the coast. He did not support Chiang's idea of moving toward the southeastern provinces on the lower reaches of the Yangtze, believing that this would lead to direct conflict with the imperialists too soon. This concept of Borodin's seemed to be the basis for his later proposal, brought forward during the Wuhan period, of the idea of "Northwestism." This seemed to exploit the experiences of the revolution in Turkey where the capital was established at Ankara, though it might also have involved some elements of consideration for the interests of the Soviet Union.

The dispute between the route along the Canton-Hankow and Peking-Hankow railway lines and the route calling for simultaneous development along the southeastern coastal areas became the major conflict between Borodin and Chiang. It seemed at the time that Chiang had already secretly entrusted his friends in Canton and Shanghai to devise measures for the establishment of contact with such powers as Britain and Japan. Borodin probably got wind of this, although Chiang had kept it a close secret. Since Chiang did not attach importance to Borodin's theory about avoiding direct conflict with imperialism prematurely, he seemed to be revealing traces of a reorientation of his foreign policy. According to Borodin's view, if the policy of opposing imperialism were annulled, the movement would not be a national revolution at all.

The CCP comrades in Canton thought that the Northern Expedition should not merely be a military action, but should also help to achieve the goals of the revolutionary political platform. They held that consolidation of the Kwangtung base and launching of the Northern Expedition should receive equal attention simultaneously. It would of course be wrong simply to remain in Kwangtung, but it would also be wrong if the Northern Expedition were to lead to the undermining of Kwangtung's solidarity. These views of ours also had the support of certain KMT leftists.

Generally speaking, the CCP comrades in Canton actively supported the Northern Expedition. Early in May the Independent Regiment of the Fourth Army, commanded by the Communist Yeh T'ing, left for Hunan; and I gave Yeh the greatest encouragement. Yeh T'ing was originally a middle-ranking officer of the Cantonese army system. He was also a CCP member (although it was kept a secret), and at the time he was the only member of the CCP to have command of an army unit. After March 20 the CCP had secretly transferred more than forty members of the Party to the army, as junior and middle-ranking cadres in this regiment, and so this regiment was one that the CCP could secretly control. It was also the basic capital for the later military development of the CCP. I had called a meeting of the CCP members in this regiment, encouraged them to fight courageously, and raised a considerable sum of money for the regiment to purchase ammunition, bayonets, and other supplies that they lacked. I also directed them to establish contact with underground CCP organs in various localities, so that they might receive help en route in such matters as sources of recruitment to replace lost manpower and supplies.

In June, CCP comrades in Canton were all exerting their efforts toward the success of the Northern Expedition. They led the mass organizations of workers and peasants and continued to wield actual power in the political work of the different armies. So their activities were concentrated on promoting fraternal relations between army personnel and civilians and mobilizing the masses to support the army with manpower and material resources. The Northern Expeditionary Army had put up such slogans as "abstain from press-gang activities," "abstain from harassing the people," and "deal fairly with the people." However, in the armies within the territory of Kwangtung and in those that were en route to the north, there were still individual cases of military men employing the barbarous practice of the press gang to get laborers. So the CCP Kwangtung District Committee felt that the present military action did not enjoy the same support from the people as had the earlier campaign for the unification of Kwangtung. The committee therefore stressed the idea that the Northern Expeditionary Army should first of all be the people's army, if it were to fulfill the task of opposing imperialism and suppressing the warlords.

Concerning this issue, I had paid a visit to the deputy chief of the general staff, General Pai Ch'ung-hsi. He was responsible for the actual preparations for the Northern Expedition. I proposed to him that in order to enable the masses in the North to "welcome the righteous army with food and water," the Northern Expeditionary Army should draw up detailed plans for implementing the political program laid down by the CEC of the KMT and should order their rigid enforcement. But he was chiefly concerned about such matters as the mobilization of railway workers and the sabotage of communications at the rear of the enemy forces—issues connected with actual military operations.

The above-mentioned differences of opinion on the Northern Expedition led to another disagreement between Chiang and the Communists. There was no disagreement then between the Russian advisers and the CCP comrades. We made fun of Chiang, who had just emerged from obscurity, on the count that his actions were all taken on the spur of the moment and only took care of the more ordinary and more general problems. We also felt that this self-crowned Napoleon might possibly be marching toward the goal of anticommunism. In Chiang's eyes the discussions on the part of the Communists were not practical; and he probably even had fears that the Communists had "ulterior motives." As a matter of fact, Chiang had completely occupied the limelight, and the Communists had been reduced to unimportant cheering squads. But the Communists were not resigned to being considered weak. In working for the Northern Expedition, they forged blindly ahead, implying "just you wait and see."

After July 1, 1926, when the mobilization order for the Northern Expedition was issued (possibly it was the eve of July 9, the day when an impressive oath-taking ceremony was held for the launching of the Expedition), I had been in Canton for nearly four weeks, and again I returned to Shanghai hurriedly. The Northern Expedition had become an established fact, and so the two-party Joint Conference was shelved. I had to return to Shanghai to attend the Enlarged Conference of the CC of the CCP, which was to discuss the overall policy vis à vis the Northern Expedition.

On July 12, 1926, the Second Enlarged Conference of the CC of the CCP was held in Shanghai. The meeting heard my report on my trip to Canton. The majority, including Ch'en Tu-hsiu and P'eng Shu-chih, had too low an estimate of the Northern Expedition—they thought it was doubtful that the army could reach Wuhan. This view was even more conservative than that of the veteran military man General Galen. They seemed to attach too much weight to the shortcomings and conflicts among the participants in the Northern Expedition, who slept in the same bed but dreamed different dreams, and they underestimated the role that could be developed by the traditional revolutionary spirit. Perhaps they were influenced by the views of the Shanghai newspapers, most of which carried reports that were unfavorable to the Northern Expedition. They might also subjectively have envisaged the fact that the successful progress of the Northern Expedition was tantamount to the rise of the anti-Communist fervor of Chiang Kai-shek. Unconsciously they tended to ignore the facts a little, and gave way to thoughts that smacked of being subjective.

The political resolution adopted at the meeting pointed out that the dispatch of troops by the National government was only a defensive campaign to prevent the entry into Hunan and Kwangtung of the anti-Red armies and not really a Northern Expedition filled with revolutionary zeal.[17] This view in fact led the CC of the CCP to adopt a passive attitude toward the Northern Expedition.

At that time membership in the CCP had increased to about thirty thousand. The peasant associations in Hunan already had two hundred thousand members and were being developed vigorously. The passive resolution adopted by the CC of the CCP was clearly not in keeping with this encouraging situation. Though the meeting also adopted resolutions on such issues as unity with the leftists, attacking the Chiang Kai-shek group, stressing the national united front, mobilizing the peasants to fight for rent and interest reduction, capturing local governments, and gradually developing the armed forces of workers and peasants,[18] they were more statements on paper than practical decisions. The CC of the CCP did not grasp the opportunity to expand its own influence in the course of the Northern Expedition.

These things had led to dissatisfaction on the part of T'an P'ing-shan, Ch'ü Ch'iu-pai, and myself. We felt that opposition to Chiang Kai-shek and the adoption of a positive attitude toward the Northern Expedition were not mutually exclusive. We held that the Northern Expedition was on the offensive and that Wuhan could be seized; it was not on the defensive. We castigated P'eng Shu-chih and other scholarly-type persons for controlling the central machinery and knowing only about writing meaningless articles, while neglecting the realities of the day. We demanded positive participation in the Northern Expedition. We felt that lagging behind a single step in the race of the Northern Expedition would be the worst thing possible. These views of ours were considered "the open expression of the allied opposition."

At the same time, the Kwangtung District Committee expressed views that differed from those of the CC. Those of the Kwangtung District Committee stressed that the CC resolution on peasants was not thorough. They advocated that during the progress of the Northern Expedition we introduce the land revolution slogan "distribution of land among the peasants," so as to mobilize the peasants for the realization of the Expedition. Such disputes prepared the ground for later disintegration of the leadership of the CC of the CCP.

Shortly afterward, facts proved that the estimate of the majority of the CC of the CCP was wrong. The Northern Expeditionary Army occupied Changsha on July 11, occupied Yochow on August 22, and then went forward to Wuhan, using the strategy of breaking up different units of the enemy separately. It was only in the midst of these drastic changes that the CC of the CCP gradually changed its viewpoint on the Northern Expedition and adopted a more positive policy. But it had fallen one step behind at the crucial moment.

During this period I was the only person in the CC of the CCP responsible for mobilizing members of the Communist Party to participate in the Northern Expedition. Up to this time I had been traveling to and fro between Shanghai and Canton, taking on emergency missions, and naturally I had no time to attend to the routine affairs of the CC of the CCP. It was not until August that I relinquished my duties as chairman of the Labor Movement Committee of the CC of the CCP, handing over the post to Li Li-san, so that I could work exclusively as the head of the Military Department of the CC, which I regarded as having the task of mobilizing the CCP organizations and mass organizations of workers and peasants for participation in the war. However, the Military Department was an obscure department at the time, with only two young comrades engaged in the collection of military information from the newspapers.

The CC of the CCP was then far from being a headquarters for military command. In our direction of the mass movements of peasants and workers, we had accumulated considerable experience; but in the matter of warfare, we were outsiders. On this point, we were very backward compared with the KMT. We did not possess communications equipment such as radios, nor did we have intelligence data that could be of use. We had to start from scratch. The transition from an organization engaged in the leadership of mass movements to an organization for the leadership of war required a long period of preparation. In the tense period of the Northern Expedition, the Military Department, which I led, had only started to transfer a small number of comrades with military knowledge, dispatching them to areas where they were needed during the Expedition, and to make some preliminary plans for the mobilization of the masses of workers and peasants.

I remember that an important task carried out by my Military Department at the time was the organization of an insurrection corps, which was dispatched to Wuchang. It consisted of eight members and was led by Comrade Yü Hsi-tu, a student of the first class at Whampoa. Their task was to join forces with comrades in Hupeh in order to harass the rear lines of the enemy, to incite desertions and uprisings, and to seize the arms of the enemy troops in order to arm ourselves. To other less important areas Yü could only send individual comrades to work. Local organizations of the CCP also were adept at work in the mass movements. I insisted that in accordance with experiences in Kwangtung, they should mobilize the masses of workers and peasants to coordinate with the actions of the National Revolutionary Army.

On September 6 and 7 respectively, the forces of the Northern Expedition occupied Hanyang and Hankow, and Wuchang was under siege. The staff of the Military Department of the CC of the CCP, under my leadership, immediately rushed to Hankow to deal with the war directly. The routine affairs of the Military Department naturally had to be laid aside for the moment. Soon Chou En-lai arrived in Shanghai from Kwangtung to take over from me the duties of head of the Military Department. He brought with him a group of comrades engaged in military work; and this branch of our activities was reorganized and expanded. For this reason, it can be said that during the course of the Northern Expedition, the central machinery of the CCP gradually adapted itself to the war situation. It was also the starting point of work that later enabled it to stage numerous uprisings and to engage in guerrilla warfare.

THE PERIOD OF THE WUHAN GOVERNMENT

CHAPTER

The First Stage of the Wuhan Government— Under Military Occupation

Early in July, 1926, the National Revolutionary Army launched its Northern Expedition. Military victory followed upon military victory, and the influence of such warlords as Wu P'ei-fu and Sun Ch'uan-fang was rapidly destroyed. The provinces along the Yangtze River basin were occupied one after another. What emerged was the period of the Wuhan government, which was known to the world for its leftist and Communist tendencies. Yet there were rivalries and conflicts among the various cliques that made up the revolutionary camp. Thus disagreement over where the new capital should be located swelled into animosity between Nanking and Wuhan, while the purge of Communists in Nanking and Kwangtung developed into an extensive breakdown in KMT-CCP relations. The Wuhan government, under pressure both from within and without, eventually collapsed; and this led to the victory of General Chiang Kai-shek, who made a turn to the Right. In this historical drama, because its policy of cooperation within the KMT had reached an impasse, because its own strength and experience were inadequate, and especially because of the endless mistakes made over the years on the instructions from Moscow, the CCP, which was then plunged into the difficult situation of not being able to issue commands and not being willing to accept orders, met with a disastrous defeat. Perhaps the historical facts of this defeat provided valuable experience which enabled the CCP to stage a comeback later. Nevertheless, as I describe the past and recall the heads that were lost and the blood that was shed by innumerable comrades and compatriots, I cannot help still being filled with pain.

When the news reached Shanghai that the Northern Expeditionary Army had captured Hanyang and Hankow one after the other, there was an emergency meeting of the CC of the CCP, and I proposed that the CC immediately prepare to move to Wuhan. My reason was that the CC of the CCP could not be located forever in an "attic" in Shanghai, issuing written directives on the revolution and the war in different areas. It should move to the central locality of Wuhan and firmly seize the opportunity to direct affairs on the spot. I pointed out that this was in keeping with the strategic concept of the CC of the CCP and with Borodin's ideas of making Wuhan the base of the Northern Expedition and of having the Expedition develop northward along the Peking-Hankow Railway. Moreover, once Wuhan became the political center, the responsibilities of the Hupeh District Committee would be increased. If the CC remained in Shanghai, troubles such as those that had occurred in the past because of differences between Canton and Shanghai would unavoidably be repeated between Shanghai and Hupeh. But Ch'en Tu-hsiu and the majority of the others still thought that the situation at Wuhan was not yet stabilized and that Shanghai was the center that could take care of the whole country. On the strength of these reasons, my proposal was shelved. Instead, a decision was reached to send me to Wuhan as the plenipotentiary of the CC of the CCP to assume alone the responsibility for directing affairs at the front.

I reached Hankow on September 11, 1926. My mission was to direct the work of the Hupeh District Committee, to develop the forces of workers and peasants, to unite with the KMT leftists, to strive for the victory of the Northern Expedition, and so forth. It was not until December of 1926, when Borodin and some members of the National government arrived in Wuhan to prepare for the establishment of the capital, that the period of the Wuhan government really began. Up to that time Wuhan was in a state of military occupation, and everything was carried out with an eye to winning a victory. It could also be said that during this period I was directly responsible for the work of the CCP in Wuhan.

When Hankow was first occupied, it presented a wartime scene. The troops of Liu Yu-chun under Wu P'ei-fu were holding the city of Wuchang, which was under siege and surrounded by the Fourth Army. Fighting was intermittent. Water communication between Wuchang and Hankow was naturally cut off. And farther out, fighting was in progress in all of the surrounding suburbs. Though the Northern Expeditionary Army was fully confident of victory, most of the citizens adopted a waiting attitude, feeling that the situation had not yet been definitely settled.

I had visited Hankow before. Since the spring of 1923, when the February Seventh Strike failed and I left the place secretly, three years and seven months had elapsed. Needless to say, in some areas there had been changes that served as reminders of the transformations that had taken place. The CCP Hupeh District Committee was still marooned inside the city of Wuchang. Its office in Hankow was located in the original Hou-hu *ch'u* (ward) in an alley near the general headquarters of T'ang Sheng-chih. In 1922 this area had been an expanse of green waters, forming a part of the Hou Hu (Rear Lake). I had then taken boat rides on the lake, taking in the scenery in the company of lawyer Shih Yang, who was killed in the February Seventh Incident. I listened as Shih, who was an old Hankow resident and knew all about the city, talked endlessly about the stories and traditions of the lake. Very little time had passed, but the grave of the lawyer Shih Yang had already been shadowed by trees that had grown up, and much of the lake had been filled up to become land on which scattered houses of the Western type had been built. The building used as the Hankow office of the CCP Hupeh District Committee was one of these houses.

Except for the quiet foreign concessions, the old city that was Hankow had donned the new clothes of revolution. The yamen of Wu P'ei-fu had changed its master. The flag with the blue sky and the white sun was fluttering everywhere. The various military units and political departments of different levels had put up signs of different sizes and various colors that could be seen everywhere. In their midst were also found the official proclamations of the parent organizations. There were all kinds of moving proposals and statements that were pleasant to the ear. It seemed that the cheques of the revolution were being written at random, and there was no thought of whether they could be cashed. Revolutionary organizations of all descriptions mushroomed, emerging from underground, one after another. On the large roads and small alleys one often discovered the signboards put up by such organizations. The majority of the responsible members of the CCP Hupeh District Committee were marooned inside the city of Wuchang, so the Hankow office felt the lack of personnel greatly, and all work seemed to be at loose ends. As a new arrival, I was busy working to create order. I paid the greatest attention to the work of winning a military victory. And so I shall start with this point.

In comparison with the Northern Expedition led by Dr. Sun Yat-sen, this Northern Expedition had a stronger force and was conducted at a more propitious time. Although the present expeditionary forces were outnumbered and not yet very adequately prepared, nevertheless the primary fact was that the Peiyang warlords, who were the enemy, were already beginning to disintegrate. At an early stage in the Northern Expedition many of the miscellaneous army units in the Peiyang warlord system had turned around and defected to the side of the revolution. The troops of Ho Lung (which originally garrisoned western Hunan), of Yüan Tsu-ming in Kweichow, of Liu Tso-lung in Hupeh, and of Lai Shih-huang in Kiangsi had followed in the wake of T'ang Sheng-chih and had accepted appointments in the National Revolutionary Army. Their action not only swelled the ranks, but actually also paved the way for the advance of the Northern Expeditionary Army. The number of armies in the North that later defected to the side of the revolution was even greater. One example was the Shansi Army of Yen Hsi-shan.

At the beginning the Northern Expedition developed as Ch'en Tu-hsiu thought it would, in that it was a defensive action against the attack of Wu P'ei-fu and Yeh K'ai-hsin. But when the expeditionary forces assembled in southern Hunan for an attack on Changsha, the situation changed into an offensive war taking large strides. This attack also did not develop in the way that had been planned by Borodin in Canton, for after the defeat of Wu P'ei-fu, the expedition not only marched northward along the Peking-Hankow Railway, but also allotted a portion of the army to enter Kiangsi. This portion then marched down along the Yangtze to liquidate the men under Sun Ch'uan-fang, who occupied the Nanking-Shanghai zone. This added measure seemed necessary because of the military situation that obtained at the time and because of internal disputes within the Northern Expeditionary Army.

The Northern Expeditionary Army captured Changsha on July 11, 1926, and Chiang arrived at Changsha from Canton on August 12 to discuss the military plans for the second stage of the expedition with the generals at the front. T'ang Sheng-chih advocated dividing the army into two branches for the march, having one branch advance on Wuhan and the other attack Kiangsi.[1] T'ang's intention seemed to be to occupy the spheres of influence separately. That is to say, he himself wanted to occupy the two provinces of Hupeh and Hunan and use them as a base for future operations, while he hoped that Chiang would attack Kiangsi and use it as a bridge to march on the southeastern provinces. Though Chiang had already conceived of the plan for taking Kiangsi and Fukien, nevertheless at the time he advocated that forces first be concentrated to capture Wuhan and to destroy the influence of Wu P'ei-fu north of Wu-hsing-kuan before marching eastward. It is possible that Chiang did not want T'ang Sheng-chih to exploit the opportunity of creating a situation in which he would be independent. Although Chiang's views carried in the discussions, this difference in military viewpoint nevertheless marked the beginning of later disputes between Chiang and T'ang.

The Northern Expeditionary Army captured Yochow on August 22, and riding on this victory, it advanced toward Hupeh. One after another, it defeated the stubborn enemy troops that held the strategic points of Ting-ssu-chiao and Ho-hsing-chiao, and then it reached the walls of Wuchang City on August 31. Because the Northern Expeditionary Army lacked artillery, the Fourth Army, which was responsible for the attack on the city, could not take it after repeated onslaughts. On the other hand, the Eighth Army under T'ang Sheng-chih, which crossed the Yangtze, occupied Hanyang on September 6 and Hankow on September 7. Riding on its victory, this force followed the Peking-Hankow Railway, pursuing remnants of Wu P'ei-fu's defeated army. So Wuchang became an isolated city, surrounded on all sides.

Before I reached Hankow, Chiang Kai-shek had decided that Wuchang could not be captured easily; and since he was anxious to ride on the victory and develop toward Kiangsi, he returned to Changsha and entered Kiangsi via P'inghsiang. Military affairs in Hupeh Province were entrusted to T'ang Sheng-chih, while political affairs were placed in the responsible hands of Teng Yen-ta, director of the General Political Department.

Everybody's attention was focused on the possibility of the early capture of Wuchang. On the second day after my arrival at Hankow, I took a detour via the upper reaches of the river above Wuchang, walked for an entire morning, and reached the front line for observations. Yeh T'ing's Independent Regiment assumed responsibility for the encirclement and siege of Wuchang City. The headquarters of his regiment was located at Tung-hu, a few li south of Wuchang City and within the range of artillery fire from the city. I lingered at the front for the entire afternoon and stayed overnight at Yeh T'ing's headquarters. Yeh's regiment had only one portable 7.5 centimeter mountain gun. Yeh T'ing told me that if he used the cannon to shell the city, the enemy would send more shells to the vicinity of the regimental headquarters. The only scouting plane that the Northern Expeditionary Army possessed often flew over the skies of Wuchang. In the city there were several antiaircraft guns that would fire at the plane, and clouds of black smoke would appear around the plane.

I held meetings and individual talks with some of the CCP comrades in Yeh T'ing's regiment. They told me that since reaching southern Hunan in May, the Independent Regiment had gone through eight important battles. Although it had suffered heavy casualties, each time it had achieved brilliant military results.[2] This regiment had consistently fought on the right flank together with the Tenth and Twelfth divisions of the Fourth Army and had always shouldered the task of making the main attack. The comrades there took pride in defeating Wu P'ei-fu, and they also felt that the Fourth Army had contributed more effort than the other armies and had registered the best results. During the attack on the city a few days previously, the regiment had suffered great losses, and plans were under way to find replacements.

These men all praised the Hunan labor and peasant movements led by the CCP for having achieved very good results. They pointed out that along the entire route of their march they had been welcomed by the peasants. The peasant organizations had supplied them with the needed transport corps, helped them in the fighting, served them as guides, and supplied them with intelligence. The dead and wounded of the regiment had been replaced all along their march. About four hundred colliers of Anyuan Mine had joined the regiment. In addition, miners of Shui-kou-shan and peasants of various counties also joined the regiment in groups. Thus the combat personnel of the regiment had actually increased rather than decreased in number, although it had been the middle- and lower-level cadres that were replaced. They added that other regiments of the Fourth Army had received similar assistance from the masses of workers and peasants.

A few days later, in hand-to-hand combat below the city walls of Wuchang, the Independent Regiment again suffered severe casualties, and regiment commander Yeh T'ing was greatly moved by the development. Comrade Chou Shih-ti, who served as chief-of-staff of the regiment, was very alarmed and hurried to Hankow to tell me that commander Yeh T'ing had secretly left for Shanghai without reporting to the division's command headquarters. Prior to his departure, Yeh had said ruefully, "The Independent Regiment has suffered very heavy casualties, and it seems that nobody cares for the regiment. It is really impossible for me to carry on." I immediately pointed out that during a critical stage of fighting, secret departure from the troops was an act that violated military discipline. A member of the Communist Party performing such an act also violated Party discipline. Whatever the reason for such action, it was not permissible.

This incident provided the first test of the CCP's ability to keep its members from inheriting the evil practices of the army in generally disregarding discipline. First I told Chou Shih-ti to take over the duties of regiment commander temporarily, and then I resorted to various measures to recall regiment commander Yeh. About a week later Yeh T'ing was successfully recalled. I insisted that at a meeting of CCP members of the Independent Regiment, he openly admit his mistake in violating discipline. Yeh T'ing did so. Afterwards I addressed the meeting of about fifty members of the CCP in the regiment. I emphasized the importance of army discipline and Party discipline, and demanded that they make themselves the model for all armies in this area. The more important post a comrade held, the more important it was for him to set an example. Since Comrade Yeh T'ing had returned and had also admitted his mistake, all comrades should continue to have trust in him as usual and obey his commands. This living example served as an important lesson in self-discipline for the military comrades that were members of the CCP, and it strengthened the leadership of the CCP over the Independent Regiment.

We did our best to obtain replacements for the Northern Expeditionary Army. Needless to say, immediate replacements were found for the casualties of the Independent Regiment. Even for the other armies, the CCP organizations in Hupeh and Hunan ceaselessly canvassed the worker and peasant masses to find replacements. These activities increased the importance of the role of the CCP during the Northern Expedition.

On October 10, 1926—National Day—Wuchang City was finally taken. The defending general, Liu Yu-chun, was taken prisoner, and his men were completely disarmed. This city, which had been isolated under a long siege, faced a growing shortage of food and was cut off from outside help. The various activities of the revolutionaries both inside and outside the city led the enemy to lose confidence in being able to successfully defend the city. Early that morning, some of the enemy troops opened the gates of the city and surrendered, and so no serious fighting occurred. Thus this famous city of the 1911 Revolution was recovered. Afterwards the situation evolved so that Wuhan became the center of the revolution.

On National Day, I accompanied the troops into Wuchang City and met Ch'en T'an-ch'iu and other comrades of the CCP Hupeh District Committee, as well as the team led by Yü Hsi-tu that I had dispatched from Shanghai for insurrection activities there. Meeting after a war, our joy was greater than usual. They told me that they had been marooned inside the city for about forty days, carrying out many activities such as the secret distribution of pamphlets, the posting of slogans and proclamations, the dissemination of news on the victories of the Northern Expeditionary Army, and the incitement of the military and the police to defect and surrender. Yü Hsi-tu and his men also threw bombs several times to undermine the morale of the people. The defending army was overawed by the revolutionary influence that threatened both from without and within, and was at a loss about what should be done. The authorities did not even dare to take effective action in suppressing the sabotage activities of the KMT and CCP elements inside the city. Only a very small number of them were arrested, and they were released safely on the day the city was captured. Most of these comrades took pride in having contributed a share to the Northern Expedition while they were inside Wuchang City.

After the capture of Wuchang City, the CCP Hupeh District Committee continued to work hard inside Wuchang. At the time Wuchang was garrisoned by the Fourth Army, but Hankow was garrisoned by the troops of T'ang Sheng-chih. The CCP was closer to the Fourth Army, feeling that its men were veteran revolutionaries. The Hupeh District Committee was more at ease psychologically because it was located in an area garrisoned by the Fourth Army. The office of the Hupeh District Committee was located at the time in an alley that was confiscated enemy property. I cannot remember the name of the street, but can only recall that in the alley were several houses, all controlled by the Independent Regiment. The largest of these buildings was occupied by the Hupeh District Committee, which used it as its office. I was assigned a smaller building to be used as an office for myself and the military personnel I had brought with me. Yeh T'ing's family occupied a house opposite mine. The several organs under the District Committee and the CYC were also located in this alley or in its vicinity.

Before I assumed the post of secretary of the Hupeh District Committee in November, I spent most of my time handling negotiations connected with the military field. Teng Yen-ta, director of the General Political Department, became concurrently chairman of the Hupeh Provincial Political Committee and director of the Wuhan headquarters of the commander-in-chief in Wuhan. After the capture of Wuchang, he moved his office from Hankow to Wuchang. The Hupeh Provincial government, the Hupeh Provincial Headquarters of the KMT, the General Political Department of the headquarters of the commander-in-chief, and other important organs were all located in Wuchang City. Thus Teng Yen-ta suddenly became the highest authority, and he was my main contact.

My relations with Teng Yen-ta were quite cordial. Though I had known him in Canton, it was only after I arrived in Wuhan that I worked with him in dealing with various matters. He came from a peasant family. After graduating from the eighth class of Paoting Military Academy, he had served as a regiment commander and had gone to Germany on a military observation mission. Before the Northern Expedition, he had served as dean of studies at Whampoa Military Academy. When the headquarters of the Commander-in-Chief of the National Revolutionary Army was established, he was immediately made director of the General Political Department. He was a military man who had a high opinion of himself and spoke with an arbitrary tone, but he was also a little soft-hearted. Though he prided himself on claiming to be a faithful disciple of Dr. Sun Yat-sen, he was also inclined toward socialism, and most of the major cadres of his Political Department were members of the CCP and leftists. For a long time he had had close relations with the Fourth Army, but he had no sympathy for T'ang Sheng-chih of the Eighth Army. At this time, he seemed to be thinking of restraining T'ang Sheng-chih and of concentrating in himself the military and political powers in Wuhan.

T'ang Sheng-chih's actual strength was quite formidable. For the time being, he was superior to the heads of the other units of the Northern Expeditionary Army. After the capture of Wuchang, his troops were not actually involved in direct fighting, and so he had an opportunity to attend to expansion. His troops greatly increased in number, and in order to reinforce his military cadres, he operated a branch military academy of considerable size in Changsha. The troops of some defectors such as Liu Tso-lung were also under his command. He controlled the whole of Hunan and the major portion of Hupeh and was concurrently chairman (governor) of the Hunan Provincial government. The mayor of Hankow was his subordinate Liu Wen-tao. In addition, he could directly and indirectly collect some revenue in the various counties of Hupeh. For this reason he had no trouble with supplies for his troops and with replacement of manpower.

T'ang had ambitions of competing with Chiang, and his activities were evident on all sides. He and his subordinates played up Buddhism to show that they differed with the Three Principles of the People of Kwangtung. He united with the Paoting clique in an attempt to vie with the Whampoa clique for supremacy. He had close connections with the Japanese consulate at Hankow, and his aim appeared to be the acquisition of useful information from the Japanese side. At the same time he was very courteous to the Russian advisers. Although most of his subordinates were conservative, he nevertheless earnestly expressed his friendship toward the CCP. People thought that his policy of cultivating all sides and factions was principally aimed at dealing with Chiang.

The measures he used in cultivating the CCP were also singularly ingenious. When the director of his Political Department, Liu Wen-tao, became mayor of Hankow, T'ang immediately accepted the suggestion that he appoint as Liu's successor in the Political Department, Comrade P'eng Tse-hsiang, who was also secretary of the CCP Hupeh District Committee. T'ang unconditionally supported the labor and peasant movements and also maintained normal contacts and friendly relations with the responsible members of the CCP in Hunan and the trade-union chiefs in Hankow. Furthermore, he solemnly asked to be admitted to membership in the CCP; and he requested that Ch'en Tu-hsiu go to Wuhan to help guide his work. He was also very courteous to me and even indicated that when he had to proceed to the front line on duty, I should assume full power in directing his troops.

For its part, the CCP still felt that conservative military men continued to be the major pillars of support of T'ang Sheng-chih's troops. Thus his manifestations of friendliness were all acts to cultivate us. The CC of the CCP rejected his request for membership, pointing out that this action was not then expedient for him. I also felt that he merely wanted to be personally friendly with the CCP, but did not wish the influence of the CCP to spread to his troops. For this reason we felt that, viewed from any angle, he could not be compared with Teng Yen-ta in his sincerity toward the revolution.

In Wuhan the influence of the CCP ranked just below the influences of Teng Yen-ta and T'ang Sheng-chih. Although the actual military strength that the CCP could control was very small, it nevertheless possessed very great potential in the political work of the various armies and in the provincial headquarters of the KMT in Hupeh and Hunan. In labor, peasant, and youth organizations, it alone occupied the position of leadership. In the struggle for power among the different cliques in the Northern Expeditionary Army, the CCP all along had held a position of considerable importance. As the CCP spokesman in Hupeh at the time, I maintained that in the interests of all-out victory for the Northern Expedition, the cleavages between the different cliques must not be aggravated. All that I could do was to increase the relative influence of the workers and peasants.

Teng Yen-ta was rather jealous over the friendship between the CCP and T'ang Sheng-chih. On one occasion he assumed the position of representing the revolutionary orthodoxy and asked me why P'eng Tse-hsiang did not report to him on conditions in the Eighth Army. I explained to him that P'eng had just gone to work in the Eighth Army and everything was new to him, so that I myself had not received a report from him. I felt that he definitely did not lack respect for the leadership of the General Political Department. I went on to tell Teng that the CCP would consult him on everything before making a decision, but that it also attached importance to the friendship of T'ang Sheng-chih and would not reject T'ang because of his tendency toward doing good. I felt that we should both adopt the same attitude.

Teng Yen-ta seemed to endorse my view. And later in handling finances, the personnel problems of Hanyang Arsenal, and the allotment of arms in order to meet Chiang's needs on the Kiangsi front—issues on which he originally would have come to odds with T'ang—my attitude seemed to influence him, and he generally resorted to a conciliatory attitude in reaching a temporary solution of these issues. Generally speaking, the internal conflicts within the revolutionary camp at the time could not be considered sharp.

On the basis of my Kwangtung experience, I exercised care in deal-

ing with problems related to military affairs. I was a man behind the
scene, and did not hold any position openly. Nevertheless those people
who sought to make connections with the revolution were especially
perceptive, and when they found it was not so easy to contact Teng Yen-
ta or T'ang Sheng-chih, they often came to me directly. I received many
representatives of army units stationed around the Wuhan area that were
anxious to defect to the revolution. I also read many documents relating
to such matters. I always referred these cases to Teng Yen-ta. The most
I would do was provide him with some opinions that he could refer to
in disposing of the issues. Both comrade Chu Teh, who had returned
from Germany, and Comrade Liu Po-ch'eng, who had come from Szechwan, were introduced to Teng by me, and they were officially appointed
by Teng to go to Szechwan and other areas to stir up the troops of Yang
Shen and Teng Hsi-hou. These incidents made Teng Yen-ta feel that I
had clearly shown my respect for his authority.

Chiang arrived in Kiangsi territory on September 22, and until
Nanchang was captured on November 7, his situation was very difficult.
At the time that the revolutionary army reached the city of Wuchang,
Li Tsung-jen's Seventh Army had proceeded eastward down the Yangtze
to deal with the vanguard of Sun Ch'uan-fang, which had advanced to
Huang-shih-chiang, and also to develop toward the Kiukiang area. The
entire Second, Third, and Sixth armies and the Second Division of the
First Army were converging on Nanchang from different directions, and
a portion of the Fifth Army had advanced from Kwangtung to Kanchow
in southern Kiangsi. On September 19 Ch'eng Ch'ien's Sixth Army ef-
fected the first capture of Nanchang, but was forced to withdraw from
the city by Sun Ch'uan-fang's superior forces. Chiang was still on his
way to Kiangsi, and Ch'eng Ch'ien, who assumed responsibility for
directing operations, had charged that the loss of Nanchang after its first
occupation was due to failure of the First Army, personally led by
Chiang, to give timely support.

After that, the fighting in the vicinity of Nanchang and Kiukiang
was personally directed by Chiang. For a time a seesaw situation developed. Sun Ch'uan-fang's main strength was concentrated along the
Nanchang-Kiukiang line, and Chiang encountered a formidable foe.
Chiang's direction of the war showed signs of not being very effective,
and the various armies adopted a hesitant attitude, so that action was
not unanimous and some reverses were suffered. The First and Third
divisions of the First Army, led by Ho Ying-ch'in, were marching on

Chekiang from Fukien; and progress was slow. This had some effect on Chiang's prestige.

The revolutionary heroes of Wuhan were ridiculing this commander-in-chief, who considered himself unsurpassable. In a sarcastic tone T'ang Sheng-chih indicated that the commander-in-chief personally led such a large army that it was indeed strange that he should meet with defeat below the city of Nanchang. Some generals of the Fourth Army felt all the more that without their "Ironsides" (Fourth and Eleventh armies) taking part, the position was untenable. Some people adopted the attitude of watching a fire from the opposite bank in waiting for Chiang to be ridiculed. Most people were anxious over the failure to capture Nanchang after prolonged attack; and Chiang himself showed that he was at his wits' end. However, General Galen, his adviser, was traveling hastily to various points on the front, working as liaison between the different armies in order to achieve unanimity of action.

In mid-October, Galen came to Wuhan to ask for help in the Kiangsi fighting. He told me painfully about the actual situation on the front line in Kiangsi and pointed out that the crux of the trouble lay in the lack of unanimity of action among the various armies. He warned that should Sun Ch'uan-fang win, Hunan and Kwangtung would both be threatened and the entire Northern Expedition might collapse. I supported his view and gave him effective assistance. I felt that it was not the time for parting ways with Chiang because of internal conflicts. If the Kiangsi front suffered defeat, the entire Northern Expedition would be affected. The revolution of the Taiping "Heavenly Kingdom" had been defeated because of an internal battle of wits; and we should learn from this example.

General Galen had great prestige, and because of his efforts to smooth over the situation, sincere support was received from all quarters. The Fourth Army proceeded to the flank of the Nanchang-Kiukiang line to help Li Tsung-jen's forces, which were already there, make a major attack. One section of T'ang Sheng-chih's army also proceeded eastward to give support. Wuhan was thus mobilizing both manpower and material resources to support the war in Kiangsi. General Galen returned to the front line in high spirits and demanded that the several armies unanimously take serious action. The report circulated in Wuhan at the time was that the actual commander of the Kiangsi war was not the nominal commander-in-chief, but rather the guest commander, General Galen. And so it happened that on November 2 the forces of Li Tsung-jen and others on the Nanchang-Kiukiang line routed the main force of Sun Ch'uan-fang, occupying Kiukiang on the fourth, followed by Nanchang on the seventh. Sun Ch'uan-fang was dealt a severe blow in the first round.

Because Chiang was harassed before reaching the city of Nanchang, a wave of opposition against him arose. In October the joint meeting of the CEC of the KMT and representatives of KMT headquarters in various provinces and municipalities that was held in Canton[3] clearly indicated the rise of leftist influence. At the meeting there was an atmosphere of direct opposition to the inefficiency and senility of Chang Ching-chiang, of welcome to Wang's return to the country to resume his post, and of indirect attack on Chiang Kai-shek. After Chiang had occupied Nanchang and Kiukiang, he started his counterattack. Later he persisted in having the National government and the KMT central headquarters moved temporarily to Nanchang, and this marked the beginning of the internal conflicts.

The work of the CCP developed rapidly with the victory of Northern Expeditionary forces. The CCP Hupeh District Committee had operated underground over a long period of time, so all work had to be carried on with great care and could not be vigorously pursued. When there was suddenly an opportunity for open activities, the committee found itself in a state of confusion because of established habits and shortage of personnel. Fortunately, it was possible to gradually assemble in Wuhan a group of energetic Party members from various localities. To help in the labor movement, for instance, the CC of the CCP sent Li Li-san and Liu Shao-ch'i after they sent me. In the field of military work, most comrades had accompanied the army from Canton. In the General Political Department, Li Ho-lin, Chang Po-chün, and Chu Tai-chieh held important posts. Military comrades actually directing army units ranged downward from Yeh T'ing and, later, Fan T'ai-ying, who was senior political instructor at the Wuhan branch of the military academy. Not much later Mao Tse-tung also came to Wuhan from Hunan to prepare another Peasant Movement Institute. Most of the personnel for various other tasks was obtained from local talent. The Hupeh District Committee was busy augmenting its organization, increasing the number of Party members, and training Party members to improve their work capacity.

After the capture of Wuchang the CCP Hupeh District Committee had a large number of members for that time. Though P'eng Tse-hsiang was busy in the work of the Political Department of the Eighth Army, he was still concurrently secretary of the Hupeh District Committee; Ch'en T'an-ch'iu was in charge of the Organization Department; Lin Yü-nan headed the Department of Propaganda; and Tung Pi-wu, Ch'ien Chieh-p'an, and Liu Po-ch'eng were members of the committee for work with the KMT; Li Li-san, Liu Shao-ch'i, Hsiang Ying, and Hsü Pai-hao were members of the Labor Movement Committee; Lu Shen, Ch'en Yen-lin, and Liu Tzu-ku were members of the Peasant Movement Committee; Ts'ai Ch'ang and Huang Mu-lan were members of the Women's Movement Committee; Li Chu-shih and Li Shu-ch'u were members of the CYC Committee and also assumed responsibility for the student movement. I, as representative of the CC of the CCP, regularly attended the meetings of the Hupeh District Committee and also had charge of military work.

Needless to say, the CCP Hupeh District Committee was the nerve center of all the activities of the CCP in Wuhan. It held two meetings a week, one to discuss policy and the other to discuss routine tasks. About twenty persons usually attended these meetings. The agendas were extremely long; emergency proposals brought forward on the spur of the moment were the most numerous. So P'eng Tse-hsiang, the secretary, had difficulty coping with the situation. Although P'eng was a capable youth, he was nevertheless too busy, and his experience was not adequate. At a meeting the secretary especially had to consider how urgent the different problems were and make adjustments on the spot to produce a schedule. Some important problems needed to have formulae for solving them prepared in advance and brought forward at the meeting for approval, if we were to take advantage of the time element. P'eng Tse-hsiang was often unable to handle such matters smoothly; and this often led to unnecessary disputes. As the representative of the CC, I sometimes had to stand up and take over his job. There were even occasions when I could not attend a meeting for some reason, and it would not reach a satisfactory conclusion.

The inadequacy of the leadership of the Hupeh District Committee led to the dissatisfaction of some of its members. Ch'en T'an-ch'iu, who was very experienced, commanded high respect, and was well known for his sense of righteousness, brought this problem to my attention. He was dissatisfied with Ch'en Tu-hsiu for appointing returned foreign students, who were inexperienced, to such important and busy posts as secretary of the Hupeh District Committee; he felt that it expressed lack of confidence in the old cadres. He wanted to go directly to the CC and ask the committee to designate me as secretary of the Hupeh District Committee. I told him that I was asking the CC of the CCP to move to Wuhan. This would naturally remedy the problem we had encountered; so it seemed to me that there was no need to make any changes in personnel at the moment. Nevertheless Ch'en T'an-ch'iu presented his recommendation to the CC of the CCP; and the CC accepted it. And so in November I also became secretary of the Hupeh District Committee. This job took the greater part of my time. I not only had to attend to matters of policy, but I also had to handle a large number of routine tasks.

Important personages in Wuhan were busy attending meetings, attending banquets, and making speeches. This became the vogue. Even the cadres of the CCP were no exception. The principal members of the numerous revolutionary and people's organizations not only had on their hands endless meetings of their own departments, but also various kinds of joint meetings. Some important persons spent almost their entire days in meetings. P'u-hai-ch'un—the large hotel situated on Chiang-han Road in Hankow—was the place most frequently used by important people for banquets. After surfeiting themselves with food and drinks, they would give vent to big talk. On such occasions views would also be exchanged on certain important problems, so that hasty decisions were sometimes unavoidable. Speechmaking was not only in vogue, but the more leftist the content of such talk became, the better. Even the big bosses of industry and trade would shout, "Long live the world revolution!" But such meetings, discussions, and speeches were mostly idle talk that brought no good and lacked practical content. I participated in such meetings on lesser occasions. Generally speaking, compared with that of other revolutionary organizations, the work of the CCP Hupeh District Committee was more efficient.

During the first stage after the occupation of Wuhan, the peasant movement led by the CCP was only beginning and had not as yet attracted people's attention. But the labor movement was truly outstanding. On September 14, one week after the Northern Expeditionary Army had occupied Hankow, a fraternal meeting of workers was held at the Hankow Municipal Headquarters of the KMT. More than four hundred workers attended as representatives of more than one hundred trade unions. The headquarters of the Commander-in-Chief of the Northern

Expeditionary Army, the General Political Department, the Front Line General Command, the Hupeh Provincial Headquarters of the KMT, and the Hankow Municipal Headquarters of the KMT—all important organs—sent representatives to the meeting. The meeting adopted three important resolutions: first, punishment of traitors to labor; second, urging the immediate reopening of factories; and third, organization of the Hupeh Provincial Trade-Unions Council. It was also decided that the General Political Department would be requested to deal with the first and second resolutions, and the various trade unions would look after the third resolution. Those from the CCP attending this meeting included such important trade-union leaders as Hsiang Ying and Hsü Pai-hou, who played a leadership role in it.

The three resolutions actually constituted urgent tasks for the labor movement of the day. After the "February 7" suppression by Wu P'ei-fu, the trade-union organizations in Hupeh were broken up, and the former Hupeh Provincial Federation of Labor Organizations had actually ceased to exist. Its only survivors were a few trade-union secret groups led by the CCP. Some of the former labor-peasant leaders had submitted to the threats and inducements of Wu P'ei-fu, and some of them had even undertaken sabotage of the trade unions on his behalf. They were the so-called labor traitors. The most notorious labor traitor at that time was Kuo P'ing-pai. He was a rightist member of the KMT, who at one time had been an important staff member of the Hupeh Provincial Federation of Labor Organizations. After the February Seventh Strike, it was widely rumored that he had become a lackey of Wu P'ei-fu. Because of his secret reports, many labor leaders were killed. Public hostility against him had mounted, and he was finally arrested by the General Political Department of the Commander-in-Chief. The punishment of labor traitors was an issue to which the trade unions attached very great importance. At first, in accordance with Chiang's wishes, the General Political Department had advocated magnanimous treatment; but many trade-union leaders argued their cases convincingly before the General Political Department, and Kuo P'ing-pai was finally given the death penalty and was executed.[4]

The resolution urging the various factories to resume operation speedily was even more difficult to implement. Some of the factories in Wuhan had suspended operations, some had reduced production, and others were struggling reluctantly. This economic depression was of course an unavoidable phenomenon in a war area. On the one hand the workers wanted the factories to resume operations so as to do away with unemployment, and on the other hand they brought forward certain urgent economic demands that made it difficult for the factories and businesses to operate. In urging the factories to resume operations, the General Political Department had no means at its disposal beyond the application of political pressure. Military needs were multitudinous, and the financial authorities were busy finding ways to increase revenue to satisfy them. They had no means for attending to the resurrection of industry and trade. Generally speaking, military quarters only knew how to get more funds. Although they were unable to understand anything about financial and economic policies and even less able to understand the need for loans to help industry and trade, their opinion was decisive.

I had stressed the need for the National government to establish firm wartime financial and economic policies. The needed revenues should be sought from contributions of landlords and wealthy people in all counties, and earnest consideration should be given to measures for encouraging industrial production in the big cities, stimulating markets, and issuing loans for relief. Li Li-san, on the other hand, emphasized the proposal that workers participate in management and production, claiming that only this would make it possible to reopen factories and businesses and make the workers pay attention to labor discipline and carry out production zealously. These constructive proposals were restricted by actual conditions, and their enforcement was not easy. Accordingly, most of the people who were generally enthusiastic over the revolution felt that although there had been military progress, there were no effective measures to be carried out in the fields of politics and finance.

The organization of the General Trade-Union Council was a complex job within the trade unions. Wuhan was just a commercial center in the hinterland of China, and modern industry had not been developed there. For this reason, the majority of the workers were still handicraftsmen and coolies. Naturally, such masses of workers were imbued with the concept of guild organizations and were influenced by the concept of the gangsters of secret societies. It was unnecessary to recall their evil conditions in the past. In the concessions of Hankow, there had been incidents of police killing ricksha pullers, and cases of coolies being "kicked by foreigners" were of even more frequent occurrence. When the tides of the revolution had reached Wuhan, they naturally aroused in the workers in general such feelings as "revenge," "giving vent to hatred," and "standing on their own feet." The saying "make money out of the foreigners," for example, was very common. The implications of this saying were very complex. It was related to the concept of "robbing the rich to help the poor," only in this case the rich to be robbed were the foreign capitalists. Although the workers had been baptized by the February Seventh Strike, there were still many difficulties in the way of organizing a modern trade union and of protecting the workers' interests in accordance with the economic conditions of the day.

The Hupeh Provincial General Trade-Union Council was officially inaugurated on October 10, 1926—National Day. On that day the broad masses of workers first participated in the grand celebration meeting. This was followed by the meeting inaugurating the trade-union council and the issuance of the manifesto on its founding. Hsiang Chung-fa, who was elected chairman of the General Trade-Union Council, and Li Li-san and Hsiang Ying—the vice-chairmen—headed the General Affairs, Organization, and Propaganda departments respectively; and Hsü Pai-hao served as secretary general. Under the trade-union council, workers' picket corps were also organized, creating a setup that was no less elaborate than that of the Canton–Hong Kong Strike Committee. That day also happened to be the day that Wuchang was captured, and the workers at the meeting were as jubilant as they were angry.

Trade-union organizations were expanding rapidly, and they spread to the counties and towns outside Wuhan. By the end of 1926 the trade-union council had a membership of 300,000.[5] Although the CCP could completely control the trade-union council, it could not exercise effective control over the branch trade unions under the council, so that certain instances of leftist deviations and harsh acts occurred. The CCP comrades responsible for the labor movement were primarily engaged in strengthening the organization of branch unions; in selecting suitable cadres to assume the duties of leadership in the various branch unions; in admitting members to the CCP in order to build up CCP cells in the different unions, factories, and businesses; as well as in training these new hands to understand their current responsibilities.

Numerous labor-capital disputes and waves of strikes resulted from the development of the trade-union organizations.[6] In addition to calling on capital to recognize the collective agreements with the trade unions, the General Trade-Union Council set forth conditions for workers. The standards stipulated were: a minimum wage of thirteen Chinese dollars per month for each worker; a maximum work period of ten hours a day, with an additional work period, if necessary, of not more than two hours; and a twenty-four-hour period of rest each week.[7] These demands were indeed pitiably low in comparison with international standards, and even considering the actual situation in Wuhan at the time, they were not excessive. In the labor-capital disputes, actual demands presented by branch trade unions were sometimes lower than the standards set forth above. In the matter of wage increases, the workers in some industries demanded only an increase of two or three dollars a month; and when this amount was added to their original wages, the standard of thirteen dollars was not yet reached. On the matter of rest, some of them only demanded a day's rest every two weeks. This was clearly being realistic about the possibilities of the situation.

Many labor-capital disputes were settled by means of arbitration. During November the Hupeh Provincial Headquarters of the KMT, the Hupeh Provincial Trade-Union Council, the Wuhan Chamber of Commerce, the Hupeh Provincial Political Committee, the General Political Department of the Commander-in-Chief, and the Wuhan Garrison Headquarters jointly organized an arbitration committee for handling labor-capital disputes. The first requirement of this committee was that both labor and capital submit to its arbitration authority. It advocated that capital should generally accept the labor conditions stipulated by the Hupeh Provincial Trade-Union Council and that during working hours the workers should maintain labor discipline.

The owners of industrial and commercial enterprises generally felt that the demands of the workers were difficult to effect. They blamed their difficult circumstances, claiming that the war had plunged them into an economic depression; that the government authorities were practically killing the goose for its egg when they only asked them for money; and that the trade unions were also playing havoc at the lower levels in presenting various demands. All this would make their future just a dark mess. They did not dare oppose the government authorities and would more or less accede to their demands. But they also utilized the opportunity afforded by the government's demands for money to complain about their dealings with the trade unions.

What aroused the reaction of the owners of industrial and commercial enterprises most were certain direct actions taken by the trade unions. During the labor-capital disputes the workers often adopted the measure of applying pressure to force the capitalists to accept their demands; and there were some incidents of the capitalists being insulted. When the capitalists did not abide by a labor-capital agreement, or when they took certain actions to undermine the trade unions, the workers often counterattacked. Sometimes management personnel would be arrested and made to wear tall hats and parade through the streets. In the eyes of the capitalists, such activities of the workers' picket corps were inexcusable.[8] Furthermore, it was even more universal for the workers to disregard labor discipline, and responsible members of trade unions often neglected their regular tasks in the factories because of activities in the trade unions. It was also common to find other workers and shop assistants not working efficiently during working hours and disobeying the instructions of the capitalists.

These facts shocked the municipality of Wuhan, and the rumor "communism is being practiced" was circulated everywhere. The cry "opposition to communism" also rose in its wake. On the basis of such a situation, Voitinsky had published an article in *Hsiang-tao Chou-pao* (Guide Weekly), advocating severe punishment of the counterrevolutionaries. As a matter of fact, such a proposal could not be carried out at the time, principally because the inner story of the national revolution was too complicated. The militarists that held the actual powers had had to seek the help of the owners of industrial and commercial enterprises and had even shielded the counterrevolutionaries, so how could punishment be talked of? The CCP was plunged into a delicate situation. While it had to consider the situation as a whole, working for the victory of the Northern Expedition and thus not merely looking after its own platform, it also had to protect the interests of the working class and could not allow itself to be used as a tool for restraining the workers. It was thus facing difficulties from both sides and was unable to take care of both sides adequately. If the counterrevolutionaries were really to be severely punished, then the CCP had to act like Trotsky in introducing the slogan for the establishment of the Soviet: in effect, in the midst of the national revolutionary camp it had to launch a Communist revolution. And this was not permitted by the Comintern.

By referring briefly to the foreign relations and internal chaos of the national revolution of the time, we can more easily find out what the cruxes of several problems were.

The national front directing the national revolution was after all built on the main theme of dealing with imperialism; and the forces of imperialism actually constituted the greatest obstacle to the national revolution. Although almost all of the province of Hupeh was occupied by the Northern Expeditionary Army, the threat of imperialism still existed. Large numbers of foreign warships regularly anchored on the river at Wuhan; at the highest count, there were no less than thirty-six of them at one time. The guns of these warships were pointed toward the central area of Wuhan. The sailors from these vessels, using the concessions as bases, overtly or covertly held themselves ready for emergencies. Furthermore, within China's territory the imperialists possessed formidable power politically, economically, and also in the molding of public opinion. This often made us feel that there was a strong hand impeding our progress.

Revolutionary elements generally felt that a practical approach to the Northern Expedition was to defeat the reactionary warlords one by one and then liquidate them. They supported the use of all types and forms of anti-imperialist propaganda, but they were also very anxious to avoid conflict with the imperialists too soon. So they did not want to have incidents of encroachment on the life and property of foreigners, which would give the foreigners a pretext to intervene. However, at a time when the indignation of the masses ran high, a cool head was needed to explain situations if trouble was to be averted. We—the responsible members of the CCP—often made such explanations before the masses of workers, calling on them to refrain from retaliatory measures against the foreign concessions or foreign individuals. We pointed out that imperialism had to be opposed; but since the guns of the foreign warships were pointed toward us, it would not be difficult for this revolutionary center of ours to be destroyed in a very short time. Our own military forces were not yet strong enough, the organization of the workers was not yet perfect, and the broad masses of peasants were not yet organized; and so, at such a moment we must definitely not act rashly and involve ourselves in difficulties.

Internally the leadership of the revolution was virtually in a state of chaos. Usually the numerous organizations and the important persons, when they were not busy attending meetings and making speeches, were moving in different directions when things had to be done. This presented obstacles in everyone's way, some of which were disputes among the different armies, between military authority and Party authority, and disputes among the cliques within the KMT. These disputes were varied and too numerous to be counted. Disputes between peasants and landlords were also beginning to rise and were assuming increased political importance.

People were becoming more and more dissatisfied with the fact that the authority of the commander-in-chief superseded everything. Some military leaders with actual power stood on their own and secretly resisted the situation. The authorities in the different provinces had been appointed by orders of the commander-in-chief. After the occupation of Nanchang, I myself was appointed by Chiang to membership in the Kiangsi Provincial Political Council and the provincial government (because of my duties in Wuhan, I did not assume the post). His orders were all-inclusive, and he interfered in the most minute affairs. And there was no system or legal code to serve as a guide. In Wuhan, Teng Yen-ta, who represented the authority of the commander-in-chief, had a similar work style in this respect.

Since military authority exceeded Party authority, the responsible members of the Party organs of the KMT were first reminded of Dr. Sun Yat-sen's principle of "using the Party to rule the state," and they felt that the position that now prevailed was not desirable. In the Hupeh Provincial Headquarters of the KMT and in the provincial government, the important posts were held by leaders of Hupeh Province, most of whom were KMT leftists or CCP members. Tung Pi-wu, for instance, was an important figure among them. They stressed the need for increasing Party authority, and they also paid attention to protecting the immediate interests of the people of Hupeh. This led to disputes with Teng Yen-ta, who did everything with military needs as the primary consideration. I mediated these disputes and advised Tung Pi-wu to temporarily suppress the provincialism of the Hupeh people; and we got into a heated argument over this. It was my opinion that Teng Yen-ta could not be compared with Chiang and that he possibly tended to gravitate toward our side, so it would be unwise for us to force him to go over to Chiang's side.

The activities of the trade unions were even more helpful in implementing the policies of the CCP. On September 20, when the Second Labor Congress of Wuhan was held, the representative of the General Political Department had declared that it would adopt an attitude of helping such mass organizations as trade unions, but demanded that the trade unions submit to the leadership of the General Political Department. The leaders of the trade unions also declared their readiness to promote relations between the trade unions and KMT headquarters and to accept the leadership of the General Political Department and KMT headquarters. At the same time they introduced a proposal for holding a national assembly. In the view of the CCP, its leadership position over the trade unions was indisputable, and nominal acknowledgment of the leadership of the KMT did not mean sacrifice of the leadership by the CCP, but rather made it possible to argue directly with such people as Teng Yen-ta. The reason we brought forward the proposal for holding a national assembly was to increase the political status of the workers.

The problem of a national assembly was occasionally mentioned in the documents of the KMT after the death of Dr. Sun Yat-sen, but actually the issue was dead. Needless to say, Chiang, with his principle of military affairs above everything, had no desire for any national assembly. On the other hand the CCP had given serious consideration to the problem at its enlarged conference in July, 1926, and the CCP leadership in Hupeh attached particular importance to the issue. Accordingly, the proposal for the convocation of a national assembly was introduced at the Labor Congress.

The First Congress of the Hupeh Provincial Trade-Union Council, which opened on January 1, 1927, had adopted a resolution on calling an assembly of the people in the province. The content of the resolution was: "For the realization of democratic politics and the consolidation of the foundation of the revolution, the Congress especially recommends to the government immediate convocation of an assembly of the people of Hupeh Province. After the establishment of the provincial assembly, the provincial government should abide by and carry out all the decisions of the assembly. The workers of organizations in Hupeh will, under the leadership of the Hupeh Provincial Trade-Union Council, participate in the provincial people's assembly."[9] At the time our policy was to exploit a set of institutions like a national assembly and the provincial people's assembly as a means of curbing military authority and the party authority of the KMT and of solving KMT-CCP disputes.

This policy had the support of the CC of the CCP, but Borodin did not attach importance to it; so it did not lead to an extensive movement. During the time of the Shanghai uprisings, the CC of the CCP had directly advocated the establishment of the Shanghai Citizens' Assembly[10] to organize the municipal government. The Hunan Provincial Trade-Union Council had also passed a proposal to convene the Hunan Provincial People's Assembly.[11] All these were expressions of concern over this issue. Later, after arriving in Wuhan, Borodin continued to advocate increasing the party power of the KMT as a means of opposing Chiang's growing arrogance. Borodin felt that the method of using a national assembly was impractical. When the National government was officially moved to Wuhan, the telegraphic instructions from the Comintern did not make a single reference to a national assembly, it only ordered the CC of the CCP to adopt the policy of staying within the KMT to participate in the National government and the provincial governments. This was the basis for the participation in the National government by T'an P'ing-shan and Su Chao-cheng, who held the posts of Minister of Agriculture and Minister of Labor respectively. Even now I feel that whether or not a national assembly could have been successfully convened, it was a bad mistake for the CC of the CCP not to persist at the time in its advocacy of this issue.

In the handling of all important matters during the first period of military occupation in Wuhan, too many departments had their fingers in the pie. The responsible members of our party in various quarters had extensively used the method of consultation in seeking compromises. Generally they had succeeded in reducing the internal contradictions and building future foundations for the Northern Expedition. At the time there was not a single high-ranking organization of the revolution located in Wuhan. The National government and the Central Headquarters of the KMT were still in Canton. The headquarters of the commander-in-chief was in Kiangsi territory. The CC of the CCP was in Shanghai. Under the conditions of war, there was considerable difficulty in making connections between Kiangsi, Canton, Shanghai, and Hankow. And so, on the basis of Wuhan's geographical location, the people in Wuhan insisted that the National government be moved there immediately to make the leadership effective. This problem of moving the capital and the various conditions I have discussed above all formed the background for the subsequent developments of the "Wuhan Period."

After Borodin's Arrival at Wuhan

The anti-Chiang movement in Wuhan started only after the arrival of Borodin at Wuhan. Borodin had previously been dissatisfied with the various arrangements made by Chiang after March 20, which I touched upon earlier. But generally he was still being tolerant and accommodating toward Chiang, attempting to remedy the near-collapse in relations between the KMT and the CCP. In October a joint conference of the Central Headquarters of the KMT and representatives of its various provincial and municipal headquarters was held in Canton.[12] It was at this time that signs of opposition to Chiang first began to appear, and this seemed to have the support of Borodin. When Borodin arrived at Wuhan, it was felt that the time was ripe for the anti-Chiang movement, and he no longer concealed his determination to oppose Chiang. This anti-Chiang movement naturally was based on the anti-Chiang trends in all quarters. It started with the restriction and reduction of Chiang's powers and developed into conflict between the Wuhan camp and Chiang.

About December 10, 1926, Borodin arrived at Wuhan, accompanied by Soong Ch'ing-ling, Hsu Ch'ien, Sun Fo, T. V. Soong, and Eugene Ch'en. These leaders came as a delegation of the KMT Central Headquarters and the National government to prepare for moving the national capital. T'an Yen-k'ai, chairman of the National government, and others were then following them to Wuhan, leading the entire working personnel of the KMT headquarters and the National government.

When I arrived at a splendid foreign-style building in the former German Concession of Hankow to call on the newly arrived Borodin, he was receiving guests in his reception hall. I went to his office and first talked with Comrade Chang T'ai-lei, who had accompanied him to Wuhan. Chang first said to me, "Borodin has a few tricks up his sleeve. In a single conversation he won over T'ang Sheng-chih." He followed this by saying that as soon as Borodin left the boat, he had accompanied T'ang Sheng-chih, who had come to welcome him, to his headquarters. They had started to converse, and Chang had acted as their interpreter. Borodin at the very outset said to T'ang, "Whoever can faithfully carry out the proposals of Dr. Sun Yat-sen will become the greatest figure in China." When T'ang Sheng-chih heard this, he seemed overjoyed and twisted his body several times. He then replied pleasantly, "I am prepared to do so." Borodin continued explaining how the proposals of Dr. Sun could be faithfully carried out and in a roundabout way suggested that he no longer had confidence in Chiang and was placing his trust in T'ang. Thereupon T'ang earnestly said to Borodin, "I am ready to follow all of your directives."

Chang T'ai-lei felt that Borodin spoke these extraordinary words to T'ang Sheng-chih not as a diplomat, but rather that he was expressing his personal decision to ally with T'ang to oppose Chiang. He also pointed out that while he did not know if Moscow concurred with Borodin's opinion, he did know that Borodin's dissatisfaction with Chiang was continually increasing. When they were passing through Kiangsi on their journey, Borodin had met Chiang at Lushan on December 7; and judging from Borodin's looks, Chang conjectured that the interview was again unsatisfactory. When Borodin could be so outspoken with T'ang Sheng-chih, whom he was meeting for the first time, his deep hatred for Chiang could well be imagined.

Borodin very soon stepped into the office. He grasped my hand warmly and sighed, "Very good, we now meet again in a new place. We shall begin a new life—write a new book." When we talked of the general situation in Wuhan, he said repeatedly, "I am tired of living in Canton. I am greatly interested in Wuhan. But what bothers me is that Wuhan is still under the threat of fire from foreign gunboats."

Our conversation turned to the situation of foreigners in Wuhan. Borodin expressed satisfaction with everything in Wuhan; but he indicated that in the future even greater attention should be given to the movements of foreigners. So I recommended to him a young CCP member who knew English, a Mr. Li (I have since forgotten his given name), to serve on his staff. Later this youth undertook the investigation of the movements of foreigners for Borodin. The CCP Hupeh District Committee had felt that its funds were inadequate, and so it was glad to let Borodin assume direct responsibility for this work.

Not only were new arrivals like Borodin undertaking the task of establishing a staff, but the CCP Hupeh District Committee was also busy doing this. The committee was moved again, from Wuchang to Hankow. Borodin felt that with the move of KMT Central Headquarters to Hankow, the scope of the work of the CCP Hupeh District Committee was no longer limited to handling affairs of the one province of Hupeh. He insisted that we move immediately to Hankow in order to establish regular contacts with the important leaders of the KMT, who had recently arrived there, in order to exercise control over the development of the situation as a whole. We accepted this recommendation of Borodin and carried out the new arrangements.

It was after December 13, when the Joint Conference between the KMT Central Headquarters and the National Government Council (hereafter referred to as the Joint Conference) was held, that Borodin and I discussed general policies. Before the event, Borodin never mentioned to me why the Joint Conference was so hurriedly organized, what its tasks and powers were, or whether Chiang had agreed to it. Only after the Joint Conference had been held did Borodin tell me that while he was in Canton he had talked of the possibility of the separation of the KMT and the CCP after the Northern Expedition had reached Peking, but from what he could now see, it was possible that the separation of the KMT and the CCP might not have to wait until the army reached Peking. I asked him why he held such a view. He said it was from his sense of smell, which was especially sensitive.

He made the following points to me: First, after Chiang had occupied Kiangsi, he was bent on developing the southeastern area, with the object of seizing Nanking and Shanghai. Such a policy of eastward march would take him farther and farther away from the Soviet Union and lead him to a compromise with the imperialist powers and the comprador bourgeoisie of Kiangsu and Chekiang. These activities of Chiang were carried out with Huang Fu, Niu Yung-chien, and others as intermediary string-pullers.

Second, Chiang had consistently wanted to establish his own personal military dictatorship and to place the National government and the KMT entirely within his grasp; and he had opposed having Wang Ching-wei return to resume his post. These things had already aroused the opposition of the majority of the members of the CEC of the KMT. The members that had accompanied Borodin to Wuhan now unanimously opposed such ambitions on the part of Chiang, and so a joint conference was organized so that the powers of the central authority would not be manipulated by Chiang alone.

Third, if Chiang did seize Nanking and Shanghai, it was very possible that he would launch an anti-Communist movement to please the imperialists and the bourgeoisie.

Borodin was one who attached great importance to actual military strength. He said that the majority of the armies were not satisfied with Chiang. The anti-Chiang attitude of T'ang Sheng-chih was taken for granted. Teng Yen-ta and the majority of the generals of the Fourth Army would actively support Wang Ching-wei. The Second Army of T'an Yen-k'ai, the Third Army of Chu P'ei-te, and the Sixth Army of Ch'eng Ch'ien had all along been dissatisfied with Chiang. The Seventh Army had also had many disagreements with Chiang during the development of the military situation. Moreover Feng Yü-hsiang had relieved the siege of Sian,[13] and as soon as his army could break out of Tungkwan, he would provide a personality that would effectively compete with Chiang. Thus from the viewpoint of actual military strength, the future of Chiang's dictatorship was beset with thorns.

These views of Borodin's provided the rallying point for his opposition to Chiang. I felt that this was a great change in our policy. The basic policy of opposition to Chiang was like an arrow in a bow that was ready to be shot off momentarily; and no further hesitation was possible. But comparing the strength of the two sides, I felt that Borodin's viewpoint was a bit too optimistic. I pointed out to him that from the viewpoint of the people of Wuhan in general, T'ang Sheng-chih was worse than Chiang. T'ang was a warlord who had defected to the side of the revolution, and his subordinates were old-type militarists. Chiang was after all a veteran member of the KMT, and he had the revolutionary young officers from Whampoa to back him. The relations between Chiang and the other armies were truly not good; but the relations between T'ang and the other armies were also defective. Ill-feelings had developed between T'ang and the Second and Sixth armies; and T'ang had differences with the Fourth Army based on provincialism. If T'ang were called upon to unite the anti-Chiang military leaders, I feared that extra efforts would be needed and results would be only partially successful. Although the leftists possessed an overwhelming force in KMT headquarters and among the masses, nevertheless they lacked effective leaders. It was still problematical whether Wang Ching-wei could return to China and, if so, whether he could act with a strong hand. There was need, therefore, to study the extent to which the anti-Chiang movement should be carried and whether the movement should be promoted quickly or by gradual measures.

Borodin had no answers to the problems that I posed. He could only stress the core of the problem at the time, which was that we could not but act as we did. For since we had seen the counterrevolutionary aims of Chiang clearly, we could not afford to stand by and do nothing. He justified the policy of alliance with T'ang by saying that T'ang was better than Chiang in that T'ang sympathized with the labor and peasant movements. He anticipated that Wang Ching-wei would return to China at the appropriate moment, and that he would surely not be as weak as he had been in the past. As to the point of uniting the anti-Chiang forces, he had confidence in his own flexible talent being able to get results.

Borodin was very strong in his individual character. While in Canton, he never consulted the Kwangtung District Committee of the CCP on any matter, but acted arbitrarily. After his arrival in Hankow, his attitude was a little more polite. He held in his hands the supreme power to make policy decisions, and he very rarely revised his decisions because of our views. At most he would ask for my concurrence as a gesture of politeness. He did not interfere, however, with the labor and peasant movements led by the Hupeh District Committee of the CCP. Perhaps he did this because he was only adept at the use of strategy and had no talent for other matters. And as a matter of fact, the situation in Wuhan could not be understood all at once by a new arrival, which he was.

It was very clear that under Borodin's policy the Wuhan situation would undergo an important change. I could only report these facts to the CC of the CCP and ask for its careful consideration, in order that we might achieve unanimity in the steps that we took. I explained that I could not proceed to Shanghai, and I requested that the CC be moved to Wuhan immediately. But the CC of the CCP did not seem to pay enough attention to the possible repercussions of the anti-Chiang movement. The directive it gave me did not bring up any new view other than its concurrence with the policy. But what the CC of the CCP did in Shanghai later was not completely in step with the actions of Wuhan.

I shall have occasion to refer to these matters later. Here let me proceed chronologically to talk about certain changes in Wuhan at the time.

When the Joint Conference was first organized, its primary task was to prepare for the establishment of the national capital at Wuhan. In no sense was it an anti-Chiang center. At most it more or less had a tendency to consider itself the central authority. The members of the Joint Conference felt that in the course of moving the capital, the powers of the central authority would be temporarily interrupted, so that the opportunity should be grasped of temporarily assuming the responsibilities of the central government in addition to the work of preparing for the establishment of the capital. However, in Chiang's eyes, this was tantamount to resisting his authority.

Hsu Ch'ien was elected chairman of the Joint Conference. This man of the Christian faith had originally been elected a member of the National government because he was in the position to represent Feng Yü-hsiang; he did not have deep connections with the KMT. He was a zealous orator, but he did not seem to be an outstanding politician. In the beginning, the work of the Joint Conference seemed to be at loose ends. The members were busy attending meetings and making moving speeches.

The numerous speeches made by these members generally explained the significance of the removal of the National government to Wuhan and called upon people to support the leadership of the National government and the CEC of the KMT. On the basis of the resolution of the Joint Conference of the KMT Central Headquarters and its provincial and municipal headquarters that was held at Canton, the KMT headquarters and the mass organizations went further and introduced such slogans as: "Welcome Wang Ching-wei's Return to China"; "Demand Wang-Chiang Cooperation"; and "Increase the Authority of the Party." These voices aimed at a slight curbing of the excessive powers of Chiang. But in Chiang's eyes, welcoming Wang's return and his resumption of posts was tantamount to direct opposition to himself.

Teng Yen-ta, who exercised the powers of commander-in-chief in Wuhan, adopted an attitude of supporting the Joint Conference. He was director of the Wuhan headquarters of the Commander-in-Chief and originally acted under Chiang's orders. But he was a noted KMT leftist, and he could not be completely controlled by Chiang. Like T'an Yen-k'ai, he felt that the national revolution should not be the monopoly of the militarists. Perhaps he had some reaction toward certain orders issued by Chiang in the past. He respected the decisions of the Joint Conference; and so some changes were made in certain propaganda work undertaken by the General Political Department. For example, the slogan "Support Commander-in-Chief Chiang" was changed to "Support the Leadership of the Central Government." For this reason Chiang's wrath was first directed against the General Political Department under Teng Yen-ta, and he started to take the General Political Department to task for its inadequate propaganda efforts.

The anti-Chiang campaign, which Borodin had told me about, did not seem to have been made public yet. He was busy helping the Joint Conference establish political order and authority. He paid the greatest attention to such matters as foreign relations and finance. And T. V. Soong, who was responsible for finances, and Eugene Ch'en, who was responsible for foreign relations, were both good friends of his, so that he could talk freely about these matters. The rectification of the chaotic financial situation as well as the handling of the difficult foreign relations problems were real problems urgently in need of being solved by the Joint Conference. Borodin started to work on these problems so that the Joint Conference would make positive moves that would lead to increasing its authority. In actual fact, of course, this also meant reduction of the powers of the commander-in-chief.

The taking back of the British Concession in Hankow provided the first test for the Joint Conference. Relations with Britain had been a thorny problem for the National government. On September 5, 1926, there was the incident of the shelling of Wanhsien by British gunboats, which resulted in thousands of casualties among the Chinese population.[14] This had aroused anti-British feelings in Wuhan. The British policy had always been one against the National government, while the anti-imperialist movement of the National Revolution had Britain for its primary target. "Among foreigners there are good ones and bad ones: the Soviet Russians are the best, the Germans come next, while the British are the worst" had been a common saying among the people of Wuhan at the time. Under the slogan "concentrate on the target of opposing Britain" even anti-Japanese sentiments had relaxed. In Wuhan there had never been a movement to boycott Japanese goods.

On December 26 an anti-British meeting of citizens was held in Hankow. This meeting had been motivated by acts of suppressing the KMT in the British concessions in Tientsin and Shanghai. The authorities of the British Concession in Tientsin had closed down the municipal headquarters of the KMT there and had arrested seventeen KMT members, who had been turned over to Chang Tso-lin. Seven of them had been executed by Chang. In Shanghai the authorities of the British Concession had closed down the *Min-kuo Jih-pao* (Republican Daily News), the organ of the KMT. Furthermore, the report was circulated that the Inspector General of Customs, the Englishman Edwards (?), was lending guns to Chang Tso-lin so that he could deal with the Northern Expedition. So, the citizens' rally in Wuhan adopted anti-British resolutions and issued an anti-British manifesto, so that anti-British feeling suddenly grew intense.

On the first three days of January, 1927, meetings were held in Wuhan to celebrate the northern transfer of the National government and victory in the Northern Expedition. Everywhere in Wuhan, activities of the propaganda corps were evident, among which was propaganda against Britain. At about 3 P.M. on January 3, the propaganda corps of the Wuhan branch of the Central Military and Political Academy, which was under the control of the General Political Department, had assembled considerable numbers of people on the square adjacent to the British Concession for a lecture meeting. The British marines stationed at the Hong Kong and Shanghai Banking Corporation came out to intervene, and many people were killed or wounded.[15] The incident immediately shocked Wuhan.

About one hour after this incident started, I reached the scene. By that time the conflict had ended, and the British marines had retreated to the rear of the defense works at the British Concession. I saw with my own eyes a group of British marines sheltered by the defense works, with their rifles aimed at the masses assembled on the square and in a shooting posture. Hsu Ch'ien stood on a table temporarily placed in the center of the square, with his back to the defense works of the British Concession. Disregarding the threat of the rifles of the British marines, he made a rousing speech in front of the masses, announcing the anti-imperialist and anti-British decisions of the National government and appealing to the masses to leave the scene singly to await the settlement of the incident by the government through diplomatic channels. But the public had become aroused, and there were loud cries of "rush into the Concession." It was possible that more serious conflicts would occur. I was fully aware that at that time we must definitely not come into conflict with the British Concession, so on the spur of the moment, I sought out responsible members of some mass organizations on the square and persuaded them to obey the instruction of Hsu Ch'ien and lead the masses away from the square. In this way the situation gradually calmed down. The indignant masses shouted some anti-British slogans and marched in groups to the National government to lodge their appeals.

That evening, to avoid any additional incidents, we notified each of the various mass organizations individually that for the time being their propaganda activities should not be carried into the concessions. Unexpectedly, at about 9 A.M. on January 4, a comrade telephoned me to report that some of the propaganda corps of the trade unions had entered the British Concession and that large groups of citizens had rushed into the Concession. I immediately telephoned Li Li-san to ask about this, but he and other responsible members of the trade unions had not yet heard about the incident. He indicated that the responsible members of the General Trade-Union Council would immediately rush to the British Concession to prevent the occurrence of any incident. I also telephoned a member of the Joint Conference to explain the situation and the measures that I had adopted to deal with it. He expressed agreement with my action and immediately sent people to the scene to maintain order.

After I put down the telephone, I immediately drove to the British Concession. The streets in the British Concession were filled with crowds of people marching toward the British Consulate, but nothing drastic had yet occurred. By the time I arrived at the front of the British Concession, a considerable crowd had gathered there. They were shouting,

"Restore the British Concession to China!" and other slogans. I found some leaders among the people at the scene and called on them to restrain the masses and refrain from any rash acts. I said that they should not damage the life and property of foreigners or come into conflict with the police, and so forth. I then entered the British Consulate and found between ten and twenty heads of public organizations assembled in the hall of the consulate, as if waiting for instructions from a higher level. I told them likewise that they must observe order strictly. The staff members of the British Consulate appeared to have escaped to the second floor of the building. On the stairs stood a British staff member, whose attitude did not reveal any serious alarm. I went up the stairs and shook hands with him. I told him that there would not be any untoward incidents, and he transmitted my views to his colleagues on the second floor. In this way the tense situation, which seemed about to explode any moment at a touch, seemed to ease up.

Very soon Li Li-san and others also arrived. They told me that inside the British Concession there were no violent agitations. Along the route they only saw a few cases of broken windows. They had notified the responsible members of various trade unions to persuade the citizens to withdraw from the Concession. They also heard that the marines stationed at the Hong Kong and Shanghai Banking Corporation had been withdrawn to the gunboats. So they thought that no serious incidents would occur. Very soon after this, Sun Fo and other members of the National government arrived. I briefly told them what had transpired up to that time; and they went upstairs to talk with the British consul.

This was the very first scene of the direct action of the people of Wuhan in the retracting of the British Concession. After this, Sino-British negotiations were begun. Under the fiery wrath of the nation, the masses of Wuhan were able to maintain strict order, exhibiting their strong determination to the British, so that the imperialists could not but look at them in a different light. This proved that the national movement in China had entered a better-organized stage. British diplomacy had always been flexible. The lessons that the British learned from the May Thirtieth Movement in Shanghai and the Canton–Hong Kong Strike seemed to show them that if they persisted in the adoption of a heavy-handed policy, they would create a deep hatred and animosity between China and Britain that would be unfavorable to Britain. Perhaps they felt that they could exploit the conflicts within the national revolution to cause the disintegration of this national front, so that there was no need for them to keep on using their previous tactics.

I saw with my own eyes that we already had the situation in our own grasp, so I left the British Consulate and drove to see Borodin. After he found out what had happened on this occasion, he pleased me by saying, "Lucky that a conflict has been averted." He also pointed out that although there were no signs of similar demonstrations against the Japanese Concession, he nevertheless thought that the various people's organizations should be notified to severely restrain the masses in order to prevent any kind of action that might encroach on the Japanese Concession. These words of Borodin actually agreed with our established policy, and further discussion was not necessary. As a result of our policy the people of Wuhan did not exhibit any signs of anger toward the Japanese afterwards.

This diplomatic victory also raised the prestige of the Joint Conference. On January 4 the Conference accepted the four conditions brought forward by the people's organization for retracting the concessions.[16] It pacified the aroused feelings of the people and at the same time furthered negotiations with the British. As a result of Foreign Minister Eugene Ch'en's negotiations with the British consul, an agreement was reached about the organization of a provisional administrative committee for the British Concession of Hankow, and for the dispatch of Chinese military and police personnel to maintain order in the British Concession.

The act of retracting the British Concession in Hankow greatly aroused the hearts of the people throughout the country. On January 6, in the vicinity of the British Concession in Kiukiang, an incident occurred involving a conflict between workers and British marines. Teng Yen-ta hurried from Hankow to Kiukiang for negotiations with the British consul at Kiukiang. This resulted in the precedent set at Hankow being followed, and a small number of Chinese military and police personnel took over the British Concession at Kiukiang on January 8. Later, on February 19 and 20, 1927, Eugene Ch'en signed with O'Malley, the representative of the British Minister to China, agreements for retracting the Hankow Concession and the Kiukiang Concession respectively, and there was also an exchange of notes. By this time the British concessions at Hankow and Kiukiang were officially returned. This could be considered an important achievement of the Joint Conference.

The tense situation in relations with Britain did not ease the disputes within the ranks of the revolution at the time. On December 5, 1926, the

National government in Canton announced the suspension of operations and carried out the move to the north. On December 31 T'an Yen-k'ai, Chang Ching-chiang, and others leading the staffs of the National government and the KMT Central Headquarters arrived at Nanchang. On January 1, 1927, the National government officially announced that the capital had been moved, and it immediately started to function. On January 3, however, Chiang suddenly telegraphed Wuhan, advocating that the temporary location of the National government be at Nanchang. This precipitated the outbreak of the well-known incident over the question of establishing the capital at Nanchang or Wuhan.

The moving of the capital and the retracting of the British Concession of Hankow occurred almost simultaneously. The important personages of the Joint Conference in Wuhan were really amazed over this proposal of Chiang's. They told each other that moving the capital to Wuhan had been decided long ago. Moreover, since the foreign relations situation was so tense and Wuhan was the fund-raising center, how could the National government be located in Nanchang? As the result of discussions at the Joint Conference, a telegram was sent to Chiang, expressing disagreement with such a sudden change.

Chiang was in Wuhan from January 10 through 18, attempting to persuade the leaders in Wuhan to his view; but he was disappointed and returned to Nanchang. Chiang's argument was that the location of the capital should be determined by developments of strategy and military progress. At the time, military operations were in progress in the lower reaches of the Yangtze, and so the National government should be temporarily located at Nanchang. When Nanking had been captured, the wishes of Dr. Sun Yat-sen should be complied with, and the capital should be located at Nanking. He also declared that this was the unanimous decision of the Central Political Council of the KMT when it met at Nanchang; and he demanded that the leaders of the Joint Conference comply with the decision.

The important members of the Joint Conference, however, claimed that the establishment of the capital at Wuhan had been proposed by Chiang on October 22, 1926, had been decided with the concurrence of the CEC of the KMT and the members of the National government, and had furthermore been officially announced. From the standpoints of foreign relations, finance, military affairs, and even the psychological state of the people, they felt that such a change should not be made at this time. If the capital eventually had to be moved from Wuhan to

Nanking, the decision to do so could be made later at a plenary session of the CEC.

Chiang, because of the deadlock in this dispute and also because on his visit to Wuhan he had received a big welcome, but not one that could be considered overenthusiastic, found unpleasant to his ears such cries as "Support the leadership of the Kuomintang Central Headquarters" and "Welcome Wang Ching-wei to return to the country to resume his posts." Because of these incidents and because of the deadlock in the dispute about location of the capital, Chiang returned to Nanchang with a depressed feeling and began to present difficult problems to the Wuhan authorities. So telegrams to T. V. Soong asking for funds came in shoals. These things further increased the distance separating the two sides.

The dispute over moving the capital developed into an unofficial propaganda battle between the two sides. One rumor in Wuhan was that T'an Yen-k'ai was detained at Nanchang and was not permitted to come to Wuhan to exercise his authority. Another was that Chang Ching-chiang was afraid to come to Wuhan, where the revolutionary atmosphere was high, and so lingered at Nanchang, secretly plotting to sabotage the policy, which had been decided upon, of establishing the capital at Wuhan. Chiang was determined to exercise his dictatorship in attempting to place the National government under his control. In Nanchang the rumors were that the Joint Conference in Wuhan was an illegal organization, that the Communist Party was playing havoc there by attempting to oppose Chiang and undermine the revolution, and so forth. It was very clear that the internal disputes of the revolution had brought it to the brink of disaster.

Toward the end of January the CC of the CCP at Shanghai sent Comrade Wang Shou-hua as its representative to Wuhan, to hold important talks with me. His object was to find out about the internal situation at Wuhan and what we were doing to cope with it. I told him in detail about the inner story of the dispute between Wuhan and Nanchang and about its seriousness, and I insisted that he transmit the information to the CC so that it could make a quick decision on the strategy for dealing with the situation.

I pointed out to Wang Shou-hua that the dispute between Wuhan and Nanchang could lead to a split in the KMT, a split between the KMT and the CCP, and even to armed conflict. Both parties had gone to extremes, and judging from his past performance, Chiang would disregard everything and act arbitrarily. Nor would Borodin adopt measures of compromise. The time had come for the CC of the CCP to rise up and cope with the situation. It was a most important opportunity.

I explained to him that there were still two courses to follow. One was for the CCP to assume the role of the impartial mediator, easing the tension caused by the dispute between Wuhan and Nanchang and keeping it within the bounds of negotiations. In view of the actual situation, this course would be difficult to follow. If it were tried, a minimum requirement would be for the entire CC of the CCP to move quickly to Wuhan, to hold talks with Borodin before proceeding with the plan. The second course was for the CC of the CCP to agree completely with the established policy of Borodin and actively prepare forces for the resolute implementation of that policy. I told Wang that in my opinion, whether or not the CC of the CCP was willing to do so, it had to pursue the second course.

I also told him that the steps currently being taken by the CCP were rather confused. There were already many problems in Wuhan that could not be solved easily. In Hunan the peasant movement was developing rapidly, and this had led to unrest among the masses in Wuhan. This did not coordinate with Borodin's policy of easing the internal conflicts of Wuhan so that concerted action could be taken against Chiang. In Kiangsi the CCP organization was located in the front line of the struggle against Chiang. Its leadership was weak, but I had no means of improving the situation. Kwangtung was an even more important base, but I had no way of establishing close ties with it from where I was. And all along I had not contacted CCP members working with Feng Yü-hsiang. In order to resolve all of these problems, it was necessary for the CC of the CCP to move to Wuhan immediately.

I recommended that the CC of the CCP not attach too much importance to the work in the Shanghai area, since, after all, it was a strong base of imperialism. If Chiang occupied Shanghai, it was possible that he would massacre the CCP members. At least the CC of the CCP could not do very much there. If the CC of the CCP moved to Wuhan, it could strengthen its leadership over work in Hunan, Hupeh, Kiangsi, Kwangtung, and even the Northwest and actively arm the masses of workers and peasants to cope with this life-or-death struggle.

This young comrade, Wang Shou-hua (whose original name was Ho Chuang-liang), had been a student in Russia and had spent several years in trade-union work among the Chinese laborers at Vladivostok. He returned to Shanghai in October, 1926, and succeeded Li Li-san as chairman of the labor movement committee of the CC of the CCP, undertaking directly the leadership of the labor movement in Shanghai. Though he was very capable, he was also young and impetuous and took an easy view of things. He boasted to me about the importance of the 800,000 organized Shanghai workers and the first uprising of the Shanghai workers on October 23, 1926.

He also described to me the fairly good attitude adopted by Niu Yung-chien, Wu Chih-hui, and others of the Shanghai KMT toward the CCP and toward the organization of a KMT-CCP joint conference. All work was discussed and settled through consultations of the Joint Conference. The CCP also maintained very good relations with Tu Yüeh-sheng, the head of the Green Gang, and others. Wang met Tu Yüeh-sheng almost daily. In Shanghai, there were no incidents of gangsters interfering with the trade unions. He explained that the CC of the CCP had pinned great hopes on the work in Shanghai and believed that if the Northern Expeditionary Army reached Shanghai, the city would be within the control of the Communist Party. These words of his showed clearly that he did not fully understand the seriousness of the dispute between Wuhan and Nanchang nor the actual conditions of Shanghai society. I solemnly warned him that his was a very dangerous illusion—one that did not recognize the great power of imperialism and also fell for the deceptive mask worn by Chiang Kai-shek.

Wang Shou-hua agreed to transmit my views to the CC, and he personally gave his unqualified support to them. Before he left, I also told him that many problems could not be resolved through the medium of correspondence. On several previous occasions travelers between Shanghai and Wuhan had failed to fulfill their missions, and I hoped that this time his journey would not be wasted. I was surprised that after Wang Shou-hua's return to Shanghai, my recommendations again did not receive sufficient attention. The most ironic thing was that this innocent Wang Shou-hua himself was, I am told, summoned by Tu Yüeh-sheng to his home on the eve of the April 12 Party purge, was seized in the reception hall of Tu Yüeh-sheng's residence, and lost his life.

In February, Voitinsky followed Wang Shou-hua, coming to Wuhan from Shanghai. This seemed to be the only reply I had from Shanghai. He came to discuss with me and Borodin the policy to be used in dealing with Chiang. Except for a quarrel with Borodin, his visit was uneventful and unproductive. Such trips back and forth for discussions not only failed to clear up the internal chaos of the CCP, but also produced delays in coping with the situation.

Voitinsky observed general conditions in Wuhan and seemed to be influenced particularly by Russian advisers like Galen who brought forward views opposed to those of Borodin. He indicated to me that the various elements composing the revolutionary camp should avoid breaking apart too quickly, for otherwise it would be impossible to counter the formidable forces of the northern warlords and imperialism. It would also be unfavorable to the CCP and to the labor and peasant movements. He said that some of the Russian advisers in Wuhan did not agree with the work style of Borodin. He also said one thing that had deep implications, "Chiang Kai-shek is after all not Ch'en Chiung-ming; and Borodin certainly is not Sun Yat-sen." He proposed that he pay a visit to Nanchang to seek an understanding with Chiang in order to avoid a separation in the ranks of the revolution.

I told Voitinsky that I doubted that such a plan would work, although there was no harm in trying it. I pointed out emphatically that the anti-Chiang group included some unreliable old-type militarists and vacillating leftist politicians, so that even if victory were won, the situation was not optimistic. If his trip to Nanchang would ease even a little bit the antagonistic feeling between Wuhan and Nanchang, so that the CCP would have a little more time for preparations, it was worth the try. However, since the situation had developed as far as it had, we could not hold our hopes for salvaging it too high.

On his return from Nanchang a few days later, Voitinsky said to me simply, "The situation is beyond salvage." In the office of Borodin, the two again began to argue. Borodin seemed to think of himself as Lenin, and he took Voitinsky to task as having played the role of such labor traitors as Kamenev and Zinoviev, who opposed the October Revolution. He said that Voitinsky's trip to Nanchang not only failed to attain its objective, but it also stirred up the anti-Chiang front, increased Chiang's arrogance, and damaged our own prestige. Voitinsky counterattacked, pointing out that Borodin's acts were not at all Bolshevik, but rather those of politicians manipulating the situation, so that the result would not benefit the Chinese revolution or the position of the Soviet Union in it.

Borodin knew that I supported Voitinsky's action, so he carefully pointed out the differences between my views and those of Voitinsky to reduce the obstacles to his own proposals. He said that although I also was against the too rapid division in the ranks of the revolution, nevertheless I knew that the anti-Chiang movement had advanced too far for us to retreat, so that I had long since asked the CC of the CCP to move to Wuhan in order to concentrate forces that could cope with the situation. Voitinsky, on the other hand, was merely singing the opposition's tune and was vacillating and undecided. Borodin finally told Voitinsky that the facts had proved that his tune was already obsolete and that there was no longer any choice in what we could do. If all would unite and cooperate in carrying out his own policy, it was possible that the situation would not end up as badly as Voitinsky imagined.

Finally, Voitinsky found that he had no means with which to change Borodin's action, and he returned to Shanghai sulkily. Before he left he said that since the CC of the CCP was not on the spot, there was no way to control Borodin's actions. He definitely realized the need for having the CC of the CCP move to Wuhan rapidly and for preparing immediately for the Fifth Congress of the CCP. He regretted that he had come so late that he could do nothing. He agreed to carry out detailed discussions with the CC of the CCP on his return to Shanghai and to seek an appropriate solution to the problems.

Facts that I discovered later proved that after his return to Shanghai, Voitinsky also failed to quickly rectify the tendency of the CC of the CCP to support the position of "Shanghai first." It still lingered in Shanghai. When it moved to Wuhan later, it was already after the great Shanghai tragedy of April 12, and by then Wuhan had reached the state of "the beautiful dusk" and could hardly carry out any program. To sum up, in the later fierce bout between the KMT and the CCP, the inefficiency and internal dissension of the CCP leadership were fully exposed. General Chiang Kai-shek, on the other hand, was fully in control of the initiative and acted arbitrarily. The outcome of the struggle was too obvious to need study.

The Party Purge and the Split Between Nanking and Wuhan

The incident over moving the capital to Wuhan or Nanchang rapidly developed into a quarrel between military authority and Party authority. This was followed by the development of antagonism between the anti-Communist front led by Chiang and the anti-Chiang front led by Wuhan. The evolution of this fierce struggle led to the gradual assumption of supremacy by Chiang, with Wuhan occupying a correspondingly lower position. Chiang not only held the reins of military power, but he also possessed as his foundation the conservative influences of the old society. After the occupation of Nanchang, it was clear that Chiang also had support from foreign powers. The anti-Chiang front in Wuhan, on the other hand, was prenatally shaky in character, and dissenting views had been evident from the beginning, so that it was easily defeated by the anti-Communist campaign of Chiang.

When the Wuhan side originally developed its anti-Chiang offensive over the issue of moving the capital, it had an imposing position. On February 24, 1927, the KMT headquarters of the three cities making up Wuhan held a congress, at which Tung Pi-wu, serving as chairman, delivered the opening address. Hsu Ch'ien, chairman of the Joint Conference, attended the meeting and addressed the gathering, stressing such issues as saving the Party and making the military leaders subservient to the leadership of the Party. The meeting adopted the following resolutions:

(1) To strengthen the powers of the central authority
(2) To unify the Party's leadership organs
(3) To immediately convoke a plenary session of the central committees to resolve the Party's problems
(4) To welcome Wang Ching-wei's resumption of duties
(5) To get the stupid and senile leaders to step aside
(6) To support the foreign policy of the National government and oppose the attempt of the reactionaries in the Party to seek a compromise with imperialism.

The meeting also shouted loudly such slogans as "Down with Chang Ching-chiang!" and "Oppose reactionaries!" This moving episode, needless to say, was a masterpiece of work carried out jointly by the KMT leftists and the CCP.

Both Wuhan and Nanchang had advocated the convocation of the Third Plenum of the second central committees of the KMT to settle internal disputes of the Party. But on the point of a location for the meeting, each side insisted on having it held within its sphere of influence. In other words, Chiang proposed Nanchang, and the Joint Conference proposed Wuhan. Furthermore, both sides put up the slogan "Save the Party," and they took each other to task for violating Party discipline. Chiang pointed out that Hsu Ch'ien had usurped the powers of the Party and had belittled Chiang's authority as chairman of the Standing Committee of the central committees of the KMT.

The dispute over the location for this meeting led to victory for Wuhan. This was because at the time the majority of the members of the KMT central committees were assembled in Wuhan, and they unanimously favored Wuhan as the location for the meeting. This seemed to make Chiang feel that if he persisted in his own view, it would be tantamount to showing people that he was a dictator. At the same time, he was already determined to develop the Southeast and had cultivated the idea of real power above everything, so that basically he did not care about the decisions of any sort of meeting. Moreover, T'an Yen-k'ai, chairman of the National government, was in Nanchang, doing his best to mediate; and he strongly advised Chiang not to go to extremes. As a result, the dispute was settled. T'an Yen-k'ai finally arrived in Wuhan accompanied by Ch'en Kuo-fu and others. Chiang and Chang Ching-chiang remained in Nanchang and did not attend the Plenum.

T'an P'ing-shan, who had returned from Moscow, had arrived in Wuhan by the end of February.[17] He actively supported the anti-Chiang policy of Borodin and became the most important responsible person from the CCP to participate in the work of the KMT. He was optimistic about cooperation between the CCP and the KMT leftists. He stated that Stalin did not support the tendency of the CC of the CCP to leave the KMT and seek independent development, but Stalin did attach importance to T'an P'ing-shan's personal ability to cooperate with the KMT leftists. T'an supported the Comintern's proposals on the participation by CCP members in the work of the National government. Accordingly, during this particular stage, he and Borodin walked the same road.

The Third Plenum of the KMT,[18] held from March 10 through 17, was clearly a victory for the leftists. On the basis of the report of Hsu Ch'ien, this meeting first approved the work of the Joint Conference and ratified all of its decisions. This was tantamount to a direct reply to Chiang's repudiation of the Joint Conference. The meeting also adopted important resolutions on such issues as "Unification of the leadership of the Party" and the "Organic Outline of Military Structures Under the Central Executive Committee." On the basis of these resolutions, the meeting elected Wang Ching-wei, T'an Yen-k'ai, Chiang Kai-shek, Ku Meng-yü, Sun Fo, T'an P'ing-shan (a CCP member), Ch'en Kung-po, Hsu Ch'ien, and Wu Yu-chang (a CCP member) as members of the nine-man Standing Committee of the CEC. Wang Ching-wei, Ku Meng-yü, Teng Yen-ta, Ch'en Kung-po, Ch'en Chi-yüan,[19] Ho Hsiang-ning, and Peng Tse-min served respectively as directors of the departments of or-

ganization, propaganda, peasants, workers, merchants, women, and overseas Chinese, in KMT Central Headquarters. This abolished the positions in the Central Headquarters of the KMT that had been held by
Chiang Kai-shek, Chang Ching-chiang, and Ch'en Kuo-fu. To the Central Political Council of the KMT six leftists were added, namely T. V.
Soong, Eugene Ch'en, Teng Yen-ta, Lin Tsu-han (a CCP member), Wang
Fa-chin, and Soong Ch'ing-ling; and Wang Ching-wei, T'an Yen-k'ai, Sun
Fo, Ku Meng-yü, Hsu Ch'ien, T. V. Soong, and T'an P'ing-shan were
elected to the seven-man presidium of the Political Conference. The
membership of the Military Council was fixed at fifteen persons. Chiang
Kai-shek was among those elected to the Council, and Chiang Kai-shek
and Teng Yen-ta were elected chairmen of the presidium of that council.
The membership of the National Government Committee (State Council)
was fixed at twenty-eight, and Wang Ching-wei was one of the people
elected to that committee. Wang Ching-wei, T'an Yen-k'ai, Sun Fo, T. V.
Soong, and Hsu Ch'ien were elected to the five-man Standing Committee
of the National Government Committee.

These resolutions clearly constituted a reversal of the decisions of
the Second Plenum of the KMT held on May 15, 1926. Principally they
attacked Chiang's attempt to build up a personal military dictatorship.
In addition to the personnel changes mentioned above, the meeting also
formulated the Basic Regulations of the Headquarters of the Commander-in-Chief of the National Revolutionary Army, stipulating that the
commander-in-chief should be responsible to the Central Headquarters
of the KMT—an important expression of the principle of placing military
authority below Party authority. Chiang had still been elected to the
Standing Committee of the central committees of the KMT, the National
Government Committee, and the presidium of the Military Council; but
compared with the powers he had established for himself in the past, his
authority had been greatly weakened.

The adjustment of KMT-CCP relations was also an important item
on the agenda of the meeting. The meeting adopted a resolution on
"unification of revolutionary forces." Its contents included: the KMT and
CCP should organize a joint conference to discuss measures of cooperation; and on the invitation of the Third International, three representatives should be sent to the meeting of the Comintern to discuss the basic
problems of the Chinese revolution.[20] This was at variance with the
spirit in which Chiang in the past simply restricted the activities of CCP
members. However, positions as heads of departments in the Central

Headquarters of the KMT remained closed to members of the CCP, and this to a greater or lesser degree abided by the Party Affairs Readjustment Program of the Second Plenum of the KMT.

KMT-CCP relations started with cooperation within the KMT and progressed to cooperation within the National government. This seemed to have been first proposed by Borodin, for on his arrival in Wuhan, he had brought up this point with me. Later the Comintern issued a directive on the need for CCP members to participate in the work of the National government, with the intention of strengthening the leadership position of the CCP in the national revolution. The KMT leftists concurred with this proposal. In his address on February 24, Hsu Ch'ien had touched on this point. The present plenum decided on the addition of five ministries—labor, agricultural administration, education, industry, and public health—to the National government. CCP members Su Chao-cheng and T'an P'ing-shan were appointed Minister of Labor and Minister of Agricultural Administration respectively. In addition, the Plenum decided on the acceptance of CCP members in the various provincial governments and also approved the proposal made by people's organizations of Hunan for the convocation of a people's provincial assembly.

These matters clearly constituted an important change in KMT-CCP relations. In the eyes of the KMT leftist leaders these moves were tactically necessary in order to consolidate the anti-Chiang front. In the eyes of the CCP they were regarded as progress in KMT-CCP cooperation. In some of the documents of the CC of the CCP "unite with the leftists" was mentioned at times, while at other times "leadership of the leftists" was mentioned. Actually the participation of CCP members in the work of the National government was still considered by Communists to be an action in support of the leftists. The object of the CCP was to support leftist opposition to Chiang; there seemed to be no intention of gradually replacing the leftists. It could also be said that such measures indicated that KMT-CCP cooperation within the KMT had changed to cooperation of the two parties in the political machinery of government. It also seemed to be a way to settle the brain-twisting problem of KMT-CCP relations.

There was no doubt that Borodin was the director of this scene. His object was to join together the KMT leftists, the generals of the different armies, and the labor and peasant influences of the CCP and knead them into a single anti-Chiang front. He had taken a lot of pains to realize this objective. Take as an example the participation of the CCP in the work of the National government. He had stressed to KMT leaders the explanation that with CCP members holding responsibility for the ministries of labor and agricultural administration, the labor and peasant forces could be placed on the proper tracks of KMT leadership and that excesses of the labor and peasant movements could be rectified. But when he explained the issue to the responsible members of the CCP, he stressed the explanation that the participation of CCP members in the work of the National government would gradually increase the proportionate influence of the CCP in the government's political machinery and would tend to turn the National government toward the Left. This was also a way by which the proletariat could seize leadership power, and after that, the CCP would no longer have to serve as the coolie of the revolution.

The statements of the Third Plenum of the KMT painted the most attractive picture of the high point in the anti-Chiang movement of Wuhan. However, things could not be settled by resolutions alone; there had to be a backing of real strength. Wuhan's specialty seemed to be writing attractive articles, and the resolutions of the meetings were many-splendored. Propaganda work was also carried out with great fanfare. But empty words were often more numerous than actual deeds, the strength that existed was not sufficient, and views were divergent. These defects could not be remedied all at once. Accordingly, after the Third Plenum, Wuhan immediately gave indications that its strength could not keep pace with its desires.

General Chiang Kai-shek, who was praised by Chiang Pai-li[21] as "the military man with determination," attached the greatest importance to real action. His desire to dictate was very strong. He also had up his sleeve the means to attain such an end; but when the opportunity was not ripe for him to take action, he could wait more or less patiently. For example, he denied opposing Wang Ching-wei and said he did not basically oppose alliance with Russia and toleration of the Communists. He denied more vehemently that he had made attempts to join forces with Fengtien[22] and with the Japanese.[23] Generally he looked upon himself as the successor to the tradition within the KMT that complied with the wishes expressed by Dr. Sun Yat-sen in his will and as the opponent of the heretics of Wuhan. He seemed to have assumed this posture in order to maintain the prestige he enjoyed at the time in the revolutionary camp.

While the Third Plenum of the KMT was being held, Chiang started to act. He no longer concealed his determination to oppose communism, and he immediately resorted to extraordinary measures to deal with the CCP and Borodin. The standard of "anticommunism" was truly an efficacious treasure in winning victory in this struggle. It was not only capable of gathering together the conservative forces inside and outside the KMT, but it was also successful in playing the important role of breaking up the Wuhan camp. Furthermore, it provided a means of getting help from the Powers. In contrast, the standard of "Party authority" put up by Wuhan paled into insignificance. In the eyes of the general public this only represented a struggle within the KMT and did not relate to them personally. In the eyes of KMT members the anti-Chiang and party-salvation movement of Wuhan, whether it was correct or not, was influenced by the Communist forces.

Chiang's anti-Communist actions started in Kiangsi. On March 11, 1927, Ch'en Tsan-hsien, chairman of the Kanchow General Trade-Union Council, was executed. This was the first CCP member to be sacrificed in the anti-Chiang movement. On March 16 Chiang ordered the dissolution of the KMT Nanchang Municipal Headquarters, which supported Wuhan, and delegated his own confidants to reorganize the municipal headquarters of the Party. On March 19 Chiang again used force to dissolve the leftist KMT Kiukiang Municipal Headquarters and the Kiukiang Trade-Union Council. Furthermore, in Foochow and Anking and other places under Chiang's authority, incidents occurred involving the murder of CCP members. Chiang's standard opposing bolshevization of Wuhan was thus unfurled openly under his orders and by use of iron and blood.

A drastic split occurred within the revolutionary camp. People that did not support the anti-Chiang movement began to leave Wuhan, while leftists, finding the lower reaches of the Yangtze uncomfortable, began to assemble in Wuhan. For example, Ch'en Ming-shu, commander of the Tenth Division, who did not support the anti-Chiang position, resigned and left during the holding of the Third Plenum. He later became active in the Shanghai area and played an important role in uniting the forces with real strength, like those of Chiang Kai-shek, Li Chi-shen, and Li Tsung-jen, for joint efforts in purging the Communists. The political workers under Teng Yen-ta that were operating in the lower reaches of the Yangtze and some workers for party organs who had been expelled escaped to Wuhan, where they recounted their experiences suffering from persecution.

Since an antithetical position had evolved between the two parties, there was no more room for reconciliation. By that time General Galen, who had been working with Chiang, had also left Chiang's headquarters and had brought his assistants to Wuhan, where he continued his duties as military adviser to the National government. From the CCP camp, Comrade Chiang Hsien-yun, who had worked alongside Chiang, also resigned and returned to Wuhan via Nanchang. Ch'en Kuo-fu and others that had accompanied T'an Yen-k'ai to Wuhan to participate in the Plenum left at the conclusion of the meeting to return to Nanchang and report to Chiang. And so all ties between Wuhan and Nanchang were cut off.

Special mention may be made here of Chiang Hsien-yun, the young military figure. His feeling of depression seemed to be shared by youths in general at the time. He was an honor student in Whampoa's first class. Before joining Whampoa, he had participated in the SYC in Hunan. Not much later he was officially admitted to membership in the CCP and had led the miners' strike at Shui-kou-shan in Hunan. He was generally respected and loved by our comrades at the time, and he had a deep friendship with me. He was a student whom Chiang liked, and so he had been appointed a secretary at the commander-in-chief's headquarters. He worked with Chiang, and Chiang's business with the CCP was often handled by him.

Comrade Chiang Hsien-yun was a sincere Communist and loved everything about the CCP. He was a young military figure with lofty ideals. He respected the president of his academy, Chiang, and he also loved everything in Whampoa. He consistently embraced the naive view that both the CCP and Whampoa were the cream of the revolution; so that if the misunderstandings between the two could be removed and they would continue to cooperate, the future of the Chinese revolution would be brilliant—otherwise the future would be unthinkable. At that time he had traveled many times between Nanchang and Wuhan, attempting to heal the split between the two sides. He not only talked to me repeatedly about the importance of cooperating with Chiang, but also spoke many times to Chiang, urging him to continue the policy of alliance with the Soviet Union and toleration of the Communists. But he was after all very naive and did not truly understand Chiang's real intentions. At the same time he was a person in a lowly position, and his words carried little weight. He was no match for Chang Ching-chiang and the others that surrounded Chiang.

The fiery flames of the fierce struggle plunged Comrade Chiang Hsien-yun into a dilemma. After he returned to Wuhan from Nanchang, he seemed to be at a loss. He demanded active combat service, determined to contribute his fresh blood to the revolution. Very soon he was appointed a regimental commander in the Fourth Army. Later, in the fierce battle with the Fengtien Army in Honan, he courageously charged at the enemy and made unforgettable contributions to the victory of that battle. However, he himself was killed on the firing line on that occasion, carrying his melancholia with him.

Chiang's anti-Communist actions immediately brought a counter-attack from the Wuhan side. On March 15, to protest the killing of Ch'en Tsan-hsien, the Hupeh Provincial General Trade-Union Council issued a manifesto condemning Chiang's actions as counterrevolutionary. On March 16 the Hupeh Provincial Headquarters of the KMT issued a circular telegram in support of the resolutions of the Third Plenum, stressing that Party power could not be usurped by Chiang. On March 25 the Wuhan *Min-kuo Jih-pao*, an organ of the KMT, carried an editorial under the captain "Unite, Masses, to Overthrow Chiang Kai-shek," declaring that Chiang was no longer the faithful disciple of the *Tsung-li* (Sun Yat-sen), but was rather a counterrevolutionary. It also listed his many crimes and demanded his dismissal and punishment.

The break between Wuhan and Nanchang was loosely connected with the military developments of the time. After the capture of Nanchang, Chiang's military operations in the provinces of Kiangsu and Chekiang achieved considerable results, and this effectively supported his resolute anti-Communist stand. From the outset Chiang ignored the opposition views of Borodin and Galen and devoted his entire efforts to the military march on the southeastern provinces. On October 16, 1926, the Governor of Chekiang, Hsia Ch'ao, announced the independence of Chekiang in order to safeguard his territory and pacify his people. This was the first achievement of Chiang in breaking up the forces of Sun Ch'uan-fang. Ho Ying-ch'in, commander of the First Army, led his Eastern Route Army to capture Foochow on December 18, and then he continued his march on Chekiang. On February 19, 1927, Ho again occupied Hangchow. During January of that year, the Second, Sixth, and Seventh armies proceeded eastward along the Yangtze, heading directly for Nanking. Ch'en T'iao-yuan, *Tupan* of Anhwei Province, which was under the jurisdiction of Sun Ch'uan-fang, announced his defection to the side of the revolution, and this removed an obstacle to the eastward advance of the Northern Expeditionary Army.

While the Third Plenum of the KMT was being held, the Northern Expeditionary Army was advancing toward Shanghai and Nanking along two routes via Chekiang and Anhwei. This was an operation in accordance with Chiang's military plans. When the Northern Expeditionary Army advanced to Lunghwa in the vicinity of Shanghai, the Shanghai workers launched a general strike on March 21 and carried on street fighting with the Chihli-Shantung Allied Army. On March 22 the Chihli-Shantung Allied Army evacuated Shanghai in disorder. Thus the Northern Expeditionary Army was able to occupy Shanghai with ease on March 23. On the same day the Second and Sixth armies led by Ch'eng Ch'ien occupied Yu-hua-tai and other heights outside the city of Nanking, and the enemy troops that were in the city withdrew toward Pukow, north of the Yangtze. Early on the morning of March 24 the revolutionary forces occupied Nanking, the strategic center of the southeast. The center of the internal struggle within the revolutionary camp was thus also moved to Nanking and Shanghai.

The Wuhan authorities were convinced that Chiang would make Nanking and Shanghai his bases for developing operations against Wuhan, so they resolved not to give Chiang the opportunity to completely control Shanghai and Nanking. The concrete measure taken was to immediately dispatch T. V. Soong, who was the Special Finance Commissioner of the Central Government, to Shanghai in order to assume direct control of the finances of Shanghai—the economic center. Orders were also issued to Ch'eng Ch'ien to have his forces garrison Nanking for the purpose of obstructing the establishment of an anti-Wuhan center in that area.

One or two days after the conclusion of the Third Plenum, Lin Tsu-han told me that the National government had issued a secret order for the arrest of Chiang Kai-shek should an opportunity present itself; and this order had been sent to Ch'eng Ch'ien for execution. He told me that as a result of the meetings of a few important persons over the past few days, it had been decided to call on the Second and Sixth armies to assume control of the Nanking area, so as to prevent the realization of Chiang's plot to create a new center in Nanking. If Chiang resisted, Ch'eng Ch'ien, the director-general of operations on the right bank of the Yangtze, was to arrest Chiang on the strength of the secret order issued by the National government.

Lin Tsu-han also said that this important measure seemed to be Borodin's idea and was unanimously agreed to by all the important persons. It was because he was the Party representative to Ch'eng Ch'ien's army that he came to know of this secret. He maintained that although Ch'eng Ch'ien, who was rather sincere in his opposition to Chiang and was about to proceed to the front lines, had fully accepted this all-important mission, nevertheless he secretly also revealed signs of hesitation, because he was being placed at the very front of this plot. So it was still problematical whether he could carry out a secret order in the future. Although I had no prior knowledge of this incident, nevertheless I still gave encouragement to Comrade Lin Tsu-han who was about to proceed to the front lines with Ch'eng Ch'ien and to shoulder such a heavy responsibility. I also immediately used secret methods of informing the CC of the CCP in Shanghai to give Ch'eng Ch'ien the needed help there.

Ch'eng Ch'ien, the director-general of operations for the army on the right bank of the Yangtze, was directing the operations of his own Sixth Army and the Second Army of Lu Ti-p'ing. (The commander of the Second Army was T'an Yen-k'ai, but he had remained at Wuhan as chairman of the National government, and Lu Ti-p'ing, his deputy, was in command of the army.) In conjunction with the army on the left bank of the Yangtze, commanded by Li Tsung-jen, and a portion of the First Army of Chiang on the right flank of the Soochow-Hangchow front, Ch'eng was advancing on Nanking. As a result, the task of occupying Nanking was a failure.

Early on the morning of March 24, when the forces of Chu Yu-po of the Chihli-Shantung Allied Army had retreated northward toward the Yangtze, the vanguard of the Northern Expeditionary Army entered Kuan-tou, inside Nanking city. Some remnants of the enemy army that had not completely withdrawn took the opportunity to engage in plunder, and there was confusion inside the city, including incidents of attacks on foreign consulates and residences of foreigners. The British consul and some other foreign nationals were injured. The British and Japanese gunboats anchored on the river at Nanking shelled the city and caused many casualties. After the main force of Ch'eng Ch'ien's army entered Nanking, it got busy restoring order, suppressing the plunderers, escorting the foreign consuls and residents out of the city to board the foreign gunboats, and other such tasks.

The incident of the shelling of Nanking by foreign gunboats placed Ch'eng Ch'ien in a disadvantageous position. At the time, the policy of the Powers was to exploit Chiang Kai-shek's opposition to the bolshevization of Wuhan. In this policy, Japan played the leading role. On March 26 Chiang boarded a gunboat and sailed from Anking to Shanghai. He immediately received the support of some members of the CEC and SEC of the KMT that were in Shanghai, and he had the economic assistance of the Kiangsu and Chekiang financial magnates[24] as well as help from foreign quarters. Simultaneously the anti-Communist front, which Chiang was forming of such parties with real strength as Li Chi-shen and Li Tsung-jen, was ripening. He exploited these favorable factors and the strength of the First and Seventh armies to apply pressure on Ch'eng Ch'ien to evacuate Nanking. During the early part of April, Ch'eng Ch'ien had to withdraw from the Nanking area. After that, Nanking was under the control of Chiang, and Wuhan's plans against Chiang suffered their first serious setback.

P'eng Shu-chih had personally taken part in some of these changes, and he had given me a clear account. When Ch'eng Ch'ien was marching on Nanking, P'eng had carried orders from the CC of the CCP in Shanghai and had hurried to Nanking on March 24 to help Lin Tsu-han, Li Fu-ch'un (then director of the Political Department of the Second Army), and other comrades take charge of work in that area, in order to realize the goal of controlling Nanking. Later, because of the withdrawal of Ch'eng Ch'ien's forces from Nanking, he had come to Wuhan early in April. He told me about his experiences in Nanking and explained at the outset that the acts of the encroachment on foreign residences and consulates had been perpetrated by remnant enemy troops, who had not yet evacuated the city, in the midst of general confusion and acts of plunder.

He also stated that after the Nanking tragedy happened, the wrath of the anti-imperialists was immediately aroused. The Northern Expeditionary Army and the masses in Nanking—baptized in the anti-imperialist movements of successive periods, stimulated by the retracting of the British Concession at Hankow, and now witnessing the brutal shelling by the foreign gunboats—naturally had their anti-imperialist feelings aroused to great heights like waves in a storm; and at any time incidents could occur that would bring about foreign intervention. While he was busy stirring up such an anti-imperialist movement, he also had to prevent continued incidence of acts that encroached upon the life and property of foreigners. Other comrades and the heads of the Second and Sixth armies likewise had their attention focused on this area.

He also said that it was not until several days later, when he turned his attention to the military situation in Nanking, that he discovered that the strategic military positions around Nanking had all been occupied by the trusted troops of Chiang Kai-shek and that defense works had been constructed. The greater portion of the Second and Sixth armies were scattered inside Nanking city, carrying out the task of maintaining order. It was clear that militarily the position against Chiang was unfavorable. Later Chiang transferred more troops to areas surrounding Nanking, increasing the pressure so that Ch'eng Ch'ien's troops had to withdraw from Nanking. Because the situation in Nanking had already been lost, he himself had to come to Wuhan to make further plans.

When P'eng Shu-chih described these experiences, he shamefacedly admitted his lack of experience in the handling of military struggles; and I angrily castigated him for his failure, pointing out that one wrong move could affect the whole situation. How could he, because of an incident in the anti-imperialist movement, relax his efforts to make military preparations for the control of the Nanking area? As a matter of fact, my castigation of him at the time was rather excessive, because the authority for handling these matters was in the hands of Ch'eng Ch'ien.

Ch'eng Ch'ien's hesitancy was an important factor leading to the loss of Nanking. After all, he was not a member of the Communist Party and could not be as resolute as the CCP members in his opposition to Chiang. Moreover, most of the men of the Second and Sixth armies were from Hunan, and their families were threatened by the peasant movement in Hunan; so they also had feelings of dissatisfaction with the leftist measures of Wuhan. They did not have harmonious relations with T'ang Sheng-chih, and they did not have any deep-rooted hatred against Chiang, so they could hardly be expected to undertake for others the task of picking chestnuts from the fire, holding on to Nanking for a drastic showdown with Chiang. Borodin had not fully considered these conditions, and thus he made his serious mistake. And because Ch'eng Ch'ien was not resolute enough in his stand against Chiang, Lin Tsu-han left the Sixth Army. It has been said that these two old friends parted ways after a heated quarrel during which there was much banging on desks.

Viewed from Wuhan, the loss of control over Nanking was a very depressing development. This was defeat in the first round of its anti-

Chiang campaign. Borodin was especially troubled over this point. As a matter of fact, the situation involved more than people, and victory or defeat on either side was not decided merely by the loss of Nanking.

Chiang Kai-shek, who arrived in Shanghai on March 26, developed a drastic anti-Communist program. He started to use terroristic measures to destroy the CCP. On April 12, 1927, the campaign to purge the Party was launched by the KMT in Shanghai with the large-scale massacre of members of the CCP. This campaign was rapidly extended to areas under Chiang's influence. At the same time he wiped out the bases of the Wuhan government on the lower reaches of the Yangtze. Early in April, for instance, the Second and Sixth armies were forced to evacuate Nanking. On April 20 the Shanghai office of T. V. Soong's Ministry of Finance was dissolved on Chiang's orders. He also established in Nanking a center to oppose the National government in Wuhan. On April 9 Chiang moved from Shanghai to Nanking and convened a meeting of the KMT central committees. On April 18 another National government was formally established in Nanking. The deep split in the internal ranks of the revolutionary camp became well known to the world as the split between Nanking and Wuhan.

Looking at these changes from the angle of the CCP, the CC of the CCP actually was too inexperienced and lacking in vigilance. It naively implemented the policy of KMT-CCP cooperation and had too optimistic illusions about a national united front. As a matter of fact, the dictatorial character of militarists, the stubbornness of conservative feudal forces, the reactionary character of the bourgeoisie, and the shaky nature of the petty bourgeoisie are all characteristics of the social structure of China. On the anti-imperialist platform, these components could exhibit the consciousness of the national revolution, but on the question of social reform, they were all forces obstructing the revolution. The CC of the CCP had to approach the problem from the side favorable to the revolution and plunge itself into a state of self-satisfaction. While it could not see clearly the limit that could be accepted by the national revolution, it also failed to observe accurately the essential nature of Chiang's influence.

Before the capture of Shanghai, the CCP had led the Shanghai workers in staging three armed insurrections. The first was in support of the independence of Chekiang declared by Hsia Ch'ao, which took place on October 24, 1926, but was suspended because of Hsia Ch'ao's defeat. The second uprising was staged on February 19, 1927, in support of the occupation of Hangchow by the Northern Expeditionary forces. This was also defeated because the Northern Expeditionary Army could not march on Shanghai immediately. On March 21, which was the eve of the occupation of Shanghai by the Northern Expeditionary Army, the CCP finally succeeded in organizing the third insurrection, which led to the occupation of Shanghai by the workers.[25]

All of these insurrections resulted from the policy of KMT-CCP cooperation. The dates of the uprisings were decided by Niu Yung-chien, Chiang's representative, on the basis of the progress of the military situation; but the CCP was completely responsible for the organization of the uprisings. At the time the KMT and the CCP had organized a joint conference in Shanghai, and the participants from the KMT side were Niu Yung-chien, Wu Chih-hui, and others; while those from the CCP side were Lo Chüeh, Wang Shou-hua, and others. They cooperated very satisfactorily, because the KMT needed the assistance of the Shanghai workers and was extremely friendly to the CCP and the Shanghai workers. The CCP held that every additional effort put forth by the Shanghai workers would give them added power in the future. The CCP's wish was that after the occupation of Shanghai a congress of citizens could be convened to elect a municipal government and the workers would have an appropriate place in the government. Niu Yung-chien and Wu Chih-hui had gladly agreed to this proposal and had given their guarantee that it would be implemented.

After Shanghai was occupied, the citizens' congress was convened. The members of the municipal government (council) were elected; but the attitude of the KMT changed. First of all, the major responsible representative of the KMT—Niu Yung-chien—feigned illness, refused to meet the CCP representatives, and rejected any form of consultation. Following this, the representatives elected by Shanghai industrial and commercial circles to participate in the municipal government made excuses not to attend meetings of the municipal government. The CCP, however, continued to act on the basis of a united front and urged the absentee representatives to participate actively in the work of the municipal government. Unexpectedly, after Chiang's arrival in Shanghai, he disregarded the agreement of the KMT-CCP Joint Conference, and declared that the municipal government was illegal, since its members had not been designated or approved by him. He also prohibited meetings of the citizens' assembly.

These matters did not make the CCP sufficiently vigilant. The anti-

Chiang measures in the Wuhan camp had been known to the CC of the CCP. The Comintern had also telegraphed instructions to the CC of the CCP in Shanghai to conceal the arms of the workers, clearly anticipating that Chiang would suppress the Shanghai workers who naturally could not resist the oppression of a regular army. However, the CC of the CCP seemed to think that the situation would not deteriorate to such a state, and so it not only failed to abide by the instructions of the Comintern, but also failed to make adequate preparations.

Exactly contrary to the CCP's expectations, the anti-Communist actions of Chiang were rapid and resolute. The CSC of the KMT held a meeting in Shanghai, and Wu Chih-hui introduced a proposal to impeach the CCP, demanding that military leaders in all localities adopt extraordinary emergency measures to deal with the situation, putting members of the CCP under separate detention and surveillance. Chiang Kai-shek, Li Chi-shen, Li Tsung-jen, and Huang Shao-hsung held a military conference at the headquarters of the commander-in-chief in Shanghai to discuss concrete measures to carry out the proposal brought forward by Wu Chih-hui for purging the Communists. On April 3 a rally was held in Foochow in support of the KMT, and it issued a circular telegram that listed sixteen measures, including the elimination of those with dual party membership. On April 5 Chiang ordered the closure of the Shanghai office of the General Political Department and arrested many of its workers. On April 8 the Shanghai Political Committee of the KMT, appointed by Chiang, was officially established, and it held the power of controlling the municipality of Shanghai. On April 9 Ts'ai Yuan-p'ei and other members of the CSC of the KMT issued a circular telegram on national salvation and party salvation, expressing open opposition to Wuhan. On the same day the Nanking municipal headquarters of the KMT was raided, and Comrade Hou Shao-chiu and other members of the municipal party committee were arrested. These events all proved that the anti-Communist offensive launched by Chiang was one that was developed on an overall basis with the greatest of speed.

The joint declaration by Wang Ching-wei and Ch'en Tu-hsiu still had a slightly hypnotic effect on the CC of the CCP. Wang Ching-wei, who had been convalescing in France, returned to China via Moscow and arrived in Shanghai on April 1. He had consultations with Chiang and Wang's old friends Wu Chih-hui, Li Shih-tseng, and Ts'ai Yuan-p'ei. Chiang insisted on two points: the immediate expulsion of Borodin and the purging of the Communists. Wang, however, advocated holding the

Fourth Plenum of the KMT central committees in Nanking to settle all disputes.[26] Wang's proposal had been condemned by Wu Chih-hui and others as not being permitted by Party tradition, since it rejected their own proposals that extraordinary measures be adopted in opposing the Communists. So Wang had an interview with Ch'en Tu-hsiu and attempted to win the support of the CC of the CCP in order to augment his own political capital. So the two of them issued a joint declaration.

On April 5 Wang Ching-wei and Ch'en Tu-hsiu, as leaders of the KMT and the CCP respectively, issued a joint message to comrades of the two parties. The contents explained that the CCP had consistently, frankly, and sincerely accepted the KMT and the Three Principles of the People of Dr. Sun Yat-sen as the basis for the national revolution. They called on the comrades of the two parties to continue their close cooperation. In view of the armed oppression of the enemy and of rumors that had been started, they should immediately abandon mutual suspicions and sincerely consult on all matters. Although their political views might not all be identical, the basic views had to be held unanimously. This document did not lessen Chiang's determination to oppose the Communists, and Wu Chih-hui even criticized it as "Wang's preposterous act."

However, this document led to a misapprehension on the part of the CC of the CCP. Ch'en Tu-hsiu and others seemed to linger over the good old days of their past cooperation with Niu Yung-chien and Wu Chih-hui. When Chiang first arrived in Shanghai, he had praised the workers of Shanghai for their contributions to the occupation of Shanghai. He also presented the Shanghai Trade-Union Council with a banner inscribed "Common Struggle." This made the CC of the CCP feel that Chiang would not resort to any rash actions in persecuting the workers. Moreover, the various expressions of sympathy expressed for the Shanghai workers by such people as Hsueh Yueh,[27] commander of the First Division of the First Army, which was stationed at Shanghai, also caused the CCP to keep its hopes too high. Now there was the joint declaration by Wang and Ch'en, and the CC of the CCP thought that it would ease the situation.

As a matter of fact, the return of Wang to China and the joint declaration of Wang and Ch'en not only failed to ease the situation, but instead accelerated Chiang's action. When Chiang first arrived in Shanghai, although outwardly he expressed the attitude of friendship for the trade unions, secretly he was actively preparing to destroy this thorn in his flesh. From the very beginning, he established contact with leaders of the gangsters in Shanghai, such as Huang Chin-jung, Tu Yüeh-sheng, and Chang Hsiao-lin, to organize the gangsters into the China Mutual Progress Society, a force wearing blue uniforms, in readiness to adopt action to sabotage the trade unions.

Early on the morning of April 12, when the blue-shirted forces of the China Mutual Progress Society launched the attack on the Shanghai Trade-Union Council, the picketing workers that were stationed in the trade union were still asleep and had to rise hurriedly to meet the challenge. A few hours earlier Wang Shou-hua, chairman of the trade-union council, had gone to the home of Tu Yüeh-sheng, one of the principal responsible leaders of the China Mutual Progress Society, to carry on a friendly consultation and had fallen into a trap. At the same time Pai Ch'ung-hsi, the Shanghai Garrison Commander, under secret orders from Chiang to use the pretext of pacifying internal struggles among the workers to disarm both sides, sent a large number of troops to completely disarm the Workers' Picket Corps, which was preparing for a fight; and many arrests were made. Thus in an instant the workers' organization in Shanghai, reportedly 800,000 strong, with its picket corps of 5,000, was destroyed. This was the beginning of the famous KMT Party purge of April 12.[28]

With the situation developed to such serious proportions, the CC of the CCP still did not seem to wake up completely. At the time Chou En-lai, the deputy commander of the Workers' Pickets Corps in Shanghai, was still given instructions to exploit his old relationships in Whampoa to contact the military authorities in an attempt to secure the release of the arrested workers. He himself was imprisoned for a time and nearly lost his life. On April 13 the CCP led workers in a mass rally in Chapei that was prepared to demonstrate before the Shanghai Garrison Headquarters to demand the release of the arrested workers. When this force marched forward and reached the corner of Hung-hsing Road, the military and police released machine-gun fire on them. Numerous unarmed workers were instantly killed and lay dead on the road. Thus Shanghai workers, who had sacrificed their blood to the Northern Expedition, suddenly became shooting-practice targets for the Northern Expeditionary forces.

By this time the CC of the CCP had come to realize that the whole world had really changed; but it was too late. The seriousness of the aftermath of the April 12 episode could never be accurately assessed. Even with regard to Chiang Kai-shek, while he no doubt achieved victory in this encounter, from the long-range view it will be up to history to pass judgment on whether it was a profit or a loss for him. At least, this incident aroused in the Communists a hatred toward him that could not be erased. As for the Communists, the policy of the Comintern calling for the CCP to remain inside the KMT to pursue KMT-CCP cooperation was not rejected by a lesson written in blood. In the CC of the CCP the leadership and prestige of Ch'en Tu-hsiu had fallen, and this led to his eventual downfall.

The sudden change in the Shanghai and Nanking area immediately aroused to varying degrees the wrath of our CCP comrades in Wuhan and of certain KMT leftists. They all started to study plans for coping with the situation. Borodin revealed great anxiety. He advocated that the CCP exercise even more restraint on the excessive acts of the labor and peasant movements, in order to reduce the internal conflicts in Wuhan. At the same time he stressed the use of force in taking punitive action against the rebel Chiang Kai-shek. But after all Borodin had no actual power to go through with his proposals, which were not possible to implement.

On April 10—two days before the Party purge of April 12—Wang Ching-wei arrived in Wuhan from Shanghai. In the midst of the grand welcome given him, he made a rousing speech, as he had done in the past. He mentioned to me that during the past year of the tense period of the revolution, he had been away from the country for convalescence. Now that he had returned, he must shoulder responsibilities to work for the party and the state so that the teachings in the will of the late leader would not be undermined. He did not reveal to me fully the seriousness of the situation in Shanghai; but he showed signs of discomfort and did not seem as brilliant as he had in the past.

Wang Ching-wei's return to the country seemed to come too late. The opportunity to eliminate conflict had already been lost, and he could no longer control development of the situation of the time. Indeed, as the saying goes, he had no strength to save a situation that had collapsed. Before his return to China, people had pinned very great hopes on him. During the first two days after his arrival in Wuhan, he also played the role of raising the morale of the people; but the good times were not to last long. In a few days, like the others, he found himself plunged into the abyss of a dilemma in which he could do nothing. In a word, his role had been reduced, and he could no longer be instrumental in forging the unity of the leftists. He even made the Wuhan camp shakier. The crux of the problem was clearly that with weapons of war prominent, empty words were after all of no practical help.

After the bad news from Shanghai and Nanking reached Wuhan, cries of "Punish Chiang Kai-shek" and "Step over to the Left, Revolutionists" came from the mouth of Wang Ching-wei and were disseminated everywhere, the noise from them piercing the skies. On April 17 the CEC of the KMT in Wuhan resolved to dismiss Chiang Kai-shek from the party and to dismiss him from the military post of commander-in-chief. At the same time anti-Chiang mass rallies and demonstrations were in vogue. But when it came to real action such as an eastward expedition to punish Chiang, views continued to be varied and no decision could be reached.

Most of the KMT elements and the general social celebrities in Wuhan were divided in their views on Chiang's actions. Some held that Chiang's actions had basically undermined the three great principles of Dr. Sun Yat-sen and that Chiang was truly a rebel. Others held that Chiang did not hesitate to use any means—killing his comrades-at-arms and even involving his own colleagues—and that this was tantamount to destroying the foundation of the revolution. Others stressed the fact that opposition to Chiang's action had been shown in establishing another center, and they held that this had been an act splitting the KMT. Others felt that the conflict between Chiang and the CCP involved rights and wrongs on both sides. Still others secretly praised Chiang's resoluteness in opposing the Communists. And so, on top of the lack of real strength, there was the problem of disunity in the minds of the people.

After Chiang had launched his anti-Communist actions in Shanghai, the movement soon spread to all areas under his influence. On April 15 the Party-purge measures adopted by Li Chi-shen in Kwangtung were even more cruel than those of Chiang. On that day in Canton, Li mobilized the army and the police, imposed a curfew, arrested about two thousand Communists and their sympathizers, and closed down more than two hundred trade unions and other organizations. It was on this occasion that noted CCP members such as Hsiung Hsiung, political instructor at Whampoa, were killed. In other areas, such as Chekiang and Fukien, the cruelty with which the Party purge was carried out was also very terrible. Those that suffered were not limited to members of the CCP, but also included many of the so-called KMT leftists.[29]

The one thing that gave Wuhan a little satisfaction was the fact that the Kiangsi authorities adopted the attitude of giving support to Wuhan. Chiang's anti-Communist action had originally started in Kiangsi, but very soon he left Kiangsi; and Chu P'ei-te, commander of the Third Army, as governor of Kiangsi, grasped the controlling power in the province. At the time Chu P'ei-te was closer to Wang Ching-wei and was not satisfied with the arrogance of Chiang. So after Chiang left Kiangsi, he turned to give support to the Wuhan leftists and attacked the people of the Chiang clique. But even this attitude of General Chu P'ei-te was temporary, and it could not drown the cries of "opposition to the excesses of the labor and peasant movements," which were rampant in the provinces of Hunan, Hupeh, and Kiangsi.

Chiang's anti-Communist operation appeared to be a "righteous cause receiving plenty of help." On March 1 the Soviet vessel *Pamiat Lenina* left Shanghai for Wuhan. While passing Pukow, she was searched by the troops of Chang Tsung-ch'ang; and Mrs. Borodin and several other Soviet passengers were detained. This cut off communications between the Soviet Union and Wuhan. On April 6, with the permission of the Diplomatic Corps of Peking, Chang Tso-lin sent troops and police to search the Soviet Embassy and the Soviet-owned Far Eastern Bank as well as the office of the China Eastern Railway, arresting Li Ta-chao and more than sixty others who had been in hiding in the Soviet Embassy. On April 28 twenty northern leaders of the KMT and the CCP, headed by Li Ta-chao and Lu Yu-yü, were put to death by strangulation. This incident greatly influenced Wuhan. For the Russian advisers, it meant loss of the general machinery of contact. For the KMT and the CCP, it meant destruction of their headquarters for activities in North China. A severe blow was also dealt to the morale of the people. Needless to say, what was disadvantageous to Wuhan was helpful to Chiang.

Added to all this, the financial and economic difficulties of the Wuhan camp were hard to overcome. All along, because of the large volume of military supplies, the increase in taxes, the economic depression, and the rise of the labor and peasant movements, Wuhan had seen the flight of capital, the soaring of commodity prices, and such phenomena. On April 17 the Wuhan government was forced to promulgate "Regulations Governing the Concentration of Cash" and took the course of issuing paper money to cover expenditures. Wuhan not only failed to obtain economic support from Shanghai, but banking circles in Peking and Shanghai on April 21 jointly announced the severance of relations with the banks in Hankow. Along the lower reaches of the Yangtze under

Chiang's occupation an economic blockade of Wuhan was also enforced. On May 3 the Nanking authorities officially banned the circulation of bank notes of the Central Bank in Wuhan. These various developments forced prices in Wuhan to soar and its bank notes to depreciate in value and plunged its economic and financial situation into extreme chaos, so that effective measures of salvaging the situation were impossible.

The major developments described above placed Wuhan in a position of extreme hardship. Viewed from the Wuhan side, all this had been directly or indirectly caused by the malicious hands of imperialism. Certain important personages of Wuhan held that Chiang Kai-shek, Chang Tso-lin, and even the Diplomatic Corps in Peking were coordinating their efforts for unanimous action. That it had been possible for the men with real power, such as Chiang Kai-shek, Li Chi-shen, and Li Tsung-jen, to join forces against the Communists was not only due to the efforts of the imperialists behind the scene to bring them together, but also was only possible with their actual support. Such things as the shaky position within the ranks of Wuhan and its economic difficulties were also the result of manipulations by the imperialists.

In the midst of attacks from all sides, Wuhan for a time wanted to deal Chiang a blow by the use of force, in an attempt to seek a way out. During those few days Borodin's attitude seemed to border on madness. He told me that in every revolution in history it had been necessary to purge the internal ranks. Now that a second Ch'en Chiung-ming had appeared within our ranks, how could we talk of the Northern Expedition? If Wuhan was to continue to exist, we had to exploit the opportunity presented by Chiang's position not yet being firmly established to carry out an eastern expedition rapidly and remove this ulcer. These views of Borodin at least superficially had the enthusiastic support of the important personages of Wuhan. Such support, in turn, seemed to stimulate Borodin's courage.

General Galen held a different view on this question. One day in the latter part of April he arranged for an interview with me in his home. Facing a map, he pointed out to me that in China at that time, there were three forces: the first was Chang Tso-lin in Peking; the second was Chiang Kai-shek in Nanking; and the third was Wuhan. In the eyes of foreigners, Chang's forces were the strongest, with Chiang's next, and Wuhan's the weakest. Chang of Fengtien was at the moment reinforcing his army in Honan, preparing to march southward. If we could first wipe out Chang Tso-lin, the strength of Wuhan would be promoted to first place. These words of General Galen indicated that he advocated temporary shelving of plans for the eastern expedition against Chiang and continuation of the Northern Expedition.

On the basis of conditions that I had come to know, I could not but support Galen's view. I said to him, "Attending first to an eastern expedition to punish the internal rebels of the revolution is correct in principle; however the present problem is not what we should or should not do, but whether or not we can do it. Today, although the important figures in Wuhan superficially support attending first to the eastern expedition, it is rather problematical if their outward expression and inner belief are the same. The most important thing is who among them will undertake to fight the tough battle. By withdrawing from Nanking, the Second and Sixth armies have shown that they have not been sufficiently resolute in their anti-Chiang stand. The Third Army is defending Kiangsi, and its strength is limited. Will its men undertake to fight as vanguards? It is reported that certain generals of the Fourth Army have considered that our major enemy is after all Chang Tso-lin and so have indicated their unwillingness to carry out the eastern expedition first. T'ang Sheng-chih seems to be resolute in his talks, but it does not seem that he will really fight it out with Chiang seriously. For this reason the eastern expedition may not escape the actual fate of being abortive, perhaps even leading to our internal disintegration; and this will instead give Chang Tso-lin the opportunity to attack Wuhan. . . ."

After hearing what I had to say, Galen grasped my hand tightly and said, "While everyone is so excited, it's really wonderful that you can remain calm." He went on to tell me that on the previous day, when he met the generals of the Fourth Army, all of them had advocated attending first to the Northern Expedition and overthrowing Chang Tso-lin before attending to other issues. They even stated that in the matter of an eastern expedition to punish Chiang Kai-shek, the middle- and lower-ranking officers in general considered it a fight among our own people, and enthusiasm could not be aroused. Galen then indicated that although he hated Chiang Kai-shek very much, he nevertheless considered an eastern expedition a most dangerous adventure. There was greater prospect for victory in a northern expedition. Moreover, Feng Yü-hsiang, who was lying in wait behind Tungkwan at the time, could use his forces to cooperate with such a move. So he wanted me to persuade Borodin and others.

After leaving Galen's residence, I immediately called on Borodin. He still indicated his insistence on prior attention to an eastern expedition. In a light vein I said to him, "Are we to carry out an eastern expedition first? Then we must see if we can actually do so. I fear that it is necessary for us to consider carefully the actual conditions of the different armies first. Otherwise, it may not be possible to avoid repetition of the incident of the retreat from Nanking of the Second and Sixth armies." Hearing these words, Borodin seemed at a loss and said no more. It appeared that he would reconsider the situation.

A few days later Borodin's views clearly changed. At a meeting of the CC of the CCP, the majority of whose members had by now arrived in Wuhan, he indicated that since Chang's Fengtien Army was then marching south toward Hsinyang along the Peking-Hankow Railway, carrying out an eastern expedition at the time would leave Wuhan open to danger of attack by Chang. For this reason the troops in Wuhan should first cooperate with the troops of Feng Yü-hsiang to wipe out the Fengtien Army in Honan, before a decision could be made on the second step. The plan for an eastern expedition was thus temporarily shelved. The Wuhan papers also suddenly conducted an extensive propaganda campaign on the threat posed by the southward march of the Fengtien Army and the importance of continuing the Northern Expedition. After this the troops of T'ang Sheng-chih and Chang Fa-k'uei immediately massed for the march on Hsinyang along the Peking-Hankow Railway to carry out the Northern Expedition.

Toward the end of April both Nanking and Wuhan felt the military pressure of Chang Tso-lin. Sun Ch'uan-fang and Chang Tsung-ch'ang led their armies from Hsuchow toward Pukow, while Chang Hsueh-liang's army marched southward along the Peking-Hankow Railway to menace Wuhan, seemingly to exploit the split in the revolutionary forces and to down the two quarreling sides one by one. On the Nanking side, although talk of an expedition against Wuhan had not been aired to any great extent, nevertheless actual movements against Wuhan were more active. On April 25 Li Tsung-jen's army, sent by Nanking, and Chu P'ei-te's army, which was stationed at Kiukiang, built defense lines against each other. The Second and Sixth armies on the southern section of the Tientsin-Pukow Railway expressed obedience to Wuhan and moved toward Anking. The Twenty-ninth Division of Ch'eng Ch'ien's army in the vicinity of Nanking was even disarmed by Chiang. These developments gave the troops of Sun Ch'uan-fang and Chang Tsung-ch'ang a favorable opportunity for advancing to the Pukow and Yang-chow area. The threat against Nanking was very imminent. So Chiang had to raise high the cry for continuation of the Northern Expedition. On May 14 Li Tsung-jen and Chu P'ei-te met at Hukow and decided on mutual nonaggression and on continuation of the Northern Expedition along separate routes. By this time the antagonism between Nanking and Wuhan had eased.

On Wuhan's part, the proposal for prior attention to an eastern expedition all at once became only an illusion. This was the second important defeat for Borodin's anti-Chiang plans. It also showed that Wuhan had no strength to return the blow delivered by Chiang in his anti-Communist offensive. Borodin was now in an unfavorable situation, and though he maintained an outward calm, his views were no longer as optimistic as they had been. He seemed to think that if he could not now remove Chiang, who was the main source of trouble, there would be endless trouble in the future. Furthermore, the outcome of the battle against Chang Tso-lin of Fengtien was still uncertain.

Early in May, Borodin once more brought forth his plans for the Northwest, but clearly there was implication of a withdrawal. He stated that the imperialist influence in China was too great and that the Northwest was an area beyond the power of the imperialists. In that region there would not be the sharp social-class conflicts like those in Wuhan, while it was also close to the Soviet Union and Outer Mongolia, and access to foreign aid would be easy. The Northwest plans that he brought up at this time had clearly the object of moving to Shensi and Kansu. It was different from what he had propounded as the Great Northwest Theory while in Kwangtung, in which he had stated that advance along the Peking-Hankow Railway would lead to control of the Northwest and the Southwest. This naturally meant that he was pinning his hopes on Feng Yü-hsiang. Little did we know that world events could not be anticipated, for later Feng Yü-hsiang, besides providing him with facilities to return personally to the Soviet Union, proved himself to be the abettor of crime in the destruction of Wuhan.

The Peasant Movement

During the Wuhan period the activities of the CCP in rural areas had developed from the lower levels up to the higher levels and had ignited the fiery flames of the peasants' struggle. The flames were fiercest in Hunan Province. Because the CCP lacked both knowledge and experience in this field, the steps taken by its leaders at the start of launching the movement were not quite in unison. When the flames spread, they could not be controlled. And so this fiery flame which was the peasant movement developed into a major factor leading to the destruction of KMT-CCP cooperation and the leftist regime of Wuhan.

With regard to this problem, the differences within the ranks of the CCP were focused not on whether the peasants' struggle should proceed in a drastic or a moderate manner, but rather on how KMT-CCP cooperation could be maintained after the launching of the peasant movement. Should the CCP resolutely adhere to the policy of cooperation with the KMT leftists? And especially if it were to maintain the anti-Chiang front and support the leftist government of Wuhan, should it restrain the peasants' struggle within the scope that was permitted by the major forces constituting the Wuhan camp? If this limit were exceeded, the CCP would have to establish a worker-peasant-soldier soviet government, such as was advocated by Trotsky. At the time, the Communist side—from Moscow to the leaders of the CCP at all levels (including Mao Tse-tung)—generally supported the first course. However, some of them advocated rectification of the excesses of this movement in order to maintain the Wuhan camp; while others did not consider the movement excessive and thought that it would not produce any serious obstacle to KMT-CCP cooperation.

The so-called excesses of the peasant movement originally referred to the barbarous leftist actions that had occurred in the movement; but by this time the connotations of the term were quite complex. Generally speaking, some "excesses" were exaggerations by opponents of the movement, some were justifiable demands of the peasants and could not be basically considered excesses at all, some were actual leftist deviations in practices, and some were acts rising out of the narrow consciousness of the peasants, which should not have occurred or could have been avoided. At the time our mistake was in failing to strictly differentiate these various kinds of problems and find specific solutions for them individually. The delicate situation of the CCP in the Wuhan government was an additional factor in the failure to carry out timely adjustment of the movement. Many CCP comrades felt that although the Minister of Agricultural Administration was a member of the Communist Party, the government was nevertheless that of the KMT; and so we did not want to assume the position of being the established authority in restraining the actions of the masses. But the general policy of the CCP caused its own fate to be closely linked up with that of the Wuhan government; and if this movement should bring harm to the Wuhan government, then the CCP would likewise suffer.

The majority of the leaders of the CCP, although recognizing that the excesses of the peasant movement called for correction, nevertheless consistently took pride in our ability to organize such a colossal peasant movement, even though we generally had misgivings also. Now that the peasants had been organized and the peasants' struggle had already developed, the influence of the CCP could be firmly planted on the foundations of the rural areas; and while it could not be easily destroyed, it could be further developed to undertake the solution of the land problem of the peasants. In fact, this was not enough. If the influence of the peasants was to be made firm and the land problem was to be solved, the most essential need was for protection that could be provided by a government supporting the interests of the peasants. At least the peasant organization should be made very strong, with adequate armed forces at its back, if the government authorities were to be forced into making concessions to the demands of the peasants. Otherwise it would mean ignoring the primary issues and merely going after the secondary problems; so that a peasant movement possessing only an imposing front must eventually be dealt a blow.

The peasant movement led by the CCP was far more progressive than the peasant uprisings that had occurred previously in Chinese history. Most of the peasant uprisings in the past had been influenced by an antiquated background of superstition, feudalism, and secret societies; and they had often been exploited by ambitious people trying to realize their individual campaigns to become ruler, if successful, or brigand, if defeated. The CCP was influenced by new cultural ideas and by the theory of the Comintern that the proletariat should lead the broad masses of peasants. Its organizational measures were not in keeping with traditional concepts, but rather were in the modern "democratic" forms. The CCP had as its goal, of course, seizure of the government; but it was very conscious of the need for improving the living standards of the peasants. The peasant movement during the Wuhan period was a large-scale experiment in the history of the development of the CCP. Although the movement was defeated at the time, later facts proved that the CCP did gain many valuable experiences from the lessons of this defeat.

To facilitate the explanation of the peasant movement of the Wuhan period, it is necessary to review a bit the development of the history of the peasant movement during the national revolution. In the CCP, Ch'en Tu-hsiu was the first to pay attention to the peasant problem. In his writings during the May Fourth Movement, he had pointed out that the Boxer Rebellion type of movement was conservative and backward and filled with superstitious concepts.[30] Later he consistently used these views as starting points in expressing his unwillingness to have the sacred and modern ideals of the CCP come under the influence of such reactionary concepts. However, the leaders of the CCP, including Ch'en Tu-hsiu himself, had not made any penetrating study of the history of international and domestic peasant movements, and so the CCP could not quickly evolve a clear-cut policy for the peasant movement and the land revolution.

Of the comrades of the CCP, P'eng P'ai was the first to engage in the peasant movement. In 1921 this intellectual youth from a good traditional family, under the influence of the teachings of Ch'en Tu-hsiu, first started to organize peasant associations in Hai-feng and Lu-feng in Kwangtung. His first aim was not the achievement of any kind of land revolution, and he had no thoughts of an armed uprising of peasants. His only thought then was the relief of some of the personal suffering of the peasants. Since then, the peasant movement in Kwangtung developed gradually, and this was followed by the discovery of many new problems.

On the eve of the Northern Expedition, in July, 1926, the CC of the CCP held an enlarged conference. On the basis of the fact that the peasant movement had been developed on a fairly large scale in Kwangtung, the meeting adopted a resolution on the peasant movement. The principal points of this resolution provided, in the economic field, for the reduction of rent and of interest rates—demanding that the income of the peasant should not be less than fifty per cent of the harvest and that the annual interest on loans should not exceed thirty per cent—and for opposition to the advanced collection of the grain tax and the levy of exorbitant miscellaneous taxes. In the political field it provided for freedom of assembly and organization for the peasants, election of county magistrates, and prohibition of the arrest and adjudication of peasants by the people's militia corps. In the organizational field it stressed a rural united front, stipulating that the peasant association would not admit as members large landowners and usurers, but that hired farmhands, farmers that cultivated their own land, and medium and small landowners should be united, that large landowners who did not actively perpetrate evil deeds should be considered neutral, and that only large landowners that were evil members of the gentry and local bullies should be opposed.[31] These decisions constituted the attempt of the CCP to mobilize the peasants as an important force of the national revolution in a realistic manner.

CCP comrades in Canton expressed opposition to the peasant-movement policy adopted by the CC of the CCP in July. On the basis of accumulated experiences in KMT-CCP cooperation and the peasant movement in Kwangtung, the Kwangtung District Committee advocated that KMT-CCP cooperation not be allowed to obstruct the peasants' struggle, which should be developed regardless of anything to the higher stage of solving the land problem. They stressed the importance of land revolution, maintaining that within the KMT only those supporting land revolution could be considered leftists, and such leftists were very few. Such a view implied that the focus of the revolution had shifted from the issue of national revolution to the issue of land revolution. The CC of the CCP, however, continued to uphold the basic policy that the national revolution remained the central task of the day and rejected this more drastic proposal of the Kwangtung District Committee.

The Comintern had attached very great importance to the problem of land for the peasants. This was characteristic of Leninism. In the view of the big shots of the Comintern, land revolution was the realistic and yet mystical inherent trait of the Chinese revolution. In the address that he delivered before the Congress of Toilers of the Far East in 1921, Safarov had emphasized this point; but Moscow had consistently failed to clarify itself on the actual situation in the Chinese peasant land problem and its relationship to the national revolution. Soviet land-problem experts had visited such areas as Kwangtung and Wuhan to make on-the-spot observations of this problem; but at the time of the collapse of the Wuhan government, they still had not come to a clear conclusion.

The views that Borodin expressed on the peasant land problem generally changed with China's political climate. Early in 1924 he had proposed to Dr. Sun Yat-sen such plans as confiscation of the property of landlords and nationalization of land; but they were not accepted by Sun. In 1925, following establishment of the National government, Borodin's entire efforts were directed toward close cooperation of the CCP with the KMT leftists to consolidate the revolutionary dictatorship in Kwangtung, and so he stopped talking about the land revolution. On May 15,

1926, after the Second Plenum of the KMT, he was no longer optimistic over the future of KMT-CCP cooperation, and so he again stressed the land revolution. The view of the Kwangtung District Committee described above had his support. Toward the end of 1926, after his arrival at Wuhan, his attention was devoted to developing the anti-Chiang front, and once more he ceased to attach importance to the peasant land problem.

In China, Borodin was the one who could best represent the views of Stalin. After he arrived in Wuhan, he talked with me about the peasant problem, indicating that the danger to the revolution at the time was that there were people that wanted to abandon Dr. Sun's three great principles. If they should succeed, then everything would be finished. He stated firmly, "Today the time for land revolution is not yet ripe; we must first develop the conditions that are absolutely necessary for the land revolution." He devoted all of his energy to planning the anti-Chiang campaign, and so he advocated correction of the excesses of the peasant movement. This attitude expressed by Borodin showed only that he himself had revised his stand since the days in Kwangtung (second half of 1926), but that directives from Moscow to the CCP also consistently made fulfillment of the national revolution the important focal point and obviously left the policy of land revolution unclear and vacillating.

The KMT attached greater importance to the peasant problem than to the labor problem. Much earlier, in his Three Principles of the People, Dr. Sun Yat-sen had brought forward the moderate policy of equalization of land rights. When the KMT was reorganized in 1924, although Sun had not accepted Borodin's drastic proposal for land revolution, he nevertheless formulated a political platform calling for protection of the interests of workers and peasants and issued the slogan "Let the Tiller Have His Land." Many KMT members felt that they should win wide support from the peasants, and they more or less accepted the idea of giving greater weight to the peasants and less weight to the workers. (The documents of the KMT, for example, invariably put the word "peasant" before the word "worker" and referred to the "peasants' and workers' movements." The documents of the CCP, on the other hand, placed workers before peasants and referred to the "workers' and peasants' movements.")

There were many expressions of KMT policy that attached importance to the peasant movement. The major points of the organizational regulations for the peasant association had been approved by Dr. Sun Yat-sen in the spring of 1924. At an early date Central Headquarters of the KMT had a department of peasants (very much earlier than the peasants' department was organized in the CC of the CCP), and similar structures were formed at the different levels of Party headquarters. The CEC of the KMT had time and again allotted considerable funds for the operation of the Peasant Movement Institute. Many special delegates of the peasant movement were sent to different localities to promote the movement. However, in point of fact, the peasant movement of the KMT was for the most part actually carried out by members of the CCP assigned to the job, especially those at the local level.

On the issue of the peasant movement, the KMT had consistently been in competition with the CCP. Although there were not many points of divergence in the peasant programs of the two parties, nevertheless KMT people generally felt that the peasant movement should be led by the KMT both in name and in fact, while the CCP, although outwardly respecting the KMT's leadership, actually took it upon itself to attend to the task. Then again the KMT stressed working from the National government on top, proceeding downward by using laws and orders to effect the improvement of living conditions of the peasants, whereas the CCP stressed launching the peasants' struggle by starting right at the bottom and working upward to strive directly for improvement in the living conditions of the peasants. Generally speaking, the KMT people, including the leftists, were afraid of the peasants' struggle and considered the land revolution even more threatening. This was especially related to the fact that most KMT members came from the ranks of middle-class families.

The above description is a general review of the endless stream of arguments over the insoluble problems involving the national revolution and the land revolution, both within the CCP itself and between the KMT and the CCP. They were precisely the hidden rocks that prevented the satisfactory solution of the peasant movement during the period of Wuhan.

The peasant movement in Hunan developed the fastest and was also on the largest scale. The peasant associations were organized from the bottom up to the top, spreading over the different *hsiang, ch'u, hsien,* and finally the entire province, developed at different levels successively. On the eve of the Northern Expedition, the peasant associations of this province had a membership of more than 200,000. On December 1, 1926, the peasant associations in all Hunan held their first congress, and of the seventy-nine hsien and municipalities in the entire province, peasant associations had been organized in fifty-four hsien and municipalities, with a total membership exceeding 1,360,000.[32] In February, 1927, membership further increased to more than two million. According to later statistics of the Ministry of Agricultural Administration of the National government at Wuhan, at the time when membership in peasant associations in Hunan was at its highest (the figures were for May), it exceeded 4,510,000.[33] Although these figures were not necessarily accurate, it was nevertheless common for the people at the time to look upon the peasant association in Hunan as a monstrous thing.

The peasant movement was more widespread in Hunan than in the provinces of Kwangtung and Hupeh. There were many reasons for this. For example, Hunan had gone through the upheavals of war between the North and the South; and the sufferings inflicted on the peasants were very severe. Most of the people's militia forces built up by the landlords had been taken over by the Army, and so the obstacles encountered in developing the peasant associations were not so great. Moreover, the KMT and the CCP in Hunan had been properly organized and were leftist in inclination. The Hunan District Committee of the CCP also could exert the greater part of its energy to the peasant movement. For example, Mao Tse-tung, the founder of the CCP organization in Hunan, consistently attached importance to the peasant movement, made repeated investigations of the rural areas, and had carried out some preparatory work for the peasant movement in Hunan.

The peasant movement in Hunan to some extent inherited the experiences of the Taiping Rebellion. In the spring of 1927 an old Hunanese scholar, who sympathized with the revolution, had described to me the general situation of the peasant movement in Hunan. He pointed out that in modern history the peasants of Hunan had gone through the experience of standing on their own feet two times—the first was during the Taiping Kingdom and the second was at the present time. The two instances of standing on their own feet had similarities, but the extent of the change was far more marked at the present, when the skies were virtually overturned and the earth was shaken up. He hoped that on the present occasion the defeat suffered during the Taiping Kingdom would not be repeated and that some of the problems of the peasants could really be solved.

The peasant movement in this province was developed right in the wake of the excellent opportunity afforded by the advance of the Northern Expeditionary Army. In order to win support for the Northern Expedition, the branch and subbranch organs of both the KMT and the CCP in the various counties and villages of Hunan actively expanded the peasant associations, while the peasants made marked contributions to the Northern Expedition and won the praise of all sides for a time. The various county governments relied heavily on the support of the peasant associations to fulfill their wartime task of mobilizing manpower and material resources. The assets of the people's militia of the landlords in different counties and villages were transferred for the most part to the hands of the peasant associations. The latter not only owned a small number of rifles, but also organized spear squads numbering hundreds of thousands. And so the peasant movement also swelled suddenly with the strengthening of such organizations. After the Northern Expeditionary Forces entered Hupeh, normal conditions were restored in Hunan, and the struggle waged by the peasant associations concentrated on the heads of the local bullies and evil gentry as their targets. At the end of 1926 the report that the Hunan peasant movement had resorted to excesses began to circulate in Wuhan.

Mao Tse-tung, the spokesman for the Hunan peasant movement, was the first to rise and oppose the claim that the Hunan peasants had been excessive in their fight against local bullies and evil gentry. In December, 1926, he participated in the First Congress of Hunan Peasant Associations. On his return to Wuhan he immediately introduced two famous slogans, namely, "Anyone with land is a bully; no member of the gentry is not evil" and "In correcting a wrong, we must be excessive in upholding the right." This was clearly a defense of the Hunan peasants, who were extensively attacking the local bullies and evil gentry. Although he admitted that the peasant movement in Hunan was a little "excessive in upholding the right," he maintained that this was necessary in "correcting a wrong." This theory of his represented the leftist feelings of comrades in Hunan. His later report on the peasant movement in Hunan was written on the basis of such a concept.

I had posed a series of questions to satirize this theory of his. What I asked him was essentially as follows: Did the statement "anyone with land is a bully" imply that a self-employed peasant with only a small plot of land was also a bully? He himself could be considered a member of the Hunan gentry; was he then also evil? With regard to the statement "in correcting a wrong, we must be excessive in upholding the right," why should we exceed in upholding the right? How far should we exceed in upholding the right? Were the excesses to be temporary or permanent? A man who would not admit his own mistake, Mao merely laughed aloud for a while and said that his words were only spoken to meet the needs and realities of the day.

Most of the CCP comrades in Hunan were similar to Mao Tse-tung. With the development of the peasant movement, they cultivated leftist and radical views. Among them, some really tried their best to push the peasant movement toward the Left, with the attitude of "exceeding the right in order to correct a wrong" and indignation over "every landlord being a bully and no member of the gentry not being evil." Even more people felt that at the very outset it was necessary to use more drastic methods if the struggle of the peasants were to advance. By the time the struggle had developed on a large scale, they would not change the situation in the interests of KMT-CCP cooperation. Furthermore, CCP comrades had a kind of traditional mentality—"turning to the Right is simply unthinkable, and turning to the Left generally cannot be bad." They would not realize that in the surging tides of revolution, the prevention of rash leftist action was not easy but nonetheless necessary. By the time such "rash leftist action" had become a kind of habit, its rectification was not easy. Moreover, the CCP comrades in Hunan lacked the power to control completely the activities of the peasant associations in the entire province.

The excesses of the Hunan peasant movement were principally expressed in such policies as "opposition to local bullies and evil gentry," "rent reduction and interest reduction," "blockade of grain and rice," and "abolition of old customs."

What the Hunan peasant associations had carried out with great fanfare and color was first of all the work of "attacking local bullies and evil gentry." The measures adopted to attack local bullies and evil gentry included "arrest, imprisonment, trial, reckoning of accounts, fines, parading them through the villages with tall caps on, slaughter of hogs, taking over grain stocks, etc." The executions of local bullies and evil gentry were also frequently reported, the most famous case being that of Yeh Te-hui, the old Hunanese leftover from the Manchu dynasty, who was known for his classical scholarship. There were also numerous instances of destruction of sedan chairs of landlords and gentry, tearing up of their gowns, and other insulting acts. The trials of local bullies and evil gentry were usually carried out at mass rallies. Very often at such rallies, so long as there was a single witness that firmly accused the defendant of being a local bully or evil gentry, no one would dare to dissent. As to the penalty imposed, the more drastic it was, the more easily it would be passed. This was very similar to scenes in the French Revolution when the National Assembly staged trials of aristocrats.

Opposition to local bullies and evil gentry was originally the common policy of both the KMT and the CCP. The rise of the peasant movement also had to have as its perquisite suppression of the influence of local bullies and evil gentry. However, if the policy were carried out spontaneously and extensively by the peasants, starting from the bottom and proceeding up to the top, then not only would the situation be as Mao Tse-tung described it—"There was a little bit of rash action"[34]— but it would lead to a state of anarchist terror. I need only give one example to prove the point.

Li Li-san's father had been executed by a village peasant association as a local bully or evil gentry. In January, 1927, Li Li-san's father, already advanced in years (he looked more than sixty years of age), came to Wuhan. On several occasions I had eaten meals with the old man in the Li home and had talked about his adventures. I had the impression that he was gentle of manner, solemn in attitude, and kind of heart. He did not deny that he had escaped to Wuhan to take refuge. He also indicated that he was willing to follow the views of his son and would not oppose the peasant association in anything. Soon afterward he took with him a letter, written personally by his son, which was addressed to responsible comrades in Hunan, guaranteeing that the old man would not oppose the peasant association or perpetrate acts against it. He returned to Hunan in high spirits. Unexpectedly, reports were received later to the effect that Li Li-san's guarantee had had no effect at all and that this old man had been destroyed by the "rash actions" of the peasant association of his own village.

If even the father of Li Li-san suffered such a fate, there is no need to refer to other cases. Li Li-san was a noted Communist whose home province was Hunan. His letter guaranteeing his father also apparently was forwarded to the peasant association of Liling County through the Hunan District Committee; but still it produced no effect. This not only showed clearly that the CCP Hunan District Committee exercised very little control over the peasant associations, but also proved that the movement against local bullies and evil gentry had reached a state of madness. When Li Li-san met this calamity, he was very crestfallen for a time; but he gritted his teeth and never mentioned the incident again.

I myself was depressed over the incident for a long time. I also thought that if such an incident had occurred to a member of the KMT or an officer of the Northern Expeditionary Army, his hatred against the peasant association would have been insurmountable.

With the swelling influence of the peasant association, refusal to pay rent and to discharge debt obligations replaced the demand for reductions in rent and interest. This became a universal practice. The policy of the KMT, the CCP, and the peasant association did not call for nonpayment of rent and nondischarge of debt obligations, but only advocated the reduction of rent and interest and laid down the rent scales so that a tenant farmer would receive at least fifty per cent of his harvested crop, while interest on monetary loans would not exceed ten per cent.[35] The realization of such demands to reduce rent and interest would lead to actual improvement in the standard of living of the peasants. On the basis of conditions that obtained at the time, this was reasonable and rational. But the development of the situation often made it impossible to halt at the right place, and this was all the more true when nobody stressed the need to pay rent and interest. For this reason, rent and interest reduction gradually were transformed into nonpayment of rent and failure to repay debts.

The refusal to pay land rent plunged rural landlord-tenant relations into a state of confusion. The landlords naturally felt that their rights as landowners had become a problem, while the tenants also felt uncertain over the future disposal of the rents they had withheld. This would produce repercussions on both the preparations for production and the production mentality. In individual areas, such as Hsia-yu village in the vicinity of Changsha, the situation even developed to the point where land plots were surveyed and signs were put up with poles in readiness for the redistribution of land, which was clearly beyond the ability of the Wuhan government to accomplish at the time. The nonrepayment of debts plunged rural finances into a state of strangulation, and people in the rural areas that had money to lend took their capital funds with them and escaped to outside areas. The small-property owners that stayed behind refused to issue further loans, since they were now deprived of protection. Thus the rural areas of Hunan in which capital was seriously lacking lost the circulation capital with which production could be maintained.

The "blockade of grain and rice" was a traditional aspiration of the poor people in rural areas who lacked food, because of the resulting decrease in grain prices. Their narrow-mindedness had led them to hope that local grain supplies would not flow outward, so that they could buy food at cheap prices. They did not realize that it was also necessary for them to have a normal state of commodity circulation maintained. Such a "blockade" was not supported by the CCP comrades in Hunan, but in the beginning they did not try their best to stop the development of the "blockade" trend. When the evil results of the act had already appeared, they tried to stop it; but by then they had already given the people an excuse for criticizing them.

The "blockade of grain and rice" was considered an effective means of stopping the landlords from shipping grain out of local areas, thus effecting the flight of capital, and the measure was in effect for a while. At the time, a ban was usually placed on taking grain out of the locality, between different counties, and between subcounty districts. Shipments out of the province had to have the approval of the provincial peasant association. But Hunan, a rice-producing province, needed to export grain in exchange for various daily necessities, such as salt and cloth. Under a situation in which grain could not be exported, the rural peasants had no means with which to purchase other things; and this was tantamount to cutting off their own economic arteries. Moreover, urban commerce, the supply of grain for the army, and even smuggling of food for military personnel were obstructed by the measure. The result was not only that the army officers, government officials, and merchants all hated the measure intensely, but that even in the rural areas there were many peasants that harbored misgivings.

The abolition of old customs in the countryside was something that the CCP thought had to be carried out. But it also knew that this had to go through a long-term, persuasive process of education before it could become effective. In undertaking the abolition of old customs, the various rural peasant associations in Hunan resorted somewhat to use of force and barbarous action. The demolition of temples, destruction of idols, overthrow of the system of ancestral temples and clan chieftains; ban of the use of sedan chairs, and encouraging women to oppose the authority of their husbands, forced remarriage for widows, and forced cutting of their long hair were all considered revolutionary tasks, and they were carried out with rigidity universally. There were even acts such as a ban on the use of grain to feed chickens as an economy measure and a ban on theatrical performances to practice thrift, all of which were rather irrational.

The drastic and forceful measures mentioned above aroused considerable dissatisfaction among the peasants, and this gave the people opposed to the peasant movement additional effective excuses. They loudly proclaimed that the peasant association was an organization that did not practice filial piety to ancestors, deceived the gods, destroyed righteousness, advocated the system of common wives, and so forth. This stemmed from the same idea as using the charge of the destruction of China's established traditions as a weapon to attack Hung Hsiu-ch'üan. The CCP also had not expected that the radicalism born of the consciousness of the peasants would develop to such proportions in Hunan, and for a time it was thrown into a state of confusion.

These excessive acts of the peasant movement in Hunan must be considered the most prominent; in the other provinces the movement was less intense.[36] The peasant association in Hupeh was not as well developed as that in Hunan, but compared with those in Kiangsi and other provinces, it was more advanced. At the end of 1926, membership in the peasant associations in Hupeh was more than 280,000; in March, 1927, it had increased to 800,000; and in May it had further increased to 2,500,000. From these statistics one can see not only that the membership lagged behind Hunan in number, but that the time of development was also later. The KMT and CCP organizations in Hupeh paid more attention to correcting the excessive acts of the peasants. While the peasant associations at the county, subcounty, district, and village levels also engaged in many direct acts against local bullies and evil gentry, the cases were usually handed over to the Local Bullies and Evil Gentry Trial committees organized by headquarters of the KMT for attention; there were few cases that were disposed of directly. In other matters, such as rent and interest reduction, the blockade of grain and rice, and the abolition of old customs, action was also not as fierce as in Hunan. Therefore the charge of excesses in the peasant movement was principally directed at Hunan.

Local bullies, evil gentry, and other people who were attacked by the peasant movement escaped in large numbers to Wuhan and other large cities to tell of their experiences and what they had seen and heard. The cries over the excesses of the peasant movement rose higher than the clamors for opposition to Chiang. By March, 1927, although the upper strata in Party and government circles still talked most about the anti-Chiang issue, most of the discussions by people on the streets related to stories of the excesses of the peasant movement. Some people main-

tained that since the peasant movement had become excessive, the movement was basically undesirable. The CCP thought that these views had
originated with the local bullies and evil gentry; but many KMT elements came under the influence of these stories, and to a greater or lesser
extent they reacted unfavorably to the peasant movement. Comrades of
the CCP and some people with firmer revolutionary convictions, while
not denying that there were excesses in the movement, nevertheless held
that the incidence of some excessive acts should not lead to basic opposition to the movement; and consciously or subconsciously they tempered
down the propaganda about the excesses.

T'ang Sheng-chih, who was then governor of Hunan, was caught
between two fires as he was confronted by the high tide of the peasant
movement. Most of his subordinates in Hunan informed him that the
peasant association had virtually become a second government. It interfered with the administrative and judicial systems of the governments at
all levels. Within Hunan Province one could not move an inch without
the approval of the peasant association. Some military personnel complained that the grain they needed could not be taken out of the province
because of obstacles imposed by the peasant association and that the
funds needed by the army could not be raised because of the drastic
reduction of revenue in the different counties under the influence of the
peasant association. A larger number of army officers and civil officials
told T'ang that their family dependents in the villages were hit in one
way or another by the peasant association. Needless to say, the reaction
of this governor against the peasant association increased with time, but
in order to maintain the anti-Chiang front, this pillar of strength in the
anti-Chiang camp had to be patient for the time being. He often indicated that he believed the excesses of the peasant movement could be
corrected with measures devised by the party headquarters of both the
KMT and the CCP.

A more serious reaction was the one bred among army officers as a
result of the blows dealt to their dependents in the peasant movement.
Most of the officers in the Northern Expeditionary forces were natives of
Hunan, some of them coming from well-to-do families in the countryside; and some, with the money and authority that came to them as
officers, had purchased land in their home districts, thus becoming landlords and suddenly waxing rich. Some army officers also had dependents
that exploited the situation of having relatives in command of armies by
throwing their weight around in the villages. A saying currently circu-

lating in Wuhan was "In the National Revolutionary Army, the ranks are mostly peasants and the officers are mostly landlords." This seemed to tally with the facts. These officers not only received many bad reports from their villages, but some of their dependents had fled from the villages to the army and were filling civilian jobs therein. As a result, a series of cries arose among the army officers against the excesses of the peasant movement.

Because of the need to unite with the anti-Chiang forces, Borodin paid great attention to the feelings of the army officers. He stressed the point that the peasant movement and the land revolution should not encroach upon the dependents of revolutionary army personnel and their land and property. The various related departments also expressed agreement with this proposal of Borodin's. But when the problem was studied further, it was found to involve a very large area and to face many difficulties. For example, the term "dependents of revolutionary army personnel" had a narrow interpretation and a wide one, and the two were quite different. The narrow interpretation included only the direct linear relatives of the revolutionary army personnel; whereas the wide interpretation took in a large scope that included relatives of subsidiary connections by marriage. Borodin's proposal aroused the dissatisfaction of the activists, who felt that if the dependents of army personnel were excluded from the category of local bullies and evil gentry—and especially if the wide interpretation were adopted—then basically there would be no local bullies and evil gentry in Hunan to oppose. Another problem was that some dependents of army personnel had already been encroached upon by the peasant associations, and it was very difficult to remedy the situation. The responsible members of the peasant associations felt that if all such cases were reversed, it would mean the collapse of the peasant associations.

As a result, the situation was being discussed and argued, and generally it was allowed to follow a natural course of development, with no one in a position to effectively alter the situation or control it.

Early in 1927 I discussed these problems with Hsia Hsi-pang, Kuo Liang, and other members of the CCP Hunan District Committee who were visiting Wuhan on business. I pointed out to them that although the peasant movement in Hunan had been developed with great fanfare, nevertheless it was not backed by armed force, nor were there plans for the organization of a peasants' soviet. At the time the subordinates of T'ang Sheng-chih, under the threat of the peasant movement, were turning more and more toward the Right, while the peasant movement was heading toward the Left. With each party going to the extreme, there would be trouble. If cooperation between the peasant association and military people were to be maintained, the peasant movement had to reduce the number of local bullies and evil gentry attacked and to correct other deviations. They supported these recommendations of mine at the time; but after they returned home, either they did not have the strength or else they did not exert their utmost effort in order to realize these proposals.

In April, 1927, after the CC of the CCP had moved to Wuhan, there was still a variety of arguments over this issue and no agreement could be reached. Summing up the views, there were the following two lines of thought. The first was advocacy of a thoroughgoing revolution, taking the opportunity to push the peasant movement forward to the stage of land revolution and not wavering because of the theory that the peasant movement had become excessive. The second view was that in order to facilitate the smooth development of the peasant movement itself, there was need to correct certain excessive acts. The CC of the CCP finally adopted a resolution to take action to correct certain excessive acts. It notified the Hunan District Committee to enforce the resolution, but it did not adopt effective measures quickly, such as sending capable representatives or a delegation to Hunan to urge its implementation. And so the effects of this resolution proved negligible.

Since the CCP did not take the initiative in reversing the tendency of the peasant movement to develop toward the Left, other organizations, needless to say, were even less effective. Under the direction of T'an P'ing-shan, the newly established Ministry of Agricultural Administration was busy investigating the situation in the peasant movement and drafting certain relevant regulations. The Land Commission created by the National government discussed the problem of confiscating land— whether it should be economic confiscation (meaning confiscation of the land of big landlords for distribution among the peasants) or political confiscation (meaning confiscation of the land of local bullies and evil gentry only). At the Joint Conference of the KMT and the CCP there was some discussion of the excesses of the peasant movement, but no one brought forward a concrete plan for solving the problem. And so all thoughts of rectifying the excesses of the peasant movement turned out to be inadequate to meet the urgency of the situation or else proved to be just empty talk.

The views of the people on the streets of Wuhan about the peasant movement were many and varied. People that opposed the movement either described how the dependents of T'an Yen-k'ai, Chairman of the National government, were injured in their village by the peasant association or they told how the father of Ho Chien, a divisional commander under T'ang Sheng-chih, was arrested by the peasant association. These various rumors were intended to prove that the peasant association was cutting the throats of revolutionaries. The spokesman for the radicals among the peasants—Mao Tse-tung—besides writing his noted report on the investigation of the peasant movement in Hunan, busied himself training cadres for the peasant movement and preparing for the First National Congress of Peasants,[37] with the intention of leading the peasant movement of the whole country to follow the example of Hunan and to march forward toward land revolution with great fanfare.

The CCP Hunan District Committee was, after all, under the influence of Mao Tse-tung. Although the members of the committee had indicated to me that deviations must be corrected, actually they consistently turned toward the Left with the leftist turn of the peasant movement. On February 12, 1927, Liu Yüeh-chih, director of the Peasant Department of the KMT Hunan Provincial Headquarters, published a plan for the peasant movement. He advocated the use of peaceful constructive methods to solve the rural disputes and called on the peasant associations in all areas to accept the leadership of the KMT and devote all their efforts to increasing agricultural production and improving agriculture. Liu Yüeh-chih was a noted leftist at the time, and he had organized a group inside the KMT called the "Leftist Society." All along he had cooperated very well with CCP comrades in Hunan, and that was why he could hold the post of director of the Peasant Department. His proposal naturally implied dissatisfaction with the guidelines of the CCP peasant movement, for the increase of agricultural production and the improvement of agriculture were actually items that were neglected in the peasant movement policy of the CCP in Hunan. It was reasonable to expect that the proposal would be accepted with good grace. But the CCP Hunan District Committee criticized this proposal of Liu Yüeh-chih as a rightist view and attacked it severely. The majority in the KMT Hunan Provincial Headquarters took advantage of this situation, and Liu Yüeh-chih and his colleagues were openly expelled from the KMT.[38] This incident proved that the members of the Hunan District Committee crudely violated the policy of the CC of the CCP with regard to cooperation with the KMT leftists and that they overlooked the importance of production increase in their leadership of the peasant struggle.

The CCP comrades in Hunan rejected proposals like those of Liu Yüeh-chih for easing the rural struggle, but they continued to uphold the Three Principles of the People of Dr. Sun Yat-sen and to develop the peasants' struggle. Like the CCP comrades in other localities, they were revolutionary idealists and primarily devotees of the mass movement. They supported the so-called KMT-CCP cooperation and supported T'ang Sheng-chih's rule in Hunan; but they did not seem to realize clearly what repercussions there would be after the peasant movement had shaken the foundation of the rule of T'ang Sheng-chih in Hunan. They did not think about replacing T'ang Sheng-shih, and they also failed to plan for what should be done if T'ang Sheng-chih or his subordinates resorted to the use of force in opposing the peasant movement. They seemed to be naively enjoying their position of having large numbers of followers and thus seeming to constitute a great force. They believed that their opponents definitely would not dare to take any rash action.

This was clearly reflected in the failure of the Hunan Peasant Association to make preparations for an armed struggle. Though the peasant association had "door to door corps" by tens of thousands and "spear corps" by hundreds of thousands, their weapons were outmoded and they did not have the necessary military organization. The armed forces of the peasants were very provincial in character. The general workers in the peasant associations only paid attention to using such weak armed forces for the protection of the local associations and never thought of making them into fighting units, either with equipment or with training and leadership. The CCP Hunan District Committee also failed to attach importance to strengthening the armed forces of the peasants, and it did not fully mobilize the military comrades to assume control of these armed forces of the peasants and to build them into effective commands. So, later in the internal review of work of the CC of the CCP, the peasant movement in Hunan often received the following criticism, "The effort was truly enormous, but preparations for the armed forces were backward." This seemed to be an accurate description of actual conditions at the time.

This heaven-and-earth-shaking peasant movement, promoted by the peasant association with the participation of more than half the population of the province, was hit by the Ma-jih Incident. This incident, which was directed by the garrison commander of Changsha—regimental commander Hsü K'o-hsiang, who controlled only about one thousand rifles—started the process of disintegration of the peasant movement. This swift current of water—the peasant movement in Hunan—which had arrived with the force of a deluge, was dissipated in an instant. When the causes and effects are studied, it is easy to see that this really was no accident. From this bloody lesson the CCP learned that "only armed force can deal with armed force." So, later the CCP devoted its attention to building the Red Army and persisted in the policy of guerrilla warfare. The foundations of the peasant movement in Hunan and other provinces were thus also transformed into the foundations of the guerrilla wars of a later date.

Chaos Within the Chinese Communist Party

During the Wuhan period, workers in the Political Bureau of the CC of the CCP held very divergent views, and this plunged them into a state of extreme chaos. I had consistently advocated that the CC of the CCP move rapidly to Wuhan, because some differences of opinion had developed within the CCP. If the members could gather at an important place, it might be easier to seek internal unity and thus strengthen the leadership of the CCP. We failed to foresee that things would not turn out this way. Each of the Communist leaders that came from Moscow and Shanghai proved to have his own ideas; and the CCP reached the point where the vessel was in danger of capsizing because of the abundance of pilots. I have already touched upon some of the arguments between Borodin and Voitinsky and upon the divergence of views between Borodin and Galen; but these were not all. When the leaders had gathered in Wuhan, their disagreements became increasingly numerous.

Viewing these differences of opinion from the angle of practical politics, they could generally be divided into two major categories: support for, and doubts about, the traditional policy laid down by the Comintern that provided for the CCP to remain within the KMT. Among the supporters of this policy there was also a lack of unanimity. Some advocated that since we had to maintain the Wuhan situation of KMT-CCP cooperation and the anti-Chiang front, we could not talk of promoting the revolution, but had to correct the excesses of the labor and peasant movements. Others held that only by promoting the revolution and proceeding to solve the land question could we strengthen KMT-

CCP cooperation and carry out the campaign against Chiang. As to those who doubted the traditional policy, some advocated that we should no longer hold on to the illusion of KMT-CCP cooperation and that the CCP should establish a soviet regime. Others suggested that the CCP should not remain within the KMT, but should continue to uphold its primary aim of thorough implementation of the national revolution and establishment of a truly democratic republic in order to pave the way for the future building of a soviet.

At the time Dalin, the Communist Youth International's representative in China, was one who supported the views of Trotsky. In 1922 he had started directing the work of the SYC in China. He was a model scholar and was somewhat removed from practical politics. Although he was implementing Stalin's policy, he personally sympathized with the views of Trotsky. He arrived in Wuhan from Shanghai in March, 1927. One day he and I were taking a walk along the bank of the river in Hankow, and he fully revealed his innermost thoughts.

He indicated to me that he supported Trotsky's theory of permanent revolution and believed that this theory was also applicable to the Chinese revolution. He looked upon the KMT as a political party of the bourgeoisie that was not anything like a revolutionary alliance between the workers, peasants, the petty bourgeoisie, and the national bourgeoisie. He criticized Borodin's policy of alliance with T'ang Sheng-chih against Chiang. He advocated the withdrawal of the CCP from the KMT, the independent development of the labor and peasant movements in order to turn them into a workers' and peasants' soviet, and replacement of the leftist regime in Wuhan by seizing power at the proper time. He definitely did not support the highly dishonorable act of correcting the excesses of the labor and peasant movements.

Dalin knew that I had always disagreed with having the CCP remain within the KMT, and that was why he spoke to me in such a vein; but my answer must have disappointed him. I pointed out to him that China was a semicolony and that merely looking at the foreign warships anchored on the river should make one realize that the principal target of the revolution was still imperialism. Neither in theory nor in practice had the time come for talk about a workers' and peasants' soviet regime. While I did not support the policy of having the CCP remain within the KMT and becoming involved in the latter's internal disputes, neither did I support using the cloak of the KMT as a cover for the campaign against Chiang. I advocated CCP-KMT cooperation outside either party, thorough opposition to imperialism and reactionary warlords, the winning of national independence, and establishment of a truly democratic republic through a national assembly. In developing this national revolution, the forces of the workers and peasants must be strengthened before we could talk of land revolution and socialist revolution.

On hearing my words, Dalin seemed disappointed. He said, "Then you are still a believer in the theory of revolution by stages." I did not deny this statement and added that the revolution should have stages that were clearly demarcated. At any rate, it was not rational for the CCP to remain within the KMT—this policy had already shackled the CCP.

Dalin's views no doubt represented the spread to China of the dispute between Stalin and Trotsky over the China problem. He further said to me, "Among the Russian advisers in Wuhan, there are also some that support Trotsky's views." He added that among these Russians an argument had developed over the theory of revolution in stages and the theory of uninterrupted revolution. Later Jen Pi-shih, who was then secretary of the SYC, often expressed certain leftist views at meetings of the Political Bureau of the CC of the CCP, and it is possible that he had been influenced by Dalin. Although the views of Trotsky did not have the support of most of the leaders of the CCP, nevertheless the shadow cast by them was a factor leading to the disputes among us.

Roy's arrival in Wuhan plunged the various meetings of the CCP into an abyss of extensive theoretical debates. He had arrived at Wuhan in the company of T'an P'ing-shan toward the end of February. He was the first Asian to participate in the Comintern, a star of Asia with a long-established reputation. Among his missions to give guidance in practical politics, the present assignment was perhaps the most important. At first he enjoyed the respect of the Chinese and Russian leaders in Wuhan. But his special talent seemed to lie in the review of theories, and people sometimes had the feeling that he was just reciting the doctrines he had digested so well.

In my own view, Roy's ideas compounded the two different proposals of Stalin and Trotsky. He supported strengthening the leftist regime at Wuhan and participation of CCP members in the Wuhan government. These positions agreed with the views of Stalin. He attached special importance to the revolutionary character of the petty bourgeoisie and had high expectations of such KMT leftists as Wang Ching-wei, seeming to think that land revolution could be realized through the hands of such people. As to military men like T'ang Sheng-chih, he looked upon them as feudal warlords who should not be included among the KMT leftists. He was not restrained by the theory of revolution in stages, but stressed promoting the revolution, and advocated pushing the peasant movement toward land revolution. Such viewpoints clearly came from the theoretical arsenal of Trotsky. Though he did not give a clear and detailed explanation of his proposal for "promoting the revolution," he nevertheless did not touch on the measure of pushing the Chinese revolution to the path of the soviet.

These views of Roy's were in conflict with the methods pursued by Borodin, and so the two of them were continuously involved in an endless argument. Looking at the situation from the viewpoint of practical politics, Borodin considered the relative strengths of the revolutionary and counterrevolutionary camps and planned concrete measures with the aim of winning victory. Roy's approach, on the other hand, stemmed from an analysis of theory, and he often attached importance to whether an act should be carried out in principle, not seeming to bother much about gains or losses. Between the two of them there was no relationship of superior and subordinate. Roy was a member of the ECCI, and at the time was the supreme representative of the International in China. Borodin had the support of Stalin and the Soviet government. So, very often the two were at loggerheads. But Borodin had after all been an adviser to the KMT for a long time; and riding on his experiences, he could easily go his own way. Still he had to spend a lot of time in endless debates with Roy.

The chaotic situation in the Moscow leadership and the conflict of views between Stalin and Trotsky exerted influence all over Wuhan; and they were also intertwined with the internal disputes of the CCP. Defeat often added to internal differences. After the April 12 incident, the differences within the CC of the CCP became more serious.

Ch'ü Ch'iu-pai was the first to introduce opposition to the leadership of Ch'en Tu-hsiu. Although at the time this opposition had not been translated into action, it did arouse psychological unrest among the comrades of the CC of the CCP. During the process of moving the CC of the CCP to Wuhan, Ch'ü Ch'iu-pai and Voitinsky had arrived early. A few days after April 12 (before Ch'en had reached Wuhan), Ch'ü Ch'iu-pai called an important meeting of the four of us—Ch'ü, Roy, Voitinsky, and myself. During the conversation Ch'ü Ch'iu-pai indignantly expressed the view that a grave crisis existed in the CC of the CCP. While the Wuhan comrades were actively opposing Chiang, the CC still held illusions about Chiang, thus inviting the severe blow of April 12. The Kwangtung comrades had long since advocated land revolution, but the CC did not support it. All these factors contributed to a grave crisis due to the loss of prestige of the central leadership. But the crisis had been covered up (he was referring to Voitinsky) so that Moscow had no means of knowing the details. Self-criticism within the Party had also been suppressed.

These words of Ch'ü Ch'iu-pai's were pointedly aimed at Ch'en Tu-hsiu, but they also implied criticism of Voitinsky. The latter had met repeated reverses; and the recent tragic defeat in Shanghai especially had produced in him a depressing feeling of deep responsibility. So he merely defended himself lightly, to the effect that he did not detect the existence of a grave crisis in the CC of the CCP and that he had not known of important differences in the past within the CC of the CCP.

To a certain extent I supported Ch'ü Ch'iu-pai, maintaining that we not only had to discuss the internal crisis of the CC of the CCP, but also had to undertake an extensive review of the crisis of the Chinese revolution. Nevertheless at the time I persuaded him to attach importance to the development of the general situation, to differentiate between matters of greater and less urgency, and not to bring up the issue of reorganization of the CC for the time being. After the meeting I learned that Borodin had also used the seriousness of the situation as an argument in persuading Ch'ü Ch'iu-pai that the time was not suitable for the discussion of internal issues; and so this matter was shelved. But Ch'ü Ch'iu-pai's actions in convening the meeting of the four of us left marked traces.

A few days later Ch'en Tu-hsiu arrived in Wuhan. He faced greater difficulties than any other person. Arriving after the disaster in Shanghai, he was greatly pained over the killing of the large number of comrades in Shanghai, Canton, and Peking. The various reprimands from within the CCP came in shoal and were concentrated on his person. Such irresponsible criticism as that offered by Ch'ü Ch'iu-pai added especially to his depression. He was not in the mood to defend the charges made against him by comrades, such as lack of vigilance, failure to take preventive measures, ineffective leadership, and rightist ideology. He tried his best to produce a remedial program; but his strength was inadequate, and no miracles dropped from heaven. He spent whole days thinking and worrying and working diligently; but the ogre of melancholy always held him tight.

In view of the gravity of the situation, I also felt that all the responsibility for failures should not be borne by Ch'en Tu-hsiu alone. I attempted to temper his feeling of depression and hinted that he should rouse himself to cope with changes. Ch'en did not wish to shirk the responsibility of bearing the blow, and he indicated that the CC could not be absolved from blame for the damage to the work of the CCP in all localities. For example, in the April 12 incident in Shanghai, the CC actually lacked vigilance. Not only was he, the secretary, guilty; but other members of the CC, such as Ch'ü Ch'iu-pai, were likewise guilty of neglect. He pointed out that among the members of the CC at the time no one pointed out the need of being prepared for Chiang Kai-shek's change of face. They concentrated their attention on the Shanghai Citizens' Assembly and organization of the municipal government. If at the time some member of the CC had brought up the matter, the sacrifices might possibly have been reduced a bit.

Ch'en went on to say that since the situation had developed to the present state, the CCP would confront many difficulties in the future. He pointed out that the Comintern had consistently wanted us to remain within the KMT, and so we could only maintain the present measure of cooperation with the leftists. There could be no talk of a soviet. If we violated the views of the Comintern by actively developing the land revolution and directly organizing the worker-peasant soviet, then we would be left isolated and standing alone. We would meet with the same failure as the Paris Commune. On the other hand, if we wanted to maintain the Wuhan situation, then we should correct the excesses of the labor and peasant movements and thus avoid aggravating the reaction of the leftists. But would such a course achieve the practical results of the anti-Chiang campaign and push forward the national revolution? This was also something that could not be foreseen. These words of Ch'en's seemed not only to reveal the crux of his dilemma, but also to explain the fact that the CCP had already arrived at the crossroads and did not know whether to turn to the left or to the right.

After Ch'en Tu-hsiu and other members of the CC had arrived one after another in Wuhan, meetings of the CC were held regularly, and preparations for the Fifth Congress of the CCP were made. There were seven participants in the meetings of the CC. Ch'en Tu-hsiu, Ch'ü Ch'iu-pai, T'an P'ing-shan, Ts'ai Ho-sen, Li Li-san, Chou En-lai, and myself. Jen Pi-shih also attended the meetings regularly in his capacity as secretary of the CC of the CYC. By that time I had been relieved of the duties of secretary of the Hupeh District Committee (Chang T'ai-lei was my successor), and I was devoting my time exclusively to policy-making work in the CC. Because of criticism by the majority, P'eng Shu-chih no longer participated in the meetings of the CC, engaging exclusively in a portion of the work of the Department of Propaganda (Ts'ai Ho-sen had by then taken over the post of director of the Propaganda Department). Roy, Borodin, and Voitinsky also regularly attended the meetings of the CC of the CCP. This arrangement for the meetings of the CC was later approved by the Fifth Congress of the CCP and was officially named the Political Bureau of the CC of the CCP, with the same constituent personnel.

The make-up of the newly organized Political Bureau of the CC of the CCP no doubt included the best selection of the day, but its work efficiency was not satisfactory. It turned out to be a conversational group that could not shoulder the task of policy-making in name and in fact. Ch'en Tu-hsiu, who was the chairman, seemed very democratic. While he naturally did not want to draft resolutions in advance, he did not even want to determine in advance the agenda of a meeting. When a meeting started, Roy would usually give a lengthy talk, which would be followed by a refutation by Borodin. Then Ch'en, Ch'ü Ch'iu-pai, and Voitinsky would all get involved in the debate, and there would be an endless general argument. The many concrete problems needing attention would only be hastily decided upon after hours of theoretical argument, when those present were tired from listening.

The Fifth Congress of the CCP, which opened on April 27, 1927, did not improve the state of internal chaos of the Party. About eighty delegates, representing 57,967 Party members, attended the Congress. This was an unprecedentedly large gathering. KMT leaders Wang Ching-wei, T'an Yen-k'ai, Hsu Ch'ien, and others attended the meeting to offer congratulations, showing that there was further development in the cooperation between the KMT and the CCP.

However, these scenes of enthusiasm could not cover up our inner sufferings. Before the Congress was opened, we had lost the district committee organizations in the three important cities of Shanghai, Canton, and Peking. The headquarters of these areas had been almost destroyed, and large numbers of comrades had been massacred. The organs that were left either lost contact with others or else had to struggle for existence under the most difficult conditions. Nearly all of the delegates to the Congress were greatly pained over these developments and did not dare feel optimistic over the situation, since they were helpless to improve it. All ambitions for further achievements were thus virtually annulled.

Many of us felt the need for a drastic review of the past if life in the future were to be restored. But as soon as we came into contact with concrete problems, we felt that a practical start had to be made. Ch'en Tu-hsiu's position had been shaken, but who could succeed him at this critical moment was a great problem. It was even more difficult to foresee what would be the make-up of a new CC which such a successor might organize and what tasks it would be able to perform. And with a big enemy before us, it was possible to lower our confidence by a self-evaluation and thus add to our difficulties. And then a review of the past had to involve the question of the correctness of the guidance given to the Chinese revolution by the Comintern. The prestige of the leadership of the Comintern was ebbing. Some other comrades and I felt that the Comintern had made a mistake in the basic policy, in which it persisted, of making the CCP stay inside the KMT, and we felt that all of the blame should not be placed on Ch'en Tu-hsiu. There were other people that were dissatisfied with the representatives sent to China by the Comintern. Ch'ü Ch'iu-pai, for instance, felt that Roy's empty talk did more harm than Ch'en Tu-hsiu did. Borodin, who did not interfere much with the internal affairs of the CCP, reasoned that the current leadership should not be shaken. He advocated less review of the past, but more planning for the future. Under the influence of Borodin, Ch'ü Ch'iu-pai temporarily halted his original plan of having a review offensive against Ch'en Tu-hsiu.

So the Congress spent much time listening to long reports from delegates and brought forward, in fragments, reviews and proposals of this or that nature. The really critical problems continued to be argued endlessly at meetings of the central Political Bureau held in Borodin's home, and the Congress appeared to be a decorative piece of no real consequence. Most of the people felt that certain critical problems of a confidential nature should not be discussed at the Congress, which had so many people and voices. Others also felt that at such a critical moment, all things should be decided immediately, on the spur of the moment, to cope with the emergency and that it was basically improper to discuss them leisurely at a Congress. So Borodin, who attached the utmost importance to reality, never attended the Congress and did not consider it important. As a result, the Congress did not make a thorough review of the past, nor did it bring up resolute and unshakable proposals for the future.

The Congress adopted resolutions on the political question, the land question, and on acceptance of the directive on the China question of the Seventh Plenum of the Comintern. A manifesto was also issued. These were the products of a considerable amount of time spent by Roy, Voitinsky, Yurin (then a Soviet land expert in Wuhan), Ch'en Tu-hsiu, and Ch'ü Ch'iu-pai. With regard to the political question, the Congress stressed that the proletariat should lead the Wuhan leftist regime—which represented the alliance of workers, peasants, and the petty bourgeoisie —against the revolt of Chiang Kai-shek—the representative of the upper middle class. But what the CCP actually did varied with the wavering attitude of the KMT leftist politicians (the so-called representatives of the petty bourgeoisie). On the land question, the Congress resolved to confiscate the holdings of the large landlords and to distribute them equally among the poor and suffering peasants. But what the CCP actually did was to correct the excesses of the labor and peasant movements. All these acts, which did not conform to the wishes of the Congress, were based on the wishes of Borodin. At the time Borodin was the one man who could best influence the actions of the CC of the CCP.

The fabrication of a revolutionary atmosphere consistently seemed to be the greatest talent of the Communists. On May 24, 1927, the Pan-Pacific Labor Congress was held in Hankow.[39] In the same locality, on June 19, the Fourth All-China Labor Congress was held.[40] For a time the revolutionary spirit of the people was stimulated. Many foreign guests also came to Wuhan, such as Chairman Lozovsky of the Red Workers' International and representatives of trade unions in Britain, the United States, France, Japan, the Soviet Union, Korea, and Java. They received a big welcome from the trade unions and other people's organizations in Wuhan. The atmosphere of "Unite, Proletariat of the World" spread everywhere.

The Political Bureau of the CC of the CCP, which served as the center coordinating these various activities, was thrown into a state of increasing paralysis. Opposed to each other were Roy's advocacy of promoting the revolution, consolidation of the Wuhan line, and land revolution and Borodin's advocacy of extensive alliance, the northwest development line, and the correction of excesses in the labor and peasant movements. Roy's empty talk was abhorrent to us, but his views were protected by the resolutions of the Fifth Congress and could not be easily rejected. Though Borodin had a hard time reconciling his views with theory, he nevertheless grasped reality and often could introduce programs for the solution of problems; and so his words found more willing ears. On this point Ch'en Tu-hsiu and Ch'ü Ch'iu-pai came quite close together, and they often used the argument that Roy did not understand the realities in China as a reason for adopting Borodin's specific recommendations. I and the majority of the other members more or less avoided these arguments and merely sought individual methods of solving the professional problems under our respective controls. But Jen Pi-shih, representative of the CYC, maintained that it was undesirable for the CCP to act differently from the principles decided by the Fifth Congress. Thus theory varied from practice, and resolutions were not in keeping with acts. The situation of the day seemed to have been vividly depicted by the statement we made at the time, "The CC of the CCP is standing irresolutely at the crossroads."

It was in the midst of arguments before "a full court" that the CC of the CCP neglected to adopt various concrete steps, "small matters," such as intensifying the strength of its own combat forces. When the tides of the countercurrent spread from the internal ranks of Wuhan to flood the situation, the CCP gradually found itself without the resources needed to deal with it effectively.

The Split

The encirclement and attack by Chiang Kai-shek and the domestic and foreign reactionary forces combined to cause the internal ranks of Wuhan to be filled with conflicts, such as I have already mentioned above: conflicts between labor and capital; struggles between landlords and peasants; differences of opinion between the CCP, the KMT leftists, and the military leaders; and internal chaos in the CCP. We were gradually marching toward a state of disintegration and collapse. This led to a complete split between the KMT and the CCP and the universal suppression of the labor and peasant movements, so that the so-called Wuhan leftist regime was declared lost in the midst of the movement for the alliance of Nanking and Hankow. In the eyes of the CCP this defeat of the Chinese National Revolution of 1925-1927 was entirely due to the revolt of Chiang Kai-shek. After that time the Chinese Communists took the path of armed uprising to oppose the rule of Chiang Kai-shek.

The Wuhan leftist regime was very weak to begin with; and the leftist leader Wang Ching-wei had consistently been a symbol of vacillation and unsteadiness. He opposed the military dictatorship of Chiang Kai-shek, but he also feared the revolutionary aggressiveness of the CCP. He was prepared to abide by the testamentary teachings of Dr. Sun; but after returning from his tour of Europe, he seemed to feel also that the forces of the Soviet Union in the international arena were, after all, fragile and could not be relied upon for victory. Perhaps he could not forget the fact that during the March Twentieth Incident, Borodin and the CCP had not supported him resolutely. Although he never revealed such feelings to me, nevertheless some of our comrades guessed that he had such thoughts. His later statement that he had consistently fallen into the midst of the combined attacks from both the leftists and the rightists seemed to describe such feelings.

After Wang Ching-wei reached Wuhan on April 10, 1927, signs of a gradual shift toward the Right in his attitude were very clear. In the very beginning he raised high the standard of "Party authority" and resolutely opposed the dissident acts of Chiang Kai-shek. The resolution of April 17 dismissing Chiang from the KMT had been adopted at the meeting presided over by Wang. After Ch'en Tu-hsiu arrived in Wuhan (about April 20), he actively promoted the holding of the KMT-CCP Joint Conference. The KMT participants in this conference were Wang Ching-wei, T'an Yen-k'ai, Sun Fo, Hsu Ch'ien, and Ku Meng-yü—five in all. Those from the CCP were Ch'en Tu-hsiu, T'an P'ing-shan, and myself—three in all. Wang was the chairman. At the time Wang appeared to be enthusiastic over uniting the KMT with the CCP in order to resolve the internal disputes in Wuhan and to stabilize the anti-Chiang front.

Only a few days later, however, his statements at the two-party Joint Conference began to change. Perhaps after he had come to understand the situation in Wuhan, he felt that the future of the anti-Chiang campaign was not optimistic and that he had to be prepared for the future. So he no longer advocated "an eastern expedition for the punishment of Chiang" but rather called for "correction of the excesses of the labor and peasant movements." And so this conference also became a conversational meeting in nature. Often Wang Ching-wei would describe some facts about the excesses of the labor and peasant movements, and the voluble Ch'en Tu-hsiu would rise and re-echo his words, making some defense of Wang's charges.

At first the CCP pinned some hope on this Joint Conference solving some specific problems. At the meetings I had introduced the idea that we needed to affirm guidelines for the labor and peasant movements and to determine what acts were excessive and what were not, so that both the KMT and the CCP would take the same measures in leadership and correction. But Wang Ching-wei was rather cool toward the idea, maintaining that specific problems should be decided in detail by the competent organs, whereas the so-called competent organs never did produce any concrete measures from start to finish. So we already felt at the time that Wang was not really serious about solving problems and that he did not want to assume responsibility for the leadership of everything; he was merely beginning by expressing his opposition to the labor and peasant movements.

So the KMT-CCP Joint Conference "met without discussion, discussed without decision, and decided without acting," as the Chinese saying goes. Such an unsatisfactory state of affairs naturally could not result in stabilizing the situation. By the time of the Ma-jih Incident, Wang's attitude turned toward castigating and satirizing the Chinese Communists. The meetings of the Joint Conference became more infrequent, and finally they were suspended. In the eyes of the CCP, this change of attitude on the part of Wang Ching-wei was only an expression of the vacillation of the petty bourgeoisie. Such people were basically incapable of leading the revolution. However, the so-called Wuhan regime of the workers, peasants, and petty bourgeoisie was not led by the Chinese Communists, but was led primarily by the wavering petty bourgeoisie. Since the CCP was aware that the petty bourgeoisie was wavering and yet wanted to place reliance on the leadership of the petty bourgeoisie, thus abiding by the views of Moscow and giving the regime the attractive name of "the democratic dictatorship of the workers, peasants, and petty bourgeoisie," it therefore seemed to be guilty of deceiving others as well as itself.

As a matter of fact, the so-called Wuhan leftist regime of the workers, peasants, and petty bourgeoisie was built upon the foundation of mutual conflicts between the landlord-bourgeoisie and the labor-peasant elements; and the armies led by the landlords served as its main source of power. Some of these military leaders had reasons for temporarily tolerating a rise in labor-peasant influences, but most of them had become agitated and restless. Those military figures that particularly abhorred the labor-peasant forces had long harbored the intention of overthrowing the regime. They realized that this government had lost its center of support and that all of its structures and meetings, like the two-party Joint Conference, were largely given over to discussions and were not very effective. They felt that if action were taken against it, this government would have no power to deal with it.

It was under such circumstances that the military revolt of Hsia Tou-yin was staged. He commanded the Fourteenth Independent Division of the National Revolutionary Army, which was originally stationed in the I-chang area on the upper reaches of the Yangtzekiang. Most of the officers had come from the ranks of the landlords in Hupeh, and the Army also served as protection for the refugee landlords and local bullies from Hunan and Hupeh that had been hit by the peasant movement. At the time when the main forces of T'ang Sheng-chih and Chang Fa-k'uei were fighting bitterly with the Fengtien Army and the outcome was yet to be decided, Hsia thought that the defenses of Wuhan had been left open; so he secretly launched an attack on Wuchang, in an attempt to overthrow the Wuhan government with a single effort.

This action of Hsia Tou-yin was doubtless masterminded by Chiang Kai-shek as an attempt to break up the internal ranks of Wuhan. Although Nanking and Wuhan had reached agreement to continue the Northern Expedition on separate routes and to refrain from attacking each other for the time,[41] nevertheless with increasing force Chiang Kai-shek had consistently proceeded with the work of overthrowing the Wuhan government from within. It was widely rumored in Wuhan that Hsia Tou-yin had accepted an appointment from Chiang and had received his economic support. On May 13 Nanking had enthusiastically published Hsia's circular telegram announcing his opposition to communism and punitive action against Wuhan; and high hopes had been placed in Hsia.

The action launched by Hsia Tou-yin was naturally not isolated, but had extensive support. The miscellaneous army units in Hupeh territory, such as Liu Tso-lung's Fifteenth Army stationed in Shashih and the units of Chang Lien-sheng and Yü Hsüeh-chung in northern Hupeh, all gave him secret help. The Twentieth Army of Yang Shen in Szechwan also moved toward I-chang to give him support from the rear, and he had ties with the subordinates of T'ang Sheng-chih. For example, division commander Ho Chien, who was at the Honan front, and T'ang's subordinate Hsü K'o-hsiang, stationed in Changsha, both seemed to have an understanding with Hsia on the anti-Communist move. But Hsia's action on this occasion did not seem to have been anticipated by T'ang Sheng-chih himself, for it was contrary to the thorough implementation of the anti-Chiang policy of the Wuhan group, which at the time was supported by T'ang. It would seem that Hsia Tou-yin wanted to present a *fait accompli* that he himself had perpetrated, in order to force T'ang to make concessions. The Fourth Army of Chang Fa-k'uei was looked upon by Hsia as the most important army supporting Wuhan; and it was thus the target of his attack.

On May 17 the forces of Hsia Tou-yin occupied a strategic line in the vicinity of Ting-ssu-chiao, south of Wuchang, and marched on the Chih-fang area near Wuchang. Comrade Yeh T'ing, who was responsible for the defense of Wuchang, was making preliminary preparations for meeting the attack. At about two o'clock that afternoon he hurried over to Hankow to see me; and he told me that the National government had called on him to attend a meeting immediately to discuss punitive measures against Hsia Tou-yin. At the time he had been promoted to commander of the Twenty-fourth Division, which had been organized for less than two months. New troops made up more than three-quarters of his men, equipment was not yet complete, and there was a lack of middle- and lower-level cadres particularly. (I had helped him operate a model battalion and had transferred certain activitists among workers and peasants to be trained as squad and platoon leaders there.) When army commander Chang Fa-k'uei led the main force of the Fourth Army, which included the Independent Regiment originally commanded by Yeh T'ing (whom Chou Shih-ti had succeeded as regiment commander), on its march to the Honan front, Yeh's newly organized division still had not built up its full combat strength and therefore had to remain in Wuchang.

I immediately indicated to Yeh T'ing that he should resolutely assume responsibility for repulsing the attack of Hsia Tou-yin, because this revolt was part of the plot of the reactionaries as a whole. If we could rapidly annihilate Hsia's army, his fellow conspirators might not dare to rise up in support lightly. The landlords and local bullies that were lying low in the triple cities of Wuhan were all elated about Hsia Tou-yin, and they circulated rumors to the effect that Hsia's capture of Wuhan would be instantaneous. The leaders of the National government were also a bit alarmed and restless. While they could not be sure that the division of Tang's army under Li P'in-hsien, which was still stationed in Hankow, already had an understanding with Hsia, nevertheless they felt that Li could not be expected to resist Hsia's attack. The Second and Sixth armies were far away in Kiukiang and Anking and could not be brought back to deal with an emergency. So Yeh T'ing was the only one left to assume the task of fighting this battle; and I encouraged him to express before the leaders of the National government his confidence in being able to suppress the revolt.

At five in the afternoon Yeh T'ing came back to tell me the results of his meeting with the National government. The government had appointed him Director-General of Operations in the front lines of the expedition against Hsia Tou-yin and had directed him to proceed to the front immediately with the entire Twenty-fourth Division and about fifteen hundred cadets of the military academy at Wuchang. The government also had ordered the Second and Sixth armies to return to Wuhan immediately to suppress the revolt. Yeh added that most of the leaders attending the meeting were worried, perhaps because they felt that Hsia Tou-yin's forces were superior. There were even people who thought the worst would happen and wondered what should be done then. I thereupon told Yeh that now it was only a case of going forward —retreat could not be afforded—for it was vitally necessary that Hsia Tou-yin be defeated. I would mobilize all the forces that I could to give him support from the rear.

Yeh T'ing immediately crossed the Yangtze to carry out his combat duty. I went at once to the home of Ch'en Tu-hsiu and gathered all the members of the Political Bureau of the CC that I could find to tell them about the critical situation. I reported that I had notified some comrades in Hankow to quickly mobilize the workers' picket corps to meet the emergency. I asked them to investigate conditions in Hunan, Hupeh, and Kiangsi; to notify comrades in all areas; and to prevent the reactionary forces from exploiting the opportunity by staging uprisings. I also asked the CC to send me to Wuchang to assume the responsibility of supporting Yeh T'ing. These proposals of mine were approved by them without dissent.

At about six in the evening I reached the bank of the Yangtze and found that the ferry boats had ceased to operate. I could not see a single motorboat or lighter on the bank of the river. By inquiring, I found that some of them had been requisitioned by the army and others had been retained by certain organizations and important officials for use in escape. It was not known where they had been hidden. This situation had perhaps been created within the past two or three hours, with rumors spreading about the emergency on the front lines. I and a comrade who was with me could only find a sampan, and on the rapid currents of the great river we managed with great difficulty to cross the river, arriving on the other side well below Wuchang. By the time we landed and hurriedly entered Wuchang City, it was already eight o'clock. One after another the stores inside Wuchang City were closing their doors, and pedestrians on the streets were saying, without the least care, "Hsia Tou-yin will enter the city tomorrow."

I decided to make Hu-shang-yüan my temporary headquarters; and I immediately proceeded there to issue orders. Hu-shang-yüan was a garden residence facing a large pond, surrounded by high walls, and built like a fortress. It had been used as the office of the Russian military advisers, and its military communications facilities were fairly complete. By that time all the Russian military advisers had gone to the Honan front and to various army units, and inside the garden there remained only a platoon of guards. The leader of this platoon was a Communist whom I could control.

I obtained the help of Chang Po-Chün (who had been chief of the organization section of the General Political Department and was then acting for the director of that department, Teng Yen-ta, who had gone to the Honan front) and the comrades of the CCP in different organs under the Hupeh provincial government; and I immediately enforced a curfew. I pointed out to my comrades that since the troops were being sent to the front line, the defenses of Wuchang were left open and the people's confidence was shaken. It was said that many supporters of Hsia Tou-yin were also in the city; and for this reason it was a matter of urgency to consolidate the rear in Wuchang. I insisted that within Wuchang City all the Party, government, and military organs, as well as people's organizations, be placed under my control and that the city be divided into districts for the strict prevention of sabotage by the sympathizers of Hsia Tou-yin. My words were immediately accepted by my comrades and were strictly enforced.

The largest armed force left behind in Wuchang City consisted of the ranks of students in the Peasant Movement Institute. There were more than four hundred students, and each one had a rifle. I immediately looked up Mao Tse-tung, head of the Institute, and requested his help. I pointed out that the force under his control was the largest force within Wuchang City. A small portion of this force should be used to carry out the enforcement of the curfew order; and the larger portion should be assembled as a task force to give aid on all sides as needed. At first Mao Tse-tung was worried because the peasant-movement students had old, worn-out rifles, lacked ammunition, and were not sufficiently trained. But when I told him that the situation was so critical that not only the peasant-movement trainees had to participate in combat, but even we ourselves might have to proceed to the front to risk our lives, he realized the seriousness of the situation and gladly took up the task that I gave him.

I also talked with him about the influence that the revolt of Hsia Tou-yin might have on Hunan. According to him, if Hsia Tou-yin should be rapidly suppressed, Hunan would probably not be in trouble. Developments turned out later to be beyond the expectations of Mao Tse-tung—who thought that he was familiar with the Hunan situation—because the Ma-jih Incident occurred. This incident alone was enough to show how naive my young friends were at the time, including even such a smart man as Mao Tse-tung.

That whole night I did not stop working. The tense situation made me forget about being tired. I encouraged the officers and political workers that had to proceed to the front that very night, asking them to concentrate at the front all forces that could be mobilized and not to worry about the defense of the rear at Wuchang. I also insisted that they all accept orders from Yeh T'ing, so as to win a total victory. I led the platoon of guards at Hu-shang-yüan and the small number of troops that I could gather on the spur of the moment and used motor cars to patrol various areas personally, making observations about precautionary measures to be taken on the important communications routes. In this way, order was gradually established; and although enveloped by fear and speculations about the war, Wuchang that night gradually returned to a state of calm.

On the eighteenth I continued to be very busy, constantly using the military telephone to contact individually those people that were directing the fighting at the front, such as Yeh T'ing. I told them that Wuchang City and its environs were well guarded and that the local bullies and evil gentry no longer dared to exploit the opportunity to start trouble, while conditions in other areas were also favorable to us. This was to encourage them to fight resolutely. As to the communications routes leading to the front lines, I urged the masses of workers and peasants to work their hardest to keep them open and unobstructed. So the supplies and the manpower needed at the front were being provided continuously, and there was no fear of a shortage of either.

Early on the morning of the nineteenth, at a point some twenty kilometers south of Wuchang, Yeh T'ing used his entire force and routed Hsia Tou-yin's army. The latter withdrew in disorder toward eastern Hupeh; but because the defenses of Wuchang were left open, Yeh T'ing obeyed the order of the National government and halted the pursuit of the fleeing men. He concentrated his forces at important points south of Wuchang, in readiness to deal with other possible revolts. Because Hsia Tou-yin's forces were defeated so rapidly, his sympathizers had to remain inactive for the moment, and Wuhan once more resumed an atmosphere of high-spirited enthusiasm.

For the time being, I—who had no official appointment of any kind and had volunteered my services—was looked upon by comrades in Wuchang as the temporary commander-in-chief, who had contributed importantly to this war. On the evening of the nineteenth, some officers who were KMT members returned from the front line and offered me their congratulations. They maintained that had it not been for my occupying the central position and making plans for support, the victory at the front might not have been so rapid. I finished making the war arrangements in Wuchang; then the CC of the CCP urged me to return to Hankow to attend a meeting of the Political Bureau. Just at this point my wife, with my first son, returned to Hankow from Moscow via Vladivostok and passed through terror-stricken Shanghai. There was need for me to give her some attention; so on the morning of May 20 I left Hu-shang-yüan to return to Hankow.

First I went to the National Government Building to call on Wang Ching-wei, with the intention of fulfilling formalities by making a supplementary report on my activities in Wuchang. He did not wait for me to open my mouth, and asked, "Why haven't I seen you these last few days? Where have you been?" I felt that his tone might imply criticism of me for acting in excess of my authority, and so I explained to him, "Since I had no time to get your instructions, I went to Wuchang to help comrades in the war; and there I carried out certain expedient measures. They have now been wound up, and normality has been restored. Today I have come especially to report to you." It was only then that he seemed very pleased and grasped my hands, saying, "Thank you for your efforts. You don't seem to have slept properly for days. Wait until you have rested properly, and then we shall talk in detail."

At two o'clock that afternoon the Political Bureau of the CC of the CCP met at Borodin's house. My comrades were generally elated over my efforts in Wuchang City during the past few days. We talked about the fact that Hsia's army had not been annihilated and that there could possibly be other incidents to follow. We could utilize the experience of fighting in Wuchang to alert comrades in all areas to increase their vigilance in coping with possible developments. But even such a big stimulus did not suppress Roy's empty talk. He continued to play his set of old, worn-out tunes, lightly setting aside the realistic struggle and engaging even less in any realistic thinking about exploiting the opportunity to expand our own strength and to continue attacking the reactionaries.

On May 21, 1927, the famous Ma-jih Incident occurred in Changsha. This was a successful action taken by the Hunanese army to suppress the labor and peasant movements. On May 19 Commander Ho Chien of the Thirty-fifth Army, which was under T'ang Sheng-chih, while he was fighting at the front in Honan, issued a circular telegram charging the labor and peasant movements in Hunan with sabotaging the rear lines of the Northern Expedition. In such counties as Lin-hsiang and I-yang, the local defense corps and the troops stationed locally had already started action and had occupied the premises of the labor and peasant organizations, arresting and killing many of their responsible members and disarming their military outfits.[42] Early on the twenty-first, the regiment of Hsü K'o-hsiang, who was under Ho Chien and was garrisoning Changsha, started military action. The headquarters of the Hunan Provincial Trade-Union Council, the Provincial Peasant Association, and other important mass organizations in Changsha City were all occupied by the troops; thousands of the armed troops of the workers and peasants were disarmed; and more than one hundred members of the CCP and leaders of labor and peasant organizations were killed.

The action of Hsü K'o-hsiang and other military leaders represented the counterattack launched by the landlords. It was reported that at the beginning of the siege, Hsü K'o-hsiang had felt that the force he commanded was weak and that he was afraid to pitch it against the powerful forces of the labor and peasant organizations. The CCP Hunan District Committee had also received earlier reports on action about to be taken by Hsü K'o-hsiang, but it did not take strict precautions. The members seemed to think that T'ang Sheng-chih would not undermine the anti-Chiang front he himself supported and that Hsü K'o-hsiang, being T'ang's subordinate, would not act contrary to T'ang's wishes either; and so they did not believe the reports. Such naive thinking made it possible for Hsü K'o-hsiang to achieve unexpected success very easily.

What happened in Changsha immediately shook up Wuhan. Hsü K'o-hsiang cut off communications in the Yochow area on the Hunan-Hupeh border, and so we in Wuhan did not have access to the actual facts. The Hunan District Committee, plunged into chaos and blockaded, had no means of reporting immediately to the CC of the CCP. All of the news circulated in Wuhan referred to victories scored by Hsü K'o-hsiang and even claimed that he had controlled Hunan completely, that the labor and peasant forces were all make-believe in nature and could not stand a single attack, and so forth. Such exaggerated reports made the Wuhan authorities hesitate in reaching a decision. We CCP comrades also dared not place high hopes on altering the Hunan situation.

The Political Bureau of the CC of the CCP was extremely indignant over this affair. Some of its members stamped their feet and beat their breasts, saying, "Hunan has more than four million organized peasants, more than three hundred thousand organized workers, armed forces of workers and peasants with more than five thousand rifles, and hundreds of thousands in the spear corps; but now they actually sit tight, waiting for death. Can the Hunan District Committee be so lacking in vigilance that it does not give thought to the effects that might be produced in Hunan by Hsia Tou-yin's revolt? Have they not received notification from the CC demanding that they increase their vigilance? In Changsha City itself there are labor and peasant armed forces with about one thousand rifles. Had they been vigilant, they could even have exploited the opportunity and annihilated Hsü K'o-hsiang. Now the thing to do is to issue strict orders to the Hunan District Committee to suppress the forces of Hsü K'o-hsiang quickly." Other members of the Political Bureau of the CC of the CCP felt that after Hsü K'o-hsiang had taken the first step to control his opponents, a counterattack might not be successful and that it might be best to clarify the situation first, before deciding on actual steps to be taken.

Most KMT elements, from Wang Ching-wei right down to the primary cadres, adopted the attitude of watching the fire from the opposite bank of the river; and many even maintained that the trouble had been started by the Chinese Communists. They blamed the CCP for causing the present incident by not having corrected in time the excesses of the labor and peasant movements, so that the rights and property of families of military men might not be encroached upon. They criticized the

Hunan labor and peasant organizations for being, though colossal, just assembled gatherings without organization that could not stand a single blow. They did not support the idea of having the National government restrain Hsü K'o-hsiang, since this might lead to its loss of support from the military elements. This was truly a key consideration, and the so-called KMT leftists were forced to reveal their rightist tendencies. They felt that other than going along with the military elements, who represented the interests of the landlords, there was no course for them to choose.

For Borodin, the Ma-jih Incident was virtually a bomb that scored a direct hit. He was greatly shocked, and yet there was nothing he could do. He indicated to the Political Bureau of the CC of the CCP that the matter had been messed up, principally because Hsü K'o-hsiang had got the upper hand. If we launched a counterattack, we would be in a war with no assurance of victory, but would only aggravate the crisis of the Wuhan situation. Fortunately T'ang Sheng-chih had not yet supported Hsü K'o-hsiang's action, and Hsü had also expressed obedience to T'ang, so there was still room for a reconciliation. Borodin suggested that he accompany representatives of the National government to Changsha for a preliminary investigation in order to seek a settlement by peaceful means and thus maintain the general situation in Wuhan. Under the circumstance of not being able to do anything else, our CC had to accept this recommendation of Borodin's.

On the day following the incident in Changsha, Borodin told the leaders of the National government that it was only a local affair and that it seemed likely the National government would dispatch high officials to the scene to investigate. He said that he was willing to go along and try to calm down the two sides in the dispute. Having nothing better to suggest, the leaders of the National government decided that this was a fairly satisfactory measure, and so the Wuhan press widely publicized the statement "Adviser Borodin personally proceeds to Hunan to investigate the Changsha incident." This was a dose of medicine that was supposed to calm the people. But Hsü K'o-hsiang rejected the proposal, and Borodin's trip to Changsha failed to materialize. A few days later T'an P'ing-shan, Ch'en Kung-po, and others sent by the Wuhan government to investigate the situation in Changsha were turned back by Hsü K'o-hsiang when they arrived at Yochow.

Hsü K'o-hsiang was a military man-of-action, and he disregarded these moves by the Wuhan government. With the spirit of seeing something through that he had started, he continued to develop his offensive. He took the opportunity to contact all five regiments in Hunan for concerted action against the Communists. He moved to occupy the Hunan Provincial Headquarters of the KMT, and he organized an independent "Party Protection Committee"[43] to enforce the Party purge. His methods were the same as those used by Chiang Kai-shek in Shanghai and elsewhere. He appointed a large number of local bullies and evil gentry to serve as rural pacification commissioners in assisting the army to proceed to the different counties and carry out the pacification of the rural areas. He retaliated with measures that far surpassed in stark cruelty those used by the peasant associations in dealing with local bullies and evil gentry.

After the Ma-jih Incident the CCP Hunan District Committee issued orders to peasant associations in all counties to lead the armed forces of the peasants in a counterattack on Changsha to punish Hsü K'o-hsiang. Later, because of the order of the CC of the CCP saying that the incident "should be peacefully settled by the National government," a directive was issued for the attack to be halted. In the Ping-chiang and Liu-yang areas the peasant forces did not receive the order to halt the attack, and so they marched on Changsha according to the original plan. But their steps were not coordinated, and they were defeated by Hsü K'o-hsiang. This matter later became a great bone of contention within the CCP. The Hunan District Committee stated that it had been resolute in taking up the struggle, but was halted by the order of the CC. Some comrades on the CC criticized secretary Li Wei-han and others of the Hunan District Committee for not having taken advance precautions against the Ma-jih Incident and called it an example of opportunism.

On May 29 T'ang Sheng-chih openly issued a circular telegram revealing his change of attitude and expressing opposition to the Communists. His telegram pointed out that "Party affairs in Hunan were all under the manipulation of the brigands that had dual party membership and the undesirable elements of our own Party [KMT]." That he should at this juncture change his hitherto consistent attitude of tolerating CCP activities in Hunan was superficially due to pressure from demands of his subordinate officers and the influence of the Ma-jih Incident. Actually it seemed to be due to the force of circumstances in the general situation that he was not able to make public his true personal intentions, which had previously lain hidden in his heart. He still hoped to use Wang Ching-wei as a front for the campaign against Chiang Kai-shek. It was of course still doubtful whether he had obtained agreement from Wang before revealing his anti-Communist attitude. But it was clearly a fact that after that time Wang began to turn toward the Right. The transformation of the entire situation in Wuhan was also affected by this development. T'ang Sheng-chih was no longer a supporter of Borodin, but had become a strong man under Wang Ching-wei and was being "squeezed in by attacks from both sides."

Just at the time when the CCP had been severely hit and plunged into a position of being encircled, a famous order from the Comintern reached Wuhan on June 1. This message was sent to Roy and Borodin in accordance with the wishes of Stalin. It ordered the CCP to act on the following policies:

1. The practice of land revolution, with the confiscation and distribution of land leading from the top to the bottom and then leading from the bottom to the top, but without encroaching on the land of army officers.
2. The correction of excesses in the labor and peasant movements by the Party's organ of authority.
3. The elimination of existing unreliable generals; the arming of 20,000 CCP members, and the selection from Hupeh and Hunan of 50,000 workers and peasants to organize new armies.
4. The placement of representatives of the new labor and peasant elements on the central committees of the KMT to replace the original CCP members.
5. The organization of a revolutionary tribunal, with a noted KMT member as president, to try reactionary officials.[44]

When this telegram was read at a meeting of the Political Bureau of the CC of the CCP, everyone present had the reaction of not knowing whether to cry or to laugh. They unanimously felt that it was impossible to implement the order. Some expressed the view that Moscow was too uninformed about conditions in Wuhan. How could we talk at this time of eliminating unreliable generals? Some stated that to realize the various points laid down in the telegram, the CCP would have to single-handedly organize a soviet. But Moscow still hoped that the KMT leftists and the National government could carry out these measures. Some said the telegram had come a little too late and that it smacked of "firing the shot after the horse had galloped away" in order to leave a loophole for the Comintern to shirk its own responsibility; for Moscow should surely have known that the peasants in Hunan were shedding their blood at the moment.

I myself said that the Wuhan situation as a whole was turning to the Right and that the policy of KMT-CCP cooperation was due to collapse soon; so it was truly a fairy tale from overseas to hold on to the illusion that the Wuhan government could carry out such heroic deeds. Borodin and Voitinsky both stated clearly that this directive could not be implemented for the time being. Roy also said at the meeting that it would be difficult to carry out. And so the people at this meeting unanimously decided to send a reply to Moscow saying that there was no way to implement its order.

The Political Bureau of the CC of the CCP seemed to think that in accordance with the Comintern's policy of continuing to cooperate with the KMT leftists, an attempt should be made to salvage the crisis caused by the rightist tendency in the Wuhan regime, the possibility of which was then enveloping Wuhan. At the time T'ang Sheng-chih still adopted a two-faced attitude. On the one hand he issued a circular telegram opposing the Communists, and on the other hand he expressed to KMT and CCP leaders in Wuhan his dissatisfaction with the unruly action taken by Hsü K'o-hsiang and said that he himself would continue to abide by Dr. Sun's three major policies. The attitude of Feng Yü-hsiang was still not clear. We still hoped that Feng would support the leftist policy of Wuhan. Furthermore, Wang Ching-wei and others did not seem to have gone completely over to the anti-Communist stand; and so we felt that the tune played by Moscow was not timely. If we could maintain the anti-Chiang front and if Wuhan did not openly reject the Communists, then the CCP would have to make some concessions in order to maintain KMT-CCP cooperation, provided that the labor and peasant movements would not continue to be suppressed. Otherwise we could only radically change the policy, and the CCP would have to stand alone, not only in opposition to Chiang, but also in opposition to the vacillating elements in Wuhan.

Unexpectedly, at this critical stage Roy did something that was hard to understand and that caused further deterioration in the situation. Without previously consulting anybody, he gave this secret Comintern telegram to Wang Ching-wei to read; and at the latter's request, Roy provided him with a copy. The message from Moscow seemed to show that Moscow had failed to understand that the Ma-jih Incident had plunged the CCP into a position of being besieged by enemies on all sides and that it thought Borodin and the others could still influence the situation; so it had ordered Roy and Borodin to direct the CCP to rouse its forces for a counterattack and to seize the leadership of the national revolution. Needless to say, this telegram could not be made public. Roy himself had participated in the meeting of the CCP Political Bureau at which the message was discussed, and he was well aware that a reply had been sent to Moscow saying that it was not being implemented at the time. And yet he handed the message to Wang to read. It was really difficult to understand his motive.

Why exactly did Roy do such a thing? At the time we felt that he was too much "the scholar." In the Political Bureau of the CC of the CCP he consistently had no means of carrying out his proposals; and this must have depressed him. But all along Wang Ching-wei had played ball with him, and Wang's outward sincerity and generous, spirited revolutionary statements were convincing. In keeping with his naive way of thinking about the implementation of the Comintern's instructions, it is quite possible that Roy did not see the change in Wang's attitude and thus hoped to perform some miracles through the person of Wang. He might also have thought that by his lone action he could prove the correctness of his own views and the incorrectness of the views of Borodin and the others.

But Wang Ching-wei's reaction was beyond Roy's expectations. Wang pointed out to him that the content of the telegram violated the Sun-Joffe Declaration, because this declaration clearly stated that the Communist organization and even the soviet system were in fact not applicable in China; whereas this telegram wanted China to go Communist. Wang also circulated his copy among the important leaders around him and indicated that this was not the KMT failing to carry out alliance with the Soviet Union and toleration of the Communists, but rather it was the Comintern going back on its promise and having "the diabolical plot of annihilating the Kuomintang."[45]

When this strange action of Roy's was brought up for discussion at the Political Bureau of the CC of the CCP, we were very indignant with him. Some took the Comintern to task for sending such an ignorant person as Roy to direct the Chinese revolution. Some pointed out that Roy had messed everything up. Some held that Roy's action was either foolhardiness in the extreme or willful rebellion. We felt that making a public defense of the telegram would lead to a sudden split that we were not prepared for; and this was not what the Comintern wanted.

After this incident Roy, Voitinsky, and some others disappeared from Wuhan. Perhaps Moscow urgently telegraphed them to leave Wuhan at once and let Borodin deal with everything. But Borodin also appeared despondent and declared that he would go to Lushan for a rest. He also told us that Moscow would send other representatives to direct the work of the CCP.

Dealt such a blow, the CC of the CCP was hard-pressed to know how to cope with the situation. Pessimism and despair increased. Moscow had not replied to our request to postpone implementation of the telegraphic order of June 1, nor did it issue any directive on how we should explain Roy's strange action to outsiders. It seemed to realize that what it had expected of the Wuhan leftists, whether in theory or in practice, had turned out to be a joke. The pitiable infantilism of its representative Roy had provided people with a weapon, and it had now become difficult to say anything. The CC of the CCP could not find out exactly what decision the Comintern had made, and it could not take any public stand by itself; so it was clearly in the difficult position that any move would bring blame upon itself. On the grounds of health, Chü Ch'iu-pai also indicated his desire to go to Lushan for a rest. Ch'en Tu-hsiu maintained that Moscow had messed things up and could not remedy the situation; so he took a passive attitude. Most of the other members had the sensation of "lingering in a leaky house with a rainstorm raging at night."

By this time a split between the KMT and the CCP seemed only a question of time. The Ma-jih Incident and the attitude of such people as T'ang Sheng-chih had led Wang Ching-wei and others to turn toward expulsion of the Communists; and Roy's strange action provided a very good pretext for doing this. Although Wang Ching-wei had not yet issued the slogan "expel the Communists," the trend was clear in his writings. Actually he was gradually making arrangements.[46] Having obtained concrete evidence, he was in the position to speak with conviction. It seemed now that he was not an appendage of Chiang Kai-shek nor an echo of T'ang Sheng-chih, but that he was fighting for the salvation of the KMT.

The clear expression of Feng Yü-hsiang's attitude of alliance with Chiang against the Communists caused further deterioration in the position of the Wuhan government, and it also forced the leaders of Wuhan to follow in Chiang Kai-shek's footsteps in expelling the Communists. In comparing the policy of peaceful separation from the Communists advocated by Wang with the policy of purging the Communists advocated by

Chiang, one sees that although they were different in method and interpretation, they were the same in that both opposed the Communists.
From the KMT viewpoint, the breakdown of KMT-CCP relations represented a kind of restraint put on the CCP for usurping the authority of
the KMT. From the viewpoint of the CCP, it represented violation by
KMT elements of Dr. Sun Yat-sen's testamentary teaching—an act of
betrayal for the national revolution. Whatever the views held by the
two sides, the first period of KMT-CCP cooperation following the reorganization of the KMT in 1924 had now come to an end.

The overall breakdown of KMT-CCP relations closely followed the
change in the military situation. Nanking, Wuhan, and Feng Yü-hsiang's
army, which had marched from Shensi, combined to launch a three-
pronged attack against the Fengtien Army and scored victory after victory. On May 16 the Ironsides, led by Chang Fa-k'uei, first routed the
right wing of the Fengtien forces at Shang-tsai in Honan, and the Fengtien Army retreated north of Huang Ho. On May 27 Feng Yü-hsiang
occupied Loyang; on June 1 T'ang Sheng-chih occupied Kaifeng; and on
June 2 Chiang Kai-shek occupied Hsuchow.

In the fighting against the Fengtien Army, the Wuhan troops under
T'ang Sheng-chih and Chang Fa-k'uei contributed the most. The Fourth
Army of Chang Fa-k'uei, especially, threw itself into the thick of the
fighting and made the greatest sacrifices to bring about victory over the
Fengtien Army. There were more members of the CCP in Chang Fa-
k'uei's army, and a very large number of them were sacrificed in this
battle. The army of Ho Lung, who was under the control of Chang
Fa-k'uei, included Chou I-ch'un and other members of the CCP, who
engaged in political work to help him; and so Ho also made a considerable contribution to the fighting. However, contrary to the expectations
of Borodin and Galen, the one who reaped the benefits of this was not
Wuhan, but rather Chiang Kai-shek, who was opposed to Wuhan.

The role of the war in Honan was principally to bring Feng Yü-
hsiang's army out from Tungkwan. But the chips held by Feng Yü-hsiang
were actually added to the stake of Chiang Kai-shek, so that the scale
weighing Nanking and Hankow was further out of balance.

Feng Yü-hsiang, who at one time held sway over Peking, was originally the confirmed enemy of Chang Tso-lin of Fengtien, and he had
advocated cooperation within the revolutionary ranks to continue the
Northern Expedition to wipe out Chang Tso-lin. But when he came out
of Tungkwan and got possession of the bases of Honan and other prov-

inces, he felt that the suspicion of being a Bolshevik would not be helpful to his political future and that military strength was the only factor that was reliable. So in making his political selection, it was only to be expected that he would tend to side with Chiang Kai-shek.

In the eyes of Feng Yü-hsiang, Wuhan had become a poor relative, who could not provide his daily needs. On June 1 the most powerful of the Szechwan warlords, Liu Hsiang, assumed the post of director-general of the Fifth-Route Army, to which Chiang Kai-shek had appointed him, and he declared that he would lead an army to attack Wuhan, with Yang Shen as director of operations for the vanguard forces. He also obtained the support of the Kweichow warlord Chou Hsi-ch'eng and others. As to Wuhan, after the revolt of Hsia Tou-yin, the defenses on the upper reaches of the Yangtze had been vacant, and there was now the military threat from Liu Hsiang. On June 6 Chu P'ei-te of Kiangsi, under pressure from Chiang Kai-shek and influenced by the attitude of Wang Ching-wei, carried out the expulsion of CCP members from the province. The Nanchang municipal headquarters of the KMT, the General Trade-Union Council, the peasant association, the student association, and other similar organizations that had come under the influence of the CCP were subjected to search by the army. The Nanchang *Min-kuo Jih-pao* (Republican Daily News), which was operated by members of the CCP, was also closed down. The Wuhan government and the CCP were hit by these blows, coming one after another, and this all the more made Feng Yü-hsiang, who was always sensitive to the political climate, feel that there was no need to share the pains of other people.

On the other hand, the influence of Chiang Kai-shek was rising like the sun at noontime. For example, Yen Hsi-shan, who had occupied Shansi for many years, had always constituted the balance of power in the North. After the Northern Expeditionary forces had occupied Wuhan, his representatives had been traveling back and forth between Nanking and Hankow, to negotiate over his defection to the side of the revolution. On June 6 Yen Hsi-shan accepted the appointment of the Nanking government and assumed the post of Commander-in-Chief of the National Revolutionary Army in the North. He issued a circular telegram expressing allegiance to the Three Principles of the People. This naturally added greatly to the influence of Chiang Kai-shek. And it appeared to Feng Yü-hsiang that Yen Hsi-shan was his most powerful neighbor and that if he should go against this neighbor, the consequences would be serious.

Before he left Tungkwan, Feng Yü-hsiang had not made his stand clear. He had representatives at both Wuhan and Nanking, and he carried out liaison with both centers in the same way. His Wuhan representative was Hsiung Pin, and his Nanking representative was Li Ming-chung. At the time Hsiung Pin had told people in Wuhan, "Whatever we ask from Nanking we get. But when we want something from Wuhan, we do not get it." His principal intention was to show that Chiang could supply Feng with the cash he needed, but that Wuhan was not in a position to do so.

After Feng Yü-hsiang came out of Tungkwan, though now and then such words came from his lips as "Long live the Communist International!" he had actually tended to be anti-Communist. He had been to Moscow for help, and in his difficulties he had received practical aid from the Soviet Union. This was of course necessary for the realization of his personal ambitions. But as times changed, he came to feel that Soviet aid was not only unnecessary, but would actually injure his relations with the outside and give him trouble from within. So he abandoned his revolutionary ideals and switched sides, thus following the natural path of the realist. In this regard Chiang Kai-shek was in the lead, and Feng and Wang Ching-wei merely walked in Chiang's footsteps.

After the victory in the Battle of Honan, the leaders of the Wuhan government had an appointment to meet with Feng Yü-hsiang at Cheng-chow on June 10. The meeting resulted in the promotion of Wuhan's plan for expelling the Communists. Wang Ching-wei's anti-Communist ideas and Feng Yü-hsiang's need to oppose communism were merged into a big current at the meeting, and it burst the dam of KMT-CCP cooperation. Furthermore, Feng Yü-hsiang's contacts with Chiang Kai-shek had started the trend toward a merger between Nanking and Hankow.

The CC of the CCP, realizing how dangerous the situation was, no longer was optimistic about the Chengchow conference. The course being followed by Wang Ching-wei and his group had already become clear, but Feng Yü-hsiang's intentions had not yet been expressed; so I was still thinking about making a final effort to save the situation. I asked the Political Bureau of the CC of the CCP to allow me to make the trip to Chengchow. I explained, "My task is to go to Honan and make some arrangements so that the CCP organization there can exist underground. I shall also try to investigate the status of the Chengchow meeting; and if possible, I hope to influence the meeting so that it won't hurt us too much." The Political Bureau considered my task colossal, but felt there was no harm in my making a try.

On June 8 I boarded a train especially provided for me by the General Trade Union of the Peking-Hankow Railway. The railway had then suffered damage from the war, and there were many obstructions en route. But as I was an old comrade-in-arms of the workers of the Peking-Hankow Railway during the February Seventh Strike, I obtained their special help and was able to travel at greater speed, so that I arrived in Chengchow on the afternoon of June 9. The railway workers had already prepared the office of the Lunghai Railway as my temporary headquarters and had provided me with a guard.

My special train and the train carrying Feng Yü-hsiang's important officers from Loyang reached Chengchow station at the same time. The hall of the Chengchow Station was furnished with only one long table, and more than ten generals, including Chang Chih-chiang, Lu Chung-lin, Sun Liang-ch'eng, Han Fu-chu, and others, sat around it. I was the only person that had arrived from Wuhan. One of Feng's generals said, "Our commander-in-chief really can get things done. See—we have suffered enough in the Northwest, and now we are in Chengchow. It looks as if we may be able to fight our way to Peking for the New Year." Someone else especially mentioned to me that Commander-in-Chief Feng Yü-hsiang was a faithful disciple of the KMT, that he abided by Dr. Sun's policy of alliance with Russia and tolerance of the Communists, that he obeyed the Wuhan government, and so forth. It seemed that they did not know what was stored in the mind of Feng Yü-hsiang.

From my temporary headquarters I at once tried to find the responsible members of the CCP organization in Chengchow to get a better understanding of the local situation. Very soon I met a comrade of the CCP Honan District Committee that had recently come from Loyang. He transmitted to me a verbal message from Comrade Liu Po-ch'eng, who was at the time director of the Political Department in Feng's army. The message said in general that Feng's attitude toward Wuhan was not good and that he tended to favor Chiang of Nanking. He also mentioned that Feng Yü-hsiang had prohibited his subordinates, including Liu Po-ch'eng himself, from carrying on independent activities outside. For this reason it was not convenient for Liu and other comrades to contact the CCP organization in Honan, and Liu had therefore wanted an intermediary to report the fact to the CC of the CCP at Hankow.

Liu Po-ch'eng's information proved that the situation was already very bad. I guessed that if I called personally on Feng Yü-hsiang, whom I had never met, no good would result. And if I looked up Liu Po-ch'eng and Teng Hsiao-p'ing (then deputy director of Feng's Political Department), they would be inconvenienced. So I sent a message to Galen and Teng Yen-ta, expressing my wish to contact them.

On the morning of June 10 I called on Wang Ching-wei at his quarters. There I met T'an Yen-k'ai, Sun Fo, and others that had come for the Chengchow conference. When T'an and Sun saw me, they made some excuse and left. This reflected the fact that relations between KMT and CCP leaders had already become somewhat strained. Wang Ching-wei continued to receive me with every courtesy. He told me that Feng Yü-hsiang was on his way from Loyang by train and that they were planning to meet Feng at the railway station.

I immediately told Wang of my intentions. I pointed out that the Chengchow conference affected the crisis of the Party and the country and his own political future. I advocated strenuous efforts to win Feng's support for Wuhan, as otherwise the future would be unthinkable. The internal problems of Wuhan, such as KMT-CCP relations and the labor and peasant movements, could all be resolved appropriately, and there should not be undue worry over them. If Feng Yü-hsiang had any demands, we should satisfy them in appropriate ways. I hoped that Wang would make an effective statement to get Feng to openly support the legitimacy of the Wuhan government. The form could be a communique from the Chengchow conference, or Wang could convene the Fourth Plenum of the CEC of the KMT and ask Feng to proceed to Wuhan to participate in it, thus showing his sincerity in supporting Wuhan.

Outwardly Wang expressed enthusiastic agreement with my proposals, especially with regard to winning the support of Feng Yü-hsiang. He also seemed interested in my reiteration of the support of the CCP for the Wuhan government. But at times his statements were ambiguous. He dared not believe in Feng's support for Wuhan. He stated that many Russian advisers had been at Feng's side over a long period and should have been able to influence Feng's attitude. If the Russian advisers could not do so, it meant that Feng had his own intentions and that no matter how much he (Wang) talked, it would be useless. But he told me clearly that he was still willing to try and that he would transmit my views to T'an and Sun for discussion.

The participants in the Chengchow conference, in addition to Feng Yü-hsiang, included Wang Ching-wei, T'an Yen-k'ai, Hsu Ch'ien, Sun Fo, and Ku Meng-yü, all from Wuhan. Generals from the front included T'ang Sheng-chih, Chang Fa-k'uei, Teng Yen-ta, and the Russian adviser General Galen. From the very opening of the conference, the situation was not optimistic. The leaders from Wuhan, including Wang Ching-wei, all aired their grievances before Feng. Their talks were all concerned with Wuhan's financial difficulties and the "troubles" created by the CCP and the workers and peasants. Invisibly Feng was elevated to the position of an arbitrator, and it seemed that these poor children from Wuhan were appealing to the great Marshal Feng to give them relief. There was no semblance of an effort to win Feng over to support of Wuhan.

Teng Yen-ta, who was running about in different parts of the Wuhan area, was a leading KMT leftist at the time. He had become dissatisfied with Wang's recent views and felt that Wang's criticism of the Comintern on the grounds that the June 1 telegraphic order was an attempt to eliminate the KMT was making a mountain out of a molehill. He was very anxious to maintain the Wuhan situation, and he had spoken to Wang about preserving Dr. Sun's three major policies; but Wang did not pay much attention to his words. Teng saw the situation for himself at the Chengchow conference and became all the more disappointed. A confidential secretary of Teng's told me on June 11 that Teng had said that in order to cater to Feng's whims, Wang Ching-wei had expressed many anti-Communist views at the meeting and that Teng only hoped that Feng could respect Wuhan and his own status. Feng, however, in addition to enjoying the anti-Communist views, seemed to hold Wuhan in contempt. Under such circumstances, it seemed that the expulsion of Communists was a natural outcome. Teng wanted to return to Wuhan to attend to the post-mortem.

My last political negotiation with Wang Ching-wei was thus a failure. I had no more hopes for the Chengchow conference. Except for making some emergency arrangements about the work of the CCP Honan District Committee, I had no more work to do in Chengchow. So without waiting for the close of the Chengchow conference, I hurriedly returned to Wuhan on the evening of June 11. On my return journey I reminisced about my contacts with Dr. Sun Yat-sen and the tragicomical acts I had experienced during these past years of KMT-CCP cooperation; and I regretted more and more that the revolutionary Three Principles of the People and the Three Major Policies had now been abandoned by the faithful disciples of Dr. Sun.

On my return to Wuhan a meeting of the Political Bureau of the CC of the CCP was held; and basing my opinion on what I had learned in Chengchow, I said that the time had come for us to withdraw from the KMT. What we had to consider now was whether there should be a peaceful withdrawal or a withdrawal in the form of an open split. I felt that we could no longer have illusions about the upper strata of the KMT leftists. But with reference to the large number of middle- and lower-level elements of the leftists, I felt that we should continue to have links with them in order to win their support. Borodin and the other members of the Political Bureau, while not expressing opposition to my proposal, nevertheless felt that we should wait for complete clarification of the results of the Chengchow meeting and also for receipt of Moscow's concurrence before we made a decision.

Wang Ching-wei and his party returned to Wuhan on June 13. They exuded an air of optimism and said that the results of the Chengchow conference were very good and that Feng Yü-hsiang supported Wuhan. What was publicly announced included the return to Wuhan of the armies of T'ang Sheng-chih and Feng Yü-hsiang and the takeover of defenses in Honan by Feng Yü-hsiang. Although the Wuhan government officially announced the organization and personnel of the provincial governments of Honan, Shensi, and Kansu, they were nevertheless all placed under the control of Feng Yü-hsiang in his position of chairman of the Political Council Branch for the North, including Honan, Shensi, and Kansu provinces. The full details of the conference were kept secret, and we did not have access to the full story.

In reality, Wang Ching-wei and his colleagues were actively working on their program of expelling the Communists. The news was released that Borodin had been relieved of his duties as adviser by the Central Political Council of the KMT.[47] Since March of that year, when Chiang Kai-shek had openly expressed his desire to expel Borodin, stories of his dismissal or resignation had circulated; and now they had been translated into reality. Borodin himself faced this development very calmly; and on the grounds that he wanted to save his wife, who was still detained in Peking, he declared that he could not leave China immediately. Actually, in his role as the agent of Moscow, he was making some final preparations and was also awaiting the arrival of a new agent from Moscow.

When we learned of the meeting on June 19 between Feng Yü-hsiang and Chiang Kai-shek in Hsuchow, we felt this could have been one of the results of secret understandings reached at the Chengchow conference. It was possible that Wang Ching-wei and the others were seeking a compromise with Chiang through the arbitration of Feng Yü-hsiang, or at least that Wang Ching-wei had prior knowledge of the development. Although Wang kept things closely to himself, he did say that he had not expected the meeting between Feng and Chiang.

A few days later the facts about the Hsuchow conference gradually reached Wuhan, and the telegram that Feng had sent to the Wuhan government became known to the outside world little by little. Later it was proved that Feng had sent a telegram to the Wuhan leaders on June 21.[48] Its contents were generally as follows: the views of the Chengchow conference were summed up, and great dissatisfaction was expressed over the acts of the Communist elements in Wuhan. It had been decided that Borodin, who had already been relieved of his post, should return home. All of the members of the National government at Wuhan, except for those who would take trips abroad to rest, should be merged into a single body with those members then at Nanking, thus reuniting the party and the government. This decision had been communicated to the Nanking leaders, who unanimously expressed their agreement. Wang, T'an, and the others were requested to make their decisions quickly. T'ang Sheng-chih was requested to transfer his troops to Chengchow to assist in the Northern Expedition. This, therefore, represented victory for Chiang and the surrender of Wuhan; it also was a clear indication of Feng's anti-Communist attitude.

On learning of the happenings of the Chengchow conference, Moscow had telegraphed orders to Borodin to adopt appropriate measures of concession to avert the danger of having the Communists expelled from Wuhan. On June 20 the CC of the CCP issued an eleven-point political manifesto.[49] The main points were: recognition of the leadership of the KMT in the national revolution; all CCP members participating in the work of governments at all levels did so as members of the KMT; to reduce difficulties in the political situation, members of the CCP could withdraw from the government at any time; labor and peasant organizations should accept the leadership and control of the KMT; demands of workers and peasants must not exceed the decisions of the KMT nor the scope of law and order, but the KMT should still protect the labor and peasant organizations and their interests; in accordance with the principles of the KMT, the people could be armed, but the armed forces of workers and peasants should be trained and controlled by the government; the Wuhan Picket Corps could be reduced or incorporated into the regular army; workers' picket corps must not interfere with judicial and administrative matters, and must not summarily arrest, try, or punish anybody by such measures as parading people in the streets; and so forth. This manifesto was drafted by Borodin on the basis of Moscow's orders, and it was passed at a meeting of the Political Bureau of the CC of the CCP. This was the way in which Moscow corrected its telegraphic order of June 1; and it also seemed to be the final limit in the policy of concession.

The CC of the CCP insisted that members of the Party implement this declaration explicitly and also persuaded the masses of workers and peasants to abide by revolutionary discipline. But these efforts could not alter the outcome of the split between the KMT and the CCP.

Wang Ching-wei was now busy summoning military and governmental leaders to meet and discuss concrete steps for expelling the Communists. Sun Fo and others issued statements directly attacking the labor and peasant movements for their continued encroachments upon the interests of industry and commerce, branding them counterrevolutionary acts; and it seemed that any demand for reform made by the masses of workers and peasants was inappropriate. In dealing with the destruction of labor and peasant forces in Hunan, besides vesting full authority in T'ang Sheng-chih to handle the situation, the Wuhan government adopted an attitude of indifference, but strictly banned illegal acts by workers and peasants. After T'ang Sheng-chih's troops had returned from Honan to Wuhan, the rumor spread more and more that the army would directly restrain the CCP and the labor and peasant organizations in Wuhan.

On June 28 another Ma-jih incident was brewing in Hankow and Hanyang. At the emergency meeting of the Political Bureau of the CC of the CCP, Borodin first pointed out that the situation was extremely serious and that it was necessary for the workers' picket corps in Wuhan to choose between voluntary surrender of arms and preparation for resistance. His own inclination was in favor of the voluntary surrender of arms. Ts'ai Ho-sen spoke against such a voluntary surrender by the workers, maintaining that it was not an act typical of Communists. Chou En-lai maintained that most of the little more than one thousand rifles of the Wuhan workers' picket corps were old weapons and not worth too much attention; and so he advocated surrender. The other members also felt there was no good policy other than voluntary surrender; and so the decision was made.

Chou En-lai then directed Ch'en Keng, the commander of the Workers' General Picket Corps of Wuhan, to surrender the weapons of the Corps to Li P'in-hsien, garrison commander of Wuhan, who thus peacefully occupied the major trade unions in Wuhan. Because of this incident, the CC of the CCP was later condemned by the Comintern for being guilty of "shameful opportunism." But actually it was Moscow's agent Borodin who proposed the measure; and Borodin had acted in accordance with the principles of Moscow's directive calling on him to cope with the situation as best he could. The majority of the members of the CC of the CCP were dissatisfied with this decision. Although they were not as indignant as Ts'ai Ho-sen, they felt they had been forced by circumstances to make this decision, and their inward suffering was very noticeable.

Early in July Borodin informed the CC of the CCP that the Comintern had called on Su Chao-cheng and T'an P'ing-shan to withdraw from the National government in protest. It seemed that Moscow felt that with the growing suppression of the labor and peasant movements by the Wuhan government, it would be rather awkward for members of the CCP to remain in such a government and share responsibility along with the perpetrators of the suppression. The CCP Political Bureau immediately accepted this directive. Most of us felt that this was one act that had some reason for being endorsed.

The CC of the CCP did not have time to discuss fully the way in which the two should withdraw from the government, since it felt that the withdrawal itself was a protest against the KMT. But, unexpectedly, T'an and Su differed in the way they chose to act. T'an resigned on the grounds of illness, and in his letter of resignation he even mentioned his "inability to put the peasant movement on the right track." Su Chao-cheng, however, frankly indicated that he could not promote the welfare of the workers, and so he did not want to carry on. At the time we already felt that T'an's expression was too weak. Later the Comintern also criticized T'an for not acting in accordance with its directive and stated this was an expression of opportunism.

On July 13 the CC of the CCP issued a declaration[50] condemning the Wuhan authorities. This was the signal for the CCP to rise in resistance, because its policy of making concessions had reached a dead end. This declaration pointed out, "The political situation during the past few months has greatly disappointed all revolutionary elements in China. . . . The CEC of the KMT and the National government only serve the reactionary army officers who rose from the ranks of local bullies and evil gentry . . . and oppose the interests of the great majority of the Chinese people as well as Sun Yat-sen's fundamental principles and policies." And so it solemnly declared that the CCP "forever struggles for the interests of the broad masses of workers, peasants, soldiers, intellectuals, and petty bourgeoisie and absolutely refrains from taking responsibility for the current policies of the CEC of the KMT."

Another reason for the CCP issuing this declaration was because of criticism by the Comintern that T'an P'ing-shan's letter of resignation did not truly represent the wishes of the CCP, and so this declaration would remedy the defect. As a matter of fact, the actual function of this declaration was to hasten the arrival of the overall split between the KMT and the CCP.

On July 15 the Wuhan CEC of the KMT decided to convene a plenum of the CEC to discuss the expulsion of the Communists and at the same time to adopt a resolution to restrain the words and deeds of CCP members which violated the principles of the KMT. On July 16 the CEC of the KMT issued a declaration[51] accusing the Comintern's June 1 telegraphic order of being "tantamount to a basic injury to the life of our Party" and saying that withdrawal of CCP members from the National government and the CCP declaration of July 13 had undermined the KMT's "policy of tolerance of Communists." On July 18 Soong Ch'ing-ling (Madame Sun Yat-sen) issued a statement opposing Wuhan's acts against the CCP, maintaining that they were in violation of the principles and policies of Dr. Sun and declaring that she would not assume any responsibility for them. This expression on the part of Madame Sun may not have been without effect in the later development of the Chinese political situation, but at the time it did not result in easing the expulsion of the Communists.

After this, the curtain on the drama of the split between the KMT and the CCP was raised by Wang Ching-wei. On July 23 the KMT at Wuhan published the following resolutions of its Political Council: (1) All members of the Communist Party that also hold membership in our Party [KMT] and have duties in the Party headquarters at all levels, the government at all levels, and in the National Revolutionary Army should immediately announce their withdrawal from the Communist Party, as otherwise their duties will all be suspended; (2) during the period of the national revolution, members of the Communist Party cannot engage in activities detrimental to the national revolution and cannot use the name of our Party in doing the work of the Communist Party; and (3) members of our Party cannot join another party without the permission of the CEC of the Party, and a violator shall be dealt with as a betrayer of the Party. On July 24 Wang Ching-wei sent a telegram in reply to Feng Yü-hsiang, stating that "the Chinese Communist Party and Borodin have been dealt with, and we are willing to move the capital to Nanking and carry out the merger of Nanking and Hankow."

These happenings were the major events in the gradual trend toward an overall split in relations between the KMT and the CCP, with the Chengchow conference as the key to developments.

During the drastic turn of events surrounding the expulsion of Communists by the KMT at Wuhan, the internal ranks of the CCP suffered such heavy blows that a state of collapse and division immediately followed, and the Party nearly disintegrated. After Roy had shown Wang Ching-wei the June 1 telegram from the Comintern, the Political Bureau of the CC of the CCP, sensing the seriousness of the situation, wanted to avoid the least dissension within its ranks. The directives of the Comintern were complied with in all matters whether large or small. But we were all people who had our own views, and under the restraint of the Comintern, we could not help suffering from the pain of not being able to pour forth our accumulated grievances. And so, pessimistic and despondent, some resorted to active struggle, and some sought individual ways to escape the dilemma.

During the critical period, when KMT-CCP relations were on the brink of collapse, the Comintern had consistently wanted the CCP to stay within the KMT. On June 20 the declaration of the CC of the CCP only stated that members of the CCP could withdraw from the government at any time and did not touch upon the question of withdrawal from the KMT. Early in July, when members of the CCP did withdraw from the National government, the Comintern still wanted the CCP to remain in the KMT, but did not give any instructions on how the CCP should cope with the situation if the KMT should proceed directly with expelling the Communists. Why did it want this? Did it want the CCP to join forces with some remnant leftists to put up the standards of the KMT and Sun Yat-sen in opposition to Wang Ching-wei and the other rebels? Or did it want the CCP to pay an even greater price in concessions to check Wang Ching-wei's act of expelling the Communists? The Comintern had never explained.

We felt that the intention of the Comintern in giving these directives was to demand that the CCP remain within the KMT, without consideration for success or failure, so that Wang Ching-wei and his colleagues would not find it convenient to expel the Communists all at once. But we held that this was a one-sided love affair, for Wang Ching-wei and his cohorts would definitely not hold off because of this. There were also some among us who felt that in calling on the CCP to do as it directed, the Comintern wanted to prevent having to evacuate all Soviet Russians from China—an action that would further aggravate the unfavorable international image of the Soviet Union. Even if this result could not be achieved, the Soviet advisers would at least be able to return home in safety. Therefore we felt that Moscow's principal concern was for the position of the Soviet Union and not for the current urgent problem or the future of the CCP.

When the CC of the CCP was forced to issue its declaration on July 13, we all felt the impending arrival of the tempest. Although by that time Wang Ching-wei had freely allowed certain reactionary officers to oppress the CCP and labor and peasant organizations everywhere, he nevertheless still paid lip service to the "peaceful expulsion of the Communists." Now that the CCP had made this expression of resistance, it was easy for Wang to change immediately to measures of open oppression. So we adopted emergency measures to enable the central organization of the CCP to safely go underground. In considering what policies should be adopted in the future at the meeting of the Political Bureau of the CC, Borodin no longer dared to make drastic proposals, and this increased the uncertainty of the CC of the CCP.

On the evening of July 13 Borodin and Ch'ü Ch'iu-pai quietly left Wuhan for Lushan. I had no prior knowledge of this move of theirs; apparently they did not tell anybody about it. On the morning of the fourteenth I went to Borodin's residence. There I saw Teruni, and only then did I know that Borodin and Ch'ü Ch'iu-pai had left. Teruni was sorting out the various documents of Borodin, to close up this office of the adviser. I had known Teruni very well, for he had all along been serving as adviser to Teng Yen-ta of the General Political Department and was also an important assistant to Borodin and General Galen. Because of this, during such a critical period he was in a position to wind up the unfinished affairs of Borodin.

Teruni was a military man with a literary flair, but at this time he also showed some confusion of mind and was unable to control himself. In a hasty manner he talked about his personal views. He advocated supporting Teng Yen-ta as leader of the KMT leftists in order to openly oppose Wang Ching-wei, who had betrayed the revolution. I told him that I had not seen Teng Yen-ta for several days and that it was rumored that he wanted to leave Wuhan. Under the circumstances I did not think that he would come out at this time to take drastic action. I went on to explain that from a strategic point of view, we were not going underground. The one who could influence the Fourth Army was no longer Teng Yen-ta, but rather Wang Ching-wei. If we immediately took to supporting Teng and opposing Wang openly, not only would our own safety be jeopardized, but CCP members in the Fourth Army would also be open to immediate and unavoidable attack.

Teruni was very impatient with my words and he questioned me, "Are you still a Communist?" I had to explain to him, "Teng Yen-ta is fully recognized by us as a leftist personality with capabilities, and Wang Ching-wei is generally discredited by us. Our question today is how to take proper steps in the struggle. In other words, is the CCP to work independently, or is it to work by the method of backing a KMT leftist leader? But no matter how precarious the circumstances are, whether or not Teng Yen-ta is willing to come forth and take drastic action, or whether there are KMT leftists willing to struggle with us, the CCP must continue its struggle."

It was only then that Teruni had no more to say. Nevertheless, his outburst was a considerable stimulant to my feelings at the time. I was thinking of our efforts during the past stage in opening up virgin territory with so much hardship and of how these efforts were being nullified by the policies of Moscow and other subjective and objective factors. Would Moscow, who was leading us, place responsibility for the failure entirely on our heads? I was in a dilemma.

The hurried departure of Borodin indicated that he could no longer influence the Wuhan political situation and had to attend to the various formalities connected with returning home. But it also implied that he was intentionally avoiding the crisis of the split between the KMT and the CCP. Ch'ü Ch'iu-pai, who was closest to Borodin, had left with him for Lushan because his health was poor and he needed a rest. But Ch'ü's departure at such a critical moment, without taking leave of his comrades, generally led people to suspect that he was shirking his responsibility. The facts later proved that he was principally engaged in discussing with Borodin the question of reorganizing CCP leadership for the future.

After Roy and Voitinsky had left, Borodin had been especially rigid in complying with the directives from Moscow. During this period he established close relations with Soong Ch'ing-ling, Teng Yen-ta, and Eugene Ch'en, in an attempt to develop a new leftist clique that would check the action of Wang Ching-wei and others in expelling the Communists. He also was well aware that it was impossible to have Teng Yen-ta and the others replace Wang Ching-wei. Had there been such a possibility, he perhaps would not have hesitated to plunge into one more new adventure. So his object in establishing close contact with Madame Sun, Teng, and Ch'en was still passive in nature; but it showed that he was inwardly depressed and that he no longer possessed his former high-spirited manner of talking freely. His departure also interrupted communications between the CCP and Moscow for a time.

On July 14 Ch'en Tu-hsiu hid himself in a secret residence and no longer appeared in public. When I left Teruni, I went to see Ch'en, but he was no longer to be found. His secretary, Comrade Jen (pardon me for no longer remembering his given name), told me that it was not wise for Ch'en to appear in public and that he would undertake to make all contacts. This scene of a crowd dispersing at the end of a show made me feel very bad. I indignantly said, "Is the CCP to be dissolved like this? I for one will not be resigned to such a fate."

On July 15 Ch'en Tu-hsiu sent a simple letter to the CC of the CCP, expressing his inability to continue his work and asking to be relieved of his duties as secretary.[52] According to what Comrade Jen told me, Ch'en held that the split between the KMT and the CCP had put an end to the national revolution. The Comintern had consistently refused to allow the CCP to withdraw from the KMT, and so there really was no way out. He himself had exhausted his efforts and could therefore only resign and take the blame. He hoped that I and the other comrades would continue the struggle. I thereupon asked Comrade Jen to tell Ch'en that at such a critical moment it was very inappropriate for him to adopt such a passive attitude.

From what Ch'en said at the time and later, his depression had reached its lowest point about July 12.[53] Reminiscing, he said that he had found that the so-called leftist military and political leaders of the KMT were one after another opposing the Communists and that large numbers of comrades and of the labor and peasant masses were being killed. Within the CCP, divergence in views grew more and more drastic. All of this seemed to be the result of the mistaken formula that called for the CCP to stay inside the KMT in order to combine all revolutionary forces. The CCP had endured a great deal of humiliation, but beyond issuing a declaration to give vent to some accumulated indignation, it had no practical measures for saving itself from the fate of destruction. This no doubt had made Ch'en feel that the national revolution was finished and that it would be difficult to get it back on its feet. Before him was an expanse of darkness, and so he himself would have to resort to the course of giving up his position to more capable persons.

When Ch'en Tu-hsiu, Ch'ü Ch'iu-pai, and Borodin almost simultaneously left their positions, I felt that I could not shirk the responsibility of strengthening this precarious situation. I summoned Chou En-lai, Ts'ai Ho-sen, Li Li-san, and other members of the CC to a meeting of the Political Bureau. I declared painfully, "At this critical moment between life and death, let those who cannot stand the strain go for a rest, but we must continue to struggle. Even if the Comintern does not have a representative at our meetings, or if it does not care for us anymore, we must not despair, but must continue to work on independently." These words of mine aroused the same feelings in all of those present. We immediately decided that the Political Bureau of the CC should be moved temporarily to Wuchang, because Wuchang was garrisoned by the leftist Fourth Army and it would be safer to arrange dispersal from there in an emergency. Our primary tasks were to have organs at all levels go underground; to intensify the dispersal of Party members, sending the comrades assembled at Wuhan to different areas; and to control the labor and peasant forces, in preparation for resistance against the reactionary oppression of the KMT.

The political situation at Wuhan was very delicate. After the Hsuchow conference, Chiang Kai-shek on the one hand applied pressure against Wuhan through Feng Yü-hsiang, and on the other hand transferred forces from Nanking to proceed up the Yangtze, striking the pose of using armed forces to settle the Wuhan problem. Faced with this situation, in addition to attending energetically to expulsion of the Communists, Wang Ching-wei still worked to preserve his traditional status within the KMT, clamoring loudly for the launching of an eastern expedition against Chiang. And so the troops of Wuhan were still moving toward the lower reaches of the Yangtze. The Fourth Army (including Yeh T'ing's troops) was the army on the right flank of the river in the anti-Chiang forces, and it was moving toward Nanchang. In implementing Wang's policy of peaceful expulsion of the Communists, the various armies in Wuhan acted with varying degrees of strictness. Most of T'ang Sheng-chih's troops applied cruel measures in opposing the Communists; the Third Army of Chu P'ei-te carried out the "ceremonious dispatch of the Communists out of his territory"; the Second and Sixth armies declared that they would not endanger the lives of the Chinese Communists; while the Fourth Army hinted that it would protect the Chinese Communists and would not allow them to be harmed.

The expulsion of the Communists at Wuhan on July 15 led to marked disintegration in the ranks of both the KMT and the CCP. Wang Ching-wei attempted to break up the CCP; and he used the theme of peaceful expulsion of the Communists to further the split in the Communist ranks. Most of the KMT leftists went along with Wang Ching-wei, and they exploited their friendly relations with the Chinese Communists to do their best to lure them into leaving the CCP and becoming KMT members, pure and simple. Among the leftists there were a few people who felt that abandoning Dr. Sun's testamentary teachings and expelling the Communists would after all be detrimental to the revolution, and they expressed pessimism and despair. Some even were prepared to continue cooperating with the Chinese Communists as individuals in order to further the revolution. As to the CCP, the leadership of the CC had been shaken up, and some of its members showed their uncertainty and indecision. Some became inactive, some escaped, and there were also some who defected to the side of the KMT.

But the CCP had after all been steeled. Most of its members, especially those who formed the backbone of the Party, would not bow their heads in the face of oppression. They held the action of Wang Ching-wei in contempt, and they criticized him for being a hypocrite who betrayed the revolution. They had long been dissatisfied with the policy of the Comintern, and they also blamed the CC of the CCP for its inefficiency. They were sincere revolutionists and took pride in having contributed their bit to the national revolution, though they also were pained because their efforts did not achieve results. They did not despair, and many even wanted to disregard success or failure and to go forward in a hard and determined fight. At a time when the organization had been split and broken up, it was due to encouragement from these spirited elements that I, Chou En-lai, and the others could place safety and danger, success and failure, out of our thoughts and continue the struggle to preserve the life of the CC of the CCP. Later the insurrection led by Ch'ü Ch'iu-pai could also trace its source to this spirit of putting up a stubborn fight.

We planned measures for continuing the revolution. The labor movement in Wuhan had been destroyed. It was no longer possible for the General Alliance to launch a strike. Much less could we in Wuhan lead a political coup that could overthrow the Wang regime. The peasant movements in Hunan, Hupeh, and Kiangsi had been subjected to the combined attack of reactionary armies and the forces of local bullies and evil gentry, and they had also been split and broken up. The armed forces of peasants that remained had been concentrated in the more desolate areas, where they only carried out some feeble resistance. The reliable capital remaining to us consisted only of the division commanded by Yeh T'ing and the Independent Regiment of Chou Shih-ti; and these troops were on their way to Nanchang for transfer. We treasured greatly this bit of capital, and we hoped to use it as the nucleus which, coordinated with the peasants' armed forces in different localities, would carry our standard of resistance.

With the staff members scattered, the CC of the CCP, which temporarily moved to Wuchang, was considerably decimated. Only Chou En-lai and I were actually in charge of affairs. We decided to discharge our duties as members of the Standing Committee of the CC. Ts'ai Ho-sen was ill and could not undertake heavy work; furthermore he was preparing to go to Shanghai secretly. Such important members of the Party as Li Li-san, T'an P'ing-shan, Lin Po-ch'ü, Fan T'ai-ying, and Wu Yu-chang had gone to Nanchang. Large numbers of CCP members and even some KMT leftists that still cooperated with the CCP gathered in Nanchang. The object of the trip for some was to take advantage of the cover provided by Chou Shih-ti in order to proceed via Nanchang to other areas to start to work underground, while for others it was in order to be hidden among the troops of Yeh T'ing in readiness to carry out resistance when necessary.

Our work was intense and heavy, and our difficulties were numerous. Funds were lacking, and we were busy urging our comrades that held posts in the government to resort to all means to procure some cash for use in dispersing members of the Party. A large number of CCP comrades had to proceed to different localities within a few days, according to their own choice, the needs for work, and their ability to exist underground. The tasks of these people and their communications and other problems had to be solved for each one individually.

Mao Tse-tung exhibited his fighting spirit and voluntarily chose Hunan, where he assumed responsibility for the leadership of the armed forces of the peasants. We had originally assigned him to Szechwan, chiefly because of concern for his safety and also because we considered Szechwan an area of great possibilities, particularly with reference to developing the peasant movement. But this "major Communist criminal," who was a native of Hunan, wanted to brave the danger in going to Hunan, because he was not resigned to an abrupt end for the peasant movement that he had led. We very gladly accepted his request to go to Hunan. This was the starting point of his forced sojourn at Ching-kang-shan at a later date.

Chou En-lai was a tireless worker who did not talk much. He dealt very calmly with complex affairs, both day and night. He took on both work and blame, disregarding criticism. He was responsible for handling most of the work connected with dispersing comrades. This period also marked the beginning of his being treated with respect by comrades in general and of the growth in importance of his status.

Most of our time was spent in holding conversations with comrades. The emergency dispersal could not help making these comrades feel that they were fleeing to escape. I felt that it was very necessary to raise their spirits. I pointed out to my comrades individually that although the CCP had suffered a reverse, it still had a victorious future. The KMT had abandoned the revolutionary ideals of Dr. Sun, and it would be split up into numerous sects. In the future there might emerge a number of KMT factions identified as the Wang clique, the Hu clique, the Chiang clique, and so forth. The militarists of the KMT would suffer the same fate as the Peiyang warlords by continuing to engage in chaotic civil wars; they were incapable of fulfilling such revolutionary tasks as unification of China, opposition to imperialism, and relief of the people's sufferings. As long as we accepted the lesson of defeat, were united around the CC of the Party, and continued our efforts, we could shoulder the revolutionary tasks and see them through to victory.

Because of our tireless efforts during those few days, the general morale within the Party was gradually stabilized, and it seemed that the spirit of the CCP had revived and was growing rapidly. Moreover, the work of our CC became more orderly, and everything could be pushed forward according to schedule.

So Chou En-lai brought forward a recommendation for an aggressive offensive. He pointed out that at the moment a large number of comrades were moving with the Fourth Army. Should the generals of the Fourth Army, such as Chang Fa-k'uei, be forced by circumstances to turn against the Communists, then our comrades in the Fourth Army would be completely trapped. He felt that rather than being controlled by others, it would be better for us to take the initiative and have others under our control. He said he had just received a letter from Li Li-san and others in Kiukiang, advocating the launching of an armed insurrection in the Nanchang-Kiukiang area. Chou accordingly supported an uprising in Nanchang which would be launched by the troops of Yeh T'ing and others and would join up with the masses of workers and peasants in the Hunan, Hupeh, and Kiangsi areas to develop a center opposed to both Wuhan and Nanking. He thought that Nanchang was an area that could be attacked from four sides and could not be easily defended; and so he advocated that the army be transferred to the East River region of Kwangtung. Using this area as a base was the main point in Chou En-lai's proposition, and he adhered resolutely to this point. He had worked in the Chaochow and Swatow area and was more familiar with conditions in that region. He maintained that in that area the enemy force was smaller, the peasant movements in the Hai-feng and Lu-feng counties were very effective, and moreover that Swatow was a seaport through which contact could be established with the Soviet Union. He asked the CC to decide immediately on the name to be used for the Nanchang insurrection, its political platform, and certain important strategies—especially the strategy for winning the cooperation of friendly armies and the KMT leftists. He also earnestly asked us to make plans for mobilizing the labor and peasant forces in Hunan, Hupeh, Kiangsi, and the East River region of Kwangtung, so that they would rise at the time of the insurrection, and for requesting that the Comintern quickly supply arms and other means of support via Swatow. All these things were needed in order to win a victory. In the eyes of Chou En-lai, supplies from Moscow would be the most important.

Time was pressing, and the matter could not be discussed at length. The two of us, as the Standing Committee of the CC, decided that Chou En-lai should proceed rapidly to Kiukiang and Nanchang to organize a Front Line Committee, with Chou En-lai as secretary and T'an P'ing-

shan, Li Li-san, Fan T'ai-ying, and Yeh T'ing as members. On the basis
of the plans brought forward by Chou En-lai, described above, the committee would deal with everything as the occasion demanded. Chou
En-lai left for Nanchang on about the twentieth. I was left in charge of
the CC of the CCP. This was another important action taken by the CC
of the CCP without the prior concurrence of Moscow.

The situation at the time was too delicate to be understood. With
regard to the generals, after victory had been won in the second stage of
the Northern Expedition and T'ang Sheng-chih and Chang Fa-k'uei had
returned to Wuhan with their armies from Honan, the idea of returning
to Kwangtung was secretly brewing among the leftists, especially those
who were natives of Kwangtung. Speaking of the group of generals in
the Fourth Army, most of them were depressed at heart and were somewhat like Shih Ta-kai during the period of internal strife in the Taiping
Rebellion. Most of these generals were natives of Kwangtung and had
joined the revolution at a relatively early date, imbued with the revolutionary tradition of Dr. Sun Yat-sen. During both of the stages of the
Northern Expedition, they had exerted the greatest effort and contributed
the greatest merit, so much so that the Fourth Army earned the name of
the Ironsides. They now witnessed the split of the revolutionary camp
into four or five sections. Feng Yü-hsiang and T'ang Sheng-chih smacked
richly of warlordism. Chiang Kai-shek, Li Chi-shen, and others were
acting in a ridiculous way. Everything was a thorn in their sides. They
themselves felt like orphaned sons of the revolution, adrift on the ocean,
with no one to rely on and depressed beyond description. The idea of
returning to Kwangtung, in addition to being prompted by homesickness
and negative thinking, was also prompted by the desire to leave the dirty
environment, to undertake first the improvement of the Kwangtung situation and then to seek further developments. This was also the basis of
the proposal at the time for a southern expedition.

For the Fourth Army, the talk about expulsion of the Communists
seemed unnecessary. A few of the generals of that army had membership in the CCP, such as Yeh T'ing and Chou Shih-ti. Most of them had
risen from the ranks of the old Fourth Army and were old comrades-in-
arms of the many generals with membership in the KMT, always fighting
shoulder to shoulder and never revealing the special colors of Communists. The Fourth Army all along had the assistance of the labor and
peasant movements in Hunan and Hupeh, while the excesses of these
movements had not the slightest effect on the dependents of these mili-

tary men from Kwangtung. And so the Fourth Army was not enthusiastic about expelling the Communists, and there were even men who felt that the expulsion of Communists would only weaken the revolutionary forces and would especially impair the combat power of the Fourth Army. There was therefore no necessity to create trouble.

Chang Fa-k'uei was the head of the Fourth Army, and his attitude toward the situation received important attention from the general public. Before the Northern Expedition he was commander of the Twelfth Division of the Fourth Army, and after the first stage of the Northern Expedition he was promoted to commander of the Fourth Army. After the second stage of the Northern Expedition he was further promoted to Commander-in-Chief of the Second Front Army of the National Revolutionary Army. At the time he was young and capable and did not have the flavor of a warlord. He qualified as a model soldier, being both of the revolutionary orthodoxy and also courageous in fighting. So people worshiped him as the hero of the Ironsides. Both the KMT leftists and the Communists respected him highly. He loved and protected his fellow fighters, made no distinction between Communists and non-Communists, and clearly indicated that the Fourth Army would protect the members of the CCP. At the critical period of the expulsion of Communists in Wuhan he expressed support for Wang Ching-wei, and because of this he started to stay away from Teng Yen-ta, who still advocated the toleration of Communists. This seemed to be the force of the mainstream, and he had to support peaceful expulsion of the Communists, but he opposed and would not tolerate acts of killing Communists, and so he stressed talk of protecting them. Although Wang Ching-wei openly declared that he was in favor of the peaceful expulsion of the Communists, people all felt that it would be "peaceful expulsion" in name and "toleration of killings" in fact. And so people began to conjecture about the extent to which Chang would go along with Wang Ching-wei. The Russian advisers that had close relations with Chang, such as General Galen, had already placed considerable confidence in this rare revolutionary military leader and felt that the CCP could and should maintain friendship with him and that there would not be any trouble between the two.

The Nanchang Insurrection, which was planned by Chou En-lai, director of the Military Department of the CC of the CCP, and others, had for its backbone the forces of the Twenty-fourth Division of Yeh T'ing and the Independent Regiment of Chou Shih-ti, both offshoots of

the Fourth Army system. This implied direct conflict with Chang Fa-
k'uei. The theory of taking advance action to restrain the other party
also implied disregard for success or failure—a last gamble and adventure without concern for the consequences. Although General Galen had
not directly opposed this venture, he nevertheless felt that its chances
for success would be greater if we could return to Kwangtung with the
entire Fourth Army led by Chang Fa-k'uei, or even proceed further with
the launching of the so-called southern expedition.[54]

I, Ch'ü Ch'iu-pai, and the others had also never opposed Galen's
views, although we had great doubts about the possibility of realizing
them. We maintained that the best strategy would be to have the troops
of Yeh T'ing and others return to Kwangtung with the entire Fourth
Army; second best would be to stage an insurrection at Nanchang (it
would even be better if we could reduce conflict with Chang Fa-k'uei);
and the worst strategy would be to hold our hands tied above our heads
to await death. This was the reason why General Galen, when the Nanchang insurrection was about to be launched, still officially proposed
that the CC of the CCP plan the return to Kwangtung with Chang Fa-
k'uei's entire Fourth Army.

On July 21 Ch'ü Ch'iu-pai returned to Wuhan from Lushan, and he
immediately brought up the problem of reorganizing the leadership of
the CC of the CCP. In his secret, newly furnished residence in the
French Concession of Hankow, he told me that Borodin and the others
could return to Moscow via the Northwest, which was controlled by
Feng Yü-hsiang, and that the Comintern had sent a new representative
in the person of Lominadze, who would arrive in a day or two. According to what Borodin told Ch'ü, Lominadze was noted as a leftist and
had risen from the ranks of the Young Communist International, but he
did not know about China's conditions. Borodin wanted us to establish
good relations with him.

Following this, Ch'ü Ch'iu-pai told me that during the past few days
he and Borodin had studied and held discussions in the coolness of
Lushan and had decided that since the Chinese revolution had failed,
the question of responsibility had to be settled. Although the CCP had
actually done everything in accordance with the directives of the Comintern, the latter could not be made to bear responsibility for the failure,
because a loss of prestige for Moscow would affect the world revolution,
would abet the Trotskyites in their attack on Stalin, and would also make
members of the CCP lose confidence in the leadership of the Comintern.

To enable the Comintern to continue its leadership of the world revolution in the future, the CC of the CCP had to stand up straight and bear the responsibility, for this would be avoiding the heavier in taking up the lighter burden.

Ch'ü Ch'iu-pai proceeded to state more specifically that if responsibility for the failure were borne by the whole body of the Political Bureau of the CC of the CCP, the leadership of the CC would go bankrupt, and the loss would be too great. To begin with, Ch'en Tu-hsiu committed serious errors during this defeat and had now gone further by adopting the incorrect passive attitude. So it might be well for us to put on this one person the entire responsibility for the failure. We ourselves should take the position of voicing support for the Comintern and opposing Ch'en Tu-hsiu's rightist opportunism. Only thus could we stabilize the leadership of the CC of the CCP. He also told me that Borodin had hoped that he and I could continue to lead the CC of the CCP, having Ch'ü take charge of theoretical research and me take charge of practical operations.

These words of Ch'ü Ch'iu-pai's aroused a very great reaction in me. I felt that it would certainly be a joke if at such a critical juncture, instead of making practical efforts to save the CCP from destruction, we resorted to a battle of wits over the question of responsibility. So I told him indignantly that the policy of the Comintern was the primary cause of this failure and that it would not be something to be proud of if we did not sincerely review the situation, but instead shirked our responsibility. I thought that the entire body of the CC of the CCP should share the responsibility jointly. It would not be just to place all the blame on Ch'en Tu-hsiu alone. Furthermore, comrades in general would look upon us as people without morals, so what prestige would be left for us to continue the leadership?

We talked over this question all night. Besides giving vent to our indignation, we needed to find a solution for this important matter, so that we would know how we should act in the future. I was really aroused and had a notion to pay no more attention to the Comintern and allow the CCP to pursue its own course. Ch'ü was calmer and took many opportunities to bring up difficult issues, pointing out that our efforts were not up to our intentions and that we could not afford to be expelled from or even to stand far away from the Comintern. Ch'ü stressed that his agreement with Borodin was a political necessity that could not be put under the restraint of morals. I did not agree, and I

advocated equal consideration for practical needs and truth and righteousness.

I seemed to have difficulty controlling myself. I felt that I could
not rest until I had poured out my accumulated grievances; nor did I
consider the possible consequences of my words. Our talk covered a
wide range of issues, and naturally there were many words unpleasant
to the ear. After the lapse of so many years, what I can roughly remember now is that the following were the major points of our discussion:
The mistakes in the directives of the Comintern could in no way be
washed clean. CCP comrades often said, "The Communist International
does not understand the China situation." This statement was very true.
As a matter of fact, within the entire circle of communism or even
socialism, from Marx through the present, distant Asia had been unfamiliar. All of Moscow's actions in China were rash, done with a desire
for immediate results and profits, and smacked of speculation and adventure. Based on the viewpoint of world revolution, the Comintern generally wanted to create a big revolution in China in order to attack
imperialism and to give support to the Soviet Union. Naturally it was
not easy for it to reach an appropriate understanding, and it was even
possible that it overlooked what the Chinese revolution needed and could
produce. And so it committed all of the deviations, including "the blind
man riding a blind horse," "producing a vehicle behind closed doors,"
"cutting the feet to fit the shoes," and "pulling up the sapling to enhance
its growth."

These mistakes of the Comintern in giving guidance were principally
expressed in the policy of having the CCP join the KMT. We had all
along been reluctant to become involved in too many issues, and our
dissatisfaction with the guidance of the Comintern was concentrated on
this point of opposition to having the CCP join the KMT. The Comintern should not have discarded so quickly the resolution of the Second
Congress of the CCP, which was based on the guiding principles of
directives from the Comintern and at the same time was so rich in
Chinese flavor. Next, it should not have exploited Dr. Sun Yat-sen's
desire to embrace and lead the CCP, nor should it have taken the opportunity to force the CCP to join the KMT in an all-out manner in an
attempt to fish in troubled waters. And when defects appeared in this
policy, it persisted in repeating the mistake over and over, disregarding
everything else, forcing the CCP to remain within the KMT until the
situation deteriorated to the stage that it was beyond salvaging.

The leadership personnel of the KMT, such as Wang Ching-wei, Chiang Kai-shek, and Hu Han-min, were generally quite zealous in taking up the revolution, and they were deeply imbued with its traditions. They were generally ready to be friends with the Soviet Union or even "look upon Russia as the teacher," but they would not allow Moscow to lead them by the nose. On the road of the national revolution, they were prepared to take the CCP along as a junior member, but they would not permit the CCP to create trouble within the KMT. These truths, once bared, were very obvious. But the heroes of Moscow had to step out of bounds, destroying everything, and single-handedly attempt to "revolutionize the Kuomintang," "ally with the Left to oppose the Right," and "support Wang to overthrow Hu" in order to create "the Whampoa center" and "the revolutionary dictatorship." When things were all messed up, they continued to further "welcome Wang to oppose Chiang." All of these actions on the part of Moscow were either superfluous, bringing trouble to itself, or else were foolish, injuring other people without benefiting itself.

These mistakes were principally rash leftist actions in nature, with their source generally Moscow. Its agents in China, moreover, at different times carried out numerous foolish and silly acts. These mistakes resulted in the sacrifice of the Chinese revolution. The entire KMT revolted sooner or later, and both the domestic and international reactionary forces rose up. The CCP was a bloody mess and was in the situation of "the rat crossing the street, with everybody going after its skin." Under the circumstances, it was impossible to say on what day, what month, and what year it could restore its power. Moreover, at the end of the chase the knife was out, and the counterattack of the reactionaries had now reached the Soviet Union itself. This was the result of a policy of looking forward without protecting the rear and of taking blatantly leftist actions. When things had reached such a state, we had to openly and frankly undertake a self-review to seek the roots of our mistakes as lessons acquired in exchange for fresh blood, or there would truly be no justice under heaven.

We could not say that because direction of the Comintern was incorrect the CC of the CCP had committed no error; much less could we resort to the idea of shirking our responsibility. The major point was that the infantile CCP was immature in every respect, and it had consistently grown up in an atmosphere of being fooled and learning tricks. Mistakes arising out of infantilism could not be totally overlooked, because this would obstruct learning. The inability to learn lessons from defeat was the greatest of all mistakes. Somebody has said that had it not been for the direction of the Comintern, the CCP would not have stood up originally, the Chinese revolution would not have developed with such fanfare, and there would have been more mistakes. This theory is correct, but we cannot use this as an excuse for refusing to review the mistakes in the guidance given by the Comintern. A strict review of the mistakes of the Comintern and the CCP would mean the learning of lessons at the international level as well as within China, so that we could march toward maturity and avoid repeating mistakes.

The leadership of the CC of the CCP also made mistakes that were serious and varied, and we who personally experienced them knew the situation very clearly. It likewise lacked an adequate knowledge of the Chinese revolution; it could not introduce its own proposals; and much less could it influence the decisions of the Comintern with regard to the Chinese question. When it diligently and carefully carried out directives, it could not discover mistakes rapidly. Even when we had independent views, we did not dare to believe in them ourselves, nor could we strive to have our views respected by presenting strong reasoning; so all the time we merely obeyed directives. In the course of the national revolution and the labor and peasant movements, we had committed many mistakes of leftist infantilism. The CC always excused them to a greater or lesser degree, and things were hushed up and allowed to accumulate. This led to the excesses of the labor and peasant movements during the Wuhan period. At the critical period—that is, when Shanghai purged the Communists and Wuhan expelled the Communists—we again showed ourselves weak and ineffective. The result of this was confusion and retreat and even failure to hold the situation together. This was truly the exposure of rightist opportunism.

What we could still take pride in was the loyalty and courageous struggle exhibited by members of the CCP in general toward the Party and the revolution. This was the capital for our comeback, and it had to be treasured and protected in the minutest detail. Take Ch'en Tu-hsiu, for example. He admittedly had committed the most mistakes, so that he could no longer be the leadership core of the CCP, and he deserved reprimand. But his fighting spirit and his services to the CCP could not be obliterated. In strictly reviewing the mistakes of the CCP leadership, we definitely must not impair the glory of the Party. The slightest disregard for right and wrong and the use of trickery would both greatly endanger the CCP. The CCP was like an army, and the Comintern was its general staff. If the army was sacrificed, what point would there be in preserving the general staff? The sacrifice of the CCP would be the greatest loss, and it was definitely not a case of avoiding the more serious issue for the lighter issue.

My uncontrolled talk, which centered around the above-mentioned viewpoints, made Ch'ü Ch'iu-pai, who did not fully agree with my views, feel that I had reason to back me up and was therefore forceful and that my righteous indignation was irresistible. On his depressed and ashen face some signs of reluctance appeared at times, but on the whole he agreed with me. Sometimes he would also touch on his own mistakes, and at other times he, too, felt indignant and made drastic comments. Only the tense situation invisibly restrained us and led us back to reality, to the path of finding a solution to the emergency.

We first decided to move the CC of the CCP back to Shanghai under the utmost secrecy and to convene an emergency meeting of the CC at an opportune time. The work of dispersing CCP members in Wuchang had changed from a state of tension to normality. The Fourth Army was moving down the Yangtze, and the garrison of the city would immediately be turned over to the troops of T'ang Sheng-chih, who was an active anti-Communist. So there was no need to remain in Wuchang. We decided at the time to move the CC back to Hankow, both to confuse people and also to facilitate the return to Shanghai. Emergency arrangements would be made first, to be followed immediately by an emergency meeting of the CC, because the reorganization of the CC could not be delayed.

We two also reached some understanding on the major political questions. I declared that the responsibility for defeat of the revolution would be borne by the CC of the CCP, which would face the issue standing up, and that we definitely would not impair the good relations between the CCP and the Comintern, in order to maintain the prestige of the leadership of the International among members of the CCP. Ch'ü Ch'iu-pai also agreed that we should make a joint statement to the Comintern, for it to use in its review of the experiences and lessons of the Chinese revolution, explaining that deviations had occurred in implementing the concrete policy of KMT-CCP cooperation, and that the strategy used was also not sufficiently flexible. Naturally this was done so that we would profit from our experiences and at the same time lighten the responsibility of the CC of the CCP, so as to arouse a spirit of courageous struggle in the Chinese comrades. As to the reorganization of the CC of the CCP, we agreed that Ch'en Tu-hsiu, having become inactive, could no longer serve as secretary. If the other members of the CC were to continue with their leadership duties, they could definitely not shirk their responsibility but would have to take the blame and carry out self-criticism, swearing to contribute services while under the weight of their guilt. We felt that only by doing this could we satisfy both righteousness and reality, and this would be our common stand in establishing contact with Lominadze, who was due to arrive soon.

We did not anticipate that this conversation would produce a great upheaval, which was to affect the political life of myself and Ch'ü Ch'iu-pai and certain future activities of the CCP. Lominadze later learned my views from the mouth of Ch'ü Ch'iu-pai, and so he treated me as the thorn in his flesh, the number two rightist opportunist after Ch'en Tu-hsiu. Of course Ch'ü Ch'iu-pai should have interpreted my views in presenting them to Lominadze, but exactly what he said was unknown to me. At least he did not express the view that he would share responsibility with me.

What was even worse, my relations with Ch'ü Ch'iu-pai deteriorated after that time. Over the policy of the CCP joining the KMT, our views had always differed. Perhaps my emphasis on righteousness obstructed his realistic ideas, and so he took the initiative in pursuing a course contrary to mine. After that, we two personalities in the CC of the CCP, who ranked only after Ch'en Tu-hsiu, both suffered. I became the oppositionist whom the Comintern was most wary about, and I was attacked repeatedly and continuously until I was ultimately forced to leave. Although Ch'ü Ch'iu-pai gained power for a time, his record was not altogether clean, and moreover he was forced to resort to putschism. Not only did he fail to win confidence, but he was never free from suspicion. This point alone should lead to the conclusion that dictatorship harms everyone on earth.

On July 23 Lominadze arrived in Hankow. That evening he held a conversation with me and Ch'ü Ch'iu-pai. It was the worst conversation in my memory. Lominadze first stated that he was the plenipotentiary of the Comintern, ordered here to correct the many mistakes committed in the past by the personnel of the Comintern and the CC of the CCP in the Chinese revolution. After this he did not ask us about the current situation, but immediately declared that the CC of the CCP had committed the serious error of rightist opportunism and had violated the directives of the Comintern. The International had decided to reorganize the leadership of the CC of the CCP. Ch'en Tu-hsiu could no longer serve as secretary and might even be expelled from the Party. As to the two of us, if we could rid ourselves of opportunism, we could still participate in the work of the leadership. If opportunism was not opposed immediately, other issues could not be taken up.

When I asked him exactly what mistakes had been committed by the CC of the CCP, he replied to the following effect. Most important was the fact that the CC of the CCP had abandoned efforts to obtain proletarian leadership of the Chinese revolution. For example, it had rejected the Comintern's June 1 directive about arming of workers and peasants and had also voluntarily disarmed the workers' pickets of Wuhan. The basic reasons for the incidence of such mistakes were the facts that the CC of the CCP was controlled by certain petty-bourgeois intellectuals who lacked class consciousness and revolutionary determination and that over a long period of time the correct directives of the Comintern had been distorted in an opportunist manner. The Comintern could no longer rely on these vacillating intellectuals and had to boldly promote some steadfast worker-comrades to assume the leadership of the CCP, having them constitute the majority of the CC of the CCP.

These words of Lominadze actually aroused the flame of anger in me. I felt that his castigation was not in keeping with the facts. At least the responsibility for these mistakes should not be entirely placed on the CC of the CCP, for the Comintern and its representatives should also share the blame. At the time I thought that perhaps he was too young; his character seemed to be that of a Teddy boy after the October Revolution, while his attitude was that of an inspector-general of the Czar. He had greatly belittled the intellectuals of the CCP, who were not altogether unequal to the test of the revolution and could much less be treated as serfs under the Czarist rule.

I suppressed my indignation and said to him, "From what you say, blame for the mistake of opportunism should be placed on the entire Central Political Bureau. We, the members, should take the blame and resign, or even be lined up before the firing squad, and a new group of persons should be found to organize a new CC." Our conversation was thus deadlocked. Ch'ü Ch'iu-pai said something of a mediating nature; he seemed to hope that we would not go to extremes.

So I laid this question aside and brought up instead a matter that needed urgent attention, asking that it be discussed at once. I reported to them that according to a secret report from people just arrived from Kiukiang, Comrade Chou En-lai and others felt that the plan for launching an insurrection at Nanchang, which he and I had drawn up, could be realized. It was expected that participants in the insurrection would include the troops of Yeh T'ing, the troops of Ho Lung, and the model regiment of Chu Teh in the Third Army. They requested me to immediately issue a directive as a guideline for the insurrection, including such things as the name of the organization leading the insurrection, its political platform, and major organizational points, and the strategy to be adopted. They also requested the CC to mobilize the labor and peasant forces of all areas to respond to the action in Nanchang. They further asked if the Soviet Union would give practical support to the Nanchang insurrection. They urgently needed the assistance of Soviet military advisers and a large amount of cash. They also hoped that when they arrived in the East River region, they would obtain support in arms and material supplies from the Soviet Union.

The youthful Lominadze (it was stated that he was only twenty-nine years old at the time) showed himself at a loss when confronted with this practical problem. He was recording my report and declared that he had to ask Moscow for instructions on everything. I repeatedly explained that it was a matter that could not wait, but had to be decided at once; and I suggested that we could work out some measures, informing Chou En-lai on the one hand and asking Moscow for instruction on the other. He then stated briefly that we could tell Chou En-lai and the others to make active preparations with regard to the mobilization of labor and peasant forces in different areas, saying that we could deal with the matter in accordance with present conditions. As to the other points, he had to ask for instructions from Moscow before making a final decision.

At the conclusion of the talk Ch'ü Ch'iu-pai also expressed disappointment. He asked me why the Comintern should send as its representative such a young and inexperienced man, who knew only about opposing opportunism, but was at a loss as soon as the Nanchang insurrection was mentioned. I said to him that apparently the misfortune of the CCP was not yet ended. After suffering under the oppression of Chiang Kai-shek and Wang Ching-wei, it would now be subjected to oppression by Lominadze. Unfortunately this statement of mine later proved to be correct. Lominadze's blind method of working almost completely destroyed the CCP that we had built up with such great difficulty.

After Lominadze had had a long talk with Ch'ü Ch'iu-pai alone, he seemed to have a little understanding of the condition of the CCP. Ch'ü Ch'iu-pai had told him of my views and had advised him against reaching an impasse in arguing with me. So when we met the next day, although he was still not satisfied with my views, his attitude had become more polite. He reiterated the need for absolute support of the Comintern and for the immediate convocation of a meeting to reorganize the CC of the CCP. But his tone was no longer that of the previous day, when he had assumed the attitude of "reading an imperial edict." For my part, I advocated first settling the many urgent problems in hand, particularly the question of the Nanchang insurrection. The problems of opposing opportunism and reorganizing the CC could be settled a little later at an enlarged meeting of the CC. Lominadze could do nothing about my proposals, and so he just kept quiet.

At the suggestion of Lominadze, the Standing Committee of the CCP held a secret meeting in a house in Hankow at 4:00 P.M. on July 26. Participants included two members of the Standing Committee—Ch'ü Ch'iu-pai and I; two members of the CC—Li Wei-han and Chang T'ai-lei; Lominadze and another representative of the Young Communist International; the Russian advisers Galen and Fan-ko; and two interpreters.

When the meeting started, General Galen made a report first. He stated briefly that he had seen General Chang Fa-k'uei that morning and had discussed military problems with him. Chang had agreed to mass the Fourth Army, the Eleventh Army, and the Thirtieth Army—the three armies under his control—at Nanchang and the Nanchang-Kiukiang line. He would not proceed further east, but would gradually change his course and return to Kwangtung. Galen's idea was that if Chang would agree to the two conditions of taking his men back to Kwangtung and not forcing Yeh T'ing and the others to withdraw from the CCP, then we could return with Chang to Kwangtung. He pointed out that the situation was extremely favorable for returning to Kwangtung with Chang. If we separated from Chang at Nanchang, there would be only from five to eight thousand men participating in the insurrection. Facing a superior enemy force, they would find it difficult to reach the East River region. If Chang would not agree to the two conditions, we would have to take action in Nanchang.

Lominadze spoke next. He first stated that at the moment there were no funds available for use in the Nanchang insurrection and that Moscow had sent a telegraphic order prohibiting the Russian advisers from taking part in the Nanchang insurrection under any circumstances. In addition to these two unfavorable items, he reported that the telegram from the Comintern stated that if the insurrection had no hope of success, it would be best not to launch it. The Communists in Chang Fak'uei's army could all be withdrawn and sent to work among the peasants.

The young rascal Lominadze, who was given to rash action, had also learned some bureaucratic tricks. He said that it seemed the two facts and the order from the International could not be communicated to the comrades on the front by letter and that we would have to send a dependable comrade to tell them verbally. As he said this, he looked at me and asked if I could be sent. Lominadze was a little embarrassed when he said these words. Perhaps he thought that from the beginning no one had hoped for success from the Nanchang insurrection, but that all had considered it an act of resistance that was unavoidable and that disregarded success or failure—an act supported by responsible comrades in Hankow and Wuchang and one that he himself had clearly not opposed. Now Moscow would not permit the participation of the Russian advisers and would not issue funds, both of which were anxiously awaited by the comrades at the front. Furthermore, it sent a telegram to stop the scheme; and this made people lose spirit all the more. This "hero," who consistently opposed opportunism, now had to stop the launching of an insurrection; and this certainly did not taste right. So he spoke ambiguously and would not state flatly that comrades at the front must obey the order of the International and immediately stop the launching of the insurrection.

When I saw the situation, I immediately replied that since the mission was only to deliver a message, there was no need to send me. Moreover, since the enlarged meeting of the CC was due to open soon, I could not leave. It was also best that I not be allowed to leave my work in the CC. Comrade Wang I-fei could undertake the task, and it was best that he be asked to go. (At the time Wang I-fei was doing important work in the secretariat of the CC.) Lominadze was a bit nervous and said that the man to be sent had to leave that very evening and that Comrade Wang could not be found. Even if he could be found, it was not easy to brief him on the mission in a short time and to have him leave immediately. Lominadze's tone indicated that he was urging me to go. And so both Ch'ü Ch'iu-pai and Li Wei-han said to me that it was best if I went. They said that the responsibility was not merely to deliver a message, but to observe the situation and participate in policy decisions. These words, spoken in a light vein by the two, produced the same result in a different way as the words of Lominadze.

At the time I also felt very awkward. First, I felt that it was after all improper for me to carry out the order to stop something to which I had agreed. Next, I really did not want to leave the CC at this time and to miss the enlarged meeting of the CC. I consistently held that the Nanchang insurrection had no hope of success, and I had worried about this fact. Now the Comintern clearly wanted to place itself outside the project, not only prohibiting the Russians to be involved, but also being unwilling to give secret financial help. This would plunge the Nanchang insurrection into the abyss of destruction. Furthermore, since Moscow had given an order to stop the act, if the Nanchang insurrection should be a drastic failure, the Chinese comrades would further have to bear responsibility for the crime of violating the order and acting in a rash manner. Thinking along such lines, I was deeply worried over the future of the CCP and the large number of comrades that were working so hard in the Nanchang and Kiukiang areas. I also thought that General Galen's proposal might be feasible and that only by acting in accordance with Galen's proposal could all sides receive consideration. To speak frankly, had I resolutely rejected the mission, there was actually no other person at the time who could shoulder this heavy responsibility. And so I felt that I was duty-bound to take up the job.

To clarify my mission, I spoke to Lominadze in a questioning tone, "The Communist International persists in labeling us as guilty of opportunism and incapable of resolutely taking up the revolution. Now preparations are ripe for the Nanchang insurrection, and a telegram comes stopping it. What is the idea? Is it that hopes are still pinned on the Kuomintang leftists, or that there are illusions about Soong Ch'ing-ling, Teng Yen-ta, Ho Hsiang-ning, and Eugene Ch'en being able to produce new tricks?"

When Lominadze heard my words, he looked a bit jolted and said that he actually had a telegram stopping the Nanchang insurrection—a serious order personally dictated by Stalin and dispatched in the name of Bukharin. How could we refuse to obey it? He also felt that the matter was beyond what he anticipated; but even if the directive was wrong, we still had to carry it out. He then switched and continued by saying that we in Hankow approached problems on the basis of conditions in our area alone, whereas the Comintern had to decide its action on the basis of the international situation as a whole. What it had to consider included international relations, Sino-Soviet relations, and many other factors unknown to us. If we did not act in accordance with the directive of the Comintern, not only would we suffer defeat, but we would also commit a violation of discipline. In the past the mistakes of the CC of the CCP were caused by its inadequate understanding of this point; and so in the future the mistake should not be repeated.

After Lominadze had clearly expressed his view on obeying orders and stopping the Nanchang insurrection, Ch'ü Ch'iu-pai and all others present at the meeting expressed their support. In the discussion they also unanimously maintained that the proposal of General Galen was feasible and that as much as possible should be done to promote its realization. If this could not be achieved, then we could only dispatch the comrades in the Fourth Army and those assembled in the Nanchang-Kiukiang area to work in the midst of the peasants in various localities.

The meeting decided that I and the Front Line Committee should immediately handle all matters in an appropriate manner. After they had been dealt with, I should rapidly return to the CC. So I finally agreed to hurry to the front that very evening. I also asked the question of what I should do if because of lack of time or other reasons I could not stop the Nanchang insurrection in time. Beyond indicating that I should resolutely stop the insurrection, Lominadze was not disposed to take any responsibility by answering this question.

The Nanchang insurrection was not stopped, but finally broke out. Within the circle of the CCP no one felt that it was in good taste to express the opinion that the insurrection should not have been launched, much less would they mention that its stoppage had been attempted. The Comintern and its agents and leaders of the CC of the CCP, such as Ch'ü Ch'iu-pai, all felt that it was after all not something to be proud of for them to have tried to stop the insurrection. If this fact were revealed among the different branches of the Comintern, it could only give rise to innumerable disputes; so they would not mention the incident any more. The foolish Ch'ü Ch'iu-pai and others even twisted things around and denied the incident. They distorted it with unacceptable reasoning, and implicated me, although I was acting on orders, charging me with delivering a bogus order and trying privately to stop the Nanchang insurrection. This was a great scandal—the first to occur within the CCP—and I shall have cause to refer to it later.

On the evening of July 26 I hurriedly boarded a Yangtze steamer after the meeting and left Wuhan, which had the designation of the "Red Capital." It was also close to the time when the curtain would fall on the Wuhan government. The "separation" of Communists had developed to the stage of "expulsion" of Communists. CCP members in the KMT, the government, and military organs at all levels had been gradually removed. The CCP organization had already gone underground. On the streets of this "Red Capital" some pamphlets were still being secretly distributed by the Communists, and there were certain desultory acts of resistance by the masses of workers and peasants to decorate the final scenes of the revolution.

One day after I had left, in the midst of a ceremonious send-off by the Wuhan leaders, Borodin, who had been a leading player in the drama of the Wuhan period, boarded a train of the Peking-Hankow Railway at Ta-chih-men Station and proceeded toward the northwest. On his journey from Lushan westward via Wuhan, he did not see the CCP leaders, and it seemed that he no longer wanted to be involved in the affairs of the Wuhan government and the CCP. His feelings must have been very melancholy. In the Chinese revolution this strategist, with his sharpened wits always on the alert, was indeed all-powerful for a time. But the "green stuff" in his pocket was after all limited, and Moscow's "magical spell enforcing restraint" did not permit him to develop freely. The Chinese, on the other hand, treated him as a "foreign devil" with doubtful antecedents. All this somewhat hampered his actions, and finally he had to leave China as a failure.

The few brilliant figures among the KMT leftists, such as Soong Ch'ing-ling, Teng Yen-ta, and Eugene Ch'en, also silently left this city, the color of which had faded. For the sake of safety, Teng Yen-ta had to disguise himself as a chauffeur, in order to smuggle himself and Teruni through the areas controlled by Feng Yü-hsiang—a highly dramatic episode. These people had no prior knowledge of the Nanchang insurrection, but their names were all included in the Revolutionary Committee of the uprising, their concurrence with which had never been obtained. Politically, however, they were clearly opponents of both Nanking and Wuhan.

By this time KMT-CCP cooperation was declared ended. In 1927 the great tidal wave of the Chinese revolution receded into the mist of the split between the KMT and the CCP. When the Yangtze steamer carried me away from Hankow, I stood on the deck, and looking back at the lights of this city, I could not help being filled with myriad thoughts. I was reciting silently the well-known verse:

The yellow crane has left with someone in the past,
And here is left the empty Yellow Crane Tower.

NOTES

Chapter I

1. According to Feng Tzu-yu, *Chung-hua min-kuo k'ai-kuo-chien ko-ming shih* (History of the Chinese Revolution before the establishment of the Republic of China), 2 vols. (Shanghai, 1928), I, 246, "The Hung Chiang Society originally planned a large uprising for December of that year [1906]. Before it could occur, however, a leak of information caused the Manchus to hunt down Li Chun-ch'i, a Society leader, who drowned in White Egret Pond in Liling County while trying to escape. Hsiao K'o-ch'ang [another Society leader] was trapped and executed by the Manchus. Kung Ch'un-t'ai and others could delay no longer. The uprising as a result was staged ahead of schedule."

   Li Chien-nung, in his *Chung-kuo chin-pai-nien cheng-chih shih* (Political history of China in the past hundred years), 2nd ed. (Shanghai, 1948), I, 136, also stated that news of the uprising leaked out before the planned date. As a result the Liuyang forces staged the uprising on the nineteenth and twentieth days of the tenth moon. But corroborating accounts do not often appear in other histories.

2. According to Chang Ch'i-yün, *Chung-hua min-kuo shih-kang* (An outline history of the Republic of China; Taipei, 1954), I, 136, the troops in this rebellion were "called collectively the Revolutionary Army." No source is given. Two manifestoes reprinted in the work by Feng Tzu-yu referred to in note 1 above (I, 247-54) differ from one another in the names by which the rebels referred to themselves. The first manifesto was issued by "The *tu tu* [commander] of the Revolutionary Vanguard of the South Army of the Chinese National Army." The body of the manifesto, however, states that it was issued "under the authority of the Government of the Republic of China." In the other manifesto the rebels called themselves "The South Insurrectionary Army of the Great Empire of New China."

   Careful scrutiny of these two manifestoes casts doubt on their authenticity. It is not necessarily true that the rebels called themselves the Revolutionary Army.

3. According to Ch'en Hsü-lu, *Hsin-hai ko-ming* (The 1911 Revolution; Shanghai, 1940), p. 40, "Society leaders . . . utilized the opportunity to instigate an insurrection by miners at Anyuan in P'inghsiang, who were struggling along on the verge of starvation. Six thousand miners were the mainstay of this rebellion."

   Feng Tzu-yu (I, 247) has written that "most of the rebels in P'inghsiang were coal miners." But the joint memorial on the Rebellion submitted by the governor of Liang-Kiang (a territory along both sides of the Yangtze River) and the governor of Kiangsi (Feng Tzu-yu, I, 262-68) mentioned only that the trouble was caused by Hung Chiang Society bandits. Of the Anyuan Coal Mine they said only that during the rebellion "there was no interruption of the daily work." After the rebellion "miners were strictly screened . . . those with no guarantee were dismissed and sent back to their homes"; and their number was only something "over one hundred." Since reports made by local officials on such happenings generally exaggerated their size and scope to win credit for coping with them, the report just cited would not have treated the miners so lightly if six thousand of them had been involved.

In addition, one source states that the Society "planned the uprising for the twelfth moon. Their force was to be divided into three units, one to occupy Liuyang first and then Changsha, one to hold Anyuan in P'inghsiang as a base, and one to move eastward to attack Juichou and Nanchang from Wantsai in order to relieve the forces along the Yangtze." See P'eng Ch'u-heng, *Hu-nan kuang-fu yun-tung shih-mo-chi* (An account from beginning to end of the Hunan liberation movement), in *Ko-ming wen-hsien* (Revolutionary documents; Taipei, 1953), II, 68. Similar accounts appear in Tsou Lu's *Chung-kuo kuo-min-tang shih-kao* (A draft history of the China Kuomintang), 3rd ed. (Shanghai, 1941), II, 695, and in Chang Ch'i-chun's *Tang shih k'ai-yao* (An outline of party history), 2nd ed. (Taipei, 1951), I, 93. But it is difficult, in view of the dearth of primary source material, to decide whether or not the Hung Chiang Society laid such plans before the rebellion. In fact, however, the attack on Liuyang was the most dramatic aspect of the rebellion.

4. Court robes used during the Manchu dynasty bore insignia on the front and back which indicated official rank. Civilian ranks were designated by birds and military ranks by animals.

5. Ch'ing officials whose status derived from passing regular examinations were called *cheng t'u* (regulars). They were differentiated from the *chuan pan* (donated rank), officials that achieved their status by making donations to the state, and from *en tz'u* (gracious bestowal), officials that received their degrees by special Imperial decree. However, even in the regular examinations, it was decreed in the early reign of K'ang Hsi (1661-1722) that "students may gain entry to state schools by donating one hundred taels of silver." This policy was abandoned after a short time. *Hsiu ts'ai* (excellent talent) were students that had passed the examination at the county level.

6. The so-called chuan pan system during the Ch'ing dynasty was started in the reign of K'ang Hsi, when money was needed to put down the "Three Kings." Military expenditures were large and the state was in financial straits. So, in order to raise money, official positions and titles were sold in the name of donations to meet military needs. However, this move stirred little enthusiasm and court receipts were small, so the system was abandoned. After Hsien Feng (1851-1861), however, financial need forced its revival, this time with two restrictions: first, official positions thus sold were reserve appointments—active positions could not be purchased; and second, the importance of the rank purchased depended upon the purchase price, and the reserve rank of *tao* was the highest that could be purchased.

7. The Ch'ing system required that every twelve years the *hseuh cheng* (administrator of schools) should select from among the students in *fu* schools those who were hsiu ts'ai and should send them to the capital. Such candidates were called *pa kung* (selected tribute). After taking an Imperial examination there, First Class students were appointed Grade Seven Petty Capital Officials (ch'i-p'in hsiao ching-kuan); Second Class students were appointed county magistrates; and Third Class students were given teaching appointments. Those who failed

the examination were sent home and were called *fei kung* (discarded tribute).

8. *Pao cheng* and *lu cheng* were popularly elected to take charge of village affairs and to carry out tasks handed down by the authorities. They formed a bridge between the people and the government. It was their duty to please government agents. Since the average honest, straightforward villager was not up to such things, and since scholars and the gentry would not condescend to undertake them, most of the jobs were filled by people that were fond of meddling in other people's affairs and that were well-to-do compared with the average villager. They derived a small income from the local community by handling public affairs.

Generally speaking, the pao cheng and lu cheng in those days stood on the people's side and spoke for the people in handling their affairs. This marked them as different from the hsiang and pao chiefs of Republican days, who generally bullied the villagers.

9. Details of the Ch'ing method of suppressing this incident, according to the joint memorial on the rebellion submitted by the governors of Liang-Kiang and Kiangsi (Feng Tzu-yu, I, 267), were: "Bandits were classified into three categories. The bandits that induced people to join the Society, started fires, looted, robbed, or killed were put in class one and were not subject to amnesty. A large reward was offered for their arrest. The bandits that joined the rebellion on the spur of the moment and that were not rebels by premeditation were placed in class two. They were allowed to redeem their crimes by assisting in the arrest of leaders. Those who did not thus achieve merit, however, were severely punished according to law. The bandits that were coerced into joining the Society and were not truly bandits were put in class three. They were permitted to surrender their membership cloth and to swear that they were penitent, and upon producing a guarantee, they were allowed under special permit to return to their homes and professions."

10. The slogan "Overthrow the Ch'ing and Restore the Ming" was considered inappropriate by the time of the Taiping Rebellion. Hung Hsiu-ch'üan expressed this viewpoint in quite clear words. He said, "To advocate this [overthrowing the Ch'ing and restoring the Ming] really was not wrong in the days of K'ang Hsi. But by now more than two hundred years have passed. We may still talk of overthrowing the Ch'ing, but we can no longer talk of restoring the Ming. Whatever the case, if we are able to restore the empire of the Han people, we should do it in the form of creating a new dynasty. If at this point we still use the slogan of restoring the Ming, how can we rally the hearts of the people?" See Han Shan-wen, *T'ai-p'ing T'ien-kuo ch'i-i chi* (The rise of the Taiping Heavenly Kingdom), in Chien Yu-wen, ed., *T'ai-p'ing T'ien-kuo tsa-chi* (Miscellany on the Taiping Heavenly Kingdom; Shanghai, 1935), p. 64.

11. When Hung Hsiu-ch'üan started the Taiping movement, his followers all let their forelocks grow long and changed their dress and hats in defiance of the Ch'ing. Official documents, as a result, referred to them as "hair bandits" and the populace called them "long hairs."

12. The eight insurrections that took place between the time the T'ung-meng Hui was established and the 1911 Revolution were: (1) The P'ing-Liu Campaign

in December, 1906; (2) the Campaign of Huangkang in Chaochow and Wai-
chow in 1907; (3) the Campaign of Ch'in, Lien, and Fangch'eng in 1907; (4)
the Campaign of Chennankuan in 1907; (5) the Campaign of Ch'in, Lien, and
Shangshih on the third day of the third moon, 1908; (6) the Campaign of
Hok'ou in Yunnan on the twenty-ninth day of the third moon, 1908; (7) the
Canton Campaign on Lunar New Year's Day, 1910; (8) the Huanghuakang
Campaign of March 29, 1911.

In addition, there was the heroic incident on May 26, 1907, when Hsü
Hsi-lin, an official of the Anhwei Police Academy, led a group of students in
an uprising. He assassinated En Ming, the governor of Anhwei. They attempted
to occupy the arsenal to get arms for a large-scale rebellion, but failed, and
Hsü Hsi-lin was killed. Earlier, during the time of the Hsing-chung Hui, Sun
Yat-sen started the Canton Campaign in 1895 (the ninth day of the ninth moon
in the twenty-first year of Kuang Hsü) and the Waichow Campaign in 1900.

Chang Ch'i-yün, in his *Tang shih k'ai-yao*, I, 22-114, says that there were
ten insurrections before the 1911 Revolution. He does not, however, include the
P'ing-Liu Campaign of 1906. Instead, he lists the Huangkang Campaign in
Chaochow and the Waichow Campaign in 1907 as two campaigns. He omitted
the P'ing-Liu Campaign because, he says, it was not planned in advance by the
T'ung-meng Hui headquarters. Yet it is quite obvious that this campaign was
influenced by the T'ung-meng Hui. Also, when Sun Yat-sen, who lists it as the
first of the T'ung-meng Hui insurrections, heard about it, he rushed a number
of comrades to take part in it. Many T'ung-meng Hui members sacrificed themselves in this campaign. The best known of them, Liu Tao-i, was the first man
to be executed as a result of this campaign, and Sun Yat-sen wrote an elegy to
him. Thus it cannot be said that this was not the first rebellion instigated by
the T'ung-meng Hui. In 1907, moreover, the Waichow Campaign and the
Huangkang Campaign in Chaochow were not only started at the same time but
were part of the same operational plan. Each was to support the other. Thus
they can be considered as only one insurrection.

13. Sun Yat-sen in his autobiography said, "Unfortunately, the P'inghsiang uprising
was a spontaneous move led by our members. Our headquarters knew not one
single thing about it before the incident, and we were caught unprepared. . . ."
See Sun Yat-sen, *Memoirs of a Chinese Revolutionary*, in *Tsung-li ch'uan-chi*
(Complete works of Tsung-li; n.p., 1943), p. 340.

14. Huang Hsing was originally named Huang Chen, with the courtesy name
Ching-wu. Later he changed his name to Huang Hsing and used the courtesy
name K'o-ch'iang. He was a native of Shanhua, Hunan, and was an honor
student at the Lianghu Academy in Hupeh. Later, he went to study in Japan,
where together with his fellow-provincials Liu Kuei-i and Yang Tu-sheng, he
launched the Hua-hsing Hui, a strong revolutionary organization that was outside the Hsing-chung Hui. When he returned to China, Huang Hsing worked
as a teacher in the Mingteh School at Changsha. He contacted Ma Fu-i, the
Great Dragon Head of the Hung Chiang Society, and together they launched
the Changsha Incident of 1904. After that he went to Japan again, and there
he joined Sung Chao-jen in publishing the well-known magazine *Er-shih Shih-chi*

Chih-la (Twentieth-Century China), which promoted the revolutionary cause. When Sun Yat-sen organized the T'ung-meng Hui, Huang Hsing immediately joined it and was elected its general affairs officer, the leadership position second only to that of the president (*tsung-li*). As soon as the Wuchang Insurrection broke out, Huang Hsing went there as commander-in-chief of the revolutionary army on the Hupeh front. For further details see Li Chien-nung, *Chung-Kuo chin-pai-nien cheng-chih shih,* I, 238,39, or the English version, *Political History of China* (Princeton, 1956).

15. The Changsha Incident of September, 1904, was sponsored jointly by Huang Hsing and Ma Fu-i, Great Dragon Head of the Hung Chiang Society. The purpose of the uprising was to overthrow the Manchus. When it failed, Huang Hsing left for Japan, while Ma Fu-i escaped to Kiangsi. The following spring, Ma returned to Hunan to undertake another uprising; but he was arrested and executed by Tuan Fang, the governor of Hunan. Kung Ch'un-t'ai, one of the leaders of the P'ing-Liu Campaign, was a disciple of Ma Fu-i. The Hung Chiang Society branch he commanded also was under Ma Fu-i. It is therefore obvious that the P'ing-Liu Campaign was influenced by the revolutionary group.

16. The Chinese educational system from the end of the T'ang dynasty to the end of the Ch'ing dynasty was built around the Academy system (Shu-yuan chih). During the Hundred Days of Reform, however, the first thing the Emperor Kuang Hsü decreed was the establishment of modern schools. The old academies at all levels in the provinces were converted into modern schools teaching both Chinese and Western subjects. After that, more and more schools of the modern type came into being in China. But this new policy was abolished when the Hundred Days of Reform came to an end. And not until the second day of the eighth moon (September 14, 1901) was the following decreed: "All academies in provincial capitals are to be reorganized into universities. All academies in *chou* directly governed by the provincial or national capital and in *fu* are to be reorganized into middle schools. All academies in other *chou* and in *hsien* are to be reorganized into primary schools. . . ." (See Sheng Lan-hsi, *Chung-kuo shu-yüan chih-tu* [The Chinese academy system; Shanghai, 1934], pp. 235-36). Modern schools then came officially to the entire country, and the original examination system was abolished altogether in July, 1905.

17. Most people believe that the Chinese began wearing queues during the Ch'ing dynasty. Actually they were first adopted in the northern Sung dynasty, when the Chin people conquered half of China. In 1129 Emperor T'ai-tsung of Chin ordered all Han Chinese in the occupied area to wear barbarian (hu) dress and hair style. Volume five of the *Great Chin History* records: "In June of the year, Han clothes and haircutting are banned for the population. Violators are to die." Thus, queue-wearing in China was long regarded as a humiliating sign of foreign enslavement. The cutting of queues in the late Ch'ing dynasty was, therefore, naturally regarded as a rebellious act.

18. Mourning in those days was indicated by wearing a white band tied on one's queue. To mourn the death of an emperor, everyone was required to wear this band for one hundred days.

19. In the Ch'ing examination system, all *Chin-shih* who passed the court examinations to become *Shu-chi-shih* were called *Han-lin*.

20. *Pu-cheng-shih* was the chief administrative official of a province during the early period of the Ming dynasty. He had charge of civil and financial affairs for a whole province. Later, new official posts, such as those of viceroy, governor, and inspector-general, were created above the rank of pu-cheng-shih, and his authority gradually shrank. By the Ch'ing period the pu-cheng-shih of a province had become the subordinate of the provincial governor, and he handled only civil affairs.

21. The date and cause of the Emperor Kuang Hsü's death remain mysteries to this day. But to judge by Yun Yu-ting, the official recorder of the emperor's activities, in his book *Ch'ung-ling chuan-hsin lu* (The true story of the Emperor Kuang Hsü), in Tso Shun-sheng, *Chung-kuo chin-pai-nien tzu-liao hsü-pien* (Source material for a history of China in the past hundred years, supplement), 2nd ed. (Shanghai, 1938), it seems quite obvious that the Emperor Kuang Hsü died at the venomous hands of the Empress Dowager's clique.

22. Details of the increased power of court nobles during the late Ch'ing period can be found in Li Chien-nung, *Chung-kuo chin-pai-nien cheng-chih shih*, I, 280-86.

23. For details of the "save the railroads" campaign, see *ibid.*, I, 295-98.

24. These are the famous words of General Ma Yuan, a national hero of the eastern Han dynasty.

25. Sun Yat-sen also believed that "a small portion of members, finding themselves in danger because the organization was uncovered, decided to take the risk and gamble for success. They did not expect to fell their opponents with one blow." (See Sun Yat-sen, *Fundamentals of National Reconstruction*, in *Tsung-li ch'uan-chi*, Chap. 8.)

26. *Tu tu* was an official title first created in the Wei Wen Ti period. All officials governing subkingdoms bore the title tu tu, in addition to their other official titles, to indicate that they also had military responsibilities. After the middle of the T'ang dynasty the title changed to *chieh-tu-shih*. Although there were Great Tu Tu and Tu Tu of the Five Armies in the Yuan and Ming dynasties, these were official titles for military commanders of the central government. They differed, therefore, from the tu tu in the Wei and Chin dynasties. In the 1911 Revolution the chief military officer of a province was not the only one called tu tu. Even several counties together might have their own tu tu when they had their own independent military force. For example, there was a Kiukiang tu tu, a Nanchang tu tu, a P'inghsiang tu tu, and others just within the province of Kiangsi. These tu tu, in addition to their military commands, had responsibility for civil affairs. It was only after the establishment of the Republic that tu tu was used to designate the highest official in a province. In 1916, however, the title tu tu was changed to *tu chun*, and it then carried with it military duties exclusively. From then on the term tu tu was used only in histories of the bureaucracy.

27. For details of P'inghsiang's break with the Manchus see Chiang Chun-yang,

Hsin-hai chiang-hsi kuang-fu chi (The liberation of Kiangsi in 1911), in *Ko-ming wen-hsien* (Revolutionary documents; Taipei, 1953, 1955), IV, 74-88.

28. Both the mast and the banners were tokens of merit awarded to the family by the court.

29. The seventeen provinces were Fengtien, Chihli, Honan, Shantung, Shansi, Shensi, Kiangsi, Anhwei, Kiangsu, Chekiang, Fukien, Kwangtung, Kwangsi, Hunan, Hupeh, Szechwan, and Yunnan. For names of the delegates, see Tsou Lu, *Chung-kuo kuo-min-tang shih-kao*, II, 945.

30. The Terms of Special Treatment included three categories. One applied to the Ch'ing emperor and consisted of eight articles. The second applied to the royal clan and consisted of four articles. The third applied to the ethnic minorities—Manchu, Mongol, Moslem, and Tibetan—and consisted of seven articles. These were given in official documents, and the diplomatic corps was notified of them by the government of the Republic of China.

31. Full text of the abdication decree is in *Cheng-fu Kung-pao* (Government Gazette), January, first year of the Republic.

32. T'an Ssu-t'ung was appointed *Chun-chi Chang-ching* during the Hundred Days of Reform. Yang Jui, Lin Hsu, Liu Kuang-ti, and he were known as the Four Officials of *Chun-chi*. They handled all memorials and decrees connected with the new policy, and Emperor Kuang Hsü relied upon them implicitly. On the third day of the seventh moon of that year (1898) T'an, knowing that the Empress Dowager planned to dethrone the Emperor while he reviewed a parade in Tientsin, tried to persuade Yuan Shih-k'ai to use his army to support the new policy and protect the Emperor. Yuan was then head of the Peiyang militarists and a member of the Society for the Protection of the Nation (Pao Kuo Hui), which was organized by K'ang Yu-wei and others. Yuang agreed to T'an's proposal, but betrayed the secret by reporting to Jung Lu, governor of Chihli and the man the Empress Dowager trusted most. This led to the coup d'état on the sixth day of the eighth moon (1898), when the Empress Dowager imprisoned Kuang Hsü and took over the administration herself. T'an was arrested, and on the thirteenth day of the eighth moon (1898), he was executed in Peking, together with Yang Jui, Lin Hsu, Liu Kuang-ti, Yang Shen-hsiu, and K'ang Kuang-jen. They are known historically as the "Six Gentlemen of 1898." For details of T'an's life and studies see T'an Ssu-t'ung, *T'an Ssu-t'ung ch'uan-chi* (The complete works of T'an Ssu-t'ung; Peking, 1955).

33. Liang Shih-i, the vice-minister of finance, published an open letter to the country in May, 1913, while acting as minister. In it he gave a rather concise explanation of the financial difficulties of the Republic's first two years. The full text is in Liang Shih-i, *San-shui Liang Yen-sun hsien-sheng nien-p'u* (Chronology of the life of Mr. Liang Yen-sun [Liang Shih-i]; n.p., n.d.), I, 137-42.

34. Sung Chiao-jen, whose courtesy name was Tun Ch'u, was a native of Changteh, Hunan. Huang Hsing and he were leaders of the Hua Hsin Society. While studying in Japan, he edited a magazine called *Er-shih Shih-chi Chih-la* (Twentieth-Century China); and there he joined the T'ung-meng Hui when it was formed. He was in charge of its public relations; only Sun Yat-sen and

Huang Hsing ranked above him. When the provisional government was set up in Nanking, he was appointed chief of its Legislative Bureau; and he wrote most of the initial legislation, orders, and regulations for the provisional government.

35. The KMT had 269 of the 596 seats in the House of Representatives, and 123 of 274 seats in the Senate. 173 seats in the House of Representatives and 82 seats in the Senate went to people that belonged either to more than one party or to no party at all. The KMT, therefore, was obviously the major party in Parliament.

36. The inside story of the assassination of Sung Chiao-jen was revealed by the investigation conducted by Ch'eng Te-ch'uan, tu tu of Kiangsu, and Ying Teh-hung, head of the Department of Civil Affairs in Kiangsu. The evidence they gathered was released in an open letter dated April 26, 1913, the full text of which appears in Tso Shun-sheng, *Chung-kuo chin-pai-nien shih tzu-liao hsu-pien*, pp. 523-27.

37. A loan of twenty-five million pounds was agreed upon on April 26, 1913, by the consortium of Britain, the United States, Germany, Russia, and Japan. Yuan raised the loan without asking for the consent of the parliament as required by the provisional constitution.

38. Although Anhwei, Kwangtung, Fukien, and Hunan responded to this campaign, it failed quickly because Yuan's army moved south rapidly and also because of differences between the provinces. However, the Battle of Kiangsi, which ended August 18, and the Battle of Nanking. which ended September 1, continued after the others had failed. The campaign is therefore known as the Kiangsi-Nanking Campaign.

39. Yen Fu, whose courtesy names were Chi-tao and Yu-lung, was a native of Houkuan, Fukien. In 1876 he went to England, where he studied naval science in addition to logic, economics, and social science. His mastery of both Chinese and English literature was impressive. After returning to China, he devoted most of his time to translating, although he also taught at the Naval Academy and was president of National Peking University during the first year of the Republic.

Yen Fu translated what were known as the Eight Great Books: *On Evolution,* by Thomas Henry Huxley, a woodblock edition of which appeared in 1898 and which was set in type and republished in 1909 by Commercial Press; *The Study of Logic,* by John Stuart Mill, Commercial Press, 1902; *Sociology,* by Herbert Spencer, Commercial Press, 1902; *Man and Society,* by John Stuart Mill, Commercial Press, 1899; *The Wealth of Nations,* by Adam Smith, Nanyang Public School Press, 1902; *Esprit des lois,* by Montesquieu, Commercial Press, 1902; *A History of Politics,* by E. Jenks, Commercial Press, 1903; and *Fundamentals of Logic,* by William Stanley Jevons, Commercial Press, 1908. These beautiful, smooth translations not only strongly influenced thinking people in China at that time, but they also were excellent examples of classical Chinese writing. For more information about Yen Fu, see Benjamin I. Schwartz, *In Search of Wealth and Power: Yen Fu and the West* (Cambridge, 1964).

40. The Twenty-one Demands were divided into five groups. The first group

included four articles defining Japanese claims in Shantung Province. The second group included seven articles that defined Japan's claims in southern Manchuria and eastern Inner Mongolia. The third group contained two articles stipulating that Japan be given the right to operate jointly with China the Hanyehp'ing Coal Mining Company, while restricting China's right to dispose of its part of the company and prohibiting other coal mines from operating in the area. The one article in the fourth group stipulated that China could not cede or lease to a third power any harbors, bays, or islands along the China coast. The fifth group contained seven articles stipulating that the Chinese government should engage Japanese as political, financial, and military advisers; that the police in China should be jointly administered by China and Japan; that Japan should be allowed to establish arsenals in China; and that Japan should be given the right to construct railroads linking Wuchang with Hangchow and Chaochow.

41. The boycott was used as a popular means of protesting foreign oppression. The first major boycott was against American goods in 1905. It protested discrimination against Chinese workers in the United States. After the May Fourth Movement in 1919, every time China suffered a diplomatic defeat by Japan, a boycott of Japanese goods was touched off.

42. Among the so-called Six Gentlemen of the Ch'ou An Society, Sun, Hu, and Li were included because of their qualifications as veteran revolutionists. Liu Shih-p'ei was selected because of his fame as a master of Chinese literature. However, in a letter to Hsiung Yu-hsi, Yen Fu said that he was listed by Yang Tu as a member of the Ch'ou An Society without his own consent. The real leader of the Society was Yang Tu. In the late Ch'ing dynasty, Yang worked in the Institute of Constitutional Study (Hsien-cheng Pien-ch'a Kuan) and was closely associated with Yuan Shih-k'ai. Later he was an intimate of Yüan K'e-ting. Confidently believing that the Great Constitution dynasty would make him its first premier, he was most enthusiastic in the movement to restore the monarchy.

43. The Chung-hua Ko-ming Tang held an election in Tokyo on June 22, 1914. Delegates from eighteen provinces elected Sun Yat-sen director-general of the Party; and its first official meeting was held on July 8 at Ching Yang Hsuen, in the Chu Ti district of Tokyo (romanizations are from the Chinese). The Party was thus officially formed.

44. The full text of the oath required of members of the Chung-hua Ko-ming Tang was: "_____, the taker of this oath, in order to save China from its crisis and liberate its people from difficulties, is willing to sacrifice his life, liberty, and privileges in order to affiliate with Mr. Sun in starting another revolution, which aims at implementing the People's Principles of Livelihood and Democracy and creating and putting into effect the Five-Power Constitution so that the country will be governed in an orderly and honest way, the people will be happy and prosperous, the country will be placed on a sound foundation, and the peace of the world will be upheld, hereby take the following oath: (1) to implement aims, (2) to obey orders, (3) to carry out my assignments with complete faithfulness, (4) to keep strict secrecy, (5) to live and die together. I will from now

on follow this oath forever and not change until death. If this oath I betray, I am willing to accept the supreme punishment.

_____ of _____ county, _____ province
Republic of China
(fingerprint)"

Huang Hsing felt that "By pledging one's affiliation with Mr. Sun in starting another revolution, one pledges loyalty to an individual and help to that individual in starting a revolution; one's placing a fingerprint on an oath is the same as a criminal's placing his signature on a confession. The former represents inequality. The latter is an insult." Huang Hsing refused to join and left Japan for America. Li Lieh-chün, Po Wen-wei, Ch'en Chiung-ming, and others left for Southeast Asia. The above-quoted oath and details of Huang Hsing's dissent can be found in Shao Yüan-ch'ung (as told to Hsü Shih-shen), *Chung-hua ko-ming-tang lueh-shih* (A brief history of the Chinese Revolutionary party), in *Ko-ming wen-hsien* (Revolutionary documents; Taipei, 1953), V, 96-106.

45. Lu Chien-chang was head of secret agents for Yuan Shih-k'ai.

46. The Imperial Capital Academy, the predecessor of National Peking University, was founded in the twenty-fourth year of the Emperor Kuang Hsü, 1898. Sun Chia-nai was the first minister in charge of the Academy. Since officials with Imperial examination degrees were the only students, the bad odor of yamen permeated it. In the eleventh moon of the first year of the Emperor Hsuan T'ung, 1909, it was divided into seven departments: the Five Classics, law, the arts, natural science, agriculture, engineering, and commerce. With the establishment of the Republic it became National Peking University, with Yen Fu as its first chancellor. It was China's first national university. Hu Jen-yuan succeeded Yen, and when Hu went to the United States in 1916, Ts'ai Yuan-p'ei succeeded him.

47. Ku Hung-ming, courtesy name T'ang-sheng, 1857-1928, a native of Amoy, Fukien. He studied literature in England in his early years, and his accomplishments in Western literature were considerable. His English-language writings include *The National Spirit of China*. For seventeen years he was a member on the staff of Chang Chih-tung. Advocating restoration of the monarchy, he not only retained his queue but he praised the institutions of bound feet and concubinage. He was a tower of strength for conservative intellectuals.

48. K'ang Yu-wei's *On Cosmopolitanism* was serialized in 1913 in the magazine *Pu-jen Tsa-chih* (Impatient Magazine). In it he advocated, primarily, abolishing national boundaries, destroying the family and clan institutions, and abolishing private property in order to bring all human beings into one cosmopolitan world. In those days this was perhaps the extreme of the radical thoughts.

49. Hsu Shu-cheng, secretary-general of the State Council and Tuan's close associate, quarrelled constantly with Sun Hung-i, the Minister of Interior Affairs, over the appointments of provincial governors. Sun was a close personal friend of Ting Shih-i, who was secretary-general of the president's office. The quarrel, consequently, developed into a conflict between President Li Yüan-hung and Premier Tuan Ch'i-jui. It continued until November 20, 1916, when as a result of mediation by Hsu Shih-ch'ang, both Sun Hung-i and Hsu Shu-cheng were

relieved of their offices. The conflict between Li and Tuan, as a result, appeared to abate for the time being.

50. For material on the birth of the corps of provincial warlord governors that was called the Tuchun Corps and its interference in the government, see T'ao Chu-yin, *Tu-chun t'uan chuan* (A history of the Tuchun Corps; Shanghai, 1948).

51. Ni Ssu-ch'ung, for example, was made tuchun of Anhwei Province and concurrently Commander-in-Chief of the Southern Route Army because he pledged allegiance to Tuan after the re-enthronment incident. Yet Ni, who was a prominent member of the Tuchun Corps, had played an important role in the re-enthronement.

52. The Anfu clique consisted of the members of Parliament belonging to the Anfu Club, and it was nominally led by Wang I-t'ang and Liu En-ke. Actually, however, it was controlled by Tuan Ch'i-jui through his trusted associate Hsu Shu-cheng. There were more than three hundred and thirty Anfu Clique members in the new Parliament, an absolute majority. The new Parliament was thus known as the Anfu Parliament.

53. There were two cliques within the Communications clique—the new and the old. Liang Shih-i headed the Old Communications clique. But when Ts'ao Ju-lin became Minister of Communications, he formed an empire of his own, known as the New Communications clique. With more than one hundred seats in Parliament, it was an ally of the Anfu clique.

54. These were the so-called Nishihara Loans.

55. On the eighth day of the fourth moon in the twenty-first year of the Emperor Kuang Hsü, K'ang Yu-wei, along with more than twelve hundred *chu-jen* from various provinces who were in Peking to sit for the Hui Examinations (Shih), signed and tendered a petition to the emperor, urging reforms. For its text see *Wu-hsu pien-fa* (The 1898 Reforms; Shanghai, 1953), II, 131-36.

56. For further information on the Society for Mass Education see *Chin-tai-shih tzu-liao* (Reference materials on modern Chinese history), No. 2 (Peking, 1955), pp. 124-60.

57. At the Paris Peace Conference, Japan utilized as an argument for taking over the German Shantung interests the notes exchanged between China and Japan on th Chiao-chi Railway in September, 1918, in which the Chinese Minister, Chang Tsung-hsiang, indicated his "delighted concurrence." In Peking, at the same time, on Japanese instigation pro-Japan elements secretly prevented the Chinese delegates to the Peace Conference from making statements damaging to Japan. As a result, when the Conference voted on the Shantung issue, the Chinese delegates did not make a last-ditch fight for their country's cause. For further details see *Shan-tung wen-t'i hui-k'an* (Documents on the Shantung question; Shanghai, 1921).

58. The Peking People's Foreign Relations Association, a group made up chiefly of prominent political and academic figures that were interested in foreign affairs, had proposed a mass rally to be held in Central Park on May 7. It was to commemorate National Humiliation Day, the day in 1915 when Japan delivered to China its ultimatum on the Twenty-one Demands.

59. According to the reminiscences of Ts'ao Ju-lin serialized in the *Ch'un Ch'iu*

magazine, Hong Kong, Chang Tsung-hsiang happened to be in Ts'ao's house when the students entered it and thus became the target of the student attack. Fortunately, a Japanese was there to protect him, and Chang managed to escape by the back door. The Japanese, though he was versed in jujitsu, was injured.

60. The note Ts'ai Yuan-p'ei left on May 9 for the teachers, staff members, and students read: "I am weary. 'The one who killed your horse is the boy by the roadside.' 'The people are tired, a little rest is in order.' I want a little rest. I have officially resigned as chancellor of Peking University. As of May 9, I do also sever all my connections with the various schools and organizations with which I have been associated. I make this statement in the hope that those who know me will understand my motives."

On May 11 the Peita Student Union received another letter from him, written on his journey. It read: "I fully believe that your act on May 4 was motivated entirely by patriotic zeal. And since I also am a citizen, how can I be dissatisfied with you? But I cannot overlook my position at the university. It is natural that I, as chancellor of a national university, should take the blame and resign. The only reason that I did not resign immediately on May 5 was because a small number of students were detained by the police As chancellor of their university, I felt bound to do the best I could for them. Fortunately, because of support from the Minister of Education and the Inspector-General of Police, and because of assistance from the heads of other schools, the students that were arrested have all been released on bail. I have discharged my responsibility. If this was not the time to resign, when should I resign? As to why I resigned and left Peking without informing people of my whereabouts, I did so to escape the convention of having my resignation rejected and to make it possible for my successor to be named at an early date. There was no other reason. The Faculty Council of Peking University has been successfully formed and departmental deans have been established in office. So the change of chancellors will definitely not affect the work of the university. I feared that you might not understand my motives, that you might think my departure was caused by dissatisfaction with you, and so I have written this hasty letter, hoping that you will excuse me."

61. Delegates of the Northern and Southern governments opened their peace conference at Shanghai on February 20, 1919. There followed lengthy, but fruitless, discussions of such issues as abolition of the Sino-Japanese Military Agreement, dissolution of the War Participation Army, suspension of the war loan, the free exercise of power by Parliament, reduction of the armed forces in the country, and the rehabilitation loan. When the May Fourth Movement broke out, T'ang Shao-yi, the delegate from the South, took advantage of the nationwide opposition to Tuan Ch'i-jui and the pro-Japan clique. On May 13 he presented the following Eight Conditions at a session of the peace conference: (1) That the Shanghai Peace Conference absolutely reject the terms that the Paris Peace Conference had made on the Shantung issue, namely, that Japan succeeded to Germany's rights in Shantung; (2) that all secret agreements between China and Japan be declared null and void, and that those responsible for contracting such agreements be punished in order to satisfy the people of the country; (3) that the War Participation Army, the National Defense Army, and similar

groups be dissolved; (4) that Tuchun and civil provincial governors that had conspicuous criminal records and that were not acceptable to the people be replaced; (5) that the peace conference declare null and void the order of Li Yuan-hung of June 13, 1917, dissolving Parliament; (6) that the peace conference elect prominent persons of national standing to a political council, which would supervise the implementation of decisions reached at the conference until Parliament resumed full power; (7) that all matters raised at the peace conference be reviewed and that matters requiring final decision be settled; and (8) that upon implementation of the above conditions, Hsu Shih-ch'ang be recognized as temporary president.

62. Li Hsin-pai, director of the General Services Office of Peita, first advocated using National Salvation Units of Ten as part of the May Fourth Movement. A friend of Ts'ai Yuan-p'ei, Li Shih-tseng, and Li Ta-chao, he was known as a practical revolutionist. He personally paid the publication costs of a set of rules for the Units of Ten and of a weekly called *New Life* (Hsin Sheng-huo), which urged people to form themselves into ten-man units. These Units of Ten were intended to form a national organizational pyramid of groups of one hundred, one thousand, ten thousand, etc. And in this way mass opinion was to be directed against the government to force it to accept the people's patriotic demands and to improve the people's livelihood. The Units of Ten drive was not, as some writers have suggested, directed particularly at the proletariat nor was it regarded as an undertaking of the workers' movement.

63. The movement by which Chiang Kai-shek sought to modernize the habits of the Chinese people in the nineteen-thirties used the same name.

64. Teng Ying-ch'ao gives a detailed description of the Tientsin Student Federation and the All-Circles National Federation in October, 1919, in her article "Wu-szu yun-tung ti hui-i" (Recollections of the May Fourth Movement), which appears in *Wu-szu yun-tung san-shih chou-nien chi-nien chuan-chi* (Special publication on the thirtieth anniversary of the May Fourth Movement; Shanghai, 1949). In it, however, she says that the citizens' rally on October 10 in Tientsin had as one of its objectives the dismissal of Ts'ao Ju-lin, Lu Tsung-yü, and Chang Tsung-hsiang. This must be a lapse of memory, for the three had already been dismissed by the Peking government on June 10, 1919.

65. The Foochow tragedy of November 16, 1919, was the result of an organized rising of Japanese hoodlums. Many students who were participating in the patriotic movement were killed by them. Moreover, the Japanese government, in a show of force, dispatched gunboats to Foochow and landed marines.

66. Chin Yun-p'eng, who became premier on September 24, 1919, was concurrently minister of war. Yet he had no control over the Frontier Army commanded by Hsu Shu-cheng, and this led to constant disputes between Chin and Hsu. Chin resigned four times between September, 1919, and May, 1920, the period during which he held office, an indication of the difficult position that he was in.

67. After the May Fourth Movement began, Wu P'ei-fu issued a condemnation of the treason of Ts'ao, Lu, and Chang and expressed readiness to move his army against foreign aggressors. During the North-South peace conference, he issued his first message directly taking the Peking government to task. After that he

repeatedly issued circular letters opposing the government's compromises with Japan and clamoring for a patriotic stand. He clearly hurt the pro-Japan Tuan Ch'i-jui and the Anfu Club, as did the patriotic student movement. (See T'ao Chu-yin, *Wu P'ei-fu chiang-chun ch'uan* [A biography of General Wu P'ei-fu; Shanghai, 1941], pp. 20-27.)

68. Wu P'ei-fu began collaborating with the Kwangsi clique of the Southern government when he was stationed in Hunan Province. On September 9, 1919, together with Mo Jung-hsin, T'an Yen-k'ai, and T'an Hao-ming, Wu issued an open message opposing the appointment of Wang Chih-t'ang as chief Northern delegate to the North-South peace conference. This had the effect of greatly alarming Peking and of displeasing KMT members.

69. This started an argument between Shao Li-tzu and me which lasted until 1923, when Wang Ch'ing-wei smoothed it over.

70. In his "Three National Heroes in the Construction of the Italian Nation" (in *Yin-p'ing-shih ho-chi* [Collected works and essays of the ice-drinkers' studio], 40 vols. [Shanghai, 1936], IV, 1-61), Liang Ch'i-ch'ao praised Camillo Benso di Cavour highly. He also wrote: "There is no need for me to be bashful and refrain from comparing myself to this great *Shun*. One who has the capacity will achieve things." It would appear that Liang likened himself to Cavour.

71. The seven directors-general of the Military government were Sun Yat-sen, T'ang Shao-yi, Wu T'ing-fan, Ch'en Ch'un-hsuan, T'ang Chi-yao, Lin Pao-tze, and Lu Jung-t'ing.

72. Political refugees from Korea had gathered in Shanghai in large numbers, and with agreement from Korean refugees in other places, a group of them organized a provisional refugee government in 1919, on the eve of the Conference of Paris. Kim Kyu-sik, in the name of the Provisional government, sent a demand for Korean independence to the peace conference. While nothing came of the demand, it did attract some attention. Chu Chih-hsin translated the text of the message in full and included it in his article entitled "Appeal of Korean Representatives to the Peace Conference." (See *Chu Chih-hsin chi* [Collected works of Chu Chih-hsin; Shanghai, 1921], I, 291-319.)

73. Huang, a well-intentioned but thoroughly impractical idealist, was unable to make much of his party. It included a weird conglomeration of people who had nothing in common, and soon it disintegrated. An original member of the KMT, Huang was in close touch with members of the Korean Provisional government. In December, 1920, he and a Korean named Kim, who claimed to represent the Comintern, convened a meeting at Shanghai that purported to be a Congress of Far Eastern Socialists.

74. I cannot recall with certainty the names of all the leading Socialist figures at Peita then, but according to Chang Hsi-man, the Guild Socialist Research Society was led by Kuo Meng-liang and Hsü Lu-chi; the Syndicalist Research Society was headed by Ch'en Ku-yüan; and the Anarchist Research Society was headed by Chu Chien-chih. (See an article entitled "Wu-szu ti she-hui-chu-i yun-tung" [The Socialist movement during May Fourth], included in *Li-shih hui-i* [Historical reminiscences; Shanghai, 1949], pp. 136-48.) However, Chang's remembrances and my own differ in many instances. For example, he describes

a Socialist Study Group (She-hui Chu-i Yen-chu-hui) organized by Li Shou-ch'ang and others. But whether or not such a group ever really existed needs to be checked. The inclusion of my name in its alleged membership is definitely an error. I have no knowledge of such an organization, and I certainly was not a member. In any event, the Marxists in China had not yet formally organized themselves at that time. Of this I am certain.

75. Li Ta-chao translated *Outline of Tolstoyism* in 1912. In March, 1917, he published the article "Effects of the Great Russian Revolution" in *Chia Yin* magazine. Many articles on socialism and Marxism followed in *Weekly Review, New Life, New Youth, New Tide,* and *Young China.* He may be considered one of the earliest students of socialism among those who started the Communist movement in China. Details of his writings are given in Chang Tsu-chi, *Li Ta-chao hsien-sheng che shu nien-piao* (Chronicle of the writings of Mr. Li Ta-chao), included in *Chung-kuo hsien-tai ch'u-pan shih-liao* (Contemporary publications of historical data; Peking, 1945), pp. 458-68.

76. When Li introduced Voitinsky and Yang to Ch'en Tu-hsiu it does not appear that Li knew of their secret mission. Neither Li nor Voitinsky ever mentioned to me any initial discussions between them. Perhaps Li treated Voitinsky as a news reporter. In any case, Voitinsky concealed his true identity when he first contacted Ch'en; and this may substantiate my belief that Li did not connect his introduction with the possibility of forming a Communist party.

77. *Ma-k'o-szu hsueh-shuo yen-chiu hui.* This Marxist study group was not actually formed until September of 1920, and I am convinced that it was the first formal Marxist group in Peking, although numerous published sources date its formation much earlier. Maurice Meisner, in *Li Ta-chao and the Origins of Chinese Marxism* (Cambridge, 1967), p. 116, states that Li Ta-chao organized the Marxist Research Society (Ma-k'e shih chu-i yen-chiu hui) some time around the last months of 1918, but gives no date. I am absolutely certain that I belonged to no Marxist group prior to the one organized in September of 1920.

Chapter II

1. In 1895, after the Sino-Japanese peace agreement, Prince Shun and Prince Ching together with Li Hung-tsao, a member of the Privy Council, submitted a memorial to the throne advocating a change in the military system and proposing that a new army be built at Tientsin. Yuan Shih-k'ai was recommended to be superintendent of training. The memorial was approved. The Ting Wu Army under Yuan set up the structure that trained the New Army at Hsin Nung Chen, a small station seventy li from Tientsin, known more popularly as Hsiao Chan—the area it had garrisoned. Tuan Ch'i-jui, Feng Kuo-chang, Wang Shih-chen, Hsu Shih-ch'ang, Wang Chan-yuan, and Ts'ao K'un, all of whom became powerful militarists in the Peiyang warlord group during the early days of the Republic, were trained in Yuan's army. This gave rise to the expression "military training at Hsiao Chan, the cradle of the Peiyang military clique."

2. The Anhwei clique was routed on July 18. On July 20 Tuan Ch'i-jui issued a message announcing his retirement. I arrived at Shanghai on July 19 or 20.

3. In April, 1919, he published some forceful and effective articles sympathetic to the Russian Revolution. These included: "Russian Revolutions of the 20th Century," in *Tu-hsiu wen-ts'un* (Works by Tu-hsiu; Shanghai, 1926), II, 29; "Kerensky and Lenin," in *ibid.*, II, 26; and "Radicals and World Peace," in *ibid.*, II, 66. In May, 1919, his *New Youth* issued a special number on Marxism (vol. VI, no. 5), which by and large treated the subject with sympathy.

4. According to Kuo Chan-po, "Mr. Ch'en was born in 1880. In his early days he studied in Japan. Dr. Sun Yat-sen had then organized the T'ung-meng Hui. But Ch'en objected to its ultranationalistic stand in exalting the Han Chinese and deriding the Manchus; and so he did not join the party. When he broke off his studies and returned to China, he stayed at Shanghai on Shou Chang Lane with Chang Shih-chao. With Chang Chi and Hsieh Hsiao-shih, he started the *Kuo-min* (National Daily), which advocated that a 'democratic' revolution be thoroughly carried out and that despotism be opposed. Later he joined Po Wen-hui as a staff member. The 1911 Revolution broke out, and he followed Po, serving as Commissioner of Education in Anhwei. In 1913, because the campaign against Yuan Shih-k'ai was defeated, he fled to Japan." (See Kuo Chan-po, *Chin-wu-shih-nien Chung-kuo szu-hsiang-shih* [A history of Chinese thought in the past fifty years; Peiping, 1936], p. 100.) According to my recollections, however, Ch'en first served as chief secretary to Po Wen-hui. I cannot remember whether or not he later served as Commissioner of Education in Anhwei.

5. *Kung-ch'an-tang Yueh-k'an* (Communist Monthly) first appeared on November 7, 1920. A total of six issues was published.

6. The first issue of this weekly magazine, called *Lao-tung-che* (The Laborer), appeared on the first Sunday of September, 1920.

7. Correspondence between Ts'ai Ho-sen and Ch'en Tu-hsiu apparently started in February, 1921. It is possible, however, that Ch'en had earlier contact with other "working students" in France, since during 1920 and 1921 his two sons, Ch'en Yen-nien and Ch'en Ch'iao-nien, were both "working students" in France. I have in hand only a letter from Ts'ai Ho-sen to Ch'en dated February 11, 1921, from Montpellier, France, and Ch'en's reply dated August 1, 1921 (in *Tu-hsiu wen-ts'un*, II, 290-301).

8. Ch'en Tu-hsiu subsequently described to me the inauguration of the Chinese Communist nucleus at Shanghai. In addition to the material given in the body of this book, I remember that at the inaugural meeting each participant formally expressed his wish to join. Tai Chi-t'ao, however, stated that his personal relationship with Sun Yat-sen was too deep to allow him to become a member, and he wept, for at heart Tai believed in the Communist movement and desperately wanted to be a part of it. Shao Li-tzu expressed no such sentiments. He officially joined the nucleus.

9. Chiang K'ang-hu, a native of Kiangsi Province, was a relatively early advocate of socialism. Late in the Ch'ing dynasty he published an article entitled "The Relationship Between Girls' Schools and Socialism," as a result of which the Ch'ing Court "placed him under the surveillance of the district official" by way of punishment. On the tenth day of the seventh moon of the third year of the

reign of the Emperor Hsun T'ung (Sept. 2, 1911), he organized a Socialist Propaganda Association at Shanghai and published the *Socialist Star* (She-hui-chu-i Ming-hsing Pao). On November 5 of the same year he formally reorganized the Propaganda Association into the Socialist Party and called its first national congress at Shanghai. The main points of its platform were public ownership of land, public ownership of the means of production, adoption of a republican form of government, abolition of the navy and army, and active participation in parliamentary activities. (For further details see "Economic Thought of China in the Past Twenty Years" by Li Chuan-shih, in *Tung-fang Tsa-chih* [Eastern miscellany], the twenty-first memorial issue, pp. 201-21.) Chiang's party claimed between 40,000 and 50,000 members. On August 13, 1913, however, the party was disbanded, and it quickly died out.

10. I cannot clearly remember the names of the other two. One of them was Yüan Ming-hsiung, according to *Chung-kuo hsien-tai ke-ming yün-t'eng-shih* (Modern history of China's revolution), edited by the Modern China History Research Committee, 2nd ed. (Hong Kong, 1939), p. 127.

11. According to *Chin-tai-shih tzu liao* (Reference materials on modern Chinese history), No. 2 (Peking, April, 1955), pp. 161-73, the Peking University Marxist Study Group was formed in October of 1921. But one of the Group's announcements, quoted in this source, dated November 17, states, "This society was started last year (March, 1920)." I definitely remember that the group I have described was formally organized in October, 1920, and that the words "Peking University" were not part of its name. In fact there were several unsuccessful attempts to start such an organization. One was proposed as early as 1919. Perhaps after its formation in October, 1920, the group I have described suspended activities for a period. By October of 1921 the CCP had been officially formed, and with the resulting expansion of Marxist study work, perhaps study groups of this type were formed within individual schools, and the Peking University Marxist Study Group was one of these.

12. Teng Chung-hsia (in *Chung-kuo chih-kung yün-tung chien shih* [A brief history of the Chinese labor movement; Peking, 1953], p. 15) says: "On January 1, 1921, the Peking Party headquarters began establishing an Adult Education Labor School at Ch'anghsintien. . . . There was only one teacher in the beginning, and he was Wu Nu-ming. . . ." His account is not correct. The school was established as I have described it. On January 1, 1921, however, the Ch'anghsintien School for Workers' Children (Ch'ang-hsin-tien Kung-jen Tzu-ti Hsueh-hsiao) was formally renamed the Ch'anghsintien Adult Education Labor School (Ch'ang-hsin-tien Lao-tung Pu-hsi Hsüeh-hsiao), at which time the school was expanded and greater stress was placed on adult education. Adult education had, however, been a program of the school from the start. Wu Nu-ming went there to teach shortly after this expansion. Soon after that, Li Shih left Ch'anghsintien for Tsingtao, and Wu Nu-ming was placed in charge of the school.

13. Liang Shan-chi, a native of Shansi Province, was elected a member of the Advisory Council (Tzu Cheng Yüan) during the latter part of the Ch'ing dynasty. In the fifth year of the Republic (1916), when the old Parliament

reconvened, Liang Shan-chi, Liang Ch'i-ch'ao, T'ang Hua-lung, and others organized the Constitution Research Society (Hsien-fa Yen-chiu Hui), generally referred to simply as the Research clique. It had some political influence during the reign of Tuan Ch'i-jui.

14. Before Karakhan's Manifesto, G. V. Chicherin, People's Commissar of Foreign Affairs, on July 4, 1918, announced to the Fifth Congress of Soviets that Russia had repudiated the imperialistic Tsarist privileges and policies in China. (See Robert C. North, *Moscow and Chinese Communists* [Stanford, 1953], p. 45.) The Chinese people did not hear about this declaration, however. Even the Karakhan Manifesto reached them some time after it was made, and then only a few heard about it. But it impressed a small circle of intellectuals favorably.

15. Ch'ü Ch'iu-pai had just graduated in 1920 from the Peking Russian Language School (Pei-ching O-wen Chuan-hsiu Kuan). He went to Russia as a correspondent for the *Peking Morning News* (Pei-ching Ch'en Pao).

16. On February 10, 1921, the following appeared in *Izvestia*: "Japanese newspapers issued in Tokyo have been aroused by news of a joint conference of Socialists of the Eastern countries held in one of the Chinese towns in the middle of December, 1920. The Conference was attended by 18 representatives from Japan, three from Korea, forty from China, and one from the island of Formosa. All participants at the Conference were representatives of the extreme revolutionary trend. With a view to initiating activities by the enumerated socialist organizations the Conference decided to set up a Central Bureau in China which would act in contact with the world proletariat. A representative from India will shortly joint [*sic*] the membership of this Bureau." (Quoted from North, *Moscow and Chinese Communists*, p. 56.)

17. The weekly *Hsiang-chiang P'ing-lun*, which Mao edited, was the organ of the Hunan Students Association. Its first issue appeared on July 14, 1919. After four issues, however, the military forces in Changsha closed it down in mid-August for publishing articles against the warlord Chang Ching-yao. Its fifth issue was printed but could not be circulated.

18. Shih Ts'un-t'ung established the weekly *New Chekiang Tide* (Che-chiang Hsin Chao) in 1919, when he was studying in the Chekiang First Normal School. In it he published his famous article "Against Filial Piety," as a result of which the principal of the school, Ching Tzu-yüan, was dismissed and the students launched a movement to retain him. This incident focused national attention on the magazine.

19. Mao Tse-tung has admitted that Ch'en Tu-hsiu influenced him greatly. (See the autobiography that Mao dictated, in Edgar Snow, *Red Star Over China* [New York, 1938].)

20. The Federation of Autonomous Provinces movement sponsored by Hunan was first proposed in a statement by T'an Yen-k'ai, the commander-in-chief of the Hunan Army, issued on July 22, 1920. It outlined the objectives of autonomy for Hunan. In November of the same year Chao Heng-t'i became commander-in-chief of the Hunan Army, and he drafted "Regulations for the Preparation of the Constitution for an Autonomous Hunan." This provincial constitution was promulgated and put into effect. Chekiang, Kiangsu, and Fukien provinces all

voiced support for it. But the movement died out with the entry of the Northern Expedition Army into Hunan.

21. After forming the Hunan Labor Society in 1920, Huang and P'ang became well-known leaders of the trade-union movement in Hunan. They joined the Hunan SYC in 1921. In January of 1922 workers in the Hua Shih cotton mill at Changsha staged a strike after their demands for bonuses and year-end double pay proved unsuccessful. The governor of Hunan, Chao Heng-t'i, ordered them both executed on charges of colluding with bandits, inciting the strike, and attempting to undermine public security.

22. The spelling "Nicolaevsky" is an attempt at romanizing the name by which he was known in Chinese, "Ni-k'ou-lou-fu-sze-chi."

23. I cannot remember fully the four points which Ch'en Tu-hsiu expressed. According to the *Brief History of the Chinese Communist Party* (contained in *Su-lien yin-mou wen-ch'eng hui-pien* [A collection of documents of the Soviet conspiracy—the documents that Chang Tso-lin seized from the Soviet Embassy at Peking and published], II, 1-47), they were:

(1) The recruiting of Party members [The term "recruiting Party members" was the term used invariably in the organizational period of the CCP. It included the concepts of educating and training as well as actually recruiting members.]

(2) Guidance in accordance with democratic principles [By "democratic principles" Ch'en Tu-hsiu meant the principles of democratic centralism as advocated by Communists. This is not to be construed as principles of democracy in its usual sense.]

(3) Discipline [Observance of the major points of discipline for that period. The term "discipline" has been interpreted differently by Communists in the past and present.]

(4) Caution in handling the problem of the seizure of state power by the masses [The major task at that time was to win the masses over to the Party in preparation for the future seizure of state power.]

These four points appear to me to be correct. This is not an easy problem to cope with, however, because the original meaning has been altered through several translations—from Chinese into Russian and then from Russian back into Chinese (neither of these translations is very good) and then from the Chinese or Russian into English. Point four, for example, has been translated by C. Martin Wilbur and Julie Lien-ying How (*Documents on Communism, Nationalism and Soviet Advisers in China, 1918-1927* [New York, 1956], p. 53): "Need of caution in approaching the masses with a view to bringing them into the Party fold."

24. Ch'en T'an-ch'iu later wrote a detailed account of this incident in his "Reminiscences of the First Congress of the Communist Party of China," published in the October, 1936, issue of *Communist Internationale* (quoted by North, *Moscow and Chinese Communists,* p. 57). I consider this account reliable. Ch'en Kung-po also has described the incident in "Wo yu kung-ch'an-tang" (I and the Communist Party; in Ch'en Kung-po, *Han feng chi* [A cold wind collection; n.p., 1944], pp. 191-267). Here Ch'en Kung-po stated that the Congress

met at the home of Li Han-chün four days in succession, and that he considered this a mistake in the arrangements I had made. This is not in keeping with the facts. For the meeting at which this incident occurred was the one and only meeting held in the home of Li Han-chün.

25. This is the date I remember. It may, however, be off by one day.

Chapter III

1. The Council on Propaganda and Action formed by the Congress of Peoples of the East at Baku in September, 1920, presented the idea to the ECCI in its first report. (See Edward Hallett Carr, *The Bolshevik Revolution, 1917-1923* [London, 1953], III, 267-68). But not until August, 1921, did the ECCI decide to convene the Congress; a provisional date of November 11, 1921, was set, and it was to be held at Irkutsk (*ibid.,* III, 525). Preparations for it could not be completed in time, however, especially because of the considerable difficulty of establishing contact with Far Eastern countries by way of Siberia, and so the Congress of the Toilers of the Far East was not actually convened until January, 1922.

2. The Soviet Union was not one of the powers invited to the Washington Conference. The calling of the Congress of the Toilers of the Far East was an obvious effort by the Comintern to make its first move to counteract the activities of the Western powers in the Pacific and Far Eastern area. This was, of course, closely related to the Soviet Union's foreign policy in the Far East.

3. The Party may have received some financial help before that time. Voitinsky, for example, donated some money to run the Foreign Language School at Shanghai, but it could not be regarded as regular Comintern help.

4. The Ch'ing Pang was the most influential secret society among the masses of the lower reaches of the Yangtze River.

5. To denote the various "generations" of mentors and disciples within the group, a single character was used. Members at that time generally fell into the "generations" of *ta, tung, chieh,* or *wu;* only a few "old men" belonged to the generation of *ta* or *tung.* Besides the "generations," there were a multitude of ranks and positions.

Chapter IV

1. J. V. Stalin, *Works* (Moscow, 1953), V, 144, which attributes the interview to *Pravda,* No. 261 (Nov. 18, 1922).

2. Su Wu was a Han-dynasty figure who was appointed envoy to the Hsiung-nu during the reign of the Emperor Wu Ti. The Khan wanted Su Wu to defect and serve him, but Su refused. He was thereupon detained and sent to an uninhabited region called Pei Hai. Sometimes compelled to subsist on a diet of snow and sheep skin, he refused to comply with the Khan's wishes. Only after working as a shepherd for nineteen years did he succeed in getting home. Even now a song popular among the Chinese people is entitled "Su Wu Tending

His Sheep." He is known throughout China for his loyalty towards his government.

3. V. I. Lenin, *The Tax in Kind,* in his *Selected Works in Two Volumes* (Moscow, 1952), II, Pt. 2, 541.

4. *History of the Communist Party of the Soviet Union (Bolsheviks), Short Course* (Moscow, 1952), p. 384.

5. *Ibid.,* pp. 384-85.

6. Details in *Lieh-ning sheng-p'ing shih-yeh chien-shih* (Short biography of Lenin's life; Moscow, 1953).

7. *Lieh-ning chuan-chi* (Complete works of Lenin), 3rd ed. (Moscow), XXVI, 317-52.

8. To refresh my memory of the Congress, I have consulted an English-language transcript of it, kindly made available on microfilm by Hoover Library. This transcript, published in Moscow, seems to me to contain a good many errors, and I have used only material from it that struck a responsive chord in my memory. Among other things, it often presents garbled versions of Chinese speeches. No doubt this was the result of faulty translating. During the early sessions, Ch'ü Ch'iu-pai translated Chinese speeches into the official Russian-language record. It was presumably from this record that the English-language transcript was in turn made. Ch'ü, whose translations were frequently riddled with errors, had to abandon the Congress and return to the hospital, however. Thereafter a Russian, who spoke hardly any Chinese, tried to translate Chinese speeches for the record, but without much success.

   The handling of Chinese names in the transcript is unreliable, too. Most Chinese delegates used either assumed names or merely their family names. Yet the transcript does not use even these with any consistency. Both Chang Ch'iu-pai, the KMT delegate, and I, for example, are at times listed as "Tao," perhaps because of our identical family names. Although we both were on the presidium, only one Tao is listed on it. Speeches attributed to Tao on pages 54, 61, 148, 154, 181, and 184 of the transcript were probably made by Chang Ch'iu-pai. On the other hand, it was I who made the speech attributed to Tao on page 11, and it was I who presided at the tenth session of the Congress (p. 192).

   The transcript seems to be unreliable in other aspects as well. On page 239 the figure of fourteen given for the size of the Chinese delegation is too small. The composition of the Chinese delegation given on that page, moreover, is obviously wrong. It lists no KMT or anarchist delegates, whereas both were present. There are additional discrepancies in the transcript.

9. Kim Kyu-sik may not have attended this Congress as a representative of the Provisional Korean government at Shanghai, of which he was premier. Harsh denunciations of that "Government" by Korean speakers at the Congress, and the statement by one (on p. 117 of the transcript referred to above) that the "Government" had turned down invitations to the Congress in order to attend the Washington Conference, make it seem unlikely that he did. My memory is not clear on the matter. While he may have attended in some other capacity, I am absolutely certain that Kim-Kyu-sik was a delegate. I knew him in Shanghai before the Congress, saw a good deal of him while we were at

Irkutsk, traveled on the same train with him, and we were together when we saw Lenin.

10. English-language transcript of the Congress, p. 11, where I am identified as Tao.
11. *Ibid.*, pp. 21-38.
12. *Ibid.*, pp. 156-74.

Chapter V

1. According to *Chung-kuo kuo-min-tang ta-shih nien-po* (Chronicles of the reorganization of the Kuomintang), in *Ko-ming wen-hsien* (Revolutionary documents; Taipei, 1955), VIII, Maring reached Kweilin on December 23, 1921.
2. According to the Shanghai *Shun Pao* of March 5, 1922, more than 2,000 strikers were returning to Canton on foot. When they reached Shatin, in the New Territories, British troops attacked them, killing three and wounding eight.
3. In 1916, when I began associating with KMT people at Shanghai, I got to know Lin Po-ch'ü, who was an important KMT figure in Hunan Province and a close follower of Sun Yat-sen. His elder brother, Lin Hsiu-mei, was a division commander in the army of T'an Yen-k'ai. Nevertheless, Lin himself was friendly with Ch'eng Ch'ien, who was struggling for power in Hunan against T'an Yen-k'ai. On the occasion of our meeting at Canton, he supported Sun Yat-sen with more zeal than most KMT members, although he was a member of the CCP.
4. "A list of presidium members was drawn up by the CCP and proposed by the delegate of a building trade union. In order to promote an alliance of the various groups, all of them were on the list. Among them was Hsieh Ying-puo, a member of the KMT and a politician. At the time, he was president of the Canton Federation of Mutual Aid Societies, which included scores of handicraft-workers unions. Certainly he was an appropriate candidate for membership on the presidium. Yet his name aroused great dissension. The anarchists, who opposed the KMT, were especially set against Hsieh Ying-pai, this politician-type of man." (Teng Chung-hsia, *Chung-kuo chih-kung yün-tung chien shih* [A brief history of the Chinese labor movement; Peking, 1953], pp. 69-70.) Of the candidates for the presidium nominated by the CCP, Huang, Lin, and Hsieh were from the KMT. Teng and T'an were Communists. When opposition to Hsieh arose, the matter of a presidium was simply shelved for the sake of expediency. In fact, however, T'an P'ing-shan himself carried out the duties of chairman of the Congress.
5. A more detailed description of the manifesto of the Anti-Christian Student Alliance and of the expansion of the Alliance into the Antireligion Alliance may be found in Wang Chih-hsin, *Outline of the History of Christianity in China* (2nd ed.; Shanghai, 1948), pp. 257-66.
6. Ch'en Kung-po gives a brief account of the trip Ch'en Tu-hsiu took to Weichow in an article entitled "Wo yu kung-ch'an-tang" (I and the Communist Party), which is included in his *Han feng-chi* (A cold wind collection; n.p., 1944), pp. 220-22. On the whole, though, Ch'en Kung-po writes evasively in this article.
7. In January, 1922, Wu P'ei-fu issued three statements attacking Liang Shih-i as a traitor who was giving away the Kiaochow-Tsinan Railway. The statements

appear in *San-shui Liang Yen-sun hsien-sheng nien p'u* (Chronology of the life of Mr. Liang Yen-sun; n.p., n.d.), II, 181-82, 184-86.

8. The Liang cabinet was forced to resign on January 25, 1922. Yen Hui-ch'ing (W. W. Yen) then acted as premier.

9. An English-language translation of this document appears in Brandt, Schwartz, and Fairbank, *A Documentary History of Chinese Communism* (Norwich, 1952), pp. 54-63. Extracts from it also appear in Robert C. North, *Moscow and Chinese Communists* (Stanford, 1953). Both of these sources state that the manifesto was issued on June 10, 1922. However, Hu Hua (*Chung-kuo hsin-min-chu chu-i ko-ming shih* [First draft of a history of the Chinese new democratic revolution; rev. ed.; Peking, 1953], p. 42) gives the date as June 15. I cannot recall now whether it was June 10 or June 15.

10. I personally invited Li Ta-chao to attend the Congress when I was in Peking, and he promised to attend, although he did not make the trip soon enough. Mao Tse-tung forgot the address of the meeting place and so could not be present, according to the autobiography he dictated to Edgar Snow (*Mao Tse-tung tzu-ch'uan* [Autobiography of Mao Tse-tung; 3rd ed.; Hong Kong, 1949], p. 33). The Canton delegate could not attend because of communications difficulties arising from the revolt of Ch'en Chiung-ming.

11. The full text of the "Manifesto of the Second Congress of the CCP" appears in Hu Hua, ed., *Chung-kuo hsin min-chu chu-i ko-ming shih ch'ang k'o tzu-liao* (Reference materials on the Chinese new democratic revolution; 9th ed.; Shanghai, 1951), pp. 69-83.

12. See also Harold R. Isaacs, *The Tragedy of the Chinese Revolution* (rev. ed.; Stanford, 1951), pp. 58-59.

Chapter VI

1. *Hsiang-tao Chou-pao* covertly started publication on September 13, 1922. Every time the Settlement authorities discovered copies of the journal, either in the press or on sale, they imposed a substantial fine on the printer or bookseller. The CC recompensed such financial losses.

2. The headquarters of the Secretariat was closed in September, 1922. I cannot recall the exact date.

3. Chinese Communist efforts, exerted in many different directions, were responsible for the fact that Li Ch'i-han escaped a death sentence at the hands of the military tribunal. Li did, however, receive a sentence of life imprisonment in the military prison. But happily, in October, 1924, Lu Yung-hsiang and Ho Feng-lin of the Anhwei clique went to war with Ch'i Hsieh-yuan of the Chihli clique. Meanwhile the KMT had entered into the so-called Sun-Tuan-Chang Triple Alliance—an alliance of the KMT with the Anhwei and Fengtien cliques. Li-Ch'i-han was regarded as having connections with the KMT, and so Ho Feng-lin released him.

4. On March 2, 1914, Yuan Shih-k'ai promulgated the Public Security Police Law by a presidential decree. It banned political assembly, meetings of societies, other meetings, and public demonstrations. Clearly, it was an "illegal" law.

5. The Fourth Congress of the Comintern opened in Moscow on November 6, 1922.
6. For the full text of this Draft Labor Law see Teng Chung-hsia, *Chung-kuo chih-kung yün-tung chien shih* (A brief history of the Chinese labor movement; 2nd ed.; Peking, 1953), pp. 76-77.
7. For details of the British intrusion upon the Kailuan Mine see the recent collection of relevant data compiled by Wei Tzu-ch'u, *Ti-kuo-chu-i yü k'ai-lüan mei-k'uang* (Shanghai, 1954).
8. The mine accepted the following demands: (1) A ten-percent wage increase for workers making less than $15 per month; (2) the equivalent of half a month's wages as a year-end bonus; and (3) medical expenses and some compensation to workers that were wounded during the strike and could not work.
9. These strike demands are taken from the "Strike Declaration of the Entire Body of Peking-Hankow Railway Workers," the full text of which appears in the article "Er ch'i kung t'ou" (The February seventh workers' suppression), published by the Hupeh Provincial Council of Trade Unions and reproduced in *Chin-tai-shih tzu-liao* (Reference materials on modern Chinese history), No. 1 (Peking, February, 1955).
10. On the basis of this order, the Hupeh Provincial Council of Trade Unions prepared its emergency notice, which appears in *ibid.*, pp. 84-86.
11. The day after the railway strike began, Wang Heng and other members of Parliament, acting on the assumption that the military and police had violated the provisional constitution by interfering with the assembly of workers, put several questions to the Government. More than one hundred members of both houses met on February 11 and discussed the February 7 tragedy. They concluded that the strike had been improperly handled and expressed the hope that both houses would propose to the Government a formula which they had worked out for settling the strike. Their formula included the following main points: (1) In accordance with Article 6, Section 4, of the Provisional Constitution, which gives the people the right to assemble and to organize, the Government should permit the existence of trade unions; (2) people that had been arrested should be released; (3) compensatory payments should be given the families of the dead; (4) the military and police sent to suppress the strike should be withdrawn, and work on the railways should be resumed. This proposal was presented to a meeting of Parliament the next day, but it was not passed.
12. Teng Chung-hsia, *Chung-kuo chih-kung yün-tung chien shih,* p. 112.
13. For example, early in 1923 the ECCI stressed the need for the CCP to retain its own "special political characteristics" and not to merge with the KMT or "fold up its own banner." See Robert C. North, *Moscow and Chinese Communists,* p. 72.
14. More than seventeen delegates may have been present, but I distinctly remember that only seventeen had votes.
15. Most writers in mainland China since 1949 have given the number of CCP members represented either as 420 or around 430. See, for example, Hu Hua, *Chung-kuo hsin min-chu chu-i ko-ming shih,* p. 44. He gives the number as 432. See also Wang Shih, Wang Ch'iao, Ma Ch'i-ping, and Chang Ling, *Chung-*

kuo kung-ch'an-tang li-shih chien-pien (A brief history of the Chinese Communist Party; Shanghai, 1958), p. 42, who place the number at 420. On the other hand, *Chung-kuo chin-tai chieh-min wen-t'eng shih*, p. 166, gives the number as 300. I cannot state definitely that there were 432 Party members at the time, but according to my memory, Hu Hua's figure seems to be close to the true one.

16. For the full text of the "Manifesto of the Third Congress" see Hu Hua, ed., *Chung-kuo hsin min-chu chu-i ko-ming shih ch'ang k'o tzu-liao*, pp. 86-87.

17. See, for example, Hu Ch'iao-mu, *Chung-kuo kung-ch'an-tang-ti san-shih nien* (Thirty years of the Chinese Communist Party; 1st ed.; Peking, 1951), pp. 9-10, or p. 13 of the 4th English-language edition (1959). See also Hu Hua, *Chung-kuo hsin min-chu chu-i ko-ming shih*, p. 45.

18. See note 2 above.

19. All preparations for the KMT organization had been made by June, 1923, when militarists of the Chihli clique made use of Li Yuan-hung to put Ts'ao K'un in the presidency. When Parliament could not decide whether the term of office of Li Yuan-hung had expired, Chihli militarists forced him to step down in a series of maneuvers. The cabinet was overthrown on June 6; on June 7 the military and police directly approached the president to demand payment of their unpaid back wages; and on June 9 the Peking police went on strike. Then a "Drive out Li" corps was formed, and both the telephone and water supply to his residence were cut off. On June 12 Wang Huai-ch'ing and Feng Yü-hsiang, who were responsible for garrisoning the metropolitan area, submitted their resignations and declared that they could not be responsible for maintaining order. Li Yuan-hung had no choice but to have some members of his family hide the presidential seal in the French Concession of the Legation Quarter and to leave Peking. He departed for Tientsin at 2:00 P.M. on June 13. But troops led by Wang Ch'eng-pin, the Chihli governor, surrounded Li's special train at Yangtsun station and forced Li to relinquish his seals and to issue a statement of resignation. That is a brief account of how the Chihli clique forced Li to step down from his office as president.

20. The bribing of members of Parliament began with the practice of sending each of them a subsidy of two hundred dollars a month as "gifts for [buying] ice [in summer] and charcoal [in winter]." These were issued through Kao Ling-wei, the Minister of Agriculture and Commerce. At the time, an article in *Nu-li chou-kan* (Endeavor), No. 38, referred to this practice. Subsequently, on October 5, Parliament held the presidential election. On that occasion, Ts'ao K'un openly bought votes from members of Parliament at five thousand dollars a vote, and thereby had himself elected president. The members of Parliament, as a result, were dubbed "Slave M.P.'s," one of the most abhorrent designations in modern Chinese history.

21. "A place for talking" (t'an hua ch'u) was the name used by some establishments in which people could gamble and take narcotics. They were run by certain militarists who took a big percentage for the alleged purpose of supplying their armies.

22. The text of this secret communication is carried in *Ko-ming wen-hsien* (Revolutionary documents; Taipei, 1955), IX, 65-67.

23. The full text of the statement by Li Ta-chao is carried in *ibid.*, IX, 37-48.
24. In his article entitled "Criticism of the Criticisms of the KMT" (originally printed in the *Min Kuo Jih Pao* supplement commemorating the reorganization of the KMT, published in 1924, and included in *Ko-ming wen-hsien*, IX, 49-64) Hu Han-min stated that one foreign friend had told him that there seemed to be a Left and a Right Wing within the KMT. That so-called foreign friend was Borodin.
25. After this Plenum I never again encountered Shen Ting-i. I do not know the details surrounding his departure from the CCP, but by 1925 he did participate in the West Hills Conference, which opposed communism.
26. Teng Chung-hsia, *Chung-kuo chih-kung yün-tung chien shih*, p. 113.
27. The impeachment was brought up by the three Supervisory Committee members on June 18, 1924. The full text of it is contained in *Ko-ming wen-hsien*, IX, 72-80.

Chapter VII

1. On May 15, 1924, someone left a bomb at the home of Wellington Koo, saying that it was a gift. Servants in the Koo household opened the parcel. The bomb exploded, wounding three of them. The incident was reported in the Peking newspapers at the time, but now I have before me only the record of the case as it was reported in the daily news column of *Eastern Miscellany*, Vol. XXI, No. 11. The account of the episode in this source is oversimplified, and the reasons for it are not given. But I am certain that it had nothing to do with the Peking Executive Department of the KMT or the CCP.
2. When Shao P'iao-p'ing, the well-known reporter on the Peking *Ching Pao*, was released from his first prison term, he brought out with him a bottle of bugs that he had collected in prison, handed them to some judicial officials, and called their attention to the need to improve prison conditions. The incident created a sensation.

Chapter VIII

1. For the full text of the resolution see Tsou Lu, *Chung-kuo kuo-min-tang shih-kao* (A draft history of the China Kuomintang; 3rd ed.; Shanghai, 1941), I, 421-22.
2. For the full text of the manifesto for the trip to the North see Sun Yat-sen, *Tsung-li yi-chiao chu'an-chi* (Complete works of the Director-General; Chungking, 1943), pp. 757-58.
3. After forcing Ts'ao K'un out of office, Feng Yü-hsiang used his name to appoint Huang Fu, who was, relatively speaking, close to the KMT, to form a regency cabinet to take temporary charge of the central government organs. Huang planned a banquet for the diplomatic corps on November 14. But the corps refused his invitation, and Huang had to cancel the function. As a consequence, Feng concluded that the diplomatic corps disliked his undertakings.

4. For the full text of the manifesto for the trip to the North see Sun Yat-sen, *Tsung-li yi-chiao chu'an-chi*, pp. 760-63.

5. There was no legal basis for Tuan's assumption of office. The military leaders Chang Tso-lin, Feng Yü-hsiang, Hu Ching-i, and Sun Yueh promulgated a joint statement on November 15, electing him "Provisional Chief Executive of the Chinese Republic." It was only after assuming office that he promulgated the so-called Organic Code of the Provisional Government.

6. Provisions for the Rehabilitation Conference were passed by the State Council on December 2, 1924, and promulgated on December 4. These specified that the Conference's constituents were to be: (1) people who had contributed significant services to the state; (2) the highest military leaders who had quelled the revolt in the fight against election by bribery; (3) military and civilian leaders of provinces and other administrative areas; and (4) people particularly invited or designated by the Chief Executive because of their special prestige, attainments, or experience.

7. Wang Ching-wei also made reference to this point in his "Address to the Second Congress: A Report on the Political Situation," which is included in *Wang Ching-wei yen-chiang-lu* (Lectures by Wang Ching-wei; 2nd ed.; n.p., 1927), pp. 31-58.

8. At the time, Sun Yat-sen personally presided over the Central Political Council of the KMT. In addition to Sun Yat-sen, it initially had three members on its standing committee—Hu Han-min, Liao Chung-k'ai, and Wu Ti-yun (C. C. Wu). Wang Ching-wei was soon added, which made five members in all of the standing committee. The Political Council, which was organized in Peking after Dr. Sun's arrival, involved the designation of a few members to deal with political issues in his behalf during his illness and was of a temporary nature.

9. Li Chien-nung, moreover, has stated: "Wu Ching-heng [Wu Chih-hui], at the request of Lu Yung-hsiang of Chekiang, asked Dr. Sun to tolerate Ch'en Chiung-ming." Li Chien-nung, *Tsui-chin san-shih-nien Chung-kuo cheng-chih shih* (Political history of China for the past thirty years; Shanghai, 1930), p. 583.

10. This was the famous "January 17th Telegram" which held the attention of the nation. For its full text see Liang Shih-i, *San-shui Liang Yen-sun hsien-sheng nien p'u* (A chronology of the life of Mr. Liang Yen-sun; ed. by Liang's students; n.p., n.d.), II, 375-77.

11. For the full text see *ibid.*, II, 378-79.

12. For the full text see *ibid.*, II, 379-80.

13. Feng Yü-hsiang, too, has said that he had many contacts with Wang Ching-wei at the time. Feng Yü-hsiang, *Wo-ti sheng-huo* (My life; Shanghai, 1947), p. 521.

Chapter IX

1. Regarding the number of CCP members at the time of the Fourth Congress, Hu Hua states that there were 980. Hu Hua, *Chung-kuo hsin min-chu chu-i ko-ming-shih* (A history of the Chinese new democratic revolution; Peking, 1953), p. 55. Miao Yung-huang states that there were 950 members. Miao Yung-huang, *Chung-kuo kung-ch'an-tang chien-yao li-shih* (A short history of the

Chinese Communist Party; Peking, 1956), p. 26. Mif states that membership approached the one thousand figure. Pavel Mif, *Heroic China* (New York, 1937), p. 24. I cannot remember the actual figure, but the view that it was near the one thousand mark is surely correct.

2. I cannot recall the full list of CC members elected by the Fourth Congress. However, I do know that the following ten people were among them: Ch'en Tu-hsiu, Li Ta-chao, myself, Ts'ai Ho-sen, Ch'ü Ch'iu-pai, T'an P'ing-shan, P'eng Shu-chih, Lo Chang-lung, Hsiang Ying, and Wang Shu-po. Li and Lo were in Peking at the time, and T'an in Kwangtung.

3. The Han-yeh-p'ing General Trade Union was organized as an amalgamation of the Anyuan Coal Miners' Union, the Hanyang Iron and Steel Workers' Union, and the Tayeh Iron Miners' Union. At the time it was the major labor union in the central reaches of the Yangtze River.

4. Mif makes a similar statement in *Heroic China*.

5. The KMT Comrades Club was organized on April 1, 1925. See Lo Chia-lun, ed., *Ko-ming wen-hsien* (Revolutionary documents; Taipei, 1955), IX, 215.

6. For details of the strike and a full text of the conditions see Teng Chung-hsia, *Chung-kuo chih-kung yün-tung chien-shih* (A brief history of the Chinese labor movement; 2nd ed.; Peking, 1953), pp. 130-42.

7. The Workers' Congress of Canton was organized by the Workers' Department of the KMT. Nominally it included all trade unions in Canton, although actually the rightist Canton Engineering Union opposed it.

8. According to *Hsiang-tao Chou-pao* (Guide Weekly), No. 155 (May, 1956), the First National Labor Congress represented only 200,000 organized workers.

9. Ma Chao-chun, *Chung-kuo lao-kung yun-tung-shih* (History of the Chinese labor movement; Chungking, 1942), p. 99.

10. For an account of the First Kwangtung Provincial Congress of Peasants and the formation of the Peasant Association see *Ti-i-tz'u kuo-nei ko-ming chan-cheng shih-ch'i ti nung-min yun-tung* (The peasant movement in the period of the First Revolutionary Civil War; Peking, 1953), pp. 178-97.

11. Foreigners seemed given to kicking Chinese coolies without explaining why they did so, and the public referred to this as "tasting foreign ham."

12. The Mixed Court of the International Settlement was organized on the basis of the Regulations for the Yangchingpang Mixed Court of 1868. Initially its jurisdiction was limited to Sino-foreign disputes, and when the accused was a Chinese, the Chinese authorities had jurisdiction. But the foreigners gradually encroached upon Chinese rights, so that by the time of the Republic even purely Chinese litigations were heard by foreign authorities. The Chinese judiciary had no control over the Mixed Court, and a Chinese who lost a case had no place to which he could appeal. This dreadful judicial system, which no independent people could tolerate, was not abolished until January, 1927, when Chinese judicial authorities opened a provisional court in Shanghai.

13. A more detailed account of the agreement of Fang Chiao-pai to the proposal for a merchants' strike is given by Hu Yü-chih, *Wu'-sa shih-chien chi-shih* (Facts of the May Thirtieth Incident), which was issued as a special supplement to *Tung-fang Tsa-chih* (Eastern Miscellany; Shanghai, July 1925).

14. For the full text of these seventeen conditions see Liang Hsin, *Kuo-ch'ih shih-yao* (Brief history of national humiliation; 6th ed.; Shanghai, 1933), pp. 227-30.

15. See Hu Yü-chih, *Wu'-sa shih-chien.*

16. The effect of the strike on the economy of Hong Kong is shown by import-export, shipping, stock exchange, and government revenue figures for Hong Kong that are cited by Teng Chung-hsia, *Chung-kuo chih-kung yün-tung chien-shih,* pp. 231-33.

17. For the full text of the CCP's "Message to the People," see Hu Hua, ed., *Chung-kuo hsin min-chu chu-i ko-ming shih tsan k'o tzu-liao;* 9th ed.; Shanghai, 1951), pp. 122-26.

18. For the full text of the thirteen conditions of the General Chamber of Commerce see Liang Hsin, *Kuo-ch'ih shih-yao,* pp. 234-35.

19. For the full text of this declaration see *ibid.,* pp. 247-48.

20. The conditions relating to the reopening of Japanese mills, which consisted of six articles, were issued as a statement by the Japanese Mill-owners' Association. For the full text of this statement see Teng Chung-hsia, *Chung-kuo chih-kung yün-tung chien-shih,* pp. 211-12.

21. In addition to these, the most important of the conditions referred to the abrogation of extraterritorial rights. On January 12, 1926, a conference on extraterritorial rights opened in Peking. The Powers, procrastinating methodically, organized an investigatory group, which devoted nearly one year to its labors, and finally, in November, 1926, produced a report. In a counterdemand, it insisted that China improve its judiciary before any steps could be taken toward abolishing extraterritoriality. So the Powers agreed only to improve the Shanghai Mixed Court system (see note 12 above), which had exceeded the bounds of extraterritoriality in any event, but left the question of extraterritoriality itself untouched. As to the tariff issue, concerning which the Powers had induced the Peking government to make concessions, the representatives of the Powers also used procrastination as their approach to the problem at the Tariff Conference, which opened in Peking on October 26, 1925. A resolution was adopted, recognizing the tariff autonomy of China, but making recognition conditional upon China's first abolishing *likin,* which was then beyond the power of the Peking government to do. It may therefore be said that the Peking government achieved no diplomatic gains at all as a result of the May Thirtieth Incident.

Chapter X

1. The official name of this school was "China Kuomintang Army Officers School," later renamed "Central Military and Political Institute." Because the site of the old Whampoa Naval Academy was used for the school, it was generally referred to as Whampoa Military Officers Academy. At first there was a Preparatory Committee of seven, and on January 24, 1924, Sun, as the generalissimo, appointed Chiang Kai-shek chairman of the Preparatory Committee. In May, 1924, the school was officially established, and the headquarters of the school was

provided with a *Tsung-li* (Director General), a president, and a party representative. Sun was Tsung-li, Chiang was president, and Liao Chung-k'ai was party representative.

2. Ch'en Tu-hsiu had verbally told me the inside story of Chiang's resignation. According to his story, Chiang visited Russia to study military affairs and did not bring back a good impression. On his return to China, he did not agree with Sun's policy of alliance with Russia and tolerance of Communists, and so he did not want to serve as Whampoa president. Then later Tai Chi-t'ao advised him to gain control of some real power first, to temporarily refrain from expressing differences of political opinion, and to wait until he grew strong before proceeding further. Chiang was convinced by this advice and gladly returned to Canton to assume the post.

3. Whampoa admitted 350 students in the first class, which entered the school on May 5, 1924. They were organized into the first, second, and third companies. There were 120 reserve students, who entered the school later, on May 10. They were organized as the fourth company. The total enrollment was 470. Actually only 460-odd came to the school.

4. This was the famous Battle of Mien-hu during the First Eastern Expedition. The date was March 13, 1925.

5. The National government adopted the committee system, using a sixteen-member committee composed of Wang Ching-wei, Hu Han-min, Sun Fo, Hsü Ts'ung-chih, Wu Ch'ao-shu, Hsu Ch'ien, Chang Chi, T'an Yen-k'ai, Tai Chi-t'ao, Lin Shen, Chang Ching-chiang, Ch'eng Ch'ien, Liao Chung-k'ai, Ku Ying-fen, Chu P'ei-te, and Yü Yu-jen. Wang Ching-wei was chairman. Under the National Government Committee (State Council) there were the ministries of foreign affairs, military affairs, and finance, headed respectively by Hu Han-min, Hsü Ts'ung-chih, and Liao Chung-k'ai.

6. In his political report at the Second Congress, Wang Ching-wei also stated that this Special Committee "had plenipotentiary powers to deal with finances, military affairs, and the police." The extensive authority of the committee could thus be gauged. It actually replaced the Central Political Council.

7. This incident was described by Ch'en Tu-hsiu on December 10, 1929, in his "Message to Comrades of the Whole Party." He said, "In that year [1925], in October, at the Enlarged Plenum called by the CC of the CCP at Peking, before the Political Decisions Committee, I brought forward the proposal that Tai Chi-t'ao's pamphlet [referring to *The Chinese Revolution and the China Kuomintang*] was not an accidental product of himself alone, but was the expression of the bourgeoisie in its attempt to consolidate its own class influence, to control the proletariat, and to proceed toward reaction. We should immediately prepare to withdraw from the KMT and become independent, if we are to preserve our own political face, lead the masses, and not be harassed by the policies of the KMT. At the time the representative of the International and the responsible comrades of the CC of the CCP unanimously and strongly opposed my proposal, saying that this hinted to the masses of CCP members to take the road of opposition to the KMT. . . ."

8. In his political report to the Second Congress, Wang Ching-wei stated that the organization of this Special Committee was decided upon at the joint meeting of the CEC, the National Government Committee (State Council), and the Military Council. As a matter of fact, this was only a formal decision. The inside story indicates that it was Borodin's idea. Hu Han-min's article "Ko-ming ko-cheng chung chih chi-chien shih-shih" (Several historical facts in the course of the revolution, in *Eastern Miscellany,* twentieth anniversary special issue) stated: "At the time, Wang Ching-wei was also in the home of Yü-wei (that is, Hsü Ts'ung-chih), and proposed calling Borodin over. He said, 'We must have Mr. Borodin here, and discuss the matter together.' After Borodin came, he said, 'We should organize a special committee to handle this case.' And so a provisional meeting was called, and Borodin proposed that Wang, Hsü Ts'ung-chih, and Chiang Chung-cheng [Chiang Kai-shek] be members of the special committee and that the power of the party headquarters, political council, and departments of the national government all be transferred to the control of the special committee." This report is reliable.

9. Here I mention only the conditions first brought forward by the Hong Kong trade unions. Later the basic resolution adopted by the Canton–Hong Kong Strike Committee listed twelve conditions for the resumption of work by the Hong Kong strikers, eight conditions for the settlement of the strike by the Shameen workers, and six demands of the Hong Kong Students' Federation. For details see Ch'en Ta, *Chung-kuo lao-kung wen-t'i* (China's labor problems; Shanghai, 1929), p. 208.

10. The special-license system provided "Regulations Governing Coastal Navigation by Foreign Vessels," which were promulgated by the National government on August 16, 1925.

11. According to Yang Yü-chiung, *Chung-kuo cheng-tang shih* (History of China's political parties; Shanghai), p. 166: "This congress was completely under the manipulation of the CCP, and of the whole body of 256 delegates, CCP members constituted about two-thirds." This is not only contrary to what I remember, but is also at variance with the policy of the CC of the CCP at the time.

12. At the end of 1925 I issued an open letter to KMT members that was published in the Canton papers. Today I do not have the original text and can only remember that its main theme was to deny the charge that the CCP wanted to monopolize the work of the KMT, to change it into the Communist Party. I also held that existence of the CCP and CYC units within the KMT was for the purpose of encouraging and directing CCP members to work positively for the revolution and to support the revolutionary policy of the KMT. So the CCP and CYC units were not harmful, but beneficial.

13. Sun, Yeh, and Shao did not attend the Congress. They were not delegates, nor were they specially invited by Wang Ching-wei.

14. Hu Han-min was elected by a unanimous vote of the delegates. Wang and Chiang each had one vote less than Hu. Hu should have been placed at the top of the list of the central committee. Later the secretary general of the Congress, Wu Yu-chang, with Wang Ching-wei's concurrence, placed the name of Hu after those of Wang and Chiang.

Chapter XI

1. After that Hsiang Ching-yu no longer worked as a leader in the CC. Late in 1927 or early in 1928 she was executed by the KMT.
2. See Feng Yü-hsiang, *Wo-ti sheng-huo* (My life; Shanghai, 1947), pp. 519-52.
3. On March 23, 1926, Chiang Kai-shek requested disciplinary action against himself. See *Ko-ming wen-hsien* (Revolutionary documents; Taipei, 1955), IX, 86-87.
4. When Wang Ching-wei was about to leave Canton, Chiang Kai-shek sent a letter to Wang and mentioned this. (Original letter published in *Letters of Five Great Chinese Personages* [Shanghai, 1939], pp. 246-53.) Later Ch'en Tu-hsiu also mentioned the incident to me.
5. This statement was made by Dr. Sun in a letter from his Canton headquarters to Chiang Kai-shek in 1924 (month and day not given). The full text is included in *Complete Works of Chung-shan* (Sun Yat-sen), "Letters Throughout the Years" section (Shanghai, n.d.), p. 42.
6. The full text of Chiang's address on this incident at Whampoa is included in *Ko-ming wen-hsien* (Revolutionary documents; Taipei, 1955), IX, 87-94.
7. On April 29 Hu Han-min, Borodin, and others arrived at Whampoa, Canton. Hu saw Chiang first. Borodin saw Chiang the next day, or later the same day. The exact arrangements for the meetings are not known.
8. In a letter to Ling Po-sheng sent on May 18, 1928, Wang Ching-wei said, "Borodin . . . Hu Han-min . . . only returned to Canton at the end of April, and by that time I had already left China." (Entire text of letter appears in *Letters of Five Great Chinese Personages* [Shanghai, 1939], pp. 308-22.) It is possible that his memory was faulty. Wang and Hu took the same boat in leaving Canton. I was told this by a friend who went to the boat to see him off. In addition, *Eastern Miscellany* (vol. XXII, no. 12), in its daily chronology of current events, recorded that Wang and Hu secretly left Canton together on May 9.
9. The Party Affairs Readjustment Plan included four resolutions in all. The full texts are rarely found in books on sale. Even *Revolutionary Documents,* edited by the China Kuomintang Party History Materials Editing Committee, only carried a portion. Readers can consult a longer record (also incomplete) that is found in *Complete Works of Chang Pu-chuan* (Taipei, 1951), notes section, pp. 420-22.
10. The Party Affairs Readjustment Plan contained provision for the KMT-CCP Joint Conference, so some KMT elements at the time held that this was changing the policy of "toleration of the Communists" into "alliance with the Communists." Actually this was just a superficial statement.
11. Both Chiang Kai-shek and Chang Ching-chiang are natives of Chekiang.
12. The disagreement between the Comintern directive and the policy of withdrawal from the KMT was explained by Ch'en Tu-hsiu in his statement to all comrades in the Party on December 10, 1929. He said, "After the March Twentieth Incident, I stated my personal views in my report to the International. I advocated the change from cooperation within the Party to alliance outside the Party. Otherwise, we would not be able to enforce our independent policies

and win the confidence of the masses. When the International read my report, it published in *Pravda* the essay by Bukharin severely criticizing the CCP for having the idea of withdrawing from the KMT, saying that withdrawal from the yellow trade union and withdrawal from the Anglo-Russian Workers' Committee had been two mistakes, and now there was a third mistake—the CCP's proposed withdrawal from the KMT. The International also sent Wu Ting-kang [i.e., Voitinsky], director of its Far Eastern Department, to China to rectify the CCP tendency to withdraw from the KMT. At the time, out of respect for international discipline and the views of the majority of the CC, I did not persist in my proposal."

13. This house was rented by the CCP Kwangtung District Committee for use as the office of the representative of the CC.

14. When the Kuominchun (National Army) was about to lose power, Tuan secretly colluded with the army of T'ang Chih-tao, which garrisoned the metropolis, to serve as an ally of the Fengtien Army inside Peking. He did this to try to get the support of the Fengtian clique. The National Army unexpectedly saw through the plot, and on April 9 the incident occurred in which Lu Chung-lin, Feng's aide, disarmed the guard of the Executive government at Peking. Tuan fled to the Legation Quarter and issued a telegram announcing the coup, thus dissolving his government.

15. See Chang Ch'i-chün, *Tang shih k'ai-yao* (An outline of party history; Taipei, 1951), II, 519.

16. The full text of Article 8 of the Organizational Outline for the Headquarters of the National Revolutionary Army reads: "After the promulgation of the Mobilization Order for the expedition, the country shall enter into a state of war. To facilitate military operations, all military, civilian, and finance departments and organs under the National government shall be subject to the direction of the commander-in-chief and shall attend to their work in compliance with his wishes."

17. See *Su-lien yin-mou wen-ch'eng hui-pien* (A collection of documents of the Soviet conspiracy; n.p., n.d.), section on the CCP, II, 63.

18. For full text of resolutions of this Enlarged Conference, see *ibid.*, II, 60-121.

Chapter XII

1. This proposal of T'ang Sheng-chih's was presented and passed at the July 24 Changsha meeting of generals of the Fourth, Seventh, and Eighth armies.

2. The brilliant war record of the Independent Regiment was later described in greater detail by Chou Shih-ti in "Reminiscences of Comrade Yeh T'ing," in *Biographies of Chinese Communist Party Martyrs*, Hua Ying-shen, ed. (Hong Kong, 1949), pp. 175-82.

3. This joint conference was held from October 15 through October 28.

4. On the question of the disposal of Kuo P'ing-pai, there was disagreement within the General Political Department. For details, see Kuo Mo-jo, *Ko-ming Chun-chia* (Revolutionary annals; Shanghai, 1951), pp. 383-92.

5. The manifesto of the first congress of the Hupeh Provincial Trade-Union Coun-

cil, January, 1927, also said, "In less than three months, the organized workers of Hupeh increased from 100,000 to 300,000." (See *The Labor Movement During the Period of the First Revolutionary Civil War* [Peking, 1954], p. 400.) The "period of less than three months" refers to October 10, 1926, to the end of the year.

6. From the occupation of Wuhan by the revolutionary army through the end of that year, many strikes were staged in factories in Wuhan. Of them, the more important recorded strikes numbered thirty-six (see Chen Ta, *China's Labor Problems* [Shanghai, 1929], p. 219).

7. This is based on "Resolution on the Economic Struggle" adopted by the first congress of the Hupeh Provincial Trade-Union Council (see *The Labor Movement During the Period of the First Revolutionary Civil War* [Peking, 1954], p. 416).

8. The Wuhan General Chamber of Commerce held a general meeting on December 3 over this issue, and decided on three proposals: (1) It is reasonable for workers to demand wage increases because of a rise in living costs, but we cannot agree to strikes for unreasonable demands. Moreover, the question of a wage increase can be directly negotiated between the workers and the management, and there is no call for interference by a third party. (2) The arrogance of the picket corps has reached its apex lately, and such brutal acts must be strictly banned. (3) The Political Affairs Committee should reveal what measures it has for dealing with the two above questions. If remedial measures are not produced by December 6, the commercial circles will adopt the method of calling a strike in self-defense. (See Chen Ta, *China's Labor Problems* [Shanghai, 1929], p. 225.)

9. See *The Labor Movement During the Period of the First Revolutionary Civil War* (Peking, 1954), p. 424.

10. On February 25, 1927, the CCP addressed a letter to the public on the general strike in Shanghai. It proposed that "all powers should be vested in the congress of citizens." See *Hsiang-tao Chou-pao* (Guide Weekly), no. 189.

11. See *The Labor Movement During the Period of the First Revolutionary Civil War* (Peking, 1954), p. 364.

12. See note 3 for this chapter.

13. After its defeat at the hands of the Fengtien-Chihli Allied Forces in the spring of 1926, Feng Yü-hsiang's Kuominchun retreated to the Northwest, while Feng himself went to the Soviet Union to study. The Second Army under Li Hu and the Third Army under Yang Hu withdrew to Sian and were encircled by Wu P'ei-fu's troops. It was only when Feng Yü-hsiang, accompanied by Soviet advisers, returned to China that he decided to join the national revolution. On September 17, 1926, when Feng took the oath of the revolution and dedicated his armies to its cause, Sian had been under siege for eight months. According to Feng Yü-hsiang, his military strategy then had consisted of two parts: first to attack Peking from Nankow, and second to march from Tungkwan to relieve Sian. Later, on the suggestion of Li Ta-chao, he adopted the course of coming out of Tungkwan and proceeded to Sian. On January 27, 1927, the siege of

Sian was lifted. See Feng Yü-hsiang, *Wo-ti sheng-huo* (My life; Shanghai, 1927), p. 619.

14. On July 8 and August 2, 1926, respectively, the British vessels *Wan Liu* and *Chia Ho* sank Chinese vessels in the vicinity of Wanhsien and drowned many people. Yang Shen, commander of the Wanhsien garrison, ordered the detention of the British vessels involved, pending negotiations. British warships thereupon sent more than three hundred volleys at Wanhsien, causing more than five thousand casualties, including dead and wounded. This, briefly, is the story of the Wanhsien tragedy, which shocked both China and the world.

15. In his article "Who Killed Whom?" (in *Hsiang-tao Chou-pao*, no. 183) Ch'en Tu-hsiu gave a more detailed account of this conflict. However, he said that the conflict led to the wounding or death of more than thirty Chinese. According to my memory, the casualty figures were not so high.

16. For the full text of the Treaty, see Sung Yun-ping, *History of China for the Past One Hundred Years* (Hong Kong, 1928), pp. 247-48.

17. T'an P'ing-shan returned to Canton from Russia on February 16, 1927, and proceeded to Wuhan from there.

18. At the opening of the Third Plenum of the second central committees of the KMT, thirty-three were present and T'an Yen-k'ai presided.

19. Ch'en Chi-yüan was elected Minister of Peasants on March 11, and he was relieved of his post by the meeting on March 17 (the closing date of the Third Plenum), when Wang Fa-chin was elected to succeed him.

20. The text of this resolution is in *Tung-fang Tsa-chih* (Eastern Miscellany; Shanghai), vol. XXIV, no. 9, p. 91.

21. Chiang Pai-li was an outstanding military scientist of modern China who had served as President of Paoting Military Academy and of the Army College. For his life, see Tao Chu-yin, *Biography of Chiang Po-li* (Shanghai, 1948).

22. In February or March, 1927, the major newspapers and news agencies both in North and South China all reported a compromise between Chiang and Chang Tso-lin of Fengtien, and the people who acted as go-betweens were Li Shih-tseng on Chiang's side and Yang Yu-t'ing on Chang's side. At the time P'eng Shu-chih collected these reports that appeared in the Northern and Southern papers and put them together in an article entitled "The Problem of North-South Compromise," which was published in *Hsiang-tao*, no. 191. In addition, Liang Shih-i, on January 16, 1927, had a talk with the British Minister to China, Sir Miles Lampson, in which he mentioned this incident. (See Liang Shih-i, *San shui Liang Yen-sun hsien-sheng nien p'u* [Chronology of the life of Liang Yen-sun], II, 502-6.)

23. Early in 1927 Wu T'ieh-ch'eng proceeded from Nanchang to Japan to make arrangements with Japanese Foreign Minister Shidehara. Tai Chi-t'ao also went to Japan in February on Chiang's orders, while the Japanese Ching-pu-tso-fen-li and others were also traveling between Nanchang and Canton, making open statements to the press and declaring that Japan had reached some understanding with the stable elements in the South.

24. According to Tung Hsien-kuang, *Biography of President Chiang* (Taipei, 1952), I, 90, after Chiang arrived in Shanghai, most of the merchants and bankers

supported the purge of Communists, and a three-million-dollar loan was immediately arranged to meet Chiang's urgent needs.

25. With reference to details of the three insurrections of the Shanghai workers, see Ch'u Ching-pai, "First Uprising of Shanghai Workers," and Shih Ying, "Second Uprising of Shanghai Workers" and "Third Uprising of Shanghai Workers." All three articles are included in *The Labor Movement During the Period of the First Revolutionary Civil War* (Peking, 1954).

26. After Wang Ching-wei arrived in Shanghai, he consulted with Chiang, Wu, Li, and Ts'ai. For details, consult Wang Ching-wei's address "The Events of Wuhan's Expulsion of Communists," which he made at Sun Yat-sen University in Canton on November 5, 1927. The text of this address was published in the *Kung Hsien* magazine (published every ten days) on December 5, 1927, being no. 1 of the magazine, pp. 3-13.

27. During the Party purge in Shanghai, Chiang suddenly ordered his trusted subordinate Liu Shih to succeed Hsueh Yueh as commander of the First Division.

28. Material about the events relating to the disarming of the workers' armed forces on April 12 and the massacre of workers the following day were collected by the Shanghai General Trade-Union Council in the article "Factual Account of the Great Massacre of April 12" (see *The Labor Movement During the Period of the First Revolutionary Civil War* [Peking, 1954], pp. 491-533).

29. During the period of the war against Japan, Ch'en Li-fu at a certain meeting recounted the Party-purge incident in Shanghai. He stated that the greatest difficulty during the Party purge was to differentiate between the Communists and non-Communists. His method was to convene meetings of KMT members in all localities and to call on those with leftist inclinations to stand on the left side, while the rest were to stand on the right side. Then the two sides would be called upon to fight each other. In this way those that stood on the left side got their due punishment. These words of Ch'en Li-fu must be accepted as facts. But at the time those that stood on the left side were not necessarily all members of the CCP, while those that stood on the right side could not definitely be considered free of leftist tendencies. There were also many that vacillated between the Left and the Right, and the red cap would be put on them.

30. See Ch'en Ti-hsiu's article "Monument of [Baron] von Ketteler," in *Hsin-ch'ing-nien* (New Youth), vol. V, no. 5 (Oct. 15, 1918), pp. 449-58.

31. For the full text of the resolution on the peasant movement, see *Su-lien yin-mou wen-ch'eng hui-pien* (A collection of documents of the Soviet conspiracy; n.p., n.d.), II, 96-115.

32. For detailed figures, see *The Peasant Movement During the Period of the First Revolutionary Civil War* (Peking, 1952), pp. 258-62.

33. *Ibid.*, p. 18.

34. See Mao's "Report on an Investigation of the Peasant Movement in Hunan," in *Mao Tse-tung hsuan-chi* (Selected works of Mao Tse-tung; Peking, 1953).

35. This is what the Sixth Congress of the CCP of Hunan District (1926) clearly laid down. (See *The Peasant Movement During the Period of the First Revolutionary Civil War* [Peking, 1952], p. 323.)

36. The peasant movement in the various provinces around Hunan was not as well

developed as in Hunan. An outline of this picture can be drawn from the number of peasants participating in the peasant associations in these various provinces. According to the statistics on members of peasant associations in the whole country, collected and compiled in June, 1927, by the Ministry of Agricultural Administration, the total number of such members in the whole country was 9,153,093, and Hunan alone had 4,517,140. With the 2,502,600 members in Hupeh added, the two provinces accounted for more than seventy per cent of the total. Kwangtung had only 700,000 members, Kiangsi only 382,617, and Kwangsi only 8,144 members. The other provinces could be gauged from this.

37. The First National Congress of Peasants was held in Wuhan in May, 1927.

38. Li Jui has written an account of the dismissal of Liu Yüeh-chih from the KMT. (*The Peasant Movement During the First Revolutionary Civil War* [Peking, 1952], pp. 286-87.) Although his point of view has led to a distortion of facts, the account can serve as reference material.

39. The convocation of the Pan-Pacific Labor Congress was decided on at the Workers Congress of New South Wales, Australia (February, 1926). The date was originally fixed for July 1, 1926, and the site was to be Sydney, Australia. By July 1 the delegates that had arrived consisted only of representatives of the Red Workers' International and of trade unions in Australia, New Zealand, and the Soviet Union. The Congress was changed into a preparatory meeting, and the date and site were changed to May 1, 1927, at Canton. Later it was changed again to May 20, at Hankow. In addition to representatives from the Red Workers' International, delegates also came from the following countries: Japan, 6; Korea, 1; France, 1; the Soviet Union, 5; China, 15; the United States, 2; Britain, 1; and Java, 1. The meeting lasted seven days, closing on May 26.

40. The Fourth All-China Labor Congress, originally scheduled for May 1, 1927, was postponed to June 19 because of inadequate preparations. More than four hundred delegates attended the Congress, which closed on June 28. The Congress adopted resolutions on trade-union organization and other subjects. (See *The Labor Movement During the Period of the First National Revolutionary Civil War* [Peking, 1954], pp. 545-52.)

41. Both Nanking and Wuhan had issued circular telegrams on this point earlier. On May 14 Li Tsung-jen personally proceeded from Wuhu to Hukou in Kiangsi to meet Chu P'ei-te. The two decided on mutual nonaggression and unanimity of action in continuing the Northern Expedition.

42. Chih Hsun has a more detailed account in his article "Recollection of the Ma-jih Incident," in *The Peasant Movement During the Period of the First Revolutionary Civil War* (Peking, 1952), pp. 381-84.

43. On May 27 at Changsha, Hsü K'o-hsiang and four other regimental commanders elected the so-called real KMT members Chiu I-shan and others to reorganize the Provincial and Municipal Headquarters of the KMT, and they circularized orders to party headquarters at all levels throughout the province to carry out their reorganization.

44. For the text of the greater portion of this document, see *Stalin on the Chinese Revolution*, Shih-chih, tr. (Shanghai, 1949), p. 174.

45. See Wang Ching-wei's address "The Events of Wuhan's Separation of Communists," in *Kung Hsien*, no. 1 (December 5, 1927), pp. 3-13.
46. *Ibid.*
47. Most publications record the date of Borodin's dismissal from office as June 5; but according to *Eastern Miscellany* (vol. XXIV, no. 16, column on Daily Events) Nanking only reported on June 17 the news that "the Central Executive Committee in Wuhan adopted the resolution to dismiss Borodin and all other Russian advisers." I no longer remember the exact date.
48. According to Feng Yü-hsiang, *Wo-ti sheng-huo* (My life; Shanghai, 1947), p. 702, the telegram mediating the dispute was drafted on his behalf by Wu Chih-hui, who volunteered for the job, and was issued after Feng had revised it.
49. The "Message to Members of the Whole Party by the August 7 Conference of the Chinese Communist Party" quoted a portion of this declaration—points four through ten. The message to Party members is included in Hu Hua, ed., *Chung-kuo hsin-min-chi chu-i ko-ming shih ch'ang k'o tzu-liao* (Reference materials on the new Chinese democratic revolution; 9th ed.; Shanghai, 1951), p. 223. But the message to Party members stated that the declaration was adopted at the Enlarged Plenum of the CC on June 30. This is at variance with the date that I remember—June 20.
50. For the full text of the July 13 declaration, see Lei Hsiao-ch'en, *San-shih-nien tung-luan Chung-kuo* (Thirty years of tempestuous China; Hong Kong, 1955), I, 81-85.
51. For the full text of this declaration, see *ibid.*, I, 85-87.
52. The reason given in Ch'en's letter of resignation was: "The International on the one hand wants us to implement our own policies, and on the other hand will not permit our withdrawal from the Kuomintang. There is really no way out. I actually cannot continue with my work."
53. See Ch'en Tu-hsiu's "Message to Comrades of the Whole Party," issued on December 10, 1929.
54. Apparently no concrete plans had been made for a "southern expedition." It was planned in secret, and the main idea was for the Fourth Army to return to Kwangtung, first reaching the North River and East River districts and then expelling Li Chi-shen, who was stationed in Canton, thus developing a new leftist center in opposition to both Nanking and Wuhan.

BIBLIOGRAPHY

Many of the entries in this bibliography are incomplete, but they were nevertheless included because it was felt that the reader would benefit from whatever information was available concerning them.

Brandt, Conrad; Schwartz, Benjamin; and Fairbank, John K. *A Documentary History of Chinese Communism.* Cambridge: Harvard University Press, 1952.

Carr, Edward Hallett. *The Bolshevik Revolution, 1917-1923.* 3 vols. London: Macmillan & Co. Ltd., 1950-53.

————. *The Interregnum, 1923-1924.* New York: The Macmillan Co., 1954.

Chang Chi-ch'un. *Chung-hua min-kuo shih-kang* (An Outline History of the Republic of China). Taipei: Chinese Cultural Publications Committee, 1954.

————. *Tang shih k'ai-yao* (An Outline of Party History). 2nd ed.; Taipei: China Cultural Service, 1951.

Chang Hsi-man. "Wu-szu ti she-hui-chu-i yun tung" (The Socialist Movement During May Fourth). In *Li-shih hui-i* (Historical Reminiscences). Shanghai: Chi Tung Book Co., 1949.

Chang Pu-chuan. *The Complete Works of Mr. Chang Pu-chuan.* Taipei: Cultural Objects Publishing Society, 1951.

Chang Tsu-chi. *Li Ta-chao hsüan chi* (Chronicle of the Writings of Mr. Li Ta-chao), included in *Contemporary Publications of Historical Data.* Peking: Chung Hua Bookstore, 1945.

Ch'en Hsu-lu. *Hsin-hai ko-ming* (The 1911 Revolution). Shanghai: People's Publishing House, 1940.

Ch'en Kung-po. "Wo yu kung-ch'an-tang" (I and the Communist Party). In *Han feng chi* (A Cold Wind Collection). N. p.: Local Administration Publishing House, 1944, pp. 191-267.

Ch'en Ta. *Chung-kuo lao-kung wen-t'i* (China's Labor Problems). Shanghai: Commercial Press, 1929.

Ch'en T'an-ch'iu [Chen Pan-tsu in reference]. "Reminiscences of the First Congress of the Communist Party of China." In *Communist International,* vol. XIII, no. 10 (Oct., 1936), pp. 1361-66.

Ch'en Tu-hsiu. "K'e Ling T'e Pei" (Monument of [Baron] von Ketteler), *Hsin Ch'ing-nien* (New Youth), vol. V, no. 5 (Oct. 15, 1918), pp. 449-58.

————. "Shuei sha le shuei" (Who Killed Whom), *Hsiang Tao,* no. 183 (Jan. 17, 1927).

————. *Tu-hsiu wen-ts'un* (Works of Tu-hsiu). Shanghai: Ya-tung Bookstore, 1926.

Cheng-fu kung-pao (The Government Gazette). Peking: Bureau of Printing and Engraving, 1912-1928.

Chiang Chun-yang. *Hsin-hai kiangsi kuang-fu chi* (The Liberation of Kiangsi in 1911). In *Ko-ming wen-hsien* (Collection of Revolutionary Documents). Taipei: Central Cultural Materials Supply Service, 1953, 1955.

Chien Yu-wen (ed.). *T'ai-ping t'ien-kuo tsa-chih* (Miscellany on the Taiping Heavenly Kingdom).

Chih Hsun. "Ma-jih shih pien te hwei yu" (Recollections of the Ma-jih Incident). In *Ti-i-t'zu kuo-na ko-ming chan-cheng shih-ch'i ti nung-min yun-tung* (The

Peasant Movement During the Period of the First Revolutionary Civil War). Peking: People's Publishing House, 1953.

Chin-tai-shih tzu-liao (Reference Materials on Modern Chinese History). Peking: Historical Research Institute of the Chinese Academy of Science, no. 1 (Feb., 1955); no. 2 (April, 1955).

Chou Shih-ti. *Hui-i Yeh T'ing chih* (Reminiscences of Comrade Yeh T'ing). In *Chung-kuo kung-ch'an-tang lieh shih chuan* (Biographies of Chinese Communist Party Martyrs). Edited by Hua Ying-shen. Hong Kong: New Democratic Publishing House, 1949.

Chu Chih-hsin. *Chu Chih-hsin chi* (Collected Works of Chu Chih-hsin). Shanghai: Reconstruction Publishing House, 1921.

Ch'u Ching-pai. "The First Uprising of Shanghai Workers." In *Ti-i-t'zu kuo-na ko-ming chan-cheng shih-ch'i ti kung-chen yun-tung* (The Workers' Movement During the Period of the First Revolutionary Civil War). Peking: People's Publishing House, 1954.

Chung-kuo chin-tai chieh-min wen-t'eng-shih (History of China's Modern Revolution). Hong Kong: New Democratic Publishing House, 1947.

Chung-kuo kuo-min-tang ta-shih nien-piao (Chronicles of the Reorganization of the Kuomintang). In *Ko-ming wen-hsien* (Collection of Revolutionary Documents). Taipei: Central Cultural Materials Supply Service, 1955.

The Communist International. Vol. XIII. New York: Workers Library Publishers, 1936.

Congress of Toilers of the East. Untitled English-language transcript of the Congress held in January, 1922. Microfilm from Hoover Institute.

Degras, Jane (ed.). *Soviet Documents on Foreign Policy.* 3 vols. London: Oxford University Press, 1951-53.

Feng Tzu-yü. *Chung-hua min-kuo k'ai chien ko-ming* (History of the Chinese Revolution Before the Establishment of the Republic of China). 2 vols. Shanghai: Shainghai ko-ming shih pien-ch'i sho, 1928.

Feng Yü-hsiang. *Wo-ti sheng-huo* (My Life). Shanghai: Educational Book Store, 1947.

Han feng chi (Cold Wind Collection). N. p.: Local Administration Publishing House, 1944.

Han Shan-wen. *T'ai-p'ing t'ien-kuo chi ni ch'i* (The Rise of the Taiping Heavenly Kingdom). In Chien Yu-wen (ed.). *T'ai-p'ing t'ien-kuo tsa-chih* (Miscellany on the Taiping Heavenly Kingdom).

History of the Communist Party of the Soviet Union (Bolsheviks), Short Course. Moscow: Foreign Languages Publishing House, 1953.

Hsiang-tao chou-pao (Guide Weekly). Sept., 1922-July, 1927.

Hsin ch'ing-nien (New Youth). Sept. 15, 1915-July 25, 1926.

Hu Ch'iao-mu. *Chung-kuo kung-ch'an-tang-ti san-shih nien* (Thirty Years of the Chinese Communist Party). Peking: People's Publishing House, 1951.

Hu Han-min. "Several Historical Facts in the Course of the Revolution." *Tung-fang Tsa-chih* (Eastern Miscellany), Thirtieth Anniversary Special Number, n. d.

Hu Hua. *Chung-kuo hsin min-chu chu-i ko-ming-shih* (First Draft of a History of the New Democratic Chinese Revolution). Peking: People's Publishing House, 1953.

———— (ed.). *Chung-kuo hsin min-chu chu-i ko-ming shih ch'ang k'o tzu-liao* (Reference Materials on the New Democratic Chinese Revolution). 9th ed.; Shanghai: Commercial Press, 1951.

Hu Yü-chih. *Wu-san shih-chien chi-shih* (Facts of the May Thirtieth Incident). In Special May Thirtieth Incident supplement to *Tung-fang Tsa-chih* (Eastern Miscellany), July, 1925.

Isaacs, Harold R. *The Tragedy of the Chinese Revolution.* Stanford: Stanford University Press, 1951.

Ko-ming wen-hsien (Revolutionary Documents). Taipei: Central Cultural Materials Supply Service, 1953 and 1955.

Kung-ch'an-tang yeuh-k'an (Communist Monthly). Total of six issues, Nov. 7, 1920-July 7, 1921.

Kuo Chan-po. *Chin-wu-shih-nien Chung-kuo szu-hsiang-shih* (A History of Chinese Thought in the Past Fifty Years). Peiping: Jen Wen Bookstore, 1936.

Kuo Mo-jo. *Ko-ming ch'un-ch'iu* (Revolutionary Annals). Shanghai: New Literary Publishing House, 1951.

Lao-tung-che (The Laborer). Began publication first Sunday of September, 1920.

Lei Hsiao-ts'en. *San shih nien tung luan* (Thirty Years of Tempestuous China). Vol. I. Hong Kong: Asia Publishing House, 1955.

Lenin, V. I. *Lieh-ning chuan-chi* (Complete Works of Lenin. 3rd ed.; Moscow: Foreign Languages Publishing House, n. d.

————. *Selected Works.* 2 vols. Moscow: Foreign Languages Publishing House, 1952.

Letters of Five Great Chinese Personages. Shanghai: Ta-fang Book Co., 1939.

Li Chien-nung. *Chung-kuo chin-pai-nien cheng-chih shih* (Political History of China in the Past Hundred Years). 2nd ed.; Shanghai: Commercial Press, 1948.

————. *Tsui-chin san-shih nien Chung-kuo cheng-chih shih* (Political History of China for the Past Thirty Years). Shanghai: Pacific Bookstore, 1930.

Li Chuan-shih, "Economic Thought of China in the Past Twenty Years," *Tung-fang Tsa-chih* (Eastern Miscellany), the Twenty-first Memorial Issue, no. 1 (Jan. 10, 1924), pp. 201-21.

Li-shih hui-i (Historical Reminiscences). Shanghai: Chi-tung Book Co., 1949.

Liang Ch'i-ch'ao. *Yin-ping-shih ho-chi* (Collected Works and Essays of the Ice-Drinkers' Studio). 40 vols. Shanghai: Chung-hua shu-chu, 1936.

Liang Hsin. *Kuo-ch'ih shih-yao* (Elements in the History of National Humiliation). 6th ed.; Shanghai: Jih Hsin Geographic Society, 1933.

Liang Shih-i. *San-shui Liang Yen-sun hsien-sheng nien p'u* (Chronology of the Life of Mr. Liang Yen-sun [Liang Shih-i]). 2 vols., compiled and published by his students.

Lieh-ning sheng-p'ing shih-yeh chien-shih (A Short Biography of Lenin). Moscow: Foreign Languages Publishing House, 1953.

Ma Chao-chun. *Chung-kuo lao-kung yun-tung-shih* (History of the Chinese Labor Movement). Chungking: Commercial Press, 1942.

Mao Tse-tung. *Mao Tse-tung hsuan-chi.* (Selected Works of Mao Tse-tung). 4 vols. Peking: People's Publishing House, 1951-53.

————. *Mao Tse-tung tzu-ch'uan* (Autobiography of Mao Tse-tung [as dictated to

Edgar Snow]). Translated by Fan Lin. 3rd ed.; Hong Kong: New Democratic Publishing House, 1949.

Miao Yung-huang. *Chung-kuo kung-ch'an-tang chien-yao li-shih* (A Short History of the Chinese Communist Party). Peking: *Hsueh Hsi* Magazine Publishing House, 1956.

Mif, Pavel. *Heroic China.* New York: Workers Library Publishers, 1937.

Mu-shu pien-fa (The 1898 Reforms). Shanghai: Shen-chou kuo-kuang she, 1953.

North, Robert C. *Moscow and Chinese Communists.* Stanford: Stanford University Press, 1953.

P'eng Ch'u-heng. *Hu-nan kuang-fu wen-ch'eng shih-ma-chi* (An Account from Beginning to End of the Hunan Liberation Movement). In *Ko-ming wen-hsien* (Revolutionary Documents). Taipei: Central Cultural Materials Supply Service, 1953.

Schwartz, Benjamin. *Chinese Communism and the Rise of Mao.* Cambridge: Harvard University Press, 1951.

Shanghai General Trade-Union Council. "A Factual Account of the Great Massacre of April 12." In *Ti-i-t'zu kuo-na ko-ming chan-cheng shih-ch'i ti kung-chen yun-tung* (The Workers' Movement During the First Revolutionary Civil War). Peking: People's Publishing House, 1954.

Shan-tung wen-t'i hui-k'an (Documents on the Shantung Question). Shanghai: European-American Returned Students' Association of Shanghai, 1921.

Shao Yüan-ch'ung (as told to Hsu Shih-shen). *Chung-hua ko-ming-tang leuh-shih* (A Brief History of the Chinese Revolutionary Party). In *Ko-ming wen-hsien* (Revolutionary Documents). Taipei: Central Cultural Materials Supply Service, 1953.

Sheng Lan-hsi. *Chung-kuo shu-yuan chih-tu* (The Chinese Academy System). Shanghai: Chung-hua Bookstore, 1934.

Shih Ying. "The Second Uprising of Shanghai Workers" and "The Third Uprising of Shanghai Workers." In *Ti-i-t'zu kuo-na ko-ming shih-ch'i ti kung-chen yun-tung* (The Workers' Movement During the First Revolutionary Civil War). Peking: People's Publishing House, 1954.

Snow, Edgar. *Red Star Over China.* New York: Random House, 1938.

Stalin, Joseph V. *Stalin on the Chinese Revolution.* Translated by Shih-chih. Shanghai: Epoch Publishing House, 1949.

⸻. *Works.* 13 vols. Moscow: Foreign Languages Publishing House, 1952.

Su-lien yin-mou wen-ch'eng hui-pien (A Collection of Documents of the Soviet Conspiracy).

Sun Yat-sen. *Tsung-li ch'uan-chi* (Complete Works of Tsung-li). Political Department of the Military Commission, 1943.

⸻. *Fundamentals of National Reconstruction.* In Sun Yat-sen. *Tsung-li ch'uan-chi* (Complete Works of Tsung-li).

⸻. *Letters Throughout the Years.* In *Tsung-li ch'uan-chi* (Complete Works of Tsung-li).

⸻. *Memoirs of a Chinese Revolutionary.* In Sun Yat-sen. *Tsung-li ch'uan-chi* (Complete Works of Tsung-li).

Sun Yun-pin. *The History of China for the Past One Hundred Years.* Hong Kong: Hsin Chih Bookstore, 1948.

Tai Chi-t'ao. *Kuo-min ko-ming yu Chung-kuo kuo-min-tang* (The Nationalist Revolution and the Chinese Nationalist Party). Shanghai: n. p., 1925.

T'an Szu-t'ung. *T'an Szu-t'ung ch'üan-chi* (The Complete Works of T'an Szu t'ung). Peking: San-lien Bookstore, 1955.

T'ao Chü-yin. *Tu-chun t'uan chuan* (A Biography of the Tu-chun Corps). Shanghai: China Bookstore, 1948.

———. *The Biography of Mr. Chiang Po-li.* Vol. II. Shanghai: Chung-hua Book Co., 1948.

———. *Wu P'ei-fu chiang-chun ch'uan* (A Biography of General Wu P'ei-fu). Shanghai: China Bookstore, 1941.

Teng Chung-hsia. *Chung-kuo chih-kung yün-tung chien shih* (A Brief History of the Chinese Labor Movement). 2nd ed.; Peking: People's Publishing House, 1953.

Teng Ying-ch'ao. "Wu-ssu yun-tung ti hui-i" (Recollections of the May Fourth Movement). In *Wu-ssu yun-tung san-shih chou-nien ch-nien chuan-chi* (Special Publication on the Thirtieth Anniversary of the May Fourth Movement). Shanghai: Hsin-hua, 1949.

Ti-i-t'zu kuo-na ko-ming chan-cheng shih-ch'i ti kung-chen yun-tung (The Workers' Movement During the Period of the First Revolutionary Civil War). Peking: People's Publishing House, 1954.

Ti-i-tz'u kuo-na ko-ming chan-cheng shih-ch'i ti nung-min yun-tung (The Peasant Movement in the Period of the First Revolutionary Civil War). Peking: People's Publishing House, 1953.

Tong Hollington Kong. *Chiang Kai-shek* (The Biography of President Chiang). Rev. ed.; Taipei: China Cultural Publishing Committee, 1953.

Tso Shun-sheng. *Chung-kuo chin-pai-nien shih tzu-liao hsu-pien* (Source Material for a History of China in the Past Hundred Years, Supplement). 2nd ed.; Shanghai: China Bookstore, 1938.

Tsou Lu. *Chung-kuo kuo-min-tang shih-kao* (A Draft History of the China Kuomintang). 3rd ed.; Shanghai: Commercial Press, 1941.

Tung-fang Tsa-chih (Eastern Miscellany). Shanghai: Commercial Press, published fortnightly, 1904-1947, monthly, 1947—.

Wang Chih-hsin. *Outline of the History of Christianity in China.* 2nd ed.; Shanghai: YWCA Press, 1948.

Wang Ching-wei. *Wang Ching-wei yen-chiang-lu* (Lectures by Wang Ching-wei). 2nd ed.; n. p.: China Printing Press, 1927.

———. "Wu Han fen kung chih ching kuo" (The Events in Wuhan's Separation of the Communists), *Kung Hsien,* no. 1 (Dec. 5, 1927), pp. 3-13.

Wang Shih, Wang Ch'iao, Ma Ch'i-ping, and Chang Ling. *Chung-kuo kung-ch'an-tang li-shih chien-pien* (A Brief History of the Chinese Communist Party). Shanghai: People's Publishing House, 1958.

Wei Tzu-ch'u. *Ti-kuo-chu-i yü K'ai-lüan mei-k'uang* (Imperialism and the Kailan Mines). Shanghai: Cheng-chou kuo-kuang she, 1954.

Yang Yu-ch'iung. *Chung-kuo cheng-tang shih* (A History of Chinese Political Parties). Shanghai: Commercial Press, Ltd., 1936.

Yun Yu-ting. *Ch'ung-ling chuan-hsin lu* (The True Story of the Emperor Kuang-hsu). In Tso Shun-sheng. *Chung-kuo chin-pai-nien tzu-liao hsu-pien* (Source Material for a History of China in the Past Hundred Years, Supplement). 2nd ed.; Shanghai: China Bookstore, 1938.

LIST OF CHINESE NAMES

This list includes the names of all Chinese referred to in this volume for which the Chinese characters could be ascertained.

張 繼	Chang Chi	張 彪	Chang Piao
張之江	Chang Chih-chiang	章柏鈞	Chang Po-chün
張之洞	Chang Chih-tung	張伯根	Chang Po-ken
張靜江	Chang Ching-chiang	張申府	Chang Shen-fu
張敬堯	Chang Ching-yao	章士釗	Chang Shih-chao
張秋白	Chang Ch'iu-pai	張太雷	Chang T'ai-lei
張發奎	Chang Fa-k'uei	張德惠	Chang Te-hui
張厚生	Chang Hou-sheng	張特立	Chang Te-li (Chang Kuo-t'ao)
張西曼	Chang Hsi-man		
張嘯林	Chang Hsiao-lin	張作霖	Chang Tso-lin
張學琅	Chang Hsüeh-lan	張宗昌	Chang Tsung-ch'ang
張學良	Chang Hsüeh-liang	章宗祥	Chang Tsung-hsiang
張 勳	Chang Hsün	張東蓀	Chang Tung-sun
張昆弟	Chang Kung-ti	趙繼賢	Chao Chi-hsien
張國燾	Chang Kuo-t'ao	趙恆惕	Chao Heng-t'i

722

趙秉鈞	Chao Ping-chun	陳贊賢	Ch'en Tsan-hsien
趙士彥	Chao Shih-yen	陳獨秀	Ch'en Tu-hsiu
陳其琬	Ch'en Chi-yüan	陳望道	Ch'en Wang-tao
陳喬年	Ch'en Ch'iao-nien	陳爲人	Ch'en Wei-jen
陳劍修	Ch'en Chien-hsiu	陳蔭林	Ch'en Yen-lin
陳烱明	Ch'en Chiung-ming	陳延年	Ch'en Yen-nien
陳春煊	Ch'en Ch'un-hsüan	陳友仁	Ch'en Yu-jen (Eugene Ch'en)
陳鐘凡	Ch'en Chung-fan		
湛小岑	Ch'en Hsiao-ts'en	陳雲	Ch'en Yün
陳賡	Ch'en Keng	鄭超麟	Ch'eng Chao-lin
陳顧遠	Ch'en Ku-yüan	程潛	Ch'eng Ch'ien
陳公博	Ch'en Kung-po	鄭潤琦	Ch'eng Jun-chi
陳果夫	Ch'en Kuo-fu	齊燮元	Chi Hsieh-yüan
陳立夫	Ch'en Li-fu	蔣中正	Chiang Chung-cheng (Chiang Kai-shek)
陳銘樞	Ch'en Ming-shu	江浩	Chiang Hao
陳璧君	Ch'en Pi-chün	蔣先雲	Chiang Hsien-yün
陳炳棍	Ch'en Ping-kun	蔣介石	Chiang Kai-shek
陳炳生	Ch'en Ping-sheng	江亢虎	Chiang K'ang-hu
陳潭秋	Ch'en T'an-ch'iu	蔣夢麟	Chiang Meng-lin
陳德榮	Ch'en Te-jung	蔣百里	Chiang Pai-li
陳天	Ch'en Tien	江紹源	Chiang Shao-yüan

錢介盤	Ch'ien Chieh-p'an	鐘　巍	Chung Wei
錢玄同	Ch'ien Hsüan-t'ung	范鴻劫（傑）	Fan Hung-chieh
靳雲鵬	Chin Yun-p'eng	范石生	Fan Shih-sheng
秦邦憲	Ch'in Pang-hsien	范體仁	Fan Ti-jen
經子淵	Ching Tzu-yüan	方椒伯	Fang Chiao-pai
周恩來	Chou En-lai	方　豪	Fang Hao
周佛海	Chou Fo-hai	馮菊波	Feng Chü-p'o
周詒春	Chou I-ch'un	馮國璋	Feng Kuo-chang
周炳琳	Chou P'ing-lin	馮自由	Feng Tzu-yu
周世弟	Chou Shih-ti	馮玉祥	Feng Yü-hsiang
周達文	Chou Ta-wen	馮　雲	Feng Yün
朱執信	Chu Chih-hsin	傅秉常	Fu Ping-ch'ang
朱卓文	Chu Chuo-wen	傅斯年	Fu Ssu-nien
朱寶廷	Chu Pao-t'ing	韓麟府	Han Lin-fu
朱培德	Chu P'ei-te	賀　昌	Ho Ch'ang
朱代杰	Chu Tai-chieh	何　鍵	Ho Chien
朱　德	Chu Teh	賀衷寒	Ho Chung-han
朱務善	Chu Wu-shan	何豐林	Ho Feng-lin
褚玉樸	Chu Yu-po	何香凝	Ho Hsiang-ning
居　正	Chü Cheng	賀　龍	Ho Lung
瞿秋白	Ch'ü Ch'iu-pai	何孟雄	Ho Meng-hsiung

何葆貞	Ho Pao-chen	徐　謙	Hsü Ch'ien
何世楨	Ho Shih-chen	徐錫麟	Hsü Hsi-lin
何叔衡	Ho Shu-heng	許克祥	Hsü K'o-hsiang
何應欽	Ho Ying-ch'in	徐梅坤	Hsü Mei-k'un
夏　超	Hsia Ch'ao	許白昊	Hsü Pai-hao
夏　曦	Hsia Hsi	徐世昌	Hsü Shih-ch'ang
夏斗寅	Hsia Tou-yin	徐樹錚	Hsü Shu-cheng
向警予	Hsiang Ching-yü	徐德珩	Hsü Te-heng
向忠發	Hsiang Chung-fa	許崇智	Hsü Ts'ung-chih
項　英	Hsiang Ying	宣中華	Hsüan Chung-hua
蕭楚女	Hsiao Ch'u-nü	宣　統	Hsüan T'ung
蕭耀南	Hsiao Yao-nan	薛　岳	Hsüeh Yüeh
謝　持	Hsieh Ch'ih	胡景翼	Hu Ching-i
謝曉石	Hsieh Hsiao-shih	胡漢民	Hu Han-min
謝紹敏	Hsieh Shao-min	胡毅生	Hu I-sheng
謝英伯	Hsieh Ying-puo	胡仁源	Hu Jen-yüan
咸　豐	Hsien Feng	胡鄂公	Hu O-kung
熊克武	Hsiung K'o-wu	胡　彪	Hu Piao
熊　斌	Hsiung Pin	胡　適	Hu Shih
熊秉坤	Hsiüng Ping-k'un	黃　愛	Huang Ai
熊育錫	Hsiüng Yü-hsi	黃介民	Huang Chieh-min

黃建中	Huang Chien-chung	高尙德	Kao Shang-te
黃金榮	Huang Chin-jung	高崇煥	Kao Tsung-huan
黃郛	Huang Fu	高語罕	Kao Yü-han
黃復生	Huang Fu-sheng	顧正紅	Ku Cheng-hung
黃興	Huang Hsing	辜鴻銘	Ku Hung-ming
黃煥廷	Huang Huan-t'ing	顧孟餘	Ku Meng-yü
黃日癸	Huang Jih-k'uei	顧維鈞	Ku Wei-chün (V. K. Wellington Koo)
黃凌霜	Huang Ling-shuang	古應芬	Ku Ying-fen
黃木蘭	Huang Mu-lan	光緒	Kuang Hsü
黃紹雄	Huang Shao-hsüng	龔春台	Kung Ch'un-t'ai
黃紹谷	Huang Shao-ku	郭亮	Kuo Liang
黃殿辰	Huang Tien-ch'en	郭隆貞	Kuo Lung-chen
洪秀全	Hung Hsiu-ch'üan	郭聘帛	Kuo P'ing-pai
易克嶷	I K'ei-i	郭壽華	Kuo Shou-hua
易禮容	I Li-jung	郭松齡	Kuo Sung-ling
任弼時	Jen Pi-shih	賴世潢	Lai Shih-huang
阮嘯仙	Juan Hsiao-hsien	李振瀛	Li Chen-ying
甘乃光	Kan Nai-kuang	李濟琛	Li Chi-shen
康白情	K'ang Pai-ch'ing	李啓漢	Li Ch'i-han
康有爲	K'ang Yu-wei	李之龍	Li Chih-lung
高恩璸	Kao En-hung	李景林	Li Ching-lin

李求實	Li Ch'iu-shih	李維漢	Li Wei-han
李富春	Li Fu-ch'un	黎元洪	Li Yüan-hung
李漢俊	Li Han-chün	梁啓超	Liang Ch'i-ch'ao
李和林	Li Ho-lin	梁鵬萬	Liang P'eng-wan
李辛白	Li Hsin-pai	梁善濟	Liang Shan-chi
李　虎	Li Hu	梁士詒	Liang Shih-i
李鴻章	Li Hung-chang	廖仲凱	Liao Chung-k'ai
李　瑞	Li Jui	廖化平	Liao Hua-p'ing
李瑞清	Li Jui-ch'ing	廖伯英	Liao Po-ying (Miao Po-ying)
李立三	Li Li-san		
李烈鈞	Li Lieh-chün	廖石溪	Liao Shih-hsi
李　斌	Li Pin	林長民	Lin Ch'ang-min
李品仙	Li P'in-hsien	林祥謙	Lin Hsiang-ch'ien
李韶九	Li Shao-chiu	林修梅	Lin Hsiu-mei
李　實	Li Shih	林　紓	Lin Hsü
李石曾	Li Shih-ts'eng	林　虎	Lin Hu
李守長	Li Shou-ch'ang	林葆懌	Lin Pao-tze
李書渠	Li Shu-ch'ü	林伯渠	Lin Po-ch'ü
李　達	Li Ta	林　森	Lin Shen
李大釗	Li Ta-chao	林祖涵	Lin Tsu-han
李宗仁	Li Tsung-jen	林偉民	Lin Wei-min
		林育南	Lin Yü-nan

林柏生	Ling Po-sheng	羅章龍	Lo Chang-lung
劉昌群	Liu Ch'ang-ch'ün	羅家倫	Lo Chia-lun
劉震寰	Liu Chen-huan	羅覺	Lo Chüeh
劉清揚	Liu Ch'ing-yang	羅漢	Lo Han
劉湘	Liu Hsiang	羅綺園	Lo Yi-yüan
劉華	Liu Hua	陸建章	Lu Chien-chang
劉仁靜	Liu Jen-ching	鹿鐘麟	Lu Chung-lin
劉光弟	Liu Kuang-ti	魯迅	Lu Hsün
劉伯誠	Liu Po-ch'eng	陸榮廷	Lu Jung-t'ing
劉少奇	Liu Shao-ch'i	陸沉	Lu Shen
劉峙	Liu Shih	魯士毅	Lu Shih-i
劉師培	Liu Shih-p'ei	魯滌平	Lu Ti-p'ing
劉佐龍	Liu Tso-lung	陸宗輿	Lu Tsung-yü
劉崇佑	Liu Tsung-yu	陸友予	Lu Yu-yü
劉子谷	Liu Tzu-ku	盧永祥	Lü Yüng-hsiang
劉維漢	Liu Wei-han	馬君武	Ma Chün-wu
劉文松	Liu Wen-sung	馬福益	Ma Fu-i
劉文島	Liu Wen-tao	馬敍倫	Ma Hsü-lun
劉玉春	Liu Yu-chun	馬謖	Ma Yuan
劉岳峙	Liu Yüeh-chih	毛澤東	Mao Tse-tung
劉雲松	Liu Yün-sung	繆伯英	Miao Po-ying (Liao Po-ying)

莫 雄	Mo Hsiüng		沈 兼 士	Shen Chien-shih
莫 榮 新	Mo Jung-hsin		沈 志 遠	Shen Chih-yüan
聶 榮 臻	Nieh Jung-chen		沈 玄 廬	Shen Hsüen-lu
紐 永 建	Niu Yüng-chieh		沈 定 一	Shen Ting-i
歐 陽 格	Ou-yang K'o		沈 雁 冰	Shen Yen-ping
白 堅 武	Pai Chien-wu		沈 尹 默	Shen Yin-mo
白 崇 禧	Pai Ch'ung-hsi		施 存 統	Shih Ts'un-t'ung
龐 人 銓	P'ang Jen-ch'üan		史 文 彬	Shih Wen-pin
包 惠 僧	Pao Hui-seng		施 洋	Shih Yang
抱 扑	Pao P'u		宋 慶 齡	Soong Ch'ing-ling
彭 澤 民	Peng Tse-min		蘇 兆 徵	Su Chao-cheng
澎 湃	P'eng P'ai		蘇 甲 榮	Su Chia-jung
彭 述 之	P'eng Shu-chih		孫 家 鼐	Sun Chia-nai
彭 澤 湘	P'eng Tse-hsiang		孫 傳 芳	Sun Ch'uan-fang
彭 永 和	P'eng Yung-ho		孫 科	Sun Fo
柏 文 蔚	P'o Wen-wei		孫 洪 伊	Sun Hung-i
卜 士 奇	Pu Shih-ch'i		孫 逸 仙	Sun Yat-sen
溥 儀	P'u Yi		孫 岳	Sun Yüeh
邵 力 子	Shao Li-tzu		孫 雲 鵬	Sun Yüng-p'eng
邵 飄 萍	Shao P'iao-p'ing		宋 教 仁	Sung Chiao-jen
邵 元 冲	Shao Yüan-ch'ung		宋 子 文	Sung Tzu-wen (T. V. Soong)

戴季陶	Tai Chi-t'ao	丁維汾	Ting Wei-fen
譚　振	T'an Chen	戴　澧	Tsai Li
譚植棠	T'an Chih-t'ang	蔡　暢	Ts'ai Ch'ang
譚平山	T'an P'ing-shan	蔡和森	Ts'ai Ho-sen
譚延闓	T'an Yen-k'ai	蔡　鍔	Ts'ai O
唐繼堯	T'ang Chi-yao	蔡元培	Ts'ai Yüan-p'ei
唐之道	T'ang Chih-tao	曹汝霖	Ts'ao Ju-lin
湯爾和	T'ang Erh-ho	曹　錕	Ts'ao K'un
湯化龍	T'ang Hua-lung	曹亞佰	Ts'ao Ya-po
唐紹儀	T'ang Shao-yi	曾擴情	Tseng Kuang-ching
唐生智	T'ang Sheng-chih	曾國藩	Tseng Kuo-fan
鄧中夏	Teng Chung-hsia	鄒　魯	Tsou Lu
鄧恩銘	Teng En-ming	杜月笙	Tu Yüeh-sheng
鄧錫侯	Teng Hsi-hou	段祺瑞	Tuan Ch'i-jui
鄧小平	Teng Hsiao-p'ing	段芝貴	Tuan Chih-kuei
鄧　培	Teng P'ei	段錫朋	Tuan Hsi-p'eng
鄧本殷	Teng Pen-yin	董鋤平	Tung Ch'u-p'ing
鄧澤如	Teng Tse-ju	董必武	Tung Pi-wu
鄧演達	Teng Yen-ta	王振翼	Wang Chen-i
鄧穎超	Teng Ying-ch'ao	王承斌	Wang Ch'eng-pin
狄君武	Ti Chün-wu	王盡美	Wang Chin-mei

汪精衛	Wang Ching-wei	吳鐵城	Wu T'ieh-ch'eng
王　俊	Wang Chun	吳廷康	Wu Ting-kang (Voitinsky)
王寵惠	Wang Ch'ung-hui	伍庭芳	Wu T'ing-fan
王法勤	Wang Fa-chin		
王荷波	Wang Ho-po	吳玉章	Wu Yü-chang
王懷慶	Wang Huai-ch'ing	楊闇公	Yang An-kung
王會吾	Wang Hui-wu	楊劍虹	Yang Chien-hung
王一飛	Wang I-fei	楊子華	Yang Chih-hua
王揖堂	Wang I-t'ang	楊希閔	Yang Hsi-min
王若飛	Wang Jo-fei	楊　虎	Yang Hu
王光輝	Wang Kuang-hui	楊人杞	Yang Jen-chi
王樂平	Wang Le-p'ing	楊明霽	Yang Ming-chai
王麗魂	Wang Li-huen	楊匏庵	Yang P'ao-an
王　明	Wang Ming	楊　森	Yang Shen
王士珍	Wang Shih-chen	楊德甫	Yang Te-fu
汪壽華	Wang Shou-hua	楊子烈	Yang Tzu-lieh
王有德	Wang Yu-te	楊宇霆	Yang Yü-t'ing
伍（吳）朝樞	Wu Ch'ao-shu (C. C. Wu)	葉　舉	Yeh Chü
		葉楚傖	Yeh Ch'u-ts'ang
吳稚暉	Wu Chih-hui	葉開鑫	Yeh K'ai-hsin
吳汝明	Wu Nu-ming	葉佰衡	Yeh Po-heng
吳佩孚	Wu P'ei-fu	葉　挺	Yeh T'ing

嚴　復	Yen Fu	于學忠	Yü Hsüeh-chung
閻錫山	Yen Hsi-shan	于樹德	Yü Shu-te
顏惠慶	Yen Hui-ch'ing (W. W. Yen)	虞維鐸	Yü Wei-to
		于右任	Yü Yu-jen
尹　寬	Yin Kuan		
虞洽卿	Yü Cha-ching	袁世凱	Yüan Shih-k'ai
喻兆藩	Yü Chao-fan	袁達時	Yüan Ta-shih
于方舟	Yü Fang-chou	袁　帶	Yüan Tai
余洒度	Yü Hsi-tu	袁祖銘	Yüan Tsu-ming
俞秀松	Yü Hsiu-sung	惲代英	Yün Tai-ying

INDEX

Abbreviations:

C   Chang Kuo-t'ao
CC   Central Committee of Chinese Communist Party
CCP Chinese Communist Party
CEC Central Executive Committee
KMT Kuomintang (The Nationalist Party of China)